PRENTICE-HALL, INC.
PRENTICE-HALL INTERNATIONAL, INC., UNITED KINGDOM AND EIRE
PRENTICE-HALL OF CANADA, LTD., CANADA
J. H. DEBUSSY, LTD., HOLLAND AND FLEMISH-SPEAKING BELGIUM
DUNOD PRESS, FRANCE
MARUZEN COMPANY, LTD., FAR EAST
HERRERO HERMANOS, SUCS., SPAIN AND LATIN AMERICA
R. OLDERBOURG VERLAG, GERMANY
ULRICO HOEPLI EDITORS, ITALY

SECOND EDITION

Executive Decisions and Operations Research

DAVID W. MILLER and **MARTIN K. STARR**

Professors, Graduate School of Business
Columbia University

PRENTICE-HALL, INC., Englewood Cliffs, New Jersey

13-294538-X
Library of Congress Catalog Card No. 78-83353

Current Printing (last digit)

10   9   8   7   6   5

Printed in the United States of America

To Renée Miller

From women's eyes this doctrine I derive:
They sparkle still the right Promethean fire;
They are the books, the arts, the academes,
That show, contain, and nourish all the world;
Else, none at all in aught proves excellent.

And Polly Starr

Preface

We reject the approach that identifies operations research with a heterogeneous assortment of mathematical techniques. Operations research is an executive responsibility. We believe that the relationship of operations research to executive responsibility can be presented meaningfully only in terms of a basic decision-theory foundation and orientation. In our conception of it, operations research is a continuum of *methods embedded in concepts.* It is based on philosophies and principles that underlie *model-building* and model use. The methodology constitutes a *fundamental program of model-building*—not just the means to manipulate data within the decision theory framework. This continuum of methods reflecting the widest spectrum begins with useful but crude qualitative models and reaches to the most highly refined forms of mathematical expression.

This book examines the structure of decision problems from the viewpoint of an integrated theory of decisions. Within this framework, a logical, rational approach is blended together with the scientific methodology of operations research. Using elementary mathematics, the reader learns:

1. How to determine when an operations research problem exists,

2. How to recognize the appropriate decision classification for that problem,

3. How to approach problems of each class in accord with present theory,

4. When it may be worthwhile to seek specialized assistance, and

5. How the results may be evaluated.

The reader is given an up-to-date overview of the wide range and value of tools which have been developed and applied over the past 20 years to aid executive resolution of decision problems. The classification of decision problems that we establish is pragmatically satisfying and theoretically significant. It enables a manager or an administrator to visualize his activities in a new way. Using this logic, quite complex decision problems can be resolved. Certainly, there are times when the assistance of a specialist may be warranted—for both problem formulation and the evaluation of results. However, the nonspecialist can always obtain guidance and enlightenment by referring to the decision theoretic structure.

With this in mind, the reader should come away from this book with the realization that decision theory is broadly powerful and highly evolved. He discovers (with some surprise) that although the relevant principles of decision theory are logical and scientific it is not necessary to use complex mathematics to explain them.

Decision-making is a root process. It is intertwined with all human activity. These roots are so fundamental to accomplishment that they take on a vital organic meaning without reference to the "real" detail of any particular problem. This is why a book such as this one could be written. Few who have not dwelt deliberately and at length on the nature of deciding are aware of how sensibly and straightforwardly decisions lend themselves to theoretical formulation. With a few strong principles we can organize the critical decision elements into basic sets that repeat themselves over and over again in every problem.

The new methodologies (called by such various names as operations research, management science, and cybernetics) are focused upon the decision process. We view these new arrivals to the decision-making scene as totally expected results of the evolving interest in *applied* decision theory and its application. This positive viewpoint is confirmed at every turn. Without such progress many decision problems would not be able to be formulated and even more of them could never be resolved.

We do elaborate in this book on the specific techniques of operations research, cybernetics, and other new methodologies. However, the reader who then wishes to pursue further such goals in greater detail and depth must continue with his studies of the structure and nature of decision-assisting *tools*. Having read this book, he can avoid the mistake of thinking that the new methodologies are simply a new set of tools.

Part I   develops the theme of the relation of the *executive and the organization to decision-making.*

Part II   outlines the interrelationships between *operations research and decisions.*

Part III explains the essential *nature of model-building and categorizes models* in different ways that are suitable for different purposes.

Part IV is then built on the foundation of the first three parts: it deals with the *treatment of problems* by specific models (or paradigms) as they occur in particular functional areas.

Part V completes the loop of operational necessity which moves us from model-building through implementation by presenting the executive's relation to operations research and by analyzing the executive's special problems of evaluation, implementation and control of the solution.

We have classified the problems analyzed in Part IV not by the techniques of analysis used (linear programming, queuing theory, and the like) but by the business area in which the problem arises: marketing, production, and finance. The reader will be familiar with this traditional business classification and with the kinds of decision problems that arise in each area. Thus, he can devote his full attention to the methods used in attacking these problems. One soon discovers that seemingly different problems in widely dissimilar areas are susceptible to similar formulations and methods of solution. Here too, our business area break-down sheds some very useful "comparative" light.

In making revisions for this second edition we have given careful consideration to the many comments offered by colleagues who have used this book for their courses. There was one topic that was frequently mentioned—about equally divided between pro and con. Namely, that our paradigms, in Part IV, should be organized by *technique* rather than by *functional area of business.* We have repeatedly debated the merits of this approach and have repeatedly rejected it. There seems to be an important conceptual difference involved—so we would like to state our position.

This book is *not written primarily for specialists in quantitative methods.* Future practitioners may choose to read this book because it is addressed to business management. Presently, one of the major concerns of management science is how to improve communications between practitioners and management. But practitioners are not our primary audience. If this book were directed towards specialists it probably would be better organized in terms of techniques. We do not believe that this is the case for a book directed towards executives who may be only occasional users of these scientific techniques but *regular users of the underlying thought processes.* This is intended to be an executive's book and, hence, it is organized according to their needs. While we might be tempted to argue further in favor of our position, a preface is not a suitable place to do so. Therefore, for those who remain unconvinced we sincerely believe *de gustibus non disputandum est.*

In accord with the above discussion, this book has been designed to satisfy the requirements of the relatively uninitiated business student or executive. We do not expect these individuals to spend time and energy developing complex mathematical models and solving demanding statistical problems. The book has been structured to obviate such needs and to respond to the varying levels of mathematical sophistication of the reader. From our experiences with the first edition, we have seen that even those who lack extensive formal training in mathematics can get insights from this book that are presently available only to practitioners from highly technical treatments of operations research.

We have bent every effort to present a clear, unified, and comprehensive approach to business decision problems. Management must make the decisions; that is its function. This book should enable the executive to utilize the *rich resources* which are available to help him achieve optimal decisions.

We express our gratitude to Young & Rubicam, Inc., and J. Walter Thompson Co. for the opportunities to have developed, in conjunction with the respective research departments of these companies, portions of the marketing material that appear in Chapter 11. With great perseverance, John Clapp and Ami Krause have worked through the problems that follow each chapter. We thank them and also John Stewart, who has helped us to render clarity to several flow diagrams and who has made supporting computer runs in the queuing area. And we reserve our most special thanks to Judy Dumas whose incredible ability with both typewriter and temperament is deeply appreciated.

Our "appreciations" for comments on the first edition extend well beyond any list of names that we could conceivably write down. For basic material, all of us are indebted to those brilliant thinkers and practitioners who have so earnestly contributed to progress in the operations research field and in its application to business problems.

DAVID W. MILLER
MARTIN K. STARR

Contents

3

THE OBJECTIVES OF DECISIONS   41

Part **II**

THE THEORY OF DECISION

4

THE STRUCTURE OF DECISIONS   69

Part **III**

THE NATURE OF MODELS

8

DESCRIPTIVE MODELS 165

9

NORMATIVE MODELS 208

Part **IV**

DECISION-PROBLEM PARADIGMS

10

OF PRODUCTION 247

11

OF MARKETING 371

12

OF FINANCE 449

Part V

THE EXECUTIVE AND OPERATIONS RESEARCH

13

EVALUATION OF PROBLEMS 499

PART I

ORGANIZATIONS AND DECISIONS

Chapter 1

Science
and the
Managerial Function

Management, as defined by *Webster's New International Dictionary*, is the "judicious use of means to accomplish an end." This definition may be too broad for our purposes, but not drastically so. Granted, we don't think that managing personal and family affairs is comparable with managing corporations, institutions, and other large organizations. Recently, however, there has been increasing acknowledgment that governments, hospitals, and libraries require a management team. This extension of the management concept can be traced to a growing awareness of the fundamental similarities in the basic patterns of all administrative issues.

Let us turn to the management of business. At once, we think of business as *we* know it—business in our terms and in our style. But consider the Dobuan Islander of the South Pacific who speculates in shell necklaces from the southern islands and arm-shells from the northern islands. Using *wabuwabu* (which is the name given to the strategy of a good businessman) the Dobuan accumulates his fortune while maintaining the movement of shell necklaces in a clockwise direction and arm-shells in a counterclockwise direction through the Kula ring of islands. A modern executive whose experience is limited to his own kind of management culture would feel like a fish out of water if he tried to negotiate on Dobuan terms. Similarly, in Burma when the accumulation of capital was not an overriding objective of business, and the pleasure of bargaining was even more important than the achievement of profit, we would have found the term "business management" awkward to apply. Yet, even in such unusual cases, some basic and transferable patterns have come to be recognized. The tools of economists can be employed and the knowledge of social scientists can increase our understanding. The culture rules are different but an important core of fundamentals transcends these relations.

The same reasoning applies to managements concerned with other objectives than those of business. Public administration, as well as military and institutional management, are as dependent upon sensible decision structures as are business, industry, and commerce. Transferability of the management function among the widest array of organizational contexts is now widely accepted. We have merely to note the number of individuals who have crossed successfully from one type of organization to another to confirm empirically what our logic indicates.

We shall avoid restricting our concept of management to any one type of organization. Similarly, we shall have no need to limit our considerations only to those ends which are customary in our own business, governmental, and institutional practices. We do not wish to cultivate an overly narrow concept of management, which could, in turn, produce a restricted view of the decision function. Such narrowness arises whenever we allow the *ends to eclipse the means.*

1/ *Changing Concepts of Management*

The emphasis on traditional ends or goals has imposed a veil hindering the search for those elements of management that are transferable to any management or administrative situation. Business has evolved in this environment and a great deal of business-school training has reinforced this tendency by concentrating on special situations, specific techniques, and the propagation of customs, traditions, and attitudes.

An analysis of the evolution of management thinking shows, however, that two currents run side by side. One line of development emphasizes the necessity of mastering administrative methods as they exist at any given time. The other is devoted to the determination of those elements that are common to all management situations. Progress in the latter direction has been consistent and significant for many years. Our modern manager is, in fact, better equipped to tackle Dobuan or Burmese business practices than he suspects.

This characteristic universality of management exists because certain elements and patterns can be learned and utilized independently of the specific area of application. We are now aware that managing a retail shoe store has much in common with managing an oil refinery, a library, or a hospital. The same applies to manufacturing radios or running an airline. Implicit in this notion is the ability to assess managerial efficiency on a cross-industry and cross-institutional basis; although more demanding, the same can be said for cross-cultural systems. Much work remains to be done before it will be possible to compare the managerial efficiency of a large computer firm with that of a small factory in the Congo producing wood carvings.[1] Within reason, however, a transferable science of management systems can be said to exist.

Decision theory in conjunction with operations research and management science are the present-day culmination of this aspect of management's evolution. At the moment they are the most advanced developments available for generalizing among administrative situations. At a describable level they are equally applicable to Dobu, Burma, Afghanistan, the Congo, and the United States of America.

Operations research (O.R.) has been purposely developed by and for management. Military management in Great Britain was the first to use O.R. *consciously*—one of many developments that have appeared in wartime when the urgency of the situation accelerated normal rates of progress. Today military managements all over the world use O.R. The same is true of business organizations and other institutions in the worldwide sense.

2/ Early Works[2]

The executive is our prototype of the decision-maker. Call him whatever you will (manager, administrator, team coach, captain, president, chairman, general, or head of the family), he is an individual with decision responsibilities. No matter what name *you* give him, he is the same central figure in *our* context.

Business has made more of a sustained fuss about the manager's role than any other organizational system. Both in practice and in training it has made major contributions toward furthering the understanding of the decision responsibility of executives. Examining history we find that formal training programs not connected with apprenticeship appeared as early as 1478.[3] A book on arithmetic for business was printed at Treviso, Italy, in the fifteenth century. At the end of the seventeenth century Jacques Savary wrote *Le Parfait Négociant; ou Instruction générale pour*

---

[1] See some of the attempts in this direction made by Barry Richman and Richard Farmer in *Comparative Management and Economic Development* (Homewood, Ill.: Richard D. Irwin Inc., 1965).

[2] For an interesting history see: Claude S. George, Jr.: *The History of Management Thought* (Englewood Cliffs, N.J.: Prentice-Hall, Inc., 1968).

[3] Before that, as early as Babylonian times, the institutions for business education were in the household or small merchants' shops.

ce qui regarde le commerce de tout sorte de marchandises. This book, apparently well received, was reprinted several times. In England, William Scott wrote an *Essay of Drapery, or The compleate citizen, trading justly, pleasingly, profitably.* At about the same time Jan Impyn completed the first Dutch book on accounting. His instructions were that the accounting journal should begin with the prayer, "May God our merciful Saviour vouchsafe me grace to make a profit and preserve me from all bad fortune."

These early works were important for the interest that they generated and because they led to a practice of searching and self-questioning which management has not yet completed. Some of the earliest questioning can be traced to Thomas Watts, who conducted a school on Abchurch Lane in London. Watts called for the development of principles and the comparison of principles with practice. In Watts' *An Essay on the Proper Method of Forming the Man of Business* (1716), we find the interplay of generalization with specific prescription. Watts emphasized arithmetic, accounting, mathematics (including algebra and geometry), and mensuration. The last point is particularly interesting because it seems to have been forgotten after Watts' time. Not until the early part of the twentieth century did management reawaken to the problems and importance of measurement theory. The reawakening has been gradual, and we cannot help but wonder if a session or two in Thomas Watts' class on mensuration would not prove helpful to all of us. Watts' stress on principle, generalizations, and mathematics is the progenitor of decision theory and operations research in our present day. To quote from Watts:

> The several parts of the Mathematicks are of that extensive Use and Benefit to Mankind, that hardly anything is to be done without them; Consequently, the Man of Business can have no small Share in these Sciences: For he that has a thorough Knowledge in them, must have the best Foundation laid, and a Mind exquisitely furnish'd for the undertaking of any Business.

3/ *Scientific Management*

The executive is always looking for better ways to do things. In the early 1900's Frederick W. Taylor concerned himself with the problems of production management and demonstrated that management could improve the means it used to accomplish ends. Some of his results were so startling that his methods swept across the United States. This movement, known as "scientific management," was later extended into time and motion studies and work-simplification methods. Taylor was responsible for the rebirth of interest in measurement. Undoubtedly, his work played an important part in creating interest in executive training but other forces were also at work contemporaneously.

4/ Concerning Business Education

In September 1890 Edmund James, Professor of Public Finance and Administration at the Wharton School of Finance and Economy of the University of Pennsylvania, read a paper presenting the plan and curriculum of the Wharton School. James urged the establishment of other such schools for the higher education of businessmen. The Wharton School, established in 1881, was the first university-level business school in the United States. Wharton was followed by the University of Chicago and the University of California, both of which set up business schools in 1898. It was not until 1908 that the Harvard School of Business was founded, 272 years after Harvard College was begun. In 1926 the Columbia University School of Business came into existence.

The growth of schools of business, management, and administration, both in size and number, is fair evidence of organizational support and encouragement for executive training and management research. If the importance of transferable methods and general procedure had not been recognized, it is doubtful that such schools would have grown to the preeminent position that they occupy today. Recent stress on continuing education for executives (so-called retooling) provides additional dimensions by which to judge the extent of this interest. If the quality of an administrator was determined primarily by his knowledge of ritual, custom, and tradition, apprenticeship training would have been more attractive than formal school training.

5/ Information for Decisions

Perhaps the most general characteristic of management problems is that some kinds of resources are always being used as inputs to produce some kind of outputs. These resources can be employed usually in alternative ways at differing costs, and the output, or benefit, from using the resources generally has value. Efficient management may try to minimize the costs associated with a given benefit or to maximize the benefit associated with a given use of resources. These opportunities invariably generate executive interest in some kind of cost-benefit analysis.[4]

---

[4] It is important to emphasize that one or the other or both of the sides of such an input-output analysis may not be measurable in dollars or in any obvious quanti-

This is why one of the first general methodologies management discovered was accounting, for accounting was neither limited to a specific industry nor restricted to a particular area of business. The history of modern accounting starts with a book by Pacioli, *Summa de Arithmetica*, published in Italy in 1494, which contains a descriptive statement of double-entry bookkeeping methods. The approach did not originate with him since he refers to it as the Venetian system. It was 1543, a half-century later, when Hugh Oldcastle wrote the first description in English of the methods of bookkeeping. Thomas Watts refers to this method of keeping accounts as his "darling science" and expresses contempt for those who kept single entry books.

Interest in accounting methods grew rapidly in the nineteenth century. James Bennett of New York wrote *The American System of Practical Bookkeeping* in 1824. Eighteen years later 19 editions had been published. Bennett used his book as a text for classes that he conducted for business students from his house at 97 John Street in New York City. At about the same time, Thomas Jones founded the New York Commercial Academy at 183 Broadway in New York City, and published his book *Principles and Practices of Bookkeeping*.

Our purpose in stressing accounting at this point is that accounting was one of the first generalized methods developed by management. It is significant as a pioneer quantitative method and as the first *well-structured* information available for the resolution of decision problems. The importance of accounting to the executive function was so great that it tended to crystallize in definite forms, which could be put to work on specific problems. However, accounting problems were inextricably connected with problems of observation and measurement, systems analysis, model construction, and decision theory. Certainly, operations research is not an offshoot of accounting. But the forces that brought accounting practices to the fore were not unlike the forces that have introduced operations research to the world. We shall have a great deal more to say about information for decisions in the material that follows.

6/ Change in Owner-Manager Relationship

Perhaps our discussion of management should have included some phrase relating to the delegation of authority. The end of the nineteenth century and the beginning of the twentieth was the period of enormous

tative form. For a variety of interesting discussions of the resulting problems and ways to solve them see Robert Dorfman, ed., *Measuring Benefits of Government Investments* (Washington, D.C.: The Brookings Institution, 1965).

organizational expansion in the United States, which is credited to the Captains of Industry. These Captains, with gigantic reserves of personal vitality, directed their companies' fortunes in the capacity of owner-managers, which was characteristic of smaller businesses. Gradually, as business began to move from its highly competitive, aggressive position to a more cooperative-competitive attitude, the individual owner-manager began to disappear. In his place, an organizational structure evolved that had the capacity to delegate authority for decisions and responsibility for the entire range of administrative tasks. Management had to learn how to cope with the problems that large organizational structures produced. Personnel problems appeared as a result of the complex, hierarchical arrangements of organization. Social developments emphasized the uniqueness of labor, management, consumer, and stockholder. At the same time, legal involvements and governmental controls raised new problems, which the management team had to solve. Similar structures evolved for military, governmental, and institutional systems.

7/ Development of Specialists

Part of the answer was—and continues to be—specialization. The demands of organizational growth were incontestable. Specialization set the pattern for the traditional areas of management. Specialists were required for production, marketing, finance, personnel, real estate, business law, and so on. Then, within each of these areas, further specialization was required and as a result we had time standards, quality control procedures, established foundry methods, press shop operations, specialists in advertising and sales promotion, public relations, building codes, patent law, and the multitudinous remainder.

8/ Development of Generalists

Is an operations-research practitioner a specialist? Most certainly he is. However, he occupies the unique position of being a specialist in generalization. That is why the operations-research function is frequently located high up in the organizational structure.

The twentieth century has seen research and technological development spurt ahead with such impact that organizational identity could hardly be maintained. Faced with swift and startling developments, management has had to question whether it had an existence above and beyond the products it made or the services it offered. The answer was affirmative. A fundamental core of management know-how was indeed transferable. At the same time, the separation of owner and manager engendered an executive tradition which permitted management people to shift from one organization to another. Ultimately, management realized that it had an identity which was independent of any or all of the individuals who composed the management group.

The solution to modern management's problems was the development of the *executive-generalist*. Such administrators could maintain the company's existence no matter what product was made. They could develop abstract organizational forms which were independent of the individuals who at any time happened to compose the management group. They could coordinate the contributions of all of the specialists of an organization. Their task required *the ability to employ structure before content* in coping with the extreme diversity of information produced by the organization.

9/ Management Science

Management recognized that the change in its role now required generalists. Individuals so trained could effectively operate in business, industry, city or federal government, hospitals, the armed forces, and schools, and could deal with behavioral scientists, research physicists, tax lawyers, and production foremen. To meet this challenge business schools have broadened their curriculums and have supported far-ranging research in management problems. More and more, independence from prescribed means and ends has been sought. Operations research and the decision-theory framework are part of a current, worldwide *management science* movement. They provide an important avenue for increasing the executive's ability to generalize and are a logical development in the evolutionary process of the managerial function.

Management science differs from Taylor's scientific management in many ways. It is not primarily concerned with production tasks and the efficiency of men and machines. Rather, it views efficiency as a secondary achievement which should *follow* adequate *planning*. (Both good and poor decisions can be implemented in an efficient way. A company can manufacture a high-quality product at minimum cost, but the product might not be the best choice for the company's objectives.)

Management science is concerned with both short- and long-range planning. At present, it is likely to be far more effective (directly) in short-range circumstances. Nevertheless, it attempts to establish whatever relationships exist between an organization's objectives and its resources. In this way, it cuts across the traditional areas of management. Such crossing of boundaries characterizes management science, which is *problem-oriented.* (See Chapter 13 for the discussion of what a "problem" is.)

Similarly, management science neither avoids nor overlooks the effects of behavioral problems, even though such problems cannot always be formulated or solved. Management science is essentially quantitative, although if important problems cannot be quantified they may be handled qualitatively. Whether quantitative or qualitative methods are applied, operations research is used to produce rational decisions and logical plans of action.

PROBLEMS

1. Mr. J, the President of E-Z Styles, Inc., objects when he learns that Mr. D, the chief designer, has hired management consultant Q to study the styling function. This relates to the way in which the full year's line of dresses is styled as well as to the style trends themselves. J states that the consultant Q has had no experience in the dress styling field, having previously worked for many years in the oil industry, as well as with the fabrication of metal parts.

In response, Mr. D states that it is precisely this that allows Mr. Q to come to the problem with a fresh look. He also points out that Q was hired to look at the larger management problem, including sales and production methods, the company's inventory problem, and the overall purchasing function. Furthermore, he adds that the consultant has refused to undertake this job unless the styling function is included. Mr. D says that this very fact alone impresses him.

Discuss the pros and cons of this argument between J and D.

2. The Homecraft Company manufactures a full line of work tools for the home. In recent years it has obtained many foreign affiliates and has begun a program of moving its executives around from one place to another. What basis can you suggest to support this policy? What disadvantages might exist? How would you resolve these issues?

3. In what way might a thorough knowledge of management history have any bearing on an administrator's efficiency or effectiveness? Would his time be better spent learning something else?

4. What criteria, objectives, and abilities exist for a business school (a) in updating an experienced executive? (b) in teaching concepts of transferability to students with no previous work experience? (c) in determining how much specialization should temper generalization?

What would be the likely long term result of emphasizing either generalization or specialization to the exclusion of the other?

5. Discuss: "Management had to question whether it had an existence above and beyond the products it made or the services it offered." To what extent do you think this is so?

6. Discuss: "Management realized that it had an identity which was independ-

ent of any or all of the individuals who composed the management group." To what extent do you think this is an accurate statement?

7. From the point of view of more or less transferability of the management function between different industries, how would you rate the following familiar organizational areas: production, marketing, finance, accounting, personnel, and general management?

8. From the point of view of more or less transferability of the management function between different institutions, how would you rate the following: libraries, hospitals, museums, charities, civic governments, political parties, military systems, and postal operations?

9. Some believe that an increasing number of companies will find that the controller's function is ascending to the top corporate post. What do you think of this notion?

10. Why is it said that top organizational corporate posts now require a modern-day version of Renaissance man?

11. "These are the basic figures on metropolitan New York City's overcrowded airways: 1955, a relatively manageable 12 million passengers; 1965, a booming 25.8 million. In 1966 the total rose to 28.5 million. . . . (in 1967) the figure might go as high as 34 million. [The actual figure for 1967 turned out to be 34 million, and for 1968, close to 37 million.] By 1975, the lowest prediction (the Port Authority's) is 53.5 million. The Civil Aeronautics Board, postulating an average one per cent decline in fares annually, puts the 1975 total at 65 million; the Air Transport Association anticipates millions more than that." (From "The Handwriting on the Air Terminal Wall," by Charles Leedham, *The New York Times Magazine,* May, 1967, p. 44.)

Assume that you are responsible for providing and *operating* the airport facilities that will experience the demands discussed above. Describe an appropriate group of specialists and generalists that you might assemble to advise you about what to do.

12. For the following situations discuss the pros and cons of installing a "specialist" as compared to a "generalist":

    a. The top post of a public utility.
    b. The mayor of a large city.
    c. The president of a university.
    d. The head of a government trade mission.
    e. The Chief Justice of the Supreme Court.

Chapter 2

Responsibility for Decisions

Theories of evolution are applicable to organizations as well as to species. Organizations cease to thrive when they find themselves unable to adapt to environmental and competitive changes. Unsuitable structures show up as marginal industries and unacceptable institutions, and eventually such organizations enter receivership where they either reorganize or cease to exist.

The ability of an organization to succeed in its environment and to adapt to change, or even to *capitalize* on change, is basically in the hands of management. In previous discussion it was pointed out that management's view of itself has not remained constant. Present-day management has redefined the administrative role to improve the organization's flexibility and responsiveness.

10/ Deciding and Doing

The major function of the executive is improperly indicated by the strict derivation of the word. "Executive" derives from a Latin word meaning "to do," and the Oxford Dictionary defines it in terms of "the action of carrying out or carrying into effect." Neither of these approaches would suggest that the main responsibility and function of the executive is to make decisions. Yet in modern business and industry this is precisely what is expected of him. He is rewarded and evaluated in terms of his success at making decisions. There is some incongruity in the term "manager," which we have already defined as a user of *judicious* means to accomplish an end. The emphasis is on doing, but *judicious* saves the day. The administrator is defined as one who directs the execution of the organization's affairs. This ambiguously accents yet another organizational responsibility in keeping with society's expectations for management performance.

The typical manager has functions other than making decisions. He has to *do* many things. Most organizations make continual attempts to relieve the manager of his (more or less) routine operations so that he will have time for the critical decision function. This cerebral conception of the executive does not diminish the importance *of doing*. Organizational structure is set up to provide the great variety of services required by the company, such as directing, coordinating, planning, staffing, analyzing, and controlling. However, crucial questions of what to do, as well as when, where, and how to do it, must be answered prior to the acts required for doing. These are the decision problems which must be dealt with. To the extent that management is involved in *doing* anything, it will have less time to devote to deciding about something.

The distinction we are making between doing and deciding is certainly a drastic oversimplification. Such orderly and well-defined boundaries between functions do not exist. A decision initiates actions which in turn generate the need for new decisions. The process is a never-ending one. The manager is necessarily immersed to some degree in both parts. Nonetheless, a conceptual separation of the two permits concentration on those aspects of the decision part of the process that can yield useful insights.

Although we concentrate on the decision side of the total process, we cannot afford to ignore *interaction* with the doing. If deciding and doing are strongly interrelated it can be misleading to separate them. This possibility must be considered before we can proceed to analyze the decision problem separately.

11/ *The Organization as a Communication Network*

In order to clarify the relationship between action and decision it will be useful to introduce a *model* of the organization, viewing it as a communication network. Throughout this book we shall be demonstrating the value of studying different models of organizations designed for different purposes.

A model can only be defined in terms of the purpose for which it is constructed. This model *abstracts the relevant aspects* of the organizational system and attempts to deduce how those aspects interact to produce effects related to our purpose. It must be emphasized that the only "total systems" model appropriate for *all* possible purposes (except practicality) is the organization itself. The reason for isolating and abstracting *certain characteristics* of an organization in the form of a model is to gain an understanding of the effect of the abstracted characteristics on the total organization. The risk involved in such abstractions is that other characteristics of the organization may be so important that ignoring them invalidates the model. However, even a valid model is at best a partial truth. Experience is the only final arbiter as to the success of a specific model.

A communication network is a collection of points between which information is transmitted. Any telephone system provides a good example of a communication network. As a matter of fact, it was primarily problems of the sort that arise in connection with such communication networks as telephone systems that led to the development of a *theory of these networks* and the closely related information theory.

We can consider an organization as a communication network by ignoring all of its characteristics except those represented by the existence of information and its transmission between persons and places. Although this is a rather severe abstractive simplification of an organization, it is not as extreme as it might appear. The definition of "information" is *not limited* to standard forms of communication. Written memoranda and verbal exchanges are only one form of information. Blueprints, budgets, part numbers, and inventory withdrawal slips are other forms. Materials and parts—flowing through a factory or warehouse—are also legitimate units of information. In fact, any characteristic of an operation that can be observed and *recorded* constitutes *potential* information for a communication network. The production of an item can be represented by the transmission of information that the item has been added to inventory. The sale of an item can be transformed into the transmission of information that that item has left inventory. At a later point, there can be the information transmission that a certain sum of money has been added to the organization's bank account. Most activities of the organization have such information-flow analogs.

12/ Input-Output and the Black Box

One important distinction between the kinds of information transmitted arises from the fact that the *organization is embedded in its environment*. The "outside world" consists of suppliers, buyers, competitors, tax and regulatory agencies, and other groups. The information that comes *into* the organization from the outside world is *input*.

In response to input the organization buys materials and facilities, hires labor, prices its products, advertises, floats stock issues, etc. These organizational responses are *outputs*.

It is useful, at times, to treat the organization as though it were covered by a black box and, therefore, unobservable. The "black box" is a convenient term to describe a system (organism or mechanism) whose structure is unknown—either because it cannot be observed or because it is too complex to be understood. (The notion of the black box has been borrowed by systems analysts from electrical engineers who use it to denote unspecified circuitry.) How well can the characteristics of the organization *viewed as a black box* be inferred from a knowledge of the inputs and outputs? Can reasonable predictions be made of the outputs that would occur for some hypothetical set of inputs if the properties of the black box cannot be inferred? The answers to both of these questions are a *qualified* "yes." The qualification depends upon the inherent structure of the information that appears in the inputs and outputs.

From a manager's point of view the black box does not apply to his organization, and he hardly likes to think that it covers his own be-

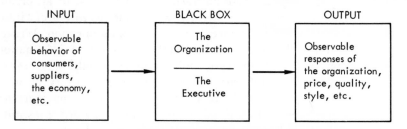

FIGURE 2.1(a) *Input-output model of the organization.*

havior [see Figure 2.1(a)]. Instead, he thinks of the black box as covering the outside world [as in Figure 2.1(b)]. The output shown in Figure 2.1(a) is transformed into the input of Figure 2.1(b), where management

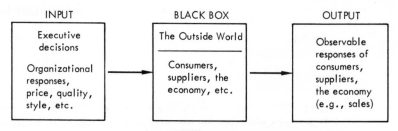

FIGURE 2.1(b) *Input-output model of managerial control.*

controls the inputs. When the black box covered the organization, only the organizational output could be observed. This output was all doing and contained no deciding. In fact, deciding was the circuitry that was hidden by the black box. By transforming to Figure 2.1(b), we have exposed the decision process and brought it into the realm of observable information.

From the standpoint of a communication network, an actuating decision consists of instructions from one point in the network to other points. As a result of the decision these other points will process the information they receive in a different manner or will change the rate of flow of information passing through them. Or, of course, the decision may result in the establishment of new points in the communication network. Deferred decisions, which are being made all the time, are far less visible. They should not be overlooked, however.

13/ *Information Storage and Memory*

A specific decision depends on the analysis, interpretation, and evaluation of information that is available to the decision-maker. Part of the information that comes to the manager is withdrawn from storage. Every organization has a *memory system* in which data can be stored. The most obvious example of these memories are the organization's files. Other storehouses of organizational knowledge are the brains and nervous systems of the personnel that comprise the organization. The time required to obtain information stored in files can in some applications be prohibitively high. The brain is not reliable for information storage; memory is perhaps its weakest faculty. Computer memories have particular advantages in this respect but even the largest computers lack the flexibility and size that characterize cerebral storage of information. The maintenance of brain-stored information, its renewal and replacement, is another critical executive problem.

It is quite apparent that the decision-maker can be deluged with information if he does not know how to select data that are pertinent to his problem. For this reason, information must be carefully categorized. *Decision problems exist as to what information should be collected and in what form; where and how long it should be stored; when and by whom it should be called for; how it should be evaluated; when it should be updated, supplemented, and so on.* Information models are intended to provide some help in answering these questions, which are essential for the *decision* activities of the manager. *Doing* would be collecting, recording, dispatching, and storing of information. It is quite clear that management prefers to minimize administrative time spent in this way.

14/ Information Feedback Channels

A decision that has been made can be countermanded or supplemented by subsequent decisions. Any such change will, presumably, be based on additional information. This additional information can result from changes caused by the *implementation* of the decision or from sources that are extraneous to the implementation of the decision. To the degree that it is the former, the decision process is closely related to the doing. To the degree that it is the latter, the decision process is relatively independent of the doing.

To make this distinction clearer, we must add an additional element to the input-output model. The new factor is called a *feedback* channel. (This term is also derived from electrical engineering, where it is used to denote an electrical signal [output] fed back into the circuit from which it emanated.) Figure 2.2 illustrates two different feedback connections, labeled (IV) and (V).

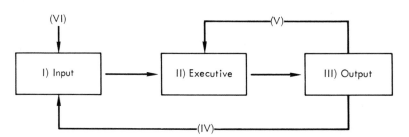

FIGURE 2.2 *Input-output model of the organization with feedback channels.*

Let us examine the implications of the feedback links, assuming that the executive occupies the position of the black box. For our purposes, the black box is not so opaque as to entirely hide his operations. Feedback channel IV indicates the executive's ability to call for certain inputs and to specify the form in which these inputs should arrive. This matter was previously discussed in connection with memories and information storage. Basically, there are three types of inputs: a) inputs that cannot be controlled, (b) inputs that are controlled by an outside agency with intelligence, and (c) inputs that an executive can control.

Link IV is the channel through which the manager exercises whatever control he has over the inputs. In all cases there is a decision and an action to effectuate control. Whenever feedback channel IV operates, we see that doing and deciding are implicitly bound together in a sequence: DECIDE → DO → DECIDE → DO, and so on. The nature of organizational control requires that most outputs should be fed back for inspection, evaluation, and follow-up, so this is a much used link.

On the other hand, the manager responds to a great range of inputs that arrive via channel VI. These are the maneuvers of competitors, the changing situation of the economy, and a variety of factors that are essentially random events of importance to the company. Inputs that do not arrive via the feedback link pose a major challenge to executive decision-making ability. These inputs are examples of situations in which deciding and doing are separate. Great care must be exercised, however, in ascertaining that hidden feedbacks do not exist.

Feedback channel V is required to show that a managerial decision can produce an output capable of modifying the future behavior of the executive. That is, the executive can *decide to decide* in a particular way in the future. A decision can alter the attitudes and values of the decision-maker. In this case, the output does not affect inputs but symbolically achieves a rewiring of the (not entirely opaque) black box. The importance of *deciding how to decide* is not trivial. There are no pat solutions to this problem but there is methodology to help decision-makers. To the extent that the manager devotes his time and attention to channels V and VI, he is relegating the doing to other areas of the organization. When channel IV is operating, doing and deciding are bound together within the managerial province.

The input-output feedback model has helped to indicate the nature of the decision process and the limitations involved in separating it from other organizational processes. Let us consider a few practical examples of typical decisions in terms of the distinction between deciding and doing.

1. The lathe operator who decides to start his lathe will promptly reverse this decision if one of the cutting tools breaks. His decision is bound up with his doing.

2. The decision to build a new hospital, plant, or library might be countermanded because unforeseen difficulties in financing arise or because of unexpected changes in the overall situation. These factors are extraneous to the implementation of the decision, which therefore can legitimately be treated separately from the doing.

3. A decision to increase production might be revoked because of a sudden slump in sales, which is extraneous to the implementation. It might also be countermanded because of production-line difficulties that are directly tied to the implementation. Here the validity of separating

deciding from doing depends on the point of view taken. In most organizations the decision-maker would be two different people, or at least it would be one man acting in the two different capacities of production and marketing management.

This last example suffices to show that no one model is adequate to describe and categorize all decisions. It also confirms that a considerable number of important decisions are sufficiently independent of the doing to permit them to be considered apart from their implementation.

15/ Cybernetic Systems

When the input-output model is fully developed with feedback links we enter the domain of integrated control systems. Many controls can be automatic and self-monitoring. The study of control systems which has been named *cybernetics*, is a rapidly growing field of research.

The classic example of a feedback control system is the thermostat arrangement that regulates the temperature of many houses. The furnace produces heat that is measured by the thermostat, which, in turn, controls the furnace. In short, the thermostat feeds back to the furnace instructions based upon a comparison of the effect of the furnace's output with a criterion for the system's performance, i.e., the temperature setting. This idea of monitoring the feedback signal in terms of deviations from the objectives of a system (or as an error measurement to correct the error) is at the heart of cybernetic theory. It is clear that this methodology of cybernetic systems can be applied to a variety of management functions which involve feedback.

Previously, we acknowledged that the inherent circularity of feedback systems would make the separation of decisions from actions purely arbitrary. In other words, the deciding and the doing are too closely related to permit a valid distinction between them. However, the cybernetic model permits the separation of deciding and doing by calling for decisions which are made only once and which determine the *design* of the organizational process. It can be recognized that the inputs arriving via the feedback channel become *repetitive* and that many of these inputs call for repeat decisions which should not require executive time. Many organizational designs permit these feedback inputs to by-pass the manager and to pass instead across an assistant's desk or into an automated controller.

In Figure 2.3, the executive transmits decision criteria and operational requirements for the construction of an automatic decision-maker (or regulator). After that, he is relieved of the responsibility of employing the same decision criteria every time a given situation repeats itself. Of course, automatic decision-makers are seldom available except in specialized and highly instrumented process industries. Nevertheless, by transmitting decision instructions to subordinates in the form of *policy* and operating rules, the executive achieves almost the same degree of freedom.

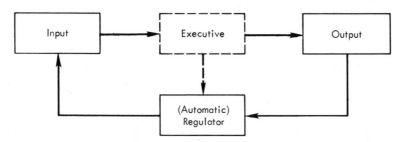

FIGURE 2.3 *Automatic decision-making bypasses the executive, but carries out his instructions.*

In the case of the simple thermostat the basic decision criteria are:

1. The desired temperature *gradients* in the heated space.
2. The *allowable fluctuations* in temperature under conditions of steady demand, or sudden changes in demand (such as a door opening).
3. The *location* of the thermostat to deliver the required temperatures.
4. The *cost of the installation.*
5. The *reliability* of the error-sensing device.
6. The *cost of maintaining* the installation.
7. The *element under control* (fuel, heat valve, or whatever).

Thus we see that in spite of the relative simplicity of the thermostat example, many difficult decisions must be made. Complex systems require far more involved decisions which, when treated in cybernetic terms, can be divorced from doing, even though they are based on feedback links that exist to control inputs. And because of our methodology it will be legitimate to treat decisions of this kind separately from their implementation.

Consideration of the different sorts of decisions made in business (and other kinds of organizations) indicates that decisions which are most clearly separate from their implementation are those made by persons who are high in the organizational hierarchy. This is in accord with the fact that most organizations make special efforts to formulate and communicate policy which can relieve their top executives of doing. A separate treatment of the decision process may, therefore, not be adequate for all decisions made within an organization, but it will certainly be relevant for many of the most important ones.

16/ The Nature of a Decision

What are the properties of a decision? The word "decision" covers such a multitude of cases that it belongs to the class of omnibus words which semanticists warn us about. There is general dictionary agreement that a decision is a conclusion or termination of a process. However, the end point of one process can also be viewed as the starting point of another. This brings us into a hall of mirrors where each mirror reflects its image onto a facing mirror in a seemingly endless progression of transformations. Consequently, when we decide to decide to decide . . . and so forth, we have left the realm of dictionary definition and have become entangled in a maze of reflexive properties which defy analysis and interpretation. There are, of course, other words and phrases with similar properties, such as the will to will . . . , to try to try . . . , or think about thinking about thinking. This reflexive property of decisions is not illusory. The organizational question of what triggers decisions is another way of asking: What causes the manager to decide to decide? In addition to this complication, the class of functions called decisions is so broad and contains such great variety that the use of a simplified definition of decision can create confusion instead of adding intelligence.

Obviously, the executive has no monopoly on decisions. Everyone makes all kinds of decisions throughout his life. What school to attend, what profession to choose, what job to take, whom to marry, how to plan for retirement—these are some of the many crucial decisions which each person must make. It is precisely the ubiquity of the decision problem which has led so many persons in so many fields to attempt to analyze it. Philosophers, psychologists, economists, sociologists, logicians, and mathematicians have all attempted to deal with the decision problem.

What is this decision problem? Simply the determination of how *people* should proceed in order to reach the best decisions. In other words, what methods can be used, what questions should be asked, what steps should be taken, what are the characteristics of best decisions? Let us consider some conclusions of the many specialized thinkers who have studied the decision problem.

17/ *Philosophers and Decisions*

Philosophers have concerned themselves with the question of what constitutes a "good" decision. In fact, this is the major concern of ethics. Mostly they have dealt with the problem of the individual: How should I act so as to lead a good life? From this they have generalized to the question: What is a good life? Philosophers approach the problem in two ways: either by defining "good" and considering a variety of values as aspects of it, or by summing up acceptable values and considering the totality to represent "good." Many philosophers have conceived this "good" to have a kind of objective, real existence. Others have maintained that values are simply those things which a particular person wants to have and that, as such, they are subjective and cannot be established in concrete terms. In either case, the philosophers deal with a particular conception of the individual's decision problem—that of the free, untrammeled person who has chosen the values he wishes to achieve and who makes rational decisions in order to obtain his objectives.

Totally involved with the question of what is "good" is the issue of what accounts for what happens. Consequently, the philosophy of decisions has always been related to the "truth" of what is known (or believed) about the fundamental laws of the universe. Primitive man, driven by fear of the unknown, appointed moon and sun gods as the source of good and bad. Even as understanding of the material world increased, the implicit association of truth and goodness was taken to be self-evident, and both Socrates and Plato staunchly advocated their inseparable existence. Science began to probe further than the evident, but faith in the connection remained, so that in the nineteenth century great optimism prevailed that by the twentieth century perfect decisions could be made because science would be able to explain the underlying truth of all phenomena. The nature of universal good was about to be discovered.

But with the birth of the twentieth century came a rash of contradictory evidence. The Heisenberg uncertainty principle, coupled with the basic concepts of quantum mechanics, reformulated truth as a probabilistic notion. By relating truth to risk and uncertainty, the fundamental connection between goodness and truth was shattered. Goodness remained a philosophical, theological, and personal matter. Individual truth came to be viewed as a property of cerebral-sensory systems; universal truth as approachable but ultimately unknowable. And so an operational philosophy of decisions developed, wherein the goodness of a decision would be measured by the extent to which its results satisfied the decision-maker's objectives.

18/ Economists and Decisions

Typically, the values with which philosophy has dealt have been nonquantitative. How, for example, can happiness be quantified? Yet there is a range of human values that seems to be already quantified. It contains all of the goods and services that are offered and purchased in the marketplace. That these things have value is apparent from the fact that people want them and are willing to sacrifice time and effort in order to get them. These values are conveniently, but imperfectly, quantified in terms of money.

The classical philosophers were cognizant of marketplace values, but relegated them to a subordinate position as compared to other kinds of values which they held constituted the "good." Adam Smith was trained in philosophy and one of his first works was on ethics. But despite his background in dealing with the higher values, it was one of his merits as an economist that he defined economics strictly in terms of marketplace values. Smith believed that these economic values played a sufficiently important role in everyone's life to justify their scientific investigation. He also felt that such an investigation could only be successful if the higher, nonquantitative values were excluded from the province of economics.

The subsequent development of economics for a long time remained circumscribed within the limits established by Smith. The decision problems which economists have explored treat both sides of the supply-and-demand relationship. How much of a commodity will a producer make at a given price? How much of a commodity will a consumer buy at a given price? These and similar questions lead naturally to the prior question: What are the objectives of the consumer and the producer? The economists' answer has been framed in terms of the *utility* which the commodity will provide to the consumer and which the production of the commodity will give to the producer.

Utility is defined as the power to satisfy human wants. The objective of the individual is held to be the maximization of the total utility he can achieve with his limited resources of time, effort, and money. The rationality of the individual is defined in terms of the utilization he makes of his scarce resources to achieve this end of maximization of utility. As we previously indicated, money is a convenient, but imperfect, measure of utility.

19/ Social Scientist and Decisions

Contemporary developments in economics have emphasized *the lack of realism* of the assumption that individuals act so as to maximize their utility. There has not been an attack on the proposition that individuals *should* act so as to achieve a maximization of their utility. Rather, there has been sufficient evidence and supporting reasons to show that *they do not act* in this way. Among the reasons suggested have been the following: the inability of the individual to duplicate the rather recondite mathematics which economists have used to solve the problem of maximization of utility; the existence of other values (the higher values originally excluded by Smith) which, though not readily quantifiable, do cause divergences from the maximization of utility in the marketplace; the effect of habit; the influence of social emulation; the effect of social institutions. Many economists have been attempting to take these various factors into account in constructing economic theories, which they feel will show a closer correspondence to the real world.

By introducing such factors, economists have been trying to incorporate aspects of behavior into choice or decision situations. This has also been the concern of psychologists and sociologists. The work of psychologists would certainly tend to confirm the assertion that human beings have a variety of diverse motivations which do not lend themselves to maximization of utility—at least so long as utility is defined in terms of the *satisfactions* resulting from marketplace phenomena. Freudian theory is only one example of a conceptualization of human motivation that relegates rational calculations in decisions to a relatively minor role. Similarly, sociologists have accumulated considerable evidence to demonstrate the enormous influence of social institutions, habit, and tradition on the choices and decisions made by individuals. The effect of these psychological and sociological factors leads individuals to make decisions and to take actions without recourse to maximization of utility in the classical economic sense. Alternatively phrased, it can be said that these factors cause people to act irrationally—but it should be noted that this is simply a matter of definition, *rationality having been defined as maximization of economic utility.*

Thanks to the subjective definition of utility, it is possible for economists to maintain that all of these factors can be incorporated into economic theory. If, for example, an individual's market decisions are affected by his desire for dignity, then it can simply be said that he is maximizing utility and he ascribes some utility to dignity. The difficulty remains, however. The utility an individual gains from a commodity or

a service can be measured, to a degree, by observable market phenomena (e.g., how much of the commodity he will buy at different
prices). But there is no convenient measuring unit for the utility of an
intangible component such as dignity. Therefore, even if these other
factors can be theoretically expressed in terms of utility, the difficulties
involved in *measuring* the utilities prevent the theory from satisfactorily
explaining observed behavior and decisions.

20 / *Logic and Decisions*

Many different approaches to the decision problem converge on one
particular model of the decision situation. Indeed, it is hard to avoid
this logical construction of the decision model once we address ourselves
to the description of a generalized decision situation.

To begin with, why must decisions be made? The answer is fairly
obvious. The executive wants to achieve something—call it his goal,
purpose, objective, or any other synonymous word. There is some state
of affairs that he desires. Of course, this state of affairs may be the same
one that presently exists for him. He may simply be striving for maintenance of the *status quo.* In either case, the decision is made to accomplish some purpose.

What does such a decision involve? The executive chooses an action
which he believes will help him most to obtain his objective. This action
will take the form of some kind of utilization of his own efforts and any
resources that he controls. If there is only one course of action available
to him we do not usually speak of a decision problem because the word
"decision" implies choice. Therefore, his decision will consist of the
specific utilization of particular resources that he controls, selected
from among all resources that are available to him. For convenience we
shall call any such specific utilization of resources under the decision-
maker's control a *strategy.* His decision will consist of the selection of
one of his available strategies.

Recognition of the notorious fact that we do not always achieve our
objectives, despite our best efforts in that direction, leads to another
question: Why may the executive not achieve his objective? The answer
is evident. Certain factors that affect the achievement of objectives are
outside his control.

There are two main classes of such factors. The first is the frequent
intransigence of society and nature. For example, an umbrella manufacturer, faced with the decision problem of how many umbrellas to make
for the coming season, knows that the final outcome of his decision will
depend in large measure on the weather conditions that occur—a factor

outside his control. Similarly, the executive of a small company that uses a basic raw material can scarcely influence the eventuality of a strike in the suppliers' industry which might close down the company. Generally, there are a great number of possible combinations of (natural) uncontrollable factors that can occur. For simplicity, we shall refer to any specific one of these *combinations* as a *state of nature*.

The second class of uncontrollable factors is the *competition of rational opponents*. For example, the final outcome of an executive's decision to capture a larger share of the market will usually be affected by actions his competitors take to frustrate his hopes. The same effects are apparent in military problems. Generally, there are a great number of different possible competitive actions. Since the specific one that does occur is usually the result of a rational decision process on the part of the competition, it will be convenient to treat these uncontrollable factors as *competitive strategies,* rather than as states of nature. Most managerial decision problems involve both kinds of factors simultaneously.

Our logical analysis has suggested that we formulate the decision problem in these terms: The decision-maker wishing to achieve some *objective* selects a *strategy* from among those available to him. This strategy, together with the *state of nature* that exists, and the *competitive strategy* that occurs, will determine the degree to which his objective is obtained.

21/ The Decision Problem

If this theoretical skeleton of the decision situation is at all reasonable, then it should fit the flesh of actual decision problems. Does it? Let us consider some simple (but realistic) examples in terms of our logical analysis.

A farmer has a plot of land and he has the objective af achieving the largest profit from it. His available strategies might consist of a variety of crops, any of which he can plant—wheat, corn, soybeans, oats, sugar beets and—no crop. His selection from among these strategies is wholly within his control and will constitute his decision. Further, the profit actually obtained will depend not only on the crop he plants but also on a number of factors that are outside his control. Weather is one important example and market price is another, although governmental supports may diminish the importance of this second factor to a considerable degree. It seems that the farmer's decision problem fits our model without much forcing.

The decision problem of an executive responsible for raw-materials inventory is similar. He might have the same objective as the farmer, which is to attain the largest possible profit. His strategies would include various amounts of inventory that he could maintain. Numerous significant factors that will determine the amount of profit actually achieved are outside his control: future availability and price of raw materials, demand for the finished products, competitive actions, general state of the economy, and so on. His success will depend on the strategy he selects and the state of nature and competitive strategies that actually occur. It appears, again, that the simple framework we have developed fits an actual decision problem.

Up to this point we have tried to discover a suitable framework for describing the general decision problem. In quest of this framework we examined the input-output model and briefly reviewed a number of approaches to the decision problem that have been used by different fields of study. We have not yet considered the basic question: How should the manager *select the one strategy* he will use from among all the strategies that he is considering? In other words, how does he make his decision?

22/ *Objectives and Utility*

The idea of utility introduced by economists proved to have general appeal to decision theorists. When utility is used as a measurement of *the degree to which satisfaction is obtained,* then (at least in theory) a number of alternatives can be compared to determine which choice yields the greatest amount of utility. Since satisfaction is not easily measured, a convenient transformation of terms changes the word "satisfaction" into the word "objective." This results in the statement that utility is a measurement of *the degree to which an objective is obtained.* If the degree of achievement of the objective can be stated in quantitative terms, then alternative choices can be compared with each other. Of course, the supposition made is that satisfaction is directly proportional to the level of attainment of the objective.

Some objectives are either attained or they aren't—with no intermediate possibilities. Examples can be found in many games. The objective in chess is to win, and, as the saying goes, "Close only counts in horseshoes." But the more general—and less frivolous—decision problems usually have objectives of such nature that there are vast numbers of degrees of achieving them. This is certainly true of such business objectives as profit or share of market.

An executive may have the objective of attaining $1 million gross profit. Naturally, he will be delighted to actually achieve $1.2 million and he may not be too disappointed if he only gets $950,000. In this case, there are an enormous number of possible amounts of profit which he might obtain. The fact that his objective of 1 million is expressed in dollars makes it simple to use the actual dollar profit to measure the degree of achievement. Similar remarks can be made about the objective of achieving some specific share of the market.

But, as previously noted, not all organizational objectives are of this nature. Some are like the game of chess. For example, management involved in a proxy fight for control can have numerous available strategies and there may be many possible states of nature and competitive strategies that affect the final outcome. This is a genuine decision problem that fits our framework. Yet there is only a "yes" or a "no" in terms of achievement of objective. Either management succeeds in retaining control or it fails.

Many organizational objectives have a broad spectrum of possible degrees of achievement but lack a means for measuring them. For example, an important objective in some decision problems may be to achieve and maintain good labor relations. Obviously there are degrees of goodness in labor relations, but how can they be measured? An administrator may have the personal objective of maximum job security. This clearly has degrees also. But how can they be measured?

We have described a range of possibilities. At one extreme, the objective may be achieved or not, with no intermediate possibilities (like a baseball team trying to win the pennant). At the other extreme are objectives that permit a whole range of possible degrees of achievement (like the attendance at a museum). For some objectives there are natural ways of measuring the degree of achievement (counting, weighing, etc.); for others there does not seem to be any obvious way to measure this degree.

23/ Forecasts and Control

Certain elements (or variables) of any input-output system can be controlled by the decision-maker. The executive's strategy is a plan of control for these variables. The reason for controlling variables is to attempt to achieve objectives. *Good strategies* must include the *right variables,* which means those variables that determine the degree of attainment of the objective. There are many examples of situations in which either the wrong variables are controlled, or not enough of the right ones are considered.

The fact that a number of variables do not lend themselves to managerial control does not mean that they should be ignored. On the contrary, it is a *management responsibility to examine all noncontrollable variables that affect the attainment of the objectives.* Although the manager cannot exercise control over these variables, he can make *forecasts* about them. The farmer can analyze records of temperature and rainfall to estimate the kind of weather he is likely to experience. The executive in charge of the raw-material inventory can read reports, talk to informed people, observe the actions of other companies that stock the same raw material, and study the history of strikes in the industry that concerns him. Usually, both states of nature and competitive strategies can be studied and estimates made to indicate that certain occurrences are more likely than others. Therefore, *a good strategy must provide control of the right set of controllable variables, which (based on reasonable forecasts) promises to cope with the right set of uncontrollable variables.* Good forecasts are seldom easy to make, nor can the methods for obtaining forecasts be quickly explained. Nevertheless, since forecasting is such a basic requirement of decision-making, and such a fundamental procedure of operations research, we must be prepared to delve deeper into this subject.

Forecasts based on the traditional behavior of a system are only useful *if the underlying causes of the system's history are unchanged.* We call this a *stable system,* recognizing that the pattern of stability may be far from simple. In some cases it might exist, but in such complex form that it hasn't been discovered. The pattern must be known (e.g., seasonal fluctuation, growth at a fixed rate of increase, an operating level that is unchanging over time, etc.) if a forecast is to have meaning.

Since forecasting involves procedures that cost money, it must be assumed that a rational manager would expect to get a return that more than compensates him (in some sense) for this expense. One great strength of decision theory is that the *value of information* generated to provide forecasts and support predictions can be compared with the cost of obtaining it. The decision of how much to spend in this way is a decision problem in its own right and is amenable to analysis—as is shown in some detail in Chapter 9.

24/ Functions and Distributions

The managerial objective is a particular kind of a variable. It must be a variable, since if it were a constant, with only one possible value, the executive would have no choice of a value for the objective and no problem to solve. The objective is called a *dependent variable* because the value that it takes depends on the values of the other variables in the system. These other variables, which are called *independent variables,* are the many controllable and noncontrollable factors which we have previously discussed.

A mathematical description of the dependent and independent variables and their relations can be written. At once, it shows both the economy of the compact mathematical form and the advantage of such representation for generalizing any situation. The equation which models this situation is $y = f(x, z)$. The letter x is an abstraction that stands for *all* independent, controllable variables. (It could be order quantities in an inventory study or an amount of fertilizer to be used by the farmer.) Our symbol z represents *all* independent, noncontrollable variables. We associate forecasts with the range of values that the z's take on. (For the inventory example this would be forecasts of demand. The farmer might choose to vary his use of fertilizer according to the forecasts of precipitation.) The dependent variable is y. It is our objective (perhaps cost to be minimized in the inventory problem or yield to be maximized by the farmer).

The equation can be written out in words, *viz.,* the dependent variable y is ($=$) a function (f) of the independent variables x and z, which are, respectively, the controllable and noncontrollable variables. The fact that we write a mathematical equation does not mean that the variables must be quantifiable, for useful information is conveyed by the equation itself. For example, consider the following statement. Customer goodwill is a function of speed of delivery, quality, and price of merchandise, and the customer's relations with our salesmen as compared with those of our competitors. Although this model *lacks quantification* of terms it *provides a systematic view of relations.*

Now let us look at a function which does lend itself to quantitative representation. We can, for example, choose profit as our objective. The generalized function would be: Total profit (p) $= f$[unit sales price (s); unit cost (c); number of items sold (n)], i.e., $p = f(s, c, n)$. In this case, we know the exact function: $p = n(s - c)$.

On the face of it, unit sales price and unit cost are controllable, while the number of items sold (n) is noncontrollable. Actually, we can exercise some control over the sales volume (n), since the number of items sold $= f$(unit sales price). Unit sales price is under our control—so to some extent we can regulate the number of items sold. Looking at unit cost, there is a threshold below which we cannot even manufacture an item. Above the threshold, cost and quality are tightly related. As we cut cost we may impair quality. Also, lower quality can result in a smaller number of items sold, i.e., quality $= f$(unit cost) and, therefore, the number of items sold $= f$(unit cost). Further, unit cost includes advertising and promotion, which means that in yet another way $n = f(c)$.

Most functions are complex in the fashion that we have illustrated above, but that is not all. Some severe accounting problems occur. Unit cost is not obvious; the appropriate measure is difficult to obtain. Fixed costs (such as advertising and administrative overhead) are not easily allocated on a per unit cost basis. Any accountant will be happy to explain why this is so, and illustrate the difficulties with dozens of cases.

It is apparent from our example of the simple profit function $p = n(s - c)$ that *dependencies exist among the independent variables.* The achievement of an objective requires the full consideration of the inter-relationships among independent variables as well as direct relationships that affect the dependent variable. Also, a penetrating understanding of measurement (e.g., accounting) problems is required before any solution can be obtained.

Degree of control is strongly affected by degree of predictability. We may, at best, have the notion that as price goes up the number of items sold goes down. (Of course this is not an inflexible rule since there are cases of items that may increase in sales volume with increasing price. Can you think of one? (See problem 16 at the end of this chapter.) Over a period of time, with an established product-line, the manager will probably have accumulated enough data to plot the relationship between sales price and sales volume. Figure 2.4 depicts a strong relationship with sales volume decreasing as price goes up.

FIGURE 2.4   *Data from past observations indicate that sales volume tends to decrease as price increases.*

The problem here is that each point represents a different month so that some points occur in the spring, which may be the best selling time. Every point has a seasonal component, and *if* seasonal variation is important, that would obscure the relationship between sales price and sales volume. Similarly, competitors' prices in each month may have affected the number of items sold. Many other factors also could influence the relationship under study. The ability to predict sales volume as a function of sales price is determined by the extent to which all the pertinent factors can be taken into account. Seldom can we expect to obtain an exact relationship.

Variables that are essentially noncontrollable can be studied initially by means of simple *frequency distributions*. The use of such distributions can result in surprisingly good forecasts. For example, an executive has collected the (hypothetical) data in Table 2.1 concerning absenteeism. It has been tabulated as a frequency distribution in Table 2.1 and plotted in Figure 2.5.

TABLE 2.1

NUMBER OF TIMES A WORKER IS ABSENT FOR A SINGLE DAY IN A SUMMER MONTH OR WINTER MONTH	NUMBER OF WORKERS WITH THE GIVEN NUMBER OF ABSENCES	
	Summer month	*Winter month*
0	2	368
1	21	368
2	136	184
3	341	61
4	362	15
-5	120	3
6	17	1
7	1	0

The shapes of these curves are well known, the summer chart illustrating a normal distribution and the winter chart showing a Poisson distribution. Many characteristics of these distributions have been carefully studied by the methods of mathematical statistics, and this large

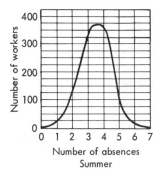 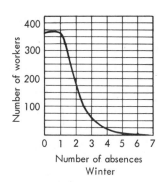

FIGURE 2.5 *A comparison of the number of times a worker is absent for a single day in a summer month and a winter month.*

body of knowledge can be put to work to achieve useful predictions of future expectations.

The *stability* characteristics of noncontrollable variables must be examined before we can put them together with measures of utility, objectives, variables, functions, and distributions in an integrated decision-theory framework. As was previously mentioned, data that are used to make forecasts and predictions are *always assumed to be derived from a stable process.* The distribution is said to describe a particular situation that holds constant throughout the period in which the data are collected and, of course, into the period covered by the forecast. Sometimes a frequency distribution gives *evidence* that a change took place during the period of observation. For example, the *bimodal* distribution shown in Figure 2.6 could have come from a process that produces such bimodal

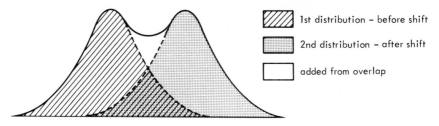

1st distribution – before shift

2nd distribution – after shift

added from overlap

FIGURE 2.6   *The bimodal distribution can arise from an unstable process.*

forms. On the other hand, it might represent two aspects of an unstable normal distribution where a shift took place during the period of observation. Predictions and forecasts based on unstable processes (where this fact is not known) can lead to serious mistakes.

25 / Maximization Principles

We are now prepared to examine the appropriate sequence of steps for the decision-maker to follow:

1. **Choose the objectives;** specify its **dimension** and **value.**

2. **Isolate all of the variables** that are **pertinent** to the attainment of the objective value, i.e., the relevant **independent** variables.

3. **Develop the relationships** that exist between the **independent** variables.

4. **Distinguish controllable variables** (which can be part of the strategy) **from noncontrollable variables** (classifying the latter as either states of nature or competitive strategies).

5. **Develop forecasts and predictions** for the **noncontrollable** variables, which should be treated as states of nature. Those variables which have (rational) intelligence behind them must be treated separately by game theoretic methods.

6. **Determine whether the forecasts and predictions** are based on **stable processes.** This determination can be intuitive but powerful methods of statistical quality control are available to assist.

7. **Develop the function that relates** the **independent** variables to the **dependent** objective variable.

8. **State the restrictions** that limit the possible values of **controllable** variables.

9. **Choose those values of the controllable variables** (i.e., that strategy) which promise to **maximize the degree of attainment** of the objective, within the limits set by the restrictions.

In step 1 above, we stated that a specific dimension and value should be chosen for the objective. For example, our objective may have the dimension of dollars of profit, and the chosen value of profit might be $500,000. Frequently it is not feasible to select a specific numerical value for the objective. Sometimes it is not even desirable. An alternative formulation is to substitute for the numerical value the requirement of a "best possible," or *optimal* value. Where the objective is a variable measured along a continuous scale, the distinguishing property of an optimal value will be direction. In other words, optimal will sometimes be the greatest possible or *maximal* value, while at other times it will be the least possible or *minimal* value.

Although it may be reasonable to select $500,000 as our profit objective, the manager would be overlooking the possibility that his company's profits might be greater. The difference between $500,000 and some larger attainable value would be an *opportunity cost.* This cost of foregone opportunity should be minimized for an optimal solution. *Opportunity costs, which we shall discuss again, are penalties suffered for not having done the best possible thing.* So, although it is perfectly reasonable to choose that strategy which will result in $500,000 profit, this type of approach is seldom likely to produce an optimal decision.

Optimal decision procedures can always be stated as a maximization problem. The quantity being maximized is the degree of attainment of the objective. Let us consider three cases. The *first case* requires no translation: Our objective is profit and we wish to maximize it. The *second case* is more complex: Our objective is to achieve some in-between scale value which is associated with a zero opportunity cost. Here are a few examples of situations where neither of the extremal points of a scale are desirable. (a) The most comfortable height for a car seat is (say) 14″. (b) 98.6 degrees is the optimal body temperature. As temperature increases or decreases from that standard, there are increasingly severe opportunity costs. (c) The optimal balance between acid and base in a carbonated soft drink is a neutral solution (i.e., pH = 7). (d) A want ad reads: Applicants for the police force should be between the following ages —— and heights ——.

In all of these cases, *deviations* from the ideal must be measured and should be minimized—which leads us to the *third case.* The dimension is cost (either type—real or opportunity) and we want to minimize the cost value. This problem is equivalent to maximizing $(K - \text{cost})$ where K is any number including zero. For example, assume that we wish to minimize the (real) cost of selling a certain product. As we find ways to lower this cost we increase the degree of attainment as measured by $(K - \text{cost})$. The minimum cost for selling the product represents the maximum attainment of the transformed objective. It is also the point at which *zero opportunity cost* occurs (i.e., "best" real cost—actual real cost). We note, however, that it is not the point of zero real cost. The nonoptimal, minimum real cost is zero. But under normal circumstances zero real cost means that no product can be made at all. This is certainly not a reasonable objective, whereas zero opportunity cost is. Therefore, the minimization of real cost is not a sensible objective until *restrictions* are placed on the means for obtaining it. In the same way, maximum dollar profit is seldom desired at the expense of goodwill, future profits, or a jail sentence.

Restrictions are a natural part of a complex objective. All real objectives are complex, because they never involve just one dimension. Whenever we say that we wish to attain some end, we do so with all kinds of if's, and's, and but's. However, it isn't an easy matter to visualize and enumerate the total set of objective dimensions at the outset of a problem. As much as possible, step 1 should specify multiple objectives. But step 8 takes into consideration the fact that certain objectives (i.e., restrictions) become apparent only *after* the full set of relationships among variables has been investigated.

Generally speaking, *degree of attainment can be maximized for only one objective at a time.* In other words, if we wish to maximize sales volume we can seldom expect to maximize profit or minimize cost at the same time. That is why we speak of *an objective* and *restrictions.* To illustrate: maximize sales volume subject to the restriction that profit does not fall below P_1, or that profit falls between P_1 and P_2.[1]

---

[1] In linear programming problems, the dependent objective variable has a symmetric relationship with another, different variable, which is automatically minimized when the objective is maximized, and vice versa. This characteristic is known as

Step 5 requires that variables belonging to states of nature should be separated from variables belonging to intelligent competitors. The reason for this is that all competing decision-makers are trying to maximize their respective degrees of attainment. Problems of conflict between rational opponents require special methods which are treated by the *theory of games*. If it is possible for a company to determine that its competitors will not behave in a rational manner, then competitive strategies should be treated as states of nature, where forecasts and predictions will be most valuable. The *value of information* for forecasting and predicting (obtained, for example, through espionage) becomes of paramount importance. Under many circumstances, if the competitor is rational no forecast is required and analysis in game theory terms is essential. This approach is particularly important when competitors are striving for identical objectives, e.g., increasing brand share. In any case, it is always important to remember that others may be trying to achieve maximization at our expense. We are seldom alone in choosing strategies and the decisions of others can seriously affect our own attainments.

PROBLEMS

1. Develop the input-output model for an electric typewriter. How does this differ from a mechanical typewriter? What control is exercised over the inputs? What feedback exists? Transform the output into the input of a corresponding system.

2. Develop the input-output model for a warehouse. Assume that the decision to reorder is made by an executive in the company's main office, which is 300 miles away from the warehouse. Design an automatic regulator to relieve management of this reorder function. How will exceptions to the procedure be handled?

3. Management has three brand names picked out for a new product, four different package designs, and four different advertising campaigns. How many different strategies are being considered? What possible states of nature could affect the choice? To what extent can competitive strategies be taken into account?

4. Using the data of Table 2.1 and Figure 2.5, draw the distribution that would apply to the fall season if the change between seasons were regular and continuous. Under these assumptions would spring and fall be the same? How many extra workers would you hire in the summer if demand for the product were constant throughout the year? How do these considerations relate to the decision framework?

---

duality. In general, the dual variable provides information about an economic aspect of the problem that might not ordinarily be considered, but which is exceedingly useful. See p. 549 for relevant discussion of this point.

5. As far as possible, apply the nine steps of the decision-maker's sequence to the following situations: management must either build a new plant or expand their present facilities; a company must replace a sales manager who is retiring; repeated complaints of bad service are received by a department store; top management requests a full report on the possibilities of bidding for government contracts; the governors of three states must agree on a site for a new airport.

6. A company that has one plant produces a variety of items for sale to the public. Their situation is conceptualized in the diagram below:

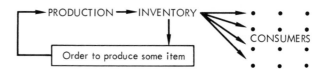

The responsible manager establishes policies which determine when an order shall be transmitted to the production department, which will require the fabrication of a specific item in a given quantity. The procedure is very much like the furnace-thermostat feedback system discussed in the text. The established policies usually require that an order be made when the inventory of an item falls to a certain level. The policy also establishes how much shall be produced. In analogy to the furnace-thermostat example, these two levels are equivalent to the temperatures at which the furnace will turn on and off.

    a. What objectives are involved in the decisions setting these two levels?
    b. Suppose demand for some item has large fluctuations around an average which is constant for a long period of time. How does this affect the levels?
    c. Suppose demand has very small fluctuations around its average but that the average is increasing steadily. How does this affect the levels?
    d. What if one item has extremely high labor costs. How does this affect the levels?
    e. Under what conditions will the inventory carried be eliminated?

7. Classify the following objectives according to whether there are degrees of attainment and whether the degree of attainment is measurable:

    a. A salesman's objective of increasing his sales enough to win a company prize.
    b. A financial executive's objective of obtaining a $1,000,000 bank loan.
    c. A salesman's objective of obtaining a large account.
    d. A salesman's objective of making a large nonrepeat sale to a customer.
    e. An organization's objective of achieving a required minimum percentage of employee participation in a health insurance program.
    f. A hospital administrator's objective of achieving the lowest possible labor turnover.
    g. An advertising agency's objective not to lose clients.
    h. The same agency's objective to gain new clients.
    i. The research department manager's belief that pure research should constitute at least 10 per cent of the R & D budget.

j. The president's announced intention to reduce government work from its present level of 80 per cent of the company's annual revenue.

8. Are there many organizational situations that you can think of which involve feedback? Name some and describe these operations.

9. How many different objectives can you think of which a sales manager might have? How many are quantifiable with regard to degree of attainment?

10. From the standpoint of advertising policies the totality of potential customers constitutes a black box. We have advertising as input and demand as output. Thus:

The effect of advertising depends on the unknown circuitry of the black box. In order to determine advertising policies we would like to know something about the effect of the input-advertising on the output-demand. If we really know nothing about the black box circuitry we can only get information by varying the input and then observing the output.

a. We can change the input or not change it, and the output can either change or not change. Thus, there are four possible combinations. Without saying anything about the size or the direction of the changes involved, what can you conclude (if anything) from each of the four possible cases?

b. Suppose the output changes in the same direction as the input but that very large input changes produce only small output changes. What does this imply?

c. Suppose the circuitry is very complicated and there is a considerable time delay before changes in input show up in the form of output changes. Suppose, further, that this time delay is unknown. What effect does this have on our reasoning? What mistakes might it produce?

Consider the analogy of controlling water temperature when taking a shower. Suppose the pipes leading to the shower are so long that ten seconds are required before a change in the amount of hot water reaches the shower. Now suppose you are impatient and only wait five seconds. What will happen?

d. In terms of this model, what is wrong with the policy of setting a regional monthly advertising budget as a percentage of the preceding month's sales for the region?

11. *Clonus* is defined as "a forced series of alternating contractions and partial relaxations of the same muscle." An eye twitch, for example, is not under the command of the brain and might be described as a runaway feedback situation. Does this model have any applicability to a business situation? What might it have to do with cybernetics?

12. Construct an input-output feedback model for an airplane under automatic control. Relate this analogy—emphasizing differences as well as similarities—to the activities of:

    a. A medical research department.
    b. A library information recovery system.
    c. A geological team searching for petroleum.
    d. The group in charge of blending paints to obtain "exact" color matching.

13. The new product manager of your company has presented an idea for a chocolate flavored toothpaste. At the product presentation meeting he offered the following rationale, "It just might *go* and the cost to the company of trying it is very low."

"Not so," you said. "You are only talking about the real costs of this attempt versus a failure. What about the opportunity costs?" Would you please explain in more detail what you mean—to the president.

14. My car can go as fast as 120 mph. The speed limit on the highway is 65. What is my opportunity cost if I'm going 50?

15. What function should be maximized if the objective is

    a. To win at bingo.
    b. To keep the house at 68 degrees.
    c. To never carry more than 2 ounces of change in one's coat pocket?

What potential strategies might be available in each case?

16. The product is silverware and Newlyweds, Incorporated has found that the price-sales volume relationship follows the "kinked" pattern illustrated below. The sales manager seems to think that this is perfectly reasonable.

    a. Can you explain why this might be so?
    b. What black box construction could exhibit such input-output characteristics?
    c. Is it likely that observational errors could account for this relationship?

17. How might the charges for computer time at a service center be calculated, taking into consideration the fact that the total demand is highly variable and a function of the per unit time charges, among other things?

Chapter 3

The
Objectives
of
Decisions

As we have seen in the preceding chapter, a rational approach to the decision problem must reflect the manager's objectives. The formulation of the problem stems from the question: Why make a decision at all? And the answer embodies the desire of the executive to achieve some future state of affairs—his objective. He must choose one strategy in preference to all other alternatives and this choice can only be made rationally in terms of the objective. Thus, the *precise formulation of the objective* is the first, major problem facing the manager. Consequently, our first concern will be with the difficulties and problems involved in formulating objectives.

We have already suggested that some objectives seem easy to quantify, others are not quantifiable, and a great number fall in the middle ground between these two types. These differences are important because *the quantitative analysis of a decision problem requires measurement*—a numerical description of each alternative strategy.[1] Only in this way can several strategies be compared. Apart from this consideration there are other paramount issues concerning objectives that require careful analysis. The various ambiguities and difficulties that characterize objectives must be explored to delineate the possibilities of using a rational approach to the decision problem.

[1] This does *not* mean that costs and/or benefits must always be measured. See, for example, "Inventory Problems with Unknown Costs," pp. 328–336.

26/ Goals, Purposes, and Rational Behavior

The formulation of objectives cannot be viewed as independent of some major ethical questions. This might be expected inasmuch as classical philosophy sought to discover the steps to be taken for a *good* life. And what is this idea of the good life if not an objective to be achieved? In fact, the classical conception of rationality was defined as the ability to select *means* to achieve goals or objectives. This line of reasoning was subsequently subjected to serious questioning.

First, extending the definition of rationality led to the interpretation of everything in terms of the purpose it fulfilled. Thus, the argument ran, if one saw a watch, one could infer the existence of a watchmaker. Similarly, if one sees an ear one must infer the existence of an ear-maker (who designed that ear to achieve its purpose of hearing). This is called *teleological* reasoning. Interpretations of this sort were what Aristotle called the "final causes" of the events. Such arguments may have their place in religion and philosophy but they tend to impede scientific analysis. One of Darwin's major contributions was the demonstration that remarkable adaption to environment could result from the interplay of a great number of essentially *random factors*. In short, he showed that it was unnecessary to assume *final* causes to understand the adaptation of organisms to their environments.

Another argument against this approach arose from the *positivistic* movement in science. A human being "introspects" and believes that he has purposefully selected means to achieve his objectives. But it is also easy to assume (similar) purposefulness in the behavior of a hungry rat. Psychological studies have thrown doubt on human purposefulness in at least some situations where humans think they are being purposeful. In any event, positivism in science required that conclusions be based *only on observable evidence*. In psychology this took the form of the ruthless elimination of introspection as a source of valid scientific information. The school of psychology that represented this position to the fullest extreme is known as *behaviorism,* from the fact that only the observable behavior of the subject is studied. (It seems apt to note that someone once said, "behaviorism is being willing to discuss the scratch—but not the itch.") The net effect of the positivistic movement was to strongly prejudice scientists against ascribing rationality to goal-seeking behavior.

27/ Open Systems

Recent developments in science serve to confirm the fact that rationality cannot be identified with purposeful selection of means to achieve desired ends. The biologist Ludwig von Bertalanffy has introduced and extensively analyzed a new class of systems, which he calls "open systems." There are many interesting characteristics of such systems. For our purposes the most important of these is the fact that such a system will *appear* to be goal-seeking, although it is not (in any sense of the word) "rational." Certain chemical solutions provide good examples of open systems. But von Bertalanffy has found even more interesting examples in organisms and higher order organizational systems which are formed of living creatures—for example, human society.

The reason that the system appears to be goal-seeking, despite the lack of pervasive cerebral rationality behind it, is that an *equilibrium* exists among its component parts. Any disturbance of this equilibrium initiates *compensating reactions* which immediately lead to the establishment of a new equilibrium. In other words, the system will *search*[2] for equilibrium *every time its balance is disturbed.*

A great many human objectives can be defined in terms of such equilibrium. To what extent can the search by humans for the satisfactory realization of their objectives be understood in terms of the dynamic equilibrium-seeking process of open systems? This kind of questioning about open systems is not purely theoretical. It has been convincingly demonstrated by W. Ross Ashby, who designed and built a device which he named the Homeostat. Ashby's machine is a complicated piece of electrical circuitry which will hunt for equilibrium whenever it is disturbed. Significantly, it will find equilibrium conditions which were not intentionally built into the device by its maker. Therefore, when the device has achieved a new equilibrium, no one, including the designer, will know what circuits it has completed in order to achieve the equilibrium. Similar devices have now been constructed by others. Some of them exhibit the most disconcertingly "lifelike" behavior while in pursuit of their objectives. And yet *there is no rationality* in any of them. It has become clear, then, that the appearance of rationality does not guarantee the actual existence of an underlying rational choice system.

These remarks may not seem relevant to the study of organizational objectives. However, upon inspection they are not at all far-fetched. The conclusion that one reaches is that an open system will find equilibrium if left alone and undisturbed. However, if the process by which the system achieves equilibrium is continually *disturbed by "rational" efforts*, it may well produce an *inherent instability* and the equilibrium may never be achieved.

The national economy, for example, is an enormously complex or-

[2] Words like search, hunt, remember, and goal-seek can be attributed to purely mechanistic systems in an anthropomorphic fashion because of the *apparent* correspondence between the observable system's actions and those of human beings.

ganization which may well have many characteristics of open systems. A frequently stated national economic objective is the achievement of prosperity without inflation. Since the quantity of money in circulation plays a fundamental role in the state of the national economy, the Federal Reserve System uses its control over the money supply to attempt to achieve the national objective. The means it uses, such as changes in the discount rate, are well known. A number of economists maintain that the rational efforts of the Federal Reserve System are of no avail and are perhaps worse than useless. Some hold that an appropriate policy should be fixed in advance and then adhered to by the Federal Reserve System. In other words, no policy changes should be made because of changing economic conditions. If, indeed, the national economy is an open system, then it would adapt to change while maintaining the national objectives as part of its own search for equilibrium. Consequently, our national objectives would have a better chance of being achieved.

Similar notions can be applied to many types of organizations and their problems. Let us examine an example of a business system that regains equilibrium after it has been disturbed. Consider the case of an established mail-order company which solicits new customers by means of direct mail. (To avoid obscuring the main point we have not introduced random variation in the hypothetical data that follows.) The company mails 800 letters every week and obtains orders from 1 per

TABLE 3.1

Generation of orders of a mail-order house.

Week Number	1	2	3	4	5	6	7	8	9	10	11	12	13	14	15	16
Number of new customers	8	8	8	8	8	8	8	20	20	8	8	8	8	8	8	8
First repeat order		4	4	4	4	4	4	4	10	10	4	4	4	4	4	4
Second repeat order			2	2	2	2	2	2	2	5	5	2	2	2	2	2
Third repeat order				1	1	1	1	1	1	1	2	2	1	1	1	1
Fourth repeat order				—	—	—	—	—	—	—	—	1	1	—	—	—
Total orders	8	12	14	15	15	15	15	27	33	24	19	17	16	15	15	15

cent of the mailing. The repeat-order rate is constant. One-half of each week's new customers reorder in the second week, one-fourth reorder in the third week, one-eighth reorder in the fourth week, and so on. Table 3.1 shows how the generation of orders, composed of new-customer orders and repeat orders, reaches an equilibrium value of 15 orders per day. Now, let us suppose that in weeks 8 and 9 the company experiences an unusually heavy response. This raises the total orders handled for a period of six weeks. At the end of that time, by the fourteenth week, total orders have returned to equilibrium. Figure 3.1 shows how the system gradually returns to equilibrium.

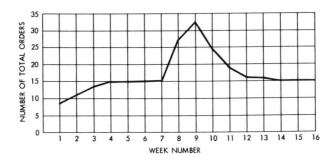

FIGURE 3.1   The system returns to equilibrium after disturbance.

Actually, a system of this type is always being disturbed by random variation in both the number of new customers and the reorder rates. However, if the *random variation* comes from a *stable process,* then the system is continually hunting for its equilibrium value. Should a basic change take place, then the system adopts a new equilibrium value as its *focus,* while continuing to respond to all random disturbances. Management's attempt to maintain total orders at 15 per week by controlling the number of letters mailed or by providing incentives to increase the repeat order rate can result in far greater fluctuation than would occur if the system were left alone. Only when management fully understands *the nature of the system* with which it is dealing can it provide *rational policy decisions* that might improve the performance of the system.

From examples such as this one, we learn that it is not necessarily the case that all objectives can be, or should be, achieved by rational selection of specific means to a given end. If we cannot identify rational behavior by observing the means that are chosen to achieve a particular goal, *can we recognize rationality by examining the objectives themselves?*

28/ Goals of the Individual

Organizational objectives coexist with the objectives of individuals who compose the organization. They are not the same. Our intention is to analyze the way in which objectives at different levels in the organization *interact* with each other. It seems reasonable to begin with the individual—the smallest entity in the organization.

The goals of individuals have been the subject of discussion and debate for many centuries. To say that *happiness is the goal* of the individual (a frequent suggestion) does not solve any problem. We cannot define happiness in operational terms. *Operationalism* is an important, underlying concept of operations research. It implies concreteness, the ability to observe, measure, and analyze. Since an analysis of the operations that must take place or be performed in order to be happy cannot be accomplished, we cannot treat happiness as an operational term. Satisfactory measurements cannot even be made to distinguish between degrees of happiness. Although each of us can testify to the fact that happiness exists, we cannot transform our awareness to concrete terms. Similar problems result from other suggested choices such as *satisfaction,* *contentment,* and *comfort* as fundamental objectives of individuals. Since life is too short to follow the arguments of philosophers in a book that is intended to be operationally useful, we must consider other ways of examining the goals of individuals.

29/ Operational Goals of the Role

People play many roles. *Each role can be associated with its own objectives.* Individuals simplify their psychological problems by establishing multiple decision objectives for themselves, instead of staking everything on just one basic objective. Most people, for example, will establish an objective for themselves in the area of their professional activities. They will have other objectives as well relating to their interpersonal relationships, e.g., the roles of father, husband, and son. They will also have objectives regarding their relationship to society as a whole, e.g., political activity or public-spirited work. They will often have some objectives regarding their leisure activities. And, of course, we can continue and obtain quite a catalogue of the areas in which people are likely to set themselves different kinds of goals.

It appears that most people handle their decision problems in a particular field of activity by ignoring the objectives of other fields of activity. A manager will solve his professional decision problems—for example, what position he will accept—in terms of his career objectives. This does not preclude other influences, but suggests that they frequently act more like *constraints than fundamental objectives.*

Within any single field of activity an individual has many different roles.[3] An administrator reports to his boss and in turn people report to him. His position in the organization determines the extent of his *responsibility* and the range and importance of the decisions he must make. The goal of the administrator is strongly tied to the complex *image* he has of his role within the organization. Although no two managers have identical situations, the similarity of goals which they share as a group allows us to generalize about managerial goals. At the same time, we cannot be blind to the differences. Similarly, we can group employee goals, stockholder's goals, salesmen's goals, and so on. There are certain relevant patterns of goal-seeking within each of these groups which hardly require expansion here. Of great interest are those cases where a significant conflict exists between the objectives of at least two groups to which the individual belongs.

30/ Conflict Between Goals

The manager has various roles and *each role has its objectives.* At the same time, the groups and subgroups to which he belongs have their own organizational objectives. Conflicts between goals can occur in a number of ways: (1) conflicts between the individual's roles, (2) conflicts between group objectives, and (3) conflicts between the individual's role and the group objectives.

Looking at *conflicts of the first type,* an individual cannot confine his attention to the objectives of one field of activities and ignore the other parts of his life. A new position that satisfies a professional objective may entail relocation, which puts stresses and strains on family relationships. In this event, the individual must attempt to weigh his different objectives, one against the other. It is difficult to do this because there is no single, underlying objective that suffices as a means of measuring the unified importance of the different objectives. Nevertheless, people have to resolve such problems many times in their lives. In some "conceptual" way they manage to evaluate their alternatives across a range of objectives. Perhaps this integration is done intuitively in terms of potential for happiness. But even if so, there are serious difficulties and possible contradictions involved in this notion of happiness.

---

[3] For an interesting psychiatric exposition of the variety of roles assumed by an individual see Eric Berne's *Games People Play* (New York: Grove Press, Inc., 1964).

Considering the *second kind of conflict,* an individual can participate in two groups that have conflicting objectives. He may not even be aware of this fact because his roles in each group are not in conflict. This point demonstrates that an individual is not compelled to identify entirely with and share completely the objectives of an organization. Furthermore, he would seldom weight the groups of which he is a member as being of equal importance. For example, an employee who participates in a stock-purchasing plan is part owner of the company in which he works. When this employee demands higher wages, he is, in effect, reducing the dividend which he can receive as a stockholder. Usually, the employee does not consider his role in the ownership group to be as important as his role as an employee. Whenever the individual's role objectives strongly coincide with conflicting objectives of the groups to which he belongs, the result is either conflict between roles (within the individual) or between the individual and (at least) one of the groups. In the latter case, which is *the third type of conflict,* the individual is likely to withdraw from the organization that he feels he is in conflict with. But he may also try to change the conflicting group's objectives.

31 / Suboptimization

If there is no conflict between objectives, the manager can proceed to solve each decision problem separately. As long as the action taken to achieve either objective is independent of the other, he can separate them. However, *when objectives are dependent,* the optimization of one can result in a lower degree of attainment for at least some of the others. This condition is known as *suboptimization.*

For example, an individual may decide to take a new executive position which advances his professional objectives. However, the post entails extremely long hours and much traveling. Although the new job is optimal in terms of the executive's professional objectives, the time he can now spend with his family is sharply reduced. This may have such adverse over-all effects that the executive will find that his optimization *in terms of one objective* has produced a total systems result *in terms of all his objectives* which is much less than optimal.

The notion of suboptimization is also involved in the effects of *time* on the decision problem. We lead our lives through time but have only imperfect ability to foretell the future. Each decision problem must be solved for a foreseeable future based on present knowledge and the situation that currently obtains. However, the action chosen is likely to have effects on the decision-maker's situation for a considerable period in the future. *An optimal action as of today* (and the near future) can turn out to produce *serious suboptimization in terms of a longer period of time.*

Consider, for example, the decision problem of an engineering student who must select a set of courses for his electives. His professional objective is to become as good an engineer as he possibly can, so he decides to use all of his electives on additional engineering courses. *At the time,* this decision appears to be a legitimate optimization of his personal objectives. Some years later the engineer may discover that stultification can result from too narrow specialization and that this may have had serious consequences on his *lifetime objectives*[4] (e.g., his ability to achieve satisfactory interpersonal relationships, his desire to have a well-rounded life, and, surprisingly, even on his career objective of professional advancement). The engineer's decision may have resulted in severely suboptimal conditions upon which to build his future.

Clearly, *we can never really achieve optimization.* Over a period of time, unexpected events can change what may have appeared to be an optimal decision into an inferior one. There is almost no *reversibility* in many important decision systems. By the time we learn that a decision was not a good one, we can no longer return to the state which prevailed before the decision was made. Consequently, decisions must be based on the best possible predictions of future expectations. In addition, *our decision procedures should not commit us to irrevocable commitments for long periods of time.* And so we reach the conclusion that a rational decision process should include the consideration of *sequence.* Such a *sequential decision process* permits maximum *flexibility* with respect to an evolution of both objectives and actions in a quasi-predictable world.

32/ *Bounded Rationality*

We have been using the notion of an "optimum" rather loosely. People rarely make a prolonged effort to achieve the optimum action in any realistic decision problem facing them. To paraphrase John Maurice Clark, *people simply don't have such an irrational passion for dispassionate rationality.* And there are good reasons why they shouldn't. These reflect the exorbitant complexity of many realistic decision problems. Three main aspects of this complexity might be noted.

First, an optimum decision, made at one point in time, is generally suboptimum in terms of subsequent times. Since we are limited in our ability to foresee the future it follows that it is useless to go to extreme

---

[4] Which are likely to have changed since his original decision was made.

lengths to search for the *"most* optimum" decision. It is complex enough to decide *how far to go.*

Second, there are frequently an enormous number of possible choices of actions (strategies). Any attempt to obtain information about all of them would be self-defeating. Consider the decision problem of the executive looking for a new job. Should he attempt to catalogue every available position in the world from which to choose the best one? If he tried he would die of old age before he got all of the necessary information. Furthermore, even as he collected the information *it would change.* While waiting for new opportunities the old ones would disappear. Until when should he defer his decision?

Third, there are virtually innumerable factors outside the control of the decision-maker. These states of nature affect the decision outcome. It would be impossible to list all of them let alone to determine the totality of their effects in order to determine the optimum action. Often *the necessary information just isn't available.* The umbrella manufacturer (generally) would not attempt to examine the effects of limited war, nuclear holocausts, prolonged depression, or an explosion of the sun on the outcomes of his decision regarding the number of umbrellas to make. He must assume some *reasonable kind of natural stability* and act accordingly.

The net effect of the limitations on human decision-making procedures has been observed and neatly summarized by Herbert Simon in his "principle of bounded rationality." According to this principle, human beings seldom try to find *the* optimum action in a decision problem. Instead, they define in a limited sense the ranges of outcomes (that probably could be delivered by their available strategies) which would be *good enough.* Then they select a strategy that is likely to achieve one of the good-enough sets of outcomes. Thus, the executive looking for a new job makes no effort to discover all possible jobs from which to select the optimum one. Instead, he decides in quite broad terms what he wants from a job. His searching will provide him with an adequate range of the things he wants, e.g., sufficient income, satisfactory working conditions, reasonable chance for advancement. He does not try to find the one job that exists somewhere in the world which will give him the *actual, present, over-all* optimum. There is always some new opportunity that may become available tomorrow. How long should he wait—for the three-, five-, or twenty-year optimum? The principle of bounded rationality is a straightforward way to describe the *actual* decision procedures of human beings. This principle succinctly reminds us *not to assume an irrational extreme of rationality.*

It is always questionable whether the optimum procedure is to search for *the* optimum value, and this is a paradox of sorts. Even looking backward, the concept of a personal, lifetime optimum is impossible to measure. Optimums are like Holy Grails; part of their existence is in the seeking. *Because of the nature of values, they may disappear as they are found.* Apparent optimums are encountered which turn out to be like reflections of bent mirrors or partial truths based on transient identifications and evanescent realities. In this sense, bounded rationality, as an approach, may bring one closer to the *ultimate optimum* than direct searches for *immediate optimums.*

This was the essence of the psychotherapeutic position known as Couéism. Emile Coué (born in France in 1857) excited widespread excitement in the 1920's with his notion that "Every day in every way, I am getting better and better." There is evidence that the actual increments were too small. Nevertheless, over time, both individuals and groups may be better off to move in incremental steps of reasonable size toward the perceived and bounded optimum than in giant strides based on long-range perceptions of where the ultimate optimum exists. *The size of a reasonable step and the amount of bounding that is rational are issues that pertain to all decision systems.*

33 / Principles and Maxims: A Reservoir of Heuristics

The difficulties involved in even simple decision problems can appear to be enormous. Yet both introspection and observation indicate that people will attempt to be rational (in the sense of achieving as much as they can) in their selection of actions, despite all the problems. Fortunately, an important source of assistance is available. Aside from outer space, today no one is the first to have to face any specific type of decision problem. Millions of people have known the same types of problems in times past. Society has accumulated an immense store of information concerning the nature of problems, their possible solutions, and approaches to these solutions. This *wisdom* is stored in many forms, including ethical rules, principles, and maxims which warn us to consider certain factors in certain ways—or to proceed at our own risk.

Maxims are no guarantee of success. Often they are *contradictory.* "Look before you leap" says one, but "He who hesitates is lost." At least, both maxims remind us that the speed with which we reach a decision may be an important factor.

Consider Kant's dictum, *viz.,* we should always treat others as ends in themselves rather than as means to our own ends. This suggests that many apparent "optimizing" actions subsequently redound to our disadvantage, i.e., turn out to have been a suboptimization. The Golden

Rule is another codification. It specifies how one should govern his choice of actions, lest he end by suboptimizing his over-all (over time) objectives. Lacking sufficient information about a situation, the Golden Rule ("Therefore all things whatsoever ye would that men should do to you, do ye even so to them . . . ," Matt. 7:12; Luke 6:31) is a good heuristic.[5] The word *heuristic* is derived from the Greek *heuriskin* meaning "serving to discover." The closest definition we can give for it—with respect to current usage—is that *a heuristic is an operational maxim. And by this we mean that it promises the best, potential suboptimization for a variety of circumstances too complex and/or too future to permit total rationality.*

Ethical maxims provide a necessary and powerful pressure that forces us to consider whether our objectives are reasonable. An eight-year-old boy's major objective may be to eat a maximum number of chocolate candies. If one speaks to him of the pleasures of marriage he may ask if it is like eating chocolates. Fortunately, society offers us a great deal of advice to the effect that we should not commit ourselves wholly to the pleasures of eating chocolates, because we may subsequently find that it was not a satisfactory over-all objective.

34/ Summary of the Individuals' Goal-Seeking Characteristics

Let us examine what we have discovered by considering the decision procedures of individuals involved in the business of living.

1. Being unable to satisfactorily describe goals in terms of one objective, **people customarily maintain various objectives.** Each is relevant to some phase of their life activities.

2. **Multiple objectives are frequently in conflict with each other,** and when they are, a *suboptimization* problem exists.

3. A particularly important aspect of the suboptimization problem is **temporal.** At best, we can only optimize as of *that* time when the decision is made. This will frequently produce a **suboptimization when viewed in subsequent times.**

4. Typically, **decision problems are so complex** that any attempt to discover *the* set of optimal actions is useless. Instead, people set

---

[5] Our statement concerning the decision-oriented view of the Golden Rule that appeared in the first edition of this book, in essentially the same form as here, has received attention unexpected by us. See *The New Yorker*, July 21, 1962, p. 68 and Jacques Barzun, *Science: The Glorious Entertainment* (New York: Harper & Row, 1964), p. 176.

their goals in terms of outcomes that are *good enough* (Simon's principle of **bounded rationality.**

5. Granted all the difficulties, human beings make every effort to be rational in resolving their decision problems. As help, they have a great store of past human **experience codified** for them in the form of ethical principles. These **principles, maxims, and heuristics** are such, that adhering to them is no guarantee of success—but they do **afford guidance.**

35/ *Organizational Objectives*

When we consider organizational objectives we find difficulties and solutions that are not unlike those applicable to an individual. Organizations certainly differ from individuals with regard to procedures for achieving rationality, the nature of suboptimization, as well as their guiding ethics. Nevertheless, the organization's problems of formulating objectives are essentially the same as those of the individual.

First, what is an organization? Most business organizations take the form of corporations, which are equivalent to legally created persons. But these fictitious persons are markedly different from real persons in several major respects. They have no appointed number of years and for all practical purposes can be considered to be eternal. The same applies to governmental organizations and other institutions.

Obviously, qualities such as happiness have no relationship to such organizations. Nonetheless, the importance of having basic overriding organizational objectives, as well as the impossibility of formulating a single objective to cover all cases, is clear. Probably the best move is to affirm the fundamental assumption that the organization is a going, continuing, and surviving entity. Phrased in terms of this fundamental objective, every organization strives to survive, to maintain its existence, and to grow.[6]

For the individual, the analog to this organizational objective would be the continuity of his life. But survival is not the all-important objective of most individuals, even though it is a singularly important subobjective. This is demonstrated by the historical fact that literally millions of individuals have given their lives (however reluctantly or cheerfully) for the sake of values and objectives that they held dear.

---

[6] Even in those cases where growth is rejected as an objective, evidence indicates that this disclaimer is suspect. Whether it be growth in prestige, accumulated earnings, power, or in size, Parkinsonian influences are evident. Parkinson states, "Work expands so as to fill the time available for its completion." (*Parkinson's Law*, by C. Northcote Parkinson, Boston: Houghton-Mifflin Company, 1957.)

This point should give us pause in the case of organizations. Perhaps they, too, have more deeply held objectives than simply continuing their existence.

Fortunately, we do not have to analyze this question. Both organizations and individuals are likely to find that the search for one underlying objective is fruitless. Even if the survival objective were accepted, it would provide little help in solving decision problems. The question would still remain: *What state of affairs ensures a continued existence?* The problem of suboptimization over time would be but one of many which would arise to haunt the administrators. For organizations, as for individuals, we find that the maintenance of multiple objectives is a practical necessity, and consequently, an analytical requirement.

36/ Multiple Objectives

As in the case of the individual, the organization will maintain objectives in the different areas of its activities. Peter Drucker lists eight such categories:

> Market standing, innovation, productivity, physical and financial resources, profitability, manager performance and development, worker performance and attitude, public responsibility.[7]

A specific organization entity can ignore any one of these areas—but only at the risk of its future performance in the others. As soon as we recognize the existence of multiple objectives we are faced with the problems of suboptimization. How does this work out in the case of the business organization? Let us follow Peter Drucker in his discussion of what may happen if a business devotes its attention exclusively to profit.

> To obtain profit today they tend to undermine the future. They may push the most easily saleable product lines and slight those that are the market of tomorrow. They tend to short-change research, promotion, and the other postponable investments. Above all, they shy away from any capital expenditures that may increase the invested-capital base against which profits are measured; and the result is dangerous obsolescence of equipment. In other words, they are directed into the worst practices of management.[8]

Any one of the objectives, emphasized to the exclusion of the rest, can lead to equally unpleasant consequences.

---

[7] Peter Drucker, *The Practice of Management* (New York: Harper & Brothers, 1954), p. 63.

[8] Drucker, *op. cit.*, p. 62.

37/ Organizational Problems
of Suboptimization

Under what conditions does suboptimization arise? We can answer that it may arise whenever an action has the effect of improving the outcomes for some objectives while simultaneously impairing the outcomes for others. If the performance of one part of a system (a subsystem) is improved and this results in an impairment of the total system's performance, we have clear evidence of suboptimization.

The best course of action in any specific decision problem is to utilize intuition, experience, and all available methodology to determine whether actions intended for one purpose are likely to have detrimental effects on other objectives. Ultimately, we wish to know how the over-all performance of the system has fared. *When the objectives cannot be measured on the same scale, it is exceedingly difficult to know what to do.* Situations involving conflicting objectives must be approached with full awareness of the fact that a most serious problem exists when it is not possible to express all of the different (but relevant) outcomes in terms of a *single utility* measure.

Fortunately, many organizations' decision problems can be framed in terms of dollars. Clearly, however, it is by no means the case that *all* organizational objectives can be expressed in monetary terms. If, to take an instance, employees' attitudes could be measured in dollars, then all outcomes affected by their attitudes could be expressed in terms of this single scale. The over-all objective might then be stated as the maximization of profit. We would not require special (nondollar) descriptions of employee morale, satisfaction, and general attitude. While no easy solution to our problem exists, we do have some procedures for dealing with such problems.[9]

Looking at the bright side, there are many important decision problems that involve objectives which are measurable on a single scale. For these we can optimize the total system's outcome without fear of producing a serious suboptimization. At the minimum, an organization should attempt to optimize its situation by improving the individual attainment of *each* of its specific objectives—in such a way that none of the other objectives are adversely affected. This construction is a variant of an idea introduced (in a somewhat different context) by the Italian economist and sociologist, Vilfredo Pareto.[10]

[9] See for example, Chapter 9, p. 236*f*.
[10] Born in Italy, 1848.

Pareto was concerned with the problem of what principles should govern the actions of society if it is assumed that the utilities of the individuals composing the society cannot be compared. By *utility* we mean the subjective value that each individual subscribes to the various goods and services available. Under these circumstances, society cannot act to achieve the greatest total utility because each individual's utility is unlike that of his neighbor. *Pareto suggested that society should try to achieve a condition such that each individual had the maximum utility possible without subtracting anything from anyone else's utility.* In other words, if society can act so as to increase one·individual's utility without taking anything away from anyone else, then it should do so. A condition where this has been accomplished is known as *Paretian optimality*.

The Pareto problem arises because there is no common standard or measure of value between individuals. And this is analogous to the problem of *multiple objectives* with which we are dealing. Our problem exists because there is no uniform and universal measure of value for the various objectives. If there were one common measure (or dimension) we could formulate a single objective rather than several. Therefore we can state (with Pareto) that organizations should at least attempt to achieve a condition of Paretian optimality with regard to their various objectives. This is a legitimate goal for both individuals and organizations; yet we can easily sense the difference that exists between them in application.

We have seen how the problem of temporal suboptimization arises for individuals. This is also true of organizations and precisely for the same reason: the limited ability to foretell the future. It must be emphasized that although the ability to forecast is limited, it does, nevertheless, exist. The decision to build a new factory requires knowledge of future sales, economic trends, costs of land and of building, and so on. The location chosen, the design of the building, the dates of construction, and many other factors taken together represent the opportunity to optimize if we could only predict the future. However, with imperfect predictions we must suboptimize. Similar statements can be made for hospitals, universities, libraries, theaters, thruways, and reservoirs.

Let us consider another illustration. Many companies manufacture products that are on the drawing boards years in advance. As much as possible, they would like to *reserve judgment on design commitments* that would inexorably fix the nature of the product. To the greatest extent that it is feasible, *decisions are made that permit a broad range of eventualities.* In this way, the degree of suboptimization can be improved over time, thereby *permitting a gradual approach to an over-all optimum.* The same reasoning applies to short- and long-range organizational planning. *If a short-range planning decision does not permit sufficient eventualities to emerge in the long-range plan, then it creates a static suboptimization, which cannot be improved upon.*

Business organizations are subject to still another kind of suboptimization problem. Whereas a real person is an entity that cannot be segmented (except in psychiatric terms) the *fictitious person* of the business corporation is usually made up of a number of departments, divisions, and branches. The successful functioning of the business demands the *integration* of the efforts of the various units that compose it. The achievement of enterprise objectives is based on the way that the various departments, divisions, and branches achieve their own objectives. By the very nature of things, the segments are likely to have considerable *autonomy*, and it can happen that the objectives they set are not in accord with the over-all objectives of the organization. The actions of one department generally have some effect on other departments. An optimal strategy for one division (in terms of its own objectives) can deleteriously affect other departments and, hence, the entire enterprise. Both of these situations represent typical variants of the suboptimization problem.

Examples of these problems are legion. Lack of accord of objectives is a major organizational problem. For example, an administrator, on doctor's orders, may accept a newly imposed objective of peace, quiet, and the avoidance of stress. This could easily be out of phase with the firm's objectives. A salesman's objective of maximizing his income may be in poor accord with the company's desired product mix or with the (long-term profit) requirement to devote time and attention to prospective customers. At yet another level, a research department can devote 90 per cent of its time to short-range projects so that its record of immediate achievement is impressive. This may be perfectly all right, but what happens if the competition does not have a similarly short-range point of view? Ultimately, the research department's short-term emphasis will cause extreme hardships for its own organization.

Suboptimization problems are very common and can be significantly harmful. We consider it worthwhile to present a more detailed example of how this kind of situation occurs. The example that we shall describe will illustrate a lack of organizational accord with respect to *inventory policy objectives.*

Assume that a leading chemical manufacturer has ten plants located at different places in the country. Four of the plants are large, four are of medium size, and two are small. Each plant requires many thousands of different spare parts. A supply of parts is stored at a warehouse adjacent to each plant. Management decides that the capital investment in spare parts is large enough to warrant doing a methodological analysis of inventories. Their objective is to minimize the total cost of inventory by taking into account the *costs associated with carrying inventory and the penalties for being out of stock.*

In the course of the analysis each plant manager is asked to specify how often each part can be allowed to go out of stock, i.e., one time out of ten demands, one in a hundred, one in a thousand.[11] The allowable outage rate is sometimes called the *alpha-level*.[12] The plant managers do their best to group all spare parts into alpha-level classes. Some parts are assigned an alpha-level of 0.001, others 0.01, and so on. *The criterion the manager uses in assigning parts to alpha-classes is the importance of the part to his operations as contrasted with the cost of stocking the part.* A part that is costly to carry, and which is not crucial to maintaining production, would be assigned a high alpha-level, such as 0.5 or even 1.0. (The value of 1.0 would mean that the part was never kept in stock and was always obtained as needed.)

We can assume that the *plant managers* will rate all parts that are in common use in about the same way. It will then fall upon *central management* to introduce differences in the alpha-level estimates based on the *relative importances of the various plants to the enterprise.* The alpha-level represents the permissible frequency with which parts can be out of stock. But the loss of goodwill and/or production that results from an "out-of-stock" in a small plant will usually be less costly to the enterprise than would be the case for one of the large plants. For example, central management might say: Our large plants are four times more important to us than our small plants. Consequently, large-plant customers account for more of our dollar volume than customers of small plants. Also, to shut down the production unit of a large plant—because of a spare part outage—would reduce output far more than a similar small-plant outage. Therefore, we might adjust the small-plant alpha-levels, say by multiplying them by four. This serves to increase the permissible frequency for small-plant outages.

Now, what does this mean to the small-plant manager? It means that he will be out of stock four times more frequently than the manager of the large plants. Is he not justified in asking: *Will central management always remember why I am out of stock more often than the large plants?* Will top management forget the underlying reasons and use my repeated outages to reinforce their belief in the greater competence of large-plant managers? Will this system spoil my chances of becoming a large-plant

---

[11] He might prefer to specify allowable outages per time period, e.g., once in a year, once in five years, etc. This can be converted to allowable outages per demand. The manager seldom has any conclusive way to assign these designations, but he usually does have an intuitive feel about them.

[12] See pp. 209–211 and compare with the Type I errors discussed there.

manager? After considerable soul-searching the small-plant manager finds an answer that satisfies his conscience as well as his desire to look as good as the next fellow. He decides to *inflate* his forecasts of demand. In other words, he protects himself from going out of stock more often than the others by indicating greater demands than he actually expects. When the alpha-level modified by central management is applied to this *inflated figure* the result may be that the manager of the small plant will go out of stock even less frequently than the manager of the large plant. Within his own organization he is certainly more respected than would be the case if he had to explain to the sales department and to his production men why they must go out of stock so often.

Let us consider further why the managers rated their respective alpha-levels in the same way while central management did not think that this was so. Was central management wrong? No, *central management was attempting to estimate the relative penalties to the enterprise as a whole* for being out of stock at each location. To accomplish this it was necessary to adjust the managers' estimates. On the basis of company-wide information they were in a position to do this, whereas the plant managers were *too localized to have the necessary perspective.* The only way that the managers could have derived the same results as central management would have been if they knew the actual cost to the *integrated company* of being out of stock at each location. Without *enterprise data* no one plant manager could succeed in correctly characterizing the total system.

The cost of carrying stock will not be identical for each location, but it is likely to be nearly the same. On the other hand, *the out-of-stock cost will differ markedly, depending on the amount of goodwill sacrificed by not filling an order and the size of the production unit that might have to close down if a single part is missing.* Specifically, the out-of-stock cost of the large plant is likely to be much larger than that of the small plant. Common sense suggests, and analysis verifies, that this means that the large plant should be out of stock less often than the small plant. Central management designs the alpha-levels to reflect this fact and approximates the optimal solution by weighting the alpha-levels according to the relative importance of each plant.[13] Generally the individual plants would not be able to do this. However, even if they were able, the small-plant manager would hardly be reconciled to the fact that he would lose more customers than his colleagues without the positive support of a progressive central management.

At the expense of digression, we have gone into this inventory situation in some detail. It is a clear-cut case of an organization attempting

---

[13] Note that it is assumed here that the true costs of being out of stock are not known, as is often the case in practice.

to optimize across all of its components. *Enterprise optimization* is often achieved to the disadvantage of the small plant. It is only natural that the small-plant manager would try to conceive of a strategy to offset the loss he would otherwise have to take. The small-plant manager's strategy is to optimize his own position and his plant's position first. The result of this conflict of objectives is suboptimization.

We have illustrated how suboptimization can occur between one part of an organization and the over-all organization. Let us now consider suboptimization where two parts of a company are in conflict with each other. For example, a division's objective of achieving the best possible profitability record may lead it to purchase parts from competitors rather than from another division of the same company. This may lower the profitability of the division that normally supplies these parts. As another aspect of the inventory problem, a sales manager's objective of maximizing sales may lead him to want a large inventory so that all orders can be filled promptly. This is likely to be in conflict with the controller's objective of tying up a minimum of capital in inventory. *Which one of these objectives is in the best interests of the business?* As a final example, a production manager may decide to use less steel by reducing the upper tolerance limit of a machined part. The foreman provides a new machine setting. This results in a greater number of pieces that are too short. The rejects are discovered at the final assembly. Eventually, *having lost track of the original causes,* a complete redesign of the product may be required with no appreciable gains in cost or quality.

These examples serve to demonstrate the crucial importance of the suboptimization problem. Being aware of the situation, we must rely on *uncommonly* good common sense to help us to discover which way to proceed. Fortunately, many suboptimization problems are not totally intractable. They can at least be approached by new methods and deeper understanding of organization and systems theory. For example, the conflicting interests of the sales manager and the controller, with respect to inventory, can generally be resolved by expressing all relevant factors as costs measured in dollars. Then the decision problem can be solved in terms of a single, unified business objective, *viz.,* the minimization of costs.

This simple statement makes the difficult seem easy. To remove this illusion we need only recall the problems of the small-plant manager. How can we express the loss of dignity that he experiences as a result of being out of stock more often than he would like? Similarly, how do we represent the loss of customer goodwill that results from being unable to deliver an item that the customer wants immediately? How do we evaluate the lack of a hospital bed or the added value of each additional library book? Despite the enormous difficulties, sometimes, these kinds of problems can be satisfactorily resolved. The future promises an ever-better track record.

38/ Bounded Rationality of the Organization

Simon's idea of *bounded rationality holds for organizations* just as much as, and perhaps even more than, it does for individuals. *First,* suboptimization problems arise because the situational complexity forces boundaries to be placed on the size of the system to be studied. For many decision problems it is necessary to assume that the action taken in one department will have no significant effect on another department. Yet we know full well that an organizational entity is a *functioning whole* and that adjustments in one area will almost always have at least some effect on other areas of the enterprise. In spite of this, the assumption of independence is usually made, and successfully. Every factor cannot be considered in a problem precisely because of the limitations of human rationality.

Second, there are sharp constraints on the availability of information needed to resolve a decision problem. *The cost of collecting, sorting, analyzing, and synthesizing information operates as an immediate constraint.* It is said that many sales promotion and advertising problems would have better solutions if detailed information were available about the sales of competitors by regions. Since this information is rarely available with any degree of accuracy we have to do as well as we can without it. Laboratory experiments, test markets, and the like are specifically designed to overcome whatever handicaps follow from information scarcity.

Third, sometimes the reverse holds; there are *enormous excesses of information* that cannot be sorted, classified, and processed in any economic sense. We have Census tapes of demographic data, financial reports, Public Health data, Bureau of Labor statistics, stock market records, store audit reports, and piles of other kinds of information which (at the minimum) have some peripheral value. How does one go about squeezing out that value? *Information inundation can be quite as debilitating as information scarcity.* Consider, for example, the promotional problems of a large mail-order house. Such an organization typically will have huge masses of information in its files concerning the addresses of past customers, what they bought, how they made payment, and various other data. Quite possibly, the accurate formulation of promotional decisions would benefit from the analysis of all this information. Yet even the assistance of large-scale computers may not prevail over the costs of programming and extracting meaningful summary data in useful form for the human user bounded in his rationality. Even if data collection and its processing were free, who would have the time to study the many thousands of results? *It is understandable that most frequently we settle for small bits and sampled pieces of the total available information.* This we blend with informed judgment, some belief in ourselves, and a sanguine hope for the best.

Fourth, there is usually an incredibly large number of possible states of nature, to say nothing of competitive actions. *No decision problem could begin to be formulated if the attempt were made to include all of these possibilities.* Almost any change in the economy, or in national and international affairs, influences the future behavior of the enterprise. Perturbations such as these mean that the search for an optimum solution of any specific decision problem ultimately must yield a *less than optimal result because some of the critical factors are not taken into account.*

Therefore, the organization is as realistic as the individual decision-maker. It is not likely to direct its executives to strive for an optimum in the total sense. Instead, a group of situations that are good enough will be selected and satisfaction will be realized when a reasonable sub-optimization is obtained. In other words, the organization will attempt to *minimize the opportunity costs of the enterprise* within the framework of the bounded rationality of the executive council.

39/ Principles and Policies

Fortunately, the organization (just like individuals coping with their personal problems) has a vast store of knowledge available. This knowledge has been abstracted by the members of the management team from the experiences of their innumerable predecessors. These generalizations and rules of thumb function for the organization in the same way that ethical principles serve the individual. And, similarly, these are not laws that can be disproved by a contrary instance. Rather, they are *means of calling attention* to aspects of the decision situation that might be overlooked and to risks that might otherwise pass unnoticed.

Consider, for example, the policy that the current liquid assets should be at least equal to the current liabilities. This policy is not invalidated because some particular corporation can be shown to have ignored it yet to have achieved success and affluence. The *policy* simply *codifies* the fact that many organizations *have run into difficulties* because they ignored this ratio. Another example is the frequently stated policy of large department stores: "The customer is always right." Do they really think that this is true? Far from it. Do they always act as if it were true? Certainly not. It serves, however, to alert the clerks and department managers to the fact that the objectives of the store demand careful attention to customer relations.

In short, it is the exceptions that must be justified, not the principles or policies that traditionally guide the organization's administration.

40/ Summary of the Goal-Seeking Characteristics of Organizations

We can summarize the important aspects of organizational objectives that we have considered as follows:

1. **Organizational goals cannot be described by one simple objective,** but rather with multiple objectives.

2. **Multiple objectives are required to understand** the organization's relationship with the **outside world.** Conflicts between these objectives lead to one type of organizational suboptimization.

3. **Multiple objectives also exist within the organization.** The fictitious entity, which is the organization, is built of many groups and subgroups which are in themselves entities. **The individual is the basic building block of the structure.** Conflicts of two basic kinds occur, but it is quite clear that many variations can appear. Conflicts between the organization and any lesser group are one cause of suboptimization. Conflicts between components of the organization also result in suboptimization.

4. As was the case for the individual, **suboptimization occurs in time.** The relationship of short-range to long-range planning requires that **short-range planning should not destoy the flexibility of the long-range plan.** Short-range planning is certainly suboptimization, but it is decision-making in a framework that is expected to include the opportunity for optimization. **Moving in steps, the suboptimization approaches optimization in the long run.**

5. Organizational decision problems are admittedly very complex. But **organizational objectives do not have the entirely tenuous nature of many individual objectives.** Frequently it is possible to find measurable quantities that represent utility to the organization. The discovery of "true" optimality is no more available to the organization than it is to the individual; nevertheless, it is frequently possible to determine a suitable or allowable degree of suboptimization.

6. The executives of organizations make every effort to be rational in their decisions. They are, of course, affected by bounded **rationality** as are all individuals. However, they have a vast body of past

experience, part of which is codified in the form of policy, to guide them.

Despite difficulties, we all know that managers strive valiantly to achieve rational decisions. No amount of emphasis on the difficulties should ever be permitted to obscure this fact. *Creativity, intuition, know-how, experience*—all these play their role in the decision process. *But the creative burst of insight precedes, it doesn't replace, the rational part of the decision-making process.* To convince others, to evaluate between two different creative insights, to subject the creative insight to the cold light of reason—all these require the weighing and evaluating of alternative strategies in terms of the objectives, the possible states of nature, and the competitive strategies. In other words, the rational decision-making process is called into play. We now turn, in the next chapter, to a consideration of how decision problems can be formulated in a manner that permits a rational approach to their solution.

PROBLEMS

1. What would be the teleological explanation of a severe drop in sales? What would be the positivistic explanation? How would an "open systems" analyst view the loss in sales?

2. Considering the example of the mail-order company, Table 3.1 and Figure 3.1, assume that new customers are obtained in an oscillating pattern as follows: 6, 8, 10, 8, 6, 4, 2, 4, 6, 8, 10, 8, 6, 4, 2, 4, 6, 8, ... Draw the graph of total orders when the repeat-order rate is: First week, $\frac{1}{2}$; second week, $\frac{1}{4}$; third week, $\frac{1}{8}$; . . . . If management can control repeat-order rates, what values should they establish in order to smooth the curve of total orders? (Notice the effect of allowing no reorders in the first, second, and third weeks.)

3. A manager of a supermarket wants to set up a test to determine how to make each aisle section yield optimal profit. In what way is the manager suboptimizing? How serious is the mistake? How can suboptimization between aisle sections be avoided?

4. Two products are manufactured on the same equipment. A decision is to be made concerning the proportion of each product that will be manufactured. Why is this not a genuine suboptimization problem? It is then learned that the wife of the president of the company favors one product over another. Why has the problem now beome a real suboptimization situation?

5. Let the cost of carrying a unit of stock for a period of time be called C_1. This cost is frequently determined by applying the interest rate that can be obtained on capital to the cost of the item plus the cost of storage, insurance, and so on. For example, $\frac{1}{2}$ of 1 per cent, or 0.005 (a yearly interest of 6 per cent), is multiplied by the combined costs of the item, if C_1 is to be determined

on a monthly basis. Therefore, an item with total costs of $100 has a C_1 of $0.50.

Use a 6 per cent interest rate to estimate the carrying costs, C_1. Also estimate the out-of-stock cost per unit for a period of time (called C_2) for the situations described below. Then determine the alpha-level that might apply for each of them, where alpha-level $= \dfrac{C_1}{C_1 + C_2}$.

    a. A new-car salesman.

    b. A used-car salesman.

    c. An airplane manufacturer.

    d. A kite manufacturer.

6. Assume that the ordering quantity specified by the inventory plan of a chemical manufacturer is given by the following formula:

$$Q = x + \frac{10(1 - 2\alpha)\sqrt{x}}{3}$$

where $Q =$ reorder quantity (number of units),

    $x =$ forecasted demand for a specified period, and

    $\alpha =$ alpha-level.

For a particular part, the small-plant manager is given an alpha-level of 0.20. For the same part, the large-plant manager is given an alpha-level of 0.02. By how much should the small-plant manager increase his reorder quantity in order to have the same alpha-level as the large plant? (Give the answer in terms of x.)

7. The sales manager of a tire manufacturer reported to the President that, on the basis of a statistical analysis just completed, the next year's dollar volume had been predicted to reach $40 million. The President said, "I'm not interested in your projections. Next year you will do $55 million of business. That's our objective and I expect you to achieve it." What does this dialogue mean? Whose approach do you subscribe to and why?

8. Frederick W. Taylor is called by many "the Father of Scientific Management." (Note: not Management Science, which traces its course from the 1940's). Taylor painstakingly studied bricklaying and prescribed in a step-by-step fashion the best way he could conceive of performing this activity. Later, time and motion analysts, belonging to the same school of thought, applied Taylor's approach to improve the productivity of many jobs. Yet, inherent in these studies was the ever-present threat of serious suboptimization. Can you explain why this is so and, additionally, what might be done to alleviate this problem?

9. Is a heat-sensing guided missile an example of an open or closed system? How about an amoeba? Explain.

10. An employee of an automobile company owns 300 shares of common stock of that company. For the past five years he has been receiving dividends of $0.90 per share. The union of which he is a member has been pressing the company for wage increases, which in his case would amount to $250 per year. Management of the company claims that the wage hike would necessitate cutting the dividend in half. This would of course decrease the value of the stock

which is presently yielding 4%. Formulating reasonable estimates, how might this employee vote at a union meeting to determine whether or not to demand the wage increase? What type of problem is this? Discuss.

11. You have been asked to prepare a plan for diversification which employs as much sequential decision flexibility as possible. Explain what is expected of you, why it is desirable, and how you intend to go about achieving this objective.

12. When you choose a vacation you generally have multiple objectives in mind. List the most important of these and explain how *you* would go about resolving the conflicts that ensue from attempting to maximize the total utility of your decision.

13. What does Couéism have to do with the statement that "bounded rationality, as an approach, may bring one closer to the *ultimate optimum* than direct searches for *immediate optimums*"? Under what kind of circumstances would this position have particular appeal?

14. Give some examples of contradictory maxims and attempt to defend the fact that both points of view are founded on reasonable grounds. How would you distinguish between maxims and heuristics?

15. Reasoning on the basis of Paretian optimality, how might you move in this direction with respect to the situations described below?

    a. Assigning final course grades to a graduating class of business students. Do your conclusions differ if these are medical students?

    b. The union's negotiations with management are at a standstill. The company is willing to provide higher retirement benefits for the lower wage scales, but lower benefits for the higher wage scales than the union demands. The union membership does not know about this but has already indicated its willingness to go out on strike.

    c. Two competing companies have been spending increasing sums on promotion and advertising in a market whose total volume is fixed and independent of marketing expenditures.

PART II

THE
THEORY
OF
DECISIONS

Chapter 4

The Structure of Decisions

Chapter 2 explained the necessity for some measure of the degree to which an objective is achieved. And in that chapter we noted that some objectives seem to permit only two possibilities: either they are achieved or they are not. Other objectives have a natural measure of the degree to which they are achieved—for example, the amount of profit. And there are still other objectives that seem to have degrees of achievement, but for which there appears to be no straightforward way to measure this degree.

For rational decision-making, we require some kind of measurement. As much as possible, our decision theory will be based on numbers and not on words. Even when numbers seem to be available as a natural consequence of a process, it cannot be taken for granted that they are the right numbers. Therefore, we must investigate in detail the means at our disposal for measuring the degree of attainment of an objective.

41/ *Development of the Payoff Measure*

In our formulation of the decision problem we have suggested that the manager has various possible *strategies* available to him; that he has one or more *objectives* which he is trying to achieve; and that a *state of nature* will occur which, together with the strategy he selected, will determine the degree to which he actually achieves his objective. Another way of saying this is that the manager's selection of a strategy and the occurrence of a specific state of nature will result in a certain outcome.

This outcome will yield some specific utility in terms of the manager's objectives. What we need is *a measure of this utility and it is called,* appropriately, *a payoff measure.*

In dealing with the idea of utility, and its measurement, we are by no means developing a new concept. It was previously mentioned that economists have long concerned themselves with these notions. However, the interest in measuring utility that resulted from various decision-theory applications has led to some new approaches to the problem. We don't need to discuss all of the developments concerning the measurement of utility, but we will need to treat some of them as we proceed.

The first point of importance is that utility must be defined in *subjective* terms. It is the utility of some specific individual or organization, not a common utility held by everyone. This results in problems that concern the comparison of the utilities of different individuals. Various aspects of this problem have led to many developments in economic theory, but for our purpose it is sufficient to note that the problem as stated is not solvable. *There is no way to compare the utilities of different individuals.*

It is worth emphasizing that utility is *defined* in subjective terms. Could it be that the inability to compare the utilities of two different individuals is simply a matter of definition? This is debatable, but in any case we will accept the current consensus that it is impossible to make such comparisons. The impossibility creates no unresolvable problems for decision theory as long as we are concerned with noncompetitive situations, i.e., there are only states of nature at work. However, as soon as we become involved in decision problems where competitive actions are part of the situation we find that the impossibility of comparing utilities of different individuals has some important consequences.

Our second point of importance requires some development. The essence of the matter is that even for those objectives which seem to have a natural measure (profit, for example) it does not follow that the *obvious* measure is a measure of the utility to the decision-maker. In other words, the state of affairs of the decision-maker that finally results (when evaluated in terms of the objective) may have an entirely different utility measure than the natural measure would indicate. This can be readily illustrated.

Suppose someone offers to gamble with you on the following terms: a coin will be tossed; if it comes up heads you will be paid $200, if it comes up tails, you must pay only $100. Now, surely, this is an excellent arrangement for you. We might even suspect the motives (or sanity) of the man who offered you such terms. However, the question is: Would you always accept the offer? It is clear that the amounts of money involved are distinctly in your favor. Half of the time you will win and thereby receive $200 increments. The other half of the time, you will lose, but only $100 increments.

In terms of utility, the question must be phrased: Is the utility that I sacrifice when I lose less than, equal to, or more than the utility I gain when I win? And, as a little thought quickly discloses, *this varies with your circumstances.* If you have a sufficient sum of money so that the loss of $100 doesn't destroy your financial situation you will probably find that the gain in utility when you win is greater than the loss in utility when you lose. (We will call this the *first case.*) Under these circumstances you would probably be happy to indulge in this particular gamble as often as your opponent would agree. But suppose, to take an extreme, that the total amount you have is $100 and you need this money to pay for transportation to the location of a new job which has been offered to you. (We will call this the *second case.*) Under these circumstances you might well feel that the loss of utility which would occur if you lost would be far greater than the gain in utility which would occur if you won.

Now, this little example is a genuine decision problem. To gamble or not to gamble are the two strategies that are available; to win or to lose are the two states of nature that can occur; and the objective is— what? Is it to maximize your total dollars? It appears that we cannot say this because it wouldn't cover the second case. Of course, we could say that this was the objective in the first case and something different was the objective in the second case. But it is certainly more convenient to formulate one objective that will cover either case, and that is easy to do. *The objective in either case is to maximize utility.* Apart from being an elementary decision problem, this example shows that *the utility of dollars is not necessarily the same as the number of dollars.*

42/ *Bernoullian Utility*

The question remains: What is the utility of a dollar and how can we measure it? A famous Swiss mathematician and philosopher, Daniel Bernoulli, had already treated this question in a paper he wrote about 1730.[1] Bernoulli did not approach this problem empirically, i.e., by measuring the utilities of different individuals for money. In common with most thinkers of his time, he was philosophically a rationalist. This means he assumed that all men, being rational, would behave in the same way under similar circumstances. Bernoulli believed that all he

---

[1] The Latin title was "Specimen Theoriae Novae de Mensura Sortis." The date is vague because the journal in which the paper appeared had one volume for the years 1730 and 1731, and this volume was not published until 1738.

had to do was deduce the fundamental laws which would govern such rational behavior. Bernoulli's argument led him to the specific conclusion that the utility of dollars (or francs, pounds, etc.) could be measured to a sufficiently good approximation by using the *logarithm of the number of dollars as the measure of utility.*

There is nothing sacrosanct about the selection of the logarithm as the measure of utility. Contemporaries of Bernoulli, who were equally rationalistic, reached some different conclusions. For example, Buffon, the famous French naturalist, concluded that the utility for money could best be represented by the reciprocal of the number of dollars.[2] A Swiss mathematician named Cramer opted for the square root of the number of dollars as the most satisfactory measure of utility.

The basic approach in each case was the same. Certain "principles" are stated which seem to the author of the argument to be essential components of the approach of any rational man. *From these principles a mathematical relationship is then deduced, which is intended to relate the utility for an amount of money and the amount of money itself.* Bernoulli hypothesized that the utility of additional sums of money to an individual must be inversely proportional to the amount of money he already has. It follows that the more money one has, the less the utility of an additional amount. Buffon's and Cramer's alternatives are in accord with the basic proposition of *diminishing utility*—but not with Bernoulli's specific hypothesis. And hence the different conclusions that are reached.

In contrast to this somewhat old-fashioned, but not necessarily false, approach of the rationalists is the contemporary empirical attack on the problem. *As empiricists we assume that utilities, being subjective, can differ, despite an identical set of external circumstances.* Therefore, it behooves us to discover means for measuring the actual utilities of a *given* decision-maker. Various methods have been developed, and we shall discuss some of them shortly.

First, however, let us emphasize the possibility that the logarithm (or a similar measure) of the amount of dollars might be a correct measure of utility (or payoff) under certain circumstances. The same can also be said for the actual amount of dollars itself. We reiterate the important fact that even where the degree of achievement of objectives seems to be measurable in dollars, it may not be so. The same decision problem presented to several individuals may have different solutions, each being completely rational. Why is this so? Because the utility that different individuals place on a given sum of money will vary.

[2] That is, if you have x dollars and you gain y dollars more, your increase in utility is proportional to $\dfrac{1}{x} - \dfrac{1}{x+y}$.

To illustrate this fact we can use the same problem with which Bernoulli was concerned, *viz., the problem of self-insurance.* But before we do this it will be necessary to introduce some concepts of probability theory. These concepts play a most important role in decision theory, operations research, management science, and many other areas. We need only some of the ideas of the probability theory, and it will be simplest to introduce them piecemeal, as they are required.

43/ Probability Theory

Probability theory deals with events of a special kind, called *random events.* These are events for which *the outcome is affected by chance.* Frequently this situation occurs when an enormous number of causes contribute to produce the final outcome, which is the event in question. A typical example is tossing a coin. Whether it lands heads or tails is a chance event because such a large number of causes contribute to the final outcome. Such factors as the force with which the coin is tossed, the amount of spin, air movements, position of the hand when the coin is caught, all act together to determine the outcome. Probability theory deals with the conclusions that can be drawn in reasoning about such events.

The basic concept is that of the *probability of the outcome.* The probability of an outcome can be most simply understood as the percentage of the times in which this outcome would occur if the event were repeated a great many times. Thus, we say that the probability of the outcome of (the event) heads in tossing a coin is $1/2$ because a great number of tosses will produce about 50 per cent heads. Similarly, the probability of rolling a 7 with two dice is $1/6$ because a great many rolls will produce 7's about $16\frac{2}{3}$ per cent of the time.

Actually, the situation is a good deal more complicated than the preceding paragraph would indicate. Probability theory is not an example of the kind of austere, settled structures of thought which seem to be represented by such subjects as mathematics, logic, mechanics, and so forth. Quite the contrary, probability theory is riddled with controversy and one of the major arguments concerns the meaning of the basic concept—the probability of an outcome.

A particularly crucial difference of opinion exists between the (so-called) *objectivists* and *subjectivists.* The *objectivists* (in a simplified sense) maintain that probabilities must relate to *long-run frequencies of occurrence.* For them, only events which can be repeated for a "long run" may be governed by probabilities. Thus, for the objectivist the fact that the appearance of a head in a coin toss has a probability of occurring of one-half is simply a shorthand way of saying that heads would be produced about half the time if the coin were tossed a great many times. The *subjectivists* (also in a simplified version) maintain that probabilities measure *degrees of belief* in the likelihood of occurrence of a given outcome. "Degrees of belief" can be roughly translated as estimates of the proportion of times that a given outcome would occur if some imaginable, but perhaps physically impossible, series of trials were performed. *For the subjectivists a probability represents a subjective appraisal of the nature of reality, while for the objectivists a probability must be an actual, countable, observable fact.* Therefore, a subjectivist can perfectly well talk about, say, the probability of war, while an objectivist would maintain that such a use of probabilities is meaningless, since the situation in question could never be examined with repeated trials.

As we shall see, this difference in conception between objectivists and subjectivists has some important consequences. In the case of coin tosses, however, the interpretations are essentially equivalent. The subjectivist would maintain that, in addition to the logic of the mechanics of coin tossing, many historical records exist of lengthy coin tosses. And since these show that heads appeared about one-half the time, then this fact constitutes a major basis for the establishment of a rational degree of belief. Consequently, the subjectivist will be willing to interpret the probabilities in this case in the objectivist's sense.

It is essential to be clear about this notion of long-run frequency of occurrence. What, after all, could it mean to say that the probability of heads is $\frac{1}{2}$, that the probability of a seven with two dice is $\frac{1}{6}$, or that the probability of being dealt a perfect bridge hand (13 cards of the same suit) is 1/158,753,389,900? In any of these cases the outcome in question will either happen or not—there is no intermediate possibility. What information, then, does the associated probability really give us? Only the percentage of times the outcome will occur if the event is repeated a great number of times. Note that the coin may show tails the first try, again on the second try, and even, perhaps, for the first ten tries. But, in the long run, we can expect to find that we have gotten about 50 per cent heads. Similarly, one might deal 158,753,-389,900 bridge hands and never get a perfect hand, or one might conceivably get one on the very first deal. Probability theory tells us, however, that if we dealt an enormous number of bridge hands—say one bridge hand for every fundamental particle in the universe (23,621,-586,204,412,503,866,408,480,941,772,333,202,067,076,871,790,675,064,049,-347,137,614,278,446,546,944 according to Sir Arthur S. Eddington)*—we

---

* This number is $\frac{3}{2} \times 136 \times 2^{256}$. See A. S. Eddington, *Fundamental Theory*, Cambridge, 1949, p. 265.

would find that we had gotten pretty nearly one perfect hand for every 158,753,389,900 deals.

All of the probability examples we have used above have been of the sort that can be calculated in advance. But this is incidental for our present point of view. Suppose we are told that the probability is $\frac{1}{10}$ that the average January temperature in New York City will be greater than 40°F. What does this mean? It means, *first,* that someone has gone over the New York City weather records and discovered that in the past, 1 out of 10 Januaries had an average temperature of more than 40°F. It means, *second,* that barring a climatological change (i.e., the process is stable), we can expect approximately the same proportion in the future. At least this is the best.information we have concerning the proportion to be expected in the future. The only difference between this case and the previous ones above is in the method of determining the probabilities, not their interpretation. If we didn't know how to calculate the probability of getting a 7 with one roll of two dice we could roll the dice a great many times and observe how often we got the 7. As a matter of fact, this is exactly how it was done, and with considerable accuracy, by gamblers before probability theory was developed in the seventeenth century.

Now, the most important use of probabilities for our present purpose is in terms of the factors that govern rational behavior when money (or, more generally, utility) is involved in chance situations. The classical gambling situation is typical. What reasoning governs a wager on the toss of a coin? Suppose the same wager is going to be repeated a great number of times. Then we know that about 50 per cent of the time the coin will show heads. This means that the gambler who bets on heads will win about 50 per cent of the time and his opponent will win about 50 per cent of the time. So, if the game is not to produce an advantage for one or the other player it is necessary that the amounts bet should be equal for the two players, assuming that they have the same utilities for money.

Suppose the coin is tossed 1,000 times. We would expect that either player would win about 500 bets and lose about 500. If as much is won as is lost on each bet, both players ought to come out approximately even. Thus, in this case, *a fair game* requires that the odds should be even—each player betting the same amount of money. It is the fact that the odds were not even that gave so much advantage to one of the players in the coin-tossing example mentioned before. If that game had been played 1,000 times, the player who received $200 when he won and who paid only $100 when he lost could have expected to win 500 times and receive $100,000 while losing 500 times and paying out only $50,000, with a net gain of $50,000.

The same considerations apply to any other probabilities. Suppose one is betting on a 7. If the dice are rolled 6,000 times, we know that there should be about 1000 7's. Thus, the person betting on the 7 would win 1,000 times and lose 5,000 times. In order to have an even game it is clearly necessary that he should receive more when he wins than he pays when he loses. In fact, he must receive $5 when he wins for each $1 he pays when he loses in order for the game to be even. Thus, *fair odds* for this game would be 5 to 1. If the odds are larger than 5 to 1, then it is an advantage to bet on a 7. If the odds are smaller, then it is an advantage to bet against a 7.

44/ Expected Value

Much of this reasoning can be clarified by introducing one concept: *expected value.* This idea is not complex. *Expected value is simply the old fashioned arithmetic average.* We shall express it with mathematical symbols, using W's (W_1, W_2, and so forth) to represent the possible numerical outcomes, and p's (p_1, p_2, and so forth) to represent the probability that each of the W's will occur. Thus, for two possible outcomes, we have

$$\text{Expected value} = W_1 p_1 + W_2 p_2$$

where $p_1 + p_2 = 1$, since either W_1 or W_2 necessarily has to occur. Generalizing to an indefinite number of outcomes (say n of them) we can write:

$$\text{Expected value} = p_1 W_1 + p_2 W_2 + \ldots + p_i W_i + \ldots + p_n W_n$$

$$= \sum_{i=1}^{i=n} p_i W_i$$

where Σ ("sigma") is the symbol for the mathematical operation of summing. This symbol gives instructions to add up what comes after it —in our case all terms of the form, $p_i W_i$. The entries "$i = 1$" and "$i = n$" show how many terms are to be included in the sum, in our case all terms from $p_1 W_1$ to $p_n W_n$ inclusive.

The W's may be all positive or all negative, or some may be positive and some negative, depending on the problem. For example, consider the executive who is certain to get one or the other of two possible bonuses. Let W_1 be one of the bonuses and W_2 the other. Then if we know the probability of getting each bonus (i.e., we have p_1, and $p_2 = 1 - p_1$) we can write the equation representing the expected value of the executive's bonus. Here both of the bonuses are positive. This is a matter of convention. We automatically think of income (in this case, the executive's bonus) as being positive and, hence, any outgo (such as taxes) as being negative. But we would reach no contradictory conclusion if the convention were reversed—as long as we remained consistent. Thus, when we analyze a problem in terms of costs it is not unusual to make costs positive. If this procedure is followed, then it is necessary to make profits negative so that our analysis can balance out.

Frequently, we will be using the expected value equation where one of two W's is positive, the other negative. This is the situation when there is the possibility of either a gain or a loss—the gambler's predicament. For example, what is the expected value of a coin toss upon which two players each bet $100? Here we can let W_1 represent the gain of $100 ($W_1$ is positive), and W_2 the loss of $100 ($W_2$ is negative). Then we have $100(\frac{1}{2}) - \$100(\frac{1}{2}) = 0$ as the expected value. What is your advantage if the other player bets $200 against your $100? Simply $200(\frac{1}{2}) - \$100(\frac{1}{2}) = \$50$. Under these conditions you should average $50 gain *on each play*; if you play 1000 times you should have $50,000 to show for it.

We are not limited to expected values of additions or subtractions such as rates of return, profits, gains, or losses. We can take the expected values of any quantities, of similar dimension, whatsoever. It is often useful to take directly the expected value of *total capital*. For example, assume you have a total capital of $500 and you are offered the coin toss of $200 against your $100. Then we can identify the W's with total capital. If you win you will have $700, and if you lose you will have $400. Therefore we have $700(\frac{1}{2}) + \$400(\frac{1}{2}) = \$550$, which is the expected value of your capital *after one toss*. Let us now consider how one might more broadly use this concept of expected value.

Suppose you have the choice of making two investments of $1,000 each. Assume that the return on investment A will be $4\frac{1}{2}$ per cent and the return on investment B will be 6 per cent. Granted the certainty of these statements and assuming that you are motivated by the objective of getting the greatest possible return, you will undoubtedly invest in B. This conclusion follows because your return from B will be $60 compared to only $45 return from A. But now suppose that you are informed that both of the investments are risky and that *the risk is greater on investment B*. Suppose, to be precise, that you are told that the probability of a return on investment A is 0.90 (90 per cent) and the probability of a return on B is 0.65 (65 per cent). We will assume that either you will get the full stated percentage return or else no return at all. How would you choose between the investments?

We can calculate the expected values for the two investments in accordance with our equation. Assume that the capital invested will remain secure in any event and the only question is whether there is a return or not. In this case the amounts won will be the return on the investment and the amounts lost will be 0—simply the fact of not receiving a return. Then, using our equation, the expected value of investment A will be $\$45(0.9) - 0(0.1) = \$40.50$. The expected value of investment B will be $\$60(0.65) - 0(0.35) = \$39$. This means that if we made a number of different investments identical in every respect to investment A we would expect an average return of $\$40.50$ on each of them. For a number of investments similar to investment B we could expect an average return of only $\$39$. We could, therefore, conclude that we should invest in A because our expected return from A is larger than it is from B.

Note that we said "could conclude" rather than "must conclude." The reasoning we followed is perfectly logical and affords complete justification for choosing investment A. However, we cannot deny that one might prefer to play a hunch and invest in B and that he might be right and we might be wrong *in this specific instance.* This in no way changes the fact that our reasoning is impeccable, granting the probabilities as given and the objective as stated. The same question arises concerning gambling. One person may play the odds correctly and lose, while another ignores them and wins. Perhaps it may be the case that some individuals have a *sixth sense* (but this is *equivalent to saying that they have more information than we do*). Those of us who don't have a sixth sense (or data-collector) can be consoled by the fact that most individuals who do think they have one and who therefore ignore the relevant probabilities eventually suffer the consequences.

In this reasoning concerning expected values we have bypassed the point with which we started—namely, that individuals do not have the same utility for money. We calculated above the considerable advantage accruing to the individual who receives $\$200$ in the coin-tossing game for each $\$100$ he wagers. Yet we have previously stated that under certain conditions (our so-called *second case*) we wouldn't accept this handsome offer. There is no contradiction. Instead of expected value we need only calculate the *expected utility.* Precisely the same procedure is used, except that we measure the utility of the amounts involved instead of the amounts themselves. This kind of calculation will be illustrated when we examine Bernoulli's problem of self-insurance.

45/ Self-Insurance

What is the problem of self-insurance? Individuals or organizations faced with the risk of loss of assets can either assume the risk themselves or pay an insurance company to assume the risk for them. The question is: When is it reasonable to do one or the other?

Let us take as an example a shipment of goods worth $10,000 that has a probability of 0.10 (10 per cent) of being destroyed or lost in transit. What is the expected value of such a shipment? Using our equation we have $10,000(0.90) + 0(0.10) = $9,000, reflecting the fact that out of 100 shipments only 90 will arrive. Put in another way, the shipper can expect that, on the average, he will sustain a $1,000 loss in value for each shipment. It would follow, on this basis, that the shipper should be prepared to pay *up* to $1,000 for each shipment as premium on insurance. In this way, he will suffer no loss on his merchandise value. Instead he will pay some amount in premiums to the insurance company.

On the face of it, only if the cost of the premium is equal to or less than the expected cost of the loss in merchandise would the shipper insure. When the costs are equal we shall call this *break even*. We may note, however, that the process is such that the shipper is going to lose money in either case. He would just like to minimize this loss. Thus, if the shipper paid $1,000 for each shipment, then he would pay a total of $10,000 in premiums for ten shipments and this would be repaid him for the one that was lost or destroyed. Consequently, he would *break even on* his premium payments. The lower the premium, below $1,000, the more advantageous it would be for the shipper to insure.

From the standpoint of the insurance company a premium of $1,000 per shipment would only enable them to break even and, since they wish to generate a profit, they would demand a higher premium, say $1,500. By our previous cost-balance criterion this premium (greater than $1,000) would seem to be disadvantageous to the shipper. Viewed in the same light as gambling games, if the shipper takes insurance at a $1,500 premium, then he has a *negative* expected value. That is, he loses on each play (shipment). Yet, under exactly this kind of circumstance, people continually insure themselves against loss. Why? Are they all being irrational? Of course the answer is no. They are not.

The explanation resides in the fact that the parties to the insurance contract have different amounts of capital and different utilities for increments of it. There is diminishing utility for money (the more one has, the less an additional amount will contribute to utility). That the diminishing utility should be measured by the logarithm of the amount of money, as Bernoulli assumed, is not necessarily the case, but it will serve to illustrate the logic of the situation. Suppose the shipper has total assets of $15,000, including the shipment, which must arrive safely for the shipper to be paid. Then, according to Bernoulli's assumption of a logarithmic measure of utility, if he does not take insurance, the shipper will have utility equal to the logarithm of $15,000 or 4.17609 with probability of 0.90 and utility equal to the logarithm of $5,000 or 3.69897 with probability of 0.10. His expected utility in this case is simply 4.17609(0.90) + 3.69897(0.10) = 4.12838 (the utility of $13,-439, since 4.12838 is the logarithm of $13,439). If he insures for a premium of $1,500 he will *always* end up with $15,000 − $1,500 = $13,500 and his utility will be the logarithm of $13,500 or 4.13033. Thus, the shipper's total expected utility is higher if he insures, so this is the course of action he should take. *This is so in spite of the fact that the cost of the premium is greater than the expected cost of the loss in merchandise.*

From the standpoint of the insurance company it is rational to offer the insurance because the company has sufficient capital so that its total utility is increased by accepting the insurance. Assume that the insurance company has assets of only $100,000. If it doesn't accept the insurance its utility will be measured by the logarithm of $100,000 or 5. If it does accept the insurance it will have the utility of $101,500 or 5.00647 with probability of 0.90 and the utility of $91,500 or 4.96142 with probability of 0.10. Its expected utility if it accepts the insurance will therefore be 5.00647(0.90) + 4.96142(0.10) = 5.00196, the utility of $100,454. The insurance company should, therefore, accept the insurance for a premium of $1,500. Thus, both parties are acting with *complete rationality*—once account is taken of the *differences in the utility of money.*

What, then, is the answer to the problem of whether to insure or not? It clearly depends on the *amount of assets* the shipper has. From the equation for his expected utility it can be calculated that he has equal utility whether he insures or not if his total assets are about $16,000. If he has more than this it is to his advantage to bear the risk himself. If he has less he should insure. Perhaps the shipper would scoff at the idea that with only $16,000 he should carry this risk himself. If so, it should be realized that this reflects the weakness of the logarithm, in this case, as a representation of the diminishing utility of money. If we had, for a specific shipper, the correct representation of his utility for money, we could use the same approach to determine at what point it was to his advantage to self-insure. Our use of the logarithm was only to illustrate the idea that it is utility that is important —not the amount of money.

The point of this discussion is that *even for objectives with a natural measure of degree of achievement it is still necessary to recognize that the natural measure may not coincide with the utility the executive receives from the degree of achievement of his objective.* And, if it doesn't, it is the *utility* that governs the decision problem, not the natural measure.

But there are many decision problems for which the amount of money involved does satisfactorily measure the utility. This would tend to be true where the amount of money involved is *small relative to total assets.* Can this be made more precise? Only if the real relation of the utility of additional increments of money to the amount of money possessed is known. For example, if the true relationship between utility and money is expressed by the logarithm of the amount of money, as Bernoulli suggested, then decision problems involving changes in money of no more than 2 to 3 per cent of the total amount possessed can be approximated with sufficient accuracy by assuming that the utility is represented by the amount of money. In short, the amounts of money involved could be used directly without worrying about the utility of the money. For decision problems involving greater proportions of total capital it would be necessary to determine the utility of the sums involved.

It is also important to note that difficulties arise as soon as a decision problem includes any risk of total loss, i.e., bankruptcy. The difficulty is indicated by the logarithm itself, since the log utility of zero is negative infinity. For some people, negative infinity, which is an infinite loss, would properly represent the situation. Other individuals, with suitable temperaments, don't look upon bankruptcy as the end of the road. For these people, it wouldn't be accurate to suppose that a small chance of complete failure would deter them. Obviously, *personality and temperament differ widely at the zero end of the log scale.*[3] Under these circumstances it is necessary to give careful consideration to each individual's measure of utility.

We have concerned ourselves so far only with objectives for which there exists a natural payoff measure of the degree of achievement. Even here we find difficulties, although they are not insuperable ones. Such natural measures exist for many organizational objectives. Since business is involved in economic activities one would expect to find

[3] If there is a 0.01 probability of bankruptcy we could represent this as (0.01) log $1.00. This would contribute zero utility, but subtract nothing from the utility obtained the remaining 99 per cent of the time. On the other hand, fractions of a dollar would subtract utility. One point of view is to take that fraction which subtracts as much utility as would be gained if bankruptcy did not result and apply the probabilities to these numbers. For example,

$$0.99 \log \$15,000 + 0.01 \log(1/15,000) = 0.99(4.17609) - 0.01(4.17609) = 4.09257$$

which is equivalent to $12,376.

Another point of view is to use as the measure of payoff a quantity called the probability of ruin. This is discussed in Chapter 13.

that various economic indices would be relevant to many business objectives. Thus, we would expect that dollars would be a natural measure of payoff for objectives concerning profits and costs *as long as the decision did not concern too great a percentage of the company's assets.* Another kind of natural payoff measure is provided by *brand share.* In the same way, volume of sales, order size, number of customers, repeat order rate, public service levels and a large number of other payoff measures may be relevant to specific organizational objectives.

46/ Payoffs Without a Natural Measure

What happens when the objective is one of the many that have different degrees of achievement—and, hence, demand a payoff measure —but for which there is *no obvious measure* of payoff? Of the eight areas listed by Peter Drucker[4] that require objectives (discussed in Chapter 3) there are four that are clearly of this type: innovation, manager performance and development, worker performance and attitude, public responsibility. (Other objectives may fall in this category also.)

Let us consider an objective in the area of worker attitude. It might well be the achievement of satisfactory labor relations. Obviously, there are all manner of degrees and dimensions of labor relations. They range from high turnover, work stoppages and strikes, poor performance, and low morale, to the case where everyone works until he reaches retirement, stoppages and strikes are unheard of, performance is excellent, and morale is tops. This example will serve to illustrate that it is possible to find some quantitative measures even for such an intractable objective as worker attitude. For instance, turnover rate, average length of service, or some index of productivity may be suitable for a payoff measure *in some cases.* But the difficulty is that usually no one of these seems to correspond to what the manager has in mind when he refers to satisfactory labor relations. If one of them is what he means, or some combination of several of them, then we need only try to discover whether there is a problem of determining the utility of various payoff measures. The more difficult case occurs when the manager isn't really sure what he means by satisfactory labor relations. He only knows that he will recognize them when he sees them.

This situation is not unfamiliar. Consider the problem of determining a quantitative measure of the *state of health* of an individual. There are an enormous number of quantitative measures involved in

4 Drucker, *op. cit.,* p. 63.

describing good health: blood sugar content, blood corpuscle count, weight, and the whole host of measures that doctors have occasion to use. For any one of them we can probably find limits such that it can be said that the individual won't be healthy unless this particular measurement lies between some specified limits. But the problem is that even if all the actual measures lie between their given limits the individual may still be unhealthy.

It is this fact that explains the need for the highly experienced *diagnostician*. If it were otherwise we could plug every individual's measurements into a computer and diagnose his condition from calculations performed on the total "model of health" with which the computer had been programmed. Work along this line *is proceeding* but it is still far from being anything but primitive. Meanwhile, wherever measurements are sufficient, doctors are quick to use them. Thus, since one of the major proofs of acute infectious mononucleosis is a change in the differential count of the white corpuscles, doctors have incorporated this knowledge as a major component in their diagnosis of this disease. And legitimately so, *for such procedures give the doctor the opportunity to devote his experienced attention to other, more intangible evidence and to concern himself with the problem of the best treatment for the particular patient in question.* The procedure is in accord with the development and use of knowledge. Some of the intangibles that one generation treats by experience are converted to measurable factors by the next generation. This process is a never-ending one because reality is far too complex to be completely circumscribed by a finite set of measurements.

In economics the same kind of problem is known as the *index number problem.* How, for example, can one achieve a quantitative measure that will describe the state of the economy? This case is particularly interesting because there are already available an extraordinarily large number of quantitative measures of different aspects of the economy. There is, quite literally, an embarrassment of riches. *Part of the difficulty is due to the underlying notion that there must be a best state. But it is impossible to define satisfactorily what constitutes the best state.* Certainly the majority of economists would recognize a good state when they saw it. There are a great number of possible relationships among all the measurable factors which would constitute a good-enough state. Perhaps this is one of the areas in which the principle of bounded rationality must operate. The question isn't really whether the national economy is optimal, only whether it is *satisfactory*.

So, recognizing that the problem we are dealing with is a general one, let us see what resources we have to deal with it. We can begin with a specific example. Suppose you are involved in contract negotiations with a union. You have, we will assume, the objective of achieving a satisfactory relationship with your workers. And, of course, you have a great number of possible strategies available to you in the form of specific offers and counteroffers to the union. Now, let us simplify the problem by assuming that there are only three possible relevant outcomes: strike, contract, or a continuation of the doubtful situation where negotiations proceed and the employees remain at work without a contract. It should be noted that under some circumstances it might be feasible to express these three possibilities in terms of dollar costs to the organization. If this were the case we could use the simpler methods discussed above, but we will assume that dollar costs cannot be determined.

47/ Ranking

Now, the first possibility available to the administrator is that he can rank the possible outcomes in order of their utility to him. Ranking the outcomes simply means that they are put in the order of their utility, the most utility first, the least utility last. Thus, in our example, the executive may rank a contract first, continued negotiations second, and a strike third, in that order. Of course, this plausible ranking is by no means a necessary one. It all depends on the utility of each outcome to the executive. Under some circumstances, he might rank a continuation of negotiations first because he anticipates a change in the economic situation which would improve his bargaining position. In any case, we are suggesting that only the executive can rank the outcomes in order of their utility to *him* in terms of *his* objectives.

Can this always be done? *Some things can't be ranked.* One cannot, for example, rank cities of the world in accordance with their distance from the equator and from the international date line. One could rank them with either one of these distances separately, but not simultaneously. Similarly, an airplane's position cannot be ranked. That is, we cannot rank it unless our objective provides a criterion other than spatial position. In airport control, for example, planes are landed according to their altitude. The lowest plane in a stack is brought in first and all of the planes in the holding pattern are then lowered by one unit of altitude separation. The criterion is not to pass any plane through an altitude occupied by another plane. So we rank these airplanes by their order of arrival starting at one and counting up from the bottom. The position of a ship does not permit ranking. However, the rules of the road rank ships according to which ones have the right of way. We cannot rank color. But we can rank position of the dominant wave length in the visual spectrum. We can also rank purity and reflectance by wave length. Any given color can be defined in terms of three variables. By means of a suitable transformation, these can be reduced to two, but the ranking problem remains.

Mathematicians refer to this situation as a problem of *dimensionality*. A ranking implies only one dimension. It cannot be used on factors that have more than one dimension, as our examples had. The sense of taste is a phenomenon that has been shown to have more than one dimension. As a result, when psychologists devised taste tests in which the individual must rank his preferences for various tastes, it was found that he cannot always do it successfully. This shows up in the form of a breakdown of the transitivity of his preferences. *Transitivity* is a mathematical word signifying that if the individual prefers A to B, and prefers B to C, then he should not prefer C to A.

Transitivity holds as long as there is only one dimension. Examples of transitive relations are *bigger, smaller, heavier, lighter, wealthier, healthier*. Its breakdown in taste tests indicates the presence of more than one dimension of taste. Might this not happen when the executive attempts to rank his outcomes? It is tempting to answer no, because the manager will reach a decision implying that he has ranked his outcomes. However, this would be *circular reasoning* with a vengeance! The modicum of truth is that *to make a decision* the manager must *believe* that he has succeeded in ranking his outcomes. We leave open the possibility that upon various occasions he might not have been able to do so.

If the outcomes can be ranked, then the *numerical* ranks can be used as a measure of the utility of the outcome—the payoff. We shall find that rankings are sometimes sufficient for analyses of decision problems involving competitive actions. They can be useful also in analyzing decision problems involving states of nature. But they are not sufficiently informative to support an extensive analysis. *The use of rankings of outcomes as measures of payoff is limited since the majority of arithmetical manipulations have no meaning in terms of ranks.* For example, we cannot tell whether the difference in preferences between 1 and 2 is greater or less than the difference in preferences between 2 and 3. *Averages of ranks,* where (responding to the various states of nature) different outcomes can occur with one strategy, have no meaning. In short, while rankings are helpful—and must serve if nothing better is available—we cannot expect to be able to use any sophisticated methods of analysis based on ranks.

It is worth investigating the arithmetical shortcomings of rankings a little more carefully. Take as an example the decision problem in labor relations mentioned above. Let us abbreviate the three alternatives by their initial letters: S for strike, C for contract, and N for negotiations. Our administrator has ranked these three outcomes in order: C, N, and S. Therefore, we assign these outcomes the ranks 1, 2, and 3, respectively. But we could equally well summarize the administrator's preferences with any other three numbers in the same order: say 1, 9, 28, or 7, 46, 259. The shortcomings become apparent when we recognize that the only arithmetical operations which can be performed legitimately on any one of these possible rankings[5] must be such that they would give an equivalent result when performed on any other of these rankings. For example, the 1, 2, 3 ranking would suggest that the difference in utility between C and N equaled the difference in utility between N and S. But this conclusion is completely contradicted by either of the other two rankings (1, 9, 28, or 7, 46, 259). Clearly, *it is not legitimate to subtract numbers that represent ranks.* Shortcomings such as this exist in the context of what we would like to be able to do. If the best measurements we can achieve are rankings, then we use them regardless of our preferences.

We have said that the arithmetical operation of subtraction is not legitimate when performed on numbers which represent rankings. This is because the answer obtained has no meaning for the outcomes being measured—utilities in our case. It can easily be verified that *hardly any of the ordinary arithmetical operations can be performed on rankings. This includes addition, subtraction, multiplication, division, averaging,* and so forth. Severe restrictions on the possibilities for quantitative analysis are obviously entailed by these limitations, which is why we stated that rankings constitute a *relatively* poor kind of measurement.

48/ Scales of Measurement

The theory of measurement deals with the use of numbers to represent certain characteristic properties of systems and their components. It might seem as if the only problem of such a theory would be how to obtain the numbers—in short, how to take the measure. This is not the case. Perhaps it is surprising that *the major problem dealt with in the theory of measurement is what can be done with the numbers once they have been obtained.* There are two main reasons for being somewhat surprised about this.

First, it is hard to resist thinking that numbers are, after all, just numbers. While numbers may represent the characteristics of systems, in the last analysis it is still true that they are *not the characteristics*—

---

[5] Or any of the infinity of other possibilities.

but numbers. Hence, one should do whatever one does with any other numbers. For the *second,* let us turn to what Humpty Dumpty said about the meanings of words, *viz.:* "The question is which is to be master—that's all" (i.e., the words or their meanings). In other words, do the characteristics master the numbers or do numbers make the characteristics subservient?

The answer is more complex than one would immediately suspect. One possible reply is that a system's properties should rule the numbers —and this approach has been consistently employed by analysts in many different areas. Despite this fact, it is an out-and-out *blunder* to reason in this way. Both of the arguments described above have a common refutation.

Alice should have answered Humpty Dumpty: "You can be the master of the meaning of your words if you want, but this does not mean that you will be understood. Assuming that you want to communicate, you have to use your words with the meanings given in the dictionary." Perhaps Lewis Carroll could have given Humpty Dumpty an answer to squelch such an argument, but we are on the rational side of the looking glass. And being in this position, we are attempting to draw *an analogy between the meanings of words and the meanings of numbers.*

Our reply to both arguments is that only those arithmetical manipulations are permissible which correspond to a *meaningful treatment of the object* being measured. With *numbers,* we can do *as we please* but with *measurements* we can only do what reality *permits* us to do. The usual conception of what is permissible comes from our familiarity with a specific kind of measurement. As an example, consider the measurement of weight. We manipulate numbers which represent weights with complete freedom. For instance, in discussing the combined weights of a 5-pound sack of sugar and a 10-pound sack of sugar we feel perfectly comfortable in saying that the total weight would be 15 pounds (by addition)—that the second sack is 5 pounds heavier than the first (by subtraction)—that the second sack is twice as heavy as the first (by multiplication)—or that the first sack is half the weight of the second (by division).

It is natural to assume that we have similar flexibility with other kinds of measurements—but this is not the case. The technical term for the type of measurement scale which permits the sort of flexibility illustrated above is a *ratio scale.* Weight is measured on a ratio scale; consequently, all the usual arithmetical operations are permissible. In contradistinction, there are common enough measurements, e.g., temperature, which demonstrate that not all measurement scales are of the ratio type. Consider two rooms with temperatures that are respectively 40 and 80 degrees Fahrenheit. It seems reasonable (in the sense that it "feels right") to refer to an average temperature of $(40 + 80)/2 = 60$ degrees Fahrenheit. It should seem intuitively wrong to say that one room is twice as hot as the other. And what does it mean to say that one room is 40 degrees (Fahrenheit) hotter than the other? The distinctions drawn by these statements are *learned* (as the meaning of language is learned).

The technical term for the type of measurement scale that applies to temperature is an *interval scale*. Only by understanding the distinctions between ratio and interval scales can one hope to understand the allowable manipulations of numbers under the varying circumstances. Let us develop the relevant differences between these scales in terms of phenomena with which everyone is familiar.

Weight, for example, can be measured equally well in units of pounds or of kilograms. We know that there should be no difference between the conclusions that would be reached about a system of objects simply because of our choice of units. This means that in establishing a ratio scale (required for descriptions of weight) the measurer has *one choice which he can freely make, i.e., the unit of measurement. Once this selection has been made*—be it pound, kilogram, or stone—*the whole scale is determined.* Algebraically, if X is the weight in some specific unit, then $Y = bX$ would be the weight on another scale—where b *units of the second kind* make *one unit of the first kind.*

On the other hand, consider the two best known ways of measuring temperature: Fahrenheit and Centigrade scales. The well-known procedure for converting from Fahrenheit temperatures to the corresponding Centigrade measurements is to use the equation: $C = -160/9 + 5F/9$, where F and C are the number of degrees on their respective scales. To some, this equation may seem more familiar in verbal form, *viz.,* subtract 32 from the Fahrenheit temperature, then take ⅝ *of the result to* get the Centigrade temperature. *The important point to notice is that there is more than one number involved.* We need only one number to convert centimeters to inches, multiplying by 2.54; only one number is required to convert pounds to kilograms, multiplying by 2.2. But here, two numbers are needed: *first,* subtract 32, *second,* multiply by ⅝. Algebraically, this is expressed as follows: if X is the measurement on *one* interval scale then $Y = a + cX$ will be the measurement on *another* interval scale, *which is identified by specific values of* a *and* c.

The difference between ratio and interval scales also can be explained verbally. *There is one "free" choice for a ratio scale; two "free" choices for an interval scale.* The one "free" choice for the ratio scale corresponds to the *"b"* in $Y = bX$. The two "free" choices in the interval scale correspond to the *"a"* and the *"c"* in $Y = a + cX$.

A ratio scale has a *natural zero,* which is why the measurer has only one choice available, i.e., the unit of measurement. *Since an interval scale does not have a natural zero, the measurer must select his zero point as well as the unit of measurement.* And what is a "natural zero"? A natural zero exists if there is a positive answer to the question: Is there a real meaning to having nothing (or none) of the quantity being measured? The notion of having no (or zero) weight has a straightforward meaning. Neither Fahrenheit nor Centigrade embody a natural interpretation of "no temperature." [6]

What are the implications of these differences between ratio and interval scales? Especially, what can be said about the allowable arithmetical manipulations on numbers that represent measurements for each type of scale? The answer to these questions follows directly from a basic principle, namely: Only those operations can be permitted which will not change any *real world characteristics* as a consequence of the units of measurement selected.

In algebraic terms this can be formulated as follows. Suppose we have two measurements, X_1 and X_2, and that we perform an arithmetical operation on them which yields a resulting number, V. Now assume that with a different choice of units the two measurements would have been Y_1 and Y_2. We perform the same arithmetical manipulations on Y_1 and Y_2 as we did on the X's, with the result W. Then we require either that W should bear the same relationship to V as the Y's bear to the X's, or that $W = V$. The latter would be the case, for example, if we take the ratio of a circle's circumference to its diameter—no matter in what units the radius is measured. If these results were to depend on the units chosen, this would violate the principle stated above.

Ratio Scale. In this case we have already seen that the relationship which must exist between the Y's and the X's would be: $Y_1 = bX_1$ and $Y_2 = bX_2$. We therefore require that $W = bV$ or $W = V$ for any permissible arithmetical manipulation. Let us try a few cases.

1. *Average.*

This operation is allowable since it is given that $(X_1 + X_2)/2 = V$, then

$$\frac{Y_1 + Y_2}{2} = \frac{bX_1 + bX_2}{2} = bV$$

It is also given that $(Y_1 + Y_2)/2 = W$; consequently $W = bV$, as required.

---

[6] The Kelvin scale of temperature has a natural zero. It is $-273.18°$C. or $-459.72°$F., called absolute zero. This follows from work in physics where both theory and experiment indicate that a limit exists to the lowest possible temperature that can be achieved, i.e., absolute zero.

2. *Difference.*

This operation is allowable since it is given that $X_1 - X_2 = V$, then

$$Y_1 - Y_2 = bX_1 - bX_2 = bV$$

It is also given that $Y_1 - Y_2 = W$; consequently $W = bV$, as required.

3. *Division.*

This operation is allowable since it is given that $X_1/X_2 = V$; then

$$\frac{Y_1}{Y_2} = \frac{bX_1}{bX_2} = V$$

It is also given that $Y_1/Y_2 = W$; consequently $W = V$, as required.

Interval Scale. For this scale the relationship between the X's and the Y's would be: $Y_1 = a + cX_1$ and $Y_2 = a + cX_2$. We require either that $W = a + cV$ or that $W = V$ for any arithmetic manipulation to be permissible. Taking the same examples as we did for the ratio scale:

1. *Average.*

This operation is allowable since it is given that $(X_1 + X_2)/2 = V$, then

$$\frac{Y_1 + Y_2}{2} = \frac{a + cX_1 + a + cX_2}{2} = \frac{2a + c(X_1 + X_2)}{2} = a + cV$$

It is also given that $(Y_1 + Y_2)/2 = W$; consequently $W = a + cV$, as required.

2. *Difference.*

This operation is *not* allowable since it is given that $X_1 - X_2 = V$, then

$$Y_1 - Y_2 = (a + cX_1) - (a + cX_2) = c(X_1 - X_2)$$

It is also given that $Y_1 - Y_2 = W$; consequently $W = cV$, not $W = a + cV$ as required.

3. *Division.*

This operation is *not* allowable since it is given that $X_1/X_2 = V$, then

$$\frac{Y_1}{Y_2} = \frac{a + cX_1}{a + cX_2}$$

It is also given that $Y_1/Y_2 = W$; clearly

$$W \neq a + cV$$

We see that our natural inclination concerning the way we talk about temperature is justified. Also, we have tried to clarify why it is that our intuition cannot resolve questions involving operations which are "impossible" for certain types of scales.

The relation of this discussion to the problem of measuring utility should be apparent. Assuming that we can measure utility, what kind of measurement might be involved? *The three major theoretical alternatives are: (1) ordinal measurement (i.e., rankings), (2) interval measurement, and (3) ratio measurement.* There has been much discussion of these questions in the literature, and it is evident that the question is a vexed one.[7] A fair summary of the positions might be as follows:

> If multiple objectives exist, then it is probable that not even ordinal measurement can be accomplished. The difficulties in this kind of situation were previously referred to as the problem of dimensionality. With only one objective there *is* general agreement that ordinal measurement can be accomplished. At the same time, there is a sizable group of authorities who maintain that more than ordinal measure, namely interval measure, can be achieved. No one maintains that utility can be measured on a ratio scale, even though there is nothing conclusive to show that it cannot be done.

A first step, if we hope to move further than rankings, might reasonably consist of some procedure for measuring utility on an interval scale. (This is the subject of our next section.) To shift from an ordinal to an interval scale represents no trivial improvement. *As an example of the implications of such a change, with ranked data as our measure of utility, we cannot calculate expected values. But if utility can be measured on an interval scale, we can base our analyses on expected values* (as previously shown). Since the use of expected values is of major importance in decision theory, it would be most desirable to achieve an interval scale measurement of utility whenever possible.

49 / The Standard Gamble

That it is often possible to achieve an interval scale for the measurement of utility was demonstrated by John von Neumann and Oskar Morgenstern.[8] The procedure they developed for doing this is known as the standard-gamble method. It is an ingenious way to determine an individual utility scale for outcomes, and we shall present the essentials of this technique in the next several paragraphs.

[7] A good treatment will be found in Tapas Majumdar, *The Measurement of Utility* (New York: St. Martin's Press, Inc., 1958).

[8] John von Neumann and Oskar Morgenstern, *Theory of Games and Economic Behavior* (Princeton, N. J.: Princeton University Press, 1947), pp. 15–30.

The idea of the standard gamble is to give the executive *pairs of alternatives between which he must choose.* Let us return to the administrator who was faced with the decision problem in labor relations. His

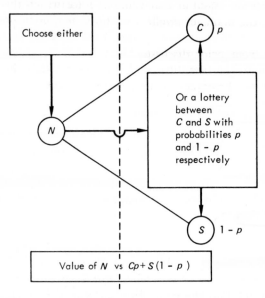

FIGURE 4.1   *The standard gamble can be used to obtain interval-scale measures of utility.*

three alternatives, it will be remembered, were ranked in order (1) C (for contract), (2) N (for negotiations), and (3) S (for strike). We have shown now why it is that almost no arithmetical manipulations are permissible on the numbers assigned as ranks for these three outcomes. It would help us greatly if we could instead determine three numbers that would measure the administrator's utilities for the three possible outcomes on an *interval scale.* This is what the standard-gamble approach attempts to accomplish.

Suppose we ask this administrator to express his preference between: Choice 1, getting N certainly; and Choice 2, a lottery in which he will get C with probability p, and S with probability $1 - p$. (The reader should meditate for a moment on exactly what we are asking the administrator to tell us, namely: *his preference between having* N *for sure and taking a gamble on* C *or* S.)

We propose to adjust p. *First,* suppose we set $p = 1$. This would mean that the executive was being asked to choose between N for sure and C for sure. We already know he will select C. *Second,* let $p = 0$. This would mean that we are asking for a choice between N for sure and S for sure. We know that the selection would be N. This indicates that as p

changes from 0 to 1, the executive's preference for N (Alternative 1) instead of the lottery (Alternative 2) *must switch* at some point to a preference for the lottery over N. It seems reasonable, then, to say that the preferences are equal at that value of p for which this switch occurs. For example, the manager might say that he has equal preferences when $p = .9$.

We know from prior discussion that for an interval scale there are two "free" choices. In the standard-gamble procedure we are instructed to exercise these choices in a particular way. We always assign 0 to the worst outcome and 1 to the best. From our ranked ordering it follows that we must set $S = 0$ and $C = 1$. In accordance with the underlying theory we now require that all other measurements (in this example there is only one other) should be measurable on the interval scale that we have now established. Von Neumann and Morgenstern proved that the measurement of utility for N is the value of p at which there was indifference and thereby equal utility for N and for the lottery (in the above case $N = .9$).

If there were more outcomes we would repeat the same procedure for each outcome. The indifference value of p would be the *interval measure* for the given outcome. So it is an easy matter to extend this procedure to any desired number of outcomes. For each outcome with an intermediate rank we find the probability at which no preference exists between certainty of that outcome and the given lottery between the two extreme outcomes. The probability determined in this way is the measure of utility for that outcome. Naturally, there are limitations to the validity of this procedure. The most important one which we should note is that *transitivity* should hold between preferences for outcomes. This means, as we have seen, that the outcomes can be ranked—which is equivalent to saying that only a single dimension is involved.

The advantage of this particular measurement technique results directly from the fact that von Neumann and Morgenstern proved that it yielded an interval scale. This means that the administrator can now utilize analytical procedures requiring the calculation of expected values. He does this knowing that he will be *entirely consistent in his actions.* There are other advantages as well. *The standard-gamble approach permits information about managerial values to be transmitted in an operational form to subordinates. And in general, the standard gamble fosters the construction of more suitable, theoretical frameworks for the decision process.* For a more detailed account of the procedure, including various other restrictions, the interested reader should see Chapter 2 of Luce and Raiffa's *Games and Decisions*.[9]

[9] R. Duncan Luce and Howard Raiffa, *Games and Decisions* (New York: John Wiley & Sons, Inc., 1958).

It should be noted that attempts to use this technique in actual practice have not always been successful. Sometimes there are inconsistencies in the stated preferences and no unique measure of utility can be constructed. But, as L. J. Savage has pointed out,[10] often this means no more than that *the individual in question is really inconsistent and, when it is pointed out to him, he will attempt to eliminate the inconsistency.* Certainly it is not always the case that inconsistencies can be blamed on multidimensionality.

Another difficulty arises if one of the outcomes is overwhelmingly bad —say bankruptcy. The possible effect of this on the standard-gamble approach can be understood by the reader if he will envision himself using the method to evaluate his utilities for the following three outcomes: make $1,000, lose $50, die. Perhaps it is the case that no rational person should prefer any lottery involving death as one of the alternatives to losing $50. One possible answer to this quandary is to note that even an entirely rational person might prefer the lottery between death and making $1,000 to the certainty of losing $50 if the probability of death were so small as to make it virtually impossible—say 1 divided by the number of fundamental particles in the universe. But one difficulty with this answer is that *people seem to be unable to distinguish realistically between small differences in probabilities that might make large differences in utilities.* It is probably more reasonable to accept the fact that a special case arises when one or more of the outcomes are overwhelmingly bad. We noted this same kind of difficulty when discussing the logarithmic representation of utility.

We see that we are not completely helpless when faced with nonquantitative objectives in a decision problem. On the contrary, there are several possible ways in which we can proceed to obtain a quantitative payoff. None of them is perfectly satisfactory. Each is subject to limitations but, nonetheless, for many typical organizational objectives that are not obviously quantifiable, a payoff can be obtained.

Finally, the standard-gamble method sometimes can be used for those cases where several different objectives are involved simultaneously. The problem in such cases is to obtain a payoff measure that incorporates the utilities of all of the objectives—each achieved to a different degree.[11] If the rankings are confused by multidimensionality there may not be much that can be done to clarify the situation. Sometimes, however, the

---

[10] L. J. Savage, *The Foundations of Statistics* (New York: John Wiley & Sons, Inc., 1954).

[11] See the multidimensional method described in Chapter 9, pp. 236–241, where the weighting factors applied to the various objects might be derived by means of the standard-gamble approach.

manager can approximate the utilities of the various outcomes to his own satisfaction by using the standard-gamble approach.

50/ Strategies and States of Nature

We have considered the need and difficulty of formulating the objectives of the executive as precisely as possible. We have also discussed the problems and possibilities of determining a quantitative measure of payoff. But our preliminary survey of the decision problem revealed the need for two additional components: strategies and states of nature. These should now be considered in more detail.

We have previously explained that strategies are based upon the resources under the manager's control. As a decision-maker, he has alternative ways in which he can use his resources. The strategy which he selects is his decision as to what he will *do* with the resources under his control. The use of the word "resources" is justifiable since some kind of disposition of resources is usually involved in all potential organizational strategies. The manager's own time and effort can be included. But it may be misleading because some decisions use up only the manager's time and effort—and no resources, in the strict sense of the word, are affected. For example, the decision problem of pricing a new product does not require allocation of resources. Neither, for that matter, does the decision to *wait and see* involve the disposition of resources. Nevertheless, in its broadest sense, *all of the talents, abilities, and experiences of the managerial staff are resources of the organization.* There is no particular need to emphasize this fact since most decision problems involve the allocation of physical resources and the executive's strategy is the plan for their allocation.

At first thought, it might appear that there are virtually an unlimited number of possible strategies in any realistic problem. Usually, there are a great many, but various factors serve to limit the number of strategies that will be considered as genuine possibilities in a given decision problem. To begin with, strategies will be considered *unacceptable if they violate any laws.* In frontier days, one of the better strategies in some competitive decision problems was to shoot your opponent. Today, the laws of the land prohibit such sharp competitive practices and we can only hope that they will be taken even more seriously. A whole range of strategies is prohibited by laws relevant to collusion between competitors. Another range of possible strategies is prohibited by the Pure Food and Drug Act. We could go on listing *restrictions to strategies that arise from legal agencies, statutes, and the common law.*

Even if there were no restrictions against "bad" practices, any organization with an eye on its public-relations objectives would hesitate to indulge in them. This indicates that a more *fundamental restriction on strategies exists in the form of social mores and public opinion.* The law, of course, is a reflection of these. Most organizations attempt to limit their strategies to those which are consonant with the socially accepted practices of their time and place. Many such self-imposed restrictions go under the name of *policy.*

Policy is applied to situations not covered by the law, except for the primary policy: not to violate the law. In Chapter 3, we discussed policy in terms of conflict of objectives. At that time, we stated that policy was a collection of principles and rules whose purpose was to guide the manager and to help him consider things which he might otherwise overlook. We can now extend this thinking to the present context. *Policy relieves the manager from having to consider a great many possibilities. It saves his time for decision elements that must be explored.* If policy were stated in details instead of principles, it would not be an effective means of ruling out vast areas of possible strategies. To illustrate, it would be virtually impossible to play a good game of chess if every conceivable arrangement of pieces on the board had to be interpreted as a unique situation. For each situation there are so many possible strategies that a player who is not guided by policy must either play by memory or by chance. It is chess policy—the existence of principles stated in terms of general configurations—that permits the player to discard a great number of undesirable strategies. He discards them as classes of strategies, not one by one. In this same manner, *the manager rejects whole classes of strategies.*

Strategies that can be eliminated in lots rather than in units are *generalized strategies.* There are a number of methods for generalizing strategies so that they can be accepted or rejected in classes. Law, social mores, and policy provide this kind of discrimination. Usually, strategies eliminated by principles are those which would result in serious conflicts between the objectives of the organization and the vital objectives of society. The type of conflict is such that the organization does not care to be placed in the situation where it must choose between its own objectives and those of society. Since the position of having to make a choice is a compromising one—even if the decision is always in favor of society—the principles are ingrained in the decision-maker. *He does not consciously reject the strategies that lead to these conflicts. He never even considers them.*

There are other situations in which the manager may eliminate a great number of possibilities, some of which are optimum solutions that in no way conflict with social, legal, or policy goals. The additional restrictions on strategic possibilities appear in two forms: (1) unthinking acceptance of the conventions and customs of an industry, and (2) an individual's reluctance to consider certain kinds of changes. In these cases, the *status quo is taken for granted,* but not with consistently desirable results. Yet there is hardly any awareness that another way might exist.

The fact that many strategies are never contemplated because of psychological deterrents is not an advantage. For example, a dress manufacturer who has been identified for years with the $14.95 line of dresses may have so profound a revulsion to the perfectly reasonable strategy of shifting to the $9.95 line that he is unable to conceive of this possibility. Similarly, the management of an organization that has been located for its entire existence in one particular area may have great antipathy to the sound strategy of moving to a new location that has lower labor costs, lower transportation costs, or some other vital advantage. *Psychological deterrents to the recognition of possible strategies cut down the size of the decision problem, but many times the saving is obtained at the expense of a simultaneous cut in the degree of achievement of the objective.*

Many trade customs are beneficial. Others, which serve as restrictions on the number of possible strategies, are neither beneficial nor harmful with respect to attaining objectives. Their consideration would add no advantage and subtract greatly from the manager's time. Therefore, in a sense, the inclusion of unusual or unthought-of strategies with high payoffs is reserved for *a creative act* on the part of the executive. There is no *direct* way in which operations research, decision theory, or mathematics can replace such creative acts. In some fortunate cases, the result of the analytic approach brings certain elements or relationships to the *attention* of the executive, and he is led to break through his barriers of bounded rationality. In fact, by introducing an external process of reasoning, analytical methods frequently act as a *catalyst for creative thinking.* This is strictly an empirical observation.

States of nature have many characteristics in common with strategies. Here, too, we want to be able to recognize as many states of nature as we possibly can. But faced with overwhelming numbers of states of nature, we want to know how to classify them so that we do not have to consider each detail in every possible form. The discovery of states of nature is less directly affected by law, social mores, policy, and custom. Psychological deterrents play a significant part. As in the case of strategies, *the discovery of the relevant states of nature requires systematic exploration, the full utilization of experience, and, if we are lucky, some creative insights which escape the confines of our bounded rationality.*

Competitive strategies are a special class of states of nature. It may seem that we should not be able to conceive of more strategic possibilities for our competitor than we can for ourselves. However, this may not always be the case. Sometimes, the competitor is in a distinctly different position than we are with respect to assets, volume, market share, product lines, and so on. Many times, *we lack sufficient information about the competitor and this seriously handicaps our efforts to predict his possible behavior.* One thing we believe is that his behavior will not be dictated by chance. The importance of this fact becomes obvious when we discuss game theory.

For the moment, it will be sufficient to say that sometimes it is possible to list all relevant states of nature and all relevant competitive strategies. At the other extreme, however, we cannot hope to consider all possible shifts in the economy, calamities in nature, technological breakthroughs, fads in society (i.e., all possible states of nature and competitive strategies).

PROBLEMS

1. Practice in calculating expected values helps to make the concept a familiar one. Here is an assortment of expected value problems:

a. A particular stock has paid dividends of $0.50 per share in 12 of the last 15 payments. The other three times it has paid $0.25. What is the expected dividend?

b. A company that sells two different models of one item finds that 65 per cent of its customers buy the cheaper model, for $95. The remaining 35 per cent of its customers pay $125 for the more expensive model. What is the expected purchase price?

c. A magazine discovers that 40 per cent of the families that subscribe are ones in which there are two wage earners. In the remaining 60 per cent of the families there is only one wage earner. What is the expected number of wage earners per subscribing family?

d. A salesman makes 35 calls without a sale, and 15 calls with an average sale of $60. What is his expected sales per call?

e. The same salesman has a particular trip of 48 miles which he often makes. Four times it takes him one hour and six times it takes him one and a half hours. What is the expected time for the trip? (Convert the data to miles per hour and calculate his expected speed. Compare the two answers. *One must be careful in calculating expected values of rates!*)

f. A small-loan company finds that 12 per cent of its borrowers default on an average 20 per cent of their loans. What is the expected percentage of default?

g. A mail-order company finds that 18 per cent of the purchases of a particular item are returned. The company estimates that each return costs $0.70

in transportation and extra handling. What is the expected extra cost due to returns per unit of this item?

h. A second-hand car lot has a mark-up of $250 on 65 per cent of its cars and a mark-up of $400 on the rest. What is the expected mark-up?

i. A department store discovers that twice as many customers buy two units at $3.95 (for both) as buy one unit for $2.15. What is the expected purchase price per unit?

j. A magazine states that the average number of cars per subscriber family is 1.2. If 20 per cent of the family subscribers have no car, what is the average number of cars per family of the families which do have one or more cars?

2. Suppose you have total capital of $5,000. You have the opportunity to make a speculative investment of $2,500 which will be either totally lost or worth $7,500 in six months.

a. Using expected values directly, what is the maximum probability of total loss for which this would be a profitable investment?

b. Using the logarithmic measure of utility, what is the maximum probability of total loss for which this would be a profitable investment?

c. Use the standard-gamble method to determine your own utilities for the three outcomes: $2,500, $5,000, $10,000. What is the maximum probability of a total loss that would be acceptable?

d. Another mathematical form which can be used to represent utility is:

$$\text{Utility of } x \text{ dollars} = \log \frac{1 + \dfrac{x}{c}}{1 - \dfrac{x}{c}}$$

where c is some constant larger than any of the x's involved. Try this form with several values of c and determine the maximum probability of a total loss which would be acceptable. How does this probability change with c?

3. A company with assets of $50,000 is considering the possibility of redesigning its product. Including new tools and dies, the total cost of the redesign job will be $12,000. The company estimates the profitability of the product for three alternatives, No Change, Design 1, and Design 2. The new designs, 1 and 2, have the same cost.

No Change		Design 1		Design 2	
Profit (per year)	*Probability*	*Profit (per year)*	*Probability*	*Profit (per year)*	*Probability*
$4,000	0.2	$8,000	0.2	$6,000	0.4
5,000	0.5	9,000	0.5	9,000	0.2
6,000	0.3	10,000	0.3	12,000	0.4

a. Compare the expected dollar values of total assets at the end of one year for each alternative strategy.

b. Compare the expected dollar values of total assets at the end of two years for each alternative strategy.

c. How long a period is required before the total assets obtained from Design 1 are equal to the assets if no change is made? How long for Design 2?
d. Instead of dollar values use the logarithmic measure of utility to answer questions a. and b. Comment on the differences resulting from the use of each method.

4. *A* reports to *B*, *B* reports to *C*, *C* reports to *D*, *D* reports to *A*, *A* reports to *C*, and *D* reports to *B*. Which relationships are transitive and which are not?

5. Determine the expected value of the executive's bonus if, for the past 15 years, he has received $200 five times and $300 ten times and the system can be considered stable. If the executive has $10,000 in the bank, what per cent increase does each possible bonus make? Using the log utility assumption, what per cent increase in utility will each possible bonus contribute? What can we say about these results?

6. Rank-order your preferences for the following business conditions (*H* = high, *L* = low):

Price	Sales volume	Cost of manufacturing	Cost of selling
L	L	H	H
H	H	L	H
L	L	L	H
H	H	H	L
H	L	H	L
L	L	H	L
L	H	L	L

How many possible rankings are there? Does it seem possible that a manager could consider all of these? What happens if we describe the condition of each of the variables with high, low, and medium? What happens if we describe each variable with any number between 0 and 100? Check each column after ranking for transitivity. What does this tell us about the manager's decision problem? What consequences are there if a manager is not transitive in his decision-making?

7. Use the standard gamble on the outcomes you have ranked in problem 6, above. First obtain *p* values for ranking numbers 1-2-7, 1-3-7, 1-4-7, 1-5-7, and 1-6-7. Then repeat the procedure for 1-2-3, 1-3-5, 1-4-6, and 3-5-7. Check your results against the first five *p* values which you derived.

8. For the self-insurance problem discussed in this chapter, the insurance company asked a $1,500 premium to insure a $10,000 shipment with a 0.10 probability of loss. The company had assets of $100,000. How much could it afford to pay the shipper above $10,000 so that it would have no gain in utility?

9. Here is an example of behavior which would be irrational if dollars always measured the utility of dollars. A lottery might involve the sale of 100,000 tickets at $.50 each, with the prize being a car worth $6,000. Many supposedly rational persons buy a ticket in such a lottery.

a. Analyze this speculation in terms of the expected dollar values of the two courses of action.

b. What relationship does this example suggest about utility scales and dollar amounts? Is this in agreement with the conclusions based on self-insurance?

10. The "numbers game" is a widely played, but illegal, gambling procedure. A given amount is bet on a three-digit number, e.g., 583. A three-digit number is drawn randomly. If it is 583 the bettor is paid 600 times the amount that he bet. Since the numbers game is commonly played by poor people in large metropolitan areas, it is a convenient political whipping boy. Do such attacks make sense?

a. Analyze this problem in terms of the expected values of dollars, assuming a $0.10 bet.

b. Contrast the numbers game with sources of small loans likely to be available to the bettors. As an example, "loan sharks," who often exact 20 per cent interest per week.

c. Contrast the numbers game with alternative ways to buy a television set on the installment plan.

d. Similarly contrast the numbers game with prepaid medical plans.

11. Compare the effects of using Bernoulli's, Buffon's and Cramer's suggested utility transformations, giving your opinion regarding when (if ever) you might prefer each.

12. What types of scales are involved in the following:

a. Frequency measures.

b. Probability measures.

c. The degree to which an executive is subjective and not objective in his assignment of likelihoods.

d. The validity of the standard-gamble technique.

e. Aptitude testing for executive ability.

Support your positions with demonstrations similar to those developed on pp. 89–90.

Chapter 5

The Analysis of Decisions

51/ The Payoff Matrix

Mathematics suggests a convenient way to present our breakdown of the decision problem. This is to put it in the form of a matrix—called the *payoff matrix*. **A matrix is simply a two-dimensional array of figures arranged in rows and columns.** A matrix representation of the decision problem is particularly convenient because we can let the rows be the available strategies (one row for each strategy) and the columns be the states of nature (one column for each state of nature). When appropriate, the columns can reflect competitive actions as well.

The entry at the intersection of each row and column is the payoff—the measure of the utility of that specific outcome which occurs for a given strategy and a particular state of nature. Thus, the payoff matrix summarizes all of the characteristics of the decision problem which we have been discussing. Symbolically, the payoff matrix looks like Table 5.1—using N's to designate states of nature, S's to designate strategies,

TABLE 5.1

	N_1	N_2	N_3	N_4	. . .	N_j
S_1:	P_{11}	P_{12}	P_{13}	P_{14}	. . .	. . .
S_2:	P_{21}	P_{22}	P_{23}	P_{24}	. . .	. . .
. . .	. . .	. . .	. . .	. . .	. . .	. . .
S_i:	. . .	. . .	. . .	. . .	. . .	P_{ij}

and P's to designate payoffs. The decision problem is always the same —to select a specific strategy. The payoff matrix provides a means of structuring and presenting the relevant information.

The payoff matrix representation of a decision problem seems so apt for its purpose that it is easy to overlook the question of whether it can always be constructed. Can every decision problem be put into a payoff matrix format? The answer is that the great majority of decision problems can be represented in payoff matrix form. However, in many instances how to do it is not obvious.

Difficulties arise as soon as it is necessary to consider a sequence of decisions as if they were one over-all decision. For example, consider the problem of sampling the quality of a production run to determine whether to accept the entire "lot." There is a preliminary decision to take a particular size sample. Then after determining how many defectives there are in the sample, a subsequent decision must be made to accept or to reject the lot. This is a typical problem involving a sequence of decisions. There are two separate decisions. (There are two sets of states of nature as well. *First,* there is the unknown percentage of defectives that are actually in the lot. *Second,* there are different possible numbers of defectives which may be found in the sample—granting any specific number of defectives in the lot.) How can a problem such as this be put in payoff matrix form? As another example, remember that the columns of the payoff matrix can represent competitive actions. Consequently, any game with a sequence of moves creates similar difficulties.

It is our purpose to analyze decision problems in such a way that we can *recommend* to the manager a particular strategy which he should select for a specific case. It turns out that the payoff matrix provides a remarkably good structure for this analysis. We shall show how the payoff matrix representation is quite generally applicable. Nevertheless, it should be emphasized that the payoff matrix is simply a methodological convenience which in no way precludes the possibility that other bases for analyses can be found. Alternatives become especially important if the payoff matrix for a particular decision problem cannot be framed.

Returning now to the example of *acceptance sampling*, a difficulty occurs because the payoff matrix format requires the selection of *one* strategy, given that *one* state of nature holds, not several. Fortunately, the difficulty can be overcome by a suitable statement of what we mean by a strategy. Then, the lot acceptance example becomes straightforward. A strategy statement for the over-all decision problem becomes something like this.

Take a sample of size 10. Reject the lot if there is any defective product in the sample; otherwise accept it.

Redefinition of the states of nature is required. The effect of this transformation of terms is to increase drastically the number of strategies that must be considered. For our immediate purposes, this is only a technical problem. Indeed, the payoff matrix for this situation can be constructed. By means of this example we have tried to emphasize that an appropriate payoff matrix can frequently be achieved—even in cases where, at first glance, it might seem otherwise.

52/ Several Kinds of Decisions

There are many ways to classify decision problems. But for our purposes there is one kind of classification which is crucial. *This is a classification based on the amount of information available to the decision-maker about the likelihood of occurrence of the various states of nature.* Five main classes of decision problems exist in accord with this taxonomy. Important procedural differences are associated with each of these classes. Therefore, we must clearly distinguish between them.

Decision-making under certainty occurs when we have a problem where we know with certainty which state of nature will occur. This means that there is *only one column* in our payoff matrix. Alternatively, this kind of decision problem considers only one relevant payoff for each possible strategy. At first, this may seem like a trivial case. How can there be any difficulty in reaching the best decision if there is only one column? Simply read down the column to find the best payoff and that will be the optimum strategy. But it isn't quite that simple. The idea behind the suggestion is absolutely correct, but the difficulty is that there may be such an enormous number of strategy rows that it would be nearly impossible to list them.

Of what use then, is a payoff matrix which can't be written down? The answer is that in some cases, *when the actual payoff matrix can't be constructed, it still remains an effective means of conceptualizing the problem.* As we shall see, one of the contributions of operations research to decision-making is in this realm. For the present, it suffices to indicate that real *and important* decision problems of this type exist.

Suppose, for example, that you run a machine shop and have 20 contracts for machined parts. You also have 20 machines, any one of which could do any one of the contracts. But since the machines are of different designs, intended for different purposes, each type would require differing amounts of time for each contract—and, hence, would be more or less expensive. Quite naturally, you would like to assign the jobs to the machines so as to minimize the total cost. The first job could be assigned to any one of the 20 machines, the second job to any one of the remaining 19, the third job to any one of the remaining 18, and so forth. So the total number of ways in which you could assign the jobs is given by $20 \times 19 \times 18 \times 17 \times 16 \times 15 \ldots \times 3 \times 2 \times 1$. If one takes the trouble to do the arithmetic he will find that the total number of ways to assign the jobs to the machines is 2.4329×10^{18} (we have rounded off the number). Each way of assigning these jobs to machines is another possible strategy, so this decision problem's payoff matrix would have only one column (because the costs of the various machines are assumed known), but it would have almost $2\frac{1}{2}$ quintillion rows.

That such a modest problem could produce so many rows in the payoff matrix may be surprising. It does serve to show that decision-making under certainty can be a genuine problem. And this sort of problem is by no means confined to machine shops. On the contrary, a great number of different kinds of organizational decision problems fall into the category of decision-making under certainty.

The *second* kind of decision problem occurs where there are a number of states of nature but where the decision-maker *knows* the probability of occurrence of each of the states of nature. This kind of situation is called *decision-making under risk.* For the purpose of illustration, consider the decision problem facing a gambler—where the possible states of nature are the various chance events, the probabilities of which can be calculated by probability theory. *Typically in many organizational problems, the probabilities of the various states of nature are known by virtue of determining how frequently they occurred in the past.* Thus, the decision problem of a manufacturer of antifreeze would involve various weather conditions. The probabilities of occurrence of these different states of nature might be determined from past experience. Similarly, inventory decision problems involving parts for factory or office equipment would include those states of nature that represent the various rates of failure of the parts, and these probabilities might be known from past experience. This kind of decision problem occurs frequently.

The *third* kind of decision problem is *decision-making under uncertainty,* where the probabilities of occurrence of the various states of nature are not known (or where, if one is an objectivist, the very idea of probability descriptions for the states of nature is meaningless). *Such problems arise wherever there is no basis in past experience for estimating the probabilities of occurrence of the relevant states of nature.* The decision problems involved in marketing a new product would include various levels of demand as states of nature. Yet there is no past experience on which to base estimates of the relevant probabilities as there is in the case of established products. Decision problems concerning expansion of facilities may have states of nature including such events as war, depression, recession, and inflation. Believable probabilities cannot easily be estimated for these states of nature. Many decision problems of major importance are of this kind.

The huge gap in the availability of information between the second and the third categories suggests the need for a *fourth* category: *decision-making under partial information.* In reaching decisions under risk, we assume that the decision-maker knows the probability of occurrence of each state of nature. Consider an inventory problem. The states of nature are demand levels; the strategies are the quantities to order. For this to be a decision problem under risk it is necessary that the demand distribution be completely known. For the same problem under uncertainty we assume that nothing whatsoever is known about the demand distribution. What, then, about the intermediate cases, where *something,* but *not everything,* is known about the demand distribution? For example, some of the standard measures of descriptive statistics (such as averages, medians, or modes) might be known without knowing the whole demand distribution, e.g., the exact form of the distribution, such as normal, binomial, or Poisson. Thus, we could know that average demand was 100 units and that the standard deviation was 10 units—but nothing else. It is such cases as these that are included in the category of decision problems under partial information. *It may be the most common category of "real" decision problems. However, since somewhat more sophisticated procedures are required in dealing with this kind of decision problem, many decision-makers act as though the problem was one of risk, with varying degrees of penalty.* Although we shall not treat these kinds of problems, it was essential for classification purposes to mention them.[1]

The last category of decision problems that we shall mention is *decision-making under conflict.* Here the columns of the payoff matrix represent strategies of *rational opponents* rather than states of nature. The essence of this kind of decision problem is that the executive is involved in a competitive situation with an intelligent opponent. Military weapon and logistic systems and marketplace brand competition epitomize this class of decision-making—but even ordinary parlor games provide perfectly good illustrations. Decision-making under conflict is the subject studied in the theory of games. *The title, "theory of games," may suggest frivolity. Nothing could be further from the truth.* The essence of games (in the sense of the theory of games) is the presence of conflict of interest between two or more rational opponents. The grimness of war, the tensions of nuclear diplomacy, and the nature of business competition are all we need consider to deny the frivolity of the concept of games. There are many important and serious exemplifications of decision-making under conflict. And it is a particularly intractable domain.

[1] This kind of decision problem is discussed at some length in Martin K. Starr and David W. Miller, *Inventory Control, Theory and Practice* (Englewood Cliffs, N.J.: Prentice-Hall, Inc., 1962).

53/ Decision Criterion Under Certainty

Now that we have outlined the various kinds of decision problems, we can turn to the basic question: How should a specific strategy be selected? In other words, how should the decision be made? What we want to investigate is the reasonable procedure or procedures by which a decision can be reached once we have developed the payoff matrix. We would like to find a *criterion* for each class of decision by which the decision-maker, given his payoff matrix, can select his strategy.

There is no difficulty, *in theory*, in determining the decision criterion under certainty. All we need do is find the strategy which has the best payoff and that is the strategy which should be selected. There is no possible reason for doing otherwise. Each strategy has one payoff, since there is only a single column in the payoff matrix when the state of nature is certainly known. The payoff (utility) represents the degree of achievement of the objective, so the largest payoff is the best one. The decision criterion, then, is: Select that strategy which has the largest payoff. The practical difficulty which arises when the number of strategies is enormous must be dealt with by such methods of operations research as *linear programming*.[2]

54/ Decision Criterion Under Risk

What happens in the case of decision-making under risk? Here we no longer have just one payoff for each strategy. Instead, there are a number of payoffs—one for each possible state of nature. So a decision criterion for risk will have to be based either on some suitable transformation of all of the possible payoffs for each strategy, or on one or more payoffs selected according to some rule.

Let us take a simple decision problem under risk as an example. Assume that a processor of frozen vegetables has to decide what crop to plant in a particular area. Suppose that the strategies are only two: to plant peas, or asparagus, and that the states of nature can be summarized in three possibilities: perfect weather, variable weather, and bad weather. On the basis of weather records it is determined that the probability of perfect weather is 0.25, the probability of variable weather is 0.50, and the probability of bad weather is 0.25. The dollar yields of the two crops under these different conditions are known and the or-

---

[2] See Chapter 10, Section 96.

ganization's utility is assumed to be measured by the dollar amounts. All of this information can be summarized in a payoff matrix:

State of nature:	N_1	N_2	N_3
Probability:	0.25	0.50	0.25
Weather:	*Perfect*	*Variable*	*Bad*
S_1: Plant peas	$40,000	$30,000	$20,000
S_2: Plant asparagus	$70,000	$20,000	$ 0

What strategy should the decision-maker select? The rational individual, under these circumstances, will govern his selection of strategies by the *expected utility* of the strategies. He will select that strategy which has the largest expected utility.

We introduced the notion of expected values earlier. Using P_{ij} to designate the payoff for the ith strategy and the jth state of nature and p_j to designate the probability of the jth state of nature, it follows that the expected value of the payoff for the ith strategy, S_i, is

$$EV\ (S_i) = P_{i1}p_1 + P_{i2}p_2 + P_{i3}p_3 + \ldots + P_{in}p_n$$

$$= \sum_{j=1}^{j=n} P_{ij}p_j$$

where EV (S_i) designates the expected payoff for the strategy denoted by S_i. (Remember that an expected value is the simple arithmetic mean or average.)

Using the equation above, we can calculate the expected payoff for each of the two strategies in our example.

$$EV\ (S_1) = \$40,000(\tfrac14) + \$30,000(\tfrac12) + \$20,000(\tfrac14) = \$30,000$$
$$EV\ (S_2) = \$70,000(\tfrac14) + \$20,000(\tfrac12) + 0(\tfrac14) = \$27,500$$

The expected payoff for Strategy 1 is larger; this is the strategy that (all other things being equal) should be selected. The food processor should choose the alternative: plant peas. Why? Because if the same decision situation were presented to him a great number of times he would average $2500 more from Strategy 1 than he would from Strategy 2.

But, one may think, aren't there other factors to consider besides the expected value? For example, let us suppose that the probabilities were different. Suppose the probabilities were $\tfrac12$, $\tfrac38$, and $\tfrac18$, respectively, for the three states of nature. Then the expected payoffs for the two strategies would be:

$$EV\ (S_1) = \$40,000(\tfrac12) + \$30,000(\tfrac38) + \$20,000(\tfrac18) = \$33,750$$
$$EV\ (S_2) = \$70,000(\tfrac12) + \$20,000(\tfrac38) + 0(\tfrac18) = \$42,500$$

And, since the expected payoff for Strategy 2 is larger, this should be the choice of the food processor.

At this point one might say: On the face of it, I disagree! Look at the difference between the payoffs. If the processor chooses to plant asparagus (S_2), the expected payoff is higher because of the much higher return on asparagus with perfect weather. But if he plants asparagus and has bad weather, he doesn't make anything at all. Whereas, if he plants peas he may not make as much when the weather is perfect, but he never risks having no return at all. So why wouldn't a perfectly rational person prefer to forego a "slightly larger" expected payoff in order to avoid the possibility of no return at all? It might be said that he was paying the difference in expected payoffs as a premium on insurance against having no return.

This argument only appears to present a valid objection to the rule that the strategy with the highest expected payoff should be chosen. In fact, the objection is misplaced. A completely rational decision-maker might well reject Strategy 2 (plant asparagus), but it is because his utility for dollars is not properly measured by the dollar amounts that we have used. In short, for this case, the payoffs are wrong.

The same kind of problem was discussed in Chapter 4—the context being the self-insurance problem. It is an important point and deserves emphasis. *Any argument against the criterion of choosing the best expected value* (for a specific decision problem under risk) *implies that the executive has some other objective than just dollar amounts.* Here it is the objective of having some *control* over his income. In the self-insurance problem it was the objective of avoiding the possibility of ruin. Criticism of the expected value criterion (for risk) is directed against the wrong part of the analysis. *It is never a question of the criterion being wrong, but rather that the payoffs have been incorrectly measured to reflect the decision-maker's utilities for the outcomes.*

If the food processor was able to utilize a procedure for measuring his utility, he should then be able to demonstrate the correctness of the expected value criterion. In our present example, suppose that the dollar amounts do not adequately represent the decision-maker's utility. Consequently, he turns to the standard-gamble procedure to measure his utilities for the various outcomes. There are five possible outcomes: $70,-000, $40,000, $30,000, $20,000, and 0. To determine this manager's utilities for the intermediate amounts we would present him with the usual choices. First, would he prefer $40,000 certainly to a lottery between $70,000 with probability $\frac{4}{7}$ and 0 dollars with probability of $\frac{3}{7}$? (Note: $\frac{4}{7}(70,000) + \frac{3}{7}(0) = 40,000$). In this particular case, he would prefer the certainty of $40,000. So, we adjust the probability upward until he in-

dicates no preference. This *might* occur at a probability of $\%_7$ of getting
the $70,000. We would proceed similarly with the other two outcomes
and *might* find the *no-preference* probability for $30,000 at $p = \%_{14}$ and
the *no-preference* probability for $20,000 at $p = \%_7$. This gives us the
utilities for the five possible outcomes as follows:

OUTCOME	UTILITY
$70,000	1
$40,000	$\%_7 = 0.857$
$30,000	$\%_{14} = 0.643$
$20,000	$\%_7 = 0.429$
0	0

Our payoff matrix would be transformed:

$$
\begin{matrix}
0.857 & 0.643 & 0.429 \\
1.000 & 0.429 & 0.000
\end{matrix}
$$

We now proceed to calculate the expected payoffs as before (assuming
that the second set of probabilities applies):

$$\text{EV } (S_1) = 0.857(\tfrac{1}{2}) + 0.643(\tfrac{3}{8}) + 0.429(\tfrac{1}{8}) = 0.723$$
$$\text{EV } (S_2) = 1.000(\tfrac{1}{2}) + 0.429(\tfrac{3}{8}) + 0(\tfrac{1}{8}) = 0.661$$

The executive should select Strategy 1, which has the larger expected
payoff. For this example, the objection that had been raised seems reasonable, and in accord with the decision-maker's utility, as measured by
the standard-gamble technique. *With a proper measure, there is no other
rational decision criterion than the selection of that strategy associated
with the largest expected payoff.*

55/ Decision Criteria Under Uncertainty

The case of decision-making under uncertainty is more complicated.
For example, take the decision problem of an investor who has the objective of achieving the maximum possible rate of return. Assume that
he has only three possible investments (his strategies): *speculative stocks,
high-grade stocks, or bonds.* Further assume that only three possible
states of nature can occur: *war, peace, or depression.* We will ignore the
many nuances of capital gains, taxes on income, and so on.

The investor has determined his payoffs for each of the nine possible
combinations of a strategy and a state of nature. He has expressed his
payoffs *as rates of return on his investment* and his payoff matrix looks
like this:

	N_1 WAR	N_2 PEACE	N_3 DEPRESSION
S_1: Speculative stocks	20	1	−6
S_2: High-grade stocks	9	8	0
S_3: Bonds	4	4	4

The distinctive difference between this case and the preceding one is that the investor has no knowledge of the probabilities of the various states of nature. He has, therefore, no way to calculate an expected pay-off for his strategies. What criterion should he use in selecting a strategy?

At the present time, *decision theory provides no one best criterion for selecting a strategy under conditions of uncertainty.* Instead, there are a number of different criteria, each of which has a perfectly good rationale to justify it. The choice among these criteria is determined by *organizational policy* and/or *the attitude of the executive.* As we shall see, *the use of different criteria can result in the selection of different strategies.* We shall discuss only some of the suggested criteria.

56/ Criterion of Pessimism

First, the *maximin* criterion was suggested by Abraham Wald. (The reason for the name will become clear as we proceed.) Wald suggested that the decision-maker should be completely *pessimistic.* He should act as if Nature would always be malevolent, i.e., for whatever strategy he selected, Nature would choose a state that would minimize his payoff. Wald stated that the decision-maker should then select his strategy so that he would get as large a payoff as he could under these circumstances.

Let us return to our example. *If* the investor selects S_1, the worst that can happen is that a depression will occur, in which case his payoff would be −6. *Suppose* he selected S_2. Again, the worst that could happen would be a depression, in which case he would have a payoff of 0. *If* he selected S_3, however, he will always get a payoff of 4, no matter what state of nature occurred. In other words, the worst that could happen to him in this case would be a payoff of 4. We can arrange these conclusions in tabular form.

STRATEGY	WORST, OR MINIMUM, PAYOFF
1	−6
2	0
3	4←

Following Wald's suggestion, the best that the investor can do, assuming that Nature will always be malevolent, is to select that strategy which has the *largest minimum* payoff—the *maximum minimum*—or *maximin.* The largest such payoff (the maximin payoff) is 4, which the investor will get if he selects Strategy 3 and invests his money in bonds. In this *particular* case the investor will always get 4 from Strategy 3. In general, the use of this criterion will *guarantee* the manager at least as large a payoff as the maximin payoff. Sometimes, of course, a larger payoff will result. The Wald maximin criterion dictates the selection of Strategy 3 —investing in bonds. (If a cost matrix is used, then the best of the worsts would yield the *minimax* solution. See the regret criterion, below.)

The argument based on pessimism can be described as a conservative approach to an intrinsically difficult situation. There is further elucidation of this criterion, stemming from its application to the theory of games. This will be encountered subsequently. It is also interesting to note that this is the criterion professed by the majority of adherents to the objectivist approach in probability and statistics. Bear in mind that *this criterion is the sole one which can be defended rigorously if the payoffs can only be ranked.*

57/ *Criterion of Optimism*

Hurwicz[3] suggested a variant of this criterion. He asks, essentially, why always assume that Nature will be malevolent? After all, we sometimes get good breaks. Suppose an optimistic decision-maker felt "lucky" in a particular case about his chances of having a good state of nature occur? How might he be rational about this feeling? First let us assume that the executive is a *complete optimist*—the exact opposite to the Wald pessimist. He assumes that Nature will treat him kindly, selecting that state of nature which will yield the highest possible payoff for the strategy he has selected. How would he proceed?

He would look at the various payoffs for each strategy and select the largest payoff for each strategy. In this case he would find:

STRATEGY	BEST, OR MAXIMUM, PAYOFF
1	20←
2	9
3	4

Since he thinks Nature will give him the largest payoff, he will select that strategy with the *largest maximum*—the *maximum maximum*—or,

---

[3] Leonid Hurwicz, *Optimality Criteria for Decision Making under Ignorance* (Cowles Commission discussion paper, STATISTICS, No. 370, 1951, mimeographed; cited in R. D. Luce and Howard Raiffa, *Games and Decisions* (New York: John Wiley & Sons, Inc., 1958).

abbreviated, the *maximax.* In this case the maximax is the payoff of 20, which he will receive if he selects his first strategy and war occurs. (Admittedly, this makes him a strange kind of optimist.)

Now, Hurwicz didn't suggest that a rational decision-maker should be completely optimistic. He did suggest that if an individual felt "lucky" or optimistic he should be able to be rational about it. For this purpose he introduced the idea of a *coefficient of optimism.* As we have seen, the complete optimist takes account only of the largest payoff for each strategy. *The coefficient of optimism is a means by which the manager can take account of both the largest and the smallest payoffs—weighting their importance to his decision in accordance with his own feeling of optimism.* The coefficient of optimism is defined in terms of a lottery between the *largest* and *smallest* payoffs. In other words, the manager assigns to the maximum payoff a probability which he would be willing to accept in a lottery between that maximum payoff and the minimum payoff. This probability is his coefficient of optimism. Suppose, for example, that the executive chooses a coefficient of optimism of $\frac{3}{5}$. This means that he would be satisfied to accept a lottery in which the maximum payoff had a probability of occurrence of $\frac{3}{5}$ and the minimum payoff had a probability of occurrence of $\frac{2}{5}$. By Hurwicz's criterion we must determine the expected payoff of each strategy, assuming that *either* the maximum *or* the minimum will occur and with the indicated probabilities. The calculations (using a coefficient of optimism of $\frac{3}{5} = 0.6$ are straight-forward:

STRATEGY	MAXIMUM PAYOFF	MINIMUM PAYOFF	EXPECTED PAYOFF
1	20	−6	$20(0.6) + (−6)(0.4) = 9.6$←
2	9	0	$9(0.6) + 0(0.4) = 5.4$
3	4	4	$4(0.6) + 4(0.4) = 4.0$

According to the Hurwicz criterion, the investor should *select his first strategy*—investing in speculative stocks. (The same procedure can be used for a cost matrix where the coefficient of optimism is applied to the best, or minimum, cost. One minus this coefficient is multiplied by the worst, or maximum cost. The criterion dictates the choice of the strategy with the lowest expected payoff.)

It may be noted that a coefficient of optimism of 1 leads to the procedure of the complete optimist, which we described above. Similarly, a coefficient of optimism of 0 leads to the Wald criterion—that of the complete pessimist. Suppose the manager doesn't know his coefficient of optimism. Luce and Raiffa suggest one way to determine what it is.[4]

[4] Luce and Raiffa, *op. cit.,* p. 283.

Consider the following simple decision payoff matrix. It reflects the values of the original matrix where the payoffs have been converted to the 0–1 utility scale:

	N_1 WAR	N_3 DEPRESSION
S_1: Speculative stocks	1	0
S_4:	x	x

The new strategy S_4 has been chosen so that *the payoffs will be the same* no matter which state of nature occurs. For example, in the present case, it might be the strategy of leaving the money in the savings bank rather than investing. (It should also be noticed that S_3 already conforms to this condition.) The strategy S_1 contains only the *maximum* and *minimum* payoffs in the original payoff matrix. Suppose, now, that the executive has a coefficient of optimism of k (an unknown which remains to be determined; we know only that, by definition, it must be at or between 0 and 1). With k as the coefficient of optimism the individual would calculate the expected values of the two strategies as before. In this case they are

STRATEGY	EXPECTED PAYOFF
1	k
2	x

For what value of x in the above payoff matrix would the executive be indifferent between the two strategies? Note that this is really the standard-gamble technique again (as illustrated in Figure 5.1). Suppose the

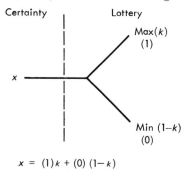

$$x = (1)k + (0)(1-k)$$

FIGURE 5.1

investor is indifferent between S_1 and S_4 if x has the value $\frac{1}{4}$. This means that the expected payoffs, in the Hurwicz sense, must be equal at $x = \frac{1}{4}$, or else the decision-maker wouldn't be indifferent. We conclude, then, that for this investor the coefficient of optimism, k, must be $\frac{1}{4}$.

Some say that this criterion is not as realistic as the one preceding or the two that follow this discussion. It may even be that the Hurwicz criterion is less likely to be used in practice.[5] Nevertheless, it is enriching for our discussion. *First,* it shows how one can attempt to include more than one payoff in the decision criterion without using all of them. *Second,* since it is a perfectly reasonable argument it demonstrates further variety and the difficulty of unambiguously selecting a criterion for this class of decision problem. *With such variety, what does it mean to be rational in the face of uncertainty? Third,* the procedure for determining the coefficient of optimism is yet another example of how one can go about obtaining quantitative measures for subjective utilities and valuations. This is such a crucial problem that any illustrations of procedures for coping with it are worthy of consideration.

58/ Criterion of Regret

A completely different criterion has been suggested by Savage.[6] This criterion requires an *alternative payoff measure* before it can be used. By "Savage criterion" we shall mean both the recommended payoff measure and the specific decision criterion applied to it.

We know that after a decision has been made and the state of nature has occurred—the executive receives the (indicated) payoff. Savage argues that after he knows the outcome the individual can experience regret because, now that he knows what state of nature occurred, he may wish he had selected a different strategy. Savage maintains that the decision-maker should attempt to minimize this regret which he can experience.

Exactly what is the nature of this regret? It resides in the fact that the best strategy may not have been selected for the particular state of nature that did occur. Savage suggests that *the amount of regret can be measured by the difference between the payoff actually received and the payoff that could have been received if the state of nature that was going to occur had been known.*

Thus, in our previous example, suppose war actually occurred. *If* the investor had selected his first strategy, he would experience no regret because he had already gotten the largest possible payoff. But if he had selected his second strategy he would have lost $20 - 9 = 11$, which he

---

[5] None of these uncertainty criteria receive much use. Managers avoid decision problems under uncertainty. They do this by ignoring the existence of such problems and by deferring these decisions. Faced with the need to reach a decision under uncertainty, knowledge of these criteria can be illuminating, but it is unreasonable to expect them to replace intuition.

[6] Leonard J. Savage, "The Theory of Statistical Decision," *Journal of the American Statistical Association,* 46 (1951), 55–67.

might otherwise have had. This measures his regret. *If* he had selected his third strategy he would experience regret of $20 - 4 = 16$.

Now, suppose peace prevailed. *If* the investor had selected his second strategy he would experience no regret because he would have obtained the largest possible payoff. But *if* he had selected his first strategy he would experience regret of $8 - 1 = 7$. And *if* he had chosen his third strategy he would experience regret of $8 - 4 = 4$.

Assuming that a depression occurred, the investor would experience no regret *if* he had selected his third strategy because it would have given him the largest possible payoff. *If* he had selected the first strategy, however, he would experience regret of $4 - (-6) = 10$. The selection of the second strategy in this case would give him regret of $4 - 0 = 4$. All of these measures can be conveniently presented in a *regret matrix:*

	N_1	N_2	N_3
S_1:	0	7	10
S_2:	11	0	4
S_3:	16	4	0

Savage then proposes to use a straightforward variant of the Wald criterion as the decision criterion for the regret matrix. Like Wald, he too chooses to be completely pessimistic about the state of nature that will occur. It will always be against the individual's best interests. The variant is required because the matrix measures regret, which (like costs) we want to make as small as possible. The original matrix represented (profit-type) payoffs, which we want to make as large as possible. But this difference is only procedural.

We ask: What is the worst that can happen to the decision-maker taking each of his strategies in turn? When we discussed the Wald criterion with respect to *profits* the answer was the minimum payoff for each strategy. Here it is *the maximum regret in each row*. We should note that this variant of the criterion is identical to that of the Wald criterion when applied to a cost matrix. We quickly obtain:

STRATEGY	WORST, OR MAXIMUM, REGRET
1	10←
2	11
3	16

The executive can insure himself against experiencing extreme regrets by selecting the strategy that has the *minimum maximum*, i.e., the *minimax*. In this case the minimax regret is 10. It is the maximum regret that the decision-maker must experience, assuming he selects his first strategy, which is to invest in speculative stocks. Of course, he may experience less regret, but 10 is the most regret he can possibly experience.

One could apply a criterion other than the minimax to the regret matrix. Either the Hurwicz or the Laplace criterion (to be discussed next) could be used instead of Wald's criterion. This is why it can be said that Savage's major contribution is the *regret measure of utility*. Nonetheless, for us the Savage criterion will describe both the development of the regret matrix and the application of the *Wald criterion* to it.

The Savage argument is applicable to either cost or profit matrices. If the original payoff matrix is expressed in "actual" dollars (whether of profits or costs), then the Savage regret calculation is equivalent to the determination of *opportunity costs* (which is a vitally important economic concept).[7] From all perspectives, *a regret matrix is an opportunity cost matrix.* This suggests that the regret matrix is rooted in fundamental economic truths which is further supported by the fact that a powerful empirical argument exists in favor of the Savage criterion. Namely, it is the only criterion that can make a "hedging" strategy optimal. *Hedging is the procedure for protecting oneself against fluctuations in the market price of commodities.* Since many businessmen hedge, we have empirical evidence of Savage's criterion in use.[8]

59/ *The Subjectivist Criterion*

All three previous criteria operated without reference to the probabilities associated with relevant states of nature. Consequently, they are well-suited for persons who subscribe to objective interpretations of probabilities. In the investor's case, this would be a crucial issue because it is clear that the states of nature in this problem do not lend themselves to objective probability assignments. After all, these states of nature are not part of a stable and repeatable system. Hence, they are not subject to frequency counts. In contrast, *the subjectivist would maintain that the manager has useful information in the form of degrees of belief concerning the likelihoods of occurrence of the relevant states of nature.* For the subjectivist, this problem is just like any other decision problem under risk.

It is evident that some problems which the objectivist considers classified under uncertainty will be considered classified under risk by the subjectivist. Are many problems affected in this way? The answer is yes —a very large number. And this explains why the dispute between objectivists and subjectivists is so important. *For the objectivist, a significant proportion of all decision problems* (particularly those which occur at higher organizational levels) *are cases of uncertainty. For the subjec-*

---

[7] See page 251 for a discussion of the opportunity cost concept.
[8] See Problem 5g at the end of this chapter.

tivist, few decision problems exist under uncertainty. To say that a decision problem is operating under uncertainty means to the subjectivist that the administrator has *absolutely no information* about the likelihoods of the states of nature. Most managers would agree that *such total ignorance is quite unlikely. So the subjectivist treats most decision problems as cases of risk. This has the important advantage that the decision criterion is not in dispute.*

There remain decision problems under uncertainty—even for the subjectivist. We shall now consider the criterion that the subjectivist recommends in this case. It is called the Laplace criterion,[9] and has been the subject of impassioned debate for many years.

The criterion is simple to state. *Since we don't know the probabilities with which the various states of nature will transpire, we will assume that they are all equal.* In other words, the inference is that every state of nature is equally likely to occur. Then we calculate the expected payoff for each strategy and select that strategy which has the largest expected payoff. That is, where there are n states of nature:

$$EV\ (S_i) = \frac{1}{n} \sum_{j=1}^{j=n} P_{ij}$$

This is straightforward. Why all the argument about it? One of the main reasons for contention is that the assumption of equal probabilities involves a famous doctrine called the *principle of insufficient reason.* The gist of this principle is: without specific cause a particular something won't happen. The relationship of the principle of insufficient reason to the problem at hand is direct. *Since we know of no reason for one state of nature to occur rather than another, we assume that one is as likely to occur as another.* The principle when used in this way *in connection with probabilities* is associated with the name of the eighteenth-century English clergyman Thomas Bayes. It is Bayes' *hypothesis* that if we have no reason to believe one probability to be different from another—we should assume them equal.

The principle has other uses in probability theory as well, and all of them are violently debated. For example, how do we know that a fair coin has a probability of $\frac{1}{2}$ of showing heads when it is tossed? One answer is that we know it because of the principle of insufficient reason. There is no specific reason why the coin should come up one way rather than another, so the probabilities must be equal (hence $\frac{1}{2}$, since there are only two possibilities). Many probabilists reject this argument. They state that the only reason we think the probability of a head is $\frac{1}{2}$ is the fact that we have observed it come up about half the time.

[9] This criterion is named after Pierre Simon, Marquis de Laplace (1749–1827), a great French mathematician who first used this criterion in important ways.

One of the best-known arguments of the Middle Ages had to do with this principle of insufficient reason. Jean Buridan, in the first half of the fourteenth century, invented an imaginary ass—known ever since as Buridan's Ass. This ass was supposed to be placed exactly in the middle between two identical bales of hay. Buridan maintained that the ass must starve to death because it would have no reason to go to one bale of hay rather than another—an interesting application of the principle.

Another famous, ancient use of the principle was with regard to the position of the earth in space. This argument ran to the effect that the earth couldn't be just any place in space because, if this were the case, God would have had no reason to put it one place rather than another. Therefore, He would never have put it anywhere. Starting from here, it was argued that the earth must be at the center of the universe.

Such uses of the principle as this sufficed to bring it into considerable disrepute. Nonetheless, the principle has many proponents who state that if used with caution, it is as legitimate as many other basic principles which underlie our efforts to understand the nature of reality.

The application of the subjectivist criterion is simple. Since there are three states of nature in our investor's example we assume that the probability of occurrence of each of them is $\frac{1}{3}$. On this basis we can easily calculate the expected payoff for each strategy:

STRATEGY	EXPECTED PAYOFF	
1	$\frac{1}{3}[20 + 1 + (-6)] = 5$	
2	$\frac{1}{3}(9 + 8 + 0) = 5.67$	←
3	$\frac{1}{3}(4 + 4 + 4) = 4$	

The largest expected payoff is that of Strategy 2. This is the strategy which should be selected according to the Laplace criterion.

Other decision criteria have been suggested, but these four are among the best-known. It is interesting to note that every strategy in our example has been selected by one of the criteria. Strategy 1 (speculative stocks) was selected by the Savage criterion and by the Hurwicz criterion with coefficient of optimism of $\frac{3}{5}$. Strategy 2 (high-grade stocks) was selected by the Laplace criterion. And Strategy 3 was selected by the Wald criterion. The selection of the decision criterion is obviously of crucial importance. So it must be emphasized that there is *no best criterion* in the sense that a conclusive argument can be offered for it. As a matter of fact, there are examples that run counter to each of the criteria. By this we mean specific decision problems for which common sense would indicate a different selection of strategy than that indicated by the decision criterion. *It should not be construed, however, that common sense is the ultimate criterion. Common sense may work well enough when reality is uncomplicated.* Trouble starts when significant complexity exists and *common sense tells us that we can no longer rely on common sense.* In such cases the choice of criterion must be left to the decision-maker. It will be determined by individual attitudes or by company policy.

60/ A Decision Criterion for Decision Criteria

A question might be raised at this point: If decision theory is so useful, why can't the problem of the decision criterion to be used be formulated as a decision problem and solved using decision theory? In other words, why not assume that the manager has four available strategies (say the four criteria discussed above), determine the possible states of nature, the objective, the payoff, and establish the payoff matrix. Then use decision theory to select a strategy—*viz.,* the decision criterion to be used for decision problems.

This question involves us with the *mirror problem* of how to decide how to decide (previously discussed in Chapter 2). Although we cannot completely unravel this knotty problem, there are several important aspects which will be worth considering. To begin with, how can we formulate the objective which is one step removed from our previous objective—to maximize the rate of return on our investment? Of course, we still want to maximize the return but we want something else in addition. In the investment example, all three strategies, under different criteria, held promise of maximizing our return. This seems like nonsense until we recognize the fact that uncertainty cannot be compromised. *Our problem in rendering decisions under uncertainty is to do it in such a way that our attitudes and state of mind are not jeopardized.*

Consequently, the formulation of our new objective must include consideration of the decision-maker's personality, attitudes, and way of life. The strategies are the four decision criteria. The states of nature become the range of values which the payoff measure (rate of return) could assume. For simplicity we can call them: win, lose, and draw. The new payoff measure must be some index of the *change* that will occur *in our state of mind* for any combination of strategy and state of nature. Let's see then what we have.

We must first characterize the individuals who would use the different decision criteria. We can call them: *cautious, adventurous, bad loser, and rational.* There are, of course, many other types of decision-makers and all shades between them. In this characterization we are taking some obvious liberties for the purpose of emphasizing the point. The four different kinds of decision-makers would now proceed to fill in the pay-off measures for the matrix below:

	WIN	DRAW	LOSE
Wald (cautious):			
Hurwicz (adventurous):			
Savage (bad loser):			
Laplace (rational):			

We can readily imagine that all four types of people will put different payoff measures into this matrix. For example, if an adventurous person decides to act cautiously and loses, he will be much more unhappy than if he had lost taking a sizable risk. The exact reverse will be true of the cautious person. The question now arises, assuming that we have filled in such a payoff matrix, how do we determine the probabilities of win, draw, and lose? Since they exist under uncertainty, we must choose a decision criterion (Wald, Hurwicz, Savage, or Laplace?), and we are back to the same problem with which we started. If we choose, we can pass on to the next mirror reflection. On the other hand, the adventurous person is likely to say: "I'm counting on luck," and he will rate "win" as more probable. The cautious person will say: "I can't count on luck," and he will lower the probability of win.

61/ Sensitivity of the Criterion

There is still another way of looking at this problem. We shall disregard the influence of attitude and turn to the Laplace criterion, introducing small deviations from the assumption of equal probabilities. In other words, we are going to presume that we are not completely uncertain and that one of the states of nature is *just a little more likely* than any other state of nature. It will be recognized that even if we make small changes in all of the probabilities of the states of nature, we are no longer making decisions under uncertainty. We are now deciding under *risk*. Yet, if the changes that we have made are small, the formulation is almost identical with the Laplace criterion.

At some point, as we add little increments to the probability of one particular state of nature, while taking away an equivalent amount from the other probabilities, the strategy chosen by the Laplace criterion can be replaced by another strategy which has a larger expected value for the payoff. *The extent of change required to achieve such a shift reflects upon the sensitivity of this aspect of the system.*

For example, the Laplace selection of Strategy 2 in the investment problem shifts to the selection of Strategy 1 when the first state of nature (war) goes from 0.33 probability to 0.37. (The other two states of nature are changed from 0.33 to 0.31.) On the other hand, the probability of depression must increase from 0.33 to 0.53 for Strategy 2 to shift to Strategy 3 (while war and peace go from 0.33 to 0.23). One way to interpret this is to say that if Strategy 1 is chosen by a particular criterion—except the Laplace—that criterion was chosen by the decision-maker because he had *more knowledge than he was aware he had.* That is why he chose a criterion other than the Laplace. In fact, he believed that war was more likely than peace or depression by an amount of 0.04. The required shift is small, and thereby *the system is sensitive to minor attitudinal biases* which support the contention that war will occur. Similarly, if the decision-maker's criterion selected Strategy 3 then we infer that he had reason to believe that a depression would occur and that he had as much as 0.20 additional belief in this outcome. This required shift is large. *The system is insensitive to minor biases* that a depression will occur.

The approach we are using is *sensitivity probing,* which is based on the question: How unbalanced must the relative uncertainties be before we stop calling them uncertainties? Since if we knew the probabilities of the states of nature we would use expected values, the Laplace criterion is the only one (of our four) that expresses *no attitude* except the desire to be rational. That is, *if we say we don't know the probabilities then we must act as if we don't know the probabilities.* That is why we characterize the Laplace criterion as rational. Therefore, the following observations about the attitude of the decision-maker seem relevant to the selection of the decision criterion.

1. States of nature may be equiprobable but it is unlikely that the individual has the chances of their occurring equally weighted *in his mind.*

2. It is possible that if you choose a criterion other than Laplace it is because you favor the probability that one or another state of nature will prevail. In any case, when it seems desirable, the Laplace criterion can permit the individual to think of the states of nature in equiprobable terms. Sensitivity testing can shed some light on the degree to which attitudes may affect results.

62/ Decisions Under Conflict

All previous discussion has been in terms of decisions against Nature. *The basic supposition has been that the state of nature which occurs will be independent of the selection of strategy of the manager.* When rational opponents are involved, we have decisions under conflict and this supposition is no longer true. On the contrary, usually the rational opponent (or opponents) will give careful thought to what the other executive can be expected to do before selecting his (or their) own courses of action. The essence of decision problems involving rational opponents is *conflict of interest.* For our discussion, the various opponents are all presumed to be rational. Therefore, they will be attempting to frustrate their opponents' wishes. As will be shown, *if one opponent exhibits nonrational behavior, he can only suffer for it.*

This part of decision theory is commonly known as *game theory.* It relates to a complex, highly developed body of knowledge. *Games* (in the general sense of game theory) *are customarily classified according to the number of opponents and the degree of conflict of interest.* The theory of games with only two opponents presents one of the simplest (but not simple!) cases. It is the variant most thoroughly developed. We shall confine our attention to this kind of game.

Games that have complete conflict of interest are ones in which what one opponent gains, the other loses. These are called *zero-sum games.* The nearest approximation to this kind of game in the business world would be a competitive battle for *share of the market.* One competitor can only increase his *share* of the market at the expense of his competitors. Political parties vying for Congressional seats is another illustration. Competitions for the award of fixed grants from foundations and for larger shares of a *given* budget also apply. Most recreational games that we play for fun are of this completely competitive type.

Games with less than complete conflict of interest are called *non-zero-sum games.* The majority of organization problems involving rational opponents are of this type. An example would be a competitive battle for sales. Here the *size* of the market is involved. An advertising campaign might result in an increased share of the market, but it could also benefit the other competitors because of the tendency of advertising to stimulate sales for the product as well as for the brand. In other words, the gain of one competitor in terms of sales volume is not necessarily completely at the expense of the other competitors. The same reasoning applies to military conflicts and to conflicts between individuals and groups within and between organizations. The theory of nonzero-sum games is fascinating, but too elaborate for discussion here. We shall confine our attention to *two-person, zero-sum games* and the explanation of the decision criterion that is appropriate for this case.

Our concern is with competitive actions on the part of the opponent rather than with states of nature. So, instead of the N's we have been using we will use C's to represent the various possible competitive strategies. Since what one competitor wins, another loses (in a zero-sum game), we need use only one payoff matrix as before to represent the decision problem. We could not do this for a nonzero-sum game. In order to analyze nonzero-sum games we need *a separate payoff matrix for each opponent.*

Let us take as an example a decision problem involving a struggle for the share of the market against one opponent. Suppose that the manager has three strategies available and his competitor has four (there is no need for them to have the same number of possible strategies). The payoff matrix will be constructed in terms of the percentage-points increase in market share accruing to the manager.

		OPPONENT'S STRATEGIES			
		C_1	C_2	C_3	C_4
MANAGER'S STRATEGIES	S_1:	0.6	−0.3	1.5	−1.1
	S_2:	0.7	0.1	0.9	0.5
	S_3:	−0.3	0.0	−0.5	0.8

This payoff matrix is read in exactly the same way as were the earlier ones. If the manager selects his first strategy and his opponent selects his third strategy, then the manager will increase his share of the market by 1.5 percentage points. And, of course, since this is a zero-sum game, the competitor will *lose* 1.5 percentage points of the market. Negative entries represent losses to the manager and gains to the competitor. The question is: How should the manager select his strategy? The difference from the cases where there was no rational opponent is that now, in reaching his decision, the manager must take into account what the opponent is likely to do. And, of course, vice versa holds.

It might appear that this would greatly increase the complexity of the decision problem and require some new kind of decision criterion. Actually, that isn't the case. In this kind of game it can be shown that the *only* rational decision criterion is the *Wald criterion*. Let us go through the reasoning to determine the strategy to be selected by using this criterion and then attempt to justify our statement that it is the *only* rational criterion.

The manager reasons, according to the Wald criterion, that if he selects S_1 he might lose as much as 1.1 (if his opponent selects C_4). If he selects S_2 he cannot do worse than to gain 0.1 (if his opponent selects

C_2). If the manager selects S_3 he may lose 0.5 (if his opponent chooses C_3). Thus:

STRATEGY	MINIMUM PAYOFF
S_1	-1.1
S_2	0.1←
S_3	-0.5

Following the Wald criterion we now select the maximum of these minimum payoffs, the *maximin*. In this case it is 0.1, resulting from selecting S_2—which should therefore be the choice.

Remember, the opponent is rational. What is he thinking? He, too, elects to use the Wald criterion. From his standpoint the worst that can happen if he selects C_1 is that he will lose 0.7 (the maximum value in the column since the payoffs are stated in terms of *his opponent*). If he selects C_2 the worst that can happen is that he should lose 0.1 (if his opponent selects S_2). Proceeding similarly we obtain:

COMPETITOR'S ACTION	MAXIMUM LOSS
C_1	0.7
C_2	0.1←
C_3	1.5
C_4	0.8

According to the Wald criterion, the competitor will want to minimize his maximum loss, the *minimax* value. This minimax value is 0.1, achieved by selecting C_2. This, then, should be his choice. Thus, the best decisions on the part of the two competitors are that the manager should select S_2, his competitor should select C_2, and the result will be an increase of 0.1 percentage points in market share to the manager.

Why can we say that this is the only *rational* approach to such a competitive decision problem? Consider the situation from the standpoint of the manager. He knows that his opponent can minimize his maximum loss by selecting C_2. Assume that the opponent uses C_2. Then if the manager selected any other strategy but his S_2, he would do worse than he would by selecting S_2. If he selected S_1 he would lose 0.3 instead of winning 0.1. If he selected S_3 he would gain nothing instead of gaining 0.1. Similarly, the competitor knows that the manager can maximize his minimum gain by selecting S_2. If he does so the opponent does best by selecting his C_2. If he does anything else he loses more. Thus, with complete conflict of interest, the opponents are driven to use the Wald criterion.

If the manager *knows* that his competitor will not use C_2, or if he has any other pertinent information about what his competitor will do —other than what is expected of him—he will establish probabilities for the competitive strategies. From these, he can determine his own optimum strategy on the basis of decision-making under risk. *In such an event, the information he has obtained has measurable utility.* It will permit him to realize a greater payoff than he could otherwise expect. On the other hand, if he is unsure of his information he can continue to use his maximin strategy and *gain the advantage which must come to him if his competitor does not act in an entirely rational manner.*

It may be noted that in this payoff matrix the maximin value for the manager equaled the minimax value for his opponent—both of them being 0.1. This is by no means always the case. When the two values are different it develops that the use of *mixed strategies*—where the specific strategy to be used is selected randomly with a determined probability—will make them equal.[9] The proof of this fact is called the *fundamental theorem* of game theory. We shall not discuss this theorem further. It won't affect our point that the existence of a rational opponent can simplify the decision problem—converting it to a strictly deterministic situation (even when mixed strategies are involved).

Often, the information required to construct a payoff matrix is difficult to obtain. This may be especially true when the payoffs must represent the utilities of various outcomes to both participants in a competitive decision system. Frequently, we have recourse to the use of ranked data. This is well-illustrated by an example in Ch. 9, p. 224.

If the competitors do not have the same approximate utility then a nonzero-sum game with *two payoff* matrices is required. And this assumes that *each* opponent is able to estimate his competitor's utilities. Otherwise, the matrix analysis loses its meaning. The common reason that competitive situations are of the nonzero-sum type is that the utilities of the opponents are not the same. Since *utilities are, by definition, subjective,* it may well be that the opponents do not know the utilities of their competitors for the various outcomes. As a matter of fact, one might expect that this would be the *usual case.*

Certain types of organizations often do have some degree of similarity in goals. In these cases, we would expect that the opponents might have some idea of the opposition's utility for the various outcomes. However, if a decision problem arose in which the executive really had no idea about the utility his opponent ascribed to the outcomes, then the decision problem would have to be treated under *uncertainty.*[10] This results because, not knowing the utilities of his opponent for the outcomes, the decision-maker has no way of knowing anything about the

---

[9] The equal value is called a *saddlepoint,* whether it arises from mixed or pure strategies.

[10] And independent of the competitor in all respects.

probabilities of the different competitive actions—which is an equivalent definition of decision-making under uncertainty.

In terms of actual organizational conditions, which decision situations are most likely to arise? It is clear that a large number of problems are primarily involved with states of nature. So the usefulness of our analysis concerning certainty, risk, and uncertainty is evident. But what about rational opponents? According to the classical conditions of *free enterprise* any decision problem is simply against nature because, by the definition of these conditions, no one business can have any effect on market conditions through any strategy which it might elect to follow. On the other hand, *wherever free-enterprise conditions do not exist in a specific market we are obliged to include competitive actions as part of the decision problem.* In short, under *oligopolistic* conditions in a particular market it is necessary to include competitive actions in the payoff matrix. Also, many problems of a *monopoly* can be construed as games against a rational opponent. In this case, they are the suppliers and consumers. Generally, *small organizations that deal in a large marketplace* can ignore the effects of a rational opponent. *This puts them in the position of deciding under conditions of risk or uncertainty. As the size of the company increases with respect to the market, the influence of rational opponents is felt.* As a rule, a particular management can evaluate its situation with respect to the importance of competition.

PROBLEMS

1. A drugstore chain has six stores. A new company policy is established which, in effect, will reassign the present six store managers to the stores in such a way as to minimize the total traveling time of the managers from home to store. How many possible arrangements (strategies) are there? Why is this decision-making under certainty?

2. A department store has four different strategies for obtaining advance information about the line of merchandise which their chief competitor will carry in the next season. The amount of information that can be obtained will depend on whether or not the competitor is aware that the department store is trying to get this information. Assume the following payoff matrix:

	N_1	N_2
S_1:	-4	10
S_2:	2	2
S_3:	3	0
S_4:	-1	6

where N_1 = competitor is aware,
N_2 = competitor isn't aware,

(Payoff measures are the utility of information obtained, and negative values represent misinformation.)

   a. If the competitor is aware (state of nature N_1), what strategy should be chosen?

   b. If the competitor is not aware (state of nature N_2), what strategy should be chosen?

   c. Assume that the probabilities are 0.90 for N_1 and 0.10 for N_2. What choice should be made?

   d. What would be the maximin choice?

   e. What would be the maximax choice?

   f. Assume a coefficient of optimism of 0.70. Which strategy will be chosen? Now, assume a coefficient of pessimism of 0.70. Does the choice of strategy change?

   g. What would be the result if we took the minimax of regret?

   h. What would be the result if we use the principle of insufficient reason?

3. Assume that the boxes of a tic-tac-toe game are numbered 1–9. How many possible combinations of the numbers (strategies) are available to the player who begins the game? How many are available to the second player? How many boxes are there in the payoff matrix? Ignoring the numbers of the boxes, how many basically different opening moves are there? How many basically different second moves are there? How large would the payoff matrix be for the first two moves?

4. Instead of tic-tac-toe boxes, consider each number to represent a sales area. Assume that whichever company gets to an area first wins that area. Each company has only one salesman. The salesman must spend one day in each area in order to win it for his company. Say that every move of one box along a row or column takes one day traveling time. Every move of one box along a diagonal takes two days traveling time. Can you devise a game to fit these rules? What would be each player's objective?

5. You are working as a consultant in a foreign country where the exchange rate is 100 units of the foreign currency for $1. You will be there for five months and your expenses are fixed in units of the foreign currency at 50,000 units per month. A sky-rocketing inflation is temporarily in check while the government is attempting to negotiate a large loan. If the government gets the loan the effect will be to lower the exchange rate by 10 per cent. If the loan is refused the exchange rate will increase by 20 per cent. In addition, a general strike has been called. If this strike is successful the government will be forced to take some economic measures which will increase the exchange rate by 15 per cent. If the strike fails the rate will decrease by 10 per cent. It can be assumed that the two events in question (loan and strike) are independent. Thus there are four states of nature:

   N_1: Loan, strike fails, rate drops to 81.0
   N_2: Loan, strike succeeds, rate increases to 103.5
   N_3: No loan, strike fails, rate increases to 108.0
   N_4: No loan, strike succeeds, rate increases to 138.0

For our purposes it will be sufficient to consider three strategies:

S_1: Immediately convert enough dollars into foreign units to meet all five months' expenses.

S_2: Wait until the events above have occurred, meanwhile holding dollars.

S_3: Hedge by converting half the amount now and holding half in dollars.

Your objective will be to minimize your dollar expenses.

   a. Determine the payoff matrix in dollars of expense.

   b. What is the minimax strategy?

   c. What is the optimal strategy if the coefficient of optimism is 0.6?

   d. What is the optimal strategy by the criterion of minimization of regret?

   e. What is the optimal strategy by the Laplace criterion?

   f. Suppose it is known that the probability that the government will receive the loan is 0.75 and the probability that the strike will succeed is 0.4. What is the optimal strategy?

   g. S_3 is the hedging strategy. Show that no hedging strategy involving the immediate conversion of a proportion k (and holding $1 - k$) could be optimal under any criterion we have covered other than the Savage criterion.

   h. Can you find an argument suggesting an optimal hedge in the sense of the optimal proportion k to convert now?

6. You are at a horse race and are considering placing a bet on a specific horse in a specific race. Thus, there are four possible strategies and four states of nature. Suppose the payoff matrix is:

	WIN	PLACE	SHOW	LOSE
BET WIN	7	−2	−2	−2
BET PLACE	3	3	−2	−2
BET SHOW	2	2	2	−2
DON'T BET	0	0	0	0

   a. What is the maximin strategy?

   b. What strategy is selected by the Hurwicz criterion with coefficient of optimism .5?

   c. What strategy is selected by the Savage criterion?

   d. What strategy is selected by the Laplace criterion?

   e. Suppose there are eight horses in the race. Criticize the assumptions underlying the Laplace criterion and solve the decision problem under risk, which results for the above payoff matrix on the basis of your criticism.

   f. What might be the subjectivist's answer to your criticism in "e"?

7. Write down the payoff matrices for the investment problem, the lottery problem, and the numbers game problem of Chapter 4 (problems 2, 9, and 10, respectively). Apply the Wald, Savage, and Laplace criteria to these decision problems.

8. As an example of some of the difficulties involved in the analysis of two-person nonzero-sum games we can use the following:

	A'S PAYOFFS			B'S PAYOFFS	
	B_1	B_2		B_1	B_2
A_1	1	-4	A_1	1	5
A_2	5	-2	A_2	-4	-2

a. What are the players' maximin strategies? Should they use them?

b. Consider the difference if the game is only played once or if it is going to be played a number of times.

c. Consider the difference if communication is allowed between the players before the game is played.

d. Suppose A and B are competitors and the first strategy in each case is to leave price unchanged. The second strategy is to lower price. Do you think payoff matrices such as these might be reasonable representations of this situation?

9. Set up a reasonable decision model for the following problem. A manufacturer of firecrackers agrees to use acceptance sampling for consecutive lots —each consisting of 1,000 units. Destructive inspection procedures are required so that clearly 100 per cent inspection is out of the question. What guidelines would you suggest and what general form will your model take?

10. It is stated that competitive decision methods for zero-sum games are equivalent to decision-making under certainty. Why is this so? Would the same statement apply when mixed strategies are used?

Chapter 6

Applied
Decision
Theory

Let us presume that the manager has been convinced by the preceding five chapters and that he is now prepared to put decision theory
to the test of practice. He is aware that many problems will stand in
his way. These difficulties in applying decision theory would eliminate
many, if not most, important applications if the manager were left to
his own resources. Fortunately, however, operations research (O.R.)
can act in his behalf. And it is our thesis that O.R. can best be understood when it is considered as an adjunct to the application of decision
theory.

63/ Definition of Operations Research

What is operations research? In common with many other fields, it
is easy to point to but hard to define. There is general agreement that
O.R. originated just prior to World War II [1] in the form of attempts by
various kinds of scientists to solve military problems. These were often
totally unconnected in substance with the specialties of the scientists.
The O.R. approach was extended to business applications after the
war, and has since become a burgeoning field with important implications and effects for industrial, institutional, and governmental systems.
It has many consultants, active professional societies, thousands of books,
monographs, and journals. Executive programs in O.R. and courses of

[1] First in Great Britain (directly related to radar) and rapidly followed by the United
States. The field is known as operational research in England.

study in colleges and universities abound. The steady growth in the number of practitioners is well beyond expectation. *Yet, no single, generally accepted definition of what operations research is exists.* This is a clue to the fact that the field is too multidimensional for any one definition to suffice.

There are three main categories of definitions. *First,* those which are variants or elaborations of the definition proposed by Morse and Kimball who published the *first* operations research text.

> Operations research is a scientific method of providing executive departments with a quantitative basis for decisions regarding the operations under their control.[2]

Any O.R. practitioner will recognize that much of his work falls within the compass of this description; nevertheless, it is not suitable. Replace "operations research" with "cost accounting" in the above definition and the new statement holds equally well. Or, replace "operations research" with "the control chart." The description still holds. We see that this definition does not distinguish O.R. from a number of other methodological approaches to organizational problems, most of which have been in use far longer than O.R. Definitions that do not clearly distinguish one field from related or different fields cannot be satisfactory.

A *second* approach to the problem of defining O.R. is to list the various techniques that have come to be associated with it. Many descriptions of the subject proceed by listing seriatim such methodological areas as queuing theory, inventory theory, linear programming, Monte Carlo, search theory, game theory, and so on. Certainly operations research often utilizes these techniques, but to define O.R. in terms of techniques is a mistake. It would be like defining medicine in terms of the collection of drugs and techniques which doctors use to cure their patients. This approach to definition is obviously ridiculous for medicine, and equally so for operations research. If there is no more unity to O.R. than the latest catalogue of techniques that can be culled from the literature, then there is no merit in giving it a name.

Third, Philip Morse (who collaborated on the first definition) has whimsically suggested that O.R. *is* what O.R. practitioners *do.* This definition has the undoubted merit of being correct; but it also suffers from the equally undoubted demerit of being uninformative. We cannot use it to communicate—even among those who use it.

The approach that this book takes is that *O.R. is applied decision theory.* There is nothing vague about this notion. But clearly, the do-

---

[2] Philip M. Morse and George E. Kimball, *Methods of Operations Research* (New York: John Wiley & Sons, Inc., 1951), p. 1.

main it encompasses is enormous. In practice, such enormity of scope is evident.

Operations research requires the use of scientific, mathematical, or logical means to structure and resolve *decision problems*. Construction of an adequate *decision model* is crucial. Questions of strategy development, recognition of states of nature, competitive considerations, outcomes and utilities, etc. are not just matters of tools and techniques. *Implementation abilities* for the decisions reached are implicit requirements for model construction. This is the decision context that enables a manager better to achieve a thoroughgoing rationality in dealing with his problems. With this in mind, let us examine some of the contributions that O.R. can make to the resolution of decision problems.

64/ O.R. Applications to Decision Theory

To begin with, there is a problem in formulating objectives. Multiple objectives, conflicts between objectives, the treatment of constraints, and the effects of suboptimization are some of the difficulties normally encountered. There are, of course, a considerable number of decision situations for which these complications are not critical. In all cases, *the identification and choice of objectives begins as a managerial function*. Operations research can provide both stimulation and guidance, but there is no way of replacing the executive responsibility for the clear definition of objectives. Where complex cases, including conflict, exist, O.R. can sometimes help to unravel the tangled skein of objectives.

Even when the objectives have been stated, it is not always an easy matter to discover the appropriate measures of utility. We have treated this topic at some length in Chapter 4. At that point, a number of possibilities were examined, including the use of *logarithms* as utility measures for "natural" payoffs. We also considered *ranking* and the *standard gamble* for payoffs that lack a natural measure. Problems of measurement concern every scientific field. Applied decision theory or O.R. is no exception. As needed, methods must be developed or borrowed for the observation, measurement, and construction of meaningful payoffs. Some help is available from the literature of other sciences (i.e., the behavioral and physical sciences). But this does not begin to exhaust the measurement and accounting problems that remain in the management sciences.

Using O.R. To Discover Strategies, States of Nature, and Competitive Strategies. The discovery and enumeration of strategies, states of nature, and competitive strategies requires *experience* and *imagination* on the part of both the manager and the O.R. practitioner. In the section on maximization principles in Chapter 2, step two stated that all variables pertinent to the attainment of the objectives should be isolated. These variables are the components that, when taken together, form strategies, states of nature, and competitive strategies. But what happens when the variables that determine the outcome are not known? What can operations research methods contribute?

Not directly, but as a by-product of its logic, O.R. has been successful in helping the manager discover relevant variables. The operations research contribution to discovery has been so considerable that there has been an observable tendency *to define the methodology of operations research in terms of this discovery function.* While the overemphasis is unfortunate, nevertheless, *the discovery attribute characterizes the generalist,* and as we have previously stated, O.R. is a generalist's specialty.

A difference should be noted between the discovery of abstract variables (such as resources, activities, origins, and destinations) and the discovery of nonabstract variables that apply to specific "real-world" problems. The ability to convert from one level to the other requires the fullest coordination between O.R. and the manager. Frequently, an O.R. practitioner endeavors to discover the relevant factors for his problem by *analogy* with problems in different areas, such as physics, engineering, biology, or ecology. This approach demands wide experience in different fields and the ability to think *creatively* about them.

Successes in this area often can be attributed to strong analogies, which stem from a similarity of verbs. Let us consider "search." A personnel department searches for new employees, an advertising campaign is a search for new customers, a plane searches for submarines or people lost at sea, a scientist searches the literature for a fact, and science searches for *true* hypotheses. Success in determining the relevant variables and their relationships in any one area may be extendible to others, with some suitable translation of terms. The verb "decide" is an excellent example in its own right. In this book we have been discussing the verb concept, "decide," in great depth, without requiring specific details to picture any one situation. Similar examples are "allocate," "replace," and "store." By finding key verbs such as these, the practitioner may be led to a suitable, and already developed, analogy in another field.

The methods by which relevant variables and their relationships are discovered must be supported with keen perception, understanding of the system, and creative insights. These attributes are not the exclusive properties of any one field. They belong to scientists and managers alike.

O.R.'s particular contribution to these endeavors lies in the *systematization of pattern formation and the subsequent logical analysis of meaningful analogies.* For example, the variables of epidemic models that describe the spread of contagious diseases can be systematically compared with those variables that describe the sales growth of a new product. The variables of addiction models can be transformed to portray the nature of brand loyalty. Prey-predator models of ecology highlight a set of variables that might be applicable to brand share analyses. Gas laws that describe the diffusion of particles may focus attention on a proper set of variables and relations for advertising a new idea or conversely for squelching a fast-spreading rumor.[3]

On the other hand, analogies can be *deceptive.* There are numerous examples of cases where a seemingly "almost perfect" fit has led to erroneous conclusions. Sometimes it is hard to resist forcing a problem to fit an analogous technique (à la Procrustes who compulsively made everyone fit his bed—the too short were stretched and the too long were cut down to size). There are also problems for which no suitable analogies are known. Under pressure, force-fits may be resorted to, but not without obvious dangers. Somehow, new forms must be found. The usefulness and cost of employing varying degrees of approximations to reality merit attention. Although we can't say much about the nature of analogic innovation, it is certain that a great deal of study concerning such creativity and the search for knowledge remains to be accomplished. All fields of endeavor share responsibility and concern in the pursuit of such progress.

Using O.R. To Handle Excessive Numbers of Strategies and States of Nature. A decision concerning inventory levels might include the full range of possibilities—from stockpiling several years' supply to operating on an order-as-you-go basis with virtually no inventory on hand. Perhaps thousands or millions of possible strategies are required to represent this situation. Similarly, the complex decision of allocating an organization's resources may easily require an astronomical number of strategies to include all feasible alternatives. We noted earlier that a machine-shop problem, of no apparent complexity, could involve 2.5 quintillion strategies. A sane manager is not going to consider seriously writing out a payoff matrix involving an incredible number of rows—no matter how enthusiastic he may be about decision theory.

In the same way, the decision-maker will often find that the number of possible states of nature is prohibitively enormous. For example, the relevant states of nature might include ten different levels of gross na-

---

[3] See Problems 1-7 at the end of this chapter for further explanation.

tional product, ten kinds of weather, ten different situations regarding interest rates and the availability of credit, twenty competitive strategies, five international situations, and ten possible levels of demand. For many problems this is not unreasonably exorbitant. Yet it already adds up to 1,000,000 (10 × 10 × 10 × 20 × 5 × 10) different states of nature. At one second per column it would take more than 11 days of continuous work to write down these 1,000,000 columns!

How does O.R. help when there are such huge numbers of strategies and states of nature? Whether the excessive number is attributable to strategies, states of nature, or both, the difficulty of size is susceptible to the same treatment—*mathematical representation.* By using mathematical models the enormous number of strategies and/or states of nature can often, *but not always,* be subsumed by a few equations. When this can be done the great number of strategies and states of nature no longer represent an insurmountable difficulty. In the past two decades, the capability for solving very large systems of equations has been tremendously enhanced by the development and proliferation of large-scale computers. Third generation computers turn out in a few hours what would formerly have taken years of analysis. These computers can solve huge systems of equations, and it is becoming increasingly feasible to represent extremely complex decision problems in mathematical form. Before the advent of powerful computers decision problems could sometimes be represented by equations, but these equations could not be solved. We have come a long way on both counts.

Of course, computers must be fed the information they use. This includes careful instructions (the *program*) concerning how to perform the appropriate operations on the information. The *program, in turn, is an appropriate transformation of the relevant *decision model.* Computers can be programmed for a variety of problem-solving and decision-making operations, but not until the model has been built. If a model does not exist for the solution of a particular problem it must be developed. This may take a great deal of time and money. However, as more analogies are found, techniques developed, and standard programs created, it has become possible to adapt this "library" for effective use at much less cost.

The operations a computer can perform are basically quite simple. For example, it can *search* for information that is *stored* in its memory; it can *compare* two numbers, accepting or rejecting the larger or the smaller; it can *combine* two numbers and thus perform addition, and so on. Computer programs are combinations of these simple operations, but the combinations are ingeniously chosen so that the result can yield complex mathematical analyses. Thanks to developments such as these, excessive numbers of strategies and states of nature are no longer *so* serious a handicap in the resolution of complex decision situations.

Using O.R. To Determine Outcomes. A major problem facing the manager who endeavors to use decision theory is the difficulty of determining the "actual" outcomes. At the intersection of every strategy (row) and state of nature (column) there is an outcome cell. Into this cell the manager must insert the appropriate payoff measure—which is not necessarily the natural measure of the outcome.

We have emphasized the necessity of determining the payoff *utility* that will result from a given *measured* outcome. Also, we have explained methods by which the manager can express his *utility* quantitatively for the various *outcomes*. But there remains the question: How is the *outcome* determined?

The word "determined" has two implications. In one sense it means: The *process* by which the selected strategy interacts with the state of nature that occurs to produce a specific outcome. In the other sense it means: The *knowledge* of what that outcome is. These two aspects are, of course, totally related. Specifically, if we know the first, we can *often* determine the second. The reader might think we should have said, "We can *always* determine the second." It would appear that if we know the process by which the strategy and the state of nature interact to produce the outcome, then we should certainly be able to determine the outcome. But a difficulty can arise.

We may not be able to solve the equations that describe the interaction (which is why we must say often instead of always). Further, even if we don't know the way in which the outcome is produced we may be able to know what it is. Sometimes this can be achieved through the analysis of past experience. For example, the meteorologist believes he knows the way various factors work to determine weather. Unfortunately, he cannot solve the equations that describe their interactions—and present-day computing equipment doesn't help. Nonetheless, he can do a pretty good job of predicting the path of a hurricane based upon the careful study and generalization of past events.

Another approach for deriving outcomes when the process is unknown is the use of *experimental methods*. The chemist may not understand the reaction between two solutions or the nature of a catalyst, but he can find out what happens in his laboratory when the two solutions are mixed or the catalyst is present. Similarly, although the consumer's mind may be a black box to the marketing manager, *test markets and surveys are his laboratory* for discovering outcomes in spite of his ignorance of the process from which these outcomes arise.

When the process that produces the outcomes is known, O.R. can usually bring to bear powerful mathematical tools to determine the specific outcomes. In fact, the determination of outcomes is an area in which operations research has made another major contribution. Let us look at some simple organization problems in this context.

Consider a manager in charge of some customer service system like toll booths at a bridge, operators at a switchboard, nurses in a hospital, or waiters in a restaurant. The manager has the problem of determining the number of personnel to have on duty to meet the demand. In decision-theory terms his available strategies consist of the different numbers of personnel he could assign. The states of nature will include the various possible levels of demand. Now, whatever the objectives may be, how does the given number of personnel (specific strategy) interact with the given level of demand (a particular state of nature) to produce an outcome? Since this is usually a question of a known process —then, can we intuitively explain what outcomes are produced? It turns out that the process by which these two variables interact is by no means obvious. Rather surprising results—*quite contrary to common sense*— emerge. In other words, in this decision problem, the ability to determine the outcomes is the crucial issue.

Consider an executive who must set the price for a new product. What outcome results for a specific price and a given potential demand curve (one of the states of nature) is a question dealt with by economic theory. However, it is by no means easy to apply this model to an actual situation. O.R. must be able to supply these outcomes in an empirically satisfying fashion. Now, consider a decision problem involving inventory level where the objective is to minimize total cost. As the inventory level is increased, carrying costs will increase—storage charges, depreciation costs, loss of interest on capital, and so on. Some costs, however, will decrease as the inventory level is increased—out of stock costs, expediting costs, loss of customer goodwill, and others. For any given level of inventory, higher demand implies a greater risk of losing sales; lower demand implies a greater risk of incurring overstock costs. With rising prices, a large inventory is advantageous—and vice versa with falling prices. These are only some of the factors affecting the cost minimization. So it is evidently not a simple matter to understand the system. In this case, O.R. makes use of straightforward mathematical methods which succeed in determining outcomes at a reasonable cost.

The situations described above are typical of a large number of decision problems in which the determination of the outcome is one of the major difficulties. Fortunately, even when the relationship cannot be worked out formally, there is still the possibility of using statistical and experimental methods.

Using O.R. To Make a Decision. Assume that the payoff matrix for a *large* problem has been completed. Undoubtedly, it would not exist in expanded form on paper. Rather, it would be *condensed* by mathematical equations. They would represent the payoff measures of all relevant strategies with all possible states of nature. The manager must now apply his selected *decision criterion* to the *mathematical representation* of the payoff matrix. The essence of the problem is to be able to search and manipulate—according to the decision criterion—billions, quintillions, decillions, or even more payoff measures. Operations research has methods available for accomplishing this feat under many different circumstances.

In summary, O.R. is an absolute necessity for the manager who wants to use decision theory as more than a toy. There are, basically, four ways in which O.R. provides assistance.

1. By the use of mathematical representation, large numbers of strategies and states of nature can be handled. Without such representation the *limitations* imposed by *bounded rationality* apply.

2. When the manager does not know the important variables, operations-research methods can help him discover them.

3. When the manager *does know* the important variables but does not know how to relate them to each other, to the outcome, and to the payoff measure, O.R. can sometimes provide the necessary framework.

4. The manager cannot use primitive search techniques if an innumerable number of payoff measures exist. Therefore, in order to apply his decision criterion, he must turn to see if mathematical methods can be devised to do this for him.

Each of the above points represents *model-building* under various circumstances and for different purposes. The applied decision approach has both weaknesses and strengths. It is in those problem areas where the executive knows that his intuition is likely to fail him that O.R. holds forth the greatest promise. Situations of great complexity will many times yield under mathematical analysis and may, in fact, become quite simple. A key to executive confusion lies in the human inability to search through millions or billions of combinations for a particular effect. On the other hand, intuition becomes more attractive as the number of relevant variables and complex relations between them increases. *The efforts required to build models for increasingly complex cases frequently goes up faster than the advantages to be gained vis-à-vis intuition.* Then, without trying to capture every nuance, O.R. can serve as a guide. It can *audit* the consultant's function in a firm (including its own) and provide management with a new source of perspective.

PROBLEMS

The best way to gain an appreciation of the advantages and difficulties of the use of analogies from other fields in solving organizational problems is to try and think one's way through some of them. Here is an assortment—with no promise that they are actually useful:

1. The number of possible relationships between pairs of people increases rapidly with the total number of people. Precisely, if there are N people then there are $N(N-1)/2$ pairs. Thus, with three people $(A, B,$ and $C)$ there are three pairs $(3 \times 2)/2 = 3$): AB, AC, and BC. Does this have any implications in terms of managing or supervising?

2. When physical bodies grow larger the relationship of surface area to volume changes. As an approximation, volume changes as the 3/2 power of the surface area. For example, when surface area increases 4 times, volume will increase $4^{3/2} = 8$ times. This simple fact serves to explain why there are no small, warm-blooded animals in the Antarctic or in the oceans and why the largest insect is about as large as the smallest warm-blooded animal. Now, organizations differ widely in size. Does this relationship between surface area and volume tell us anything about organizations?

3. A complex and interesting mathematical theory has been developed to describe the interaction between an animal predator species and its prey (one or more species) in terms of the resultant fluctuations in numbers of the two or more species. It would appear possible to construct an analogy between this situation and that of customers (the predators) and the one or more brands of some product they wish to buy (the prey). Try to define the important factors in the first case and the corresponding factors, if any, in the second.

4. We have previously mentioned some analogies connected with the word "search." Define the important factors involved when an airplane searches for an enemy submarine. Find the analogical factors in a personnel department's search for a salesman.

5. Define the factors which would be important in analyzing an inventory problem. Are there corresponding factors involved in a problem concerning total plant capacity? Are there analogical factors involved in budgeting for long-range research?

6. A mathematical analysis of a combat between two forces leads to Lanchester's law (see F. W. Lanchester, "Mathematics in Warfare," in J. R. Newman, *The World of Mathematics,* Vol. 4, New York: Simon & Schuster, 1956, pp. 2138–2157). Let:

$$N_1 = \text{units of } A\text{'s force}$$
$$N_3 = \text{units of } B\text{'s force}$$
$$\alpha = \text{hitting power per unit of } A$$
$$\beta = \text{hitting power per unit of } B$$

Then by Lanchester's law the forces are equal when

$$\alpha N_1{}^2 = \beta N_2{}^2$$

This means that the strength of a force is directly proportional to hitting power per unit and to the square of the number of units. What applicability does this result have to advertising?

7. A complex mathematical theory has been developed to describe the spread of contagious diseases or epidemics through a host population. The spread of the disease depends on such factors as the number of contacts with infected individuals, the probability of contagion through contact, the length of the period of contagion, immunity characteristics, etc. Can you find analogous characteristics in the spread of word of mouth advertising for a product? Might this mathematical theory be useful in advertising?

8. A toy manufacturer has pricing points as follows: $0.09, $0.19, $0.22, $0.29, $0.34, $0.39, $0.62, $0.74, $0.99, $1.19, $1.59. A product is being marketed for which the relationship between sales volume and sales price is known:

$$n = 2,500 - 2,000s \qquad (1.0)$$

where n = sales volume per month, and
s = sales price (in dollars) per unit.
The cost and profit functions are also known:

$$c = \frac{450}{n} \qquad (1.1)$$

$$p = n(s - c) \qquad (1.2)$$

where c = cost per unit, and
p = total profit per month.
If the manufacturer holds to his pricing points, how many of his price strategies are profitable? What is his optimum price strategy? Construct the payoff matrix and fill in the values. Assume that dollar profit is the appropriate measure of utility.

Note: If Equations (1.0) and (1.1) are solved simultaneously, and s is set equal to c, the range of profitable sales prices can be determined. When $s = c$, profit must be zero.

Equation (1.2) can be written entirely in terms of s and p. By methods of calculus, the derivative of this equation when set equal to zero can be solved directly for the s value that yields optimum profit.

This example aims to illustrate how mathematical representation can include a great number of strategies with economy. At the same time, it derives outcomes for the gamut of possible strategies and states of nature. Lastly, the mathematical form provides a means for applying the decision criterion to the entire range of possible payoffs and discovering the optimum value. What decision criterion has been applied? Why is it correct for this case?

9. In a well-known case a drug manufacturer overlooked an important state of nature. The result was tragic. Explain what might have happened, how this was possible, and what might have been done to avoid it.

10. Assume that you can conduct experiments at the rate of one per hour. There are 100 temperature gradients that must be tested against 50 different bimetallic strips for a new thermostat. If individual experiments are to be conducted for each possible circumstance, how much time must be allocated to complete the series? How might a mathematical model be used to advantage?

11. We have stated previously that the *effort* required to build models as the situations become more complex frequently goes up faster than the *advantages* to be gained from enclosing the more complex systems.

    a. Graph these relationships of efforts and gains (in approximate form).

    b. How might one determine the optimum level of complexity to use?

    c. Now, let us differentiate between complexity of two sorts, namely: the degree of detail used and the size of the system included. How do such considerations affect the prior answers?

12. Among the ways that outcomes can be derived we have mentioned: correlational procedures, experimental methods, functional relations of mathematical form, and straightforward intuitional reasoning. Discuss each of these in terms of examples derived from business, government, scientific research and personal experience.

PART III

THE
NATURE
OF
MODELS

Chapter 7

Model-Building

65/ Definition of a Model

A model is a representation of reality intended to explain the behavior of some aspect of it.

Since a model is an explicit representation it is generally less complex than the reality itself. But it must be sufficiently complete to approximate those aspects of reality which are being investigated. The use of models characterizes the O.R. approach to the problems of management.

In the original sense, models were *physical* representations of material structures. It was understood that the model was related in *scale* to the object that was being copied. Consequently, the analysis of such models required the evaluation of dimensional effects. At first, the dimensions were limited to static, physical aspects of the object such as its height, width, length, and weight. Later, dynamic characteristics were included, such as velocity and acceleration. Newton's Law of Similarity was concerned with geometric and dynamic equivalencies between the model and the system being modeled. Physical representations of this kind reached an apex of sorts with the development of fluid mechanics.

Why has this concept come to be applied to management problems? In fact, the physical and social sciences are also using it. What accounts for this apparent discovery of model-building by thinkers in various fields? This question brings to mind Monsieur Jourdain in Molière's *Bourgeois Gentilhomme* who found to his amazement that he had been talking prose for more than forty years without knowing it. So, it isn't that a totally new way of looking at problems, called model-building, has been discovered. Rather, this term *characterizes*—and thereby *emphasizes* a way of approaching reality that has always been present. It is the emphasis that is new, and what comes of it. The use of this term makes the effort to model explicit and concentrates our attention on its relevance.

Model builders can now treat all dimensions. Factors such as time, profit, satisfaction, prestige, and so on, are included as part of the model if they are significant descriptors of the subject under study. Newton's Law of Similarity does not suffice under these circumstances. To understand the nature of our present-day models, we must examine the model-building function—paying particular attention to the connection between model-building and decision problems.

There are many motivations for attempting to understand some part of reality. Thereby, it is hoped that we may be able to describe, explain, or predict the behavior of our selected part of reality. An evident fact about this process is that we can only begin with the image of reality in our heads. A lot of thoughts about it get crammed into our brains—but the reality stays outside. In other words, all of our thoughts are abstractions from reality. Nor does this mental, abstract representation differ from reality only because it is somewhat ghostlike.

Our thoughts are formed of words and concepts which correspond to reality with considerable fuzziness. From the unlimited complexity of that part of reality which we are trying to understand, we select a few aspects—represented by a few concepts. Upon this basis we erect our thought structure. So our thinking process is abstractive in *two* ways. First, the thoughts are themselves an abstraction from reality. Second, the thoughts deal with only a few aspects of the rich complexity of reality.

Before we condemn this thought process, let us note that it is the best we have and that we have done pretty well with it so far. But it does have its dangers. Continual efforts must be made to avoid confusing reality with the thoughts about it (or the concepts from which the thoughts are constructed). Philosophers refer to such confusion as the fallacy of hypostatization—assuming our concepts to be the reality. This polysyllabic mistake is exemplified by the child who said, "It's a good thing they call pigs 'pigs' because they're such dirty animals." Besides being an injustice to pigs, this is a confusion of concept with reality. A directly relevant form of this mistake arises when we assume that, because a specific explanation of some aspect of reality seems to work, it is right. Such reasoning can be fallacious, based on some form of coincidence. The explanation may not lie in the handful of concepts we have selected, but in unconsidered aspects of the reality with which we are dealing.

We see that "the thought process" corresponds to our definition of a model. We are continually building such models of reality, which explains why model-building is ubiquitous. It can be found in any organized discussion—and is bound to be there owing to the very nature of the thought process. Further, we have just been *thinking about thinking* and, in the process, have constructed a model of thinking. With every such reduction of the complexity of reality, we can only hope that we have not broken the fragile butterfly of thought on the wheel of our abstractions. Here, as in many other abstractions, we have drastically oversimplified the complex reality of thinking in the effort to understand some salient aspects of it.

Even the best possible definition of a model that we can offer in a simple statement is not satisfactory. There are too many different aspects of models to permit the essence of model-building to be captured in a really succinct way. At one extreme, all human effort is based on model-building; at the other, scientists construct explanations of reality that require highly specialized understanding in order to comprehend their meaning. That is why we will now examine models from several different points of view. In the process, the full impact of this subject on decision-making should become apparent.

66 / A Major Model Taxonomy: Normative and Descriptive

A primary distinction between models is the normative vs. the descriptive. The dictionary calls our attention to the fact that normative (pertaining to a norm of some kind) implies the establishment of *standards* of correctness or *prescription* of rules. Normative science, according to the dictionary, does not merely describe or generalize facts. So we see that normative models tend to prescribe what *ought* to be. Descriptive models, as their name suggests, describe facts and relationships. They do not contain a basis for evaluation of the system or prescription of its form.

On these grounds, the Golden Rule is a normative model for ethics. Physicians possess a normative model of health, and construction engineers, a normative model of the properties of stable structures. On the other hand, the photographic record of an event, the journalist's account of what happened at Yalta, the scale model of an airplane, or the physician's X-ray are descriptive models.

It is sometimes difficult to avoid the inadvertent inclusion of biased normative elements in a descriptive model. For example, the journalist may describe his observations in terms of his own (personal) normative model of what he thinks should have happened. Similarly, the autobiographer may see himself in a distorted mirror. A poll of political opinion or a test market result can also reflect normative biases. The disadvantage of such distortions becomes clear when we recognize the distinctly different purposes for each kind of model.

Normative models inherently possess *a criterion for choosing* one descriptive configuration from a set of alternatives. Thus, in a decision matrix, each row (strategy), with its particular set of outcomes, is another configuration of a descriptive model. The *means of selecting* between rows (strategies) is the basic property of normative models. When this criterion operates in an unbiased fashion we have an acceptable decision model.

Descriptive models are oriented to answering *"What if"* questions. As such they are fundamental to learning and generally precede the development of new strategies aimed at improving the degree of achievement of objectives. When normative biases exist in the descriptive models, our ability to understand the system is inhibited and the potential for improvement is hindered. For example, let us suppose that a thorough study of the job of a department store buyer has been done with the intent of finding out what the job entailed. No attempt to optimize this job is envisioned until the job is thoroughly understood and present performance measures obtained and evaluated. If, however, the job description is prepared by someone who thinks he knows what ought to be done, he is likely to include his own hypotheses as part of the description. An evaluation of present performance against this job description can only serve to mislead.

The normative/descriptive distinction is probably the most useful basis for classifying models. Therefore, the next two chapters continue to explore this dichotomy. This gives us the opportunity, now, to examine the nature of models in some other ways.

67/ Models Categorized by Their Degree of Abstraction

We have pointed out that abstract conceptualizations of thinking about reality qualify as legitimate models. These abstract models are based on language, or on its sophisticated variant, mathematics. The language models are obviously the most familiar to all of us because *language is our collective basic model of reality*. It has many weaknesses which we are able to sense, but cannot express. If we could express them we might be able to correspondingly modify the language. Instead, the weaknesses are continually being corrected non-consciously as society modifies its means of expression in the historical *process* of achieving a *better correspondence to reality*. Language is also changing in the direction of *more efficient communication,* and the two objectives are not always compatible. This accounts for the development of specialized uses of language based on the existence of scientific vocabularies. It also explains the evolution of logic and mathematics and the increased emphasis that progress seems to place upon them.[1]

An important question arises as to why mathematics should be called more abstract than our language of words. There are many possible avenues to follow in explaining this distinction. Perhaps the most immediate reason is that words are chosen to denote a *specific* class of objects, actions, or qualities. If two things can be called by the same name they must be carefully modified by an adjective to distinguish them. The language of mathematics, on the other hand, treats large classes in an identical fasshion. In other words, x can stand for apples, automobiles or automata. There is no reason why we couldn't have the word "x" in our language, but people would be hard-pressed to employ it. (Although mathematics is more abstract than language, nevertheless language is quite abstract in itself. The word "book" subsumes an enormous number of items and in no way resembles the object.)

At the other extreme from "x" there are concrete structures which gave birth to the term "model." Many times they look like the object they are representing. Being that close to reality frequently brings the advantages of physical manipulation. An engineer will use a small ship in a tank of mercury to predict the behavior of the full-size ship in the ocean. Model planes mounted in wind tunnels serve the same function. A step closer to abstraction are the Tinker-Toy models used by chemists to represent protein molecules, and engineers' electrical circuit model of a complex hydraulic system.

Between the extremes of abstract and concrete there is a large range of models. Industrial models run the full gamut from the highly abstract representations that exist in the research laboratory to the exacting pilot plant characterization of a process required to determine the feasibility of a larger operation. Business schools use case studies to model encounters that are likely when the student has become an executive. Executives abstract critical elements of their company's behavior in the familiar profit-and-loss model and balance-sheet model.

It is generally held that *concrete models* have advantages over abstract models for purposes of communication and observation. They are essential if the relevant variables and functions cannot be represented in any other way. *Abstract models* have greater potentialities for intensive analysis and lend themselves to normative manipulation. Concrete mod-

---

[1] "It is no paradox to assert that in cardinal respects reality now begins *outside* verbal language." From "The Retreat from the Word" in George Steiner, *Language and Silence* (New York: Atheneum, 1967), p. 17.

els are closer to facts, while abstract models are nearer to laws and general principles that can be applied over and over again. Concrete models are almost uniformly descriptive, while abstract models can be of either type.

The concrete/abstract distinction is also related to the difficulty in handling great numbers of strategies and states of nature. An insufficient degree of bounded rationality may result from too many detailed, concrete models which cannot all be put together. This will produce poor systems descriptions unless a larger abstract model can be found to contain them. But an excessive degree of bounded rationality is equally unfortunate. The abstraction level is too great to reflect *all relevant* detail.

68/ Models Categorized by the Nature of their Dimensionality

The abstract-concrete scale is one of many ways of looking at models. They can also be classified by the *kind of representation* that is used. Spatial, temporal, and both tangible and intangible symbolic dimensions of the model can be used to differentiate one type from another. In other words, we group models according to the *character of their dimensions*. Each group is associated with some degree of abstraction related to the *number* and *nature* of the dimensions of which the model is constructed.

Scale Models. For example, there are two-dimensional scale models such as maps, photographs, blueprints, and plant layouts. They are called *scale* models because they resemble the prototype *in some concrete way*. Maps and charts are variously constructed to reflect the purpose for which they are intended. A tour map shows roads, highways, mileage between cities, and points of interest. Other maps show elevation, average rainfall, population densities, and average temperatures. An organization chart is a two-dimensional map, spatially transformed to indicate hierarchical positioning. Graphs of production, turnover, cost, and profit can be viewed in similar ways. This class of diagrammatic (scale) models conveys information visually through known systems of spatial transforms. Although these models are constructed in only two dimensions they are able to transmit information about many more dimensions.

Three-dimensional models include scale prototypes of ships, airplanes, bridges, buildings, automobiles, etc. Such scaled-down models overcome the expense and difficulty of working with full-sized subjects.

Scale transformations usually can be accomplished in both directions, e.g., increasing the size of atoms or decreasing the size of ships. The results obtained from manipulating scale models must be reconvertible to terms that are commensurate with the full-scale subject.[2] Transformations linking the model and the prototype must be understood in advance of experimentation with the model if meaningful predictions concerning the behavior of the full-scale subject are to be obtained.

Operating scale models include the *dimension of time.* This brings us to four-dimensional models. There are also important three-dimensional models that include *time.* They are restricted to a plane surface, e.g., a movie screen and a radarscope. The classification of scale models as three- or four-dimensional overlooks the many other dimensions (such as color, velocity, style, attitude) which may be critical forms of information. Generally, the inclusion of *time* will change a model from a static state to a dynamic one. The difference is of major significance.

Models can have so many dimensions that it is not feasible to count them. They are then called *n*-dimensional models. Whenever the decision-maker is preparing to cope with vast numbers of strategies and states of nature, his thinking begins with *n*-dimensional modelling and then moves through bounded rationality to a countable set of dimensions. The most powerful models are those which can handle *n*-dimensional systems. The value of *n* will vary according to the specific problem.

Analog Models. As the correspondence between a *physical* model and the subject becomes more abstract, we stop calling it a scale model and refer to it, instead, as an *analog.* In other words, when the model stops looking like the prototype we frequently call it an analog model. But the modelling principle remains intact, i.e., a strong correspondence of some kind must exist between the chosen characteristics of the model and reality. Airplane and ship models look something like the full-scale airplanes and ships. The mediums in which they are tested can also be compared (e.g., air and air, mercury and water). The correspondences seem sufficient to call these scale models. If, however, their performance and behavior were represented by electrical circuitry, we would call them analog models.

All models must correspond to their prototypes in terms of the variables required for meaningful description, that is, in accord with the objectives that led to the construction of the model. For example, the righting angle of a ship (i.e., that angle of roll beyond which the ship

---

[2] For example, ship performance predictions can be made if the Reynold's number (which is a ratio of inertial to viscous forces experienced by a given body in a fluid) is equivalent for both the scale model and the prototype.

will not return upright) is determined by the physical distribution of weights in the vertical plane. But the weight distribution changes in line with the nature of the cargo and the way it is loaded. The model (to test capsizing) must reflect this fact. Many rules of correspondence exist, such as the Reynold's number (previously mentioned) which relates ship velocity and length to fluid characteristics, or Mach's number which applies to compressible flow. Only when correspondence is assured can test results derived from scale or analog models be applied to the actual system.

There are numerous examples of the use of scale and analog models in industry. The operation of a pilot plant (or semi-works) is a clear utilization of scale reduction to avoid costly mistakes. Many such models have led to important changes in design, and sometimes a pilot plant has resulted in the cancellation of an entire program. Test markets are another type of scale model which is coupled to the full-scale marketplace by means of a statistical analog. The test results must be transformed to predict the effects of the over-all marketing effort.

Statistical sampling is, therefore, another legitimate class of modelling methods which has many applications. Less than 100 per cent of all parts need be inspected. The same applies to observations of worker performance and machine down-time. Polls and surveys of attitudes can also be generalized by statistical laws to predict the composition of the total system. The behavioral sciences are replete with similar statistical models applied to hiring, training, and the human factors of product design. The productivity of small, experimental communication groups is generalized to production lines, executive decision systems, and to research methods in laboratories. Statistical analogies are used to transform experimental results into a growing body of knowledge about learning curves, incentive systems, and the like.

The organization chart is a two-dimensional analog model. The laws of correspondence with reality are the conventions for reading and interpreting it—but these laws are, unfortunately, vague. They are not clearly defined as are the laws of correspondence for fluid mechanics. Demand curves and frequency distributions are also two-dimensional analogs. Their use is precisely dictated like those of engineering scale models. Frequently, highly abstract mathematical models are re-interpreted into physical form in order to solve the equations as rapidly as possible. The most striking example is the use of analog computers to perform the symbolic operations of add, subtract, multiply, and divide. This is accomplished by means of physical components such as resistors, potentiometers, gears, levers, and heat conductors (depending on the design of the computer). Mathematical models of many different business situations have been constructed and programmed on analog computers. The computer receives information about a particular strategy or state of nature in the form of some physical input such as voltage or current. It processes this information physically in its circuits and reports output through dial and guage readings or by conversion to a printed format.

Generally, these analogs are not normative models. An optimum strategy can only be *approached* in a qualitative sense, i.e., by trying many different strategies and observing the results.

Simulation Models. Analog models that embody a clock to keep time deserve special attention. These models produce outcomes that vary over time depending upon the temporal sequence of inputs received. Often, the output is fed back as a new input which means that the next outcome may (in some way) depend upon the last one. Such a model can go on changing its state even though all external inputs have been withheld. The outcome trajectory may be composed of a continuous or discrete sequence of outputs. The analogs we have in mind belong to a general class called *simulation models*.

Simulation time can be compressed in its correspondence with real-world time. Model-running rates can be speeded up so that an hour's use of the simulation model represents (perhaps) twenty years of activity for the model of the company. This characteristic of simulation has particular significance to business. Fatigue testing, material aging experiments, and similar scale model simulations which have been used in research laboratories for years offer their own kind of time contraction. Analog simulations apply to systems that resist the look-alike representation available through scale models.

Let us examine the benefit of speeded up time. Assume that the variables pertinent to a specific decision problem and their relationships to each other have been identified. Further, suppose we cannot develop a normative, mathematical model that captures all necessary relevancy and still can be solved. So, instead, we use concise *descriptive language, flow diagrams* and other logical notations to set down a sequence of rules concerning what happens to each element in the model as a result of changes in the others. We specify, name, and label the inputs. We describe what follows from each combination of inputs, allowing them to interact with the states of the system. We detail those aspects of the system's behavior that we consider output.

Frequently, this type of (pre-computer programming) description can be efficiently converted to a quasi-mathematical form. Such "descriptive mathematics" is then suitable for translation into a digital computer language such as BASIC, FORTRAN or COBAL, or into the wiring instructions of an analog computer. The simulation can also be run by hand if the processing load is not too great—much as the game of "Monopoly" can be played by those who know the rules.

There would be no need to use simulation methods if normative mathematical equations could be written and solved. Unfortunately, even though such equations can often be written, they cannot be solved. For this reason and others of economy, simulation is generally regarded as an important method. We shall have ample occasion to discuss it again (for example, in Chapter 8). On the other hand, mathematical optimization models are no less fundamental to our studies. They will be dealt with in Chapter 9 and appear frequently thereafter.

69/ *Models Classified by Their Subject*

No one theory explains all phenomena. Not even within the highly developed field of physics is a unified theory available. Correspondingly, *no unified theory of models exists.* Therefore, we have turned to various classifications of models with the hope of affording some cumulative insight concerning their nature. Let us consider one more approach, namely, by the subjects and fields to which the models are applied.

For example, economists are concerned with a particular set of variables. However, the interrelationships of these variables have characteristics in common with those found in other fields. Accordingly, we can expect strong similarities (of the abstract models—in terms of "x") to cut across various fields, even though the economist's strategies and the effective states of nature are uniquely his own. The economist strives to predict economic developments and, ultimately, to control economic conditions. However, he is uncertain about the relevant variables. He is interested in the kind of model that will help to point them out.

Psychological studies also suffer from uncertainty as to the relevant variables. Consequently, behavioral scientists have stressed the design of models aimed at locating these variables. Whereas the economists' models treat variables of supply, demand, price, and the like, the psychologists' models are involved with such variables as motivation, reinforcement, conditioning, and *Gestalt*. Although the dimensions of the models in each field seem quite different, a development in one area can profoundly affect the other area.

Medicine is also a field that lends itself to the discussion of models. Physicians use descriptive models to obtain non-quantitative diagnoses. Yet these are based on many dimensions that yield quantitative data such as temperature, pulse, and blood counts. The medical field lacks systems models that can combine these data to yield quantitative payoffs.

Similar discussions describe the decision-making situation of meteorologists (who have an abstract model that cannot be solved) or biologists and biochemists (who know the pertinent variables but cannot formalize the relationships that describe physical patterns in mathematical terms). Chemists, physicists, electrical engineers, and architects, to name a few more fields, all have their own characteristic problems within the decision-making framework. Because of intra-field analogies, the various groups learn from the advances of the others. Business is not an exception, and, as a result, in recent years it has experienced a transformed relationship to society.

As we are particularly interested in business problems, let us now turn in that direction. An enterprise has many ways of looking at itself. Each viewpoint presents a basis for another descriptive model. The differences are usually related to alternative objectives. However, these models have an aspect in common—they provide frameworks for thinking about the problem area.

The executive tends to classify his decision problems by various familiar subject names. Of course, he recognizes the limitations of this framework. Areas interrelate and boundaries are frequently illusory. He knows there is both convenience and danger in separating areas so that "fundamentally" different organization groups can deal with them.

1. By Product Type. There are many ways in which product characteristics can be classified. For example, we contrast "consumer goods" with "industrial goods." The strategies connected with selling consumer goods contain many variables that never appear in the strategies used in the industrial area. As a rule, we have many consumers to reach, convince, and supply, whereas there are relatively few industrial users. Problems of inventory, distribution, and so on are unique to each area. Economic states of nature seem to produce different effects in the sales of "soft" and "hard" goods. Another product type classification contrasts durable goods (which do not spoil) with nondurable goods. Each requires basically different inventory management, selling procedures, and distribution policies. Fashion items also deserve special models uniquely adapted to their circumstances.

2. By Integrated Function. We have reference to manufacturers, retailers, wholesalers, salesmen, sales agents, factors, and so on. The strategic variables will differ in each of these areas. More important, the objectives of each group will not tend to concur. We note that when one organization includes several of these functions, suboptimization can become a serious problem. If the functions exist separately, any one of these organizations might have to consider the others' behaviors as relevant states of nature and/or competitive strategies.

3. By Commodity Class. Perhaps, in practice, not enough accent has been placed on this class of models. The usual consideration of what constitutes competition includes only those companies which make "very" similar products and which are directly competitive in distribution, advertising, and so forth. Yet real competition exists at far more general levels. For example, milk, beer, soda, fruit juices, and soft drinks compete not only within each subgroup but also among themselves. We would call this commodity class "beverages." Recognition of the possible importance of commodity class competition has been growing in recent years. Other such classes might be framed as textiles, transportation, fuels, electronic devices, etc. The size of the commodity class can be enlarged or diminished depending upon the extent to which relevant competitive strategies influence the behavior of our system.

4. By Economic Situation. Here we dwell on some macroeconomic descriptions, classifying by pure competition, oligopoly, monopoly, monopsony, and the rest.[3] These relate to identification of competitors. They describe legal and financial circumstances that can become critical. The economic situation that prevails will determine the extent to which a rational competitor can affect the decision-maker's outcome. Recalling our discussion (end of Chapter 5), as monopolistic conditions are approached the supplier and the consumer become "competitors" of the enterprise. Similarly, under conditions of monopsony (where there is one buyer and many suppliers, e.g., government contracts) there is complete competition among the bidders, and the special nature of such problems must be treated. These kinds of economic models represent an important classification for business. Their structures will differ significantly from other models and will lead to unique strategic choices.

5. By Operations. In this case we are referring to assembly, inspection, machining, casting, storing, transporting, and the like. We view the organization as a communication network, where parts and materials flowing through the factory or warehouse are legitimate units of information (discussed in Chapter 2). Each operation is studied separately as a transformation of information. Controllable variables can be isolated from noncontrollable ones by this procedure and important input-output relationships can be detected. When the various "operation" subsystems are interconnected for consideration of the whole this method of classi-

---

[3] All of these concepts are defined in W. Harrison Carter and William P. Snavely, *Intermediate Economic Analysis* (New York: McGraw-Hill Book Co., 1961).

fication becomes advantageous, permitting a *systems* (analysis) point of view. In general, the segmentation of operations leads to improved efficiency. The synthesis of these operations is required for improved effectiveness. The nature of the model will differ significantly according to which objective is being sought.

6. By Types of Problems. The most familiar classification is the traditional breakdown used by management: production, marketing, finance, personnel, and so on. Schools of business take a magnifying glass to this classification and arrive at a basis for their curriculums: accounting, advertising, banking, business law, corporate finance, economics, industrial relations, insurance, real estate, security analysis, statistics, transportation, and others.

What reasons are behind this breakdown? First, many of the classes coincide with employment positions. That makes hiring, training, wage-setting, delegation of authority, etc. less of a problem. Second, these categories exist like separate file drawers in which many facts can be stored. These are the historical records of customs and events, observations and negotiations. This classification provides a convenient way to file and store them.

There are many other explanations to account for the existence of this kind of classification. But from the point of view of model-building for decision-making these categories are useful only insofar as different strategies and states of nature apply to the specific areas and do not cross boundaries. They thereby signal the danger of routinely according separate status to certain business functions. Such fragmentation can lead to conflicts of objectives and suboptimization. Therefore, while these classes emphasize differences between areas, they stress neither the similarities nor the connectedness associated with the systems point of view.

Certainly there is nothing wrong with this classification. There is just something missing which is a way of integrating areas and of tracing lines that uncover dependent relationships between the areas.

7. By Types of Techniques. The classification of operations research models by types of methods—allocation, search, replacement, inventory, queuing, and so on—cuts across the boundaries of the conventional business classifications. But this O.R. breakdown is not likely to be the most useful from the point of view of the executive. At best, he may find it informative. It is far better suited to the needs of the O.R. practitioner who wishes to transfer information about models by technique. It has *disutility* if the practitioner comes to think of reality being structured in this way (see our preface for some further remarks). In this respect, classification by O.R. techniques provides another system of limited utility. The same applies to other techniques such as those of quality control, market research, statistical design, job rating, accounting, and so forth.

Ultimately, it is *decision theory* that supplies a base for developing, understanding, and evaluating any logical classification of models employed by business.

70/ Qualitative and Quantitative Models

It is not absolutely necessary that outcomes should be stated in numerical terms. The fact that the die cast department will *improve* its productivity when foreman X is transferred is a perfectly legitimate (and useful) outcome. *Improve* does not have a numerical measure, therefore any model from which it was derived or with which it is used represents a qualitative one.

Sometimes, direct quantitative observation is impossible. Nevertheless, the qualitative outcomes can be translated into quasi-quantitative payoffs by such means as ranking and the standard gamble. At other times, the outcomes may be quantitatively measurable, but the relationship between the payoff measures (which express the utility for the outcomes) and the outcomes themselves cannot be formulated exactly. Again, a quasi-quantitative result may be available.

Many models, such as verbal ones, are fundamentally not quantitative although there are various words that express measure and relation. In fact, a complex spectrum of models differentiated by completeness, rigor, and precision exists. Although we can get less ambiguous information from quantitative models, this does not gainsay the importance of qualitative models. Most thinking about reality starts with qualitative models and subsequently develops to a point where quantitative models can be used. The originating qualitative model must reach a certain degree of correspondence to reality before the quantitative step can be taken. Sciences that deal with particularly complex aspects of reality are still at the stage of developing suitable *qualitative* models. And these qualitative models afford a great deal more insight into the complexities of their subject matter than any attenuated attempt to model quantitatively.

Operations research can be a powerful source of assistance to the executive in systematizing qualitative models and developing them to the point where they can be quantified. This isn't meant to imply that operations-research methodology can be used to quantify any qualitative situation. Frequently, serious problems (such as those listed below) cannot be overcome.

1. Measurement techniques that are inadequate.

2. Too many variables required.
3. The variables are unknown.
4. The relationships between variables are unknown.
5. The relationships are too complex to be formally stated.
6. Relevant probability distributions cannot be derived.

Nevertheless, by using the logic of decision theory in conjunction with *dimensional analysis* and well thought out classification systems, O.R. can bring some helpful concepts into play.

71/ *Models Must Be Dimensionally Sound*[4]

Although decision-making is frequently restricted to qualitative or quasi-quantitative results, operations research can assist in the derivation of suitable models. By suitable, we mean a model that captures all relevant variables and combines them in a dimensionally consistent fashion.[5] Whether the model is structured for simulation or mathematical analysis; whether it is a qualitative or quantitative model—dimensional soundness is vital. It is the first test that any model should be made to pass.

This can best be seen by considering an essentially qualitative situation. Assume that a manufacturer does not have numerical data to relate profit, sales volume, price, and cost. Still, he is able to benefit from the qualitative relationships that he knows must exist. For example, he realizes that as cost goes up, profit will go down. He begins by identifying the relevant variables: *profit* (p) is a function (f) of *sales volume* (n) as well as *price per unit* (s) and *cost per unit* (c). This is more compact in mathematical form: $p = f(n, s, c)$. Furthermore, the following *qualitative* model seems appropriate:

$$\text{Profit} = \text{Sales Volume (Price per unit} - \text{Cost per unit)}$$

or
$$p = n(s - c) \text{ and in dimensional terms,}$$

$$\text{Outcome (\$)} = \text{units} \left(\frac{\$}{\text{units}} - \frac{\$}{\text{units}} \right) = \$ - \$ = \$$$

This descriptive model is dimensionally sound. The "units" dimension cancels out, leaving $'s on both sides of the equation. We should note that a clear bill of health for dimensional fitness is no assurance that the right dimension for studying the problem has been chosen. A dimen-

---

[4] For a variety of applications of dimensional analysis to economics, see F. J. De Jong: *Dimensional Analysis for Economists* (North-Holland Publishing Co., 1967).

[5] As will be seen in Chapter 9 this statement applies even when the functional relationships between the variables are unknown.

sionally sound model that measures the brightness of moonbeams would not help the manufacturer.

What if the manufacturer is better able to think about the problem in terms of *total costs?* Then it is vital that his model's structure should reflect this difference. Namely:

$$\text{Outcome (\$)} = \text{units}\left(\frac{\$}{\text{units}}\right) - \$$$

The above is also dimensionally sound.

If, however, the manufacturer had in mind yet another dimensional configuration, that is, *unit price* and *total cost:*

$$\text{Outcome (?)} = \text{units}\left(\frac{\$}{\text{units}} - \$\right)$$

then the model (on the right-hand side of the equation) would supply an outcome of meaningless dimension, *viz.,* ? = \$(1 − units). In a simple example of this sort, it may be difficult to conceive of making such dimensional errors, but in complex situations it is hard to determine how to avoid them.

These thoughts relate to both analytic and simulation models. Whether we formally write down the description of our system—or just think about it—we must use consistent dimensions. Of course, while it is easier to check the formal description it is also an onerous burden (especially for complex simulation structures). Engineers who, typically, are not put off by the demands of great detail, have employed dimensional analysis for years. Intuitive models of management cannot be examined in this light. This in no way implies that they are dimensionally sound and suggests the contrary, which should provide some incentive for formal model construction.

Let us emphasize this point by extending our example. Assume that sales volume (*n*) has a linear relationship with unit price (*s*). The characterization of the relationship as linear is a qualitative description. Lacking data, the executive can only write (or think)

$$n = a + bs$$

where *a* and *b* are the unknown parameters[6] of the system that define the exact relationship between *n* and *s*. Rewriting this expression in terms of the dimension of *n* (which is units) and *s* (which is \$/units) we obtain:

$$\text{Units} = a + b\,\frac{\$}{\text{units}}$$

---

[6] Parameter—an arbitrary constant . . . in a mathematical expression, which distinguishes various specific cases. From Glenn James and Robert C. James, eds., *Mathematics Dictionary,* 2nd Ed. (Princeton, N.J.: D. Van Nostrand Co., Inc., 1959), p. 282.

From an analytical point of view it is clear that the dimension of a must be *units* and the dimension of b must be $units^2/\$$. But what meaning do these dimensions of the parameters have?

In the first place, when the price s is zero, only a units can be given away. In qualitative terms this represents an extreme value equal to a units which is the *total market potential*. Furthermore, another qualitative feature of a has been found, namely that it has a positive sign. How about b? If b had a positive sign, then as price rises sales volume would go up. Perhaps for a certain price range this "odd" effect does hold and the executive might even be able to describe that price range in qualitative terms. However, in general b would be negative and the executive has discerned another qualitative characteristic of the model. Lastly, what is b? The answer to this question is more easily given in terms of the Figure 7.1.

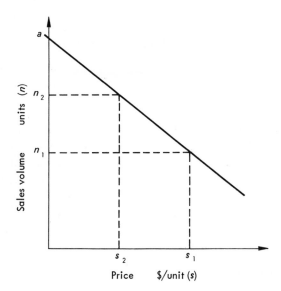

FIGURE 7.1 *Dimensional interpretation of the linear relationship between sales volume and price.*

The slope of the line is b. That means

$$b = \frac{n_2 - n_1}{s_2 - s_1}$$

In dimensional terms

$$b = \frac{units - units}{(\$/unit) - (\$/unit)} = \frac{units}{\$/unit} = \frac{units^2}{\$}$$

Therefore, b is the ratio of the change in sales volume to the change in unit price.

This too was a simple example. More complexity would have required a great deal of explanation and interpretation.[7] Figure 7.2 depicts the

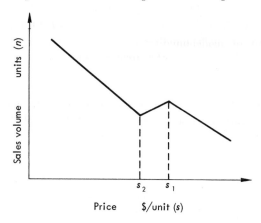

FIGURE 7.2 *There is a range of prices in which sales volume decreases as price decreases.*

situation when there is a range of prices ($s_1 - s_2$) for which sales volume increases as price increases. When an executive uses intuition to consider such relationships of sales volume to price, in some way he is attempting to perform mentally the operations we have described above. If his thinking is dimensionally inconsistent, then the model he is using is incorrect and his conclusions will be wrong. We shall return to dimensional analysis in Chapter 9, at which time quantitative measures of multiple outcomes will be viewed in a normative context.

PROBLEMS

1. A suburban retailer asks his customers where they come from so that he can find out how distance affects his potential market. He also learns that population density is almost equal for 50 miles in any direction and that most people come to his store by car. As a result of questioning over 1800 customers the following information is obtained:

---

[7] For example, if estimates of the ratio, b, were statistically distributed we might have had to use the dimensions of averages in accord with the following equation for expected sales volume:

$$E(n) = \sum_{b=min}^{max} p(b)[a + bs]$$

NUMBER OF CUSTOMERS	DISTANCE TRAVELED
640	0–2 miles
680	2–5 miles
520	5–10 miles
40	10–20 miles

The retailer concludes that, *up to 10 miles, distance has no effect* on his business. What kind of model-building error is he making? What relationship actually holds? (Remember: area of a circle $= \pi r^2$.)

2. Three machine-tool companies (*A*, *B*, and *C*) supply a special part which is used by only four aircraft manufacturers (*D*, *E*, *F*, and *G*). Company *A* has received a total of 5 orders in the year—4 came from *D* and 1 from *E*. The management of company *A* would like to know how well they are faring in comparison with their competitors. They collect the following information: *D* has placed a total of 6 orders; *E* has placed a total of 4 orders; and *G* has placed only 1 order. *F* has placed more orders than *E* but less than *D*. How many different possibilities are there for the number of orders received by *B*? If it is then learned that *C* received more than 2 orders but less than one-half of the number received by *B*, how many possibilities remain? With this information can you tell how *D, E, F,* and *G* placed their orders?

3. The following quotation describes some of the earliest work (about 1740) in the development of a theory of ship motions. Please discuss the nature of the model-building effort that was involved.

> "Examining the problem of small oscillations of a floating vessel, Euler reduced its solution to the action of a simple mathematical pendulum, which would have the same period and the same amplitude of oscillation as the rocking vessel. In so doing Euler neglected the resistance of the water, and of all the forces acting upon the oscillating vessel, he included in the equations of the motions only the hydrostatic restoring forces and the forces of inertia of the vessel itself." *

4. What kind of models do the following terms bring to mind? What purposes are they intended to serve, and how effective are they?

a. concept	f. random
b. art	g. lucky
c. technology	h. statue
d. syntax	i. method
e. to search	j. proportional

5. Thinking in terms of a broad range of models, would it be closer to the truth to say that models are invented, discovered, or both? Comment fully.

6. There is significant differentiation between the roles of nouns, verbs, ad-

---

* (From *Theory of Ship Motions*, Volume 1, p. 1 by S. N. Blagoveshchensky, translated by Theodor and Leonilla Strelkoff, Louis Landweber, Ed., Iowa Institute of Hydraulic Research, State University of Iowa. New York, Dover Publications, Inc., 1962).

jectives and adverbs as they are used and reflected in the structure of models. How would you characterize these differences?

7. Explain the character of each of the following models in as much detail as seems appropriate:

    a. "By their fruits ye shall know them."
    b. "Cogito, ergo sum."
    c. He decided to decide to decide.
    d. "Work expands so as to fill the time available for its completion."

8. What kind of model is the alphabetic order of a dictionary and how does it relate to the search for proper spelling? What are the categories of actual dictionary use and the relative frequencies of each of these? Comment.

Chapter 8

Descriptive Models

The accountant enumerates all of the variables that contribute to the cost of making a particular product. The industrial statistician, in conjunction with the industrial psychologist, designs experiments to determine whether one package is preferred to another. The quality-control engineer maintains close observation of a process in order to discern if and when the process changes. In none of these situations is the objective an optimal value.

The accountant observes the strategy that was followed and the state of nature that prevailed. They are past and recorded history. He must determine the outcome, which is a cost figure. He has no problem of risk or uncertainty. However, when the accountant is asked to estimate on the basis of a quarterly report what the annual business will be, he cannot be certain what state of nature will prevail. His prediction is necessary in order to determine an outcome. But his problem is not that of optimizing the outcome. Similarly, the statistician and psychologist who prepare questionnaires or interviews are attempting to discover the outcome that will result from a variety of strategies—different packages which are shown to groups of people with different demographic and psychological characteristics. Generally, such experiments assume that the state of nature is constant and will not undergo change in the foreseeable future. The quality-control engineer knows what outcome to expect from a stable process. As the states of nature shift they produce the random variation which he anticipates. However, what he is looking for is a change in strategy that is unintended. He spots this occurrence when a number of observed values all fall on one side of the mean value of a process—called a *run*—or when a point goes outside the limits drawn on his statistical quality-control chart. The control engineer is not trying to optimize anything. He is devoted to maintaining the company's strategy.

In Chapter 7, we introduced the distinction between descriptive and normative models. (Normative models are designed to search for an optimum system's configuration; descriptive models portray that system.) It is clear that normative models are constructed of descriptive models. The normative contribution provides an operational choice criterion for selecting the optimal, descriptive model configuration from the set.

Viewed in this light, descriptive models are the basic building blocks of normative methodology. When they are not being used in this way, what other functions do they serve? Let us begin by classifying them according to purpose.

72/ Information Models

One major function of a descriptive model is to *convey information*. Maps, photographs, and blueprints serve in this capacity. The criteria for judging the effectiveness of these models are the costs of communication and the accuracy and intelligibility of information and its transmission rate. As the information flows from "sender" to "receiver" it can be evaluated in three ways: for structural properties (the coding system used); for semantic properties (the transfer of meaning); and for its practical value (as reflected by the *needs* of the model-user). Some of these models can also *store information* whose composition changes over time. The information recovery rate tends to be inversely related to the size of the memory. Frequently, the accessibility of certain items differs from that of others. Stating an *average* information recovery rate may mask this fact. Many additional considerations apply, not the least of which is that the cost of storing and maintaining information should be offset by the information's utility, which can also change over time.

It does not seem important for our present purposes to distinguish between the kinds of information that such models transmit. But it will be useful to note that the degree of abstraction, the model's dimensionality, the field to which it applies, and the extent of quantification used —all play a significant role in determining the specific form of the model. The road map, organization chart, matrix of numbers, profit-and-loss statement, photograph, TV screen, blueprint, and the printed book are all different forms of information models. Because communication models are important to all organizations we shall consider the (mathematical) theory of information shortly.

73/ *Observation and Measurement Models*

The purpose of such models is clear, but little is known about the underlying complexities of perception, scaling, and measuring. General forms of observation precede the construction of scales which, in turn, precedes measurement. While observational models reflect reality, they are reduced in complexity. We have only limited powers of observation, being unable to perceive, understand, and measure the totality of any experience. Our senses are neither sufficient nor sensitive enough. Further, we are unable to observe an environment without changing that environment in some way. That is, the observer and his subject are bound together in some mutual relationship which alters both of them. This effect, which is known as the *Heisenberg uncertainty principle* in physics, has its counterpart in the social sciences, where it is called the *observer effect*. The principle has been the center of much discussion and it remains an important consideration to be included in even the briefest treatment of measurement models.

Ultimately, a model that lends itself to experimentation is desirable. The cycle, shown in Figure 8.1 will be developed.

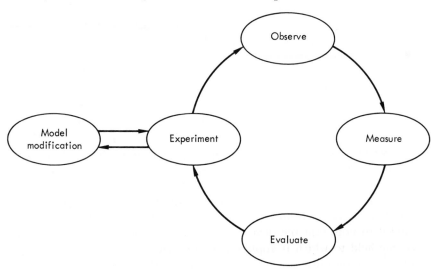

FIGURE 8.1

There are many examples of this kind of experimentation: attempts to influence weather by cloud seeding, to increase the yield of land by fertilization, to utilize rivers for power, and so forth. But no model can be initially experimental. Models begin in the mind. The *choice of what to observe* is the first link between reality and the model.

We have defined measurement models by their class, order, distance, and origin.[1] Models having only items sorted by classes—such that all members of one class are equivalent—are said to follow a nominal system of measurement. For our purposes, perhaps it would be more appropriate to call this a classification system. *Nominal measurement models play an important role in the decision systems of executives.* Many models that begin in this strictly qualitative framework always remain qualitative. Without question, there are more models of this kind in business than of any other kind. However, models for classification have been elaborately developed in many other fields, such as botany, and including logic and mathematics.

Good classification systems are not easily developed. This is especially so when the elements we want to sort and arrange have complex descriptions and coexist in several categories at the same time. (Such problems are common.) In the natural sciences the principles of taxonomy have been applied in painstaking fashion for hundreds of years. Yet the attempt to classify animals and plants according to all of their relevant relationships has not been entirely successful. Libraries arrange their books to permit rapid access and discovery. But deciding whether a particular book should be put in the economics or business section continues to cause problems for librarians. In spite of much attention, many classification problems are inadequately solved.

The typical organization filing system is essentially qualitative. Before a classification system can be created it is necessary to fully specify the variables by which the data should be sorted. The simplest classification systems involve one variable which has only two subgroups. For example, some bills are filed "paid" and others "unpaid." These subgroups are mutually exclusive, i.e., a bill cannot be both "paid" and "unpaid." However, there are always bills that require special attention. This leads to the need for additional classes, which creates problems that can be onerous to handle.

Difficulties of definition are at the core of classification problems. For example, borrowing from a census problem, when does a rural location become an urban one? Or, following another tack, how can we classify objects by shape? Both problems involve defining the variables. Accountants are faced daily with situations of this sort. How, for example, should they assign overhead to the various departments in a company? The classification difficulties become more acute as new variables are

---

[1] For an excellent discussion of these terms, see Warren S. Torgerson, *Theory and Methods of Scaling* (New York: John Wiley & Sons, Inc., 1958), pp. 15–21.

added. Arranging personnel records by age and skill, we find that within any one age group there will be many different levels of skill, and within any one level of skill there will be many different ages. Often, the degree of dependency between such variables can be recovered from data that have been properly classified. Thus, if skill improves with age, there should be a noticeable increase in the number of skilled workers that appear in the older age groups. Classes can be designed to reflect these dependencies. But lacking known relations, the classification problems become more acute. Ultimately, each individual is treated as a class in his own right and no benefit is derived from classification efforts.

The methods of information theory can sometimes be useful in developing classification systems. They help to uncover patterns of dependency. Some sense of theory must underlie any classification scheme. On the operational level, appropriate classification models must provide benefits of sufficient utility to warrant using them.

When objects and events can be sorted into classes which can then be ordered we term this an *ordinal system of measurement*. For example:

A is equivalent to *B*	or	*A* is the same as *B*
C is greater than *D*	or	*C* is preferred to *D*
E is not as good as *F*	or	*E* is not as smart as *F*.

Order (like rank) opens quantitative potentials for the first time.

Information about *distance* represents a big step forward. Knowing that *C* is greater than *D*, and *D* is greater than *E*, but that the difference between *C* and *D* is greater than the difference between *D* and *E* can have practical utility. See, for example, Figure 8.2 which shows one of many configurations that satisfy the stated conditions.

Origin
unknown

FIGURE 8.2

Assume that we have three candidates for a particular job. The executive responsible for the decision of whom to hire is likely to be able to rank these men in the *order* that best describes their abilities to do the job. But he will be hard-pressed to say how much better one is than another. In other words, he is able to invoke order but not distance. This situation is particularly acute when dealing with behavioral problems, the outcomes of complex strategies, and decision systems involving multiple objectives.

The executive described above might decide to make things easier for himself by employing a rating test to differentiate the candidates. He can then say that one man is so many times better than another man. If the test score is a measure of intelligence then the model does not have a natural origin (we prefer not to conceive of a man with zero intelligence). The use of a standard—say, "average intelligence"—does provide an origin by means of which all three men can be rated against the general population. However, this sort of origin is legitimately subject to question.

Measurement models are far more developed in the physical sciences than in the management sciences. The tractable dimensions of the universe are closer to the physical reality than are dollars to the business reality. Nevertheless, problems that *center* around dollars can have order, distance, and a natural origin (if the utility transforms are known). Such models form a basis for the quantitative measurements found in abundance in the accounting department of any company. The significance of these models for situations that involve multiple objectives or demand complex utility transforms is also subject to question.

As yet, the best possible models for many critical management problems cannot be assigned a real measure of distance or a natural origin. Their weaknesses in *economic* and *behavioral* applications are continually reflected in the attempts of executives to find superior methods of determining work standards, measurements of corporate image and enterprise efficiency, executive ability, true appraisals of costs, profits, market potential, effectiveness of advertising, creativity of research, and so forth. The development of improved measurement models requires continuous effort on the part of management in cooperation with specialized personnel who have appropriate technical skills.

74/ *Transformation Models*

They are required for predicting prototype behavior on the basis of scale model observations. In this way, map distances are converted to actual ones, and the performance of the ship model in the towing tank is extended to the ocean liner.

Isomorphic transformation models concern changes in scale which leave the nature of the dimension intact and which lose no information as a result of the transformation. They are used when the form of the data obtained from the most efficient or convenient measurement model is not compatible with subsequent analytical operations, or when the analytical operations can be performed in a more meaningful manner as a result of the transformation. For example, Fahrenheit values are transformed to Centigrade values by the symbolic transformation model: $°C = \frac{5}{9}(°F - 32)$. Inches are converted to feet by the symbolic transformation model: $x = 12y$, where x is given in inches and y is given in feet. One of the best known isomorphic transformations involves the use of *logarithms* to perform mathematical operations. Multiplication under the log-transform becomes addition; an exponent becomes a multiplier. In no way are the original data altered—except by scale. The original form is recovered by use of the *antilog*.

Another powerful transformation (which is not isomorphic, but *homomorphic*) models a population with a *statistical sample*. Characteristics of the sample are transformed into predictions about the larger population. In this way, results obtained from a test market model are applied to the entire country; or quality tests made on a few parts (using an acceptance sample model) are generalized to the entire production-lot to determine its acceptability. *Homomorphic* transformations group fine classes into larger ones, and do lose information thereby, but hopefully with compensating gains.

The importance of this class of models lies in the fact that with appropriate transformations, seemingly inadequate models can provide useful analytic benefits. For example, brand share analysis loses information about the absolute size of the market but with great conceptual advantages for the executive. To further exemplify the significance of these models, let us consider the data in Table 8.1. This table describes the number of trucks arriving at a company's loading dock.

TABLE 8.1

*Number of trucks arriving within 15-minute
periods of each hour*

	HOUR OF THE DAY																
15-MINUTE PERIODS	MORNING HOURS						AFTERNOON HOURS						EVENING HOURS				
	7	8	9	10	11	12	1	2	3	4	5	6	7	8	9	10	11
:00–:14	4	1	4	5	1	2	2	1	3	0	3	1	2	3	1	0	1
:15–:29	1	2	1	1	0	1	2	0	2	0	2	0	0	1	1	0	0
:30–:44	1	0	2	2	0	1	1	0	3	2	3	0	2	2	1	0	1
:45–:59	1	0	1	1	1	3	1	2	1	2	3	0	1	2	2	0	0
TOTAL:	7	3	8	9	2	7	6	3	9	4	11	1	5	8	5	0	2

If the data had been collected in hourly periods (corresponding to the TOTALS shown in the bottom row of Table 8.1) a frequency distribution would be obtained which would be of little help in predicting future arrivals. It is an *irregular distribution,* which means that it does not correspond to any of the *well-known* frequency distributions. (The distribution is obtained by counting the frequencies of each number that appears in the 17 entries of the TOTAL row of the matrix.)

TABLE 8.2

NUMBER OF TRUCKS ARRIVING PER HOUR	FREQUENCY WITH WHICH THIS NUMBER OCCURS	FREQUENCY CONVERTED TO PROBABILITY
0	1	0.0588
1	1	0.0588
2	2	0.1176
3	2	0.1176
4	1	0.0588
5	2	0.1176
6	1	0.0588
7	2	0.1176
8	2	0.1176
9	2	0.1176
10	0	0.0000
11	1	0.0588
	17	0.9996

On the other hand, if the *period is transformed* from an hour into 15-minute units, the new distribution, composed of 68 observations, closely approximates the well-behaved form of the Poisson distribution (see Table 8.2). (The distribution is obtained by counting the frequencies of the 68 numbers that appear in the matrix: rows 00–14, 15–29, 30–44, 45–59.)

TABLE 8.3

NUMBER OF TRUCKS ARRIVING PER QUARTER HOUR	FREQUENCY WITH WHICH THIS NUMBER OCCURS	FREQUENCY CONVERTED TO PROBABILITY
0	18	0.2647
1	24	0.3529
2	16	0.2353
3	7	0.1029
4	2	0.0294
5	1	0.0147
	68	0.9999

Figure 8.3 compares the actual distribution obtained for one-hour periods with the theoretically derived Poisson distribution (based on the same average number of truck arrivals).

Figure 8.4 represents the same kind of comparison for truck arrivals in 15-minute intervals. When based on a 15-minute period for observation, truck arrivals exhibit regularity and predictability. It is worth noting that we can transform observations based on 15-minute intervals into hourly observations—but the reverse is not true.

Two kinds of transformations have been used in this example. First, frequency counts were changed into probability estimates. Although this transformation model is regularly used, it is not immune to objection.

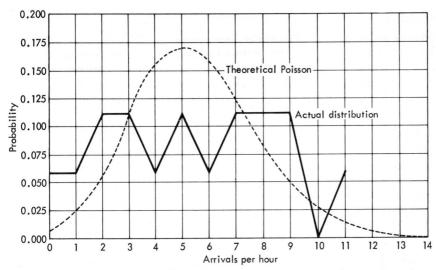

FIGURE 8.3   Comparison of Poisson distribution with the actual distribution derived from data based on
hourly truck arrivals.

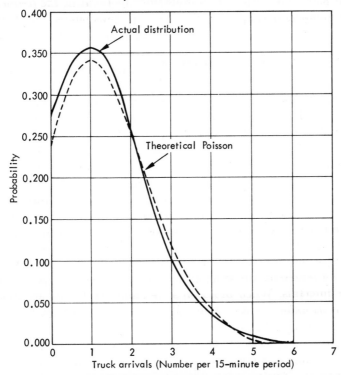

FIGURE 8.4   Comparison of Poisson distribution with the actual distribution derived from data based on truck
arrivals every 15 minutes.

Second, we transformed the arrival interval in order to achieve a close approximation to our well-known Poisson distribution. The fact is that the system possesses Poisson characteristics only in the vicinity of 15-minute intervals. The advantage of such a transformation lies in the immense knowledge we have about Poisson distributions and their behavior. So, this is a clear example of where the transformation model delivers new analytic strengths and insights.

It is critical that we don't distort dimensions when we utilize transformations. Equally important, we should try to preserve information during the transformation. When we do not, the consequences and advantages should be known. There is also a message here concerning the benefit of maintaining detailed information in storage, even though homomorphic transformation models may use only a part of it. Operations research can provide important guidance for this class of model.

75/ *Discovery Models: Variables*

One of the most fundamental purposes of models is to discover *which variables are the pertinent ones.* As previously discussed, the choosing of variables to investigate is a complex conceptual process which eventually is followed by the development of a measurement model. The basic notion is to explain the behavior of one or more variables in terms of other variables.

For example, to determine what factors influence the time required by an executive to make a decision, we can obtain from a group of executives a list of variables they consider relevant. Such a list might include the number of employees working for the executive, dollars involved in the decision, degree of reversibility of the decision, number of years that the executive has spent with the company, and so on. This list is just a list of suggestions. No one pretends to know the relationship between decision time and these other factors. If data are collected for each decision of a number of executives, then correlation analysis can be used to determine the relevance of each variable to the decision time.

Qualitative correlation goes on in our minds all the time. *Quantitative correlation,* on the other hand, is a formal, statistical means of determining the extent to which a change in one factor is accompanied by a change in another factor. Sometimes, the changes are linearly related, that is, equal changes in variable x result in constant changes in another variable, y (i.e., $y = mx + b$). Quadratic relationships exist when equal changes in variable x produce changes in another variable, y proportional to the square of x's value, plus whatever linear response exists (i.e., $y = ax^2 + bx + c$). Higher-order correlation possibilities also exist.

There are weaknesses in both qualitative and quantitative correlation methods. Nevertheless, the mind does seem to be able to relate variables which, if correlated quantitatively, result in very complex equations. Perhaps the mind does not correlate on the basis of the frequency patterns of variables in association. Rather, it may be able to discern causality in a logical sense. Correlation does not employ notions of causality. If a causal relationship produces a high measure of correlation between certain variables, the techniques for establishing correlation cannot discern in which direction the causal relationship works. Correlation is a means of isolating factors that have a tendency to appear together, for whatever reasons.

Qualitative appraisal can be useful when there seems to be no other way to determine the outcomes that result from a given strategy and state of nature. For example, day-to-day fluctuations in sales will occur although the company's strategy and the state of nature remain essentially unchanged. A company's strategy includes many elements which affect the system at different rates over time, so it is frequently impossible to tell which action brought which result. Similarly, it is hard to detect changes in the state of nature that account for specific outcome variabilities.

In the nineteenth century, J. S. Mill formulated a number of rules which are antecedents of present-day models for discovering pertinent variables. We shall discuss two of these rules, and use them to illustrate how qualitative models pertain to the problem of discerning important variables.

The *method of agreement:*

> If X is observed with $ABCD$,
> and X is observed with $ARST$
> —Then X and A are related.

Let X be a foreman in department BCD and let A represent low productivity. The production manager shifts foreman X from department BCD to department RST. After a time, he learns that the production of department RST is dropping. Therefore, he concludes that foreman X is to blame. Is this J. S. Mill conclusion justified?

The *method of difference:*

> If X is observed with $ABCD$,
> and Y is observed with $MBCD$
> —Then X and A are related.

M stands for high production. The manager notices that after foreman X is replaced by foreman Y in department BCD, the production of that department goes up. Therefore, he concludes that foreman X is to blame. Is this J. S. Mill conclusion justified?

Let us see what might be wrong with this approach. One possibility is that removing the foreman from a department with a poor production record gave the workers cause for concern and so they reacted by improving their performance. The second department, on the other hand, had a good production record; when their foreman was removed it may have lowered their morale and productivity.

What if the productivity of department BCD had not improved, having been so strongly affected by foreman X that foreman Y could do nothing to raise the production level? Or, what if the manager was rumored to favor Y over X and the departments were reacting accordingly? Such complications can lead to erroneous conclusions. It is important to remember their potential when using Mill-type models.

76/ *Discovery Models: Relationships*

The *discovery of pertinent variables* is intimately connected with the investigation of the *relationships that exist among variables.* Correlation techniques, for example, require some hypotheses to be made about the relationships of the variables with the outcomes. If the wrong relationships are hypothesized, then the chosen variables will be rejected as not pertinent.

Why then didn't we include this class of model in the previous section? The answer is that many times logic tells us which variables are important factors in determining outcomes. But since we don't know the relationships, correlation can't bear us out. We must look for other means to learn how the variables interact with each other to yield the outcomes. And this is the class of models we are now considering.

An executive believes that patience, strength, and intelligence are *the* vital factors that determine how well a "particular job" can be done. We shall assume that he has developed adequate measurement models to describe the patience, strength, and intelligence of any applicant for the job. What he must still find out is in what way these three variables are critical to the outcome. Are they equally important, or does one count twice as much as another? How do they combine to yield the outcome? A model must be developed that will relate how well a particular job can be done to the values of patience, strength, and intelligence. These outcomes that describe the doing of a job might include the speed of doing the job, quality of workmanship, employee endurance, and so on. Somehow, these multiple outcomes must be combined to yield a single payoff.

One of the first approaches is to examine the available data. The manager can attempt to fit curves to these data. Holding *patience* and *intelligence* constant, he can vary the value of *strength* and observe what effect that has on each of the outcomes. The same procedure can be followed for the other variables.

If this approach does not yield useful results, it is still possible to attempt the derivation of a model by *deduction*. Deductive reasoning starts with generalizations and moves toward particulars. A good example of this process is the discovery of analog models which can be taken from one situation and fitted to another. We have mentioned how *verbs* help to find appropriate analogs. Something we read or hear strikes us as incorporating elements that are significant to our own problem. The analogy is systematically transferred with modifications as needed. Once such a model has been created (be it in physical or symbolic form) it is necessary to test the *validity* of the hypotheses that are its foundation as well as the model's reliability.

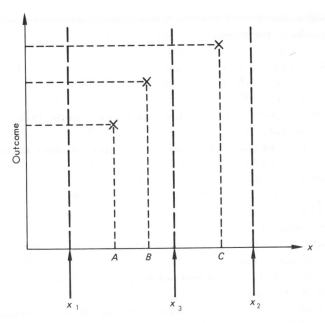

FIGURE 8.5 *Extrapolation is required to estimate the outcome values for x_1 and x_2; interpolation is needed for x_3.*

Model testing (related to the cycle shown in Figure 8.1) is not a simple process. Outcomes can occur that go contrary to reason. Yet, this is not *sufficient* evidence to reject the model. A sound testing program, composed of properly designed experimental methods, is the basic generator of believability.

There are times when the relationships between the input variables and the outcomes are known over a short range. An important problem is to determine outcomes that fall outside the range (for example, ABC . . . . . x where AB and C are known but x is not). This is the problem of *extrapolation.* If two outcomes are known but all values in between are not, we use methods of *interpolation* to find them. (For example, AB . . x . . . C where AB and C are known but x is not.) See Figure 8.5. Extrapolation frequently plays a more vital role than interpolation, especially when the relationship to be extrapolated is presumed to have a statistical form (as in most prediction models). Complex extrapolations (based on both qualitative and quantitative reasoning) are being done all the time by executives to project social and economic trends that will influence their forecasts.

77 / Simulation Models

Simulation models are a form of descriptive models with discovery or outcome-seeking properties. Previously, we categorized them by degree of abstraction but they can be typed in various other ways as well. Physical simulation models can be operating scale models such as the airplane in the wind tunnel which simulates flight conditions or the pilot plant simulation of the full-scale production system. Fatigue and wear tests are used to compress time. The scaled-down dimension is time—perhaps one model minute being equivalent to a day. Such simulation models have been used to study problems of similitude for hundreds of years. Many of the variables that influence the achievement of objectives cannot be specified. Their relationships with outcomes are vaguely perceived or unknown. But as long as the rules for similitude can be formulated, the outcome behaviors of the physical model can be transformed to their full-scale equivalents.

As stated in Chapter 7, when O.R., management science, and systems people speak about simulation models they usually have reference to the next level of abstraction, that is, analog models. Frequently, these analog models incorporate probability terms. They deal with problems that have a number of different states of nature, each of which is known to occur with some probability. *Simulation is accomplished by allowing the states of nature to appear randomly in proportion to the assigned probabilities.* The methods for embodying these random effects in models represent a significant advance in methodology which is recent, and to a large extent dependent on the existence of the computer facility.

Simulation of military problems has a long history. Complex war games have been simulated in the field, as board games, and most recently with the computer. Typically, they involve competitive strategies as well as states of nature (such as weather) that might affect the outcome of the military operation. Here too, the ability to generate random occurrences has considerably augmented the utility of these models. Some executive business games are of this same type. They involve the effects of both competitive strategies and states of nature in such complex relationships with outcomes that the model-builder does not know the result of a particular configuration until he simulates that pattern. This can be contrasted with business games that are based on normative game theory models. The objective, in this latter case, is to see how well (and how fast) the player can approximate optimum conditions.

Analog simulation models are designed with known variables and known relationships. In the non-normative class, however, the relationships are too complex to solve even though the mathematical equations can be written. Since they cannot be solved in their symbolic form, they are transformed into a flow of logical steps. A number of simulation models operate on a problem-solving sequence where the outcome of one stage serves as the input to the next stage. Models of this type, with potentially millions of steps, can be programmed for and run through high-speed computers with ease. For models that are not excessively complicated, pencil and paper can be used for running and simulation. Business board games, such as Monopoly, are surprisingly rich in alternative configurations, including the influence of chance occurrences.

Simulation can be used to reflect situations characterized by statistical distributions that are either of well-known forms (such as normal, Poisson, and exponential) or not. Frequently, several probability distributions interact with each other in irregular ways and it is not possible to solve for their combined effect in mathematical terms. Again, simulation can provide useful results.

Let us exemplify how this is done. Assume that the production manager of an oil refinery has information about the frequency with which certain components need remedial attention. When *any one* component fails, the *entire section* of the refinery composed of them is forced to shut down. The executive wants to know what the probabilities are that the entire section will be down. This same sort of problem applies to any interdependent multicomponent system where each component has its own particular failure characteristics. The method for solving such problems is based on the use of a quantitative model called the *Monte Carlo method.*

78/ *Monte Carlo Generation of Outcomes*

Specific outcomes that interest us often cannot be observed, but related phenomena can be. The reasons for this might be that it would be excessively expensive, require impossible forms of destructive testing, or be too time-consuming to collect the necessary data. We may know the probabilities of many individual factors that contribute to the outcome. How can we use this information to generate a sequence of hypothetical outcomes?

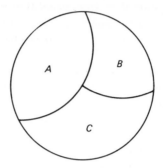

FIGURE 8.6   When one component (A, B, or C) fails, the entire
unit (A + B + C) is shut down.

The executive in charge of refinery production is installing four new units. He has no data for them since they have never been built before. However, the units are made up of components with which he is familiar. Three types of components, *A, B,* and *C,* are combined to form the four different operating units, *ABC, AB, AC,* and *BC.* When any one of the components fails to operate properly, the entire unit is shut down. At that time, crews provide full maintenance for *all* the components in the unit—not just the one component that has caused the shutdown. Data are available for the probabilities with which each component *A, B,* and *C,* fails after *x* weeks of operation.

Let x = number of weeks that elapse between maintenance and failure, and
$P(x)$ = the probability that x weeks will elapse between maintenance and failure

COMPONENT A		COMPONENT B		COMPONENT C	
x	$P(x)$	x	$P(x)$	x	$P(x)$
0	00	0	00	0	00
5	05	5	15	5	30
10	10	10	35	10	10
15	15	15	30	15	10
20	20	20	10	20	05
25	20	25	05	25	04
30	15	30	03	30	06
35	10	35	02	35	15
40	05	40	00	40	10
45	00	45	00	45	05
50	00	50	00	50	05
55	00	55	00	55	00

Using these data we can obtain the expected values of x for A, B and C. (For example, $EV(x_A) = .05(5) + .10(10) + .15(15) + .20(20) + .20(25) + .15(30) + .10(35) + .05(40) = 22.50$ weeks.) Proceeding in the same way, we find: $EV(x_B) = 13.6$ weeks and $EV(x_C) = 21.8$ weeks.

What will be the probability distributions for the combinations ABC, AB, AC and BC? That is the real issue to be resolved and it is not made obvious by knowing the expected values of the individual components. If the executive wants this information to hire an adequate maintenance crew, he can hardly afford to wait several years until each unit has failed enough times to provide the necessary data. Consequently, using the Monte Carlo method, we shall transform the available information into that which is required.

To begin with, the probabilities $P(x)$ for the outcomes x are listed with an additional column for Monte Carlo number identifications. These are best explained as follows:

Put into a bowl 5 red chips, 10 blue chips, 15 yellow chips, 20 white chips, 20 black chips, 15 green chips, 10 orange chips and 5 purple chips. We have then created a model of the failure characteristics of component A. Mix the contents of the bowl thoroughly, reach into it without looking,[2] and pull out one chip. Record the color, put the chip back in the bowl and mix thoroughly. Continue in this way: mix, draw, record, replace, mix, etc. until a large enough sample of chip colors has been obtained. This sample will approximate the failure distribution of component A.[3] If the drawings are properly done very many times, the sample results will almost exactly duplicate the actual distribution. We could use other means than colored chips to represent the sizes of the probability categories. For example, fill the bowl with 100 chips of one color *numbered* from 00 to 99. Assign 5 numbers to the first category ($x = 5$, $P(x) = 0.05$). They would be 00, 01, 02, 03, 04—the equivalent of the red chips. Similarly, in the second category we would use numbers 05 to 14, intending the same meaning as the 10 blue chips, and so forth. Each grouping of Monte Carlo numbers corresponds to a given color and hence to a given x proportional to $P(x)$. Every row in the table presents the set of Monte Carlo numbers that corresponds to the appropriate x value.

---

[2] It is necessary to assure *random* sampling.

[3] It should be noted that if we do not replace each chip after it has been drawn and recorded, we must eventually exhaust the contents of the bowl. Necessarily, the proportions of each color originally placed in the bowl will be our final result. The same is not true when we use replacement. This latter sampling technique is appropriate when the population size is large. Then, if the true population proportions are known, the results obtained from varying sample sizes can be observed.

COMPONENT A

x	P(x)	Color	Monte Carlo number
5	0.05	red	00–04
10	0.10	blue	05–14
15	0.15	yellow	15–29
20	0.20	white	30–49
25	0.20	black	50–69
30	0.15	green	70–84
35	0.10	orange	85–94
40	0.05	purple	95–99

Now we shall draw one of the numbered chips at *random* from the bowl. If we drew a chip numbered 86, we would know that this number was equivalent to an orange chip, and that an orange chip is equivalent to $x = 35$. Each number (00–99) *has an equal chance of being drawn.* Since there are twice as many numbers assigned to the category $x = 10$ as there are to $x = 5$, the probability that $x = 10$ will occur is twice that of $x = 5$. Using chips is an unnecessarily awkward procedure. Tables of random numbers are available in which any number is as likely to appear as any other. Therefore, we can put the bowl back on the shelf. (A Table of Random Numbers will be found on page 585.)

Monte Carlo numbers were assigned to component A above. We now give them for components B and C.

COMPONENT B				COMPONENT C		
x	P(x)	M.C. number		x	P(x)	M.C. number
5	0.15	00–14		5	0.30	00–29
10	0.35	15–49		10	0.10	30–39
15	0.30	50–79		15	0.10	40–49
20	0.10	80–89		20	0.05	50–54
25	0.05	90–94		25	0.04	55–58
30	0.03	95–97		30	0.06	59–64
35	0.02	98–99		35	0.15	65–79
40	—	—		40	0.10	80–89
45	—	—		45	0.05	90–94
50	—	—		50	0.05	95–99

How do we combine these distributions of the individual components to obtain the distribution for the unit ABC? First, draw a random number. Determine which value of x corresponds to that number for component A. Then do the same thing for component B. Take the next random number from the table and mark down the appropriate x value for B. Next, do the same for C. Then start again with A and repeat the process over and over until the sample size is judged sufficient. The result of working in this fashion is shown in Table 8.4.

TABLE 8.4

Using random numbers to generate outcomes

SAMPLE NUMBER	COMPONENT A Random number	x_A	COMPONENT B Random number	x_B	COMPONENT C Random number	x_C	UNIT ABC x_{MIN}
1	87	35	50	15	10	5	5
2	98	40	42	10	44	15	10
3	03	5	60	15	65	35	5
4	27	15	88	20	83	40	15
5	84	30	10	5	12	5	5
6	44	20	41	10	51	20	10
7	55	25	62	15	29	5	5
8	10	10	92	25	74	35	10
9	68	25	81	20	34	10	10
10	70	30	86	20	18	5	5
11	04	5	35	10	43	15	5
12	02	5	53	15	62	30	5
13	53	25	54	15	21	5	5
14	74	30	40	10	04	5	5
15	23	15	36	10	73	35	10
16	60	25	24	10	01	5	5
17	39	20	93	25	32	10	10
18	60	25	72	15	96	50	15
19	50	25	61	15	50	20	15
20	93	35	53	15	85	40	15
21	15	15	10	5	75	35	5
22	46	20	57	15	17	5	5
23	23	15	49	10	12	5	5
24	54	25	24	10	43	15	10
25	36	20	83	20	31	10	10

Let us look at the first *row*. The random numbers 87, 50, and 10 appeared. They correspond to x values as follows: $x_A = 35$, $x_B = 15$, and $x_C = 5$. In line with each component's probabilities of failure, we have simulated the event that A fails at 35 weeks, B fails at 15 weeks, and C fails at 5 weeks. Since the first component to fail causes the entire unit to be shut down and repaired, the failure of ABC would occur, in this case, at 5 weeks. However, if the unit were only composed of AB, the first failure would occur at 15 weeks. For units AC and BC, the simulated failure would take place after 5 weeks. The last column of Table 8.4 lists the minimum row values of x for each ABC sample (i.e., that value which dominates ABC's failure time).

These results are transformed to estimates of the probability $P(x)$ that x weeks elapse between shutdowns for unit ABC (by means of a straight-forward frequency count of the x_{MIN} column).

x_{MIN}	FREQUENCY	$P(x_{MIN})$
5	13	0.52
10	8	0.32
15	4	0.16
	25	1.00

The more x_{MIN} values obtained in the sample, the more accurate is our description of the distribution of failures. Generally, far more than 25

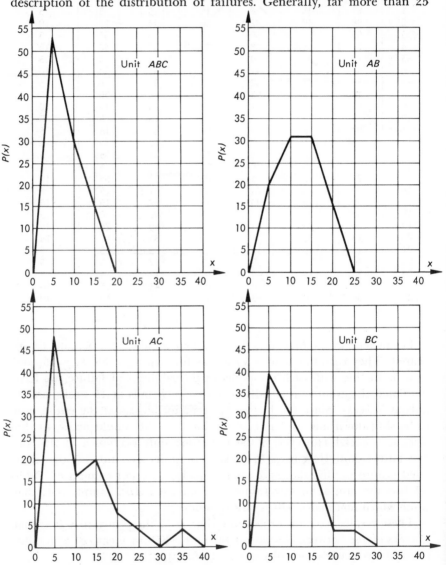

FIGURE 8.7   Probability that x weeks elapse between shut-downs for units.

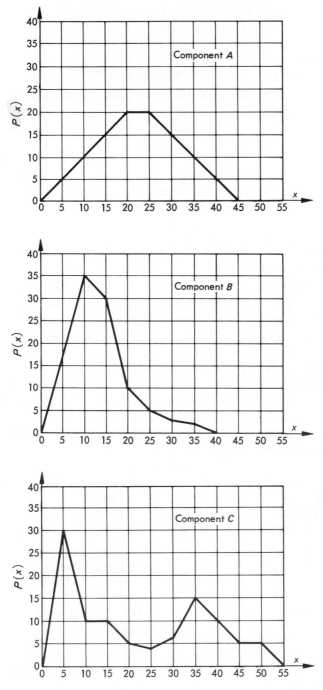

FIGURE 8.8 *Probability that* x *weeks elapse between shut-downs for components.*

results are required. Distributions that describe each unit are shown in Figure 8.7. Distributions of the individual components *A, B,* and *C* are drawn in Figure 8.8 for purposes of comparison.

The importance of the Monte Carlo procedure to simulation methodology should be evident. The technique can be applied in a great variety of situations where complex probability relationships hold, yet its use does not require advanced mathematical knowledge. It is critical, however, to relate the variables and their probabilities to each other so that the outcome is *dimensionally sound.*

79/ Heuristic Simulation of Human Behavior

One great boon of simulation models is that they permit heuristics (i.e., rules of thumb—see page 152) to be used. These informal, descriptive notions of how things relate to each other can be captured and used rigorously by simulation. The same notions do not lend themselves to representation by formal mathematical equations. The simulation approach allows very complex and interacting systems to be sculptured, including some attempts at modelling the behavior of man. To illustrate this heuristic approach we shall create our own model of the market place. Although oversimplified, it will present the essential ingredients of this form of application.

Let us propose that the behavior of many different consumers be simulated. From the marketing viewpoint, a powerful model would result from the aggregation of many individual consumer's behavior. The model would be responsive to various marketing stimuli, including price, advertising copy, brand qualities, and so forth, in the same manner as real individual consumers. Various consumer-types should be representable. We want to be able to test our model under many marketing conditions.

We shall let each individual (or group) behave in accordance with statistical evidence obtained by observation of the real world. As we try to develop useful realism in our models, the problems of observation and measurement become crucial.

Table 8.5 is intended to describe certain characteristics of a particular demographic and psychological set of consumers which we can call the α-type.[4]

It is easy to compute the average number of exposures per week of an α-type consumer to the advertising of the two brands, *A* and *B*.

$$\bar{n}_A = 0.30(0) + 0.40(1) + 0.20(2) + 0.10(3) + 0.00(4) = 1.1 \text{ exposures}$$
$$\bar{n}_B = 0.20(0) + 0.50(1) + 0.15(2) + 0.10(3) + 0.05(5) = 1.3 \text{ exposures}$$

[4] The same approach can be used for β, ∂, and other consumer types as required.

TABLE 8.5

$P(n_i)$ = Probability of n_i exposures per week for α-type individuals to the advertising of Brand i. (i = Brand A, Brand B)

(1)	(2)	(3)	(4)	(5)	(6)	(7)
	PROBABILITIES		CUMULATIVE		MONTE CARLO NUMBERS	
n_i	$P(n_A)$	$P(n_B)$	$P(n_A)$	$P(n_B)$	Brand A	Brand B
0	0.30	0.20	0.30	0.20	00 – 29	00 – 19
1	0.40	0.50	0.70	0.70	30 – 69	20 – 69
2	0.20	0.15	0.90	0.85	70 – 89	70 – 84
3	0.10	0.10	1.00	0.95	90 – 99	85 – 94
4	0.00	0.05		1.00		95 – 99
5	0.00	0.00				

Columns 2 and 3 of Table 8.5 describe the probabilities that an α-type consumer will receive the different number of exposures shown in column 1 to the advertising of Brands A and B, respectively. Accordingly, for Brand A, it is expected that in 30 out of every 100 weeks each α-type consumer receives no exposures. Similarly, in 20 out of every 100 weeks no Brand B advertising is received. Assuming that exposure to Brand A advertising is completely independent of exposure to Brand B advertising (and vice versa), then in 6 weeks out of every hundred ($0.30 \times 0.20 = 0.06$) the consumer sees no advertising at all. All reasoning about Table 8.5 can proceed in like manner.

Columns 5 and 6 are the cumulative probabilities of n_i exposures, i.e., the total probability of receiving n_i exposures or less. We have included the cumulative operation in our table because it affords computational convenience. It will be noted that the Monte Carlo assignments occupy the same numerical intervals as the respective intervals between adjacent cumulative probabilities.

Depending upon the strategies employed by Brands A and B, these α-type consumers will receive different numbers of exposures during the week. It will be noticed that Brand B has a small advantage with respect to the average number of exposures of the respective brands received by each consumer. By varying its media schedule, either brand can change its own expectation level for exposures. However, in addition to the α-group, there are β, ∂, δ, . . . , and other demographic/behavioristic groups of individuals. Each group will be reached with varying degrees of efficiency through the different media plans. Changes that will increase the number of α-type exposures might decrease the number of β and ∂-type exposures. Consequently, Brand A would ordinarily choose to have a lower number of average exposures for α-type individuals if by so doing they can be more effective on an over-all basis. In any case, the relationship of the average number of exposures to the relative success of a campaign is not obvious and can be misleading. Simulation models are particularly appealing in situations of this kind.

Columns 6 and 7 are the Monte Carlo numbers which, for the problem-solver, are as romantic as their name suggests. It will be remembered that, when properly arranged, the *numbers constitute a model* of the likelihood with which all of the pertinent *random* conditions (or states of the system) will occur.

In a *nonrandom* process, only one set and sequence of events can occur. An exact description can be given for the state of the system at any moment in time. In a *random* process, different conditions and sequences will be observed to occur with frequencies that can be characterized by an appropriate probability distribution. No exact description can be given for what will happen at the next moment in time. However, a forecast can be made. It is a statement of the *odds* that one or another type of event will occur. We must now generate two-digit random numbers or else make use of a table of random numbers such as the short one that we have generated for this book (p. 255). We recall that it is characteristic of these random numbers that any number is as likely to be drawn as any other.

Table 8.5 presents the Monte Carlo configuration that we shall use to generate various reasonable patterns of exposure to the advertisements of both brands that can occur by chance. Table 8.6 extends the model. It reflects the hypothesis that the probability of purchase is dependent upon the cumulative number of exposures that each α-type consumer has received. Reference to Table 8.6 will show that when seven exposures (representing some combination of Brand *A* and Brand *B* advertising) have been achieved, a purchase *must* occur. It will be noted that the

TABLE 8.6

Probability that a purchase will be made as a function of the cumulative number of exposures (expressed in terms of Monte Carlo numbers)

CUMULATIVE EXPOSURES $n_A + n_B$	PURCHASE	NO PURCHASE
0	—	00 – 99
1	00	01 – 99
2	00 – 02	03 – 99
3	00 – 09	10 – 99
4	00 – 25	26 – 99
5	00 – 39	40 – 99
6	00 – 69	70 – 99
7	00 – 99	—

Note: Cumulative $n_A + n_B$ is carried *until discharged* by a purchase.

Table is stated only in terms of the Monte Carlo assignments. The underlying probability distribution can be recovered without difficulty. Each row of the Table represents a specific and unique situation for the consumer. Since, for any given condition of cumulative exposures he has only two alternatives, namely, make a purchase or make no purchase, the alternative behaviors—row by row—must share between them the total number of available Monte Carlo numbers; in this case, 100 two-digit numbers.

The two charts are easily used. Let us draw three random numbers and suppose they turn out to be 62, 94 and 35. The first number, 62, tells us (from Table 8.5) that $n_A = 1$; the second number, 94, indicates (from Table 8.5) that $n_B = 3$. We add these two results in order to enter Table 8.6, i.e., $n_A + n_B = 4$. Using this sum of four in the left-hand column of Table 8.6, and the third random number drawn, namely 35, we find that no purchase will be made in the first week. (The number 35 falls in the No Purchase column.) Again, we draw three random numbers. Let us assume that they are 05, 53 and 16. The first indicates that $n_A = 0$. Consequently, the *cumulative* n_A remains unchanged at 1. Random number 53 indicates that $n_B = 1$. The original n_B, which was three —as explained above—is then increased by 1, i.e., *cumulative* $n_B = 4$. The new total for $n_A + n_B$ is now 5. The sum of 5, in conjunction with random number 16, indicates that this particular α-type consumer is going to make a purchase in the second week. It remains to determine whether he will buy Brand A or Brand B. Table 8.7 has been designed to resolve this question. Of course, all of these charts and the relation-

TABLE 8.7

Probabilities of Brand A and Brand B purchases on the
condition that a purchase will be made (expressed in
terms of Monte Carlo numbers)

$n_A - n_B$	$A'A$	$A'B$	$B'A$	$B'B$
-4	$90 - 99$	$00 - 89$	—	$00 - 99$
-3	$83 - 99$	$00 - 82$	$00 - 01$	$02 - 99$
-2	$46 - 99$	$00 - 45$	$00 - 05$	$06 - 99$
-1	$26 - 99$	$00 - 25$	$00 - 10$	$11 - 99$
0	$16 - 99$	$00 - 15$	$00 - 15$	$16 - 99$
$+1$	$11 - 99$	$00 - 10$	$00 - 25$	$26 - 99$
$+2$	$06 - 99$	$00 - 05$	$00 - 45$	$46 - 99$
$+3$	$02 - 99$	$00 - 01$	$00 - 82$	$83 - 99$
$+4$	$00 - 99$	—	$00 - 89$	$90 - 99$

Note: A' indicates that the *prior* purchase was Brand A, e.g., when $n_A - n_B = -3$, then B has achieved three more exposures than has A. If A were the prior purchase (A'), then only two possibilities exist, *viz.*, $A'A$ and $A'B$. We see from the table that these have 17 per cent and 83 per cent probabilities, respectively. If B had been the prior purchase, then the probability of $B'A$ is 2 per cent and, necessarily, 98 per cent for $B'B$.

ships among them, represent *hypothetical* constructs. With observation, experience, and experimentation the validity of such heuristics should improve, eventually yielding operational models of the market place.

Table 8.7 has also been converted to Monte Carlo numbers. Another hypothesis is introduced at this point. It might be worded as follows: If the cumulative number of exposures of Brand A is greater than the cumulative number of exposures of Brand B, then there is a greater probability that a new purchase will be a Brand A purchase rather than a Brand B purchase, and vice versa.

One further complication has been introduced. If the prior purchase was a Brand A purchase, then the probability of making a new Brand A purchase will be greater than would be the case where the prior purchase was a Brand B purchase. The addition of the prime, as A' or B', signifies whichever brand was purchased the previous time that a purchase was made.

Now it is a simple matter to complete our illustration. Our α-type consumer is about to make a purchase in the second week. Will the purchase be of Brand A or of Brand B? We must discover what the prior purchase was but we have no previous record. Only the first value of a simulated sequence of consumer purchases must be assumed. After that, the prior purchase is always the last one that has been made. We know that n_A cumulative through two weeks was equal to 1; n_B cumulative through two weeks was equal to 4; then cumulative $(n_A + n_B) = 5$; and cumulative $(n_A - n_B) = 1 - 4 = -3$. Let us *assume* that the prior purchase was a Brand B purchase. If the next random number drawn was either 00 or 01, our simulated consumer switches to Brand A. All other random numbers that could be drawn would signify that the consumer remains loyal to Brand B.

The essential features of this approach now have been shown. It is easy to see how we succeed in collapsing time. Thousands of α-type consumers can be led through years of purchase decisions in the micro-moments of computer operations. Also, we have the opportunity of sampling many different types of consumers, β's, ∂'s, δ's, . . . , and so forth, without incurring exorbitant expenses but with a good deal of heuristic probing and resolution.

Table 8.8 describes the behavior of a single α-type consumer over a 16-week period. In each simulated and compressed week—an instant of the computer's time—four random numbers must be drawn. The computations used for Table 8.8 are based on the assumed conditions of Tables 8.5, 8.6, and 8.7, respectively. When no purchase is indicated the fourth random number, which distinguishes between a Brand A and a Brand B purchase, is not used. We then proceed to the next time period, accumulating and carrying with us the prior number of exposures

TABLE 8.8

16-Week record of one α-type consumer

Time	Number of Exposures		Cumulative	Cumulative	Monte Carlo numbers drawn from a table of random numbers				Purchase* A
	n_A	n_B	$(n_A + n_B)$	$(n_A - n_B)$					
1	3	1	4	2	96	20	59	17	0
2	0	1	5	1	26	51	90	00	0
3	2	1	8	2	81	55	03	52	A
4	0	0	0	0	18	09	14	45	0
5	1	3	4	−2	60	94	68	37	0
6	2	4	10	−4	83	98	47	78	B
7	1	2	3	−1	69	82	89	76	0
8	3	1	7	1	93	66	64	68	B
9	2	0	2	2	86	19	26	39	0
10	1	1	4	2	31	50	11	36	A
11	3	0	3	3	90	06	34	45	0
12	0	0	3	3	04	01	36	33	0
13	1	0	4	4	56	12	23	17	A
14	3	3	6	0	96	94	86	42	0
15	1	1	8	0	48	35	80	37	A
16	1	1	0	0	57	36	06	53	0

* It has been assumed that the initial purchase is *A*.

until they are discharged by a purchase. In this way, the buying pattern shown in Table 8.8 is derived. The reader can follow through these computations by studying the flow chart of Figure 8.9.

Table 8.9 summarizes the results of this hand-worked simulation.

TABLE 8.9

Summary of purchasing behavior in the 16-week period

	Frequency	Per cent
Brand *A*	4 times	25.0
Brand *B*	2 times	12.5
No Purchase	10 times	62.5
	16	100.0

Brand *A* has been purchased four times. Brand *B* has been purchased twice. No purchase was made in 10 of the weeks. With respect to this particular α-type consumer, Brand *A* has obtained two-thirds of his purchases. The consumer has an average purchase cycle of 2.5 weeks.[5]

A large scale simulation, based on reasonable hypotheses and a plenti-

---

[5] Through the 15th week, $15/6 = 2.5$.

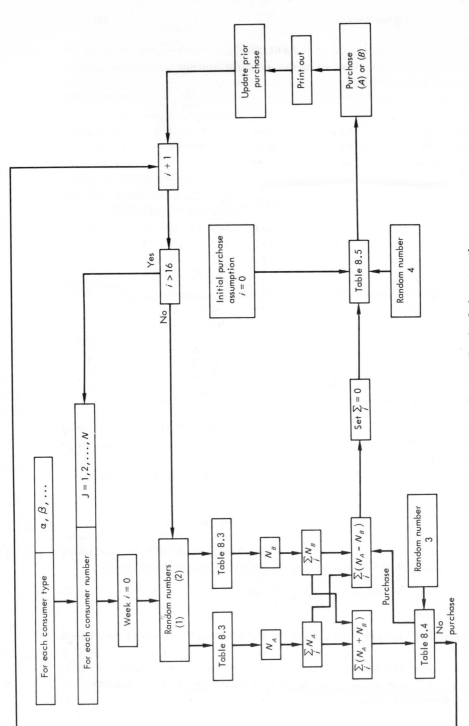

FIGURE 8.9 A flow chart of the simulation operations.

ful supply of meaningful data, can produce useful estimates of brand share, dollar volume, and so forth. The relationship of reach, frequency, product price, and copy effectiveness also can be explored in this way. Utterly oversimplified notions, such as the pure advantage of a greater exposure rate, can be examined in terms of the total effect of a specific campaign. It is generally understood that the average number of exposures achieved by Brand *A* as compared with Brand *B* cannot be used as a simple criterion of the effectiveness of Brand *A*'s market strategy. A simulation model permits the consideration of such factors as switching inertia or loyalty, advertising effectiveness, the repurchase rate and repurchase quantity, etc., some of which may play a crucial role. In addition, we can hardly ignore the fact that each strategy that might be followed has its own cost and produces a particular rate of return. Thus, this form of heuristic simulation permits consideration of a multitude of factors and relationships that could not be considered in any other way.

We have collapsed time. We do not have to wait 16 weeks to derive our heuristic results. With a computer we could have run many thousands of hypothetical consumers through a period of several generations in a matter of a few minutes. Furthermore, we can reasonably continue to add to the complexity of these simulations in an attempt to approach reality. Our 16-week period is a poor sample, even for a single consumer. By chance, strange results can occur. Any system which possesses variable behaviors, both in the real and simulated world, will, now and then, produce unusual results. Oddities are expected. But in the long run, erratic behaviors will balance out and the "true" characteristics of the system will begin to emerge.

80/ *Analytic Forms of Mathematical Models*

Because simulation models are an extremely useful, *recent* development, we have spent time with them. Now let us turn to descriptive models which are drawn along the lines of formal mathematics. Frequently, these models (which are called analytic models) possess characteristics that are confused with the properties of normative models.

Queuing Theory Models. Among many such models, perhaps the most representative class is that of queuing[6] models. Queuing theory is not normative. It does not tell us what we ought to do, but rather explains the behavior of a service facility with respect to its capacity, configuration, and load.

---

[6] We use the word *queue* (a pigtail) in the sense of a waiting line.

One or several entities come to the facility to claim service. As soon as it is able, the facility meets the demands that are placed on it. So we have a provider of service and a user of that service. This is the underlying theme of any transformation process, and accordingly, many instances of situations analogous to queuing will be found in production, marketing, R&D, organization theory, etc.

Queuing models are descriptive—not normative—because they do not provide optimum solutions to a decision problem. They are explanatory models which can be used to explore the behavior of a given arrangement of facilities within a specific environment.

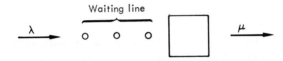

FIGURE 8.10   Single channel service system.

Let us consider a basic queuing model. Figure 8.10 shows a single channel (one service facility) system. It is an input-output model, simple enough to use when the flows in and out are deterministic, scheduled and controlled. It is far more complex, however, when the flows are subject to random arrivals and servicing times.

If demand is *exactly* 6 per hour and service is exactly 6 per hour the system is perfectly balanced. If, however, demand and/or service is irregular and subject to a statistical distribution—then *averages* of 6 demands and 6 service completions have much more complicated interrelations. Sometimes, a queue will form and units will have to wait varying intervals. At other times the service facility may be idle.

Now we introduce an additional dimension. Figure 8.11 shows a mul-

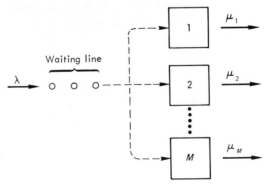

FIGURE 8.11   M-channel service system.

tiple channel (M service facilities) system. This too is an input-output model, but a more sophisticated version, especially if the flows are not deterministic, but random. To compare alternative service arrangements, it is essential that we develop relevant measures of effectiveness that can be used to evaluate the alternatives. In other words, there must be a sound basis for choosing one arrangement in preference to others.

Queuing models are concerned with stochastic situations. The system to be modelled provides specific services which are under the manager's jurisdiction. Service facilities might be composed of such diverse units as drill presses, milling machines, turret lathes, drop forges, plating tanks, airplane seats, hospital operating tables, supermarket checkout counters, bank tellers' windows, toll booths, shipping docks, airport runways, restaurant tables, telephone trunk lines, and machine repairmen.

Units arrive to receive service. These units may be materials to be machined or plated, travelers to be transported, patients to be treated, shoppers, customers, ships, airplanes, gourmets, gossipers, and machines that have broken down. The diversity of possible applications is incredible.[7] There is an expected rate of arrival of the units for servicing. For example, on the average, 3 units require service per day. We call this expected arrival rate λ. There is a *distribution of arrival rates* around this mean value. Also, there is an expected or average rate of servicing the units. For example, on the average, 5 units are serviced per day. We call this expected servicing rate μ. There is a *distribution of servicing rates* around this mean value. That is, sometimes more than 5 units are serviced per hour; at other times, less than 5 units receive service.

Because we are dealing with statistical distributions, a greater than average number of units can arrive for servicing. It is equally possible that a run of units will require longer than average servicing times. Under such circumstances a queue or waiting line can develop, even though the process has ample capacity and is capable of providing more service than is normally demanded; that is, $\mu > \lambda$. At other times, less than the expected number of units can arrive or shorter than average servicing times can occur. This produces idle time for service facilities. We have as a guide to the probable behavior of a single channel system the ratio $\rho = \lambda/\mu$. It is called the *process utilization factor.* For multiple channel systems, an important descriptive relationship would be:

$$\rho M = \lambda/\mu$$

where M equals the number of channel (or service facilities). In addi-

---

[7] For example, an entire class of important inventory models are constructed on the basis of the queuing model family. See, for example, Martin K. Starr and David W. Miller, *Inventory Control: Theory and Practice* (Englewood Cliffs, N.J.: Prentice-Hall, Inc., 1962), pp. 146–150, 242–248.

tion we must also know (or make assumptions about) the shapes of the distributions from which the expected values of λ and μ are derived.

Management must decide how much service capacity is required, what type of facility will provide optimum service, and how to arrange a group of facilities, such as machines in a production line. Decisions of this kind represent one of the major controls exercised by managers. This is especially true when resources can be shifted around to meet transient disturbances.

Whatever the specific situation, some *measures of effectiveness*, such as those shown below, are required to evaluate the service system. Many others can be found that might be better suited to particular circumstances.

- The average number of units in a queue.
- The average number of units in the system. (This includes the number in the queue and the number in service.)
- The average waiting time or delay before service begins.
- The average time spent by a unit in the system. (This total delay includes the delay before service begins and the time to complete service.)
- The probability that *any* delay will occur.
- The probability that the total delay will be greater than some value of t.
- The probability that all service facilities will be idle.
- The expected per cent idle time of the total service facility.
- The probability of turn-aways, resulting from insufficient waiting line accommodations.

Having evaluated the characteristics of a process in terms of these, or other measures of effectiveness, the executive attempts to manipulate and regulate whatever controls exist to achieve improvement in the process' performance. Thus, management will control the service function to the extent that it is possible by:

- Using additional servicing facilities.
- Rearranging existing service facilities. For example, take 3 clerks who perform specialized sequential operations on a purchase requisition and revise the job so that the clerks are specialized by types of purchase orders which are handled entirely by one person.
- Replacing existing service facilities with improved ones.
- Establishing a system of priorities whereby certain units receive attention before others do.

• Providing special service facilities for units having exceptionally long or short service times.

As we have said before, the means for achieving optimization are not inherent in queuing models. The function of these models is restricted to providing evaluations by discovering the conditions of relevant measures of effectiveness. (Some examples of how queuing models are used will be found in Chapter 10, see pp. 360–363. We shall need to discuss a number of other properties of these models before we can understand their application to appropriate situations.)

Information Theory Models.[8] When a strategy and a state of nature produce an outcome which then modifies the state of nature in such a way as to produce a new outcome, the determination of only the first outcome does not suffice as a basis for description. (So it cannot be used for decision-making, either.) We recognize that this is the description of a feedback model. The input strategy, in conjunction with the state of

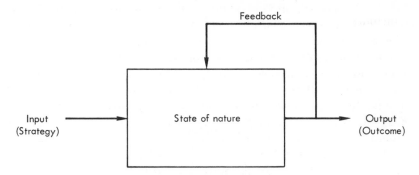

FIGURE 8.12   Decision feedback model.

nature produces an output, all, or part of which, is fed back as a new input. This input modifies the state of nature and a new output results which is then fed back, and so forth. Consequently, no one outcome describes the effect of the strategy. A whole sequence of outcomes (or states of nature) is required. In terms of the elements of our decision matrix, we can represent such a process in the following way:

TABLE OF TRANSFORMATIONS

	STARTING STATE	N_1	N_2	N_3	N_4	N_5	N_6	N_7	N_8
S_1:	OUTCOME	O_1	O_2	O_3	O_4	O_5	O_6	O_7	O_8
	NEW STATE	N_8	N_5	N_2	N_1	N_3	N_6	N_4	N_7

[8] For a variety of interesting uses of information theory in economics, see Henri Theil, *Economics and Information Theory* (Chicago: Rand McNally, 1967).

For example, let N_2 be the initial state in the sequence:

TIME SEQUENCE	STARTING STATE	OUTCOME (FEEDBACK)	NEW STATE
t_0	N_2	O_2	N_5
t_1	N_5	O_5	N_3
t_2	N_3	O_3	N_2
t_3	N_2	O_2	N_5
$\vdots$	$\vdots$		

Thus, the cycle O_2, O_5, O_3, O_2, etc. occurs repeatedly when the strategy is held at S_1 and the initial state of nature is N_2. If the initial state of nature had been N_1, the corresponding cycle would be O_1, O_8, O_7, O_4, O_1, etc.

The state of nature that results from a given feedback might be known with certainty—as in decision-making under certainty. It could just as well be subject to random variation and require a probability description, as in decision-making under risk or uncertainty. It is frequently difficult to observe the inputs or the states of nature and so all that we can get at is a sequence of outcomes. In such cases, lacking knowledge of the transformations, or the strategies and their changes, our *total information* consists only of a sequence of outcomes. We have little information and must experiment to collect more if we hope to be able to make predictions about future outcomes. That is the problem we wish to resolve by means of an adequate descriptive model.

Our analytic approach begins by observing patterns. Assume that the outcome O_2 led to the outcome O_5 the first time that it appeared. If the second time O_2 appeared it was followed by O_1, this would mean that at least two possibilities exist for outcomes that follow O_2. Since outcome O_2 can be followed by several outcomes—possibly with different probabilities—we cannot know with certainty what is going to happen. This situation has been identified as a *stochastic process*. "Stochastic" is a Greek word meaning to aim or guess. In its present-day nontechnical usage it means "skillful in conjecturing." And so we can see that the name of the process implies some ability—but not absolute certainty— in knowing what will take place.

Observations made of the outputs of a stochastic process constitute *information*.[9] It is true, we would prefer to know what strategies are being utilized and what states of nature are occurring. But if we could follow all of the pertinent variables and the relationships that connect them we would not be studying outcome data. Since we do not know the

---

[9] Many times, we can view states of nature as outcomes and vice versa. This being strictly a definitional matter, it will not affect the discussion of these models.

other important elements of the decision matrix we carefully analyze our outcome data in order to *detect arrangements, patterns, and regularities.*

The mathematical theory of information enables us to measure the degree of order that exists in a sequence of outcomes. The class of models involved is descriptive-analytic. At one extreme we can find the situation where there is no order at all. This condition of complete disorder occurs only when all outcomes appear to be equally likely. At the opposite end of the scale, we find complete order. This is the situation when only one possible outcome can occur. Between these extremes exist a countless variety of outcome patterns.

What kinds of patterns can there be in a sequence of outcome data and how do we use information theory to detect them? The *first* type of pattern we can look for is one with which we are quite familiar—the relative frequencies of the outcomes. We have previously developed frequency distributions to describe the likelihoods of states of nature. In this case, we are applying the same procedure to outcomes.[10]

A *second* type of pattern is inherent in the *sequences* of outcomes. We observe the frequencies of the *transitions* from one outcome to another. From this, the probabilities of all possible outcome sequences can be determined.

These remarks will be illustrated as soon as we have explained the *measures of information* represented by H and R. H is a measure of the inherent order of a sequence of outcomes. Frequently, it is called *entropy*, a thermodynamic term used to describe the change of available energy in a system. In our sense, it measures the amount of information that is available in a sequence of outcomes. To be an adequate measure, it must reach its extreme values when the data are completely ordered and disordered—which it does.

When completely ordered, we have decision-making under certainty (i.e., complete predictability). When completely disordered, we have decision-making under uncertainty (based on the Laplace criterion where all events are considered to be equally likely). In between these extremes is decision-making under risk. The following model accomplishes our measurement objective:

$$H = -p_1 \log p_1 - p_2 \log p_2 - p_3 \log p_3 \ldots -p_j \log p_j \ldots -p_n \log p_n = -\sum_j p_j \log p_j$$

$$p_j = \text{probability of the } j\text{th outcome occurring}$$

$$\sum_j p_j = p_1 + p_2 + p_3 + \ldots + p_j + \ldots + p_n = 1; \quad 0 \leq p_j \leq 1$$

These equations are written for n outcomes. If only one outcome can occur, then:

---

[10] See the previous footnote.

$$p_j = 1$$

and $$H = -(1) \log (1) = 0$$

This is the situation of complete order.

On the other hand, the maximum value of H occurs when each of n outcomes can appear with equal likelihood. That is:

$$p_j = 1/n \ (j = 1, 2, \ldots, n)$$

$$H_{max} = - \log \frac{1}{n} = \log n$$

This is the situation of complete disorder.

To determine the **relative** *degree of disorder* of a set of data, we can use the ratio of the observed H value to the maximum H value that can occur. When we subtract this fraction from 1, we obtain an information measure of the **relative** *degree of order* of the set of data. We call this measure *redundancy*. Redundancy illuminates the degree of structure in a sequence of outcomes in the **relative** terms of zero through one.

$$R = 1 - \frac{H}{H_{max}}$$

If H is measured as zero, then $R = 1$. This occurs when only one outcome is possible. On the other hand, $R = 0$ when $H = H_{max}$. Since $H = H_{max}$ when all states are equally likely, it is reasonable to obtain 0 redundancy. The redundancy measure ranges from 0 to 1, no matter how many outcomes are involved.

$R = 1$ (Decision-making under certainty)
$R = 0$ (Decision-making under uncertainty—Laplace)
$0 < R < 1$ (Decision-making under risk)

Let us consider the following situation. It has been designed to present a simple example with the characteristics we want to illustrate. A construction company bids on many contracts each year. If they win a contract, they record this outcome as 1. If they don't get the contract, they record the failure as 0. Over a period of time, they produce the following sequence of outcomes:

Bid
Number 1 2 3 4 5 6 7 8 9 10 11 12 13 14 15 16 17 18 19 20
Outcome 0 1 1 0 1 1 0 0 1 0 1 0 1 0 1 0 1 0 1 0

Bid
Number 21 22 23 24 25 26 27 28 29 30 31 32 33 34 35 36 37 38 39 40
Outcome 0 1 1 0 1 0 1 1 0 1 0 1 0 1 0 1 1 0 1 0

If we count up the number of zeros and ones, we will find an almost equal number of each. When we apply the H measure to the relative frequencies of the outcomes, we observe that H and H_{max} are practically equal so redundancy is almost zero. In other words, the prediction of outcomes on this basis will be hardly better than the prediction of heads or tails in a game of chance with a coin. (Redundancy for the outcomes obtained from a true coin is zero.) The appropriate calculations of H and R are shown below.

Outcome	Frequency	p = probability	$\log_{10} p$	$-p\log_{10} p$
0	19	0.475	9.67669 − 10	0.1536
1	21	0.525	9.72016 − 10	0.1469
	40	1.000		0.3005

$$H_1 = (3.32)(0.3005) = 0.9976 \text{ bits}^{11}$$

And what is H_{max}?

$$H_{max} = -\log_2(1/2) = 1 \text{ bit}$$

Therefore:

$$R = 1 - \frac{0.9976}{1.000} = 0.0024$$

Analysis of the frequency distribution does not uncover the kinds of regularities for which we are looking. So we now *analyze the sequence of one-step transitions* in order to see whether, by looking at the system in this way, we can observe regularities, dependencies, and greater structuring. We note that the first 0 is followed by 1. This 1, in turn, is followed by another 1. The second 1 is followed by a 0, and so forth. We continue in this way until we have counted the frequency of each kind of transition that can occur—in this case, four kinds. The matrix below shows the number of times that each kind of transition took place.

	by 0	by 1
0 is followed	2	16
1 is followed	16	5

This frequency matrix can be converted to probability form *where the row probabilities sum to one*. It is then called a *transition matrix*.

	0	1	
0	0.111	0.889	1.000
1	0.762	0.238	1.000

[11] Information statistics are generally written in terms of the logarithm with base 2. In order to convert from logarithms with base 10, we multiply by 3.32. We call the value derived in this form, bits.

Also, we have denoted the H measure for the initial outcome distribution by H_1. Shortly, the H measure will be applied to a transition matrix and denoted by H_2.

We have uncovered certain strong dependencies that exist in the sequence. These *transition probabilities* can be used to determine the *distribution of outcomes* that could be expected to hold in the far future, if the process came to an *equilibrium* called the *steady state*. The method of determining the limiting distribution will not be shown here since it is explained in Chapter 11. However, the probabilities of the outcomes *in the limit* are:

$$p(0) = 0.461$$
$$p(1) = \underline{0.539}$$
$$\ 1.000$$

In this example, the limiting probabilities are not very different from the probabilities derived from the original frequency count. However, in many cases, the limiting distribution will be substantially different from the initial distribution.

In any event, by using the appropriate row of the transition matrix, we now have a means for predicting the next contract outcome with far better than a 50–50 chance. Our improved knowledge represents a real *gain of information*. The H measure *for the transition matrix* is obtained by getting the expected value for H which is composed of the individual H values of each row, weighted by the limiting probabilities.

OUTCOME	p	$\log_{10} p$	$-p \log_{10} p$
Row 0: Column 0	0.111	9.04532 − 10	0.1060
Row 0: Column 1	0.889	9.94890 − 10	0.0454
	1.000		0.1514
Row 1: Column 0	0.762	9.88195 − 10	0.0900
Row 1: Column 1	0.238	9.37658 − 10	0.1484
	1.000		0.2384

$$EV(H_2) = 0.1514(0.461) + 0.2384(0.539) = 0.1983$$

Again, we convert to values expressed by log with base 2.

$$EV(H_2) = 3.32(0.1983) = 0.6584 \text{ bits}$$

This H value is equivalent to the situation where one outcome has an observed probability of about 0.16 and the other, 0.84. Comparing these values with the actual observations of 0.475 and 0.525 we see that with transition information we can make far better predictions about which outcomes will occur in the future. The estimates of 0.16 and 0.84 reveal how much we have improved our ability to predict outcomes.

The maximum value of H that can be obtained for any two-state transition matrix is 1. Using this information, we observe that the redundancy has also increased markedly.

$$R = 1 - \frac{0.6584}{1.0000} = 0.3416$$

Perhaps not enough, however, for situations where incorrect predictions are severely penalized. If this is true we might wish to probe our outcome sequences for patterns reflected by even *higher-order* transitions.

What kind of dependencies could account for the improvement that was realized in our ability to predict outcomes based on one-step transitions? One possible interpretation would be that, having obtained a contract, the construction company feels less pressure to get another one. Conversely, when their prior bid has failed to get them the contract, the executives work harder to get the next one. Estimated costs may also change depending upon how much of the company's capacity is being utilized (which is certainly affected by the past 0, 1 pattern).

Our analysis has only examined dependencies on the previous outcome. Such one-step dependencies are characteristic of stochastic processes which are called *Markov chains*. Many times, dependencies go back further than one step. In such cases, we can include two, three, or more previous outcomes in our analysis. (That is, 01 is followed by 1, 11 is followed by 0, and so on, or 011 is followed by 0, 110 is followed by 1, and so on.)

There are other methods as well for analyzing dependencies in a sequence of outcomes. But in essence they amount to the same thing—the attempt to gain information by finding regularities. There are far too many types of *correlational models* for us to deal with them here. Fortunately, there is an extensive literature treating correlation and a tradition whereby it is covered in other academic, business, and research domains. The cybernetic analysis of systems utilizes the more recently developed measures of information to determine the characteristics of a process and the effects of changing strategies. Figure 8.12 (page 197) includes most of the elements that are generally considered in the cybernetic analysis of a system.[12] To whatever extent information flow can be traced through the system, we improve our ability to control outcomes.

We have assumed throughout this discussion that the transition probabilities remain constant. If we were to modify our bidding strategy, or if our competitors altered their strategies, or if the states of nature changed, the transition probabilities in the sequence of outcomes might also change. For this reason, it makes sense to observe and analyze *the transitions of transition* probabilities.

The analysis of sequential data can yield a great deal of information that might otherwise escape us. We have tried to present a short explanation of the nature of such analysis so that the reader will be familiar with the characteristics of this kind of descriptive model.

---

[12] A clear and comprehensive treatment is given by W. Ross Ashby, *An Introduction to Cybernetics* (New York: John Wiley & Sons, Inc., 1956).

81/ Combinations of Simulation and Analytic Models

When the sequence of critical outcomes cannot be observed because it is too expensive or physically impossible (perhaps the system is not yet built or the new strategy cannot be used until it is tested), we often turn to simulation models. This was the case with the failure characteristics of refinery units ABC, AB, etc. It was also true of α-type consumers reacting to hypothetical advertisements and media plans of Brands A and B.

We should note that analytical models have *potential* for improving upon what is known about the failure characteristics of individual components and their interrelations. Similarly, by using analytic models as "pattern probes" some of the heuristic rules employed for the consumer simulation might have been raised to higher orders of effectiveness. The Monte Carlo tables might have been made more representative of the actual market place. As it was, it is likely that an analytic formulation was responsible for the estimates that were used to describe the effects of having previously purchased one or the other brand.

It is through the pieces and the parts of the model that the effects of analytic models make themselves felt. By the initial employment of models (such as those of queuing and information theory) we can frequently augment considerably the strength of the simulation system. Analytic models of various forms are always embedded in the descriptions of larger systems and it is of crucial importance to use them in as optimal a fashion as possible.

PROBLEMS

1. Using the Monte Carlo failure model of the refinery's manager (discussed on pp. 180–186) answer the following questions:

    a. What is the failure distribution for a unit composed of the four components $ABBC$?

    b. If the average down-time (for repairing a component) is 5 hours, what is the expected loss in production hours per year for units ABC, AB, AC, BC, $ABBC$?

    c. In general, what is the effect of aggregating a larger number of components within an operating unit, thus $(x_1 x_2 x_3)$ vs. $(x_1 x_2 x_3 x_4)$ vs. $(x_1 x_2 x_3 x_4 x_5)$? What implications does this conclusion have for a large system $(x_1 x_2 x_3 \ldots x_n)$? Can the system's designer help?

d. How would you change the simulation rules if maintenance is only sup-plied to the component that fails? For example, assume that after 5 hours component *A* of unit *ABC* fails. The entire unit is shut down while *A* is being repaired. *B* and *C* are not touched. Thus, when the unit is started up, *A* begins at zero time, *B* and *C* have already logged-in 5 hours of use.

2. Draw a flow diagram for the simulation of unit *ABBC*'s failure pattern. Then modify this flow diagram to satisfy the new rules described in Question 1, part d, above.

3. Using the data of Table 8.1 (p. 171), show how a distribution of truck ar-rivals per 30-minute period can be derived. What do you think the distribution of truck arrivals per 10-minute period would look like? Explain the change in shape of the curve in qualitative terms. What would the .00005-minute distri-bution look like?

4. A secretary has five items to be filed. There are two filing cabinets with four drawers in each. Assume that the items to be filed arrive randomly and that all file drawers have equal probability of being used. What would you estimate is the probability that no two items will be filed in the same drawer? After you have tried your intuition and qualitative sense, solve the following equation to check your answer:

$$P = \frac{x(x-1)(x-2)\ldots(x-y+1)}{x^y}$$

where $P =$ the probability that no two items will be filed in the same drawer, $x = 8$, and $y = 5$.

a. What kind of a model is this?

b. By analogy, see if you can now create a model to describe the probability that among y people no two would have a birthday in the same month.

5. Suppose you have the following probability distribution of truck arrivals at a loading dock:

Trucks per 15-minute interval	Probability
0	0.135
1	0.270
2	0.270
3	0.180
4	0.090
5	0.055

You want to know the probability distribution of truck arrivals on an hourly basis. One way to do this is by Monte Carlo. Assign three-digit numbers to each number of truck arrivals in the above table in proportion to the probability of occurrence. Thus, for example, we can assign the numbers 000–134, inclusive, to zero arrivals. Then use the table of random numbers to select a series of samples of four 15-minute interval arrivals. The total number of arrivals in the four intervals is the number of arrivals in one hour. Continuing in this way one can get a sample of as many hours as is desired and can determine the desired probability distribution. Take a sample of 100 hours and find the probability distribution.

6. It is often the case that, when a new system is planned for processing some work load, only the arrangement of the system is new. The components of the system are familiar and information is available concerning their performance individually. Under such circumstances it is often worthwhile to use Monte Carlo methods to determine how the system will operate as a whole. Suppose there are two processes with the following probability distributions of *time necessary to process one unit:*

PROCESS *A*		PROCESS *B*	
MINUTES REQUIRED	PROBABILITY	MINUTES REQUIRED	PROBABILITY
1	0.10	1	0.11
2	0.20	2	0.45
3	0.40	3	0.15
4	0.20	4	0.10
5	0.10	5	0.08
		6	0.05
		7	0.04
		8	0.02

The system being considered requires that each unit shall be processed first on *A* and then on *B*. The average time required on *A* is three minutes and the average time required on *B* is three minutes. A unit arrives at *A* every three minutes.

a. Use Monte Carlo procedures to run a sample of 50 units through the system. You will be interested in such characteristics of the system as the average time it takes a unit to go through and the *waiting times* before either process. (Assign numbers to *A*'s processing times in proportion to the given probabilities and do likewise for *B*'s processing times. You will need two separate samples of 50 random numbers: the first will represent *A*'s processing times; the second, *B*'s processing times. It is now only necessary to work through the sample, keeping track of the time when each unit actually starts processing on *A* and *B*.)

b. How does this simulation relate to queuing theory models?

7. Here are 65 outcomes:

  01101101001111010101101110110110111101011110111010101011011010011

a. Determine the entropy and the redundancy of the frequencies of the two outcomes.

b. Determine the entropy and the redundancy of the one-step transitions. The limiting probabilities are: $p(0) = 0.348$, $p(1) = 0.652$.

c. What processes might have generated this sequence?

8. Show that the redundancy of the transition matrix for the sequence of outcomes obtained by repeatedly tossing a "fair" coin is zero and that the same can be said for a "fair" die. What is the equivalent entropy measure in each case?

9. Explain why the models of information theory are classed as descriptive and analytic.

10. Classify the models listed below and discuss their characteristics:
    a. Paul Revere's model: "One if by land and two if by sea."
    b. Traffic lights.
    c. Genetic code.
    d. Heisenberg's Uncertainty Principle.
    e. Dictionary and Thesaurus.
    f. "Haste makes waste."
    g. Currency converter.

11. Try to build appropriate queuing models for the following situations:
    a. Airplane movement at an airport.
    b. The operation of a restaurant.
    c. Counter service.
    d. The control of inventory.
    e. The play at a gambling table.

12. Assume that a reasonable queuing model has been built to represent airport operations.
    a. How might you be able to use this model for normative purposes?
    b. If feedback is introduced into the description, how is the model transformed? What feedback usually does exist and how is its effect felt?

Chapter 9

Normative Models

Since normative models seek for what *ought to be done* from among reasonable alternatives they are also called *prescriptive*. The *criterion* for prescription must be operational and implementable. In other words, the criterion must be able to select an *obtainable, optimal,* and *applicable* configuration of the controllable variables.

Previously, we pointed out that normative models are composed of descriptive models. We can think of each individual row of the decision matrix as being a different configuration of a descriptive model. The decision criterion, operating in conjunction with the search capabilities of the model, form the essence of what we mean by normative. The decision *criterion* will differ according to the number and likelihoods of the descriptive models' states of nature. Thus, normative models may operate in a framework of certainty, risk, or uncertainty.

82/ Test Models

An important category of normative models is that which provides a *test criterion*. The function of a test model is to confirm or reject those hypotheses which underlie the model's construction. To illustrate, we can test the water of bathing beaches for pollution, agreeing to permit bathing if the count of harmful bacteria (such as coliform bacteria) is below specified levels. A descriptive *measurement model* is responsible for the numerical or qualitative determination of how many bacteria of each type are present. The measurement, if qualitative, may be nothing more than a comparison with a standard to determine if there are more or less bacteria present in the sample than in the standard. The standard and the rule for rejection function as the test model criterion.

Test models frequently incorporate *arbitrary*[1] standards. For example, the determination of piece-work rates based on some norm of performance; the decision to discontinue a TV show if the program ratings fall below a certain level; the hiring of an employee who exceeds an arbitrarily chosen personnel test score; a control chart limit which, when violated, signals for action to locate an assignable cause for a possible change in the process. While arbitrary, these rules are seldom haphazard, having been determined as carefully as possible in terms of fundamental objectives. There is no clear-cut line with respect to how many coliform bacteria can be permitted before they jeopardize health. In this regard, arbitrary standards can often be backed up with quantitative test models which determine the *degree of relationship* between the relevant factors, such as the number of coliform bacteria and their effect on health.

Test models are also used to accept or reject a sample as being derived from a specified population of elements. Assume that an executive wants to know how long it takes for two different brands of tires to wear out on fork-lift trucks. He gets a sample of ten of each kind and puts them on his trucks at the same time. As the tires wear out he obtains reports on them. These results can be compared by means of a statistical test model to determine if the tire brands are significantly different. However, can the executive be sure that the tires are representative of the two manufacturers' products? Perhaps one batch was older than the other. Were the trucks employed in the same way? These and many other similar questions must be answered if the executive is to reach a conclusion concerning which brand of tires to purchase in the future.

There are various experimental designs available to assist the executive. He can use a t test to determine whether the mean value observed in a sample set of data came from his hypothesized population. There are other tests for variation; tests for distribution shape; and tests to detect change from a stable system. Statistical tests such as these are necessary when some of the elements can introduce random variation.

Of particular importance is the distinction between two types of errors that can be made whenever an *accept or reject test criterion* is used. These are indicated as Type I and Type II errors in the matrix at the top of the next page.

The Type I error is to falsely reject the hypothesis that the state A really exists. The Type II error is to falsely accept the existence of state A when, in fact, some other state (such as B) exists. Almost unconsciously,

[1] Arbitrary is used here in the sense of individual discretion or judgment.

		1. If the True State of Nature Is:	
		A	B
2. And then, because of the test result we:	accept A	Result is correct	Type II error
	reject A	Type I error	Result is correct

management takes much greater pains to protect itself against Type II errors (which are highly visible) than against Type I errors which are not readily visible. It is difficult to evaluate paths that are never taken, to judge that which has been rejected. Figure 9.1 illustrates how we can cut

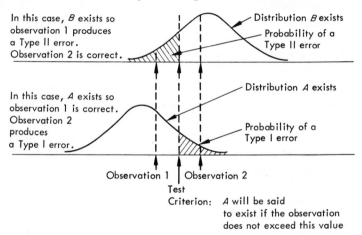

FIGURE 9.1   Relationship of Type I and Type II errors.

down on the probability of a Type I error by moving the test criterion to the right where it is a weaker reject criterion. However, we then increase the probability of a Type II error. Although they lack an awareness of the specifics of this relationship, executives frequently request that the test criterion be moved to the left, i.e., a stringent test criterion. This increases the number of rejections and is reflected in a larger probability of the Type I error. An informed and sophisticated management would prefer a better balance between these two types of errors. It would recognize that there are opportunity costs involved in rejecting potentially beneficial alternatives.

We see why intuitive qualitative models cannot be relied on to sort out the "real" state of affairs. Formal, quantitative test models are far more able to tell us what we *ought to do*. Nevertheless, we cannot apply statistical test methods to every such problem. Judgment must continue to furnish an important part of the spectrum of test models. The majority of executive decisions will continue to be based on qualitative test results.

In a real sense, every financial statement is tested by executive judgment. The decision as to when sales have fallen off so much that something should be done about it is an example of a qualitative test model of major importance in every executive's life. Similarly, at what point have sales increased to warrant building a new plant? When have costs grown too large? How much is too much absenteeism? What indicates that something should be done about pilferage? When should another salesman be hired?

Assuming that an acceptable test criterion exists, how many observations must be made for each of the above situations before we can be reasonably certain that a real change has taken place and that we are not just observing *random variation?* We must even determine a standard for reasonable certainty. All such test criteria are based on decision models in their own right.

Over-reliance on test models can produce administrative problems. Characteristically, when a test report indicates that no change has occurred, no action is taken, whereas signals of change trigger executive action. Dependency on test models can destroy executive initiative, and thus, in a roundabout way, turn the fundamental advantages of test models into disadvantage.

83/ Search Models for Successive Approximation

Having discussed accept/reject (two strategy) models, let us now consider models with many strategic alternatives. Assume we have generated all relevant outcomes and that the outcomes have been transformed into payoffs, how do we pick the strategy that yields the "best" payoff? There are both qualitative and quantitative procedures to accomplish this end.

We can enumerate some general rules to be followed in *searching* for an optimum payoff.

1. To discover the best payoff, we must know the objectives.

2. We must also know the available strategies, states of nature that can occur, and the various possibilities for competitive strategies. The decision-maker's strategies should be viewed as composed of variables whose possible values lie along a continuum.

3. By some form of reduction (such as obtaining expected values) only

one outcome must be associated with each strategy.[2] Such transformations are not required for decision models (with single objectives) operating under conditions of certainty because there is only one column to begin with, and only one payoff in each cell.

4. All possible payoffs should not be searched. That would take far too long if there are many of them. Therefore, on the basis of logic, intuition, and intelligent heuristics, we can begin our search by choosing one or more strategies that should, in our opinion, lead to "reasonably good" payoffs.

5. These payoff measures can then be compared with payoffs that would result from rather extreme conditions for the variables. The extreme conditions should be selected so that they represent strategies that are feasible, although not necessarily reasonable. If possible, the extremes should include between them the reasonable strategies that were chosen. Payoffs derived in this manner can sometimes detect that logic and common sense have failed us because the extremal payoffs are unexpectedly good. Generally, they can also indicate that one direction in which a variable is changed is superior to the opposite direction.

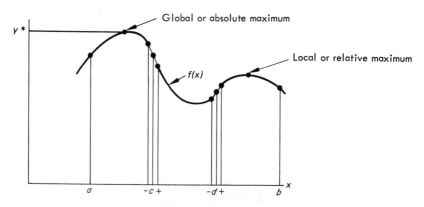

FIGURE 9.2   Locating an optimum payoff by heuristic means.

Figure 9.2 illustrates these remarks. Assume that the equation for the curved line $y = f(x)$ is unknown, but that it can be derived by conducting an experiment for each value of x. That is, for any value of x we can derive the appropriate value of y by observation and the results will eventually show us the *exact* form of the expression $y = f(x)$. How, with a reasonable amount of effort can we find the maximum value of y (indicated by $y*$)? We shall assume that it is too costly for us to compute

[2] See also, p. 239, where dimensional analysis is used to determine a single payoff.

enough (x, y) values to draw the curve. For this simple two-dimensional case, that may seem to be an unreasonable restraint. However, when it is pointed out that a realistic problem would involve a surface in multi-dimensional space, the assumption makes sense.

The payoff is y and x is the variable under our control. We are trying to locate the optimum (maximum) value of y, denoted y^*. Let us choose $x = c$ and $x = d$ as our reasonable strategies. We select $x = a$ and $x = b$ as our feasible but extreme values. For the case shown, the search problem is particularly difficult since the curve does not *monotonically*[3] decrease on both sides of the maximum value. In other words, there are two maxima shown, only one of which is the *global* or *absolute* maximum. (The same kind of reasoning can be applied to minima as well.) We find the value of y at the extreme value a about equal to the payoff of (reasonable) strategy c. This leads us to investigate some more points falling between a and c. Both y values produced by b and by d are lower than the y values produced by a and by c. This would indicate that the payoff tends to decrease as the x value increases above c.

There is no certainty in these suppositions. The curve between b and d could *suddenly* rise and within a very small range of x achieve the global maximum of the system. The fact that it does not (in this case) is in keeping with the *usual* inertial properties and momentum conditions in systems. If, however, it had run counter to expectations we would probably have to explain this behavior as an *interaction* effect related to fundamental changes that occur in a system's properties as a result of special thresholds being crossed.

6. The "reasonable" conditions should then be altered gradually in both directions to see whether improvement occurs. (The results obtained at the extremes should also be kept in mind.) If improvement is observed, another stepwise change should be made, and this process continued until no more improvement can be achieved. In terms of Figure 9.2, we have altered c and d by small $+$ and $-$ amounts. We observe significant improvement at $c-$ which leads us to continue in this direction. Hopefully, we shall eventually reach y^* (or close to it).

The advantages and disadvantages of qualitative and heuristic searching procedures are reasonably evident. It is a simple matter to overlook important peaks, even in a two-dimensional plane. With complex surfaces in n-dimensional space, the problem is enormously difficult. Nevertheless, using systematic procedures it is possible to obtain significant improvements in payoffs, although the methods are strictly cut-and-try.

---

[3] Any portion of a curve which has no changes in the algebraic sign of its slope is said to be *monotonically* increasing or decreasing (as the case may be).

Heuristic searching for optimal payoffs can be time consuming. It is essential to record all results so that directions that result in improvement can be remembered and we can avoid having to go back over the same ground.

Iterative methods apply heuristics that promise to improve the system in repetitive cycles. When the potential for further improvement disappears or becomes "sufficiently" small, the use of the algorithm is discontinued. We can see this kind of operation in the example above. Another search model of the same class which is useful enough to warrant inclusion here is Newton's Rule for finding the roots of an equation through successive approximations.

Newton's Rule.   Assume that we wish to solve the following equation: $f(x) = 3x^2 + 5x - 2$. This equation is simple to *factor* and solve. Thus: $(x + 2)(3x - 1) = 0$. The roots are -2 and $+\frac{1}{3}$. Many equations (especially those of higher order) do not lend themselves to such easy solution.

Our interest in being able to obtain the roots of an equation are many. The transformation to factors is useful for a variety of mathematical operations. It should also be noted, that if Newton's Rule is applied to the equation of the first derivative $f'(x)$, the x values for which $f'(x) = 0$ are the roots which identify the maxima and minima points of the original equation.[4] Aside from pointing out its utility, our purpose in this discussion is to further exemplify the class of iterative search models.

Let us assume that we do not know the two roots of the equation, $f(x)$. We begin by estimating their values as best we can. This gives us a starting point for each of the iterative processes—one for each root. For this example, let the roots be estimated to be -1 and $\frac{1}{2}$. We will call our estimates, x_k, and the improved approximations, x_{k+1}. Then, according to Newton's Rule,

$$x_{k+1} = x_k - \frac{f(x_k)}{f'(x_k)}$$

is applied in the following way for the first root (estimated as -1):

First Iteration
for x_k $= -1$;
$f(x_k)$ $= 3(-1)^2 + 5(-1) - 2 = -4$
$f'(x_k)$ $= 6(-1) + 5 = -1$

so $x_{k+1} = -1 - \left(\dfrac{-4}{-1}\right) = -5$

[4] The first derivative of this equation is $f'(x) = 6x + 5 = 0$. Therefore, we do not need to use Newton's rule in this simple case to determine the minimum point of the equation. It is obtained directly, $x = -5/6$.

Second Iteration

for $x_{k+1} = -5$;

$$f(x_{k+1}) = 3(-5)^2 + 5(-5) - 2 = 48$$
$$f'(x_{k+1}) = 6(-5) + 5 = -25$$

so $x_{k+2} = -5 - \left(\dfrac{48}{-25}\right) = -5 + 1.92 = -3.08$

By the third iteration, this root is evaluated as -2.26 and at the fourth it is equal to -2.02. Since -2.00 is one of the roots of this equation we see how quickly Newton's model homes in on the solution by means of its iterative hunting pattern. The same approach would now be used to approximate the second root.

All descriptive models—and especially computerized simulations—can be used effectively in this normative sense of successive approximations to an optimal. The heuristics for modifying the system's controllable variables are *external* to the model. Each new configuration of the model generates its own particular payoffs. Configurations that produce superior and inferior payoffs are interpreted in much the same sense as when we searched for a global maximum along our curve. And the same problems exist. We may never find the absolute optimum of the system and if we have, we may not always know it with certainty.

84/ Search Models for Optimization[5]

Mathematical optimization methods which are *exact* and *formal* are an integral part of many normative models. There are some highly refined methods available for searching through a great number of outcomes in order to find that one (or several) which precisely maximizes the degree of attainment of the objective.

The Derivative. One of the oldest and most generally useful techniques employs the *derivative* of a mathematical equation which is set equal to zero. In the problem section of Chapter 6, we mentioned the use of the derivative to find the optimal sales-price strategy. The equation was:

$$p = 2,500s - 2,000s^2 - 450$$

where p = profit, and
$\quad s$ = sales price.

Every point along the curve is a profit outcome p that results from a different price strategy s. The derivative of the equation is a measure of the

---

[5] For a good mathematical discussion of a variety of such methods, see D. J. Wilde, *Optimum Seeking Methods* (Englewood Cliffs, N.J.: Prentice-Hall, Inc., 1963).

slope of the curve at any point. In other words, it measures the rate of change of profit as compared to the rate of change of price.

At three places on the curve in Figure 9.3, an exaggerated derivative

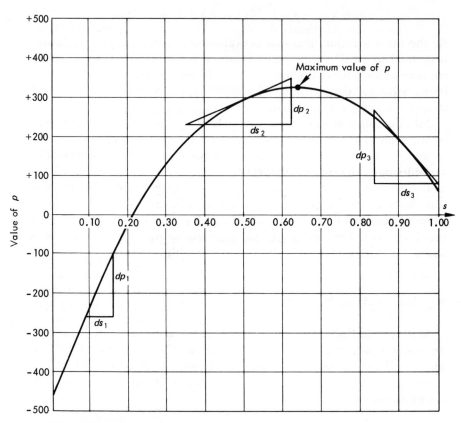

FIGURE 9.3   The use of the derivative to obtain an optimal value.

relationship is shown. The slope of dp_1/ds_1 is positive since p increases when s increases. The slope of dp_3/ds_3 is negative because p decreases as s increases. Somewhere in between, the slope changes sign from plus to minus. That occurs when the slope is zero. The slope of dp_2/ds_2 is slightly positive. As the point of tangency moves to the right, the slope approaches zero.

The derivative of the profit equation is:

$$\frac{dp}{ds} = 2{,}500 - 4{,}000s$$

Since the slope of the curve is zero at its maximum[6] point, we can set the derivative equal to zero and solve for the value of s that satisfies this condition.

$$0 = 2{,}500 - 4{,}000s$$
$$s = 0.625$$

The derivative can frequently be employed in this way to find the "best possible" outcome and the strategy that produces it from among countless possibilities.

The Optimal Vertex. A great number of optimal-value models are based on the solution of *inequations* instead of equations. An equation always has an equals sign, e.g.:

$$ax + by = c$$

An inequation can take various forms:

Greater than: $ax + by > c$
Equal to or greater than: $ax + by \geq c$
Less than: $ax + by < c$
Equal to or less than: $ax + by \leq c$

The understanding of inequations is extremely important to the decision-making process. Let us examine why this is so. Then we can show how optimal values for inequalities are determined by methodological means. To begin, assume that a confectioner is attempting to find the optimal candy mixture for a box of chocolates. There are two kinds of candy (called C_1 and C_2) that the box should contain. A matrix is drawn up for the critical characteristics of each kind of candy, i.e., those properties likely to be important for determining an optimal mixture. Thus:

	C_1	C_2	*Box*	
Number of pieces	x	y	35	(total pieces)
Weight per piece (oz.)	1.6	0.8	32	(total weight)
Space per piece (sq. in.)	2.0	1.0	65	(total space)
Cost per piece (dollars)	0.02	0.01	0.60	(total cost)

According to this, the manufacturer wants the box to weigh 32 ounces (a standard 2-pound box.) He wants 35 pieces of chocolate in each box and the cost of these chocolates is to be $0.60. Can he get *everything* that

---

[6] By setting the derivative of a function equal to zero and solving that equation we can determine that value of the control variable for which the function is either a maximum or a minimum. It is usually obvious from the form of the function whether a maximum or a minimum is obtained. When there is doubt, the question can be resolved by analyzing the second derivative or by drawing a graph of the function being studied. The confusion of global and local maxima (or minima) can also be resolved mathematically.

he wants? The broader question can also be asked: Can he get *anything* that he wants? Let us see.

There will be x pieces of the C_1 type, y pieces of the C_2 type, and the total number of pieces of candy must be 35, i.e.,

$$x + y = 35$$

Similarly, the total space used must be 65 square inches where each piece of the C_1 type requires 2 square inches and of the C_2 type, 1 square inch. Thus,

$$2x + y = 65$$

These two equations have only one solution:

$$x = 30, \quad y = 5$$

If we now put these values into the cost equation,

$$0.02x + 0.01y = \text{cost}$$

we find that the resulting cost is \$0.65, which is more than the manufacturer wanted to spend.

It is impossible for him to obtain all of his objectives *if he insists on having the exact requirements* that he has listed. However, let us ask the manufacturer to restate his requirements in terms of inequalities. He will probably recognize that the inequalities are what he really meant to say in the first place. For example, the number of pieces of chocolate can be 35 or greater. (A skimpy box would be competitively vulnerable.) So,

$$x + y \geq 35$$

As a matter of fact, the greater the total of x and y the better—*as long as* the cost per box does not exceed \$0.60. And if the cost of more than 35 pieces can be less than \$0.60, this manufacturer will be delighted. In other words, all will be well if

$$0.02x + 0.01y \leq 0.60$$

As far as weight is concerned, it must be at least 32 ounces so that the box can compete in the 2-pound market. *Perhaps* it can weigh more— as long as there are no deleterious side effects (such as increased transportation costs). We shall assume that greater weight is acceptable if the cost restrictions are met. Therefore:

$$1.6x + 0.8y \geq 32$$

Lastly, the confectioner points out that by means of fillers, the total space required by the candy in the box can range from 40 square inches to 65 square inches. Let us see what the use of these inequations means by studying Figure 9.4.

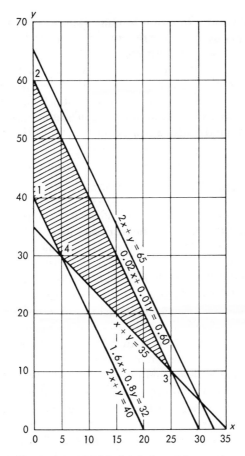

FIGURE 9.4 *Graphical solution of inequations.*

Each statement in *equation* form has been drawn on this graph. We observe that the line for the space requirement of 40 square inches is exactly the same as that of the weight restriction. Consequently, it is only necessary to draw one line on the graph to represent both requirements. If we now transform the equations to inequations, each line drawn on the chart becomes a *boundary*. All values described by the inequation $x + y \geq 35$ lie on or above the line $x + y = 35$. In the same way, all values of $1.6x + 0.8y \geq 32$ lie on the line $1.6x + 0.8y = 32$ or above that line. That is why a shaded area is filled in above these two lines. No usable values can lie below them.

Similarly, $0.02x + 0.01y \leq 0.60$ describes all points on the line $0.02x + 0.01y = 0.60$ and all points below that line. These three inequations define the entire shaded area which constitutes the *only* area in which a solution can exist. The space requirements for the candy box must fall between the two lines $2x + y = 65$ and $2x + y = 40$. We see that this statement is irrelevant since the previous restrictions have already formed the *permissible region* for a solution.

Solutions to *equations* must lie somewhere on the lines. Solutions to inequations can occur on the lines or within the areas bounded by the lines. In this way, we are presented with a much larger number of alternative solutions. Every point within the shaded area (including the lines) is a *feasible solution* to our problem.

The nature of this type of search problem, given in decision theory terms, is as follows. The decision matrix has only one column. Therefore, the model must be classed as decision-making under certainty. Each feasible point describes a possible x, y strategy. There are far too many feasible strategies to undertake the individual computation of each of their payoffs, even though there is only one payoff per strategy. And it is inconceivable to search through all of these payoffs for the optimal one.

In other words, having increased the number of possible strategies that can be employed, we have seemingly made the decision-maker's job much more complicated. Actually, we have succeeded in giving him many more *degrees of freedom* within which to find an optimal solution. Equality constraints seldom reflect the manager's *real concept* of this kind of problem. Furthermore, it turns out that the model based on inequalities has great computational advantages.

Our methodology tells us that an optimal solution *must lie on one of the corners* of the convex polygon (i.e., the shaded area) which we have constructed with our inequalities. This knowledge represents a crucial advantage. It is only necessary to search corner points to find the solution. Sometimes, however, the optimal solution will occur simultaneously at every point on one of the lines that form part of the perimeter of the polygon. But then, equivalent optimal solutions will occur at the adjacent corner points connected by the line. So this situation does not invalidate our rule, it extends it. Later, when we shall discuss linear programming models, the fundamentals that underlie this model will become apparent.

Let us look at the four corner point strategies that are shown in Figure 9.4.

Corner	x value	y value	Weight	Space	Cost
1	0	40	32	40	$0.40*
2	0	60	48	60	$0.60
3	25	10	48	60	$0.60
4	5	30	32	40	$0.40*

There cannot be a solution with a cost lower than $0.40 (indicated by *). The candy manufacturer is a reasonable man and when he sees the solution he is pleased to observe how low the cost can be made while all of his requirements are satisfied. However, he may decide that $x = 0$ (corner 1) or $x = 5$ (corner 4) represent too few pieces of C_1. He then states that there should be at least 10 such pieces in the mixture. We use the same polygon, but add the additional line $x \geq 10$. This is shown in Figure 9.5.

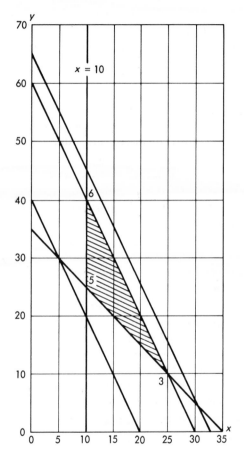

FIGURE 9.5 *Graphical solution of inequations with an additional restriction.*

The values of the two new corner points of the polygon are:

CORNER	x VALUE	y VALUE	WEIGHT	SPACE	COST
5	10	25	36	45	$0.45
6	10	40	48	60	$0.60

So he would probably choose the strategy of $x = 10$ and $y = 25$ since it offers the minimum cost.

For very complex sets of linear equations, related methods are also available which can locate the corners of the convex-shaped spaces. Thus, when many dimensions $(x, y, z, \ldots$ etc.$)$ are involved in the problem, the polygons are formed in n-dimensional space and they cannot be visually represented. Consequently, other methods are used for moving from one corner to another *in such a way as to always improve the outcome.* This iterative procedure is continued until the optimal value is discovered. It is a specific optimal that is defined by the coordinates of the chosen corner point; it is not an approximation.

85 / *Classic Competitive Models*

The classic, two-person, zero-sum game previously discussed in Chapter 5 is, in fact, a simple variant of the linear programming model. In the footnote on page 37 we referred to the dual form of the linear program. The solution of the two-person, zero-sum game is derived from a normative model that incorporates both the primal and the dual solutions of the LP format.

It is not our present intention to delve into the technicalities of this model but rather to show how *purely qualitative* information can be used in a *fully normative* sense to resolve classic competitive problems.

Let us consider the following problem. Our company, an established lock manufacturer traditionally has made replacement parts for all items which the company no longer produces. It also manufactures a new line of locks (which presently carry the cost of the replacement business). It has always been company policy to carry stock on obsolete models in the belief that the maintenance of replacement goodwill is absolutely essential for future business. If the company charged the proper amount to make a profit or to just break even on replacement parts, the cost of these parts would be exorbitant, defeating the purpose of maintaining goodwill.

The company learns through its salesmen that a competitor is considering the possibility of manufacturing a substantial part of this line of replacement parts. The motives for this move are not entirely clear. But it can be assumed that the competitor hopes to remove consumer dependency upon our company and to release a large part of the building trades presently obligated to us as the original suppliers.

Hoping to view the situation in a normative light, this decision problem is formulated by our company's O.R. group. Working in conjunction with management, they formulate three possible strategies for our company and two for the competitor. Then the sales manager of our company determines the outcomes shown below:

THE COMPETITOR'S STRATEGIES

		C_1	C_2
OUR	S_1:	O_{11}	O_{12}
COMPANY'S	S_2:	O_{21}	O_{22}
STRATEGIES	S_3:	O_{31}	O_{32}

S_1 : continue making replacements.

S_2 : announce suspension of the policy to make replacements—to become effective at some date in the far future.

S_3 : stop making replacements.

C_1 : competitor decides to make replacement parts.

C_2 : competitor decides not to make replacement parts.

O_{11}: we lose some replacement customers but gain new customers, since the competitor's prices on his present line must go up to absorb the cost of replacement parts.

O_{12}: we lose no replacement customers but continue to gain fewer new customers than our competitor does (present policy).

O_{21}: we lose more replacement customers than in O_{11}, but gain about the same number of new customers as in O_{11}.

O_{22}: we lose fewer replacement customers than in O_{11} and gain fewer new customers as in O_{12}.

O_{31}: we lose all our replacement customers and gain more new customers than in O_{11}.

O_{32}: we lose more replacement customers than in O_{21} and gain fewer new customers than in O_{31}.

These outcomes can be further simplified by a logical analysis of the statements. This produces the following:

O_{11}: lose x	and	gain y
O_{12}: lose 0	and	gain $y - a$
O_{21}: lose $x + b$	and	gain y
O_{22}: lose $x - c$	and	gain $y - a$
O_{31}: lose all	and	gain $y + c$
O_{32}: lose $x + b + d$	and	gain $y + c - e$

If our sales manager can assign values to these terms (x, y, etc.) that are appropriate to the gains and losses, he can solve this decision problem quantitatively. However, even if he cannot supply numbers, he can rank the outcomes according to his best judgment.

Assume that he has ranked the outcomes and that the numbers that appear in the profit-type payoff matrix below represent these *ranks*. (1 is assigned to the poorest payoff; 6 to the best.)

	C_1	C_2	MINIMUM PAYOFF
S_1:	4	6	4**
S_2:	3	5	3
S_3:	1	2	1
MAXIMUM PAYOFF:	4*	6	

Now applying the maximin (**) and the minimax (*) criteria, we find that the company will do best to continue its present policy. We also observe that if the competitor has about the same utilities as the sales manager, and derives approximately the same estimates for the payoffs, he will begin to manufacture replacement parts (assuming that the market is shared on a zero-sum basis).

This example illustrates the *normative* characteristics of classic competitive models and also the way in which *qualitative* information can be used to determine an optimum payoff measure. It demonstrates that normative models are combinations of many kinds of models. Data are derived from *information* models by *observation* and *measurement;* outcomes are *transformed* into the utilities for those outcomes or payoffs; strategies, states of nature, and competitive strategies require *discovery* of relevant variables; outcome statements are based upon the *discovery* of relationships among the variables; and the choice of one particular strategy is made after *searching* all possible payoffs with specific decision criteria.

86/ Value of Information

Normative models can be evaluated with respect to their informational attributes. We shall consider five levels of information completeness, starting with the least complete and moving to the most. We have decision-making:

1. under conditions of uncertainty, i.e., *no probability assignments* can be made;
2. under conditions of risk, i.e., a *believable* forecast exists;
3. under conditions of imperfect predictability, i.e., it is possible to foretell which state of nature will occur *with known probabilities of being wrong;*
4. under conditions of perfect predictability, i.e., it is possible *to foretell exactly* which state of nature will occur; and
5. under conditions of perfect control, i.e., it is possible to override prediction by *making a specific* state of nature occur.

Frequently, we can determine an optimal level (between 1 and 5) of information completeness. Only on the face of it might one think that the optimal level would always be the highest degree of completeness; a conclusion that is hardly the case. Similar insights concerning the economics of information architecture can usually be obtained from descriptive models by using appropriate heuristic procedures.

The fundamental idea is to *compare* payoffs (or expected payoffs) under differing conditions of information completeness. To generalize this notion assume that at a cost, C_j, we obtain an information level, I_j, and that with these data we can earn an expected payoff, P_j. The table below contains hypothetical data to illustrate our evaluation procedure.

INFORMATION LEVEL I_j	COST OF INFORMATION C_j	PAYOFF P_j	NET PAYOFF $P_j - C_j$
1	10	50	40
2	20	70	50
3	40	80	40
4	60	90	30

If we invest the minimum amount (10) in collecting information for our model we obtain a net payoff of $P_1 - C_1 = 40$. When more data are collected, the net payoff is raised to its maximum value of $P_2 - C_2 = 50$. We note that in moving from I_1 to I_2, an additional information cost of 10 is incurred, but the payoff improves by 20, so we prefer I_2. For the I_3 level, the incremental cost of information (above that of I_2) is 20 while the increase in payoff is only 10. Therefore, we reject this move. The net payoff of I_3 equals that of I_1, and when the I_4 data level is reached, the net payoff has decreased to 30.

We can relate these notions directly to decision models. Consider the farmer's matrix which appeared in Chapter 5.

STATE OF NATURE	N_1	N_2	N_3
PROBABILITY	0.25	0.50	0.25
WEATHER	PERFECT	VARIABLE	BAD
S_1: Plant peas	$40,000	$30,000	$20,000
S_2: Plant asparagus	$70,000	$20,000	$ 0

Base Point Level (Uncertainty). If the farmer did not have knowledge about the probabilities, he might assume that Nature is a hostile and rational opponent. Thereby, he could use the Wald criterion (maximin or minimax).

	N_1	N_2	N_3	WORST PAYOFF
S_1:	40,000	30,000	20,000	20,000 * MAXIMIN
S_2:	70,000	20,000	0	0

The *worst* result the farmer *must* anticipate is $20,000. This is his base point from which he can measure improvement as more information is collected. The indicated base point strategy is "plant peas."

Perfect Forecast Level (Probabilities).   The farmer has already obtained a forecast (0.25, 0.50, 0.25), presumably from his study of weather records. As before, we shall continue to accept its validity. Using this forecast, the farmer chose to plant peas.

$$\text{Expected Payoff (Plant Peas)} = 0.25(40,000) + 0.50(30,000)$$
$$+ 0.25(20,000) = \$30,000$$

It turns out that for this *specific* forecast, the farmer's *expectations* have been increased by $10,000 above the maximin, but he would plant peas in either case. However, the forecast value of $30,000 gives us another level from which to measure improvement.

Perfect Prediction Level (Omniscience).   Let us jump to *perfect* prediction and assume that the farmer achieves this through an unexpected opportunity. Weather Incorporated claims to have perfected a method for predicting the season's weather with 100% accuracy. The farmer is convinced that this is true and for our purposes, we shall agree. How much should the farmer be willing to pay for this information?

Our subsequent analysis is straightforward. *If the prediction is made that N_1 will occur,* the farmer will plant asparagus and obtain a $70,000 payoff. He would not choose to plant peas—it would earn him only $40,-000. As a second possibility, *if he is notified that N_2 is "what's happening,"* then he will choose to plant peas and get $30,000. Asparagus would earn him only $20,000. The third situation would be *if N_3 should exist,* he can obtain $20,000 by planting peas.

The farmer's forecast (in this case, 0.25, 0.50, 0.25) still holds. Therefore, the states of nature will occur with the same frequencies as before. The difference is that the farmer will *know in advance which state it will be.* Operating under such conditions of perfect information, he can improve his situation by choosing his strategy *after he learns* which state of nature will occur. His expected payoff will increase to $37,500.

$$\text{Expected Payoff (Perfect Information)} = 0.25(70,000) + 0.50(30,000)$$
$$+ 0.25(20,000) = \$37,500$$

This means that, given the specific forecast (0.25, 0.50, 0.25), there are savings of $7,500 available. If something less than this amount can be used to pay Weather Incorporated, a net savings will result. But if this weather predicting company intends to charge $7,500 or more for their services then the arrangement would be pointless. Should they charge, say, $5,000, the farmer stands to gain $2,500 by using the service.

Perfect Control Level (Omnipotence). Control requires the use of information. It is, in fact, a form of information management. The value of various forms of control can be ascertained. Assume that Weather Incorporated has a subsidiary called Weather Control which uses cloud-seeding methods and other new technology to *create* the state of weather.

How much should the farmer be willing to pay for perfect control over the weather? The best payoff in the matrix is $70,000. To achieve this, the farmer would ask Weather Control for the state N_1. Then, by using his strategy S_2, he would get this payoff. Total control represents the maximum level of information completeness. For it to function, Weather Control must *constantly monitor* the state of the system and, in addition to such awareness, it must have *all necessary control actions available* to override disturbances to the system. From the farmer's point of view (as measured from the value of his forecast) he can spend no more than $40,000 to obtain perfect control.

The range has gone from $20,000 under uncertainty to $70,000 under perfect control. Figure 9.6 below may help fix this in mind.

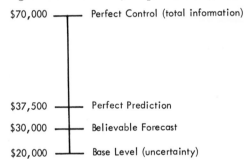

$70,000 ——— Perfect Control (total information)

$37,500 ——— Perfect Prediction
$30,000 ——— Believable Forecast
$20,000 ——— Base Level (uncertainty)

FIGURE 9.6 *Showing the range of value of information.*

We note that it is pointless to measure values from zero since improvement begins at $20,000. Also, we observe that the drive to collect more and more information may be irrational, leading one away from an optimal economic level of system's understanding.

87/ *Imperfect Predictions*

No discussion of forecasts, predictions, and the value of information (as they relate to normative models) would be complete without some treatment of Bayesian decision-making. Previously, we had mentioned the Reverend Thomas Bayes and his hypothesis (p. 118). Now we wish to talk about Bayes' Theorem.

To do so, let us return to the farmer. It was hard to believe that

Weather Incorporated could produce perfect predictions. But, for illustrative purposes, we went along with that notion at the time. Now let
us propose something more reasonable. Weather Incorporated has available various prediction models based on procedures that are not perfect, but quite good. For example, they have a correlation model for
predicting weather, whose use will cost the farmer $3,000. The reliability
of the model (based on past records) is shown in the matrix below.

		IF THE TRUE STATE OF NATURE IS:		
		N_1	N_2	N_3
THEN x PER CENT OF THE TIME	$T[N_1]$	0.8	0.2	0.0
THE TEST RESULT WILL BE:	$T[N_2]$	0.1	0.7	0.1
	$T[N_3]$	0.1	0.1	0.9

(x is the value of each entry in the matrix)

This conditional probability matrix is read in the following way. *Assume
that the weather will be N_1.* Then 80% of the time the test result will
be right—i.e., $T[N_1]$ is the prediction that will occur. However (still
assuming that the true state is N_1), 20% of the test results will be wrong.
N_2 will be indicated 10% of the time ($T[N_2]$) and N_3 will be predicted the
remaining 10% of the time ($T[N_3]$).

To make sure that this explanation is clear, let us assume that N_2 *is
the true state.* The test result will correctly indicate N_2 70% of the
time. But 30% of the "N_2 is true" predictions will be wrong. Specifically,
the test will indicate N_1 20% and N_3 10% of the time.

Each entry in this matrix of conditional probabilities can be written
in the form: $P(T[N_i]|N_j)$, which is the probability of a specific test result
(i) on the condition that a particular state of nature (j) exists. *Bayes'
Theorem* states an important relationship about these conditional probabilities, namely:

$$\frac{P(T[N_i]|N_j)\ P(N_j)}{P(T[N_i])} = P(N_j|T[N_i])$$

Inspecting this equation we see that if we multiply the conditional prob-
abilities $P(T[N_i]|N_j)$ by the forecast values for the states of nature $P(N_j)$
and divide by the probability that the ith test result will occur $P(T[N_i])$,
then we can obtain a symmetric relationship, i.e., one that is conditional
with respect to the test results, $P(N_j|T[N_i])$.

Let us carry through these calculations using the farmer's forecast for
the values of $P(N_j)$, frequently called the *a priori* probabilities.

$$P(T[N_i]|N_j)\ P(N_j)$$

$$\begin{vmatrix} 0.8\ (0.25) & 0.2\ (0.50) & 0.0\ (0.25) \\ 0.1\ (0.25) & 0.7\ (0.50) & 0.1\ (0.25) \\ 0.1\ (0.25) & 0.1\ (0.50) & 0.9\ (0.25) \end{vmatrix} = \begin{vmatrix} 0.200 & 0.100 & 0.000 \\ 0.025 & 0.350 & 0.025 \\ 0.025 & 0.050 & 0.225 \end{vmatrix}$$

Summing the columns we obtain the forecast values (0.25, 0.50, 0.25). In effect, we have distributed the probabilities in each column in proportion to these forecasts. Summing the rows we get:

$$P(T[N_i])$$

$i = 1$	$0.200 + 0.100 + 0.000 =$	0.300
$i = 2$	$0.025 + 0.350 + 0.025 =$	0.400
$i = 3$	$0.025 + 0.050 + 0.225 =$	0.300

Because $\sum_j P(T[N_i]|N_j) \, P(N_j) = P(T[N_i])$. The $P(T[N_i])$'s are the probabilities that the various test results will occur.

So the calculations shown above represent the exact steps indicated by the equation for Bayes' Theorem. If the reader will go through these computations with pencil and paper, the relationships involved will become evident in short order. (It is also recommended that problems 7 and 8 in the problem section of this chapter be worked out.)

Now we can derive the symmetric conditional probabilities $P(N_j|T[N_i])$. These are the conditional probabilities for the true states of nature, given that a specific test result has occurred. Divide all entries in the matrix by their appropriate row value of $P(T[N_i])$. Thus, reading from (1) to (2):

(2) then $P(N_j|T[N_i])$ per cent of the time the true N_j will be:

(1) if the test result is:		N_1	N_2	N_3				
	$T[N_1]$	$\dfrac{0.200}{0.300}$	$\dfrac{0.100}{0.300}$	$\dfrac{0.000}{0.300}$		$\tfrac{2}{3}$	$\tfrac{1}{3}$	0
	$T[N_2]$	$\dfrac{0.025}{0.400}$	$\dfrac{0.350}{0.400}$	$\dfrac{0.025}{0.400}$	$=$	$\tfrac{1}{16}$	$\tfrac{7}{8}$	$\tfrac{1}{16}$
	$T[N_3]$	$\dfrac{0.025}{0.300}$	$\dfrac{0.050}{0.300}$	$\dfrac{0.225}{0.300}$		$\tfrac{1}{12}$	$\tfrac{1}{6}$	$\tfrac{3}{4}$

Each row of this final matrix sums to 1 and represents a set of conditional (*a posteriori*) probabilities that can be compared with the farmer's original forecast. Consequently, we observe that the use of the test produces modifications of the farmer's original forecast. We can then determine the effect of these modifications on the decision matrix.

Thus, assuming we use the test, and:

	PROBABILITY	$\tfrac{2}{3}$	$\tfrac{1}{3}$	0	EXPECTED PAYOFF
IF $T[N_1]$ OCCURS	$\begin{cases} S_1: \\ S_2: \end{cases}$	40,000 70,000	30,000 20,000	20,000 0	36,667 53,333*

This means that if the test result is $T[N_1]$ the farmer would use his second strategy, with an expected payoff of $53,333.

	PROBABILITY	$\frac{1}{16}$	$\frac{7}{8}$	$\frac{1}{16}$	EXPECTED PAYOFF
IF $T[N_2]$	$\{S_1:$	40,000	30,000	20,000	30,000*
OCCURS	$\{S_2:$	70,000	20,000	0	21,875

Accordingly, if the test result is $T[N_2]$ the farmer would use his first strategy, with an expected payoff of $30,000.

	PROBABILITY	$\frac{1}{12}$	$\frac{1}{6}$	$\frac{3}{4}$	EXPECTED PAYOFF
IF $T[N_3]$	$\{S_1:$	40,000	30,000	20,000	23,333*
OCCURS	$\{S_2:$	70,000	20,000	0	9,167

And if the test result is $T[N_3]$ the farmer would use his first strategy, with an expected payoff of $23,333.

Previously, we had calculated the probabilities of the different test results. They are the $P(T[N_i])$, which were 0.3, 0.4, 0.3 for $i = 1$, 2, and 3 respectively. Therefore, if the test is used, the farmer's expected payoff of $53,333 should occur 30% of the time; his expected payoff of $30,000 will appear 40% of the time; and his expected payoff of $23,333 will occur 30% of the time. Thus:

$$\text{Expected Payoff (Using the Test)} = 0.3(53,333) + 0.4(30,000) + 0.3(23,333) = \$35,000$$

We could add this value of our particular imperfect prediction to Figure 9.6 and it would lie between the value of the perfect forecast and that of the perfect prediction. Thus:

$$\text{Expected Payoff (Perfect Prediction)} = 0.25(70,000) + 0.50(30,000) + 0.25(20,000) = \$37,500$$

and not using any test:

$$\text{Expected Payoff (Believable Forecast)} = 0.25(40,000) + 0.50(30,000) + 0.25(20,000) = \$30,000.$$

This test is worth (at a maximum) $5,000 to the farmer. He was asked $3,000 for it—so it looks like a good deal all around.

88/ Subjective Forecasts

It may be helpful to think of Bayes' Theorem as a means of combining forecasts and predictive tests. Figure 9.7 illustrates this.

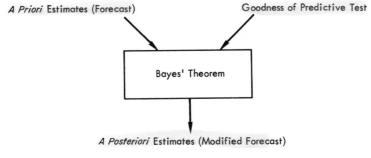

FIGURE 9.7

The farmer's *a priori* estimates were obtained from weather records. In many cases, however, there is no such convenient source of forecast data. Still, the executive can come up with some *subjective* estimates which reflect his experience with the situation. Usually, he would like to have such intuitive considerations included in the decision model.

If no predictive test can be devised (or if its development and use would be too expensive) then the executive's subjective probability estimates must play the solo part in the normative scheme of the decision model. That is, the expected value criterion for choosing a strategy under decision-making conditions of risk will operate. The result will be identical to that which would be obtained if a completely useless test were employed, namely:

1/3	1/3	1/3
1/3	1/3	1/3
1/3	1/3	1/3

On the other hand, with little belief in his own estimates, the executive is likely to invest in test development. To the degree that this test is reliable, the weight given to the executive's estimates for determining which strategy to use will become increasingly diminished. Ultimately, under conditions of the perfect (test) prediction the only role played by the executive's subjective estimates will be that of determining the probabilities of the test results, $P(T[N_i])$. (See problem 7 at the end of the chapter.)

89/ Tree Presentation[7]

A useful way of presenting the Bayesian model is in tree form. This is shown in Figure 9.8 as it applies to the farmer's problem.

[7] Decision trees are discussed at length in section 115.

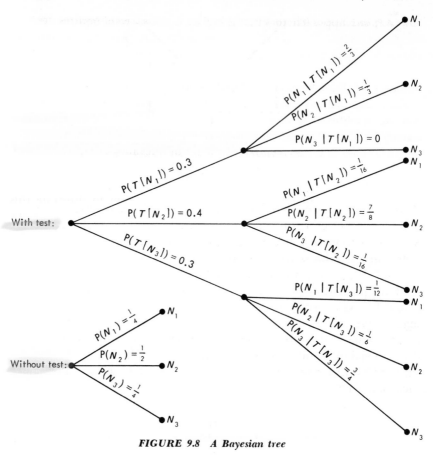

FIGURE 9.8 A Bayesian tree

Such trees are powerful descriptive models. They illustrate the various probability assignments to the states of nature and the way in which they were derived. In this case, four variants of the probabilities have been derived. Each applies to a unique set of conditions. These end results can be presented in tabular form:

	N_1	N_2	N_3
WITHOUT TEST	¼	½	¼
WITH TEST RESULT $T[N_1]$	⅔	⅓	0
WITH TEST RESULT $T[N_2]$	1⁄16	⅞	1⁄16
WITH TEST RESULT $T[N_3]$	1⁄12	⅙	¾

But the table loses the basis of derivation. Other tests might be fashioned to provide additional options. Ultimately, among all beneficial test procedures a best test will be chosen on the basis of economic superiority.

However, the approach to discovering an optimal test requires creative test design in the first place. Then, secondly, the best existing test can only be found through iteration founded upon sensible heuristics.

Degree of Dimensional Reduction. Information completeness is a relevant measure of models which permeates many aspects of model-building in addition to those discussed above. We know that an optimal strategy is found by the search procedures associated with normative configurations. It is one member of the set of relevant descriptive models. The "sense" of such an optimal solution will be dependent on the size of that set, especially as size is a function of the degree of refinement or specificity of the alternatives. Figure 9.9 is an attempt to illustrate this concept for a specific decision problem (hypothetically bounded by the circle).

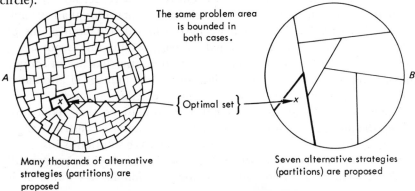

The same problem area is bounded in both cases.

{ Optimal set }

A

B

Many thousands of alternative strategies (partitions) are proposed

Seven alternative strategies (partitions) are proposed

The optimal set includes the optimal solution x

FIGURE 9.9

In *A*, the many descriptive models explain the variables with far more detail and potential precision than the seven descriptive models in *B*.

It is always relevant to inquire as to the extent that any particular situation is well-modelled. How much detail is required? The problem "embedded in reality" has a total "real" dimensionality. But only *part* of these dimensions is captured by the model. And with respect to *that part*, the measurements taken along each dimension may be fine or crude, according to one's ability to measure, as well as the costs and benefits to be derived from different levels of detail and refinement.

Some models are approximately one-for-one, such as the relationship of the positive and negative of a photograph. We have said (see p. 170) that such models of reality are *isomorphic*. However, when information reduction occurs, then the model is a *homomorphic* transformation of reality, such as the relationship between a photograph and a cartoon.

These definitions are hardly exact. Nevertheless, generally there can be consensus as to which type of relationship exists. It would be agreed that a road map is homomorphic to the actual geography represented; that a balance sheet is homomorphic to company performance; and that a blueprint is isomorphic to the product design characteristics *required for manufacture.*

The distinction between a homomorphism and an isomorphism is also illustrated by Figure 9.9. If each partition in the set space of *A* is a descriptive model, then an optimal solution can be found that is close to isomorphic with the "true" optimal strategy, *x*. If, however, the sets are modelled as in *B*, then that one of the seven partitions chosen, will be homomorphic to the solution, *x*. For example, assume that in *A* each partition represents an integer value of *x* (i.e., $x = 1, 2, 3, \ldots$), whereas in *B* the partitions stand for *x* counted by tens (i.e., $x = 10, 20, 30, \ldots$). If the optimal $x = 3.4$, then model *A* is far closer to isomorphic than is model *B*. In this particular illustration we have assumed that both of the optimal partitions contain the optimal strategy, *x*. But this is not always the case. The probability that our chosen alternative (partition) contains the optimal strategy will generally improve as the number of alternatives considered approaches the actual number of possible outcomes.

Homomorphisms always represent transformations that reduce and (generally) lose information. Such loss should not be construed as unfortunate, since there are many examples when the solution is insensitive to the reduction. An appropriate degree of homomorphism can usually be determined by invoking an economic criterion for the value of information.

In the isomorphic case, the transformations from reality to the model are one-for-one, i.e., there are an equal number of different variables (letters and numbers respectively) in each line of the transform diagram shown below.

	ISOMORPHIC TRANSFORMATION							
REALITY FACTORS	*A*	*B*	*C*	*D*	*E*	*F*	*G*	etc.
MODEL FACTORS	1	2	3	4	5	6	7	etc.

Using matrix form, the isomorphic transformation requires a square matrix wherein each row and column contains only a single entry.[8] (The entries do not all have to fall on the diagonal, but such a configuration can always be obtained by some arrangement of the rows and columns.)

---

[8] This conforms to the characteristics of the assignment method (see p. 248*f*).

MODEL FACTORS

	1	2	3	4	5	6	7	etc.
A	x							
B		x						
C			x					
D				x				
E					x			
F						x		
G							x	
etc.								x

REALITY FACTORS

For similar representation of the homomorphic case we should note that (in several instances) in the transform diagram below two or more reality factors are reduced to a single model factor. This is called a *many-one* transform. It should be contrasted with the *one-one* transforms of isomorphisms.

HOMOMORPHIC TRANSFORMATION

REALITY FACTORS	A	B	C	D	E	F	G	etc.
MODEL FACTORS	1	2	1	1	3	4	2	etc.

The matrix form of the homomorphic transform is not square. More than one entry can appear in any column. Consequently, there is a reduction of information in the model which embodies fewer variables than the reality. Furthermore, the model which is constructed in terms of the number variables cannot be used to recapture the original letter variables unless the rules of reduction from many to one are preserved.

MODEL FACTORS

	1	2	3	4	etc.
A	x				
B		x			
C	x				
D	x				
E		x			
F			x		
G	x				
etc.				x	

REALITY FACTORS

Almost all models in the business field are homomorphisms of varying degrees. While it may not be possible to prescribe the optimal degree of dimensional reduction for any specific problem, it is feasible to discuss such questions in economic terms once the nature of iso- and homomorphisms is understood.

Nature of Dimensional Soundness. When a number of critical objectives coexist in the model it is not unusual to find that a *dilemma* arises concerning which objective to maximize. They all seem important to the executive (although perhaps not equally so). Further, as the degree of achievement of any one objective is improved, those of others deteriorate. This is a typical situation occurring with increasing frequency as we consider decision domains moving from middle to top management levels.

For example, in the previous problem of the candy manufacturer (page 217), we obtained outcomes for weight, space, and cost. To *simplify* things we assumed that cost was the factor to be optimized. Accordingly, we developed the solution of minimum cost, subject to various restrictions. If our objective had also included weight, and we had wanted to maximize weight in addition to minimizing cost, *the problem could not have been solved.* The data for the corner points show that maximum weight never occurs with minimum cost. In fact, weight and cost are related to each other as Weight $= (80)$Cost.

Therefore, since as weight increases, cost will increase, what should be done? Should we settle for a little of each, and choose that strategy which brings us neither minimum cost nor maximum weight? There is only one way in which we can decide what to do, and that is *to determine how important each objective* is to the decision-maker.

It will be recognized that our *quandary* stems from *multiple objectives* that occupy different dimensions. We cannot quantitatively combine these multiple outcomes in any simple fashion. Both methods of ranking and the standard gamble are inadequate to deal with complex, multi-dimensional outcomes. Certainly, we cannot add pounds of weight and dollars of cost together and choose the sum we like the best. We cannot do this even if we first *rate* each outcome in terms of its importance to us and then use an appropriately weighted sum.

To illustrate, let us now consider the problem of the executive who has to decide between two possible locations for a new plant which the company is planning to build. To determine the "best" location, he lists six different outcomes that result for each strategy. The management considers these six outcomes as the relevant dimensions of the company's objectives. The executive rates these outcomes in terms of his considered judgment of their relative importance to the final outcome or payoff measure. (*Note:* This weighting can be attempted by ranking or standard gamble.)

OUTCOME	DIMENSIONAL UNIT	IMPORTANCE
$X1$: cost of land	dollar investment	A
$X2$: cost of building a plant	dollar investment	B
$X3$: desirability of site	preference rating*	C
$X4$: cost of labor	dollar expense	D
$X5$: community relations	cooperation rating*	E
$X6$: raw-material supply	quality and cost*	F
$X7$: transportation facilities	convenience and cost*	G

* For the asterisked dimensions, it is convenient to use a scale where 10 is poorest and 1 is best. This reflects the fact that we are dealing in costs.

Data are collected for the alternative strategies and the resulting payoff matrix will have seven outcome values in each box. For simplicity, we shall consider only one state of nature. If more than one state of nature exists, the methods previously developed for decision-making under risk and uncertainty can be applied—after the problem of combining the multiple outcomes has been resolved.

OUTCOME	STRATEGY $S1$	STRATEGY $S2$
$X1$	$400,000	$700,000
$X2$	$600,000	$800,000
$X3$	6	10
$X4$	$1.70/hr.	$1.50/hr.
$X5$	7	4
$X6$	2	8
$X7$	9	6

Measures taken along equivalent dimensions should be combined.[9] In this case, X1 and X2 (being dollar investments) lend themselves to immediate summation without any difficulty. On the other hand, although X4 is a dollar dimension, it is a per unit cost experienced over time rather than a present worth outlay of total cost. To cast X4 in the same dimension as X1 and X2 we require an estimate of man-hours per year. This would be multiplied by the per unit cost of labor to obtain a total cost for each strategy. Then an appropriate *discounting factor* must be applied to each year's expenses so that the stream of costs over time can be converted to a single present worth figure.

Instead of doing this, the executive might prefer to estimate the importance of X4 in the over-all scheme of things as compared to X1 and X2 as well as all of the other outcomes. If correct, this *importance*

---

[9] If they are not, appropriate weighting factors can be found which accomplish the same objective.

weight will reflect the size of the discounting factor acting in conjunction with the other estimates required to transform the $X4$ dimension to
that of $X1$ and $X2$. It may also express intangibles that are somehow em-
bodied in a per unit labor cost such as union relations, manpower availability, and legal and tax environments.

Let us assume that the latter course (using *weighting factors*) has been
followed.

Outcome	S1	S2	Importance Weight
$(X1 + X2)$	$1,000,000	$1,500,000	3
$X3$	6	10	4
$X4$	$1.70/hr.	$1.50/hr.	5
$X5$	7	4	1
$X6$	2	8	3
$X7$	9	6	2

(Importance is assumed to increase as the *weighting factor* number grows
larger.)

An Incorrect Method That Is Frequently Used. One method of
comparing strategies $S1$ and $S2$ is to sum the products of the weights and
outcomes from each strategy. That is,

$$O(S1) = 3(1,000,000) + 4(6) + 5(1.70) + 1(7) + 3(2) + 2(9)$$
$$= 3,000,063.50$$
$$O(S2) = 3(1,500,000) + 4(10) + 5(1.50) + 1(4) + 3(8) + 2(6)$$
$$= 4,500,087.50$$

By this method, $O(S1)$ is indicated to be the better selection. (Note that
this model is based on costs where larger numbers are less desirable.) The
following ratio provides a comparison:

$$\frac{O(S2)}{O(S1)} = \frac{4,500,087.50}{3,000,063.50} = 1.50$$

Now let us see what happens if we change the scale of $(X1 + X2)$ so that
it is read in million-dollar units instead of single-dollar units. We know
that if the method we are using is dimensionally sound, the exact same
ratio should result in spite of the scale transformation.

$$O(S1) = 3(1) + 4(6) + 5(1.70) + 1(7) + 3(2) + 2(9) \quad = 66.5$$
$$O(S2) = 3(1.5) + 4(10) + 5(1.50) + 1(4) + 3(8) + 2(6) = 92.0$$

And the ratio changes:

$$\frac{O(S2)}{O(S1)} = \frac{92.0}{66.5} = 1.38$$

This demonstrates that the change in scale introduced dimensional distortion in the ratio.

A Dimensionally Correct Method. The proper method for comparing multiple outcomes (which occupy different dimensions) has been developed by Gauss, Buckingham, and others. It is explained by P. W. Bridgeman in his studies of the dimensional properties of systems.[10] This method uses the product of the outcomes raised to weighted powers. That is, the outcome for any strategy S will be:

$$O(S) = (X1)^A (X2)^B (X3)^C \ldots (X6)^F$$

We shall now apply the million-dollar transform of the unit-dollar scale to this method.

($X1$ is expressed in unit dollars):

$$O(S1) = (1{,}000{,}000)^3 (6)^4 (1.70)^5 (7)^1 (2)^3 (9)^2 = 8.34 \times 10^{25}$$
$$O(S2) = (1{,}500{,}000)^3 (10)^4 (1.50)^5 (4)^1 (8)^3 (6)^2 = 1.89 \times 10^{28}$$

$$\frac{O(S2)}{O(S1)} = \frac{1.89 \times 10^{28}}{8.34 \times 10^{25}} = 226$$

($X1$ is expressed in million dollars):

$$O(S1) = (1)^3 (6)^4 (1.70)^5 (7)^1 (2)^3 (9)^2 = 8.34 \times 10^7$$
$$O(S2) = (1.5)^3 (10)^4 (1.50)^5) 4)^1 (8)^3 (6)^2 = 1.89 \times 10^{10}$$

$$\frac{O(S2)}{O(S1)} = \frac{1.89 \times 10^{10}}{8.34 \times 10^7} = 226$$

We see that these latter ratios are invariant to the transformation of scale. That is because the multiplicative method produces a *pure number* ratio, i.e., a number without dimensions. To illustrate this fact, let us add some amount of cooperation to an amount of convenience, and derive the ratio (for two strategies, $S1$ and $S2$) of the combined outcomes:

Ratio = ($S1$ cooperation + $S1$ convenience)/($S2$ cooperation + $S2$ convenience)

Dimensionally, this is equal to:

$$\text{Ratio} = \frac{S1 \text{ cooperation}}{S2 \text{ cooperation} + S2 \text{ convenience}} + \frac{S1 \text{ convenience}}{S2 \text{ cooperation} + S2 \text{ convenience}}$$

There is no utility to be gained from such a ratio. Its dimensionality is meaningless. On the other hand, using multiplication, all of the dimensions cancel and a pure number results. Thus,

$$\text{Ratio} = \frac{(S1 \text{ cooperation})(S1 \text{ convenience})}{(S2 \text{ cooperation})(S2 \text{ convenience})} = \text{pure number}$$

We observe that in all four of the previous cases, $O(S2) > O(S1)$, indicating that the first strategy is desirable. This kind of consistency cannot

[10] P. W. Bridgeman, *Dimensional Analysis* (New Haven: Yale University Press, 1922), pp. 21–22.

be counted upon. Frequently, the incorrect method will produce a ratio reversal and the executive will be misguided. (See problem 15 at the end of this chapter.)

Dimensional integrity is an absolute requirement of any sound analysis. When we combine a number of outcomes that occupy various dimensions in an attempt to optimize the over-all outcome, the ratio of the outcomes should be a pure number. The multiplication method will always produce a pure number. This follows from the fact that multiplication generates an area, a volume, and so on, which has the property of being common space for the participating outcomes. This common space is proportional to the importance of the values. Addition creates no such common territory and is not properly used when it attempts to combine basically different dimensions as though they were the same. The method of addition should be used only for outcome variables that are characterized by the same dimension.

It is always possible (in theory) to find a *unifying transformation* that will permit addition to be used. For example, apples and oranges can be added when both are transformed to units of fruit. Similarly, if *dollar estimates* can be placed on intangibles such as community relations, goodwill and the desirability of a plant site, these can be summed. It is not unusual to find that the attempt has been made to find a *preference measure for each of the variables.* In this case, the single outcome measure is assumed to reflect total preference as the sum of the individual preference contributions of each variable.

The soundness of such utility transformations to a single scale may be more illusory than correct. They are not easily achieved. The dimension of fruit, for example, may have no direct bearing on the problem. The dollar estimate of goodwill is known to vary greatly depending upon the purpose it is to serve and many aspects of preference, satisfaction, and other attitudinal measures are still considered to be intractable. On the other hand, a number of accepted conventions exist for equating rent, buy, or build options. Knowledge of how to treat these kinds of issues is critical for successful model-building.

If some components are to be maximized while others are to be minimized, we can use positive powers for the outcomes to be maximized and negative powers for the outcomes to be minimized. For example, let us now compare the first two strategies of the candy manufacturer, assuming that he wishes to *maximize weight* and *minimize cost*. He lists their relative importance as follows:

OUTCOME	$S1$	$S2$	IMPORTANCE
Weight	32	48	2
Cost	40	60	3

$$O(S1) = (32)^2(40)^{-3} = \frac{4}{250}$$

$$O(S2) = (48)^2(60)^{-3} = \frac{4}{375}$$

$$\frac{O(S1)}{O(S2)} = 1.5$$

On this basis, the candy manufacturer will prefer his first strategy. It is the best that he can do *in terms of his stated preferences*. In a fully normative sense, it is the optimal strategy.

PROBLEMS

1. Characterize and discuss the standards that exist for judging the quality of the following:

a. a vintage wine
b. a product-line mix
c. a nursery school
d. a new president
e. a TV program
f. a new drug
g. a test for employee aptitude

h. the finish of a manufactured product
i. the workability of an inventory model
j. a research project
k. styles of clothing
l. the family doctor
m. the company library
n. income tax rates

2. If sales drop below a specified level the company policy states that advertising will be cut in half. How might consideration of the Type II error affect this position?

3. Using cut and try methods of approximation find the value of x which maximizes the per cent change in sales volume, y. The controllable variable x equals the per cent change in advertising expenditures from the previous year. Because of company policy it is known that a decrease of no more than $\frac{1}{2}$ per cent can be accepted—and the model is not considered to be valid for values of x exceeding 1.5 per cent.

The model, developed for the advertising manager by the marketing department's O.R. group is:

$$y = 3x^3 - 4x^2 - x$$

a. Discuss the result you obtain and assess the conditions for which it might be reasonable.
b. What value of x within the stipulated range will minimize the sales volume?
c. What are the results for y at the extreme values of x?
d. Find the roots of this equation and explain how they provide useful information. (Newton's method may be of some help.)

4. In the text (p. 214) one of the roots of $f(x) = 3x^2 + 5x - 2$ was approximated by $x = -1$. Using Newton's method, it was determined that the actual

value was $x = -2$. Applying the same approach find the value of the other root.

5. For the profit model, $p = 2500s - 2000s^2 - 450$, on p. 215, what does the second derivative tell us? What has this to do with the normative form of models?

6. The lock manufacturer in this chapter (p. 222) decided, on a qualitative basis, to continue manufacturing replacement parts. His competitor, on the other hand, went through the same reasoning process but obtained numerical estimates as follows: $x = y/2 = 2a = 4b = 6c = 8d = 10e$. If the total replacement market $= 100x$, what conclusions should the competitor reach?

7. Consider the farmer's problem (p. 225). What happens if his weather forecast can be augmented by a *perfect* predictive test? Using the Bayesian approach derive the appropriate decision tree representation. Discuss your results and show that the farmer's forecast (or any executive's subjective estimates) will reflect the probabilities of the test results under these circumstances.

8. Using the same procedures as described in problem 7 above, show what happens if the test is *totally unreliable*.

9. Suggest the general lines necessary to model the following problems in queuing terms.
    a. An inventory (order quantity) decision for an expensive part.
    b. Scheduling arrivals and departures at a congested airport.
    c. The amount of service needed to provide for a large and busy restaurant.
    d. How to operate a gambling table.

10. How can queuing models be used for normative purposes?

11. Is it reasonable to state that the *congruence* of two triangles is based on an isomorphic transformation, while the *similarity* of two triangles is related to homomorphic transformation? Discuss.

12. Referring to p. 233, develop an example to show when the optimal partition would not necessarily contain the optimal strategy.

13. An executive states that his two personal objectives are income and leisure time. He spends 77 hours per week in the routine activities of sleeping, commuting, etc., so his leisure time is calculated to be $168 - 77 = 91$ hours minus the time he spends on his job. The executive is currently working 48 hours per week for $20,000 per year. He has turned down a job offer of $24,000 which would require him to work 54 hours per week, but has accepted an offer of $33,000 which requires 62 hours per week.

    What can be said about the weighting of his two objectives, assuming that the three jobs were similar in all other respects? What would be his salary requirements if a job demanded 72 hours per week?

14. A graduating business student has received a variety of job offers. He has three objectives: salary, opportunity for advancement, and location. The student measures opportunity for advancement by the number of executive positions in the company and he is interested in location only in terms of distance from his home city—the farther it is, the less he likes it. There are three job offers which he considers to be equally good:

JOB OFFER	SALARY	EXECUTIVE POSITIONS	DISTANCE
A	$7,200	200	500
B	7,500	300	2,000
C	8,500	200	1,000

How is this student weighting his objectives?

15. It has been stated that the incorrect use of addition in attempting to evaluate a system with multiple objectives can produce a result that is the reverse of the correct solution derived from the multiplicative method. *Set up* an example to demonstrate this effect. (See p. 238.)

16. Explain the nature of iterative methods and why they are important in normative procedures.

17. What is new and different about the use of heuristics in normative configurations?

PART IV

DECISION-PROBLEM
PARADIGMS

Chapter 10

Of Production

Production refers to all the areas of company operations which are concerned with the manufacture or processing necessary to supply goods or services to the consumer. More generally, any *transformation* process qualifies as production and can be treated by the methods and models that have been developed to characterize and analyze such transformations. Materials can be altered in various ways; e.g., by moulding, deformation, cutting, and assembly. Sometimes, chemical changes are involved. Many other transformations qualify as well, including growing and harvesting food, the transportation of individuals from one point to another, or the communication of information from a source to a destination. The above description is intended to indicate the subject matter of the decision problems we shall be considering in this chapter. The structural properties of the models frequently will be found to be easily transferable across different subject areas and will occur in recognizable form in subsequent chapters on marketing and finance.

As compared to the marketing area, production is characterized by the fact that it is more wholly within the control of the company. Production functions are particularly visible. For this reason, and the others that follow, production systems have been studied longer than those of other areas. The work of Frederick W. Taylor centered on the production field. The first major thrust of O.R. was production-oriented.

More relevant variables in production decision problems are subject to executive control than is the case with marketing or financial decision problems. The relevant states of nature do not often include competitive strategies and, generally, there are not so many hidden variables which may drastically affect the outcome. In production decision problems the objectives and their payoffs are likely to be more easily expressible in terms of costs or profit. The necessary cost information will be more generally available and with greater accuracy. Though generalizations these statements may serve to suggest some of the basic characteristics of production decision problems.

Any separation of the areas of marketing, finance, and production is to some degree arbitrary. Major areas of mutual interaction exist, such as between scale of the system, product quality, product price, and inventory levels. With this in mind, we have followed the traditional problem assignments to areas.

90/ *Relatively Determinate Problems*

Many of the decision problems we will consider in this chapter involve decision-making under risk. It is a fact, however, that a great number of important and costly decision problems are of the kind we have called decision-making under certainty. In other words, they require no probability descriptions to provide a *useful* basis for analysis. We can also call these "relatively determinate" problems because the precision lost by approximating risk elements as though they behaved with certainty carries a negligible penalty.

The idea that decision-making can be a problem when things are certain sometimes seems to involve a contradiction in terms. Earlier, we have tried to show that it is by no means a contradiction, but we will emphasize this fact again. A few moments' thought about the game of chess will suffice to illustrate the genuine problems of decision-making under certainty. Everything is certain in chess in the sense that there are no secrets about rational moves and there are no interrupting chance elements. Yet men have played chess for thousands of years with unflagging interest and there are no signs yet that the formidable decision problems involved are getting any easier despite all the certainty. The decision problem in chess results from the incredibly large number of possibilities that exist. Each one of them is certain enough, but there are too many to think one's way through. Exactly similar problems arise in production and other areas of business. Fortunately, a variety of methods have been developed to help the executive find his best strategies from among the enormous number that may be possible.

91/ *The Assignment Method*

A problem which arises in machine shops, paper, chemical, and other manufacturing industries, transportation and communication, as well as any multiplant operation, is that of assigning a group of jobs that must be done to a group of machines, plants, or processes. Any *one* of the processing units can do any *one* of the jobs. The jobs must be worked simultaneously. We might state, alternatively, that each process can be assigned only one job—split arrangements are not permitted. Typically, the machines, or processes, are of different efficiencies in performing the various jobs. The reason may be that the machines are of varying vintages, were designed for different kinds of jobs, or simply that one machine is slower than another. Management usually has cost data available so that it knows the cost involved in having a specific machine do a specific job. The decision problem is to assign the jobs to the machines or processes in such fashion as to minimize the total costs of doing all the jobs.

We are introducing this as an example of decision-making under certainty. Yet it is well known that cost data of this kind are not completely accurate and, indeed, can be quite unreliable. There is no reason to assume that the costs are certain, even if everything else about the problem is. This objection is true, but not critical. Management will assign the jobs on the basis of the cost data that is available. Sensitivity analysis (see p. 121) generally will show that data deviations will not affect the results. It should be noted that solutions are chosen as one out of a finite set, not an infinite one. Thus, changes take place by incremental jumps, and not continuously. We propose to accept the data as management does. We intend to ensure that the decision based on these data will be the best one possible, granted the costs. In other words, certainty exists because management will accept the costs in reaching decisions. It does not imply that there is any eternal, or even temporary, truth in the cost figures.

Suppose that a machine shop has five jobs to produce and five machines, any one of which can do any of the jobs, but at differing costs. The jobs must be assigned for simultaneous production, each job being placed on one machine. The available cost data can be presented in

| | MACHINE | | | | |
JOB	1	2	3	4	5
A	$430	$440	$465	$480	$490
B	320	340	350	375	380
C	295	300	330	320	320
D	270	290	310	275	280
E	245	240	265	280	250

matrix form. The entries in the matrix show the cost of having the given machine do the given job. Thus, it will cost $275 to have machine 4 do job *D*. The decision problem is: How to assign the jobs to the machines in order to minimize the total cost of producing all five jobs.[1]

The first thing to notice is that one cannot proceed by simply assigning job *A* to the machine which does it most cheaply, job *B* to the machine which does it most cheaply, and so on. It *can* happen that this procedure will give the lowest-cost assignment. Usually, however, as in the present example, one machine can do several of the jobs more cheaply than any other machine can do them. Machine 1 can do jobs *A*, *B*, *C*, and *D* more cheaply than any other machine. But only one of these jobs can be assigned to machine 1. Nor can we start by assigning job *A* to the machine which does it most cheaply (machine 1 here) and then assign job *B* either to the machine which does it most cheaply or, in case of conflict (as in the present example), to the second cheapest machine (machine 2 here). This procedure would result, for the first two jobs only, in assigning job *A* to machine 1 and job *B* to machine 2 for a total cost of $430 + $340 = $770. But it is evident that assigning job *A* to machine 2 and job *B* to machine 1 would cost only $440 + $320 = $760.

One might try the other approach: assign each machine to the job it does most cheaply. But this, too, generally will not work. In the present example four of the machines (1, 2, 3, and 5) do job *E* more cheaply than any other job. In short, none of these obvious attempts guarantees finding the minimum-cost assignment.

One infallible procedure for determining the minimum-cost assignment would be to try all possibilities, calculate the cost of each, and select the cheapest. Unfortunately this procedure is usually impracticable. In the present example there are only 120 different possible assignments. So it would be feasible to calculate the cost for each one of them—though it would be more arithmetic than most of us would prefer to do if we could avoid it. But the number of possible assignments increases very rapidly as the number of jobs and machine increases. The assignment of 10 jobs to 10 machines would require calculating more than 3.5 million possible assignments. And assigning 15 jobs to 15 machines involves 1.3 trillion (1,300,000,000,000) possible assignments.[2] This is too many even for a computer! It is clear that we need some procedure other than the enumeration of possibilities. What we would like to have would be some simple *algorithm* (a mathematical term meaning a systematized proce-

---

[1] Nothing would be different if the entries were of different dimension, such as seconds of time, to complete the job.

[2] $5! = 5 \cdot 4 \cdot 3 \cdot 2 \cdot 1 = 120$

$10! = 10 \cdot 9 \cdot 8 \cdot \ \ldots \ \cdot 2 \cdot 1 \approx (3.5)10^6; \ 15! \approx (1.3)10^{12}$

dure for finding a solution) which would enable us to quickly locate the optimal assignment.

Such a procedure (the desired algorithm) is available and is remarkably quick and easy to use. *It is based squarely on an economic concept* which we have already discussed: namely, the *opportunity cost* which results when we do not utilize our resources to the best possible advantage. The selection, and implementation, of any specific course of action relegates to the limbo of foregone possibilities all other alternative courses of action. If the action(strategy) followed turns out to have not been the best utilization of our resources, then we have suffered a loss of the difference between what we actually achieve and that which we could have achieved. The only course of action which has zero opportunity cost is the best one.

Opportunity cost is a real cost—even though it doesn't customarily show up on balance sheets. But how can we measure opportunity cost unless we know the value of the best strategy? To determine this we would have to know the best strategy, and if we knew it we wouldn't need to introduce opportunity costs in the first place. The answer to this quandary is that by defining the nature of the opportunity cost we will be able to discover the strategy, or strategies, for which it is zero. At first, this may appear somewhat like lifting oneself by one's shoelaces, but it will soon be seen that it really isn't.

First, let us introduce some small examples which can serve better to illustrate the argument. Suppose we have the following cost matrix:

	MACHINE		
JOB	1	2	3
X	$100	$150	$170
Y	170	120	190
Z	180	220	150

What is the opportunity cost associated with assigning a job to machine 1? *There are two ways of defining it, depending on which alternatives one considers.* As an example, we can use the assignment of job Z to machine 1. The *direct cost* of this assignment is given in the cost matrix as $180. But there are, in addition, indirect costs which result from the fact that assigning job Z to machine 1 prevents us from assigning any other job to machine 1 and also prevents us from assigning job Z to any other machine. *These assignments which are eliminated as possibilities* by assigning job Z to machine 1 *are the alternatives against which the opportunity costs are measured.*

First, an opportunity cost arises because a different job could be assigned to machine 1. The lowest-cost assignment of a job to machine 1 is job X, with a cost of $100. By comparison, the assignment of job Z to machine 1 involves an opportunity cost of $180 − $100 = $80. Similarly, and second, another opportunity cost arises because job Z could have been assigned to a different machine. Since the cheapest assignment of job Z would be to machine 3, at a cost of $150, it follows that this opportunity cost of assigning job Z to machine 1 would be $180 − $150 = $30. The first kind of opportunity cost arises because a different job could be assigned to the same machine; we can call it the *job opportunity* cost. The second kind arises because a different machine could be assigned to the same job. We shall call this the *machine opportunity* cost.

Both kinds of opportunity costs are easy to determine. The *matrix* of *job opportunity costs* is obtained by *subtracting the smallest cost in each column* from *every* entry in that column. The *matrix of machine opportunity costs* is obtained by *subtracting the smallest cost in each row* from *every* entry in that row. Thus:

Job Opportunity Cost Matrix				Machine Opportunity Cost Matrix			
	Machine					Machine	
	1	2	3			1	2	3
	Lowest Cost				Lowest		
Job	100	120	150	Job	Cost		
X	0	30	20	X	100	0	50	70
Y	70	0	40	Y	120	50	0	70
Z	80	100	0	Z	150	30	70	0

The job-opportunity-cost matrix must always have at least *one zero* in each *column* and the machine-opportunity-cost matrix must always have at least *one zero* in each *row*.

In this example, the three assignments with zero opportunity cost are identical in each matrix (X to 1, Y to 2, and Z to 3). When this happens the decision problem is solved, since we cannot do better than to have a zero *total* opportunity cost and here we are able to assign each job to a machine so that every opportunity cost is zero. However, this result will occur only sometimes. It can only happen when there is no opportunity cost arising from the necessity to work the three jobs simultaneously or without splitting assignments. In the present case we would assign job X to machine 1 whether or not we had jobs Y and Z, and similarly with the assignments of jobs Y and Z. In short, there is *no conflict* among the zero-opportunity-cost assignments. Let us now take an example where there is conflict.

Direct Cost Matrix				Job Opportunity Cost Matrix				Machine Opportunity Cost Matrix			
	Machine				Machine				Machine		
Job	1	2	3	Job	1	2	3	Job	1	2	3
P	110	120	130	P	0	0	0	P	0	10	20
Q	115	140	140	Q	5	20	10	Q	0	25	25
R	125	145	165	R	15	25	35	R	0	20	40

Here, there is no way to assign all jobs to machines which have zero opportunity cost. As a matter of fact, there is only one assignment of a job to a machine which has zero job opportunity cost and zero machine opportunity cost (job P to machine 1). Before we discuss what can be done about this situation, we shall introduce a simplification.

It is awkward to have to use two matrices for the two kinds of opportunity costs. It would be simpler if we could amalgamate both into one matrix of total opportunity costs. One method for doing this would be to simply add the two opportunity-cost matrices together to get a new matrix showing the *total opportunity cost* of each assignment. This method will work perfectly well, but it requires more arithmetic than an alternative procedure. The alternative is to calculate the machine opportunity costs *on the basis* of the job-opportunity-cost matrix rather than directly from the original cost matrix. Thus, in our example, we shall obtain one total-opportunity-cost matrix by subtracting the minimum cost in each row of the job-opportunity-cost matrix from every entry in that row. This gives:

Total Opportunity Cost Matrix

	Machine		
Job	1	2	3
P	0	0	0
Q	0	15	5
R	0	10	20

where, for example, the new row Q comes directly from row Q of the job-opportunity-cost matrix by subtracting 5 from each entry in that row (and similarly with the other rows). It is equally correct to determine the total-opportunity-cost matrix by subtracting the minimum cost in each column of the machine-opportunity-cost matrix from every entry in that column. In other words, the method does not prescribe whether to start with either row or column derivations of the opportunity costs—as long as one is followed by the other.[3]

To have an assignment (of jobs to machines) which has zero total opportunity cost it is necessary that there should be three zeroes in the matrix such that *no two of them occur in the same row or column*. This is clearly not the case for our matrix, and the fact that it isn't means that we have not yet properly defined the opportunity costs.

Opportunity costs are defined in terms of the optimal assignment, which we do not yet know. The optimal assignment will have (by definition) zero opportunity cost and this means that there will be three *independent* zeroes in the matrix (i.e., no two of them occurring in the same row or column). Since the zeroes we have in the above matrix do not fulfill this condition it follows that at least some of them have a nonzero opportunity cost and, hence, are not correctly given as zeroes. It remains to find out how to *change* them to get the *correct* opportunity costs.

The procedure for changing the opportunity costs is simple once it is recognized why they are wrong. The reason is that we have not yet taken account of the fact that *we cannot use two zeroes if they are in the same row or column*. We can use only one. But our total opportunity-cost matrix has three zeroes in one row and three in one column. If we select any zero in row P, for example, we deny ourselves the opportunity to select any other zero in the same row. This fact, then, produces an opportunity cost *which we have not yet taken into account*.

Generally, we shall have zero and nonzero entries in the rows or columns of our matrix. The same argument which applies to zeroes would apply to any nonzero entry *in rows or columns with zeroes*. Suppose the entry at $P1$ were 5 instead of 0. This 5 would be the wrong opportunity cost for $P1$ because it does not include an opportunity cost to reflect the fact that this assignment (job P to machine 1) would eliminate the possibility of selecting any zero in the same row or column.

We want, then, to change the opportunity costs of the entries *in the rows and columns in which the zeroes occur*. How do we decide which rows and columns these are? In our example, we can name row P and column 1, but usually there is some choice in selecting them. In this case one could say (as well) that there are zeroes in columns 1, 2, and 3 or in rows P, Q, *and* R. However, we follow *the rule of always naming the rows and columns which include zeroes so that the total number is the least possible*. In other words, we select the least possible number of rows and/or columns which includes all the zeroes in the matrix. The number of rows and/or columns required to do this will always be equal

---

[3] The resulting total-opportunity-cost matrix starting with row derivations followed by column derivations may appear to be different from that obtained by using rows first followed by columns. But the ultimate solution will always be the same.

to or less than the total number of rows (or columns, since the matrix is square).

If the *least number of rows and/or columns required to include all the zeroes equals the total number of rows then the decision problem is solved.* There must always be a set of zeroes in the matrix which provides an assignment of jobs to machines with zero total opportunity cost. Consider a three-by-three matrix with zeroes as follows:

	1	2	3
G		0	
H	0		0
K		0	

All of these zeroes can be included in row *H* and column 2. This shows that the problem is not yet solved. A matrix with zeroes as shown:

	1	2	3
G		0	
H	0		0
K		0	0

requires three rows or columns to include all the zeroes. And this one is solved by assigning *G* to 2, *H* to 1, and *K* to 3, with total opportunity cost of zero.

In those cases where there are various ways to choose the rows and/or columns which include all the zeroes it doesn't matter which one is selected. All selections will lead to a solution.

Why is this question of the selection of the rows and/or columns which include all the zeroes so important? Simply *because the entries in these rows and columns (when they do not satisfy the criterion for completion) have the wrong opportunity costs.* The simplest procedure for changing these costs is based on the following argument. At least one of the zeroes must be moved from the row or column in which it occurs. The smallest possible cost involved in such a move would be if it were moved to replace the *smallest nonzero entry* in the matrix which is *not* on one of the rows and/or columns containing the zeroes. In our example this is 5 at $Q3$. The least possible opportunity cost involved, then, in selecting any entry on row *P* (except $P1$) would be to move a zero to $Q3$, which would cost 5. Similarly, the least possible opportunity cost involved in selecting any entry in column 1 would be to force the move of a zero in that column to $Q3$, costing 5.

Therefore, we will add this opportunity cost, 5, to every entry in row

P and in column 1 (except for *P*1). Why the exception for *P*1? Because if we select *P*1 we will force the move of two zeroes, one in row *P* and one in column 1. This will cost *at least* twice the minimum entry in the general case, here $2 \times 5 = 10$. (Actually, it will cost more in the present case, but the assignment of an additional opportunity cost of $2 \times 5 = 10$ to *P*1 will work equally well and is simpler to do.)

These, then, are the changes: add 10 to *P*1, add 5 to every other entry in row *P*, and add 5 to every other entry in column 1. This gives:

Opportunity Cost Matrix

		Machine	
Job	1	2	3
P	10	5	5
Q	5	15	5
R	5	10	20

We now repeat the procedure of subtracting the lowest opportunity cost in each column from each entry in the column.[4] In the present case this step produces a zero in each row, so for this example it is unnecessary to subtract the minimum entries from the rows which would otherwise be required. The final matrix is as follows:

Opportunity Cost Matrix

		Machine	
Job	1	2	3
P	5	0	0
Q	0	10	0
R	0	5	15

This matrix has three zeroes which meet our requirement, *no two of which are on the same row or column.* These are the zeroes at *P*2, *Q*3, and *R*1. The minimum-cost assignment is, therefore, job *P* to machine 2, job *Q* to machine 3, and job *R* to machine 1. Referring to the original cost matrix we see that the total cost of these assignments is $120 + $140 + $125 = 385. No other assignment of these three jobs to the three machines *can* cost less than this amount.

It is not necessary to go through all of the steps of the above method. The whole procedure is equivalent to adding 5 to the entry at the inter-

---

[4] Or row subtraction first, followed, if needed, by column subtraction.

section of the row and column; leaving the other entries in row P and column 1 unchanged; and subtracting 5 from each entry in the matrix which is not on row P or column 1.

The algorithm can be boiled down to the following steps:

1. Determine the row-opportunity-cost matrix by subtracting the smallest entry in each column of the cost matrix from every entry in the column. (Alternatively, one can start with the column-opportunity-cost matrix.)

2. Determine the total-opportunity-cost matrix by subtracting the smallest entry in each row of the row-opportunity-cost matrix from each entry in the row. (Substitute column for row if the alternative procedure is used.)

3. Determine the *smallest* number of rows and/or columns which include *all* the zeroes in the total-opportunity-cost matrix. (Mark the *particular* rows and columns chosen.) If this number equals the total number of rows (or columns) the problem is solved and we may select the assignments from among the zeroes.

4. If the problem is not solved in step 3 then find the smallest entry in the matrix which is *not* on one of the *marked* rows and/or columns containing zeroes. *Add* this entry to the entry at *every intersection* of a *marked* row and a *marked* column containing zeroes. *Subtract* it from every entry in the matrix which is *not* on one of the *marked* rows and/or columns containing zeroes.

5. Repeat the process until step 3 shows that a solution has been obtained. For an $n \times n$ matrix, there must be n zeroes, no two of which are on the same row or column.

In common with many other step-by-step procedures for finding a solution, the verbal description is more difficult that the procedure, which is really simple. Let us return to the original 5-by-5 matrix and demonstrate the method on it. Our first step is to determine the matrix of job opportunity costs by subtracting the smallest cost in each column from every entry in that column. This gives:

Job	Machine				
	1	2	3	4	5
A	185	200	200	205	240
B	75	100	85	100	130
C	50	60	65	45	70
D	25	50	45	0	30
E	0	0	0	5	0

Next we determine the machine opportunity costs directly from this matrix by subtracting the smallest entry in each row from every entry in that row. Thus:

			Machine		
Job	1	2	3	4	5
A	0	15	15	20	55
B	0	25	10	25	55
C	5	15	20	0	25
D	25	50	45	0	30
E	0	0	0	5	0 *
	*			*	

We are now at step 3. We can include all these zeroes in columns 1 and 4—and row E, which we mark. The smallest entry not in columns 1 or 4 or in row E is 10 at B3. Columns 1 and 4 intersect row E at E1 and E4, so we add 10 to these entries. Then we subtract 10 from every entry not in columns 1 and 4 or in row E. This gives:

			Machine		
Job	1	2	3	4	5
A	0	5	5	20	45
B	0	15	0	25	45
C	5	5	10	0	15
D	25	40	35	0	20
E	10	0	0	15	0 *
	*		*	*	

The repetition of steps 1 and 2 doesn't change this matrix because there is already a zero in every row and column. We can include all these zeroes in four columns and rows: columns 1, 3, and 4—and row E, which we mark. The problem is, therefore, not yet solved. The smallest entry not in one of these columns or in row E is 5, at A2 and C2. The columns 1, 3, and 4 intersect row E at E1, E3, and E4, so we add 5 to these entries. Then we subtract 5 from every entry in the matrix which is not on columns 1, 3, or 4, or row E. This leads to the following result:

Job	Machine				
	1	2	3	4	5
A	[0]	0	5	20	40
B	0	10	[0]	25	40
C	5	[0]	10	0	10
D	25	35	35	[0]	15
E	15	0	5	20	[0]

A little experimenting indicates that we cannot include all these zeroes with less than five rows and/or columns. We quickly find a solution to the decision problem: assign A to 1, C to 2, B to 3, D to 4, and E to 5. These assignments have zero total opportunity cost. Referring to the original cost matrix we find that the total cost of producing the five jobs with these assignments is $430 + $300 + $350 + $275 + $250 = $1605.

The fact that the total opportunity cost is zero guarantees that no other assignments could have a smaller total cost than this. In general, it is possible that *more than one assignment can have the same total cost,* but our procedure ensures the selection of a strategy (assignment) at least as small in total cost as any other.

This procedure, with a little practice, is a remarkably quick way to solve the assignment type of decision problem. For large matrices it is necessary to use computers, as the hand computations are too onerous. Generally speaking, *the potential savings resulting from the use of this algorithm are larger when the cost matrix is larger.* For small matrices it will usually be true that the decision-maker has previously found semi-quantitative, semi-intuitive methods which give nearly optimal assignments. However, as the dimensions of the matrix increase, the strain on intuition becomes too great and strategies selected are likely to be far from optimal. In these cases the savings resulting from the use of this procedure can be considerable.

The catalogue of potential applications for the assignment method is extensive. Whenever relatively permanent types of assignments are to be made, where jobs *must* be assigned to only one facility and never split, or if the simultaneous use of all facilities is required, this kind of problem exists. For example, selecting store managers to minimize their total travel-to-work time, specifying crews for airplanes on given routes to minimize the away-from-home layover time, assigning executives to office locations in a new building to maximize[5] pleasure or minimize dis-

---

[5] To use this algorithm for assignments which will maximize profit-type matrices, simply convert the profit matrix to an (initial) opportunity cost matrix by subtracting all entries from the largest profit in the matrix. Then proceed as above. The solution will provide at least as large a total profit as any possible assignment.

pleasure, and so on. Trains to tracks, airplanes to hangars, ships to docks, even the composition of research teams can be analyzed fruitfully in this way.

92/ *The Transportation Algorithm*

The next decision problem under certainty which we shall consider will be one that frequently arises in transportation. The analogy extends much further, however. It has been found that job assignments which *can* be split are nicely handled in this way. Plant and warehouse location problems are a natural for the algorithm. And many other situations that can be transformed to the *source* and *destination* structure of the transportation model have been developed.

The major decision problem in transportation is: How can we get the required amounts of materials or products to and from the right places at a minimum total cost? In many businesses, transportation costs represent major expenditures, and sizable savings can result from any lessening of these costs.

Many transportation situations do not have any difficult decision problems. For example, a *single* plant supplying its product nationally will *have to ship to each* of the warehouses carrying the product. Usually, there will be a variety of alternative means of transportation to any specific warehouse and these will have differing costs. However, the single plant must ship to each warehouse because that plant is the only source of supply. Frequently, there will be time requirements on the deliveries which will eliminate some of the alternatives. But from among the feasible alternatives for each specific warehouse it is only necessary to select the cheapest to minimize the total transportation costs. This is not meant to gainsay the fact that difficulties can arise. For example, the probability of loss in shipping a highly perishable product may be a function of the days in transit. The reader will recognize that this would be handled by calculating for each alternative an expected loss. The transportation cost plus the expected loss would then be known for each alternative, and the lowest such amount would be the minimum-cost means of transportation for each warehouse. One can also, if it is desired, include the extra loss in interest on the capital tied up in the goods in transit owing to additional time in transit. This might be an important factor for a bank shipping currency. Generally, however, such niceties are not important factors, and when they can be handled for each warehouse separately, there is little complexity to the decision problem.

Entirely different is the common case where there are several possible origins of the goods to be transported and several possible destinations, i.e., when a number of plants located in different regions must supply various warehouses. Here we may have a decision problem of consider-able complexity owing to the fact that the various warehouses can be supplied by any one of the plants. *As the number of warehouses and plants increases, the total number of possible different ways of transport-ing the required amounts to the various warehouses increases with such rapidity that it quickly becomes impossible to evaluate the total cost associated with each of them.*

The decision problem is to select a strategy of shipping from the plants to the warehouses which satisfies the warehouse requirements and the plant capacities. A reasonable objective is to minimize total trans-portation costs. Note that we assume that the kind of analysis discussed in the preceding paragraph has already been performed for each plant-warehouse combination. In other words, we assume that the transporta-tion cost from each plant to each warehouse is already known, as are the requirements of each warehouse and the capacity of each plant. In short, all the relevant information is known with certainty and we are dealing with a decision problem under certainty. Our previous statements con-cerning the "relatively" determinate and discrete nature of the assignment problem apply here as well.

The data can be conveniently presented in a matrix. Let us consider a situation where three plants are supplying five warehouses. The trans-portation cost between each plant and each warehouse, the amount re-quired by each warehouse, and the capacity of each plant are as follows:

	Plant			
	1	2	3	Warehouse
Warehouse	Transportation Cost Per Unit			Requirements
A	$4	$7	$5	400
B	6	5	4	700
C	5	8	6	300
D	4	5	7	500
E	6	6	5	500
Plant Capacities:	1000	800	600	2400

The transportation costs, given in the body of the table, vary because of different available means and different distances involved. The decision problem is to meet the requirements of each warehouse while remaining within the capacity of each plant and to minimize the total costs of transportation.

Why can't we proceed by meeting the requirements of each warehouse from the plant with the lowest transportation cost to that warehouse?

Simply because *a plant may have the lowest transportation cost to several warehouses and be unable to meet the requirements of all of them.*[6] Thus, in our example plant 2 has its lowest transportation costs to warehouses *B* and *D*. These two warehouses have total requirements of 1,200 units and the capacity of plant 2 is only 800 units. Should we, therefore, ship 600 from plant 2 to warehouse *B* and 200 from plant 2 to warehouse *D* or ship 300 to *B* and 500 to *D*, or some other combination? The same kind of problem arises with plant 1 with regard to warehouses *A* and *D*. The situation, even with these few plants and warehouses, is too complicated to think one's way through unaided. Fortunately, we have available a relatively simple algorithm which enables us to resolve all these questions simultaneously by discovering the method of shipping with the lowest *total* transportation cost.

The statement in the last paragraph of the difficulties of the obvious approach suggests a procedure to resolve them. One problem is that by shipping, for example, 600 units from plant 2 to warehouse *B* we have foregone the possibility of shipping more than 200 units from plant 2 to warehouse *D*. There is an opportunity cost involved in making this shipment and indeed, in any specific shipment. The shipment of 600 units from plant 2 to warehouse *B* means that *B* now has 600 units which cannot be shipped to it from any other plant. We must take account of such opportunity costs in order to find the minimum-cost shipping strategy.

How can this be accomplished? Let us take the simplest possible case as an example. Suppose there are two plants and two warehouses with the relevant data as follows.

Warehouse	Plant 1	Plant 2	Warehouse Requirements
X	$5	2	300
Y	4	3	700
Plant Capacities:	400	600	1000

A possible shipping strategy would be:

Warehouse	Shipments 1	Shipments 2	Warehouse Requirements
X	300		300
Y	100	600	700
Plant Capacities:	400	600	

[6] The same kind of conflict was encountered in the assignment situation.

This strategy meets all the unit requirements. There is one specific shipment (2 to X) which is not included in the strategy. Let us note that the total transportation cost of the strategy is $300(5) + \$100(4) + \$600(3) = \$3,700$.

How can the strategy be changed to include the shipment from plant 2 to warehouse X? The final result must still balance out to meet requirements and capacities, so *compensating changes* have to be introduced. To add one unit to $X2$ while leaving the total of X at the required 300 means that we must subtract 1 unit from $X1$. Similarly, to keep the total of plant 2 at 600 we would have to subtract one unit from $Y2$. Finally, to balance the two subtractions we would have to add one unit to $Y1$. These changes are all necessary in order to ship one unit from plant 2 to warehouse X. They amount to making the following changes in shipments:

	Unit Changes					Shipments		
	1	2				1	2	
X	−1	+1	giving		X	299	1	300
Y	+1	−1			Y	101	599	700
						400	600	

The total cost of making these four changes of one unit would be simply $\$4 + \$2 - \$5 - \$3 = -\$2$, since it costs \$4 to ship an extra unit from 1 to Y and \$2 to ship a unit from 2 to X while we save \$5 by not shipping a unit from 1 to X and another \$3 by not shipping a unit from 2 to Y. So we save \$2 for every unit shipped from 2 to X. The opportunity cost of our original strategy is \$2 per unit *in terms of the shipment from plant 2 to warehouse* X. The opportunity cost is simply the amount saved by the changes.

How will we change our shipping strategy? Since we save \$2 for each unit we ship from 2 to X we will want to ship the *maximum* possible amount. What is that amount? The matrix of unit changes, above, shows that anything added to $X2$ must be subtracted from $X1$ and $Y2$. Since we *cannot ship negative amounts* it follows that we cannot ship more from 2 to X than we can subtract from the $X1$ and $Y2$ shipments. *The minimum of these two, therefore, establishes an upper limit to the amount we can ship* from 2 to X. In this case the limit is the 300 shipped from X to 1. We can ship 300 units from 2 to X by making the necessary changes in the other shipments. Thus:

	Total Changes				Shipments		
	1	2			1	2	
X	−300	+300	} gives {	X		300	300
Y	+300	−300		Y	400	300	700
					400	600	

This is the minimum-cost shipping strategy in this example. The total cost is $300(2) + $400(4) + $300(3) = $3,100.

How do we know that some combination of all four shipments isn't less costly than the last one? After all, we only tested strategies that involved three shipments. The answer to this question is an *important* one. In our reasoning, we said that since each unit shipped from 2 to X saved us $2 we would *want to ship as many units as possible*. Similarly, if a specific shipment cost us some amount extra we would want to ship *as few units as possible*. This reasoning can be generalized mathematically.

It can be proved that an optimal shipping strategy need never include more different shipments than the number of plants (P) plus the number of warehouses (W) minus one. That is, the number of shipments used equals P + W − 1.

In our case this is $P + W − 1 = 2 + 2 − 1 = 3$, so we know that the best strategy involving three shipments is at least as good as any strategy involving four shipments. In some cases, the optimal strategy may involve less shipments than this number (three here). Such situations are said to be *degenerate* and require some slight modifications in the procedure we are developing here.[7]

Basically, three steps are involved:

Step 1. *Start* with any strategy meeting the requirements and the rule $P + W − 1$.

Step 2. Evaluate the *opportunity costs* of the strategy in terms of the shipments not in the strategy.

Step 3. If all opportunity costs are less than or equal to zero the problem is solved and the strategy is optimal. If one or more opportunity costs are greater than zero, incorporate the shipment with the largest positive per unit opportunity cost in the strategy and repeat steps 2 and 3.

---

[7] For example, consider an inconsequential amount (ϵ) to be added to an appropriate "empty" cell. From the point of view of the rule ($P + W − 1$) this will set things right. The cell chosen must be appropriate so that the algorithm can be used.

Our example sufficed to show that the per unit opportunity costs were determined only for the shipments *not* in the strategy. Information about the amounts of the shipments in the strategy was used solely for deriving the total opportunity costs. It is only necessary to know the pattern of shipments in the strategy to evaluate the unit opportunity costs. Suppose then, that we were given our two-by-two matrix of costs in this form:

	1	2
X	5	$C(X2)$
Y	4	3

We are told that the three costs (given above) are those of the three shipments used in our strategy. What can we say about the cost of X2, called $C(X2)$, which is assumed unknown? Any change in our strategy to include a shipment of one unit from 2 to X must be of the form:

	1	2
X	−1	1
Y	1	−1

Therefore, we know that the cost change which will result will be:

$$C(X2) + C(Y1) - C(X1) - C(Y2) = C(X2) + 4 - 5 - 3 = C(X2) - 4$$

We can now state that *if* $C(X2)$ is greater than 4 it will cost more to include this shipment; *if* $C(X2) = 4$ the cost will be the same whether we include this shipment or not; and *if* $C(X2)$ is less than 4 we will save money by including the shipment from 2 to X. In fact, we know that this last case was true so we did include the X2 shipment in our strategy. The savings resulting from the changes will be $5 + 3 = 8$ and the additional costs will be $4 + C(X2)$. Therefore, the *opportunity cost* of the strategy in terms of X2 is simply $8 - [4 + C(X2)] = 4 - C(X2)$. Here 4 is the *calculated value* and $C(X2)$ is the *actual value*. So the opportunity cost = calculated value − actual value. If this opportunity cost is positive—if 4 is greater than $C(X2)$—we know we should include the shipment from 2 to X in our strategy.

Now let us turn to a larger matrix. Suppose we are given, analogically to the last example:

	1	2	3
R		3	
S	6		4
T		5	2

It will be noted that we have included $3 + 3 - 1 = 5$ shipments in our strategy since this number is sufficient to get the optimal strategy and will be required unless we have a degenerate case. How can we evaluate the empty cells in this matrix? Using essentially the same procedure as we did with the 2×2 matrix, we would calculate the opportunity costs. Specifically, if the actual original cost matrix was:

	Actual Costs		
	1	2	3
R	4	3	2
S	6	6	4
T	5	5	2

We would proceed by calculating, entry by entry, the quantity (calculated value − actual cost = opportunity cost) and get:

	Opportunity Costs		
	1	2	3
R	−2	0	−2
S	0	1	0
T	−1	0	0

The only opportunity cost which is greater than 0 is that of $S2$, so we would change our strategy to include $S2$.

The "stepping" patterns for calculating these unit opportunity costs are shown in the four matrices on page 267. The key, in each case, is to determine that pattern of stepping which allows the shift of a unit (to a new location) to be balanced out for all requirements and capacities of the matrix.

It is clear why this approach to solving the transportation problem is frequently referred to as the *stepping-stone method*. But, necessarily, a stone to step on must always be available. That is why *Step 1* requires that $P + W - 1$ assignments (or shipments) be made. If there are less stepping-stones than that (which we have called *the degenerate case*) all of the necessary paths cannot be traced. Examine, for instance, the following pattern:

	1	2	3
R		3	
S	6		
T		5	2

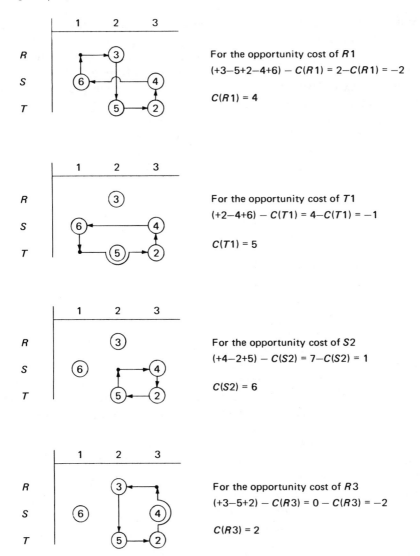

For the opportunity cost of *R*1
$(+3-5+2-4+6) - C(R1) = 2-C(R1) = -2$

$C(R1) = 4$

For the opportunity cost of *T*1
$(+2-4+6) - C(T1) = 4-C(T1) = -1$

$C(T1) = 5$

For the opportunity cost of *S*2
$(+4-2+5) - C(S2) = 7-C(S2) = 1$

$C(S2) = 6$

For the opportunity cost of *R*3
$(+3-5+2) - C(R3) = 0 - C(R3) = -2$

$C(R3) = 2$

In such cases (as we have previously footnoted) the addition of a "negligible" shipment ϵ to an appropriate empty cell will permit us to introduce the required cost so that we can trace out all paths.[8]

This stepping-stone procedure isn't too difficult for *Step 2* but it is a great deal more laborious than we would like. Fortunately, the same results can be accomplished more rapidly in an alternative way. The algebraic proof of the equivalence of these methods need not be given.

[8] An inappropriate cell would be *R*3.

Suffice it to say that they lead to precisely the same evaluation of the opportunity costs.

The new procedure ascribes costs *only* to those rows and columns of the matrix that contain the transportation costs of *the shipments in our strategy*. These costs are determined so that the transportation costs which are in the matrix (those of the shipments in our strategy) are *each equal to the sum of the cost ascribed to the row and to the column in which it occurs*. This can be done simply, since we can *arbitrarily start* by assigning a zero cost to any row or column we choose. Consider our example. The matrix of the costs for the shipments in our strategy is shown below:

	1	2	3	Row Cost
R		3		0
S	6		4	
T		5	2	2
Column Cost:		3		

Then, in addition, we have (arbitrarily) assigned a zero cost to row R. In order to have $C(R2) = 3$ we must assign to column 2 a cost of 3 [since row R cost plus column 2 cost must equal $C(R2)$]. Then, $C(T2) = 5$, so row T must have a cost of 2 [since row T cost plus column 2 cost must equal $C(T2)$].

To continue: $C(T3) = 2$, so column 3 must have a cost of 0 [since row T cost plus column 3 cost must equal $C(T3)$]. But $C(S3) = 4$, so row S must have a cost of 4 [since row S cost plus column 3 cost must equal $C(S3)$]. And finally, column 1 cost must equal 2 to have $C(S1) = 6$. Thus, the row and column costs are all determined by the formula:

$$\text{Row Cost} + \text{Column Cost} = C(\text{entry})$$

The result, in this case, is:

	1	2	3	Row Cost
R		3		0
S	6		4	4
T		5	2	2
Column Cost:	2	3	0	

All of the shipment entries in the matrix equal the sum of the row and column costs as required.

If the other entries are now filled in by taking for each cell the sum of the costs of its row and column, we get:

	1	2	3	Row Cost
R	2	③	0	0
S	⑥	7	④	4
T	4	⑤	②	2
Column Cost:	2	3	0	

where the *original entries are circled*. From all entries in this matrix we *subtract* the respective values of *the actual cost matrix,* which is repeated here for convenience.

	Actual Costs		
	1	2	3
R	4	3	2
S	6	6	4
T	5	5	2

This gives:

	1	2	3
R	−2	0	−2
S	0	1	0
T	−1	0	0

It will be seen that this last matrix of opportunity costs is identical to the one we calculated before by the more lengthy stepping-stone procedure. Thus, this much shorter method can be used for *Step 2.*

Now let us turn to Step 3. We have discovered a positive opportunity cost and know that it should be included in our strategy. How do we include it? Suppose the shipments for our 3-by-3 example are:

	1	2	3	Warehouse Requirement
R		200		200
S	300		400	700
T		500	100	600
Plant Capacity:	300	700	500	

The only shipment with a positive opportunity cost was $S2$. Each unit shipped from 2 to S saves us \$1, so we want to ship the maximum number of units possible. How can we rearrange the shipments so all requirements are met while we increase $S2$ to the maximum amount possible? We use the appropriate stepping-stone path. As before, it consists of a series of right-angled steps. They change direction *only at entries included in our strategy.* The path starts at $S2$ (moving horizontally) and ends at $S2$. The compensating changes are made along this path. For $S2$ we proceed as follows: $S2 \rightarrow S3 \rightarrow T3 \rightarrow T2 \rightarrow S2$.

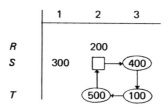

We are going to add some amount to $S2$. To balance row S we must subtract that amount from $S3$. Since we must balance column 3 we add that amount to $T3$. Then, in order to balance row T we have to subtract that amount from $T2$. And then, in order to balance column 2 we have to add that amount to $S2$, *which is what we wanted to do,* and which completes the cycle.

> *The general rule in such a cycle is: subtract from the termination of every horizontal step and add to the termination of every vertical step. The subtractions constitute the limitation, since we cannot have a negative shipment.*

Here, we are subtracting from $S3$ and from $T2$. The *smaller* of these is 400. So 400 can be added to $S2$ and all the indicated changes are made: add 400 to $T3$, subtract 400 from $S3$ and $T2$. This gives us our new strategy:

	1	2	3
R		200	
S	300	400	
T		100	500

Steps 2 and 3 would now be repeated to see whether any further improvement is possible.

Let us repeat this procedure with the other cells of the matrix although their opportunity costs are negative. For $R1$ we have the path:

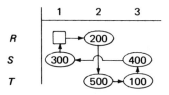

The smallest entry at the end of a horizontal step is $T3 = 100$. Therefore 100 is the largest amount that can be shipped from 1 to R. Making the necessary changes gives:

	1	2	3
R	100	100	
S	200		500
T		600	

For $T1$ we have the path:

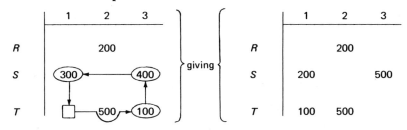

and for $R3$ we have

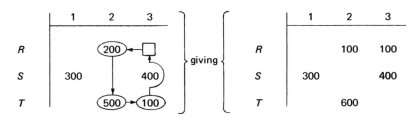

Such a path can always be found unless we have a degenerate case.[9] This is the procedure for step 3.

The method for accomplishing step 1 is easy. Let us demonstrate it on our original decision problem (p. 261). Required: a strategy which

---

[9] In which case, we add ϵ to an appropriate missing cell and proceed as before.

meets the warehouse requirements and is within the plant capacities. There are many such strategies. To get *one,* we start in the *northwest corner* of the matrix (i.e., *A*1) and work down the column, *completely meeting the requirements of each warehouse until the capacity of plant 1 is exhausted.* Then we complete the requirements of the warehouse in which we stopped by moving across the row to plant 2 and continue similarly until we end up in the southeast corner (i.e., *E*3). The following pattern of assignments occurs:

| | Northwest Corner First Strategy | | | Warehouse Requirements |
	1	2	3	
A	400			400
B	600	100		700
C		300		300
D		400	100	500
E			500	500
Plant Capacities:	1000	800	600	

This method automatically produces a strategy meeting all requirements. In our case, we have $P + W - 1 = 3 + 5 - 1 = 7$ entries, as we should, or more generally (rows + columns $- 1$) $= 7$. If a degenerate case results, it can be handled by the procedural variants previously mentioned.[10] The cost of this first (NW corner) strategy is $13,300 (obtained as follows):

$$(\$400 \times 4) + (\$600 \times 6) + (\$100 \times 5) + (\$300 \times 8) + (\$400 \times 5)$$
$$+ (\$100 \times 7) + (\$500 \times 5) = \$13,300$$

Now, *Step 2:* We determine the row and column costs so that each of the unit costs *of the shipments* in our first strategy equals the sum of its row and column costs.

	1	2	3	Row Cost
A	4			0
B	6	5		2
C		8		5
D		5	7	2
E			5	0
Column Cost:	4	3	5	

[10] Note that a degenerate case occurs if Warehouse *B*'s requirements are reduced to 600 units and Plant 2's capacity to 700 units.

Then we calculate the values of the other entries by summing the row and column costs for each entry.

	1	2	3	Row Cost
A	④	3	5	0
B	⑥	⑤	7	2
C	9	⑧	10	5
D	6	⑤	⑦	2
E	4	3	⑤	0
Column Cost:	4	3	5	

Subtracting the original, actual cost matrix from this, entry by entry, gives the opportunity-cost matrix.

	1	2	3
A	0	−4	0
B	0	0	3
C	4	0	4
D	2	0	0
E	−2	−3	0

There are several positive opportunity costs and we can put any one of the corresponding shipments into our strategy. It is generally *quickest to use the largest positive opportunity costs first.* Let us, therefore, put $C1$ in our strategy. The path to be used in achieving the change is:

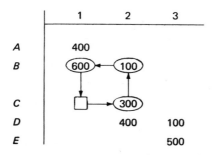

The smallest termination of a horizontal step is 300 so we can ship 300 units from 1 to C by making the indicated changes.

Repeating *Step 2:*

	Second Strategy					1	2	3	Row Cost
	1	2	3						
A	400				A	4			0
B	300	400			B	6	5		2
C	300				C	5			1
D		400	100		D		5	7	2
E			500		E			5	0
					Column Cost:	4	3	5	

	1	2	3	Row Cost			Opportunity Cost		
							1	2	3
A	(4)	3	5	0		A	0	−4	0
B	(6)	(5)	7	2		B	0	0	3
C	(5)	4	6	1		C	0	−4	0
D	6	(5)	(7)	2		D	2	0	0
E	4	3	(5)	0		E	−2	−3	0
Column Cost:	4	3	5						

The cost of the second strategy was $12,100.

Again we have positive opportunity costs and again we select the largest (*B3*) to include in our next strategy. The path to be used is:

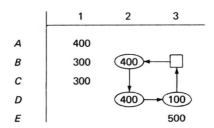

	1	2	3
A	400		
B	300	400	
C	300		
D		400	100
E			500

The smallest termination of a horizontal step is 100. This is the amount we may ship from *3* to *B*. Making the indicated changes and repeating step 2 gives:

	Third Strategy					1	2	3	Row Cost
	1	2	3						
A	400				A	4			0
B	300	300	100		B	6	5	4	2
C	300				C	5			1
D		500			D		5		2
E			500		E			5	3
					Column Cost:	4	3	2	

	1	2	3	Row Cost			Opportunity Cost		
							1	2	3
A	④	3	2	0		A	0	-4	-3
B	⑥	⑤	④	2		B	0	0	0
C	⑤	4	3	1		C	0	-4	-3
D	6	⑤	4	2		D	2	0	-3
E	7	6	⑤	3		E	1	0	0
Column Cost:	4	3	2						

The cost of the third strategy was $11,800.

Some opportunity costs are still positive so we select the largest (*D*1) for inclusion in our next strategy. The path to be used in making the necessary changes is:

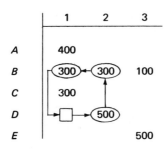

The most we can ship from 1 to *D* is 300 units. Making the indicated changes and repeating step 2:

	Fourth Strategy 1	2	3			1	2	3	Row Cost
A	400				A	4			0
B		600	100		B		5	4	0
C	300				C	5			1
D	300	200			D	4	5		0
E			500		E			5	1
					Column Cost:	4	5	4	

	1	2	3	Row Cost		Opportunity Cost 1	2	3
A	(4)	5	4	0	A	0	−2	−1
B	4	(5)	(4)	0	B	−2	0	0
C	(5)	6	5	1	C	0	−2	−1
D	(4)	(5)	4	0	D	0	0	−3
E	5	6	(5)	1	E	−1	0	0
Column Cost:	4	5	4					

The cost of this fourth strategy is $11,200. Since no opportunity cost is greater than zero we cannot do better than this strategy which is, therefore, the solution to our decision problem. Familiarity with the relatively simple steps of the transportation algorithm permits it to be done with pencil and paper quite rapidly. However, this kind of decision problem is often so large that it requires a computer (programmed for this model) to perform the computations.

When the total output of the sources does not equal the total requirements of the destinations, a dummy source or a dummy destination is used.[11] Thus, for example:

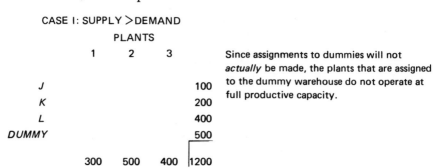

CASE I: SUPPLY > DEMAND

	PLANTS 1	2	3	
J				100
K				200
L				400
DUMMY				500
	300	500	400	1200

Since assignments to dummies will not *actually* be made, the plants that are assigned to the dummy warehouse do not operate at full productive capacity.

[11] These dummies are equivalent to slack variables. See p. 306.

CASE II: SUPPLY < DEMAND

PLANTS

	1	2	3	DUMMY		The warehouses that are assigned to a dummy plant do not get fully supplied
J				100		
K				200		
L				400		
	100	200	250	150	700	

As in the case of the assignment method, it is possible to use a matrix of profits where the objective is to maximize total profit. We require a transformation of the unit profit matrix to one of unit costs, and this is achieved by subtracting all matrix values from the largest unit profit in the matrix. For example:

UNIT PROFIT MATRIX

	1	2	3
J	5	8	4
K	6	5	3
L	2	7	4

TO BE MAXIMIZED

would become

UNIT COST MATRIX

	1	2	3
J	3	0	4
K	2	3	5
L	6	1	4

TO BE MINIMIZED

Minimizing the total cost of the transformed matrix is equivalent to maximizing the total profit of the original matrix. It is essential, of course, to reinterpret the solution in terms of profits.

93/ A Sequencing Algorithm

Another example of a "relatively" determinate and discrete situation is described below. An appropriate technique is discussed which is readily applied under the *specific* circumstances that any number of jobs are to be processed by two (or three) facilities where the order of processing by the first facility must be maintained for the subsequent facilities. Some call this a *no-passing* rule. It is most likely to arise for technological reasons. Again, it is because production problems are particularly visible that this sequencing method finds its greatest applicability in the production area.

Let us consider the (schedule) sequencing problem as it relates to maintenance. Models describing the amount of maintenance which should be done can be formulated in a variety of ways. Different maintenance strategies, including the degree to which preventive maintenance is used, the scheduling of maintenance crews, the replacement of old and worn equipment, and so on, produce different payoffs over the long run. States of nature which affect deterioration, breakage, and failures of various sorts are difficult to detect and can require a great deal of careful observation before any reasonable predictions can be made. The study of failure rates as states of nature is of particular importance in the maintenance field. The reader will recall how the Monte Carlo technique was used to determine the failure characteristics of a unit for which the failure characteristics of the components were known. Based on even limited knowledge of the states of nature, optimal replacement policies for machines, light bulbs, tool bits, and so on can sometimes be determined by analytical methods.

It is interesting to observe that in this area many techniques have been suggested and partially developed, but generalized problem-solving techniques are rarely found. The mathematical representation of replacement strategies is complex. Similarly, sequencing and routing models have not been developed to handle all general cases. Purely mathematical solutions are available for some special cases. Consequently, simulation has become an important approach for treating the complexity and many variants of the scheduling problem. The use of heuristic procedures is commonplace. In many cases, the selection of scheduling strategies remains largely a matter of intuition and hard work.

The above discussion is not meant to imply that either replacement problems or sequencing problems are solely in the province of maintenance. At certain levels, replacement problems are more nearly financial problems, and sequencing problems exist in almost every area of business. They are of particular importance in scheduling production facilities and routing a variety of jobs through a factory. Yet this same general type of problem appears in routing salesmen through a company's territory in such a way as to minimize the distance covered, or the time or expenses required. Although many interesting aspects of this last-mentioned problem have been uncovered, a general solution is lacking. Bearing in mind these remarks, we shall now proceed to develop several examples of sequencing models which can be solved. They will serve to illustrate the kinds of solutions which have been obtained as well as demonstrate the advantages to be gained by using formal analytic models.

The *first* example requires scheduling factory maintenance crews in such a way as to minimize their idle time. The company, we shall assume, has eight large machines which receive preventive maintenance. The maintenance team is divided into two crews, *A* and *B*. Crew *A* takes the machine "down" and replaces parts according to the number of hours of use the machine has accumulated up to the time of servicing. The second crew resets the machine and puts it back into operation. At all times, the *no-passing* rule is considered to be in effect. Different training and abilities are required by each crew. The machines are not alike and, therefore, the servicing times are not the same for each machine. The specific servicing times are given in hours, as follows:

	MACHINE							
	a	*b*	*c*	*d*	*e*	*f*	*g*	*h*
Crew *A*	5	4	22	16	15	11	9	4
Crew *B*	6	10	12	8	20	7	2	12

The method for *minimizing idle time* of the maintenance crews requires a few simple rules. The rules can be developed in (descriptive) mathematical terms. The algorithm interprets the formulae in the following manner:

1. Choose the single *smallest* value that appears in the *two* rows.

2. If it is in the *second row* (which is always reserved for the second operation in the two-step servicing sequence), then that machine will be serviced *last* by crew *A*.

3. If it is in the *first row* (the first operation in the two-step sequence), then that machine will be serviced *first* by crew *A*.

4. Cross out the column of the machine which has been assigned.

5. In general, from the *remaining* numbers, choose the single *smallest* value which appears in the *two* rows. If the number is in the second row, then that machine is assigned to be serviced *last* by crew *A*—if no previous assignment to the last place has been made. If a previous assignment has been made to the last place, then the machine goes into the *next to the last* place. If two previous assignments, to the last place and the next to last place, have been made, then the machine is placed into the *next to the next to the last* place. Cross out the column and proceed until all possible assignments have been made.

6. If the smallest value remaining is in the first row, then the machine is assigned to be serviced first, second, third, or whenever, depending upon how many previous assignments have been made. After an assignment, cross out the column and proceed until all possible assignments have been made.

7. If a *tie* exists for the smallest value remaining, *choose either one.* Make the assignment as described above. Cross out the column chosen and proceed until all possible assignments have been made.

Now let us apply our rules to the above example. If a machine is to be serviced last by crew A we will use the number 8 to denote this fact, since there are only eight machines. The number 7 will indicate the next to the last assignment. The number 2 will denote an assignment to second place, and so forth.

Our minimum number in the table is 2. It appears in the second row. Therefore, we make the assignment $g8$, which means that machine g will be serviced last (or eighth) by crew A. The next minimum number is 4 and it appears twice. We can choose either one; let us pick machine b. We get $b1$. It has been assigned first place since it appears in the first row. This leaves the other 4 as a minimum number, so we get $h2$. Proceeding in this fashion, we derive the sequence

$$g8, \ b1, \ h2, \ a3, \ f7, \ d6, \ c5, \ e4$$

We can arrange these in order, and put down the servicing times for crews A and B.

	CREW *A*	CREW *B*
*b*1	4	10
*h*2	4	12
*a*3	5	6
*e*4	15	20
*c*5	22	12
*d*6	16	8
*f*7	11	7
*g*8	9	2

This order of servicing the machines is the *optimal sequence.* We can represent it on a chart as shown in Figure 10.1. The solid black areas are the idle time of crew B. The result has given us 11 hours of idle time for crew B.

The method can be applied to *any number of machines,* but the number of maintenance operations *is limited to two.* However, the technique *can be extended to three* maintenance operations by means of a few additional steps which were developed by S. M. Johnson.[12]

---

[12] Johnson, S. M., "Optimal Two- and Three-Stage Production Schedules with Setup Times Included," *Nav. Res. Log. Quart.,* 1, Nr. 1, (March, 1954) pp. 61–68.

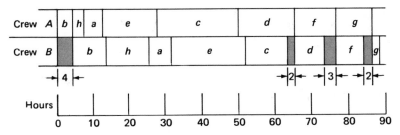

FIGURE 10.1 *Sequencing machine maintenance with two crews and eight machines*

For our *second* example, we shall consider the problem of an oil company with eight refineries located in different parts of the country. Each refinery has its own maintenance crew to do the necessary routine work. However, once a year each refinery undergoes a complete overhaul. For this work the company hires outside maintenance crews which specialize in the required kind of maintenance work. Because these crews are very expensive the company would like to minimize their idle time.

Let us assume that the yearly overhaul (or *turn-around*) procedure involves three distinct steps, *A*, *B*, and *C*, with *no-passing* permitted. Furthermore, we shall suppose that phase *B* is handled by the local refinery maintenance group while phases *A* and *C* are taken care of by crews *A* and *C* of the outside team. The problem can be set down in the following form, where the entries are the number of hours required by each crew to complete its phase of the work.

	REFINERY							
	R1	R2	R3	R4	R5	R6	R7	R8
Crew *A*	5	4	22	16	15	11	9	4
Crew *B*	4	3	2	4	3	4	2	3
Crew *C*	6	10	12	8	20	7	2	12

The sequencing algorithm requires adding the time required by crews *A* and *B* for each refinery and thereby forming a *new* row: crew *A* + crew *B*. The same procedure is used for the time required by crews *C* and *B* for each refinery and in this manner we obtain a second row: crew *C* + crew *B*. Thus,

	R1	R2	R3	R4	R5	R6	R7	R8
Crew *A* + Crew *B*	5 + 4	4 + 3	22 + 2	16 + 4	15 + 3	11 + 4	9 + 2	4 + 3
Crew *C* + Crew *B*	6 + 4	10 + 3	12 + 2	8 + 4	20 + 3	7 + 4	2 + 2	12 + 3

which is:

	R1	R2	R3	R4	R5	R6	R7	R8
Crew A + Crew B	9	7	24	20	18	15	11	7
Crew C + Crew B	10	13	14	12	23	11	4	15

To this transformed matrix we apply the previously developed rules *in exactly the same way*. The smallest value is 4, appearing in the second row. Therefore, we assign $R7$ to the last operation of crew A which means it must also be the last operation for crews B and C. Continuing this procedure, the result is:

	CREW A	CREW B	CREW C
1 $R2$	4	3	10
2 $R8$	4	3	12
3 $R1$	5	4	6
4 $R5$	15	3	20
5 $R3$	22	2	12
6 $R4$	16	4	8
7 $R6$	11	4	7
8 $R7$	9	2	2

Figure 10.2 graphically depicts this optimal sequence. There are 13 hours of idle time for crew C.

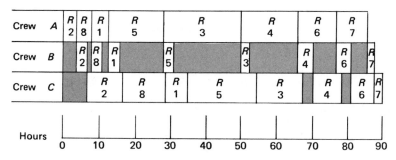

FIGURE 10.2 *Sequencing refinery turnaround with three crews and eight refineries.*

One important limitation of this method restricts its usefulness. Crew B, which is in the middle of the servicing sequence A-B-C, may not have *any* servicing times which are *greater than the minimum servicing times of both A and C* for this procedure to apply.

In other words, the *minimum* servicing time in the first row (crew *A*) is 4. The *minimum* servicing time in the third row (crew *C*) is 2. The *maximum* servicing time in the second row (crew *B*) is 4. *Since this last value is not greater than both the minimums of the other two rows, the method can be used in the manner we have shown.* However, if the maximum servicing time in the second row had been 5, this method could not have been employed.

94/ Combining Models to Fit the Problem

Minimizing the idle time of the maintenance crews is most certainly an important objective. However, if we suppose that once turnaround has begun the refinery must be either entirely or partially shut down—which is generally the case—then the objective of minimizing the idle time of the maintenance crews becomes of secondary importance. The major objective of the oil company is to *minimize down-time of the refineries.* Lost production time is the bane of this and other process industries. Therefore, the administrator of the maintenance function would reject the solution we have just found.

The same consideration might well apply to the machine problem which was our first sequencing example. If once maintenance starts on a machine, that machine cannot be used until the servicing is completed. Then the first objective would be to get that machine back into use as soon as possible. This would be particularly true when an expensive machine is involved since the cost of machine down-time would be high in relation to the cost of the maintenance crews.

To handle this objective, we shall now develop a model which *insures that each refinery will be put back into operation as soon as possible. Subject to this condition, we will minimize the idle time of the maintenance crews.* For this example, two maintenance crews, *A* and *B,* will service the eight refineries.

The sequencing methods we have introduced are composed of components which provide service and of elements which require service. The methods can be used for *any number of elements* which *require* service, but as yet there is no *general* solution available for more than two service components. Our second sequencing example involved three components and as was explained, the solution applies only when specific conditions are met. Consequently, we do not even have a general model to cover three service components. The same limitation applies to the model we are about to explain. For this reason, the example consists of two crews and eight refineries.

For convenience, we shall use the same data as were employed in the machine-servicing problem. The reader can refer to Figure 10.1 to derive the values shown below. Again, crew A precedes crew B. As soon as crew A begins to work at any refinery we assume that the refinery *must* be shut down. On this basis, the following table of information can be prepared.

	R1	R2	R3	R4	R5	R6	R7	R8
Servicing time Crew A (in hours)	5	4	22	16	15	11	9	4
Servicing time Crew B (in hours)	6	10	12	8	20	7	2	12
Total servicing time for each refinery	11	14	34	24	35	18	11	16
Unnecessary down-time for each refinery*	13	0	2	0	4	0	0	6

* For example, consider $R1$. Crew A completes working at $4 + 4 + 5 = 13$. Crew B begins on $R1$ at $4 + 10 + 12 = 26$. The difference of 13 is the unnecessary down-time for $R1$.

The total unnecessary down-time for our first solution is $13 + 2 + 4 + 6 = 25$ hours. We know from our previous results that 11 hours of idle time had resulted for crew B under the optimal idle-time condition. If we assumed that 100 men composed crew B and that these men were paid \$5.00 per hour, the idle-time cost would be \$5,500. Compared to the 25 hours of lost refinery production, the idle-time cost would be relatively insignificant.[13]

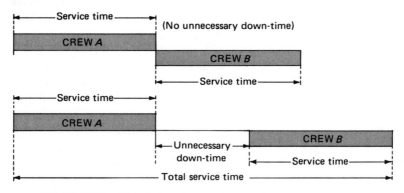

FIGURE 10.3 *Illustrating the requirement for no unnecessary down-time.*

For this reason, the administrator would be prepared to increase the amount of idle time in exchange for *no unnecessary down-time* of the

[13] The cost of lost refinery production might well be as high as a million dollars of production.

refineries. In order to obtain no unnecessary down-time, each refinery must be serviced in the manner shown in Figure 10.3, page 284.

Our problem consists of finding the optimal sequence of refineries when the condition for no unnecessary down-time is enforced. Looking back to Figure 10.1, we observe the gaps between the servicing periods of crews A and B for h, a, e, and c. (These are equivalent to our refineries $R8$, $R1$, $R5$, and $R3$.) To get rid of these gaps, we can compare the idle time for sequential pairs of refineries. Figure 10.4 illustrates several pairs of refineries: $R1-R2$, $R1-R4$, $R7-R4$.

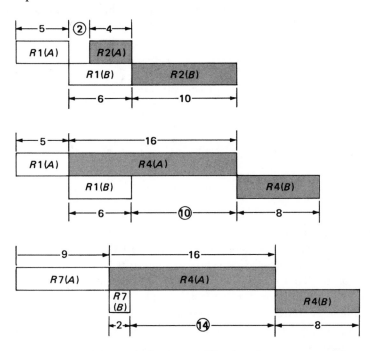

FIGURE 10.4 Determination of idle time for sequences with no unnecessary down-time.

For *every possible combination of pairs of refineries* we determine the idle time of either crew enclosed by two consecutive servicing operations. Sometimes the idle time occurs for crew A and sometimes for crew B. (We do not include any idle time which might arise at the beginning or end of the sequence.) From Figure 10.4 we find that $R1-R2$ has 2 hours of idle time, $R1-R4$ has 10 hours of idle time, and $R7-R4$ has 14 hours of idle time. It is not necessary to draw pictures for every possible sequence in order to determine the enclosed idle time. Using the original table of data, we obtain the absolute value for

$$|Ri(B) - Rj(A)|$$

where i = any one of the refineries which is serviced first, and
j = all of the other refineries which are serviced second.

Thus, for $i = 1$, then $j = 2, 3, 4, 5, 6, 7$, and 8, we get

$$|R1(B) - R2(A)| = |6 - 4| = 2$$
$$|R1(B) - R3(A)| = |6 - 22| = 16 \qquad \text{(and so on)}$$

For $|R1(B) - R1(A)|$ we obtain no value since a refinery cannot follow itself.

Proceeding in this manner we can determine the idle time for any sequence of two refineries. The idle times are presented in the matrix below:

| | FIRST | | | | | | | |
SECOND	R1	R2	R3	R4	R5	R6	R7	R8
R1	x	5	7	3	15	2	3	7
R2	2	x	8	4	16	3	2	8
R3	16	12	x	14	2	15	20	10
R4	10	6	4	x	4	9	14	4
R5	9	5	3	7	x	8	13	3
R6	5	1	1	3	9	x	9	1
R7	3	1	3	1	11	2	x	3
R8	2	6	8	4	16	3	2	x

This table shows the idle time for all possible sequences of two refineries —the first is given in the column heading and the second by the row. Thus, refinery $R4$ followed by refinery $R7$ results in idle time of 1 hour.

We would like to find the *total sequence, including all refineries,* which has *the minimum total idle time*. The reader will recognize that this problem is similar to the *assignment problem.* However, there is a *crucial difference.* In the assignment problem it was sufficient to find the total minimum-cost assignment and *any* machine could be assigned to *any* job. Here, however, there are *additional restrictions.* Suppose we found that the minimum total idle time resulted from a sequence containing $(R4–R1)$ . . . $(R1–R8)$ . . . $(R8–R4)$. This sequence would be *impossible* since it would call for servicing $R4$ twice.

Such a sequence is called a *sub-cycle,* and the additional restriction on this kind of sequencing problem is that there should be no sub-cycles in the final sequence, i.e., no cycle that does not include all refineries. The restriction makes this problem similar to the famous *traveling-salesman problem.* A salesman must start from Washington, D.C., for example, travel to each of the 50 state capitols, and return to Washington, D.C. *How should we schedule the sequence* of state capitols so that his total distance traveled is minimized? There is no *general* solution to problems such as this, and there is none to our sequencing problem. However, this does not mean that there is nothing that can be done with such problems.

One thing *we* can do is to use the assignment method. If the solution has no sub-cycles we have solved the sequencing problem. If it does have these internal cycles we cannot use the sequence. It can, however, represent a starting point from which to make changes. Let us solve the assignment problem for our matrix. The method, based on opportunity costs, was previously discussed. We subtract the minimum entry in each column from each element in the column and then do the same thing by rows (assume that the x's are of such great magnitude that we can ignore them):

	R1	R2	R3	R4	R5	R6	R7	R8
R1	x	4	6	2	13	0	1	6
R2	0	x	7	3	14	1	0	7
R3	14	11	x	13	0	13	18	9
R4	6	3	1	x	0	5	10	1
R5	5	2	0	4	x	4	9	0
R6	3	0	0	2	7	x	7	0
R7	1	0	2	0	9	0	x	2
R8	0	5	7	3	14	1	0	x

All zeroes in this matrix can be included in seven rows and columns: *viz.*, rows $R2, R5, R6, R7, R8$ and columns $R5$ and $R6$. Since this is less than eight, we know the problem is not solved. The minimum entry in the matrix, if these rows and columns are excluded, is "1" which we subtract from every entry not in one of the seven rows and columns and add to every intersection. Leave all of the other entries unchanged. This gives:

	R1	R2	R3	R4	R5	R6	R7	R8
R1	x	3	5	1	13	0	0	5
R2	0	x	7	3	15	2	0	7
R3	13	10	x	12	0	13	17	8
R4	5	2	0	x	0	5	9	0
R5	5	2	0	4	x	5	9	0
R6	3	0	0	2	8	x	7	0
R7	1	0	2	0	10	1	x	2
R8	0	5	7	3	15	2	0	x

The zeroes in this new matrix cannot be included with less than eight rows and columns, so the assignment problem is solved. There are several solutions in this matrix, which is good for our purposes because we hope to find one with no sub-cycles.

We can begin by finding the rows and columns with only one zero. Such a zero must be in the solution. Columns $R4$ and $R6$ have only one zero so we know that (R6–R1) and (R4–R7) must be in the solution. Row R3 has only one zero so (R5–R3) is in the solution. There are two zeroes in column R2 but one of them is in row R7, and (R2–R7) is impossible because we already have (R4–R7). Therefore, (R2–R6) must be in the solution.

There are two zeroes in column R1. (R1–R2) is impossible for our problem because we already have (R2–R6) and (R6–R1). Therefore, we must have (R1 − R8). But this makes (R7 − R8) impossible, so we must have (R7–R2). Since we already have (R5–R3) we cannot have (R3–R5), so we must have (R3–R4). This, in turn, requires that we have (R8–R5), which completes the solution. Putting these together we get:

$$R6–R1–R8–R5–R3–R4–R7–R2–R6$$

We have found the sequence which has minimum idle time. If we had found only sub-cycles we would have turned to trial-and-error methods, starting with the solution to the assignment problem.

Returning to the solution stated above, we see from the original table that the idle time is the sum of the entries indicated by the optimal sequence; that is,

$$
\begin{array}{ll}
(R6–R1) & 2 \\
(R1–R8) & 2 \\
(R8–R5) & 3 \\
(R5–R3) & 2 \\
(R3–R4) & 4 \\
(R4–R7) & 1 \\
(R7–R2) & 2 \\
(R2–R6) & 1 \\
\hline
17 & = \text{Total idle time (hours)}
\end{array}
$$

We can observe how the 17 hours of idle time arise by referring to Figure 10.5. There is no unnecessary down-time. The saving in down-time is accomplished at the expense of six additional hours of idle time.

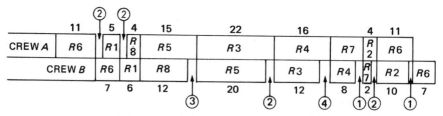

FIGURE 10.5 Optimal sequence for eight refineries with no unnecessary down-time.

Using our previous assumption of 100 men paid $5.00 per hour, we find that the administrator is paying an additional $3,000 to idle maintenance crews in return for a saving of 25 hours of refinery production. It is quite certain that the management of an oil company would gladly accept this trade.

For other types of maintenance problems, the choice might not be made so easily. Assuming that the company is able to estimate *the cost of lost production,* a balancing of these two objectives can usually be accomplished. As an additional aspect, we might require analysis of the costs of *transporting* maintenance crews between refineries to minimize transportation costs. In this case, a third objective is evident. However, the *direct* minimization of any of the three kinds of outcomes will usually result in a less than optimal value for the remaining outcomes. Therefore, it is relevant to note that the cost of transporting maintenance crews between refineries might be entered in the matrix. Idle time can be converted from hours into the appropriate dollar value, which would then be summed with the transportation cost.

All of the models that have been discussed in this chapter thus far are based on *network* considerations. Assignments and schedules lend themselves to these ideas of finding an *optimal path* through a complex network of connections. But this is not the only approach to such problems. Transportation problems, for example, also can be resolved by the mathematical programming methods frequently associated with linear programming. Similarly, scheduling models are usually far too complex to get at by strictly formal means, and so heuristic-motivated computer simulations are utilized.

95/ Critical Path Network Models

The use of network models ranges from such basic algorithms as the stepping-stone method for transportation problems to highly elaborate sociometric analyses that describe the relations of people and groups to each other.[14] One of the most important contributions of network theory has been in the field of project planning models.

The strengths of early project planning methods (such as represented by the "Gantt-type" project planning chart[15] in Figure 10.6 shown below) were that they systematically described project steps, specified the schedules for completion and tracked actual performance against the schedule. There were weaknesses, however, which stemmed from the lack

[14] See for example, Frank Harary, Robert Z. Norman and Dorwin Cartwright, *Structural Models: An Introduction to the Theory of Direct Graphs* (New York: John Wiley & Sons, Inc., 1965).

[15] Henry L. Gantt (1861–1919), an associate of Frederick W. Taylor known for his production control contributions to management.

TIMING SCHEDULE FOR A NEW CAR

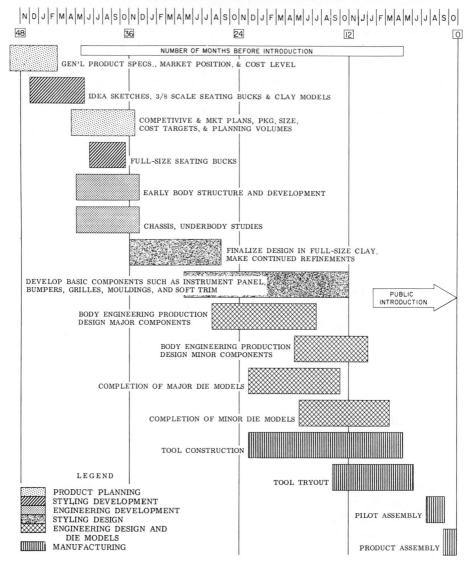

FIGURE 10.6 *Project planning chart for new car introduction.*
Courtesy Chrysler Corporation.

of interconnectedness in the design of the project stages and in the allocation of resources to the design stages.

Networks are the epitome of interconnectedness. They provided the
opportunity to consider the project as a whole relating the parts of the
network in such a way that compensating changes in resource allocations

can be made at various points so as to permit major improvements in sequencing and resource utilization.[16]

Starting about 1957, a number of approaches to this problem were begun at different locations and for different reasons. The reassuring thing about these efforts is the fact that in spite of a variety of names that emerged to label each system, they all turned out to be fundamentally alike. A rash of acronyms, such as those below, began to appear in literature devoted to the project planning area.

PERT — Program Evaluation Research Task[17]
CPM — Critical Path Method
PRISM — Program Reliability Information System for Management
PEP — Program Evaluation Procedure
IMPACT — Integrated Managerial Programming Analysis Control Technique
SCANS — Scheduling and Control by Automated Network Systems
ICON — Integrated Control
MPACS — Management Planning and Control System
PAR — Project Audit Report
PLANNET — Planning Network
RAMPS — Resources Allocation and Multi-Project Scheduling
LESS — Least Cost Estimating and Scheduling
SPERT — Schedule Performance Evaluation and Review Technique
TOES — Trade-Off Evaluation System
TOPS — The Operational PERT System

The differences among the approaches are primarily those of emphasis, arising as a consequence of the specific job for which the method was designed. PERT was developed by the U.S. Navy Special Projects Office in conjunction with Booz, Allen and Hamilton. It was one of the first of the network methods, and was used for the Polaris project. CPM was developed by E. I. duPont de Nemours and Company and Remington Rand at about the same time as PERT, and was used to plan the construction of a plant. These two approaches focus on removing similar deficiencies of the old project planning methods.

Since these network methods share in common the unifying notion of a *critical path,* we have chosen to call this section "Critical Path Network Models." PERT is one of the most familiar names to managers and we will, therefore, discuss the PERT variant of Critical Path Methods.

Three steps are required to utilize these network analytic tools.

1. All the elements, jobs, steps, tasks, activities, and so on, that are

---

[16] See Martino, R. L., *Project Management and Control,* New York: American Management Association, 1964.
[17] Also called, Program Evaluation and Review Technique.

required to bring the project to fruition must be detailed. The level of detail is to be commensurate with the degree of schedule control that is to be exercised.

2. A sequencing order must be determined which is based on technological and administrative dependencies. In other words, all necessary sequential constraints must be made explicit.

3. The time (and cost) to perform each task or activity must be estimated.

When all this information has been assembled, a PERT network can be constructed. Figure 10.7 presents an example of such a network.

PROPULSION FLOW CHART

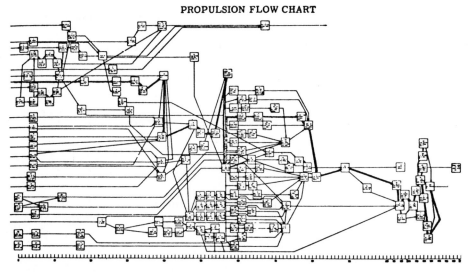

FIGURE 10.7   *An example of a complex PERT network.* From R. A. Niemann and R. N. Learn, "Mechanization of the PERT system on NORC," Technical Memorandum No. K-19/59, U.S. Naval Weapons Laboratory (Washington, D. C.: U. S. Government Printing Office, 1960).

Detail is essential for the success of the CPM's. Activities cannot be overlooked without adversely affecting the results. Various estimates are required for each activity, with the result that, for normally complex projects a gigantic amount of information is generated. Fortunately, computer programs have been developed for most of the network systems.

Many applications of Critical Path Methods can be found for management problems. Thus, an operating enterprise may wish to develop a new process, film a movie or stage a play, build a new plant (for example, see Figure 10.8), work on a government contract, provide a new

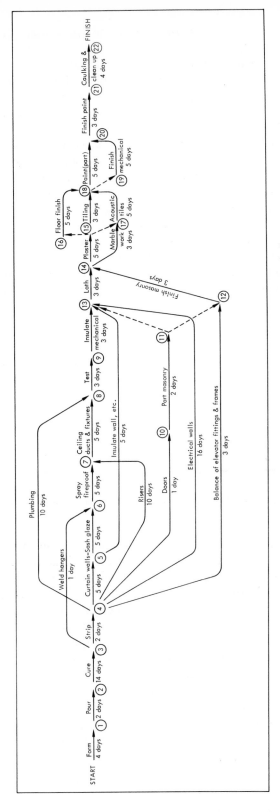

FIGURE 10.8 CPM diagram for a construction of a typical floor in a multistory building. Redrawn from Engineering News-Record, January 26, 1961, Mc-Graw-Hill Book Co., Inc.

service, or diversify into an entirely new area of endeavor. Government agencies have found Critical Path Methods so useful that they frequently require this approach from companies working on government contracts. This is particularly true when an integrated effort on the part of several companies is needed.

We recognize that the network approach is a means of unifying the totality of activities, problems, decisions, and operations that relate to management objectives. Each activity is shown as an arrow. There is nothing sacred about the arrangement of activities; good design is the criterion. The completion of an activity is called an *event* and as shown in Figures 10.9, 10.11, 10.12, etc., is represented as a circle. In planning a project, some activities go through a cycle of steps and then repeat themselves, once or many times, at increasing levels of detail. Cycles of activities (which would also be characteristic of control system functions) are not permitted in these networks. Cycles must be depicted in *extensive* form as shown in Figure 10.9.

Consider the 2–3 cycle:

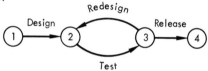

this must be treated as follows:

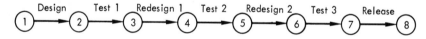

FIGURE 10.9   PERT *networks must be developed in extensive form.*

We observe many different configurations of activities and events. Some are arranged in series, meaning that the first activity must be finished before the succeeding one can begin. In other cases, several arrows emanate from a single event circle. These activities can parallel each other. Whenever materials, parts, sub-assemblies, or particular procedures come together for a new activity, an event circle must be used to signify that the previous activity has been completed. Proceeding in this way it is not difficult, although it may be tedious, to lay out the relevant network of activities and events.

The PERT system requires that three estimates be made for each activity. These are estimates of the time that will be required to complete the activity. The planner is asked to supply: (1) an optimistic estimate—called a; (2) a pessimistic estimate—called b; and (3) an estimate of what is most likely—called *m*. These three estimates are then combined to give *an expected elapsed time*—called t_e. The formula for achieving the combination is:

$$t_e = K_1 (a + b) + K_2(m)$$

where K_1 and K_2 are derived weights.[18] A possible distribution for the elapsed time estimates is shown in Figure 10.10. Some individuals seem to think that the combination of estimates provides greater accuracy in estimating, whereas others do not. Because estimates can be checked against actuality it should be possible to determine what is best for a particular kind of project. In any case, at the heart of the issue is the need to develop some reasonably good estimate for the expected elapsed time required for the completion of an activity.

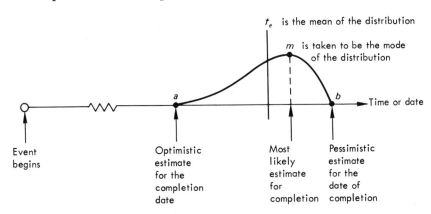

FIGURE 10.10 *A possible distribution for the elapsed time estimates. (There is no assurance that the three estimates* a, m, *and* b *fall at these positions on the time scale of the distribution.)*

In addition, an estimate of the variances associated with the expected value of elapsed time is also frequently supplied for the PERT system. The sum of the variances of a number of consecutive estimates of sequenced *independent* activities measures the variance of the total sequence. For example, if three estimates, t_{e_1}, t_{e_2}, and t_{e_3} are made, each of them having a particular variance measure σ_1^2, σ_2^2, σ_3^2, then the variance of the sum of these estimates is given by $\sigma_1^2 + \sigma_2^2 + \sigma_3^2$. This relationship is depicted in Figure 10.11. The formula for the variance of an elapsed time estimate is given by $\sigma^2 = [K_3(b - a)]^2$, where K_3 is a derived weight.[19]

---

[18] Frequently, the weights are taken as $K_1 = \frac{1}{6}$ and $K_2 = \frac{2}{3}$. These values are associated with the estimate of the mean of a Beta distribution.

[19] Generally, $K_3 = \frac{1}{6}$, which is associated with the estimate of the variance of a Beta distribution.

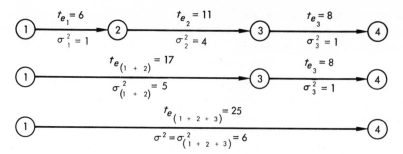

FIGURE 10.11 *The variance, σ^2, of combined estimates is equal to the sum of the variances of the individual estimates of* **independent** *activities.*

Let us take an abstract **PERT** network (see Figure 10.12) and apply the estimates which have been hypothetically obtained. We see that each arrow is labeled with an expected elapsed time. In addition, the variance is shown for each activity as a number within the parentheses.

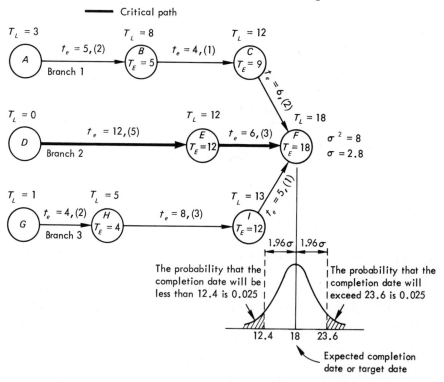

FIGURE 10.12 *An abstract* **PERT** *network with hypothetical estimates supplied for* t_e's *and* σ^2's. *(The variance is shown within parentheses.)*

We next obtain a cumulative total for each branch, moving along the particular branch from the beginning of the project to the end, and call this value T_E. This cumulative total gives the expected clock time that each event will begin. The event circles, or nodes, enclose these numbers. It will be noted that as we sum along different branches until we arrive at a junction node, that the joining branches can carry a different cumulative number to that node. Whenever this condition arises at a junction node, *we accept the largest value of* T_E. All further accumulation proceeds with this larger number. The logic behind this will become apparent in a moment. The last node in the network represents project completion. It now bears a value which is the measure of the *maximum* cumulative time, that is, the time required to perform the longest time-sequence of activities in the network. Examination of Figure 10.12 will show that the middle branch dominates the cumulative total that has been carried forward. This branch requires the longest elapsed time for completion and is called the *critical path* of the system.

Now let us see how we make use of the critical path that has been determined. Starting with the largest cumulative total, T_E, which resulted from the second branch, and which is the estimated, expected time for *job completion,* we now move backwards through the network. Then, successively, we subtract from each previously accepted T_E value all expected elapsed activity times, t_e, that immediately precede it in the network. These values, called T_L, are assigned to the event nodes that precede their respective activities. In some cases, when moving backwards, two or more branches converge on a node such that the values of T_L produced by subtraction are not equal. Then, *we accept the smallest value of* T_L.

The difference, $T_L - T_E$, can now be obtained for each event node. It describes the amount of *slack* that exists at each node. By slack we mean that the specific time estimates can slip by the amount of slack that exists, and the total job can still be completed on time. As expected, at every node of the critical path which, by definition, dominates the system, $T_L - T_E = 0$. In general, a branch has as much slack as the time required to complete the branch requirements is *less* than the time required to complete the project stages that make up the critical path. For our example, the top branch has the most slack and the bottom branch has a small amount.

This finding is not trivial because we know now that it would be wasteful to do any *expediting* on either the top or bottom branches. The critical path (middle branch), cannot be allowed to slip. If it does, it will directly affect the project completion date. Therefore, the major emphasis of project control should be assigned to the critical path which is the middle branch.

We can see from these results why this system is often called PERT/
TIME. Time is the only factor under consideration. It is the fundamental dimension of the planners' objectives. With this idea in mind,
the variance measure can now be used. (It should be noted, however,
that this procedure is not a mathematically rigorous one.) We sum the
variances, proceeding along the critical path branch. Thus, for the final
event which signals completion of the job we can obtain not only the
expected time for project completion but also an estimate of the variance around this expected value. Figure 10.12 shows a distribution with
both tails marked at the 1.96 sigma limit. Each tail contains the probabilities of an event occurring approximately 25 out of 1000 times.[20]
The upper tail contains very long completion dates. The lower tail contains very short completion dates. Thus, moving 1.96 standard deviations
(1.96σ) in either direction gives us a range of times for job completion
within which there is a 95 percent probability that the actual completion date will be met. Stated another way, we have determined, utilizing
a 1.96σ criterion, an earliest and a latest project completion date.

TABLE 10.1

Computations Associated with PERT Network
(in the general form utilized for computer systems)

Event	T_E	T_L	Slack $(T_L - T_E)$	Cumulative variance
F	18	18	0	8
C	9	12	3	3
I	12	13	1	5
E	12	12	0	5
B	5	8	3	2
H	4	5	1	2
G	0	1	1	0
D	0	0	0	0
A	0	3	3	0

The computations that have been utilized in order to determine the
critical path do not require that the network be drawn up; they can be
handled in tabular form as in Table 10.1.

[20] Assuming that a Normal distribution applies, we would have:

Number of Standard Deviations for the Specification of the Range	Probability that the Actual Time Falls Within the Specified Range
1σ	0.680
1.64σ	0.900
1.96σ	0.950
3σ	0.997

The method we have used can be further interpreted to imply that a better arrangement of resource utilization might be found. Any alteration that reduces the length of the critical path would decrease the amount of slack that has been observed in the other branches of the network. A reasonable approach would be: (1) to obtain and employ new resources toward this end, and (2) to shift resources, wherever possible, from the branches having the largest amount of slack to the critical path.

Considering the second alternative, let us assume that the length of time it takes to complete each activity is linearly related to the number of men employed on the job. Assuming that the skills required are interchangeable between branches, we could then bring the entire network into better balance by shifting manpower resources from slack branches to the critical path. This has been done for the previous example, and the results are shown in Figure 10.13. In general, we cannot hope to

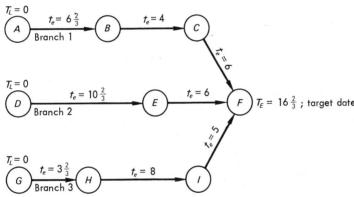

FIGURE 10.13 *A perfectly balanced PERT network is achieved —for the example in the text—by trading-off resources. (Note: We have permitted the resources to be fractionated and have used the following balancing equations: (1) for the top and middle branches, $15 + x = 18 - k_1x$; (2) for the top and bottom branches, $15 + x = 17 - k_2x$; (3) where $k_1 + k_2 = 1$; (4) then: $x = 5/3$, $k_1 = 4/5$, $k_2 = 1/5$; (5) and x = the amount of time added to the top branch, k_1x = the amount of time subtracted from the middle branch, k_2x = the amount of time subtracted from the bottom branch. All branches are critical paths—there is no slack in the system. The target date has been improved by $1\frac{1}{3}$ time units.*

achieve such perfect balance because men, machines, and other resources cannot be fractionated at will, and because all skills and facilities are not readily interchangeable between branches. But to the extent that changes can be made, we usually can achieve considerable improvement in the time performance of the system. The ability to recognize slack paths, and to trade-off resources makes Critical Path Methods significantly more useful than the older methods associated with the Gantt Project Chart. The paths of greatest slack provide the best opportunities for improving the target date of the project. On the other hand, they also point to places where effort would be wasted in expediting work to meet scheduled deadlines.

Sometimes it is possible to utilize whatever expediting and control facilities exist to improve the variance (estimates) along the critical path. By doing this, we do not change the target date, but instead we *reduce the risk* of substantially deviating from the target date.

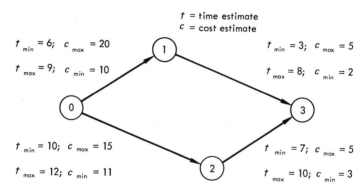

t = time estimate
c = cost estimate

$t_{min} = 6;\ c_{max} = 20$
$t_{max} = 9;\ c_{min} = 10$

$t_{min} = 3;\ c_{max} = 5$
$t_{max} = 8;\ c_{min} = 2$

$t_{min} = 10;\ c_{max} = 15$
$t_{max} = 12;\ c_{min} = 11$

$t_{min} = 7;\ c_{max} = 5$
$t_{max} = 10;\ c_{min} = 3$

FIGURE 10.14   *A PERT/COST network with hypothetical data. For minimum cost, 0-2-3 is the critical path, with $T_E = 22$ and cost $= 14$. The slack for 0-1-3 is $T_L - T_E = 5$. Assume that T_E must be no greater than 20. The best COST/TIME ratio applying to the critical path is associated with activity 2-3 (see Figure 10.15). Making the required change, we obtain: $t_{23} = 8;\ c_{23} = 4\frac{1}{3}$. This gives 0-2-3 as the critical path with $T_E = 20$ and cost $= 15\frac{1}{3}$. The slack for 0-1-3 is $T_L - T_E = 3$.*

The utilization of the Critical Path Method has been extended in a number of different ways. Of interest to project planners, in addition to the time objective, is the desire to maximize the quality of the work or the performance characteristics of the system. Another major objective is to *minimize cost*. The relationships of cost and time have received considerable investigation. Various time-cost systems have been developed and others are being developed to attempt to resolve this problem, which we recognize as one of conflicting multiple objectives.

The PERT/COST system starts in the same way as does PERT/TIME, that is, we construct the representative network of activities and events.

We shall use the hypothetical network shown in Figure 10.14. However, in this case we have developed two different estimates for each branch. These are: (1) a minimum time estimate and its cost; and (2) a minimum cost estimate and its time. Figure 10.15 shows the way in which these factors might be related for each of the branches of our network.

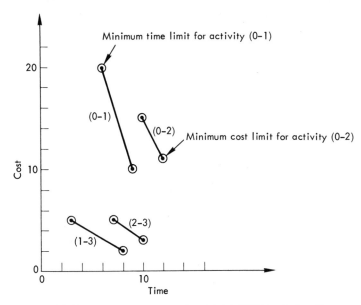

FIGURE 10.15 *Some representative COST/TIME relationships where the weak assumption is made that linearity prevails over the specified range. The end points are assumed to be limits. If all minimum times are used, we have a "crash" program; if all minimum costs are used, we have a budget-constrained program.*

The minimum cost estimate (the second of the two listed above) is used for each activity, and the critical path is determined for those data. The result will then be a completion date that is based on minimum cost requirements for completing the project. This completion date and the length of time required to complete the project under minimum cost conditions may be too great to be tolerated. Accordingly, alternative times, requiring greater costs, can then be substituted for chosen minimum cost activities along the critical path. In this way, the critical path can be shortened until such time that: (1) another branch becomes critical; or (2) a satisfactory compromise with the original critical path is achieved. As a *rule of thumb,* we make compromises for those activities along the critical path where the ratio of increasing costs for the activity with respect to decreasing time for the activity is smallest. Thus, we select that critical path activity where Δ cost/Δ time is smallest. Then the next biggest ratio is used, and so on until a satisfactory compromise between time and cost is achieved.

The PERT/COST method can be modified to meet the particular requirements of a given project. It is not an optimizing technique. Instead, it is a logical attempt to utilize reasonable trade-offs between cost and time, where they count, in order to obtain an approximation to an optimal result.

96/ A (Linear) Programming Model for the Allocation of Production Facilities

A major production problem arises in connection with the allocation of productive facilities. This kind of problem can produce large savings resulting from the determination of the optimal strategy. Some of the most spectacular results of operations research have been obtained through analyses of this class of decision problem. Again, we wish to emphasize that our approach is based on decision-making under certainty. We assume "relatively" determinate conditions and the existence of discrete possibilities from which a solution must be chosen. These are circumstances that we have come to associate with a large segment of all production problems.

It will be convenient to take a simple example around which we can develop our discussion of the powerful LP model. Consider a small plant which has two departments, grinding and plating. The plant makes two products. Each must be processed in both departments. No specific sequence of operations is required.

The capacities of the two departments are different for the two products and the profit per item is also different. The relevant data can be summarized in a table.

	CAPACITIES (PER DAY)		
PRODUCT	DEPT. I, GRINDING	DEPT. II, PLATING	PROFIT PER UNIT
A	400 units	250 units	$1.00
B	200 units	400 units	1.25

The decision problem is: *How many units of each product should be produced? The objective is to achieve the maximum profit.* We have referred to this as a decision problem in the allocation of productive facilities because we can also ask: How much of the capacity of each department should be allocated to each product?

Is this a real problem or is the solution obvious? We could produce product *A* only. In that case, we are limited by Dept. II to a total production of 250 units *and a profit of $250.* There will be *excess* capacity in Dept. I since we shall use only $250/400 = 62.5$ per cent of its capacity. But there is no advantage in using this capacity to produce product *B* because there is no capacity left in Dept. II. Similarly, we could produce product *B* only. In this case, we are limited by Dept. I to 200 units *and a profit of* $200 \times \$1.25 = \$250$. Dept. II would have 50 per cent of its capacity unused but the Dept. I bottleneck would prevent its utilization. In both cases, we have made the same profit, $250. Is this the best that can be done? The fact that each of these two possibilities leaves unused capacity is sufficient to make us wonder whether we can find a production combination of *A* and *B* which would utilize more capacity and return a larger profit. Does it exist?

In decision-theory terms the problem is clear. The available strategies are all possible combinations of the amount of *A* and *B* which are within the capacities of the two departments. The profit possibilities and capacity restrictions are known and for any given amount of *A* and *B* the outcome is *certain,* a calculable amount of profit. The difficulty is the usual one in this kind of decision-making. The number of possible strategies is exceedingly large. How can we find the optimal one?

The first thing to emphasize is the meaning of capacity. Dept. I can produce either 400 units of *A* or 200 units of *B, not both.* Of course, combinations of the amount of *A* and *B* can be produced providing the total capacity is not exceeded. How can we tell what combinations are permissible? Fortunately, this is easy to answer. It is only necessary to determine the percentages of capacity of the two departments which are used up by the production of one unit of each product. One unit of *A* uses up $1/400 = 0.25$ per cent of the capacity of Dept. I and $1/250 = 0.4$ per cent of the capacity of Dept. II. One unit of *B* uses up $1/200 = 0.5$ per cent of the capacity of Dept. I and $1/400 = 0.25$ per cent of the capacity of Dept. II. These data can be presented in tabular form.

PERCENTAGE OF CAPACITY,
REPRESENTED BY ONE UNIT

PRODUCT	DEPT. I	DEPT. II
A	0.25%	0.40%
B	0.50%	0.25%

This conversion to percentages of capacity is based on a hidden assumption, namely, that a linear relationship exists between capacity and amount produced. We have assumed that the production of twice as many units will take twice as much capacity. This is, frequently, a reasonable assumption—it is always a crucial one. If it is not true, the analysis of this kind of decision problem becomes more difficult. Fortunately, it is often so nearly true that the discrepancy does not seriously affect the analysis.

Once these percentages have been calculated it is easy to determine *which combinations of amounts* of *A* and *B* are within the capacity limitations of each department. Any combination is permissible which doesn't exceed 100 per cent of capacity. Thus, for Dept. I we could have combinations such as:

FEASIBLE DEPT. I STRATEGIES				
PRODUCT *A*		PRODUCT *B*		TOTAL PERCENTAGE
UNITS	PERCENTAGES	UNITS	PERCENTAGES	
400	100	0	0	100
300	75	50	25	100
200	50	100	50	100
100	25	150	75	100
0	0	200	100	100

All possible combinations for Dept. I can be summarized with an inequation:

$$\text{Dept. I: } 0.25X_A + 0.50X_B \leq 100.00$$

where X_A and X_B are the amounts of *A* and *B* respectively. (It will be remembered that the sign, $\leq$, is read "less than or equal to" and that we usually refer to mathematical expressions containing this symbol as *inequations*. It is symbolic representation of the fact that there is no requirement to use up the full 100 per cent of Dept. I's capacity.)

For Dept. II we could have such combinations as:

FEASIBLE DEPT. II STRATEGIES				
PRODUCT *A*		PRODUCT *B*		TOTAL PERCENTAGE
UNITS	PERCENTAGES	UNITS	PERCENTAGES	
250	100	0	0	100
200	80	80	20	100
150	60	160	40	100
100	40	240	60	100
50	20	320	80	100
0	0	400	100	100

We can summarize all possible combinations for Dept. II with its appropriate inequation:

$$\text{Dept. II: } 0.40X_A + 0.25X_B \leq 100.00$$

where X_A, X_B, and $\leq$ have the same meaning as above.

The particular *combinations of amounts* of A and B produced which are given in the above two tables represent only a few examples from the total number of possibilities for each department. Some of the possibilities given in one table are impossible in the other. For example, in Dept. I we could produce 200 units of A and 100 units of B, but the table for Dept. II shows that if we produce 200 units of A we can only produce 80 units of B. This shows that *not all the solutions of the Dept. I inequation are possible strategies. Nor, of course, are all solutions of the Dept. II inequation.* Some of the combinations in one table are, however, possible in the other table. For example, the combination 200, 80 is possible. As another illustration, Dept. I could produce 100 units of A and 150 units of B and the table for Dept. II shows that with 100 units of A we could produce as much as 240 units of B. *The smaller of the two is always limiting.* To produce 100 units of A and 150 units of B is a possible strategy.

We have, then, two problems. *First,* we must determine what strategies are possible for all inequations. In the mathematical theory which underlies our analysis the possible strategies are called the *feasible solutions* of the equations. *Second,* we must locate that particular strategy which will yield the largest profit. One could try to proceed by determining the possible strategies, calculating the profit resulting from each, and then selecting the strategy with the largest profit. This would generally be prohibitively time-consuming, if not impossible, so it is necessary to find more expeditious means.

Such means are available in the form of a procedure which requires only some repeated simple algebraic manipulations. The idea behind the procedure is to start with *any* possible strategy *(feasible solution,* in the mathematician's terms) and to determine the profit which would result from that strategy. Then a criterion is applied to determine whether it is possible to increase the profit by switching to a different *feasible* strategy. If it is possible to increase the profit another criterion tells us how to find a strategy which does increase profit. Once this is accomplished, the procedure is repeated. When the profit cannot be increased by switching to any other strategy we know that we have found the optimal strategy.

The *first* thing we need to use this procedure is a quick means of calculating the profit from any specific strategy. This is easy to achieve using the symbols we have already introduced. Since the amounts of A

and B which are produced by any specific strategy are designated X_A and X_B, we have:

$$\text{Profit} = 1.00X_A + 1.25X_B$$

where the profit is \$1.00 for each unit of A produced and \$1.25 for each unit of B. One hundred units of A and 150 units of B would produce a profit of \$1.00(100 + \$1.25(150) = \$287.50.

Second, we must include symbols for all the possible components of our strategies, i.e., the various amounts of A and B which might be produced. For any specific *combination of amounts* we might find that some of the capacity of Dept. I and/or Dept. II was unused. In mathematics (like accounting) interrelated quantities must balance. So symbols are required to represent the fact that our strategies may not utilize the full capacity of one or both departments.

We have already obtained inequations expressing the capacity restrictions of Dept. I and II. These inequations are more flexible than equations precisely because they allow for a part of capacity not to be utilized. Therefore, by introducing symbols for unused capacity we can convert the inequations to equations. Letting X_1 represent unused capacity in Dept. I we can change Dept. I's inequation

$$0.25X_A + 0.50X_B \leq 100.00$$

to an equation:

$$0.25X_A + 0.50X_B + X_1 = 100.00$$

This equation expresses the amount of unused capacity in Dept. I for any specific strategy. Thus, the strategy of producing 250 units of A and zero units of B results in:

$$0.25(250) + 0.50(0) + X_1 = 100.00$$
or
$$X_1 = 100 - 0.25(250) = 37.50$$

Thus, for this strategy there is 37.5 per cent of unused capacity in Dept. I. Similarly, let X_2 equal the unused capacity in Dept. II and convert the inequation

$$0.40X_A + 0.25X_B \leq 100.00$$

to the equation:

$$0.40X_A + 0.25X_B + X_2 = 100.00$$

For the strategy $X_A = 250$, $X_B = 0$, we see that $X_2 = 0$, which means that there is no unused capacity in Dept. II. The variables, X_1 and X_2, are often called *slack variables* because they take up the slack in the inequations, permitting them to become equations.

All necessary preliminary work is now done and we have a simple mathematical model for this type of decision problem. Our objective is to maximize profits subject to the capacity limitations of the two departments. Our mathematical model has an objective function to maximize:

$$\text{MAX } [\text{Profit} = 1.00X_A + 1.25X_B]$$

subject to the constraints:

$$0.25X_A + 0.50X_B + X_1 = 100.00$$

and

$$0.40X_A + 0.25X_B + X_2 = 100.00$$

Our outline of the procedure to find the optimal strategy suggested the following steps:

1. *Start* with a *feasible* strategy.

2. *Determine the profit* from that strategy.

3. *Use a criterion to see whether profit could be increased* by using some other strategy.

4. *If profit can be increased, use some criterion to discover a larger profit strategy.*

5. *Repeat the process until step 3 shows that no other strategy will increase profit.* The optimal strategy has, then, been found.

We shall follow these steps to find the optimal strategy for our example.

In choosing a feasible strategy with which to start the search for the optimal strategy, there is one major requirement.

It can be shown mathematically that the optimal strategy will not include more components than the number of restrictions.[21]

In our case we have *four variables which may be components* of the optimal strategy: X_A, X_B, X_1, and X_2. Since we have only *two* restrictions (the two equations expressing the department capacity limitations) we know that the optimal strategy will contain at most *two* variables. The other two variables will be zero. *The requirement for the strategy with which we start our search is, then, that it should contain only two of the variables at nonzero levels.* This still leaves a number of possible starting points.[22]

Expressed mathematically, we start with two of the four variables hav-

---

[21] This *fundamental theorem of linear programming* also accounted for the $P + W - 1$ rule encountered in the transportation algorithm. When the transportation model is set up in LP form, it becomes apparent that there are exactly $P + W - 1$ effective constraints.

[22] It will be useful to recall the northwest corner method (p. 272) which produced a first feasible solution for the transportation algorithm.

ing nonzero values. The equations must be satisfied given that the *other two* variables are zero. For example, we can start with $X_1 = 100$ per cent and $X_2 = 100$ per cent, which satisfies the equations when X_A and X_B are both equal to zero. This *starting* strategy would not produce anything. Or we could start with X_A and X_1, since $X_A = 250$ and $X_1 = 37.5$ per cent satisfy the equations when X_B and X_2 are both equal to zero. This would be the strategy of producing only A, and we have already seen that this leaves 37.5 per cent ($X_1 = 37.5$ per cent) of the capacity of Dept. I unutilized. Or we could start with X_B and X_2, since $X_B = 200$ and $X_2 = 50$ per cent satisfy the equations with X_A and X_1 both equal to zero. This is the strategy of producing nothing but B.

We start with X_1 and X_2. It is *always possible to begin with the slack variables* set equal to the maximum* constraint values, even though such strategies produce nothing. The next step is to determine that strategy's profit. In this case, there is no profit. The strategy uses only X_1 and X_2—we are producing nothing. The third step is to discover whether some other strategy would produce a larger profit. *The criterion for doing this is based on the fact that none of the variables in our equations (X_A, X_B, X_1, and X_2) can be negative.* It is meaningless to have a negative amount produced or a negative amount of capacity.

Look at our objective function. It now includes the slack variables and will change in form as we proceed.

$$\text{Profit} = 1.00X_A + 1.25X_B + (0)X_1 + (0)X_2$$

If any variables occur in this equation with positive coefficients it follows (since the variables cannot be negative) that the profit objective can be improved by increasing that variable. Both X_A and X_B have positive coefficients, so we know that profit can be increased by increasing either X_A or X_B.

The fourth step is to find a strategy which will increase profit. We know that only two of the four variables can occur at nonzero levels in the optimal strategy. Therefore, the only way we can include X_A or X_B is by *replacing either X_1 or X_2 by X_A or X_B*. To decide which to replace, we can rewrite our two equations making X_1 and X_2 the dependent variables.

$$X_1 = 100 - 0.25X_A - 0.50X_B$$
$$X_2 = 100 - 0.40X_A - 0.25X_B$$

Profit can be raised by increasing either X_A or X_B. We make only one change at a time and it may as well be that change which produces the greatest increase in unit profit. Consequently, *choose the variable with*

---

* Or minimum, using so-called "artificial variables." In this case, we could arbitrarily assign (say) X_3 and X_4 equal to the minimum values, removing them from the solution in the first steps that are taken.

the largest positive coefficient in the objective equation. It is X_B, with a coefficient of 1.25. We propose to replace either X_1 or X_2 by X_B to get a new, more profitable strategy. Which shall be replaced?

We want to make X_B as large as possible because the larger it is the more profit will be made. But neither X_1 nor X_2 can be negative, and this places a restriction on how large we can make X_B. According to the first equation above, X_B cannot be larger than $100/0.50 = 200$ because if it were larger than this X_1 would have to be negative. According to the second equation, X_B cannot be larger than $100/0.25 = 400$, because if it were larger than this X_2 would have to be negative. The actual limit to the size of X_B is, therefore, the smaller of these two limits, 200, which results from X_1. We shall, therefore replace X_1 by X_B to obtain a new, more profitable strategy.

To achieve this change in strategy, we now use *algebraic manipulation.* Later, the simplex algorithm will be presented. The simplex is a *matrix method* capable of accomplishing the same ends—in much the same way—but with far less computational demands. The algebraic approach is one of the best ways of explaining what the simplex method does.

Using algebra, solve the first equation for X_B. Then, substitute this expression for X_B in the second equation and in the objective function. Thus, from

$$X_1 = 100 - 0.25X_A - 0.50X_B$$

we get

$$0.50X_B = 100 - 0.25X_A - X_1$$

or

$$X_B = 200 - 0.50X_A - 2X_1$$

Substituting *this* expression for X_B in the next equation gives

$$\begin{aligned} X_2 &= 100 - 0.40X_A - 0.25(200 - 0.50X_A - 2X_1) \\ &= 100 - 0.400X_A - 50 + 0.125X_A + 0.500X_1 \\ &= 50 - 0.275X_A + 0.500X_1 \end{aligned}$$

and substituting the expression for X_B in the objective function gives

$$\begin{aligned} \text{Profit} &= 1X_A + 1.25(200 - 0.50X_A - 2X_1) \\ &= 1X_A + 250 - 0.625X_A - 2.500X_1 \\ &= 250 + 0.375X_A - 2.500X_1 \end{aligned}$$

These calculations have already accomplished steps 1 and 2 of the next cycle of our search. Our new strategy involves X_B and X_2. Thus:

$$\begin{aligned} X_B &= 200 - 0.500X_A - 2.00X_1 \\ X_2 &= 50 - 0.275X_A - 0.50X_1 \end{aligned}$$

If we were to use this strategy, X_A and X_1 would both be zero, so our equations tell us exactly what the values of X_B and X_2 are and also the resulting profit. This strategy has $X_B = 200$ (produce 200 units of B) and $X_2 = 50$ (leave 50 per cent of the capacity of Dept. II unutilized). The resulting profit is $\$1(0) + \$1.25(200) + \$0(0) + \$0(50) = \$250$.

We had previously calculated this particular strategy by cut-and-try methods, and we might have used it as our starting strategy. But our procedure has produced it automatically. Now, we need to apply step 3 again. Our objective function has become:

$$\text{Profit} = 250 + 0.375X_A - 2.500X_1$$

Can we increase profit by some other strategy? Since the coefficient of X_A is positive, we see that profit can be increased by including X_A. Note that we cannot increase profit by increasing X_1. An increase in X_1 would decrease profit. We want, therefore, to find a new strategy which will increase X_A. This can only be done by replacing either X_B or X_2 by X_A.

The two restricting equations show the limits of the amounts by which X_A can be increased. From the equation for X_B we see that X_A cannot be larger than $200/0.50 = 400$ since otherwise, X_B would have to be negative. From the equation for X_2 we see that X_A cannot be larger than $50/0.275 = 181.8$. The limit on the size of X_A is X_2. We shall replace X_2 by X_A in our next strategy and this is done in the same way as before. First, solve the X_2 equation for X_A.

$$X_2 = 50 - 0.275X_A + 0.500X_1$$

Rearranging gives: $0.275X_A = 50 - X_2 + 0.500X_1$

or $X_A = 181.8 - 3.636X_2 + 1.818X_1$

Then, substitute this expression for X_A in the X_B equation and the objective equation.

$$
\begin{aligned}
X_B &= 200 - 0.5(181.8 - 3.636X_2 + 1.818X_1) - 2X_1 \\
&= 200 - 90.9 + 1.818X_2 - 0.909X_1 - 2X_1 \\
&= 109.1 + 1.818X_2 - 2.909X_1
\end{aligned}
$$

and

$$
\begin{aligned}
\text{Profit} &= 250 + 0.375(181.8 - 3.636X_2 + 1.818X_1) - 2.5X_1 \\
&= 250 + 68.18 - 1.364X_2 + 0.6818X_1 - 2.5X_1 \\
&= 318.18 - 1.364X_2 - 1.8182X_1
\end{aligned}
$$

Again, steps 1 and 2 have been accomplished by our calculations. This strategy is to produce 109.1 units of B and 181.8 units of A with a total profit of \$318.18. (To get these values simply set $X_1 = 0$ and $X_2 = 0$ in the two equations and the objective equation.) In repeating step 3 we see that *profit cannot be increased any more* because both X_1 and X_2 occur in the objective equation with *negative coefficients*. The optimal strategy is, therefore, the one we have just stated. No other strategy can produce a larger profit. It will be noted that the optimal strategy *in this example* leaves no unused capacity in either department (X_1 and X_2 both equal zero). This is by no means always the case. Optimal strategies often leave some capacity unused.

Before moving on to the simplex algorithm, we should note that all of our equations (the objective function and the constraints) were of linear form—ergo, *linear* programming. This is graphically evident when we turn to the geometric resolution of our problem.[23] Since the geometric properties of our problem are representable (because it is small enough to be shown in two dimensions) we can derive the same final solution at point (*c*) in yet another way, as shown in Figure 10.16.

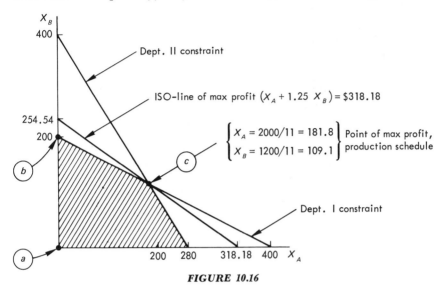

FIGURE 10.16

Many problems are treated as linear even though they are only "relatively" so. Generally speaking, a surprising amount of flexibility exists within which *approximations work quite well*. However, for those circumstances where nonlinearity clearly affects the situation, several approaches can be used. These include methods for *transforming* certain kinds of nonlinearities into linear systems. Also, nonlinear programming models have been developed which, although cumbersome, are effective—especially when programmed for the computer. An ever present alternative, frequently used, is to treat the problem with linear programming as a base, working in conjunction with sensitivity analysis and liberal amounts of intuition.

97/ The Simplex Algorithm for Linear Programming

The simplex method (or related variants) for solving LP problems has a number of distinct advantages over other mathematical techniques

---

[23] See pp. 217–222 for prior discussion of the geometric approach.

that might also be used.[24] In fact, it is fair to say that without the simplex as a means of calculating all of the steps necessary to solve large LP problems, linear programming would still be a concept, not a working method. Small LP problems are not typical of the needs of potential users of the model. The essence of these decision problems under *certainty,* it should be remembered, is the extraordinary size of the search that is required to discover the optimal strategy. But the simplex method alone could not have turned the trick. It would not have been viewed as operational had it not been for the almost simultaneous development of computer systems (both the hardware and software) that were capable of handling the simplex's computational demands.

We can begin our description of the simplex method with a set of m inequations and n unknowns. For the example that follows, let $m = 3$ and $n = 4$. Thus:

$$\text{Equation 1} \quad a_{11}x_1 + a_{12}x_2 + a_{13}x_3 + a_{14}x_4 \leq b_1$$
$$2 \quad a_{21}x_1 + a_{22}x_2 + a_{23}x_3 + a_{24}x_4 \leq b_2$$
$$3 \quad a_{31}x_1 + a_{32}x_2 + a_{33}x_3 + a_{34}x_4 \leq b_3$$

To convert the inequations to equations, we appoint the slack variables, x_5, x_6, x_7. Because there are three constraints, there are three slack variables. This gives us:

$$\text{Equation 4} \quad a_{11}x_1 + a_{12}x_2 + a_{13}x_3 + a_{14}x_4 + x_5 + (0)x_6 + (0)x_7 = b_1$$
$$5 \quad a_{21}x_1 + a_{22}x_2 + a_{23}x_3 + a_{24}x_4 + (0)x_5 + x_6 + (0)x_7 = b_2$$
$$6 \quad a_{31}x_1 + a_{32}x_2 + a_{33}x_3 + a_{34}x_4 + (0)x_5 + (0)x_6 + x_7 = b_3$$

We must also write the appropriate objective function. Let us assume that maximization is intended.[25] Then:

$$\text{Equation 7} \quad \text{MAXIMIZE } [Z = c_1x_1 + c_2x_2 + c_3x_3 + c_4x_4 + (0)x_5 + (0)x_6 + (0)x_7]$$

Since negative amounts of activities (including the slack variables) make no sense, we must specify that:

$$\text{Equation 8} \quad x_j \geq 0 \ (j = 1, 2, 3, 4, 5, 6, 7)$$

These eight equations represent an abstract algebraic formulation. We have explored, previously, the way in which LP lends itself to algebraic manipulation with such equations. *Matrix methods,* on the other hand, embody equivalent operations, but in such a way as to organize

---

[24] For example, *Lagrangian maximization under constraint* (see pp. 336–339) is a far more burdensome method. This is true in spite of the fact that the *dual variables* of *all* LP's can be shown to be *identical* with *Lagrangian multipliers.*

[25] We are only showing maximization procedures. If the problem requires minimization then the dual can be maximized. Minimization procedures with the simplex are similar to, but not identical with, the steps we shall describe. Minimization frequently requires *artificial variables* because the slack variables carry minus signs. See LP references in the Bibliography for such expanded coverage.

and simplify the steps that must be taken to reach a solution. Let us construct the appropriate matrix, which is called a *simplex tableau.*

ϕ_i	c_i	x_i	x_1	x_2	x_3	x_4	x_5	x_6	x_7	b_i
ϕ_5	0	x_5	a_{11}	a_{12}	a_{13}	a_{14}	1	0	0	b_1
ϕ_6	0	x_6	a_{21}	a_{22}	a_{23}	a_{24}	0	1	0	b_2
ϕ_7	0	x_7	a_{31}	a_{32}	a_{33}	a_{34}	0	0	1	b_3
		c_j	c_1	c_2	c_3	c_4	0	0	0	
		BFS_1	0	0	0	0	b_1	b_2	b_3	
		c_j^*	c_1^*	c_2^*	c_3^*	c_4^*	c_5^*	c_6^*	c_7^*	

There are three boxes shown above. We can call them upper-right, upper-left and bottom. First, we shall examine how to assign specific values to all of the required entries. Then we shall explain how to use them.

The upper-right box is readily seen to be another representation of Equations 4, 5 and 6. If each row entry is multiplied by the appropriate column heading, and then these products are added, we derive the equations. To illustrate for row 1 (compare with Equation 4):

$$a_{11}x_1 + a_{12}x_2 + a_{13}x_3 + a_{14}x_4 + x_5 + (0)x_6 + (0)x_7 = b_1$$

we are now ready for:

STEP 1: Enter the appropriate values for the a_{ij}'s and the b_i's in the upper-right hand box.

There are always m columns (in the upper-right hand box) which, when taken together, form an *identity matrix.* The identity matrix is square; all of its elements are zero, *except* those on the *principal diagonal,* which are all one. Thus:

x_5	x_6	x_7
1	0	0
0	1	0
0	0	1

We use the identity matrix to process information in several different ways.

STEP 2: Let us derive *the row marked* BFS_1. It is our short-hand notation for the *first, basic feasible solution.* For each diagonal element, enter the corresponding b_i value in the BFS_1 row.

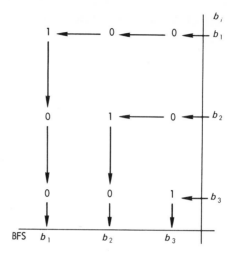

All other entries in the BFS row are zero.

STEP 3: *The column marked x_i* in the upper-left box contains a
set of x's (m of them) which represents the strategy that is
presently being evaluated. It should be noted that these
same variables head the columns of the identity matrix.
In other words, the x_i variables correspond to the unit
elements of the principal diagonal. Thus:

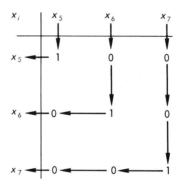

These are the same variables that have b_i values entered in the BFS row
(as in STEP 2).

At the outset, the x_i column lists the slack variables. This is always
a convenient way to begin. The first basic feasible solution, BFS_1, will
then be modified and new variables will replace the slack variables in
the x_i column. At each stage the variables in the x_i column represent
the activities or components of the strategy that is under consideration.
The corresponding b_i's are the activity levels, or amounts involved, of
each variable.

STEP 4: *The row marked c_j (top row of the bottom box) is obtained directly from the coefficients of the objective function. In this case, if we multiply each row entry by the column heading and then add the products, we derive the objective function.*

$$Z = c_1 x_1 + c_2 x_2 + c_3 x_3 + c_4 x_4 + (0)x_5 + (0)x_6 + (0)x_7$$

Since zero profit is associated with a slack variable we have zero coefficients for x_5, x_6, and x_7.

STEP 5: *The column marked c_i (upper-left box) contains the coefficients of the objective function for the corresponding x_i variables. The same values appear in the c_j row under the appropriate column headings—in this case c_5, c_6, and c_7.*

STEP 6: *Compute the c_j^* row where* $c_j^* = c_j - \sum\limits_{i=1}^{i=m} [a_{ij} c_i]$

For the first, basic feasible configuration of our example:

i	c_i	x_1	x_2	$\cdots$	x_j
1	c_5	a_{11}	a_{12}		a_{1j}
2	c_6	a_{21}	a_{22}		a_{2j}
3	c_7	a_{31}	a_{32}		a_{3j}
		c_1	c_2	$\cdots$	c_j

And:

$$c_1^* = c_1 - a_{11}c_5 - a_{21}c_6 - a_{31}c_7$$
$$c_2^* = c_2 - a_{12}c_5 - a_{22}c_6 - a_{32}c_7$$
$$\vdots$$
$$c_j^* = c_j - a_{1j}c_5 - a_{2j}c_6 - a_{3j}c_7$$

STEP 7: Select the *largest positive c_j^**. The variable heading that column is the one to put into the *next* BFS.

STEP 8: For that column, j^*, we use a ϕ test as follows:

$$\phi_5 = b_1/a_{1j^*}, \quad \phi_6 = b_2/a_{2j^*}, \quad \phi_7 = b_3/a_{3j^*}$$

Select the *smallest positive, ϕ_i*. The variable, x_i, is the one to be taken out and excluded from the next BFS.

STEP 9: We have selected a column to put in (STEP 7) and a row
to take out (STEP 8). Take the coefficient at the *intersection* of this row and column. Divide all entries of that
row—*in the upper-right hand box*—by the *intersection*
value. For example, assume that a_{22} is the intersection
value. Then our new row 2 will be:

$$\frac{a_{21}}{a_{22}} \left(\frac{a_{22}}{a_{22}} = 1 \right) \frac{a_{23}}{a_{22}} \quad \frac{a_{24}}{a_{22}} \quad \frac{0}{a_{22}} \quad \frac{1}{a_{22}} \quad \frac{0}{a_{22}} \quad \frac{b_2}{a_{22}}$$

We have in this way brought a *one* into the column of the
variable to be put in.

STEP 10: We must next reduce all other entries in the column of
j^* to *zero*. To do this *for the first row,* multiply all of
the row elements derived in STEP 9 by a_{12}. Remember
that column 2 contained the intersection value *for this
example.* Then subtract this modified row from the first
row.

$$a_{11} - \frac{a_{12}a_{21}}{a_{22}}, \quad a_{12} - \frac{a_{12}a_{22}}{a_{22}} = 0, \quad a_{13} - \frac{a_{12}a_{23}}{a_{22}}, \quad \text{etc.}$$

Call this the *new row 1*. A zero appears in *new row* 1 in
the column of the variable which is being put into the
solution. Similarly, for row 3, multiply the row elements
derived in STEP 9 by a_{32} and subtract this modified row
from row 3. Call this the *new row 3*.

STEP 11: We can now construct the tableau for BFS$_2$. Column x_i
would be changed by substituting x_2 for x_6. All of the
entries are changed in the upper-right hand box. The
old first row is replaced by the elements of the *new row*
1. The *new second row* is the one derived in STEP 9.
The old third row is replaced by the *new row 3*.

STEP 12: We can now complete all other assignments in the tableau using the rules as before. This is BFS$_2$.

Objective Z: At each step Z can be calculated by adding the products
of $c_j \times$ BFS. Thus, for the first tableau:

$$Z_1 = (c_1 \times 0) + (c_2 \times 0) + (c_3 \times 0) + (c_4 \times 0)$$
$$+ (0 \times b_1) + (0 \times b_2) + (0 \times b_3) = 0$$

The optimal solution is reached when all $c_j{}^*$'s are equal to zero or take
on negative values.

The steps outlined in the above algorithm are equivalent to a set of
well known matrix operations. Their similarity to our previous algebraic

manipulations is also quite apparent. But the individual performing these calculations need not be trained in mathematics or matrix algebra. After all, computer programs follow essentially these same steps by rote, without being aware of the power, sophistication, and intricacies of the theory that underlies their correctness. In a real sense, the more robot-like the calculator, the more dedicated his unquestioning compliance with the stated rules, the more efficient the computing procedure is likely to be. Yet, such LP resolution embodies all of the *concepts of search* we have discussed previously.

Let us complete these notions by subjecting our original example, previously solved—first by straightforward algebraic methods and then by geometric means—to the simplex algorithm. The similarities between all of these approaches should become increasingly apparent.

The simplex tableau is:

ϕ_i	c_i	x_i	x_A	x_B	x_1	x_2	b_i
ϕ_1	0	x_1	0.25	0.50	1	0	100
ϕ_2	0	x_2	0.40	0.25	0	1	100
		c_j	1	1.25	0	0	
		BFS_1	0	0	100	100	
		$c_j{}^*$	$c_A{}^*$	$c_B{}^*$	$c_1{}^*$	$c_2{}^*$	

The profit of this first tableau (STEP 12) is $(1 \times 0) + (1.25 \times 0) + (0 \times 100) + 0(100) = 0$. This solution occurs at point (*a*) in Figure 10.15. Next, to calculate which column to put in and which row to take out, we complete the $c_j{}^*$ row and the ϕ_i column. Thus:

$$c_A^* = 1 - (0.25)0 - (0.40)0 = 1$$
$$c_B^* = 1.25 - (0.50)0 - (0.25)0 = 1.25$$
$$c_1^* = 0 - (1)0 - (0)0 = 0$$
$$c_2^* = 0 - (0)0 - (1)0 = 0$$

Since $c_B{}^*$ is the *largest positive value,* we select it. This is equivalent to putting x_B into our next strategy. Then:

$$\phi_1 = 100/0.50 = 200$$
$$\phi_2 = 100/0.25 = 400$$

and since ϕ_1 is the *smallest positive value,* we choose it (which is equivalent to taking x_1 out of our strategy.

The necessary matrix changes are accomplished by means of STEPS 9, 10 and 11. The *intersection* value is 0.50.

STEP 9

	0.25/0.50	0.50/0.50	1/0.50	0/0.50	100/0.50
or	0.500	1	2	0	200

This is the *new first row.*

STEP 10

	$0.25(\frac{1}{2})$	$0.25(1)$	$0.25(2)$	$0.25(0)$	$0.25(200)$
or	0.125	0.250	0.500	0	50

This is subtracted from the *old second row*, as follows:

(old 2nd row)	0.400	0.250	0	1	100
(minus)	0.125	0.250	0.500	0	50
(new 2nd row)	0.275	0	$-\frac{1}{2}$	1	50

Now we can construct our next tableau:

ϕ_i	c_i	x_i	x_A	x_B	x_1	x_2	b_i
ϕ_B	1.25	x_B	0.500	1	2	0	200
ϕ_2	0	x_2	0.275	0	$-\frac{1}{2}$	1	50
		c_j	1	1.25	0	0	
		BFS_2	0	200	0	50	
		c_j^*	c_A^*	c_B^*	c_1^*	c_2^*	

The profit of this second tableau is $250. This solution occurs at point
(*b*) in Figure 10.15. Also, it should be noted that the new identity matrix
is composed of x_B and x_2. Proceeding in like manner, we determine which
variable to put in and which to take out:

ϕ_i	c_i	x_i	x_A	x_B	x_1	x_2	b_i
400	1.25	x_B	0.500	1	2	0	200
181.8	0	x_2	0.275	0	$-\frac{1}{2}$	1	50
		c_j	1	1.25	0	0	
		BFS_2	0	200	0	50	
		c_j^*	0.375	0	-2.50	0	

take out x_2

put in x_A

The third tableau would then be:

ϕ_i	c_i	x_i	x_A	x_B	x_1	x_2	b_i
	1.25	x_B	0	1	2.909	-1.818	109.1
	1	x_A	1	0	-1.818	3.636	181.8
		c_j	1	1.25	0	0	
		BFS_3	181.8	109.1	0	0	
		c_j^*	0	0	-1.818	-1.363	

The profit of this third tableau is $318.18. This solution occurs at point
(*c*) in Figure 10.15. The new identity matrix is composed of x_A and x_B.
And, as can be seen from the c_j^*'s, no further improvement is available.
We have derived the same final solution in three different ways. The
simplex has the advantage of being a highly routinized and compact
form of solution, ideally suited to computer operations.

Decision problems that fit the LP format occur frequently in production. The example that we have used had only two products and two departments, but precisely the same procedures would be followed if there were more products and/or more departments. And, of course, the decision problem does not have to refer to departments. Similar problems arise with machines, or for a multi-plant company, with plants instead of departments. Other restrictions than those imposed by capacity limitations can be introduced, e.g., the requirement that at least some minimum amount of a specific product be produced. The same procedure we have followed will suffice to determine the optimal strategy in any of these variants. However, as the size of the problem increases it becomes impractical to perform the necessary computations by hand. Fortunately, computers are available to handle such computations.

98/ *Relatively Determinate Inventory Models*

Inventory problems are generally assigned to the production area although marketing and financial issues are certainly involved in their resolution. We should not lose sight of the fact that inventories can consist of services, cash, energy and manpower, as well as maintenance items, raw materials, and finished and in-process goods.

No matter what the resource stored (to meet some demand), certain fundamental concepts have been developed which can guide executive decision-making. The usual issues involve when to replenish a depleting resource and how much to order or to obtain at any one time. If the demands for the resource are not "highly" variable and if the replenishment time is "relatively" certain, the inventory problem can be treated under conditions of certainty. Nevertheless, all of our previous remarks concerning approximations of certainty and "relatively" determinate systems prevail.

99/ *A Basic Model for Determining Economic Order Quantities*

This fundamental problem arises frequently in a variety of production processes and purchasing situations. Some part is produced (or purchased) in *batches* or lots[26] to meet an *anticipated* demand. In the case of produc-

---

[26] This means that *all* parts are completed *at one time*, presumably after passing through a number of stages. In the same sense, *all* parts must complete one stage before they can enter the next one. Such batch production is equivalent, in effect, to ordering from an outside vendor who ships the total order at one time so that a batch of items enters the inventory simultaneously. For the case of serial production, see the next section.

tion, the number of parts needed *does not require the full-time capacity* of the machine or machines used to produce the part. Therefore, the production of the part can be scheduled in a variety of ways. At one extreme, each day's production could be scheduled to be just enough to meet the demand for that day. The remaining machine capacity would be used to work on other jobs. At the other extreme, the part might be produced *continuously* until there was enough on hand to meet demand for a long time, perhaps a year. Then production of that item would be stopped, and the machine would be switched to another item. What is the best way to schedule production?

The essential framework of this problem arises in a great number of different situations. To illustrate, we will present a typical problem for analysis. Suppose that the part in question is a bolt which is used in an assembly and that 4,000 of these bolts are needed per day. This problem is simpler in two respects than some other inventory problems which are of the same type. *First,* we assume that demand for this part is known with *certainty,* whereas most parts being produced for sale would have a risk-type demand. Subsequently, we will find out how to deal with such problems under risk. *Second,* the part is obviously a minor one and so the objectives can safely be assumed to be the minimization of costs. If, instead, we considered a very expensive part, we might have to introduce some measure of utility other than costs. In this problem of decision-making under certainty the strategies are the various possible production lots of these bolts which might be scheduled.

The objective is to minimize costs. What are the costs? On the one hand, there is the *set-up cost* of the machine that produces the bolts.[27] When the machine is not producing bolts it is producing something else, and each time these bolts are put into production it requires time— and, hence, money—to set up the machine for production. On the other hand, there are *carrying costs* associated with maintaining the part in inventory. At the very least, there is the loss of use of the money tied up in inventory. Often, in addition, there are costs of storage space, insurance, deterioration, pilferage, obsolescence, etc.

It can be seen that *these two costs are opposed in the sense that, as one gets larger, the other gets smaller.* Thus, if a great number of parts are run with one set-up, it follows that the set-up cost per year is lower than if only a few parts are run, but the carrying cost is higher. If very few parts are run with one set-up, then the set-up cost becomes large but the carrying cost is low. The cost picture in Figure 10.17 is typical.

In the figure, curve *A* represents the annual set-up cost which decreases as the number of parts produced on one run increases. Curve *B*

---

[27] For the purchasing variant, this would be the order cost.

represents the yearly carrying cost, which increases as the number of parts produced on one run increases. Curve C represents (annual) total cost— the sum of A plus B. The objective of minimizing the total cost is fulfilled by selecting the strategy of producing X parts on one run, where X is determined from the minimum of the total cost curve, C.

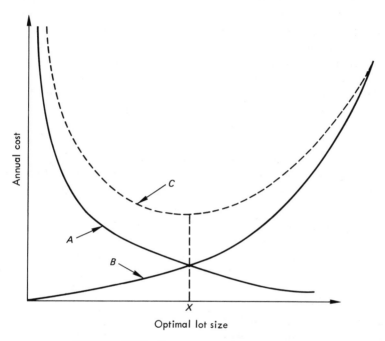

FIGURE 10.17   Cost as a function of lot size.

Such opposing costs always exist. If there were no costs which increased as the number produced in one set-up increased (curve B) then it would be most reasonable to produce an enormous amount in advance—perhaps ten years' supply. If there were no costs which increased as the number produced in one set-up decreased (curve A) then it would be most reasonable to produce each part as it was needed. The unreasonableness of these two possibilities (in almost all cases) is due to the existence of both kinds of costs.

The decision problem is solved as soon as the two curves are obtained and summed to get the total cost curve (C). The shapes of the curves in Figure 10.16 are arbitrary and only meant to illustrate the general situation. For each *specific* problem the *actual shapes* of these curves must be determined. This is the phase of the decision-problem analysis which we have called the determination of the relationship between the independent variable (the number of parts scheduled for production in one run) and the dependent variable (the associated total cost).

How do we measure the costs? The set-up cost consists, essentially, of the cost of the man-hours required for set-up plus the cost of having the facility idle while being set up. This is usually relatively easy to determine.[28] Suppose, in our case, this cost is $40. The carrying cost includes several component costs, as indicated above. The costs of deterioration, pilferage, and obsolescence must be determined from historical records. The storage costs, including insurance costs, can usually be determined from cost-accounting data. But the cost of the loss of use of the money tied up in inventory is not so straightforward—and it is often the largest single cost component in this set of carrying costs. Basically, it can be measured in two ways, each a kind of opportunity cost. It can be considered to be measured by the cost of borrowing money (either from the bank or by bonds), under the assumption that if the money were not tied up in inventory then that much less would have to be borrowed. Or it can be measured by the current rate of profit being made by the company, under the assumption that if the money were not tied up in inventory it could be invested in the other company activities and would return the usual rate of profit. Let us assume that the company in question selects the first alternative; that it borrows at 7 per cent per year; and that analyses of the other costs indicate that they total 3 per cent per year. Thus, total carrying costs would be 10 per cent per year.

To make our costs comparable we need to express them all on the basis of some fixed unit of time. Any time unit will do as long as all costs are put on an equivalent basis. Since carrying costs are already on a yearly basis ($1.00 in inventory for one year costs $0.10) we shall use one year as our unit. The demand for the bolt amounts to 1,000,000 per year (we are assuming 250 working days per year). Therefore, if we produce X bolts in one run we will need $1,000,000/X$ runs per year at an annual set-up cost of $(1,000,000/X) \cdot \$40 = \$40,000,000/X$. For example, if we produce 50,000 bolts in one run our set-up costs for one year will be $\$40,000,000/50,000 = \$800$. This equation expressing the set-up part of the relationship between our selection of strategy (choice of X) and the objective (of total cost) is curve A, graphed in Figure 10.18.

Carrying costs depend on the average inventory investment. What is the average inventory investment if X parts are produced each run? Suppose $X = 50,000$ are produced each run.[29] Then the inventory will behave as graphed in Figure 10.19. This is the typical "saw-toothed" behavior that results from constant, regular demand for inventory. Starting

---

[28] Ordering costs are more difficult to obtain. As a general rule, they are significantly smaller than set-up costs.

[29] Or requested for each purchase order.

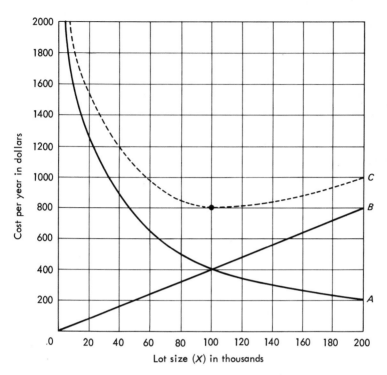

FIGURE 10.18 Costs for bolt inventory.

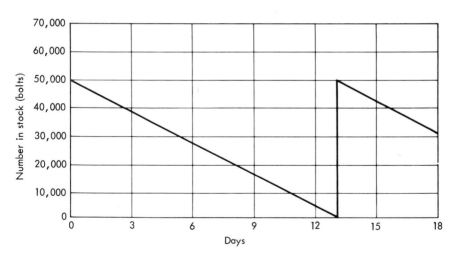

FIGURE 10.19 Inventory with constant rate of demand—and batch production.

out with 50,000 units in stock the amount on hand goes down by 4,000 (the daily usage) each day until it reaches zero. But just then, *assuming perfect timing,* another 50,000 units come into stock and the process repeats itself. It should be intuitively evident—and if it isn't, a little geometry will suffice to prove it—that there will be an average stock on hand of 25,000 bolts. The average, year-round inventory will be $X/2$.

The cost of each bolt must be determined to ascertain how much money is invested in the inventory. This cost (including the raw-material and the labor components) can usually be determined from cost-accounting data. In our case, presume that this cost is $0.08 per bolt. Then, the total carrying cost will be given by the average number in inventory *times* the cost per bolt *times* the carrying-cost rate (10 per cent). This is:

$$\frac{X(\$0.08)(0.10)}{2} \qquad \text{(curve B)}$$

For $X = 50,000$ this cost would be $200 per year; as plotted on curve B, Figure 10.18.

Our total-cost curve is the sum of these two costs:

$$\text{Total cost} = \frac{\$40,000,000}{X} + \frac{X(\$0.08)(0.10)}{2}$$

which is graphed as curve C on Figure 10.18. The *minimum point* of this total-cost curve can be achieved by producing $X = 100,000$ bolts at each run, with a total cost of $800 per year. In other words, the minimum-cost scheduling requires production of 25 days' requirements in each run.

The same result can be obtained mathematically, avoiding the chore of graphing three curves. Thus:

let X = number of parts produced in one run (or ordered in one shipment),
p = cost per part,
C_1 = set-up cost,
C_2 = carrying cost per dollar of inventory investment per year,
D = yearly demand for parts, and
TC = total annual cost.

It can readily be shown that:

$$TC = \frac{DC_1}{X} + \frac{XpC_2}{2}$$

This equation can be *minimized* by taking the *derivative of total costs with respect to X and setting it equal to zero.*

$$\frac{dTC}{dX} = -\frac{DC_1}{X^2} + \frac{pC_2}{2} = 0$$

The value of X which minimizes total costs is:

$$X = \sqrt{\frac{2DC_1}{pC_2}}$$

Putting in the numerical values from our problem, we have:

$$D = 1,000,000, \quad C_1 = \$40, \quad p = \$0.08, \quad C_2 = 10 \text{ per cent or } 0.10 \text{ per year}$$

and

$$X = \sqrt{\frac{2(1,000,000)(40)}{(0.08)(0.10)}} = 100,000$$

as was found before. Total costs for this value of X are:

$$\text{(MIN)} \ TC = \frac{\$40,000,000}{100,000} + \frac{100,000(.08)(.10)}{2} = \$400 + \$400 = \$800$$

also as before.

This general formula for X accomplishes the same purpose as the graph, is easier to use, and is more informative. From this we see that X gets larger: (1) as D gets larger (the more needed the more we must produce), (2) as C_1 gets larger (the more it costs per set-up, the fewer set-ups we want to have), (3) as p gets smaller (the less the price, the less the carrying costs and the more we can carry in stock), and (4) as C_2 gets smaller (the less the cost of carrying a dollar in inventory, the more we can carry in stock). All of these relationships are in accord with what we would intuitively expect.

An alternative procedure that could be followed in solving this decision problem involves an application of the *marginal principle,* which is basic to most economic thinking. An economist presented with this problem would immediately set out to find that value of X for which the marginal set-up cost equaled the marginal cost of carrying stock in inventory.[30] He would get the same expression for X that we have derived. The advantage of using the derivative is its ready applicability to more complicated variants of the same fundamental type.

This solution leads naturally to a consideration of inventory problems in general. More than two costs can enter the formulation of the problem. In the next section we shall explore a variant where production is serial rather than of the batch type, and again the same general ideas apply. Also, as we have indicated in several places, nothing prevents us from replacing "set-up cost" by "ordering cost," leaving the carrying cost as before. This purely verbal change does not affect the formulation of the decision problem, but it does show that the same solution is available for an organization that is ordering the item rather than producing it.

For example, suppose that all conditions of the former problem remain

---

[30] This would mean that the increased total carrying cost for a small increase in X would equal the decrease in total set-up cost for the same small increase in X, when measured from the *appropriate* value of X.

the same *except that the item is ordered* and that the order cost is $10. This order cost may be more than just the cost of processing an order. It can also include costs associated with *receiving and inspecting* the incoming items *if these costs are affected by the purchase quantity*. The decision problem to determine the minimum-cost order quantity has already been solved (being identical to that of batch production runs). The numerical solution for the purchase order quantity will be:

$$X = \sqrt{\frac{2(1,000,000)(10)}{(0.08)(0.10)}} = 50,000$$

That is, 50,000 bolts should be ordered each time. Total costs will be:

$$\text{(MIN) } TC = \frac{(1,000,000)(10)}{50,000} + \frac{(50,000)(.08)(.10)}{2} = \$200 + \$200 = \$400$$

The total costs are less in this case owing to the lower cost of placing an order as compared to the previous set-up cost.

To incorporate the relevant costs is a model-building requirement which technical facility in finding solutions cannot obviate. For example, it is essential sometimes to include purchase quantity discounts, which can be done. Storage space limitations may be represented in the form of additional carrying costs—if the quantity ordered requires more than the usual available space—and this also can be readily built into the model. When relevant, anticipated price changes can be included. Such additional factors generally require only more algebraic complexity. No basic difference in the model results from their inclusion.

100/ An Inventory Model for Serial Production

Unlike batch systems, line production entails processing a sequence of parts, each one of which is at a different stage of completion. At the beginning of the line are raw materials and/or unassembled, purchased components. At the end of the line there is a continuing output of finished goods. In between, the parts pass sequentially through a series of operations.

The scheduling problem is altered because a batch of finished goods does not enter inventory at one time. Accordingly, the "saw-tooth" diagram of Figure 10.19 must be changed. Figure 10.20 holds the key to the behavior of these systems. In this case, it is based on the data that we previously used where $C_1 = \$40$, and in addition, where the daily production rate (r) is 4,500 units per day.

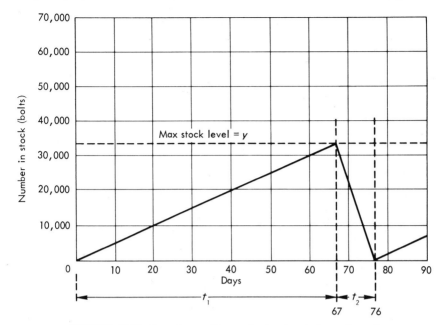

FIGURE 10.20 *Inventory with constant rate of demand—and line production.*

Assume that items enter stock continually at the rate of $r = 4{,}500$ units per day during the period of the production run ($DAYS$ 0–66). They are withdrawn at the rate of 4,000 units per day ($D/250 = d$), both during the production run and when the line has been switched over to another item ($DAYS$ 67–76). Figure 10.20 depicts the optimal, minimum-cost configuration. How is this determined?

Once again, we could graph the curves A and B; sum them to obtain curve C; and then visually determine the minimum cost and its associated run-size value, X. But we shall use the equational approach. Curve A, as before, is given by DC_1/X. Curve B, on the other hand, must be adjusted to reflect the fact that additions to inventory are being made continuously during the production run. The effect of this is to alter the average unit inventory carried.

Let the period of the production run be t_1 days. Then the number of units produced during that interval would be $X = rt_1$. However, because of the daily withdrawal rate, d, the maximum stock level, y, is equal to $(r - d)t_1$. Hence, $y = (r - d)t_1 = (r - d)X/r$. It is apparent that the average unit inventory is $y/2 = (r - d)X/2r$.

We can now write the appropriate equation for total cost, namely:

$$TC = \frac{DC_1}{X} + \frac{(r - d)XpC_2}{2r}$$

Taking the derivative with respect to X and setting it equal to zero:

$$\frac{dTC}{dX} = -\frac{DC_1}{X^2} + \frac{(r-d)pC_2}{2r} = 0$$

We obtain for the optimal run size, X:

$$X = \sqrt{\frac{2DC_1}{pC_2}\left(\frac{r}{r-d}\right)}$$

Let us now return to the numerical values that were used to determine Figure 10.20. We have:

$$X = \sqrt{\frac{2(1,000,000)40}{(0.08)(0.10)}\left(\frac{4,500}{4,500-4,000}\right)} = 100,000\sqrt{9} = 300,000$$

This is three times as large as our previous (batch) run-size. The maximum inventory level is:

$$y = (r-d)X/r = (500)\ 300,000/4,500 = 33,333$$

The production run period would be:

$$t_1 = X/r = 300,000/4,500 = 66.7 \text{ days}$$

The total cycle period $t = t_1 + t_2$ is $250X/D = 250(300,000)/1,000,000 = 75$ days, so $t_2 = 75 - 66.7 = 8.3$ days. This is rapidly checked by noting that $dt_2 = y$. Also, the minimum total cost in this case is:

$$\text{(MIN) } TC = \frac{1,000,000(40)}{300,000} + \frac{500(300,000)(0.08)(0.10)}{2(4,500)} = \$267$$

In this model, the production rate, r, is required. Its presence offers new opportunities for determining optimal equipment selection. A slow machine (say one that can *just satisfy* the demand rate) would have to be run continuously. A fast machine (where $[r/(r-d)] \rightarrow 1$) produces a solution that is essentially equivalent to the batch production result, which is in keeping with our intuition. Thus, another dimension for interpreting our models has appeared. In this case, an interaction between financial planning for equipment selection and managing the inventory has occurred.

101/ Inventory Problems with Unknown Costs

Models have been constructed to handle a variety of special circumstances which can influence inventory problems: price discounts, anticipated changes in prices, transportation costs depending on quantity, warehouse limitations, peculiarities of demand, and many others. These different models are based on the same approach that we have followed here: the isolation of the opposing costs involved, the construction of the total-cost equation, and the determination of the minimum total cost. Rather than continue to develop elaborations on this basic theme, we shall now consider some fundamental questions about the costs required in the total-cost equation.

The difficulties in obtaining many of these costs (particularly the out-of-stock cost) are often considerable. It is, therefore, important to ask whether the analysis we have developed is of any use to the executive *when these costs cannot be determined accurately*. Clearly, the costs in question are involved in every inventory decision, whether the decision-maker consciously knows it or not. These costs are not creations of the fertile imagination of the analyst. Rather, every intuitive decision concerning inventory policy *imputes* a value to the relevant costs.

In this section, we shall show that the inventory problem *can be formulated* so that the costs are left to the intuition of the decision-maker. This, at least, will ensure that the decision-maker is logical in his use of the intuited costs (which is by no means a minor achievement).

It will be helpful to employ a numerical example. Suppose that a company maintains inventories of the three different items described below:

ITEM (i)	YEARLY DEMAND (D_i)	PRICE (p_i)
A	120,000 units	$ 3.00
B	80,000 units	2.00
C	600 units	96.00

These are actual data, rounded off. They are from an inventory problem in the petroleum industry. The items were selected to provide some range in demand and price characteristics.

First, let us consider the problem of determining the *optimal order size*. We have seen that this decision problem is solved by taking the derivative of the total-cost equation. For the ith item:

$$TC_i = \frac{D_i C_1}{X_i} + \frac{X_i p_i C_2}{2}$$

This assumes that the C_1 and C_2 costs are "relatively" identical for all three items. The assumption is quite reasonable for C_2 in most cases and for C_1 under most ordering cost options. Minimum total cost for the ith item results when:

$$X_i = \sqrt{\frac{2 D_i C_1}{p_i C_2}}$$

We cannot determine the optimal value of X_i for each of the three items above without knowing the costs, C_1 and C_2. As previously discussed, frequently these costs can be approximated from cost-accounting data. However, it is also often the case that the validity of the estimates is in doubt, mainly because of the difficulty of measuring the opportunity costs involved in each of them. Thus, C_1 (as an ordering cost) will include a component based on the space occupied by the order department. But what is this space worth in terms of other ways that are available to use it? What does the manpower and money *tied up* in the order department cost the company? These and similar questions relating to C_2 (carrying cost) indicate that in some cases it may not be possible to obtain valid estimates of C_1 and C_2. What then can be done?

Returning to our equation, if we substitute the minimizing value of X_i in the total-cost equation, we get:

$$\text{(MIN)}\ TC_i = \sqrt{\frac{D_iC_1p_iC_2}{2}} + \sqrt{\frac{D_iC_1p_iC_2}{2}} = \sqrt{2D_iC_1p_iC_2} = \sqrt{2C_1C_2}\sqrt{D_ip_i}$$

From this expression for the total cost it can be seen that, *whatever the costs are,* the total cost involved in maintaining an inventory *for any particular item* will be *proportional to the square root of the product of yearly demand times price* (yearly value used). We must now show that this equation gives us the means for determining optimal inventory policies when we do not know the costs but are given some restrictions on the solution. First, we note that the minimum total cost for all i items is:

$$\sum_i \text{(MIN)}\ TC_i = \sqrt{2C_1C_2}\sum_i\sqrt{D_ip_i}$$

Second, the ratio of minimum total cost *for any item* to the minimum total cost *for all items* will be:

$$\text{(MIN)}\ TC_i / \sum_i \text{(MIN)}\ TC_i = \sqrt{D_ip_i} / \sum_i\sqrt{D_ip_i}$$

Furthermore, it can be shown quite readily that:

$$\frac{\text{(MIN)}\ TC_i}{\sum_i\text{(MIN)}\ TC_i} = \frac{\text{Optimal number of orders for the } i\text{th item}}{\text{Optimal total number of orders}} = \frac{\sqrt{D_ip_i}}{\sum_i\sqrt{D_ip_i}}$$

and

$$\frac{\text{(MIN)}\ TC_i}{\sum_i\text{(MIN)}\ TC_i} = \frac{\text{Optimal average inventory investment for the } i\text{th item}}{\text{Optimal total average inventory investment}} = \frac{\sqrt{D_ip_i}}{\sum_i\sqrt{D_ip_i}}$$

We can illustrate these relationships in terms of the three items above. Suppose that *current policy* is to order each of the three items every month. Then we can calculate the total number of orders directly, and the total average investment in inventory which will result.

Item (i)	D_i	p_i	Orders per year	Average inventory investment $(D_ip_i)/(2 \times 12)$
A	120,000	$ 3.00	12	$15,000
B	80,000	2.00	12	6,667
C	600	96.00	12	2,400
			36	$24,067

This policy requires a total of 36 orders per year and produces an average inventory investment of $24,067.

But, we know that any optimal policy must have *the total cost for each item proportional to* $\sqrt{D_ip_i}$. For these items the square roots of yearly value of usage are:

Item (i)	D_i	p_i	$\sqrt{D_ip_i}$
A	120,000	$ 3.00	600
B	80,000	2.00	400
C	600	96.00	240
		$\sum_i \sqrt{D_ip_i} =$	1,240

The sum of the square roots is 1240.

Now, suppose that we *do not know the costs* (C_1 and C_2) but are told that 36 orders per year will be *acceptable*. What should be the policy to minimize the amount of inventory, granted that there will be 36 orders per year? In the appropriate equation, above, substitute "total orders specified" for "optimal total number of orders." Lacking knowledge of the costs, we cannot hope to attain the optimal situation, but we can insist upon achieving a *rational* one. By rational we mean:

$$\text{Rational number of orders for the } i\text{th item} = \frac{\sqrt{D_ip_i}}{\sum_i \sqrt{D_ip_i}} \times (\text{Total orders specified})$$

In other words, using this relation, the final results for 36 orders per year (or any other number) must be *proportional to the square roots* of the yearly usage dollar value of the items in question. We want to make the total number of orders equal to 36 while having the orders for each item proportional to the square root of its yearly dollar usage values. This is accomplished by calculating:

$$\frac{\sqrt{D_ip_i}}{\sum_i \sqrt{D_ip_i}} \times (\text{Total orders specified})$$

In our specific case we want the rational policy for 36 orders per year so we calculate $\dfrac{36}{1240} = 0.029$. This must now be multiplied by each item's $\sqrt{D_i p_i}$ to determine the optimal order size. We calculate:

ITEM (i)	$\sqrt{D_i p_i}$	$\sqrt{D_i p_i}/\underset{i}{\Sigma}\sqrt{D_i p_i}$	NUMBER OF ORDERS PER YEAR	QUANTITY ORDERED*	AVERAGE INVENTORY**
A	600	0.484	17.4	6,888	$10,332
B	400	0.322	11.6	6,888	6,888
C	240	0.194	7.0	86	4,133
	1,240	1.000	36.0		$21,353

* This "rational" value of X_i is calculated for each item by: $X_i = D_i$/Number of orders per year.
** The average inventory is simply $X_i p_i/2$.

Thus, a rational policy based on 36 orders per year would require only $21,353 average investment in inventory as compared to the $24,067 investment required when each item is ordered twelve times. The saving was accomplished by distributing the orders in accordance with the size of $\sqrt{Dp}$. *The 11 per cent saving in inventory investment is a measure of the lack of rationality of the policy of ordering each item each month.*

Alternatively, we could ask: How many orders per year would be required if a rational policy were followed which required $24,067 (the amount under the original monthly ordering policy) average inventory investment? We want to divide the "total specified average inventory" into amounts proportional to the items' square roots of yearly dollar usage value. In the general case we do this by calculating:

$$\frac{\sqrt{D_i p_i}}{\underset{i}{\Sigma}\sqrt{D_i p_i}} \times \text{(Total average inventory specified)}$$

This will give the ordering policy which minimizes the *total number of orders* for any specified inventory investment. In our case we want the optimal ordering policy for a total inventory investment of $24,067.

ITEM (i)	$\sqrt{D_i p_i}$	$\sqrt{D_i p_i}/\underset{i}{\Sigma}\sqrt{D_i p_i}$	AVERAGE INVENTORY	QUANTITY ORDERED*	NUMBER OF ORDERS PER YEAR**
A	600	0.484	$11,645	7,764	15.5
B	400	0.322	7,764	7,764	10.3
C	240	0.194	4,658	97	6.2
	1,240	1.000	$24,067		32.0

* Number ordered $(X_i) = 2$(Average inventory)$/p_i$.
** Number of orders per year $= D_i/X_i$.

An optimal policy constructed with the intention of having $24,067 in average inventory investment would require only 32 orders per year instead of 36. And, again, *the saving of 4 orders per year is a measure of the lack of rationality in the policy of ordering each item each month.*

In other words, we are able to use the information $(\sqrt{D_i p_i})$ to improve existing inventory policies without knowledge of the true costs. If the decision-maker, for whatever reason, imposes a restriction on the number of orders per year or on the average inventory investment, then an optimal inventory policy can be determined subject to that restriction. The reason is that any such restriction implies a particular ratio between the two costs, C_1 and C_2. Thus,

$$X_i = \sqrt{\frac{2D_i C_1}{p_i C_2}} = \sqrt{\frac{C_1}{C_2}}\sqrt{\frac{2D_i}{p_i}}$$

or

$$\frac{C_1}{C_2} = \frac{X_i^2 p_i}{2D_i} = \left(\frac{p_i X_i}{2}\right)\left(\frac{X_i}{D_i}\right) = \frac{\text{Average inventory investment}}{\text{Number of orders per year}}$$

This last equation explains why we can be certain that the original policy of ordering each item once each month was not optimal. Suppose that this policy is optimal. Then we can calculate for each item the imputed value of the cost ratio. We find

ITEM	ORDERS PER YEAR	AVERAGE INVENTORY INVESTMENT	C_1/C_2
A	12	$15,000	1,250
B	12	6,667	556
C	12	2,400	200

Granting that these three items are similar with regard to carrying cost and order cost, there is no reason why these ratios should be different. The fact that they are different indicates that the inventory policy is not rational. When we fix the total number of orders per year at 36 and use the rational assignments, we are fixing this cost ratio at 593. This can be calculated from any one of the items or the totals. And when we fix the average inventory investment at $24,067 we are fixing this cost ratio at 753.

Suppose we knew that the carrying cost was $0.12 per dollar inventory per year (C_2). If the executive fixes 36 orders per year as an objective of inventory policy he is imputing a value of $593 \times 0.12 = \$71.16$ as the order cost (C_1). If, instead, he fixes the average inventory investment at $24,067, then he is imputing a value of $753 \times 0.12 = \$90.36$ as the order cost. And, of course, we have seen that a policy of one order per month per item is simply illogical, and unnecessarily costly, because it imputes different order costs for each item.

This same approach permits the decision-maker to survey *the whole range of possible optimal policies*. We have developed above two "potentially" optimal inventory policies which result from specific assignments (even though implicit) of values to the ratio C_1/C_2. In fact, for every *real* inventory situation there is only one optimal policy which would be known if the actual costs were known. This optimal policy must belong to the set of rational policies described by every possible ratio of C_1/C_2. In other terms, each possible value of the ratio C_1/C_2 determines an optimal number of orders per year and an optimal average inventory investment—for the particular yearly dollar demand values of the items.

A convenient way to present a picture of this whole set of optimal inventory policies is as follows. The optimal *number* of orders per year is obtained in terms of the costs by substituting the expression for optimal X in D/X.

$$\text{Optimal number of orders per year for the } i\text{th item} = \frac{D_i}{\sqrt{\dfrac{2D_iC_1}{p_iC_2}}} = \sqrt{\frac{C_2}{C_1}}\sqrt{\frac{D_ip_i}{2}}$$

Similarly, the average inventory investment for an optimal policy is given by substituting optimal X in $Xp/2$.

$$\text{Optimal average inventory investment for the } i\text{th item} = \frac{p_i}{2}\sqrt{\frac{2D_iC_1}{p_iC_2}} = \sqrt{\frac{C_1}{C_2}}\sqrt{\frac{D_ip_i}{2}}$$

These expressions hold for *any optimal inventory policy for any item*. If we multiply them together, the terms involving C_1 and C_2 cancel out and we get the following condition for a *rational policy*:

$$\text{Number of orders} \times \text{average inventory investment} = \frac{D_ip_i}{2}$$

However, we want to handle situations involving more than one item. Using summation, the following holds for a rational policy for any number of items:

Number of orders $\times$ average inventory investment

$$= \left(\sqrt{\frac{C_2}{C_1}}\sum_i\sqrt{\frac{D_ip_i}{2}}\right)\left(\sqrt{\frac{C_1}{C_2}}\sum_i\sqrt{\frac{D_ip_i}{2}}\right) = 1/2\left(\sum_i\sqrt{D_ip_i}\right)^2$$

For our three items:

Number of orders $\times$ average inventory investment

$$= 1/2(\Sigma\sqrt{Dp})^2 = 1/2(600 + 400 + 200)^2$$
$$= 1/2(1240)^2 = 1/2(1,537,600)$$
$$= \$768,800$$

This *rational* relationship between the number of orders and the average inventory investment takes the form of a *hyperbola*. It can be graphed as in Figure 10.21.

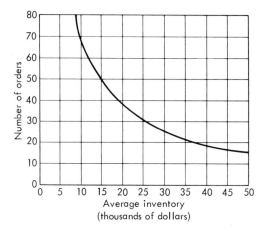

FIGURE 10.21 *Optimal inventory policies.*

We have determined two of the points on this curve in the two policies above. In the first we found 36 orders per year and an average inventory investment of $21,353, and 36 × 21,353 = $769,000 (rounded off). In the other policy we found 32 orders per year and an average inventory investment of $24,067, and 32 × 24,067 = $770,000 (rounded to the accuracy of the figures). The equation, or curve, gives *every possible* optimal policy for these three items.

The advantage of this approach is that it permits the executive to see the effects of his assumptions about limitations on the inventory policy. If, for example, he believes that the inventory investment must be held to no more than $15,000 then he must be prepared to handle 51.3 orders per year. If the order department cannot handle more than 20 orders per year then he must be prepared to have $38,440 average inventory investment. By use of this equation or the corresponding curve, the executive can utilize his knowledge about the availability of capital for inventory investment and/or limitations on the capacity of the order department without having to attempt to get reliable estimates of the two associated costs.

Let us emphasize again that the ratio of the costs, C_1/C_2, is tacitly involved in every solution represented by a point on this curve. Specifically, the cost ratio associated with any specific point on the curve is given by the relationship previously derived.

$$\frac{C_1}{C_2} = \frac{\text{Average inventory investment}}{\text{Number of orders per year}}$$

Thus, holding the inventory investment to $15,000 is equivalent to assuming that:

$$\frac{C_1}{C_2} = \frac{15,000}{51.3} = 292.4$$

or that the order cost is 292.4 times as large as the carrying cost. If the number of orders is held down to 20 per year, then the imputed cost ratio is:

$$\frac{C_1}{C_2} = \frac{38,440}{20} = 1922$$

In other words, the change from 51 orders per year to 20 orders per year implies an increase in the estimate of order cost (C_1) by a factor of more than 6, as compared to the carrying cost.

In exactly the same way, out-of-stock costs are imputed by any decision concerning reserve stocks. The decision-theory approach makes these costs explicit, but they are always involved, whether explicit or not. The demonstration of the way that out-of-stock costs are imputed by a reserve-stock decision would be longer and more complicated than that given above for carrying costs and ordering costs, but the reasoning remains the same.

We know that a rational decision concerning reserve stocks would be achieved by balancing the out-of-stock costs against opposing costs, such as carrying costs. Such costs must exist, because if there were no out-of-stock costs there would be no need to have any reserve stock, and if there were no opposing costs one would simply carry an enormous reserve stock.

Any given amount of reserve stock implies a calculable probability of going out of stock, given the demand probability distribution. Suppose out-of-stock cost were known. Then the out-of-stock costs associated with any reserve stock could be calculated. By the *marginal principle* a reserve stock would be carried of such size that the last unit added to reserve decreased the total out-of-stock cost by as much as it increased the total carrying cost. By the same token, any given reserve stock (if it is the result of a rational policy) must be such that the last unit added to the reserve equated these costs. Therefore, any reserve-stock decision establishes a ratio between the carrying cost and the out-of-stock cost even if the executive does not explicitly know these costs. Generally, the larger the reserve stock, the larger the imputed cost of out-of-stock.

102/ *The Lagrangian Approach*

The problem that we have just dealt with can also be treated by the well-known and compact Lagrangian multiplier. The odds are that any operations research study would move directly to the Lagrangian format for a solution, yet for communication with management, the more lengthy explanation (based on the proportionality factors $\sqrt{D_i p_i}$) would appeal to all conscientious O.R. practitioners. The dichotomy between approaches is so evident in this case, that we have chosen to describe briefly, at this time, the Lagrangian approach.[31] It can serve as a model for similar discrepancies that exist between "the efficient solution" of a problem and the "communication of its essentials" to management, in almost all areas of management science.

Assume that our objective is to minimize the total *number* of orders per year, given a constraint on the average dollar inventory. Since C_1 and C_2 are constants, this is *equivalent* to minimizing the total annual cost—subject to a specified (fixed) average dollar inventory carrying cost. That is: (Equation 1)

$$(\text{Constrained Minimum}) \ \sum_i TC_i = (\text{Min}) \sum_i \frac{D_i}{X_i} (C_1) + (\text{Fixed}) \sum_i \frac{X_i p_i}{2}(C_2)$$

Similarly, let the objective be stated as the minimization of the average dollar inventory, given a constraint on the total number of orders per year. This is equivalent to Equation 2 which minimizes total annual cost by minimizing the average dollar inventory carrying cost subject to a constraint on the annual order cost. Equation 2:

$$(\text{Constrained Minimum}) \ \sum_i TC_i = (\text{Min}) \sum_i \frac{X_i p_i}{2} (C_2) + (\text{Fixed}) \sum_i \frac{D_i}{X_i} (C_1)$$

The Lagrangian model permits us to achieve both of these objectives. *First* we transform each equation of a constrained minimum so that a new equation (L) equals the objective function whether or not the constraint is exactly satisfied. Thus, for Equation 1, let:

$$L = \sum_i \frac{D_i}{X_i} + \lambda \left(\sum_i \frac{X_i p_i}{2} - I \right)$$

where $I = (\text{Some})$ Fixed Average Dollar Inventory Value.

If the dependent variable L is minimized subject to the given (fixed value) constraint, I, our objectives will be achieved. The Lagrangian multiplier λ must equal zero if $\sum_i \frac{X_i p_i}{2} \neq I$, and $\lambda \neq 0$ if the constraint is exactly met. *Second*, we take the partial derivatives $\partial L/\partial X_i$ and $\partial L/\partial \lambda$; and third we set them equal to zero in accord with the familiar procedures of calculus.

---

[31] See also Starr and Miller, *Inventory Control: Theory and Practice* (Englewood Cliffs, N.J.: Prentice-Hall, Inc., 1962), pp. 93–104.

Equation 3:
$$\frac{\partial L}{\partial X_i} = -\frac{D_i}{X_i^2} + \frac{\lambda p_i}{2} = 0$$

Equation 4:
$$\frac{\partial L}{\partial \lambda} = \sum_i \frac{X_i p_i}{2} - I = 0$$

Solving Equation 3, we obtain Equation 5:

$$X_i = \sqrt{\frac{2D_i}{\lambda p_i}}$$

We substitute this value for X_i in Equation 4 and rearrange the terms:

$$\sum_i \left[\sqrt{\frac{2D_i}{\lambda p_i}} \left(\frac{p_i}{2}\right) \right] = \sqrt{\frac{1}{2\lambda}} \sum_i \sqrt{D_i p_i} = I$$

Whence:

$$\lambda = (\sum_i \sqrt{D_i p_i})^2 / 2I^2$$

This value for λ can now be substituted back into Equation 5. Thus:

$$X_i = \sqrt{\frac{2D_i(2I^2)}{p_i(\sum_i \sqrt{D_i p_i})^2}} = \frac{2I}{\sum_i \sqrt{D_i p_i}} \sqrt{\frac{D_i}{p_i}}$$

For the numbers used in our previous example, where $I = \$24,067$:

$$X_i = \frac{2(24,067)}{1,240} \sqrt{\frac{D_i}{p_i}} = 38.818 \sqrt{\frac{D_i}{p_i}}$$

$$\text{Average inventory} = \frac{X_i p_i}{2} = 19.409 \sqrt{D_i p_i}$$

Then:

Item (i)	D_i	p_i	$\sqrt{D_i p_i}$	Average inventory
A	120,000	$ 3.00	600	$11,645
B	80,000	2.00	400	7,764
C	600	96.00	240	4,658
			1,240	$24,067

which is the same result obtained by the prior approach.

Now let us derive the comparable result for Equation 2.
Let:

$$L = \sum_i \frac{X_i p_i}{2} + \lambda \left(\sum_i \frac{D_i}{X_i} - N \right)$$

where $N =$ (Some) Fixed Number of Orders Per Year.
Again we take partial derivatives and set them equal to zero.

Equation 6:
$$\frac{\partial L}{\partial X_i} = \frac{p_i}{2} - \frac{\lambda D_i}{X_i^2} = 0$$

Equation 7:
$$\frac{\partial L}{\partial \lambda} = \sum_i \frac{D_i}{X_i} - N = 0$$

Solving Equation 6, we obtain Equation 8:

Equation 8:
$$X_i = \sqrt{\frac{2\lambda D_i}{p_i}}$$

Substitute this X_i (from Equation 8) in Equation 7.

$$\sum_i D_i \sqrt{\frac{p_i}{2\lambda D_i}} = \sqrt{\frac{1}{2\lambda}} \sum_i \sqrt{D_i p_i} = N$$

Whence:

$$\lambda = (\sum_i \sqrt{D_i p_i})^2 / 2N^2$$

This value of λ is then substituted back into Equation 8.

$$X_i = \sqrt{\frac{2D_i}{p_i} \frac{(\sum_i \sqrt{D_i p_i})^2}{2N^2}} = \frac{\sum_i \sqrt{D_i p_i}}{N} \sqrt{\frac{D_i}{p_i}}$$

Returning to the numbers used previously (where $N = 36$):

$$X_i = \frac{1{,}240}{36} \sqrt{\frac{D_i}{p_i}} = 34.44 \sqrt{\frac{D_i}{p_i}}$$

Then:

ITEM (i)	X_i	NUMBER OF ORDERS (D_i/X_i)
A	6,888	17.4
B	6,888	11.6
C	86	7.0
		36.0

Once again, we obtain identical results. This confirmation of our mathematical approach is superfluous since the mathematical reasoning is in itself sufficient for those who are trained in the methodology. But the nature of the communication problem with a non-mathematical management is evident.

103/ Stochastic Models—
A Reserve Stock Problem

We now turn from "relatively" determinate systems which play such a large part in production analyses to those which require consideration of the random behavior of one or more relevant variables. Models based on certain demand, for example, suffer from a lack of realism in many

inventory problems. In other words, they are not even "relatively" determinate. This is not to say that we are stretching the allowable tolerances for approximation or taking undue liberties when we treat actual
problems as if they were determinate. On the contrary, solutions to
economic-order quantity problems have been used by industry for many
years. But a variety of inventory decision problems (whether the part
is produced or ordered) cannot be handled by such simple models. The
major cause of discrepancy is the assumption that demand is *fixed* and
known accurately in advance.

Typically, we have a good idea of about how large the demand is
going to be. But we are prepared to discover the actual demand is
smaller or larger than we had forecast. Under such circumstances how
should we determine an optimal inventory policy?

We shall assume that the objective remains the same: the minimization of costs associated with procuring and carrying stock. How does the
uncertainty about the exact level of demand affect costs? To answer this
question we must find means for expressing the demand we anticipate.
Our method for summarizing information of this kind is by means of a
probability distribution which describes the probability of occurrence
of each specific level of demand.

Probability distributions can be used to describe a host of different
kinds of phenomena for which there is no certainty about outcome. If we
toss ten coins we do not know how many heads will show. But we can
summarize our information about the likelihood of the different possible
outcomes by means of a probability distribution.

Number of heads	Probability
0	1/1,024
1	10/1,024
2	45/1,024
3	120/1,024
4	210/1,024
5	252/1,024
6	210/1,024
7	120/1,024
8	45/1,024
9	10/1,024
10	1/1,024
	1

In accord with our expectations the most likely outcome is five heads.
The probabilities decrease as the outcomes depart in both directions
from that value.

We can often express information about demand in the form of a
probability distribution. However, our information about demand is

seldom as accurate as that about the outcomes of coin tosses. Nevertheless, we group the possible demands into classes and estimate the probability for each class. For example we might have this information:

DEMAND (IN UNITS)	PROBABILITY
500–699	0.05
700–899	0.20
900–1,099	0.50
1,100–1,299	0.20
1,300–1,499	0.05
	1.00

Where does this information about demand come from? There are various kinds of demands, each one characterized by some combination of the reliability and accuracy of the information about it. At one extreme, there are highly stable demands such as those to replace worn and broken drill bits in a machine shop. The machine shop must maintain an inventory of bits to meet this demand. Here, *complete knowledge* of the population from which the demand arises exists, and frequently the historical records of demand show a high degree of uniformity. Accurate probability distributions of demand can be drawn up directly from these records. For example, 500 days might show the following frequency distribution of demand:

NUMBER OF BROKEN BITS	NUMBER OF DAYS
0	68
1	136
2	135
3	90
4	45
5	18
6	6
7	2
	500

From the *frequency distribution* a *probability distribution* can be constructed (dividing the number of days for each given number of broken bits by 500).

NUMBER OF BROKEN BITS	PROBABILITY
0	0.136
1	0.272
2	0.270
3	0.180
4	0.090
5	0.036
6	0.012
7	0.004
	1.000

As a second type, we can cite items for which the demand is relatively stable (i.e., insensitive to most significant environmental factors). Examples are lubricating oil, light bulbs, and the like. Often, in cases like these there will be trends over time in the demand for these items. The probability distribution for demand must be measured around any trend which may exist—it should not include the trend. Frequently, for basic items a relatively simple analyses of the historical data will be sufficient to produce good approximations to the probability distribution of demand.

As a third type, we can cite items for which demand is *relatively unstable* with regard to many significant factors (e.g., common stocks). In these cases it becomes difficult to separate fluctuations in demand due to changes in trend (or economic factors) from the expected behavior of the probability distribution of demand around the level established by trend (and economic factors). A variety of statistical techniques are used for this purpose but the accuracy of the resulting probability distribution is always somewhat in question.

Finally, we may have the case where a new product is being marketed and there is *no historical information.* Under these circumstances, it may often be useful to have the relevant executives pool their intuitions and *estimate the probabilities* for the various levels of demand. These probabilities will measure the *subjective* beliefs of the executives, which may be all that is available. If so, the executives will reach their decisions on the basis of these subjective probabilities anyway, so there is certainly no loss—and sometimes a gain—in making the probabilities in question explicit. After all, if one is going to be intuitive, he may as well be as rational about it as he can.

Granting the use of probability distributions to express our information about demand, we can return to our original question: How does the uncertainty about the exact level of demand affect costs? A major point is that risk considerations introduce *two new costs.* First, it is apparent that it will *generally* not be the best strategy to maintain enough stock to meet the *maximum conceivable demand.* Second, while *rare,* it is also possible that to prepare for the *minimum conceivable demand* would be the optimal stocking policy.

Looking at these in turn, the possibility exists of running *out of stock* and thus being unable to meet the demand that arises. Running out of stock has costs associated with it, for example, the *loss of profit* on a lost sale, loss of customer *goodwill,* or loss of the production and revenue of a machine if a necessary spare part is out of stock. The opposite result occurs when demand is smaller than the amount in stock. In some inventory problems this only increases the carrying costs slightly and the surplus is sold in subsequent time periods. However, in other situations a sizable loss results from *overstocks*. For example, in women's fashions, clothing overstock at the end of a season may require markdowns to far below cost. Similarly, in some lines of toys the overstock after Christmas can produce almost a total loss. Of these two kinds of costs which arise because of uncertainties in demand, the first (understock) is frequently a significant factor; the second (overstock), while of lesser importance, can be of great significance for certain kinds of items.

How are these costs determined? The overstock cost is usually fairly simple to measure. Under ordinary circumstances the loss owing to an overstock is some percentage of the amount paid for the item, and this percentage can often be determined from historical data. The out-of-stock cost is generally more difficult to measure. Such possible components of this cost as expediting costs, loss of profit from forfeited sales, or loss of output from some machine not operating for lack of a spare part are not difficult to measure. But a major *intangible* component of the cost of out-of-stock is the so-called loss of customer goodwill. How can this component be expressed in dollar form comparable to other costs? A variety of methods can be used to estimate this cost, including the judgment of informed executives. Sometimes, however, there seems to be no way of getting a reasonable estimate. But let us hasten to add that when goodwill is involved, somehow its effect must be included in the inventory policy decisions. The only question is whether the estimate will be made explicitly or implicitly.

To explain our stochastic model, we shall take a situation which (while not the most common) is well suited to highlight the decision-problem formulation. Consider the purchase of some complex and expensive piece of equipment: a large boiler or generator, a jet aircraft, a nuclear submarine, etc. Such equipment usually has a number of major component parts that have been especially designed for it. Often, extra components can be ordered at far less cost when the piece of equipment is first purchased than if the components are ordered subsequently. The reason is that the manufacturer can produce the extra component parts with his original set-up far more cheaply than if he must set up again to make them. This being the case: How many extra component parts should be ordered with the original purchase?

The purchaser wants a *reserve stock* of components to protect himself from the failure of parts in the piece of equipment. The usual decision elements exist. The *states of nature* are the various possible numbers of failures of the specific part during the lifetime of the equipment. The *strategies* are the various numbers of units of the component which might be ordered. The *objective* is to minimize total costs. Engineering information is generally available about the probabilities of these states of nature, so we are dealing with decision-making under *risk*. To determine the optimal strategy we need to find the *payoffs* in each cell of the decision matrix.

Let us develop a numerical example. Suppose a generator is being ordered for an atomic power plant and that a specific component part will cost $1,500 for each extra unit ordered *at the time* of the initial purchase. However, if an additional unit is ordered later it will cost $4,000 to have it made. What other costs must be considered? First, *carrying costs* will be involved for extra units maintained in inventory. Second, there will be "lost production" costs if the part fails and the generator cannot operate at 100 per cent of capacity while a replacement is being ordered and manufactured. We shall assume that the estimate of generator down-time cost is $20,000, and for simplicity, that carrying costs are small and can be ignored.

These data are sufficient to evaluate the total cost payoffs in every cell of the matrix. *Suppose the strategy of carrying zero extra units is followed.* Then, if no failure occurs there will be no cost. If one failure occurs there will be a cost of $4,000 to have a replacement made to order plus a cost of $20,000 for the down-time of the generator, or $24,000 total. Two failures will cost $48,000 and, similarly, a greater number of failures will cost the corresponding multiple of the $24,000 for each failure. *Suppose the strategy of carrying one extra unit is followed.* Then if no failure occurs there will be a cost of $1,500 minus the scrap value for the unit purchased and never used. We shall assume that the scrap value of the part is negligible. Therefore, the cost is $1,500. If one failure occurs the total cost is still $1,500 paid for the unit. If there are two failures the total cost will be the $1,500 spent for the extra unit plus the $24,000 cost of the second failure, or a total cost of $25,500. The remainder of the cells of the matrix can be calculated in the same way. For seven states of nature and the equivalent seven strategies we get the payoff matrix:

		STATES OF NATURE						
		N_1	N_2	N_3	N_4	N_5	N_6	N_7
STRAT-EGIES	EXTRA UNITS ORDERED	NUMBER OF FAILURES						
		0	1	2	3	4	5	6
S_1	0	$ 0	24,000	48,000	72,000	96,000	120,000	144,000
S_2	1	1,500	1,500	25,500	49,500	73,500	97,500	121,500
S_3	2	3,000	3,000	3,000	27,000	51,000	75,000	99,000
S_4	3	4,500	4,500	4,500	4,500	28,500	52,500	76,500
S_5	4	6,000	6,000	6,000	6,000	6,000	30,000	54,000
S_6	5	7,500	7,500	7,500	7,500	7,500	7,500	31,500
S_7	6	9,000	9,000	9,000	9,000	9,000	9,000	9,000

At this point, the decision problem is in familiar form. If the probabilities of the various states of nature were completely unknown we would use one of the decision criteria available for decisions under uncertainty. Ordinarily, however, we would have engineering information about the probabilities of the states of nature. Suppose that the probability distribution is given as follows:

STATE OF NATURE	NUMBER OF FAILURES	PROBABILITY
N_1	0	0.70
N_2	1	0.15
N_3	2	0.07
N_4	3	0.04
N_5	4	0.02
N_6	5	0.01
N_7	6	0.01
		1.00

We know that the decision criterion for decision-making under risk is the minimum (or maximum) *expected value*. This requires calculating the expected total cost of each strategy, using the probabilities of each of the states of nature. For S_1 we calculate:

$$0.70(\$0) + 0.15(\$24,000) + 0.07(\$48,000) + 0.04(\$72,000)$$
$$+ 0.02(\$96,000) + 0.01(\$120,000) + 0.01(\$144,000) = \$14,400$$

For S_2 we have:

$$0.70(\$1,500) + 0.15(\$1,500) + 0.07(\$25,500) + 0.04(\$49,500)$$
$$+ 0.02(\$73,500) + 0.01(\$97,500) + 0.01(\$121,500) = \$8,700$$

Proceeding similarly we find:

STRATEGY	EXPECTED TOTAL COST
S_1	$14,400
S_2	8,700
S_3	6,600
S_4	6,180
S_5	6,720
S_6	7,740
S_7	9,000

Our criterion selects strategy S_4, which has the minimum expected total cost, $6,180, so 3 extra units should be ordered initially.

The inventory problem has been solved. The optimal strategy is S_4. But it will be worthwhile to raise a question concerning the payoff matrix which we constructed. This matrix may not *seem* to reflect what we really had in mind. Consider, for example, our evaluation of the various payoffs for S_5, the initial purchase of 4 extra units. We have calculated that the total cost of this strategy is the same, $6,000, for all states of nature from N_1 to N_5. But, one might reason, for N_1 we have in some sense "wasted" the $6,000 because we didn't need any replacement units at all. Similarly, for N_3 we needed only 2 units and, in the same sense, the other 2 units were "wasted." For N_5 we needed all 4 units so none were "wasted." By this line of reasoning it seems, somehow, incorrect to have given each of these five states of nature the same payoff measure, $6,000.

Furthermore, the payoffs for the other two states of nature (still assuming S_5) seem equally wrong. If N_6 occurs we are 1 unit short and must order it, at a cost of $24,000. This plus the $6,000 for the 4 units originally purchased gives the $30,000 payoff for S_5 and N_6, as in our matrix. But consider the $24,000 component of this payoff. If we had originally ordered another unit it would have cost $1,500, so it seems that the $24,000 only represents an avoidable, cost of $24,000 − $1,500 = $22,500. Similar arguments apply to every entry in the payoff matrix except that for S_1 if N_1 occurs, which has a zero cost by any argument. The whole payoff matrix seems wrong. What can we say to this?

The answer is that both ways of reasoning are correct. Both will lead to the same optimal strategy although the payoff matrices are different for the two approaches. In the second case, instead of considering total costs we only concerned ourselves with avoidable costs. These are costs which might have been avoided had we obtained reliable advance information about the state of nature which would occur. In economic terms, we used opportunity costs instead of total costs. Consider S_5 again. We have "wasted" the $6,000 if N_1 occurs because we didn't need any replacements. The opportunity costs for S_5 and N_1 are $6,000 since we could have used S_1, which would have had zero cost for N_1 and $6,000 − 0 = $6,000. We may note that this opportunity cost is an overstock cost. If N_3 occurs, the opportunity cost for this case would be $6,000 minus the cost of the minimum-cost strategy for N_3, which is S_3 with a cost of $3,000. Thus, the opportunity cost for S_5 if N_3 occurs is $6,000 − $3,000 = $3,000.

It is easy to determine the opportunity-cost payoff matrix. We want to measure each payoff as an opportunity cost based upon the minimum total cost for the same state of nature. This amounts to subtracting the lowest cost in each column (of the total cost matrix) from every entry in that column. (Exactly the same procedure was used in constructing the Savage regret matrix for decision-making under uncertainty, see pp. 115–117.) From our previous total-cost payoff matrix we get the following opportunity-cost matrix.

	STATES OF NATURE						
	N_1	N_2	N_3	N_4	N_5	N_6	N_7
	PROBABILITIES						
STRATEGIES	0.70	0.15	0.07	0.04	0.02	0.01	0.01
S_1	$ 0	22,500	45,000	67,500	90,000	112,500	135,000
S_2	1,500	0	22,500	45,000	67,500	90,000	112,500
S_3	3,000	1,500	0	22,500	45,000	67,500	90,000
S_4	4,500	3,000	1,500	0	22,500	45,000	67,500
S_5	6,000	4,500	3,000	1,500	0	22,500	45,000
S_6	7,500	6,000	4,500	3,000	1,500	0	22,500
S_7	9,000	7,500	6,000	4,500	3,000	1,500	0

Although the payoff measures have been changed, the decision problem remains the same in all other respects. It is still decision-making under risk requiring the use of expected values.

How does this matrix differ from the preceding one? We have subtracted from every entry in each column a fixed amount (the minimum cost for that column). The amounts subtracted from the various columns were:

STATE OF NATURE	AMOUNT SUBTRACTED (MINIMUM COST)
N_1	$ 0
N_2	1,500
N_3	3,000
N_4	4,500
N_5	6,000
N_6	7,500
N_7	9,000

Therefore, the *expected opportunity costs*[32] for the various strategies will each be a *constant amount smaller* than the expected total costs we calculated previously. Specifically, the difference will be the expected value of the "amount subtracted."

$$0.70(0) + 0.15(1,500) + 0.07(3,000) + 0.04(4,500)$$
$$+ 0.02(6,000) + 0.01(7,500) + 0.01(9,000) = \$900$$

For example, consider S_7's *expected opportunity cost.*

$$0.70(9,000) + 0.15(7,500) + 0.07(6,000) + 0.04(4,500)$$
$$+ 0.02(3,000) + 0.01(1,500) + 0.01(0) = \$8,100$$

This is just $900 less than the *expected total cost* for the same strategy. The reader may verify the relationship for other strategies if he has any

---

[32] The expected values derived for the new matrix.

doubts about its validity. Consequently, we can derive the expected opportunity costs for each strategy by subtracting $900 from the corresponding value of the expected total costs.

Strategy	Expected total cost	Expected opportunity cost
S_1	$14,400	$13,500
S_2	8,700	7,800
S_3	6,600	5,700
S_4	6,180	5,280
S_5	6,720	5,820
S_6	7,740	6,840
S_7	9,000	8,100

Our criterion dictates the selection of that strategy with the lowest expected opportunity cost. It is S_4, with an expected opportunity cost of $5,280.

Whether total costs or opportunity costs are used, the strategy selected will always be the same. In decision theory terms, the minimum expected value criterion selects the same strategy whether it is applied to the original matrix or to the Savage regret matrix (not the Savage criterion).

We have ignored carrying costs in this example even though carrying units worth thousands of dollars for the entire life of a generator could be quite costly. Why ignore such costs? The answer is that these costs should not be ignored in an actual decision problem. We neglected them because their inclusion complicates the calculation of the payoffs with a lot of details that do not in any way affect the basic procedure but that instead obscure it. To include carrying costs, we require a probability distribution that describes the lifetimes of generators. Then one must have information concerning the intervals between failures (which may require several more probability distributions). Such information is necessary to determine how long the various units will probably have to be carried. The net effect of these complications is to hide a fundamentally simple and straightforward decision problem under a mass of arithmetical details. We ignored carrying costs to spare the reader, and ourselves.

104/ Stochastic Service Systems

Facilities that provide *production services* (such as machining, transporting, etc.) are at the heart of any production system's configuration. Planning for such systems becomes particularly interesting when the approximation of determinate behavior is untenable. In this case, decision problems arise concerning variable service rates and/or variable demands for that service which have many similarities to the stochastic inventory problems we have been discussing. For example, let us consider the problem associated with the servicing of machines. The *elements* of the problem are as follows: Some number of operating machines are subject to breakdown. Repairmen are maintained on the payroll to restore the machines to operation. The *decision problem* is: How many repairmen should there be? The *objective* is to minimize costs. The *strategies* are the various numbers of repairmen who might be hired. The *states of nature* are the various rates at which the machines may break down. In short, all the usual components of a decision problem are found in this situation. The only step necessary to complete the decision matrix is the evaluation of the payoffs.

This problem has striking resemblances to the inventory problems we considered above. The close relationship between the two problems becomes apparent when we rephrase the repairmen problem: An inventory of repairmen's time must be maintained to meet future demand, which consists of the breakdown of machines. There is a cost which increases as the number of repairmen increases: the cost associated with their idle time. And there is a cost which increases as the number of repairmen decreases: the cost of having machines out of operation (because there is no repairman available to service them). These two costs correspond to the *carrying costs* and the *out-of-stock costs,* respectively, in the inventory decision problem. It might, therefore, seem as if the repairmen problem could be solved along exactly the same lines as the inventory problem. This is not the case, and the reason for the difference deserves emphasis.

In the inventory problem it is necessary to have information about the probability distribution of demand to determine the probability of being out-of-stock and, hence, the cost associated *with any specific level of reserve stock.* Similarly, in the repair problem it will be necessary to have information concerning the demand for repairmen, i.e., the rate at which machines break down. But in the inventory problem, reserve stock is *immediately available* to meet any demand that occurs. Therefore, the out-of-stock cost associated with a specific level of reserve stock can be calculated readily as some straightforward function of the *excess of demand over the reserve stock.*

This is not true in the case of the repairmen. The reserve inventory is the time of the repairmen, and this will be available to meet demand *only* if one of the repairmen is unoccupied when a machine breaks down. Should all the repairmen be occupied the machine must wait until one of them is free. This is not equivalent to being out of stock in an ordinary inventory problem because it can happen even when the total inventory of available man-hours is greater, over some interval of time, than the demand. The reason is, of course, that *time cannot be stored.* The repairmen's past idle time is not available when a number of machines later break down. This difference from the inventory problem has surprising consequences.

Let us illustrate. Suppose that a machine shop has 30 machines and that the cost of *one* machine's being out of operation for *one* hour is estimated to be $40. Repairmen capable of repairing these machines are paid $5 per hour. As pointed out above, we need information about the demand for repairmen's time which results from the breakdown of machines. This information could be available in several forms; one type of record might show the numbers of machines that broke down each day. From such a record we can construct a frequency distribution and probability distribution. For example, based on 200 days of observation, we obtain Table 10.2.

TABLE 10.2

NUMBER OF BREAKDOWNS PER DAY	NUMBER OF DAYS	PROBABILITY
0	99	0.495
1	70	0.350
2	24	0.120
3	6	0.030
4	1	0.005
	200	1.000

The probability has been determined by dividing each frequency (number of days) by the total frequency (total number of days). The form of this distribution (Poisson) is frequently found in data such as these. It is characterized by having a longer tail to the right than to the left. In the present case, the mean of the distribution of machine breakdowns is 0.7 machines per day $[0(0.495) + 1(0.350) + 2(0.120) + 3(0.030) + 4(0.005) = 0.700]$. This means that, on the average, one machine breaks down every 1.429 days $(1/0.7 = 1.429)$ or every 11.432 hours $(8 \times 1.429 = 11.432)$ assuming an eight-hour workday.

Since the opposing cost in this decision problem is the cost of having machines out of operation we need information concerning the length of time it takes to restore a machine to operation. Ordinarily, such information would be available from repairmen's time sheets. Suppose that the following probability distribution holds:

TABLE 10.3

Hours to repair	Probability
1	0.021
2	0.051
3	0.099
4	0.143
5	0.165
6	0.160
7	0.132
8	0.096
9	0.062
10	0.036
11	0.019
12	0.009
13	0.004
14	0.002
15	0.001
	1.000

Often, it will be found that these data also fall in a exponential distribution. This is a reflection of the fact that many repair jobs will take some relatively small amount of time but that a few will take much longer. In the present case the average repair time can be calculated to be 5.8 hours.

It might appear that there is really no decision problem here. On the basis of the information we have been given it seems that, *on the average,* a machine will break down every 1.429 days or 11.432 hours, and that it will take a repairman, *again on the average,* 5.8 hours to fix it. Thus, one repairman can easily handle the necessary repairs and, in fact, will only work about 4 hours of an 8-hour day (5.8 hours every 1.429 days, i.e., $\frac{5.8}{11.432} \approx \frac{4}{8}$). It will cost $5.8 \times \$40 = \$232$ in lost operating time for each machine which breaks down. Certainly, one repairman seems more than sufficient. And indeed, at this point the executive might wish that labor wasn't so "lumpy" and that he could hire only half a repairman!

This conclusion, however, overlooks the outstanding characteristic of such problems. The fallacious argument of the preceding paragraph is based on the assumption that, since it takes an average of 5.8 hours to repair a machine, we can calculate the cost of the machine's being out of operation by simply multiplying 5.8 by the cost per hour ($40). The error in reasoning lies in this assumption.

Granted, it takes 5.8 hours to repair a machine—but only after the repairman can start work. What about the times when he isn't able to start work on the machine because he is already working on another one?

In this event the second machine will have to wait for service. The time it has to wait also costs $40 per hour, the same as the actual repair time. It is this waiting-time cost which we must investigate. Such situations have been studied extensively and a whole branch of probability theory has developed around it. Fittingly, it is called waiting-line, or queuing, theory.

The mathematics involved in the analysis of waiting lines is so broad-based and far-reaching that it is impossible to cover even the major categories here. We can, however, use simulation with Monte Carlo techniques to get some generalized insight into the problem. The simulation results can then be compared with those derived from the equivalent mathematical formulation, which is the procedure that we shall follow.

The reader will remember that the idea behind Monte Carlo is to use random sampling to construct a simulated version of the process being analyzed. By this means we can see what actually occurs rather than having to calculate it from mathematical equations. In the present case we want to determine what happens if we have machines that break down in accordance with Table 10.2 and a repairman who repairs the machines in accordance with Table 10.3. We can readily perform this Monte Carlo by assigning blocks of three-digit numbers to the different possibilities in proportion to their probabilities. We will need the machine-breakdown data on an hourly basis to fit these data to the repair-time data. They can be obtained by a mathematical transformation of the data in Table 10.2 (or directly from the original records). On an hourly basis the machine-breakdown data are:

TABLE 10.4

NUMBER OF BREAKDOWNS PER HOUR	PROBABILITY
0	0.916
1	0.080
2	0.004
	1.000

These data are *precisely equivalent* to those compiled on a daily basis.

In Table 10.5 three-digit numbers are assigned to each of the possibilities in accordance with the given probabilities, and similarly for the repair times. Thus, for both distributions we have assigned 1,000 three-digit numbers. For example, 80 of them (916–995) *represent* one breakdown in an hour. This is a probability of 80/1,000 = 0.080, as it should be. Using a table of random numbers (pp. 585–588) we obtain a sample of the behavior of our system. First, we start reading three-digit numbers from

TABLE 10.5

BREAKDOWNS PER HOUR	PROBABILITY	NUMBERS ASSIGNED	REPAIR TIMES	PROBABILITY	NUMBERS ASSIGNED
0	0.916	000–915	1	0.021	000–020
1	0.080	916–995	2	0.051	021–071
2	0.004	996–999	3	0.099	072–170
			4	0.143	171–313
			5	0.165	314–478
			6	0.160	479–638
			7	0.132	639–770
			8	0.096	771–866
			9	0.062	867–928
			10	0.036	929–964
			11	0.019	965–983
			12	0.009	984–992
			13	0.004	993–996
			14	0.002	997–998
			15	0.001	999

the table. Each number drawn repesents one hour, taken consecutively, hour by hour. Every specific three-digit number shows (in accord with our Monte Carlo assignments) which possibility occurred in that hour.

The first number selected was 573. Since this falls between 000 and 915 it means that there was no machine breakdown during the first hour. The second number is 608, again no breakdown. We continue reading numbers, *one for each hour,* until the ninth number read is 919, meaning that a breakdown occurred in this hour. Proceeding similarly, we can take a sample for any desired number of hours. In this case, a sample of 800 hours or 100 eight-hour days was taken.[33] A record must be kept of the *specific hours* in which each breakdown occurred.

After obtaining the sample of breakdowns it is necessary to read a new, three-digit random number *for each breakdown* to determine the repair times. For example, for the first breakdown we read the number 257. Referring to the table of numbers assigned to the various repair times (Table 10.5) it will be seen that 257 designates a repair time of 4 hours, which is then associated with the first breakdown. When the repair time has been determined for every breakdown it is possible to calculate the resulting waiting times. The hours in which the breakdowns occurred can be recorded numerically, in this case as they took place successively from 1 to 800. Our data are recorded in Table 10.6.

These are raw data. We must now calculate the waiting times of those breakdowns that had to wait for the repairman. This can be accom-

---

[33] The use of the computer greatly facilitates such work. Subsequently, we include the flow diagram and results of a computer run (of 625 days or 5,000 hours) for illustrative and comparative purposes.

plished by a routine procedure. The first step is to determine the hour at which each repair was terminated.

TABLE 10.6

BREAKDOWN NUMBER (i)	BREAKDOWN HOUR (B_i)	REPAIR TIME (R_i)	BREAKDOWN NUMBER (i)	BREAKDOWN HOUR (B_i)	REPAIR TIME (R_i)
1	9	4	37	355	4
2	26	4	38	375	5
3	35	4	39	401	2
4	59	2	40	413	3
5	62	6	41	430	8
6	75	8	42	435	2
7	94	6	43	436	6
8	104	3	44	440	3
9	110	4	45	450	5
10	111	6	46	452	15
11	111	7	47	467	5
12	135	6	48	483	6
13	153	8	49	504	7
14	156	2	50	505	7
15	157	5	51	509	7
16	171	1	52	533	6
17	173	5	53	534	6
18	187	4	54	538	6
19	189	8	55	582	9
20	223	9	56	612	4
21	224	4	57	624	3
22	226	3	58	631	3
23	232	8	59	634	7
24	241	4	60	640	10
25	244	4	61	647	4
26	245	4	62	663	6
27	250	5	63	678	10
28	260	4	64	694	9
29	298	5	65	702	4
30	299	3	66	743	5
31	307	6	67	746	4
32	309	7	68	756	6
33	313	6	69	763	9
34	316	4	70	764	10
35	318	7	71	796	13
36	320	5			

Let B_i designate the hour at which the ith breakdown occurred and let R_i designate the hours required for the repair of the ith breakdown. Finally, let T_i be the hour at which the repair of the ith breakdown was terminated. Then we have a simple rule:

$$T_i = T_{i-1} + R_i \quad \text{if} \quad B_i < T_{i-1}$$
or
$$T_i = B_i + R_i \quad \text{if} \quad B_i \geq T_{i-1}$$

The first part of the rule says simply that if the ith breakdown occurs before the end of the repair of the $(i-1)$th breakdown then the repair of the ith breakdown will not start until T_{i-1} and, hence, will end at $T_{i-1} + R_i$. The second part of the rule says that if the ith breakdown occurs at or after the termination of the repair of the $(i-1)$th breakdown then the repair of the ith breakdown can start immediately. Using this rule we can quickly determine all the T_i for our sample (Table 10.7).

TABLE 10.7 *

Breakdown hour (B_i)	Termination of repair (T_i)	Breakdown hour (B_i)	Termination of repair (T_i)
9	13	355	359
26	30	375	380
35	39	401	403
59	61	413	416
62	68	430	438
75	83	435	440
94	100	436	446
104	107	440	449
110	114	450	455
111	120	452	470
111	127	467	475
135	141	483	489
153	161	504	511
156	163	505	518
157	168	509	525
171	172	533	539
173	178	534	545
187	191	538	551
189	199	582	591
223	232	612	616
224	236	624	627
226	239	631	634
232	247	634	641
241	251	640	651
244	255	647	655
245	259	663	669
250	264	678	688
260	268	694	703
298	303	702	707
299	306	743	748
307	313	746	752
309	320	756	762
313	326	763	772
316	330	764	782
318	337	796	809
320	342		

* The arrows indicate that some waiting must occur.

We can now calculate the waiting times by finding $T_{i-1} - B_i$ for each breakdown for which this was positive. The $T_{i-1} - B_1$ (when positive) represent the waiting times since when $T_{i-1} > B_i$ then the ith breakdown would have to wait until the conclusion of the repairs on the $(i-1)$th

breakdown. The total waiting time *for this sample* with *one* repairman
was 202 hours (Table 10.8).

TABLE 10.8

Breakdown hour (B_i)	Waiting time $T_{i-1} - B_i$
111	3
111	9
156	5
157	6
189	2
224	8
226	10
232	7
241	6
244	7
245	10
250	9
260	4
299	4
309	4
313	7
316	10
318	12
320	17
435	3
436	4
440	6
452	3
467	3
505	6
509	9
534	5
538	7
640	1
647	4
702	1
746	2
764	8
	202

Let us inspect these data. We note there were two failures in one hour
(111). The probability of two breakdowns (as shown in Table 10.4) is
0.004. This is equivalent to more than three such events in the sample
of 800. Consequently, our small sample is low in this regard. We had
one repair time of 15 hours (452) even though this probability is only
0.001, or one in a thousand. But such are the ways of random samples—
the relatively unexpected is always happening—showing that it really

shouldn't have been unexpected. Since our sample covers 800 hours it is not surprising that rare events occur. On the other hand, because the sample is only 800, we cannot expect that our observations will exactly match the probabilities.

How else does the sample compare with the original data? A count shows that there were 71 breakdowns in the simulation of 100 days (800 hours). Since we know that the average number of breakdowns was 0.7 per day *in the original data,* it follows that the *expected number of breakdowns* in 100 days would be $100 \times 0.7 = 70$. Our sample result is close to what is expected on number of breakdowns. Adding up all the repair times, we observe that it took 400 hours to repair these 71 breakdowns, or an average of $400/71 = 5.63$ hours per breakdown. This compares well with the 5.8 hours average repair time of the original data.[34] It appears that our sample is a reasonably good representation of the original data.

Reference to Table 10.9 confirms this fact but sheds additional light on the relative goodness of our small sample simulation, shown in column A. Here we find several comparisons: first, with a computer simulation of 5,000 hours, based on an infinite source for breakdowns (column B); second, with a computer simulation of 5,000 hours, based on a finite source for breakdowns of $M = 30$ machines (column D); third and fourth, with similar variants of analytical forms of mathematical models (columns C and E). Before we can use Table 10.9 a few of the terms and conditions it embodies must be explained.

First, the probability distribution $\{P_n\}$ forms part of the left-hand column of performance measures. The symbol n represents the number of machines that are broken down. When $n = 0$, the repairman is idle. When $n = 1$, the repairman is busy and no broken down machines are waiting. When $n = 3$, the repairman is busy and two machines are waiting for repair. P_n *stands for the probability that n machines are broken down.* Thus, P_o is the probability of an idle repairman.

Second, the distinction is made in Table 10.9 between finite and infinite sources. The "reality" is, of course, that a finite number of machines (namely, $M = 30$) exists. However, 30 machines is a large enough number to permit us to approximate the size of the source of breakdowns as being infinite. The advantage of such approximation is a simplification of the simulation procedure, a reduced record-keeping burden and less complex mathematical equations for the analytic resolution of

---

[34] Also, since there were 400 repair hours in the 800 hour sample, necessarily, there were $800 - 400 = 400$ non-repair hours. These non-repair hours are the *idle time* of the repairman. Using probability terms, we say that P_o (which is the probability of no machines being down) $= 400/800 = 0.50$. See P_o in column A of Table 10.9.

the problem. Table 10.4, which was used as the basis for the 800 hour hand-simulation, reflects the infinite assumption since no provision is made for reducing the expected number of breakdowns when one or more machines are out of order.

TABLE 10.9

PERFORMANCE MEASURES	A INFINITE SOURCE HAND-SIMULATION RUN OF 800 HOURS OR 100 DAYS	B INFINITE SOURCE COMPUTER-SIMULATION RUN OF 5,000 HOURS OR 625 DAYS	C INFINITE SOURCE MATHE-MATICAL MODEL	D FINITE SOURCE, $M = 30$ COMPUTER-SIMULATION RUN OF 5,000 HOURS OR 625 DAYS	E FINITE SOURCE, $M = 30$ MATHE-MATICAL MODEL
P_0	0.5000	0.4737	0.4930	0.4666	0.5082
P_1	0.3200	0.2549	0.2500	0.2739	0.2579
P_2	0.1213	0.1489	0.1267	0.1484	0.1264
P_3	0.0450	0.0755	0.0642	0.0648	0.0598
P_4	0.0137	0.0368	0.0326	0.0309	0.0273
P_5	—	0.0094	0.0165	0.0090	0.0120
P_6	—	0.0008	0.0084	0.0050	0.0051
P_7	—	—	0.0042	0.0014	0.0021
P_8	—	—	0.0021	—	0.0008
P_9	—	—	0.0011	—	0.0003
P_{10}	—	—	0.0006	—	0.0001
P_{11}	—	—	0.0003	—	—
P_{12}	—	—	0.0001	—	—
P_{13}	—	—	0.0001	—	—
P_{14}	—	—	0.0001	—	—
	1.0000	1.0000	1.0000	1.0000	1.0000
L_q	0.25	0.45	0.52	0.44	0.43
W_q	6.73	5.06	5.95	4.95	5.12
TOTAL THRUPUT	71.	447.	—	445.	—
THRUPUT PER HOUR	.089	.089	.088	.089	.085
THRUPUT PER DAY	.710	.715	.700	.712	.676

The $\{P_n\}$ rows are braced together in the left margin.

To further explain this, let each machine have a breakdown rate of λ. Then, when all thirty machines are in working order ($n = 0$), the system's breakdown rate will be 30λ. If only 29 machines are in working order ($n = 1$), the (finite) source of breakdowns is reduced and the system's rate would be 29λ. As an extreme case, if all 30 machines are out of order ($n = 30$), the source size is zero and the system's breakdown rate is $(0)\lambda = 0$. We see that Table 10.4 is written so that the breakdown rate is independent of the number of machines that happen to be out of order at any time.[35]

Third, in the column of performance measures, we have listed:[36]

L_q — the average number of machines in the waiting line,
W_q — the average time spent by a machine in the waiting line,
And — throughput measures which reflect the total number of breakdowns, as well as the breakdown rate per day and per hour. (Since total throughput has no meaning for the mathematical models, the respective entries have been left blank.)

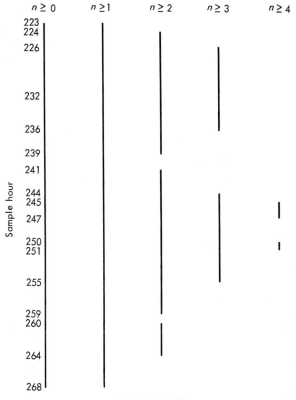

FIGURE 10.22

Now let us return to Table 10.9. The hand-simulation (column A) compares remarkably well to the larger simulations (columns B and D)

---

[35] If a finite source model is to be used, breakdown records must be maintained for the *individual* machines. For the finite source computer simulation, each individual machine's λ was assumed to be $(0.7)/(30)(8)$ and the system's λ was changed as a function of n, viz., $\lambda = (30 - n)[0.7/(30)(8)]$ breakdowns per hour. The infinite source computer simulation assumed that $\lambda = 0.7/8$ regardless of the value of n.

[36] See pp. 193–197.

with respect to $\{P_n\}$. The column B simulation fills out more of the tail values than does A, and column D is even better in this regard. However, the average number of machines waiting for service (L_q) is considerably lower in column A than it should be and the average waiting-time (W_q) is somewhat higher. (This result is in line with our previous observations concerning the probabilities of two failures in one hour [111] and a repair time of 15 hours.) Further, we note, comparing columns B and D, that the infinite approximation is not too far off from the finite results, which are based on reality.

A word is in order concerning the way in which the $\{P_n\}$ distribution was derived from the raw data of the 800 sample simulation. Using Table 10.7, a waiting-line diagram can be constructed which covers *all* 800 hours. Figure 10.22 portrays only a part of this diagram, beginning with the failure at the 223rd hour (Number 20, Table 10.6) and ending with the termination of repair at the 268th hour (Table 10.7).

We find *(for this part* of the total simulation):

$$n \geq 0: 268 - 223 = 45$$
$$n \geq 1: 268 - 223 = 45$$
$$n \geq 2: (264 - 260) + (259 - 241) + (239 - 224) = 37$$
$$n \geq 3: (255 - 244) + (236 - 226) = 21$$
$$n = 4: (251 - 250) + (247 - 245) = 3$$

Whence: $\quad n_4 = 3 \qquad\qquad P_4 = \tfrac{3}{45}$
$\qquad\qquad n_3 = 21 - 3 = 18 \qquad P_3 = \tfrac{18}{45}$
$\qquad\qquad n_2 = 37 - 21 = 16 \qquad P_2 = \tfrac{16}{45}$
$\qquad\qquad n_1 = 45 - 37 = 8 \qquad P_1 = \tfrac{8}{45}$
$\qquad\qquad n_0 = 45 - 45 = 0 \qquad P_0 = \tfrac{0}{45}$

The same procedures, when applied to the total sample of 800 hours, yield the results presented in Table 10.9.

Figure 10.23 portrays the computer flow diagram used to obtain the 5,000 hour simulations. It will be noted that the methods for deriving the performance measures are built directly into the simulation. Great flexibility exists with respect to changing assumptions and parameters in the computer program. The sample size could have been enlarged (say to 10,000) quite readily if this seemed desirable. The hand simulation, on the other hand, was onerous and any sample additions are granted reluctantly. Furthermore, the utilization of additional repairmen can be introduced in the computer simulation with a minimum of complication and the effects of these extra repairmen can be studied under a variety of conditions. While this is also possible in the hand simulation, the amount of calculation simply becomes prohibitive.

Now let us turn to the mathematical analysis of this problem. If we assume the *finite source* considerations,[37] the following equation holds for one repairman and M machines:

Flowchart for queuing simulation

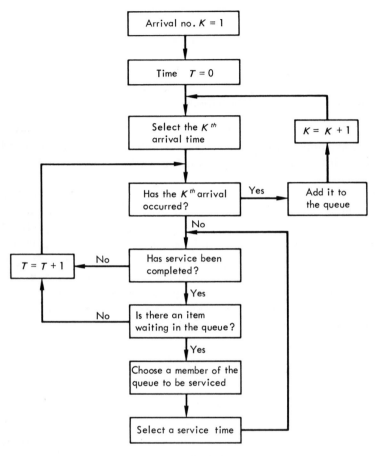

FIGURE 10.23

$$P_n = \frac{M!}{(M - n)!}\left(\frac{\lambda}{\mu}\right)^n P_0$$

Thus, when $n = 0$: $\quad P_0 = P_0 \qquad\qquad\qquad = 1.000\, P_0$

And, when $n = 1$: $\quad P_1 = M\left(\frac{\lambda}{\mu}\right)P_0 \qquad\qquad = 30(0.0169)P_0$

$\qquad\quad n = 2$: $\quad P_2 = M(M - 1)\left(\frac{\lambda}{\mu}\right)^2 P_0 = 30(29)(0.0169)^2 P_0$

$$\begin{array}{cc} \cdot & \cdot \\ \cdot & \cdot \\ \cdot & \cdot \end{array}$$

$\qquad\quad n = M$: $\quad P_M = M!\left(\frac{\lambda}{\mu}\right)^M P_0 \qquad = 30!(0.0169)^{30} P_0$

[37] Here $\lambda = 0.7/(8)(30)$ breakdowns per hour appropriate to the individual machine and $\mu = 1/5.8$ machine repairs per hour. Therefore, $(\lambda/\mu) = 0.0169$.

No more than M machines can be out of order, so $P_{n>M} = 0$. If we now add both sides of these equations, we obtain:

$$\left(\sum_{n=0}^{n=M} P_n = 1 \right) = 1.9678 P_0$$

Solving for P_0 we find: $P_0 = 0.5082$. Returning this value to the above equations, we derive $\{P_n\}$, shown in column E of Table 10.9.

The average number of machines in the waiting line is computed by the equation $L_q = \sum_{n=1}^{n=30} (n-1)P_n$. The value $(n-1)$ is used here since the first machine down will go to repair immediately and does not have to wait in line. Also, $W_q = L_q/\lambda$ which is a well-known formula in queuing theory.[38]

The degree of agreement between column E and column D is high. Nevertheless, we note that the tail of the column E distribution is more clearly delineated. Events such as $n = 8$, 9, and 10 have probabilities measured in the ten-thousands and for these our sample of 5000 is relatively insufficient. Clearly, the mathematical analysis is fast, efficient and precise. It is a preferred approach so long as the equational forms are capable of reasonably rapid and straightforward solution.

For the infinite source hypothesis an even less complex mathematical formulation is available.[39] The appropriate equations are:

$$P_n = \left(1 - \frac{\lambda}{\mu} \right)\left(\frac{\lambda}{\mu} \right)^n$$

$$L_q = \frac{\lambda^2}{\mu(\mu - \lambda)} \text{ and again, } W_q = L_q/\lambda$$

These results are shown in column C of Table 10.9. Comparison of columns C and E indicates that the infinite source assumption produces a somewhat longer tail for the distribution than would actually exist. Also, both L_q and W_q are larger when the infinite source assumption is made. Nevertheless, the results are sufficiently close to warrant the use of this approximation under most circumstances.

Of all of our methods, this last one (column C) is the least demanding computationally. However, both mathematical models that we have used are *directly based* on the assumption that breakdowns occur in Poisson fashion and that repair intervals follow the exponential distribution.

---

[38] We have used $\lambda = 0.6763/8$, which is the system's average value obtained from:

$$\frac{1}{8} \sum_{n=0}^{n=M} (30 - n)[0.7/30]P_n$$

[39] We use the system's value for λ, *viz.*, $(.7)/8 = \lambda$; $\mu = 1/5.8$ and, therefore, $\lambda/\mu = 0.5070$.

Significant complications are added for most queuing models whenever the input rate (λ) deviates from the Poisson form and the service interval ($1/\mu$) from the exponential distribution. As the problem becomes more resistant to mathematical resolution, simulation becomes increasingly attractive as an alternative approach.

Equations can be written for systems analysis of the effects of more than one repairman.[40] For the finite case, where S = the number of repairmen:

$$0 \le n \le S \qquad P_n = \frac{M!}{(M-n)!n!}\left(\frac{\lambda}{\mu}\right)^n P_0$$

$$S \le n \le M \qquad P_n = \frac{n!}{S!S^{n-s}} \cdot \frac{M!}{(M-n)!n!}\left(\frac{\lambda}{\mu}\right)^n P_0$$

Here, too, we use the fact that $\sum_{n=0}^{n=M} P_n/P_0 = 1/P_0$, to solve these recurrence relations.

When the infinite source hypothesis is used:

$$0 \le n \le S \qquad P_n = \frac{1}{n!}\left(\frac{\lambda}{\mu}\right)^n P_0$$

$$S \le n \qquad P_n = \frac{1}{S!S^{n-s}}\left(\frac{\lambda}{\mu}\right)^n P_0$$

In this case, $\sum_{n=0}^{n=\infty} P_n/P_0 = 1/P_0$ and the method of solution is similar to those we have seen before.

Using the pertinent performance measures for systems having one and more repairmen, we can proceed to determine an optimal number of repairmen. The solution will depend upon a balance of the opposing costs as they are affected by the performance characteristics of the different system's configurations. Thus, for example, with respect to the results obtained for our hand-simulation sample of 800 hours, the total waiting time was 202 hours or an average of $202/71 = 2.845$ hours per breakdown. Alternatively, there were $202/100 = 2.02$ hours waiting time for each of the 100 days represented by the sample. At the stated cost of $40 per hour for a machine which is out of operation this amounts to $80.80 loss due to waiting time per day. Since an additional repairman would cost only $40 per day it appears worth investigating whether an additional repairman would save more than $40 in waiting time.

We can use the same Monte Carlo sample for this purpose. Breakdown times and repair times remain unchanged but it is necessary to recalculate the termination of repairs for each breakdown. The rule to be followed is an obvious modification of the one we used for one repair-

---

[40] These equations assume Poisson input and exponential service times. Also, $L_q = \sum(n-S)P_n$ and $W_q = L_q/\lambda$ can be used for problem 12 at the end of this chapter.

man. Namely, a breakdown must wait for a repairman only if $B_i < T_{i-1}$ and $B_i < T_{i-2}$. In other words, a breakdown must wait for a repairman only if both repairmen are occupied with other breakdowns. The table showing the T_i will not be included here, but the table of waiting times with two repairmen is as follows:

BREAKDOWN	WAITING TIME
111	3
157	1
226	2
318	1
436	1
509	2
538	1
	11

The total waiting time of 11 hours represents an average waiting time of 0.11 hours per day. At $40 per hour this is $4.40 per day. The additional repairman has decreased the average daily waiting time cost by $80.80 − $4.40 = $76.40. This saving has been achieved at the cost of one additional repairman's salary, so the net saving is $76.40 − 40.00 = $36.40. The additional repairman should definitely be added.

This conclusion may seem surprising because of the relatively high cost of idle time for the two repairmen. In this case almost 75 per cent of the total time of the two repairmen will be idle time. However, the conclusion of our analysis is correct and results from minimizing *total costs,* in accordance with the objective of this decision problem. The conflict between our conclusion and that which one might expect is due to the fact that the obvious averages are not good measures of effectiveness in processes like these. On the average, 0.7 machines break down per day and, on the average, 5.8 hours are required to repair a machine, so, on the average, the repairman will only work 4 hours per day, therefore, why should we need another repairman? The fault in this reasoning is that it doesn't take into account another kind of average, namely, that, machines will not break down in intervals properly spaced to meet the repairmen's availability. Rather, the breakdowns will *cluster* in the way they do in our sample. This clustering of breakdowns accounts for the waiting time, which is not considered in our on-the-average reasoning above.

PROBLEMS

1. a. In our repairmen problem Monte Carlo procedures were used to obtain a sample of the behavior of the system. We drew random numbers to find the times of breakdowns and then used a different selection of random numbers

to find lengths of time of the repairs required. Why couldn't we employ the same random numbers to do both of these things simultaneously?

b. In the repairmen problem we didn't analyze what would happen if there were three repairmen. Was this an oversight?

2. Four business-school students who are fatigued by their studies decide to interrupt their labors and to spend an evening with some young ladies. Since they do not know any, they call a neighboring girls' school and, after some negotiations, succeed in finding four girls who are willing to make a collective "blind date." After introductions are made, and while the girls are getting their coats, the young men decide that since they are business students they should try to maximize their total utility. They quickly use the standard-gamble technique (or some other system) to express their utilities for each of the girls:

BUSINESS STUDENTS	GIRLS			
	BLONDE	BRUNETTE	REDHEAD	?
A	0.50	0.85	1.00	0
B	0.75	1.00	0.90	0
C	0.50	0.90	1.00	0
D	0.40	0.80	1.00	0

Note that this decision problem requires *maximization* of the total utility whereas the technique illustrated in the chapter for this kind of problem was designed for minimization. This difference causes no difficulties. As previously mentioned, simply calculate the *disutilities* by subtracting each entry from one which is the maximum value in the matrix. The minimization of the disutility matrix is equivalent to the maximization of the utility matrix.

a. Determine the set of four "twosomes" which maximizes total utility.

b. In the solution it will be found that it is necessary to have A match coins with one of the other students to see who will get the date with the redhead and who will get "?". A lost and protested bitterly. He maintained that he had been forced to take a gamble with expected utility of $0.5 = [\frac{1}{2}(1.00) + \frac{1}{2}(0)]$, whereas he would have very much preferred to have the certainty of a date with the blonde, with the same utility. He asserted that this would have meant the same total utility and would therefore not have affected the maximization. He further asserted that he had a strong aversion to gambling and if he had known that he would have to gamble he would have changed his utilities. Comment on his argument.

Postscript. In the actual case it developed that the young ladies had had a brief discussion and had agreed on an allocation of the young men which in no way corresponded to the solution found above. This, of course, they easily accomplished. The moral of this is that decision-problem solutions are of no avail if there is no control over implementation—a subject which will be treated in the last chapter of this book. Furthermore, it may be noted that the student who got "?" found her to be quite the most delightful girl he had ever met (another example of how difficult it is to measure the most essential behavioral dimensions).

3. A well-known book on operations research has a problem dealing with inventories of spare parts for generators. Each spare part is built uniquely for the specific generator and may not be used on any other generator. If the part is ordered with the generator, the cost is $500. If a part is needed and is not available, the cost of having it made plus the cost of the time the generator is out of operation will be $10,000. The probability distribution for failures of the parts is:

NUMBER OF SPARE PARTS NEEDED	PROBABILITY
0	0.90
1	0.05
2	0.02
3	0.01
4	0.01
5	0.01
	1.00

a. The authors of the book in question solve the problem in a way which in our terms would produce the following decision payoff matrix:

STRATEGIES: NUMBER OF SPARE PARTS	STATES OF NATURE DEMAND					
	0	1	2	3	4	5
0	$ 0	10,000	20,000	30,000	40,000	50,000
1	500	0	10,000	20,000	30,000	40,000
2	1,000	500	0	10,000	20,000	30,000
3	1,500	1,000	500	0	10,000	20,000
4	2,000	1,500	1,000	500	0	10,000
5	2,500	2,000	1,500	1,000	500	0

This payoff matrix is *wrong*. Try to state exactly why it is wrong and deduce the fault in the reasoning which led to the error. Note that it could have been avoided by precisely stating the objective.

b. Solve the decision problem correctly.

4. A company maintains an inventory on three items for which we have the following information:

ITEM	PRICE	YEARLY DEMAND
A	$4.00	10,000
B	2.00	30,000
C	1.00	10,000

The company estimates carrying costs at 12 per cent per year and ordering cost at $10 per order. Current policy is to order each item once each month.

a. What are the total carrying and ordering costs per year with the present policy?

b. What is the optimal ordering policy which has the same total number of orders? What is the total cost per year?

c. What is the optimal ordering policy which has the same total inventory? What is the total cost per year?

d. What is the optimal ordering policy and what is its total cost per year?

e. Find and graph the curve showing the total inventory and the total number of orders which result from the optimal policy for every ratio of ordering cost to carrying cost.

f. What ratio of ordering cost to carrying cost is implied by b? by c?

5. A company must ship from 3 factories to 7 warehouses. The transportation cost per unit from each factory to each warehouse, the requirements of each warehouse, and the capacity of each factory are:

| | FACTORIES | | | WAREHOUSE |
WAREHOUSES	1	2	3	REQUIREMENTS
A	$6	11	8	100
B	7	3	5	200
C	5	4	3	450
D	4	5	6	400
E	8	4	5	200
F	6	3	8	350
G	5	2	4	300
FACTORY CAPACITY:	600	400	1,000	2,000

a. Find the minimum-cost transportation schedule.

b. Suppose warehouse *B* goes out of business. This means that there is now excess capacity of 200 units. Find the minimum-cost transportation schedule.

Hint: Leave *B* in as a dummy warehouse with the same requirement of 200 units. Change the transportation costs to *B* from each factory to zero. A shipment to *B* now corresponds to leaving 200 units of capacity unused, which has zero transportation cost. Now solve as before.

c. How would you handle the case where total warehouse requirements exceed total factory capacity?

6. Earlier (see page 307), we mentioned that one particular kind of maximization problem involved a simultaneous minimization. The example of the allocation of productive resources illustrates this. The procedure used in maximizing profit in this example is known as linear programming, and it is a mathematical fact that to every such maximization problem there is an equivalent minimization problem, called the *dual*. For our example the dual is:

$$\text{Minimize } Z = 100W_1 + 100W_2$$
$$\text{subject to: } 0.25W_1 + 0.4W_2 \geq 1$$
$$0.5W_1 + 0.25W_2 \geq 1.25$$

This is minimized by $W_1 = 1.818$ and $W_2 = 1.364$.

a. Carefully compare the formulation of the dual with the original formulation. All the numbers are the same but they are arranged differently. Can you express in words what is being minimized and what restrictions the in-equations represent?

b. Calculate Z from the equation, using the given values of W_1 and W_2. Compare Z with the final profit obtained in the original problem. Try dimensional analysis to determine in what units W_1 and W_2 are expressed. W_1 and W_2 have an important economic significance which will be discussed in Chapter 14, see p. 550.

7. A factory with three departments makes three products. The maximum daily capacity of each department for each product, assuming it makes nothing else, and the profit for each unit of each product are:

| | DEPARTMENT | | | PROFIT |
PRODUCT	I	II	III	PER UNIT
A	333	286	500	$4.00
B	500	1,000	1,000	1.50
C	1,000	667	500	2.00

a. Using the simplex method, determine the maximum possible profit and the amounts of each product which must be produced to obtain it.

b. Try to set up the dual to this maximization problem.

c. Suppose it is decided not to produce product B. Find the amounts of the other two products which must be produced to obtain maximum profits.

8. a. What condition characterizes the transportation matrix shown below?

b. Describe precisely the steps that should be taken to permit the computations to proceed.

	1	2	3	
A	400			400
B	600			600
C		300		300
D		400	100	500
E			500	500
	1,000	700	600	2,300

9. a. Test the *sensitivity* of *total cost* for the *batch*-type production inventory model to a ±5 per cent error in the set-up cost.

b. Similarly, test the *sensitivity* of *total cost* for the *serial*-type production inventory model to a ±3 per cent error in the daily production rate.

10. In Problem 1 of Chapter 5 a drug store chain is about to reassign its present six store managers. *Create* your own numbers for this problem so that the solution requires the use of all steps of the assignment algorithm (i.e., intersection manipulations).

11. For the hand-simulation on pp. 354–356 a waiting-line diagram (Figure 10.22) was constructed to help derive the $\{P_n\}$ distribution. This diagram covers only a part of the entire simulation. Develop the remainder of the diagram and compare the values of $\{P_n\}$ that you obtain against those given in column A of Table 10.9.

12. Use the equations on p. 363 (for more than one repairman) to determine $\{P_n\}$, L_q and W_q for 2 and 3 repairmen. Working with the given cost figures of \$40 per idle machine hour and \$5 per hour for each repairman's rate of pay, what is the optimum number of repairmen?

13. The example of sequencing machine maintenance with two crews and eight machines resulted in an optimal sequence with 11 idle hours for crew *B*. Assume that there are five men in crew *B* and that they receive \$3.50 per hour.

    a. If the previous sequence followed was: *a, b, c, d, e, f, g, h,* how much was saved by the sequencing study?

    b. Assuming that each man does an equal share of the work, what result occurs if an additional man is added to group *B*?

14. A company has four departments which are to be modernized during the plant's annual summer-vacation shutdown. The work is to proceed in three stages: *A*, install new lighting fixtures and other equipment; *B*, plaster walls and make carpentry repairs; *C*, paint walls, ceilings, machines, and so on. The necessary sequence of the operations is *A–B–C*. The superintendent of maintenance decides on the size of the crews and schedules them as follows:

First to be serviced: Department 2
Second to be serviced: Department 3
Third to be serviced: Department 4
Fourth to be serviced: Department 1
Size of crew *A*:   8 men
Size of crew *B*:   6 men
Size of crew *C*:   12 men

For the stated crew sizes, the hours required for servicing are given in the chart below.

	DEPARTMENT				TOTAL CREW TIME
	1	2	3	4	
Crew *A*	20	25	45	25	115 hours
Crew *B*	10	15	5	15	45 hours
Crew *C*	30	20	35	30	115 hours

The plant is shut down for a two-week period which allows 128 hours, including the use of Saturdays, to complete the job.

    a. If the superintendent's schedule is followed, will the job be completed in time?

    b. How much idle time results from the superintendent's schedule?

    c. Is there a better schedule which can be followed?

    d. What happens to the optimal schedule if each of the crews is doubled in size?

    e. What happens if crew *B* is halved in size?

15. The Bellisima Company manufactures a full line of cosmetics. A competitor has recently brought out a new form of hair spray that shows every sign of

sweeping the market and destroying Bellisima's position in the market. The sales manager asks the production manager what the shortest possible time would be for Bellisima to reach the market with a new product packed in a new container. The production manager sets down the following PERT structure:

ACTIVITY	INITIAL EVENT	TERMINAL EVENT	DURATION
Design product	1	2	
Design package	1	3	
Test market package	3	5	
Distribute to dealers	5	6	
Order package materials	3	4	
Fabricate package	4	5	
Order materials for product	2	4	
Test market product	2	7	
Fabricate product	4	7	
Package product	7	5	

a. Construct the PERT diagram.

b. Estimate in a reasonable way the durations you think might apply.

c. Determine the critical path.

d. Neither the sales manager nor the production manager are satisfied with the way the project is designed, but the production manager insists that because of the pressure of time the company will be forced to follow this plan. In what ways does this plan violate good practice?

e. By trading-off resources would it be possible to reduce the critical path time?

16. In the example above, it was suggested that a reasonable method be employed for estimating the durations of activities. Now, employ the parameters of the Beta distribution, see p. 295. Discuss the relevancy of this latter approach in terms of the comparison between your first estimates and these new ones.

17. Draw up an appropriate PERT diagram for the following projects:

a. Organizing a community affair.

b. Computerizing the activities of a library.

c. Taking a year-end inventory.

d. Introducing the use of linear programming for a paint factory.

e. Solving the following problem with a team of three persons as rapidly as possible and with full accuracy:

$$\left[\frac{(46.222)^{1/2}}{(8.328)^2} + \frac{(9.827)^2}{(11.035)^3}\right]^{-1}$$

Chapter 11

Of Marketing

Marketing is that subject which treats all of the conditions under which the supplier meets the consumer. It is the testing ground where the cumulative effect of many previous decisions can be observed. If sales are good, then the marketing effort is said to be successful, and vice versa. Of course, it is usually understood that the marketing objective is not only sales. It is sales at a sufficiently low cost so that a good profit can be realized. At the same time, few companies are solely interested in profit today, or profit this month. The ability to continue to make profit far into the future is of prime importance. It is hard to make marketing decisions that take both present profit and future profit into account. For this reason, marketing problems are prone to serious temporal sub-optimization. But this is only one of the difficulties that management experiences in formulating marketing decision problems.

First of all, there are an enormous number of strategic possibilities. The dimensions of marketing strategies are so varied that it is inconceivable to include all of them in a formal analysis. The controls that exist for achieving different market strategies begin with the design of the product and include naming the brand, packaging the product, pricing the product, choosing types of outlets, and advertising the brand. In other words, they consist of product characteristics, price, distribution, and communication with consumers.

The second major difficulty is the effect of competition. Formulating the strategic possibilities of a rational competitor is as difficult as, if not more difficult than, formulating our own strategies. Creativity plays such an important part in the development of marketing strategies that it is quite often impossible to analyze the effects that competitive strategies will have on the outcomes. Many times, more than a single competitor exists. Each competitor has so great a number of possible strategies that the resolution of the decision problem is impossible. In the same way, the states of nature that affect the outcomes are hard to detail. The economy can change in too many ways to catalog them all. Consumer attitudes are dynamic and respond to factors that are outside the ordinary scope of consideration. All told, detection and listing of all relevant columns in the decision matrix cannot be a reasonable approach to the problem. To illustrate this, imagine that the decision-maker's strategy includes 5 possible product designs, 5 prices, 5 patterns of distribution, and 5 methods of communicating with the consumer. This is a total of 625 strategies. If there are 4 competitors, it is not unreasonable to assume that each of the competitors has 625 strategies available. Presuming that there are 5 states of nature, then the number of different conditions that can prevail is 476,837,158,203,125. Ironically, the only ludicrous thing about this number is that it is far too small to describe the actual situation.

The third difficulty is the determination of outcomes. Even if we could write down all of the important strategies, competitive strategies, and states of nature, we could not hope to find one outcome that would suffice to describe completely each box in the payoff matrix. We have already mentioned that a multiple objective exists. That is, we are interested in both short- and long-term profit. Usually, we cannot determine either of these two kinds of profit for every box. The situation is simply too complex for us to conceive of what would happen to profit if one or several factors changed. For example, suppose the decision-maker changed his package; at the same time, one competitor lowered his price; meanwhile, the state of nature changed so that it was warmer than usual; and the cost of living rose—how would the two kinds of profit be affected? Even the most deliberate and painstaking attempts to formulate this problem must result in failure.

How, then, do we handle these three types of difficulties? One approach is to consider only a few factors at a time, i.e., parts of strategies, states of nature, and so on. These few factors are related either to the profit outcomes or to suboutcomes that are believed to influence profit. For example, we relate color of the package and the expressed preferences of consumers for various colors. The connection between the consumers' preference and profit cannot be formalized. The executive believes that increasing consumer preference is a means of increasing profit. Similarly, the executive tries to minimize the cost of communicating the brand name to x number of consumers, or he attempts to increase sales volume. The profit objectives are not forgotten in these cases. The general relationships between cost and profit—between the size of an advertising campaign and profit—between sales volume and profit, and so on are kept in mind even though they cannot be included in the explicit formulation of the problem.

Another approach to the problem is to consider outcomes and suboutcomes without attempting to find relationships between them and the strategies, competitive strategies, and states of nature. We have previously discussed this kind of analysis of outcome data which treats outcomes as information. The purpose of the investigation is to find patterns and regularities that permit us to predict future outcomes although we do not know the way in which these results occur. Neither this approach nor the one that considers parts of strategies is entirely satisfactory. The use of parts of strategies results in suboptimization, and a great deal of caution must be exercised to prevent the suboptimization from producing outcomes that lower the degree of achievement of the objectives. The danger always exists that a few factors isolated from the total environment in which they appear will behave in an entirely different manner under the conditions of isolation. The recourse to suboutcomes is another cause of suboptimization. We presume that the suboutcome is related to profit in a manner that we can intuit. If we are wrong, then the achievement of the optimal suboutcome can lead to lower, rather than higher, profit. However, since we can observe only certain kinds of factors that relate to the marketing objectives, we have no alternative but to use suboutcomes. For the most part it is better than doing nothing at all. The danger in just studying outcome data arises from the possibility that significant changes might have taken place during the period in which the data were collected. Since the outcomes are not analyzed in conjunction with strategies and states of nature, the effects of changes are observed in the data without the knowledge of what caused them. Sometimes, the fact that a significant change took place can be detected and traced to its source by means of statistical control techniques. In general, however, the assumption is made that no significant changes took place during the period and that the outcome process is essentially stable. If a competitor, or the decision-maker, introduces an important change, then it is possible to attempt to determine the effect of that change by studying the outcome data before and after the change. All of the above remarks will apply in one form or another to the discussion which follows of specific marketing models.

105/ The Problem of Objectives

Our analysis of the decision process is based on the payoff matrix, and payoffs are the measure of the worth of the various outcomes in terms of the decision-maker's objectives. Generally, then, our analysis depends on our ability to define the objectives in a specific decision problem so that this kind of measurement can be accomplished. How difficult is it likely to be to do this?

The answer is that it is rarely easy to define objectives satisfactorily, and it is often almost impossible. Indeed, one of the major reasons for the earlier development of management science models in production, in contrast with other areas of business, is precisely the greater ease with which objectives can be defined. "Greater ease," of course, doesn't mean "easy," although the satisfactory definition of objectives in production might well seem "easy" in comparison to the excessive difficulties often found in defining objectives for marketing decision problems. This is a kind of problem where almost nothing can be gained by a general discussion. The reason is that the most important aspect of the problem is the lesson to be learned by considering the efforts of reasonable persons to cope with the difficulties.

A particularly good example comes from advertising. Specifically, what is the objective of magazine advertising? This objective needs to be defined in order to analyze any decision problem involving the use of magazines for advertising. How much money should be spent on magazine advertising? Which magazines should be used in a specific campaign? Should we use women's magazines or men's magazines to advertise, say, color film for cameras? These are the kinds of decisions which require specification of the objective of magazine advertising. In this section we are not going to be concerned with a specific decision problem but rather in the prior question common to any such decision problem, namely, what are we trying to accomplish with our magazine advertising?

Part of the difficulty in answering this question is related to the index-number problem, mentioned earlier.[1] What is usually wanted for a business enterprise is very much like health for a human being—it is easy to recognize when it is missing but it is terribly hard to define. But suppose that the optimal desired state of a business was defined in terms of a whole series of measurements or qualitative statements. If this existed it would then be theoretically possible to measure the effect of specific magazine advertising on the components of the ideal description and thus achieve a measure of payoff. The difficulties would still be enormous because the objectives are multidimensional and because the measurement of the effectiveness of magazine advertising along any one dimension is extremely complicated. But even this theoretical possibility is precluded because we haven't the least hope of achieving such a defini-

[1] See page 83.

tion. To return to the analogy with health, we are in the position of trying to decide between a Yucatan vacation or a vacation in the Swiss Alps. Our decision is to be based solely on health considerations, but we do not understand the effect of climate on health. Under these circumstances, what can be done?

The answer is to suboptimize. This word can mean a great many different things, depending upon the circumstances. Here it means that some one component of the definition of the optimal state of the business is accepted as an end in itself and used as the objective. Thus, this year's profit may be the objective, or the present worth of the expected profit stream over the next few years or, simply, sales. Granted the acceptance of such an objective, the payoffs are measured accordingly. This kind of approach is by no means confined to marketing problems. The same thing takes place in production problems, where we may take the minimization of costs as our objective even though it is suboptimizing in exactly this sense. But it is more difficult to define objectives for marketing problems because there does not even seem to be a way to define a suboptimal objective.

Let us return to our example, the objective for magazine advertising. Can we use profit as our suboptimal objective? If so, how can we measure payoffs? Profit depends directly on every aspect of a company's operations. How can the specific effect of magazine advertising be disentangled? It is most unlikely that this can be accomplished. To indicate some of the problems, suppose we move back one step, so to speak, and take sales as the objective for magazine advertising.

This would mean, among other things, that the advertising agency used by a company would be evaluated in terms of the sales generated by the advertising. The agency's arguments against this approach would be that they were being held accountable for matters over which they had no control. They could argue, for example, that sales depend on distribution. Why penalize the advertising agency for low sales when it may well be a question of poor distribution? Sales depend on the price. Why should advertising be penalized for low sales when it may be the fault of too-high a price for the product? Sales depend on retailers' displays, on other kinds of promotional activities, on salesmen's commissions, and so forth. How can the influence of magazine advertising be disentangled and evaluated? There is no simple answer to this question. The difficulties are so intransigent that there is only the most remote possibility of measuring payoffs along these lines.

Perhaps we should start from the other end, with the people to whom our advertising is directed. But which people? Those who are already regularly purchasing our product, or those who are brand loyal to a competitive product, or those who are switching from one to the other, or those who don't use the product at all—or what else? Obviously, a company might wish to direct different advertising campaigns to different classes of people, or it might wish to evaluate one campaign in terms of its possibly diverse effects on different classes of people. In either case, there are severe difficulties. This can best be seen by contrasting a classification of people by, say, brand loyalty with one based on some important standard demographic characteristic such as income. In the latter case it would seem a reasonable approximation to assume that the importance of a given class of people to the company was proportional to its total purchasing power. But in a classification based on brand loyalty this would not be at all reasonable because the purchasing power of the class that is loyal to the competitive brand is simply not "available" in the same way as is that of the class of "switchers." Let us pass beyond this problem by assuming that it has been handled by a combination of explicit measures while ignoring others that are too difficult to approach.

The remainder of this discussion will deal with any *one* specific class of people. This means that we are assuming that all individuals within the class are identical in terms of their potential value to the company. To simplify even further, assume that the decision problem is a simple choice between a single advertisement in magazine A and a single advertisement in magazine B. Now, what is the objective? Should the magazine with the larger circulation (subscriptions plus newsstand sales) be chosen? Or should the magazine be chosen which has the larger readership (circulation plus readers due to passing the magazine along and due to reading the magazine in barbershops, doctors' offices and so forth)? One argument for using circulation is that people who are willing to purchase the magazine are more likely to be receptive to advertising in it because they have demonstrated their interest in the magazine's contents. One argument for using readership is that interest in the magazine is equally displayed by those who bother to pick it up to read, however that is done, and that the only relevant question is whether or not an individual had a chance to be influenced by the advertisement. But perhaps the important distinction is one that cuts through the preceding argument by asserting that the objective should be at-home readership (the magazine was read in the individual's home). The argument here is that a pass-along reader who is reading the magazine in his home is just as likely to be influenced by the advertisement as is the original purchaser of the magazine, but that the casual reader in the barbershop is not nearly as likely to be receptive to the advertisements.

The argument continues—perhaps none of the above are reasonable objectives. In the preceding paragraph are several surreptitious references to advertisements "influencing" the readers. It is clear that there can be no influence if the reader did not notice the advertisement and it is certainly introspectively clear that one can read a magazine and not notice some of the advertisements. Why not, then, make "noticing" the objective? Such measures are available for magazines and are called "noting scores." "Noting" in this sense means that a reader of the magazine remembers having seen or "noticed" the advertisement. Perhaps our objective should be to obtain the maximum possible noting scores.

But if we are talking about influence, then we want to influence people to use our specific brand. To do this it is not enough that the reader should notice the advertisement. He must also associate it with the specific brand. This is called "brand registration" and measures of brand registration can be obtained from various suppliers of magazine data. Should brand registration be the objective?

Have we gone far enough? Probably not. What does "influencing" mean? An advertisement ordinarily carries some message, some statement about the brand in question. Does not "influencing" really mean convincing the individual that the statement is true? In other words, the advertiser wants to convince the reader that the claim he is making is correct. Should this, then, be the objective? The term for this notion is "claim conviction" and it appears that an argument can be offered for making some measure of claim conviction the objective of the advertiser.

Yet claim conviction is not enough. A colleague of the authors has been so convinced of the claims made by Rolls-Royce that for twenty years he has been stating that he would never own any other car. This "claim conviction" has been of modest worth to the manufacturer as our colleague has never yet owned a car. A smoker can be convinced of the claims of some brand of cigarette lighter and yet continue to use matches. The role of a nonsmoker is even more apparent. These examples suggest that what is needed is claim conviction plus an intent to take action on the basis of the conviction. The term for this is "intent to buy" and our remarks suggest that the objective should be precisely this: the definite intention to buy on the part of the reader of the advertisement.

Once we have gone this far the next step seems inevitable. Why equivocate with "intent to buy," an intent which may diminish to nothingness with the passage of time between reading the advertisement and the next opportunity to buy? What is wanted is sales, so sales should be the objective. But this is one of our starting points and we have already seen that sales cannot meaningfully be taken to be the objective for magazine advertising. So what is the objective? Which of the many possibilities should be used? It is the fact that *there is no definitive answer to this question* which led us to include this discussion.

In practice, the responsible executives of the company and of its advertising agency would use their combined knowledge and experience to select some one of the above possibilities. Although there would be a large component of arbitrariness in the choice, still it might be expected that the circumspect use of any specific objective (and its associated measures of payoff) would lead to better selections of strategies than the alternative of proceeding on the basis of guesswork. The key word in the preceding sentence is "circumspect." Since the selected objective is *not* the true objective but an intermediate one, there is always the risk of distortion from overemphasizing the selected objective. This results from the tendency to convert means for achieving ends into ends in themselves. An illustration is needed.

Suppose noting scores has been selected as the objective. It is likely to follow that the advertising campaigns, the advertising agency, and the advertising personnel are going to be evaluated on the basis of the noting scores they achieve. This being so, it is very likely that the persons who create the advertising are going to aim for noting scores and that this will tend to produce poor advertising in terms of the real objectives. For example, high noting scores among male readers are easy to achieve by showing a photograph of a scantily clad girl. High noting scores among female readers can be achieved by showing a picture of a happy, healthy baby. However, such high noting may be achieved at the price of irritation if the photograph appears to be irrelevant to the true objective of the company.

The situation can be summarized. Noting scores may be a fine measure of advertising effectiveness, but this is more likely to be true if no one has tried to achieve noting scores. It may sound paradoxical but it is not. If an advertising campaign is designed with the broad underlying objectives of the company in mind, then noting scores may be used as a measure of success. But as soon as the measure of success becomes the goal, the underlying objectives are likely to be forgotten. The general process of which this is an instance is so widespread and so serious a blunder that it deserves a name—perhaps "index number fallacy" would do. The steps leading to this fallacy are straightforward. First, an extremely complex situation is under study. Second, some kind of measurement is introduced as a partial aid in understanding the situation. Third, since the measurement is easy to talk about it is gradually taken to be the situation itself. The stage is then set for some of the most pernicious follies which otherwise intelligent men can commit. Examples can be found almost everywhere. Consider the evaluation of teaching machines. The educational process is enormously complex and the effect of it on different individuals is often mysteriously intangible (first step). Tests are introduced in specific subjects to provide a measurement to help assess the effects of the educational process on the students (second step). The test scores now become the goal rather than the intangible something which is really desired (third step). Therefore, to demonstrate that teaching machines are just as good as teachers we need only show that students get just as good scores on tests after being taught by teaching machines. The fallacy is clearly exemplified in this contemporary instance. The refutation of this kind of argument is always the same: The fact that students do as well on tests if they have been taught by teaching machines is a crushing demonstration of the inadequacy of the tests. The reader might find it instructive to observe the same fallacy in operation in the use of batteries of tests by personnel departments searching for executives, or in the use of number of publications in evaluating faculty members, or in other examples which he can find.

The difficulties in formulating a satisfactory statement of objectives for magazine advertising have been illustrated by the above discussion, but they have by no means been exhausted. Almost any advertising campaign will encounter other problems which are, at least, equally perplexing. One major source of these additional intricacies is the fact that advertising campaigns take place over time. This implies that it is necessary to decide about the effects of multiple exposures to the same advertising campaign for the same individual. To put the issue in perspective: Is a second exposure to the same advertisement for a specific individual worth more, as much, or less than a first exposure to the advertisement for another individual who is of equal potential worth to the company? Two answers to this question are sufficiently well known to have standard names. First, the assumption that all exposures (first, second, etc.) are equally valuable leads to the objective of "total tonnage." Second, the assumption that only first exposures have value, the subsequent ones to the same individual being worthless, leads to the objective of "reach." The total tonnage of a given selection of advertising media is the total number of exposures delivered. The *reach* of the same selection of media is the percentage of individuals who received at least one exposure. Obviously, there is no reason why the objective cannot vary from one company to another, but the difficulty results from the fact that equally competent individuals have different opinions about the objective in these terms even for the same company.

Couldn't the question of the relative effectiveness of successive exposures be answered by some kind of market study? In theory, perhaps yes; in practice, definitely no. There are seemingly insurmountable difficulties in disentangling the multitude of causal factors and in establishing adequate controls. But it is because of the great need to have an informed basis for selecting objectives of this kind that there is so much interest in the behavioral sciences on the part of marketing and advertising research. The same need leads to the interest in exploring certain kinds of quantitative models of consumer behavior. The construction and analysis of such models of consumer behavior is an increasingly popular pursuit in marketing and advertising research today and we can profitably discuss one such model in the next section.

106/ Brand-Loyalty Model

Faced with the complexities of consumer behavior, how can we proceed in order to gain some understanding? There are two basic methodological approaches which merit discussion here. One possibility is to try to eliminate suggested explanations. Suppose, for example, that some simple relationship is suggested between advertising exposures and purchase behavior; and, incidentally, we ought to try the simple relationships first if we accept the principle of parsimony (sometimes called Occam's Razor). Because of the great number of interacting causal factors we may not be able to discover any means of demonstrating the probable truth of the hypothesized relationship, even if it is true. However, we might very well be able to demonstrate that it is probably false, if it is false. We could do this by deducing some conclusions from the assumed relationship which are not in accord with reality. This approach is a very popular one in contemporary model building.

Another possibility might be called the devil's advocate procedure. Suppose there is some plausible theory which *is* in accord with reality. Then it is quite likely that this theory will be accepted as being true. The devil's advocate procedure is to demonstrate that the same aspect of reality has an alternative, often completely opposed, explanation. The existence of this possibility automatically renders the truth of the generally accepted theory suspect. We now want to illustrate both of these approaches.

Consider how advertising might affect consumer behavior. If we want to be able to make comparisons between any theoretical conclusions and the real world we will need to confine our attention to aspects of consumer behavior which can be objectively described in terms of some kind of feasible observations. A convenient source of data comes from the purchase diaries maintained by members of various consumer panels. From these diaries it is possible to determine the sequences of purchases, by brand, for specific product categories. Let us assume a specific market with just two brands, A and B. Suppose that the brands have 50% market shares and that the general product quality is the same for each brand. We will further assume that the advertising campaigns for the two brands are of similar size and effectiveness so that the probabilities are equal that a randomly selected individual will be exposed to either brand's advertisement. The point of these assumptions is to ensure that the two brands are equivalent with regard to all factors which affect the consumers of the product. This granted, what kinds of purchase behavior are likely to be found?

Instead of suggesting the actual distribution of behavior we might expect to find, let us ask what we could anticipate on the basis of some simple assumptions about the effect of advertising. Suppose that a consumer's purchase depends solely on the one advertisement he saw just before he was ready to purchase. In other words, the effect of all previous advertising and all previous purchases has been expunged and the most recent exposure to a brand advertisement determines the purchase of that brand. Under the terms of this model of the effect of advertising on purchases, what kinds of purchase patterns are we likely to find if we tabulate the last ten purchases, say, of our consumer panel? Since our assumptions make it equally likely that a prospective purchaser will see either brand's advertisements we are entitled to assume that the specific advertisement last seen will be randomly determined, with equal probabilities for each brand. This means, in accordance with the hypothesized relationship between advertising and purchase, that the purchases will be randomly determined, with probability of .5 for each brand. The distribution of purchases by any specific purchaser will be governed by the binomial distribution:

$$P(i) = \binom{n}{i} p^i (1 - p)^{n-i}$$

where $P(i)$ = probability of purchasing Brand A, i times
n = total number of purchases
p = probability of purchasing A = .5 here

$\binom{n}{i}$ = combination of n things taken i at a time = $n!/i!\,(n-i)!$

$$= \frac{n(n-1)\ldots(n-i+1)}{i(i-1)\ldots(3)(2)(1)}$$

Thus, if we take $n = 10$ and $i = 3$ as an example we would find $P(3) = \dfrac{(10)(9)(8)}{(3)(2)(1)} (.5)^3 (.5)^7 = .117$. This means that about 11.7% of the purchasers should have purchased A three times and B seven times—and, of course, because this example is symmetrical, there should be the same number with three purchases of B and seven purchases of A. The complete distribution would be

i	$P(i)$
0	.001
1	.010
2	.044
3	.117
4	.205
5	.246
6	.205
7	.117
8	.044
9	.010
10	.001
	1.000

How is this distribution likely to compare with the actual distribution obtained from a consumer panel? We are taking an oversimplified example for pedagogical purposes so that we cannot offer actual data for comparison. However, there is not the least doubt as to the correspondence between the above-deduced distribution and any comparable reality.

The actual distribution would be dissimilar to the one above. According to the binomial distribution few persons would show, say, 9 or 10 purchases of either brand and almost two-thirds of the purchasers would show 4 or 5 purchases of either brand. The marketing reality is likely to be contrary to this. We would probably find considerable numbers of persons who showed 9 or 10 purchases and relatively few who would show 4 or 5 purchases of one brand. This, then, is an example of the first kind of reasoning, since we would have to conclude that the hypothesized model of the effect of advertising on purchases was simply not in accord with the facts and therefore should be rejected. But what kind of explanation can be offered for the suggested actual distribution?

Any product manager would immediately offer an answer: brand loyalty. A new term, *brand loyalty*, has been used. What does it mean? Students of marketing are forced to use many phrases and terms which provide some intuitive meaning but which lack any precise definition. This is the usual situation in the beginnings of any science and most of the development of a particular science can be interpreted as a steadily improving ability to offer precise definitions for such concepts. Each of us probably has a definite idea of what it means to be brand loyal, based on our own purchasing behavior. For example, one of the authors is loyal to a specific brand of coffee. This means, in his case, that this brand has been purchased for many years, that if a store is out of the brand he goes to another store for it, and that if no convenient store has any stock he will probably drink tea instead. Or at least this is how he conceives of his behavior. The problem is, however, that even if his memory is correct this introspective conception of brand loyalty is not a suitable basis for objective studies. It is clear that a scientific analysis of "brand loyalty" cannot be accomplished by asking the respondents whether or not they were brand loyal. What is needed is some kind of behavioristic definition of brand loyalty so that its presence or absence can be deduced (say, from the purchase diaries of the respondents).

Nonetheless, it is the intuitive notion which would be the basis of the product manager's suggested answer. An essential component of any idea of brand loyalty is the fact that the brand-loyal customer would show long sequences of purchases of his favorite brand. It is exactly this pattern which is so often found in the real world and to which our binomial distribution does not conform. Obviously, brand loyalty in this intuitive sense is of great importance to companies which produce the brands. Once this kind of consumer commitment is achieved the producer has a guaranteed stream of sales for a considerable period of time, assuming that product quality, price, etc. are maintained. Therefore, most brand producers are likely to be extremely interested in inducing brand loyalty among the product consumers.

It is worth trying to clarify the concept a little because it is easy to confuse brand loyalty with other factors which are not intended to be part of what it means to be brand loyal. Thus, for example, an individual might purchase nothing but Brand *A* simply because he shopped regularly at a store which only carried Brand *A*. We have eliminated this possibility, for our example, by specifying that the two brands are equivalent in all factors affecting the consumer. This means that in our example the two brands are each carried by each store, but in the real world the inevitable imperfections of distribution cause serious problems in determining brand loyalty. This granted, it is worth considering why we would not ordinarily want to include the purchaser among those brand-loyal to *A* if the only reason for his sequence of purchases was that only *A* was carried in his store. The reason is, of course, that we intend brand loyalty to imply some kind of personal commitment on the part of the consumer, not simply the physical happenstance of availability. We want brand loyalty to be based on a choice which is the result of a genuine preference between brands, even though the preference may be the result of an imagined distinction between brands. Thus, we would consider a consumer as brand loyal who always selected one brand of beer, say, even though he was unable to distinguish this brand in a blindfold taste test. In this last context it should be noted that brand loyalty is not simply the result of superior quality. This, again, has been excluded in our example but it is obvious that the choice of a specific brand because of a marked superiority in quality is a matter separate from brand loyalty.

With all of these exclusions from the concept of brand loyalty, what is it and what causes it? We can do no better than we have done before. It is the kind of behavior of which we are often introspectively aware in making our selection from among competing brands. What causes it is exactly what we would like to be able to study scientifically. Perhaps it results from a kind of imprinting phenomenon stemming from a random first purchase of the product, or perhaps it results from the development of an ego-syntonic image created by advertising, or perhaps the image comes from identification with other purchasers observed, or perhaps—who knows?

This brings us back to the problem of defining brand loyalty in such a way that it becomes possible to determine its presence or absence objectively. A straightforward way to do this is in terms of sequences of purchases, which is certainly a major component of the notion of brand loyalty. With this approach it is clear that 100% purchases for either brand would certainly be considered as indicative of complete brand loyalty to that brand. What would be indicative of complete lack of brand loyalty? The prototype here would be a possibly imaginary consumer who might toss a coin to determine his brand purchase on each purchase occasion. This would result in purchases of each brand about half the time. By any definition this would represent total indifference and, hence, total lack of loyalty. Starting with these two ends of the scale of brand loyalty it would be straightforward to create a measure of brand loyalty. For example, suppose A is purchased by a person more than half his total number of purchases—a necessary requirement in order for there to be any brand loyalty for A. Let n be the total number of purchases and k the number of purchases of brand A $(k > .5n)$. Then a possible measure of an individual's brand loyalty would be $100(2k - n)/n$. But such a measure is unnecessary for our purposes and would probably not be adequate for any other purposes.

Instead, let us say that the 100% purchasers are brand loyal and we will allow that an occasional purchase of the other brand might still leave the consumer brand loyal to his usual choice. "Occasional" will be defined in some reasonable way according to specific circumstances. An immediate consequence of this definition of brand loyalty is that we will sometimes conclude that persons are brand loyal when in fact they are not. Consider our binomial distribution and suppose we take the purchase of 9 or 10 units of one brand as demonstrating brand loyalty to that brand. Then we would find 1.1% of the purchasers brand loyal to each of the brands. This, of course, would not be really true, although we would think it was. As a matter of fact, the model of the effect of advertising which led to the binomial distribution is exactly equivalent to the toss of a coin to determine the brand purchased—the prototype of indifference. In the case of this model no difficulties are caused by this because the binomial distribution is in such flagrant contradiction with the real world. However, it is not always so clear.

Thus, suppose we leave the assumptions of our model the same but introduce the idea that purchasers have a memory for past advertisements as was the case in our simulation example, pp. 186–193. Specifically, we will assume that each purchaser is equally likely to see an advertisement of either brand (just like a coin toss) but that he remembers all that he has seen and keeps, so to speak, an unconscious running tally of the number of advertisements he has seen of each brand. We will now hypothesize that he purchases that brand for which he has seen the larger number of advertisements. For example, suppose at the time of purchase the purchaser has seen a total of ten advertisements and that six of them have been for Brand A. Then he purchases A. (This is unlike the simulation where the probabilities favored A, but a B purchase was possible.) What kind of distribution of purchase sequences would result from this hypothesis?

Let us consider a large number of purchasers, each of whom has seen 20 advertisements. By our assumptions he will purchase A as long as the cumulative number of A exposures *exceeds* the cumulative number of Brand B exposures.[2] Under our assumptions he is just as likely to see either brand's advertisements. "Common sense" suggests that the typical purchaser ought to switch his purchases from one brand to the other frequently, thus displaying no brand loyalty, by our definition. But the reality is quite otherwise—"common sense" is misleading! Here is a typical sequence of exposures to the 20 advertisements:

$$A\,B\,A\,A\,B\,A\,B\,A\,A\,B\,B\,B\,A\,B\,A\,A\,B\,A\,B\,B$$

Each brand's advertising was seen ten times. Yet by our rule regarding the cumulative totals of exposures, this particular purchaser would buy Brand A uninterruptedly throughout this whole sequence of exposures. Why? Because the total exposures for A throughout the sequence are always greater than or equal to the total exposures for B. Therefore, in this particular sequence, a perfectly undistinguished arrangement of the exposures would result in complete "brand loyalty" to A. Is this result exceptionable? Not at all. Actually, this is the usual result. Although at first it may seem surprising, there is a high probability that for any one purchaser either Brand A or Brand B will take the lead over the other brand and never relinquish it in such a series of exposures.

---

[2] More precisely, we will assume that he will continue to purchase one brand until the total cumulative exposures for the other brand *exceeds* the total for the brand he is purchasing.

To explain this result is not difficult. One needs only to look at all the possibilities. Consider, for example, the case of a total of four exposures. There are sixteen possible arrangements of the four exposures. By a straightforward count the following breakdown is found:

	A LEADS	
4 times	*2 times*	*0 times*
A A A A	A B B A	B A B A
A A A B	A B B B	B A B B
A A B A	B A A A	B B A A
A A B B	B A A B	B B A B
A B A A		B B B A
A B A B		B B B B

Therefore, in 6 cases out of 16 Brand *A* leads during the whole sequence of exposures. Under our assumptions this means that any purchaser with this pattern of exposures would purchase nothing but *A* during this time period. Clearly, if enough purchases were made then this purchaser would be considered loyal to Brand *A* even though his purchase behavior is in fact a happenstance of the fluctuations of cumulative exposures.

The same kind of result obtains for the case of 20 exposures, the example we used above. Specifically, we find the following distribution of the 2^{20} patterns of 20 exposures:

A LEADS *i* TIMES	PROPORTION
0	.175
2	.095
4	.075
6	.065
8	.060
10	.060
12	.060
14	.065
16	.075
18	.095
20	.175

It will be noticed that one of the brands, either *A* or *B*, will be in the lead throughout all 20 exposures for 35% of the purchasers. The purchase records of these individuals will therefore show an uninterrupted sequence of purchases of one of the two brands. Yet this fact would not be an indication of "brand loyalty" in any sense which would be useful to the brand manufacturer.

Suppose he identified a group of such individuals through the analysis of purchase diaries. If he attempts to find out in what ways the "loyal" customers differ from the rest of the market, he will find no significant differences.

It is a fact that some essentially two-brand markets do show the proportions of apparently brand-loyal customers that would be suggested by the above model. The fact that this model would produce the observed proportions of apparently brand-loyal customers calls into question the assumption that they are in fact brand loyal. This is an example of the kind of argument we called the devil's advocate procedure at the beginning of this section. In addition to exemplifying this kind of argument, the model shows how misleading one's intuition or common sense can be when dealing with probabilistic relationships. Intuition would certainly suggest that the most common pattern of exposures received by each individual would be the kind for which each brand had the lead, in the cumulative sense, about half the time. Yet, in fact, this is the least common pattern.[3]

Of course, the model is purely hypothetical. There is, if anything, less reason to believe that such a relationship holds between purchase and cumulative exposures than there is to believe in a loyal customer. Perhaps no one explanation will suffice. Certainly, it is interesting to find that the distribution of apparent loyalties derived in this manner comes fairly close to a number of observed distributions. But then other hypotheses can also be used to obtain this same result, including the notion that advertising has a cumulative impact. The point is that before a concept such as brand loyalty can be used in a meaningful way to measure the effectiveness of strategies it is necessary to establish that the suggested measurement of the concept really does measure it.

107/ The Boolean Algebra of Media Data

One of the main problems of advertising is called the media allocation problem. This is the problem of determining how the total advertising budget should be spent: how much should be put into nighttime television, how much into spot radio, how much into magazines, and so forth. Of course, the complete solution of the problem requires specifics, not generalities. Which magazines should be purchased? How many times a year? Which issues? Color or black-and-white? Full-page or frac-

---

[3] This model is simply the exemplification in a marketing context of a well-known law of probability theory called the *arc-sine law*. This law states that the probability that one brand has the lead for a fraction of time $\leq x$ (where $0 \leq x \leq 1$) is approximately $F(x) = \frac{2}{\pi}$ arc $\sin\sqrt{x}$. For a discussion of the arc-sine law see William Feller, *An Introduction to Probability Theory and Its Applications*, 3rd edition (New York: John Wiley & Sons, Inc., 1968), Chapter 3.

tional page? The complete solution to the media allocation problem for a specific advertiser would detail how each dollar of the budget should be spent. This total problem is of enormous difficulty and we have no intention of trying to solve it here. Indeed, the problem has not yet been solved in its full generality.

Our interest in the media allocation problem here has to do with the data which are required in order to attempt to solve this problem. The amount of data which are needed is extraordinarily large, as will be shown shortly. As a matter of fact, it was the need to somehow process these prodigious amounts of data which first led advertising agencies to investigate the potentialities of computers for the advertising industry. And, interestingly enough, the masses of data which must be considered still exceed the capacities of existing computers. Some laymen, knowing the Sunday-supplement descriptions of computer capabilities, can hardly believe that many problems still exceed the available computer capacities. Yet this is often the case, and nowhere more so than in attempts to cope with the advertising allocation problem.

The original major uses of computers can be categorized into two types of problems. One type required a small number of calculations for a large amount of data. Examples are payroll checks and dividend checks. The other type required a large number of calculations on a small amount of data. Many scientific problems are of this sort. New difficulties arise when one finds, as in the advertising allocation problem, that large numbers of calculations are necessary on huge amounts of data. These difficulties are certainly part of the reason why the advertising allocation problem has still not been completely solved.

Why are the amounts of data so huge? Consider the data required for 20 magazines. An adult may read or not read each of the twenty magazines, independently of the rest. Therefore, the number of logical possibilities is 2^{20}, or 1,048,576. These range from not reading any of the magazines to reading all twenty of them, and include every possible arrangement of some of the magazines being read and the others not being read. Of course, a little more than a million are not very many possibilities for a computer to consider. But twenty magazines is only an example. A large advertiser may want to consider a list of 100 or more magazines. In addition, the advertiser will be interested in several hundred television shows, in hundreds of radio spots, in newspapers, and so forth. Each of the possibilities under consideration adds another logical dichotomy—an individual either does or does not read, watch, or listen to the given medium. Thus, each possibility multiplies the total number of logical possibilities by two. This quickly leads to astronomical numbers—100 magazines alone produce 2^{100} possibilities, a number with 31 digits.

The advertiser, in order to determine the optimal selection of magazines, needs to know the proportion of adults that is to be found in each of the logical classes, or at least in certain subsets of these logical classes. Nor is this all. Most advertisers define their potential customers for consumer products in terms of demographic characteristics. Thus, a specific advertiser may be interested in adult readers of a particular type: a given income, a given family structure, and a given group of professions. This means that the advertiser needs to know the proportion of each of several types of adults in each of the logical classes defined by the 100 magazines.

The mere fact that there is such an enormous number of logical classes does not establish that there is any particular difficulty associated with the data requirements. It is perfectly possible in theory that, given some relatively small amount of data, we could calculate with the computer any required proportion of adults in a specified logical class. This would be the case if the data were independent in the probabilistic sense, as defined and illustrated below. In fact, however, the data are not independent, and a difficult problem results. But regardless of the data problem, the mere existence of such a multitude of logical classes makes it essential to have an organized procedure for specifying the classes and their relationships. The natural tool for this purpose is Boolean algebra.

Boolean algebra is named after George Boole, the English mathematician of the nineteenth century (1815–1864) who discovered it. It is often called the algebra of classes because it is so useful in dealing with complex systems of logical classes. Boole developed his algebra primarily so that logical deductions could be carried out symbolically. But he did this by thinking in terms of classes. Thus, he interpreted the logical premise "All horses are animals" to mean that the class of horses is contained within the class of animals. (This is by no means the only interpretation of the premise, but it is the one which Boole used.) He introduced symbols to stand for the class of horses, the class of animals and, naturally, he also needed symbols for the class of not-horses and the class of not-animals.

The structure is directly applicable to the magazine example we are interested in: we want to talk about the class of adult readers of *Life,* and the class of adults who do not read *Life.* The same is true for the *Ladies Home Journal,* television programs, and so forth. Both examples, the magazine one and the logical statement about horses, are based on dichotomies—a thing is either X or it is not-X—and Boolean algebra is the natural tool for dealing with dichotomies.

We do not need to develop much of Boolean algebra here. For our purposes it will suffice to introduce the two basic operations of Boolean algebra and the important relationship which exists between them.

Let capital letters represent classes of things: A might be the class of animals, the class of adult readers of *House Beautiful,* the class of persons who purchased apricot jam, or any other defined class. In the Boolean convention it then follows that a capital letter with a bar over it represents the things that do *not* have the property that defines the class: $\bar{A}$ would be the class of not-animals, the class of adults who do not read *House Beautiful,* the class of persons who did not purchase apricot jam, and so forth. Now suppose that we have defined two classes, A and B. Boolean algebra has two operations which can be performed on any two classes:

$\cup$: "cup"; called "union" or "logical addition"
    $A \cup B$ is the class of all those things which are *either A or B or both*
$\cap$: "cap"; called "intersection" or "logical multiplication"
    $A \cap B$ is the class of all those things which are *both A and B.*

It is helpful to remember that these two operators were Boole's rendering into symbols of the logical connectives "or" and "and," respectively. The equivalence of $\cap$ and "and" is clear, but the relationship between $\cup$ and "or" needs comment. The English word "or" is ambiguous. In fact, it has two meanings: the inclusive—when we say that a great opera star must either have a great voice or must be a great actor but clearly both could be true, and the exclusive—when we say that one either pays one's taxes or else one goes to jail and clearly we expect that only one will be true. The symbol $\cup$ is equivalent to the inclusive "or."

It will be noted that the class given by $A \cap \bar{A}$ contains no things at all since no thing is simultaneously something and its opposite at the same time. In Boolean algebra this fact is designated by the equation

$$A \cap \bar{A} = 0$$

where 0 is the null class, the class with nothing in it. On the other hand, $A \cup \bar{A}$ contains all the things under consideration, since every thing is either A or *not-A.* This fact is designated by the equation

$$A \cup \bar{A} = 1$$

Where 1 is called the logical universe or the universe of discourse, the class of all things under consideration.

It is possible to use the definitions above to translate logical premises into algebraic form and to deduce by algebraic arguments the correct conclusions from the premises. This, of course, was the major goal of Boole when he developed his algebra. However, this use does not interest us here because our concern is with the number of individuals in a class. Let us use the sumbol $N(A)$ to represent the number of individuals included in the class designated by$A$. Then:

$$N(A) + N(\bar{A}) = N$$

where N is the number of individuals in the logical universe. It is convenient to divide this equation through by N and to let

$$\frac{N(A)}{N} = R(A) \text{ and } \frac{N(\overline{A})}{N} = R(\overline{A})$$

Then:

$$R(A) + R(\overline{A}) = 1$$

The symbol $R(A)$ can be read as the "reach" of class A. This is the meaning of "reach" in advertising data. To say that the reach of a magazine among adults is 0.2 is to say that that magazine is read by 0.2 proportion of the total number of adults. In Boolean terms we would define the class, say A, as all adults who read the given magazine. The logical universe is the total number of adults and, clearly, $R(A) = 0.2$, as it should, and:

$$R(A) + R(\overline{A}) = 0.2 + 0.8 = 1.0$$

simply expresses the fact that each adult either reads or does not read the given magazine.

The major relationship which we need is that which holds between the reaches of classes formed by the two Boolean operators and the reaches of the original classes to which the operators were applied. Thus, given class A and class B, what do we need to know in order to calculate $R(A \cup B)$? The relationship in question is almost obvious if we let areas represent reaches and draw what is called the Venn diagram for the case in question:

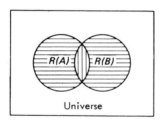

The reach of the universe is, of course, 1. The total shaded area is $R(A \cup B)$, the left-hand circle is $R(A)$, the right-hand circle is $R(B)$, and the cross-hatched area is $R(A \cap B)$. A moment's reflection will suffice to verify that

$$R(A \cup B) = R(A) + R(B) - R(A \cap B)$$

This is the basic relationship we need. From it we can develop expressions for an arbitrary number of classes.

Before doing so, however, let us see what all this has to do with media data. Consider two magazines, A and B. Suppose an advertiser is considering using both of these magazines in his media plan. Suppose, further, that the advertiser has some demographically defined group of adults as his target. He then wants to know what he will accomplish in his target audience by using the two magazines. In accordance with our discussion in the first section of this chapter, the advertiser will have to define his objective in some suitable measurable terms. We will assume that he is willing to measure the results of his magazine advertising in terms of magazine readership achieved. If the target audience is not unusually defined the advertiser will probably be able to get the information he wants from one of the major suppliers of such information.

Since the advertiser of our example is only concerned with two magazines it is quite likely that he will be able to get complete information. What is complete information in this example? From our earlier discussion it is clear that the two magazines will split the target audience into $2^2 = 4$ classes. Since the target audience is the logical universe here it follows that the reaches of the four classes must add up to 1. Therefore, the supplier of information will be providing complete information by giving the reaches of any three of the classes since the fourth one can then be obtained by subtracting the three given reaches from 1. The data is obtained by direct survey. Therefore, it would be possible for the data to be presented directly in terms of the number of persons in the sample who fell into the given class. However, for various reasons, it is almost always the case that the data is converted into the form of class reaches.

One of the problems is that there is a variety of ways in which the same data can be presented. Thus, our advertiser's information might be presented directly in terms of the four classes:

$$R(A \cap \overline{B}) = 0.28$$
$$R(\overline{A} \cap B) = 0.18$$
$$R(A \cap B) = 0.12$$

From these data we can immediately calculate that $R(\overline{A} \cap \overline{B}) = 0.42$, or 42% of the target audience will not be reached by either of the two magazines. A natural way to summarize the data, as given above, is in a two-by-two table:

		A		
		Read	Doesn't Read	
B	Read	.12	.18	.3
	Doesn't Read	.28	.42	.7
		.4	.6	

From the marginal totals of this table it is clear that $R(A) = .4$ and $R(B) = .3$. Notice that this had to be deduced from the data as given—it was not given directly. And this is an example of another problem. Any given presentation of the data emphasizes certain things and ignores others. Of course, if the data are complete, than any desired piece of information can be calculated. But this is by no means easy to do when many magazines are involved.

Data are almost never presented in the form given above, which we may call the logical form. This is because it becomes annoyingly difficult to read expressions like $R(\bar{A} \cap B \cap C \cap \bar{D} \cap \bar{E})$. Further, with more magazines in the sample this form would not be particularly convenient for the construction of the most common arrangement of the data which the advertiser is likely to want. This breakdown is called the *exposure distribution*. For our data it is:

Exposures	Proportion
0	.42
1	.46
2	.12
	1.00

This table shows the proportion of the target audience which is exposed 0, 1, or 2 times to the advertising. Note that this table is *not* a complete presentation of the data. Since it is a homomorphic transformation, as described on p. 171, we cannot work backwards from this table to reconstruct the original data. Information has been sacrificed since two distinct classes have been lumped together in the proportion with one exposure.

Nonetheless, advertising objectives are most often expressed in terms of such exposure distributions because there is insufficient knowledge of the effect of advertising to permit using more complete information. In our example there probably is some kind of difference in effectiveness for a specific campaign between the two magazines. So, if management had some accurate knowledge about effectiveness, then it might be desirable to the advertiser to distinguish between the value of the persons who read A and did not read B and the value of the persons who read B and did not read A. But this kind of distinction is not possible with the current level of knowledge. The most that can be hoped for is to distinguish the value of successive exposures.

The two extreme objectives in these terms are known as the *reach objective* and the *total tonnage objective*. The reach objective is based on the proposition that the most important thing is to achieve at least one exposure: "If you don't reach them, you can't influence them." With this objective, any exposures to a given person after the first one are treated as having no value for the advertiser. The total tonnage objective is based on the assumption that any exposure is as good as any other. The fifth exposure to one person is just as valuable as the first exposure to another. Obviously, there are innumerable intermediate possibilities, like letting the second exposure have half the value of the first, the third exposure have one-fourth the value of the first, and so on. For our example the total reach is $R(A \cup B) = 0.58$. The total tonnage is $R(A) + R(B) = 0.7$.

Because of the importance of the reach objective, one common form of presentation is directly in terms of reaches. For our data:

$$R(A) \qquad = 0.40$$
$$R(B) \qquad = 0.30$$
$$R(A \cup B) = 0.58$$

This may be called the *union form*. It has the obvious advantage that it gives the total reach of the two magazines directly. Since three reaches are given we can calculate any other breakdown of the data from this one. From the fundamental relationship we derived above it follows directly that

$$R(A \cap B) = R(A) + R(B) - R(A \cup B) = 0.4 + 0.3 - 0.58 = 0.12$$

And since $R(A \cup B) + R(\bar{A} \cap \bar{B}) = 1$ it follows that $R(\bar{A} \cap \bar{B}) = 0.42$. Further, since $R(A) = R(A \cap B) + R(A \cap \bar{B})$, we have $R(A \cap \bar{B}) = 0.4 - 0.12 = 0.28$. Proceeding in this way we can calculate any desired quantity.

Another common form of presentation of the data may be called the *intersection form*. For our example it is

$$R(A) \qquad = 0.40$$
$$R(B) \qquad = 0.30$$
$$R(A \cap B) = 0.12$$

From the fundamental relationship we can immediately determine $R(A \cup B)$ and, similarly, we can calculate any other desired quantity.

Certainly, there is no great difficulty in dealing with the data concerning two magazines. The above discussion ought to suggest, however, that there may be some problems when more magazines are under consideration, in part due to the fact that there are such a variety of ways in which the data may be presented. From our earlier arguments it follows that complete information for n magazines requires $2^n - 1$ reaches. This amount of data becomes awkwardly large even for a modest number of magazines. It would certainly be advantageous if the desired quantities could be calculated from some small amount of data. As suggested earlier, this might be possible. Under what circumstances could it be done?

If reading one magazine was independent, in the probabilistic sense, from reading any other magazine, then knowing the reach of each individual magazine (*n* pieces of information) would permit the calculation of all the rest. For the case of two magazines the definition of independence is that

$$R(A \cap B) = [R(A)] \times [R(B)]$$

Notice that this holds true for the two magazines in our example above. For those magazines we have

$$R(A \cap B) = 0.12 = 0.4 \times 0.3 = [R(A)] \times [R(B)]$$

It follows that all the information needed in this case is $R(A)$ and $R(B)$. The calculation of desired breakdowns in the case of independence can be easy. For example, to calculate the exposure distribution we introduce the idea of the *exposure-generating function*. For any magazine, X, the exposure generating function is defined as a linear function of a dummy variable, S, as follows:

$$\text{exposure-generating function of } X = E(X) = R(\overline{X}) + SR(X)$$

For magazine A we have

$$E(A) = 0.6 + 0.4S$$

and for magazine B,

$$E(B) = 0.7 + 0.3S$$

Remember, S has no independent significance; it is simply a dummy variable. It can be shown that the exposure-generating function which results from using several magazines is obtained by multiplying the individual magazine's exposure-generating functions together. The coefficient of S^i in the result is the proportion of persons having i exposures. Thus, in our example

$$[E(A)] \times [E(B)] = (0.6 + 0.4S)(0.7 + 0.3S) = 0.42 + 0.46S + 0.12S^2$$

the coefficient of S^0 is 0.42 and this means that 0.42 receive no exposure; 0.46 is the coefficient of S^1 and this means that 0.46 receive one exposure; 0.12 is the coefficient of S^2 and this means that 0.12 received two exposures. These results are identical with the exposure distribution given earlier.

The same argument applies to any number of magazines as long as they are independent in the probabilistic sense.

This would be a marvelously easy way to calculate the exposure distribution, if only magazines in the real world were independent. Unfortunately, it is far more nearly the case that no two magazines are ever independent. Hence, this theoretical possibility of eliminating the need for large amounts of data is not applicable to the real world. This forces us back to reliance on the data, with whatever difficulties that entails.

As an illustration, we will consider some actual data for three magazines. Suppose we are given the data in the union form:

$$R(B) = 0.229 \qquad R(B \cup D) = 0.490 \qquad R(B \cup D \cup G) = 0.612$$
$$R(D) = 0.383 \qquad R(B \cup G) = 0.463$$
$$R(G) = 0.310 \qquad R(D \cup G) = 0.539$$

With this form we know immediately the total reach, $R(B \cup D \cup G) = 0.612$, and the total tonnage, $R(B) + R(D) + R(G) = 0.922$. How can we calculate the exposure distribution and the other kinds of breakdowns if they are desired?

The basic starting point in such calculations is the fundamental relationship, extended to three magazines. This can be done in two directions. The arguments are simple, but only the results will be given here. They are:

$$R(A \cup B \cup C) = R(A) + R(B) + R(C) - R(A \cap B) - R(A \cap C)$$
$$- R(B \cap C) + R(A \cap B \cap C)$$

and

$$R(A \cap B \cap C) = R(A) + R(B) + R(C) - R(A \cup B) - R(A \cup C)$$
$$- R(B \cup C) + R(A \cup B \cup C)$$

The symmetrical forms of the two expressions are apparent. The first expresses the union in terms of the intersections and the second expresses the intersection in terms of the unions. Since our data gives unions, we can immediately use the second relationship to deduce that

$$R(B \cap D \cap G) = R(B) + R(D) + R(G) - R(B \cup D) - R(B \cup G)$$
$$- R(D \cup G) + R(B \cup D \cup G)$$
$$= 0.229 + 0.383 + 0.310 - 0.490 - 0.463 - 0.539 + 0.612$$
$$= 0.922 - 1.492 + 0.612$$
$$= 0.042$$

This means that 0.042 is the proportion of adults who have three exposures. We already know that $1 - 0.612 = 0.388$ is the proportion who receive no exposure.

Now we can use the fundamental relation for two magazines to deduce:

$$R(B \cap D) = R(B) + R(D) - R(B \cup D) = 0.229 + 0.383 - 0.490 = 0.122$$
$$R(B \cap G) = 0.229 + 0.310 - 0.463 = 0.076$$
and $R(D \cap G) = 0.383 + 0.310 - 0.539 = 0.154$

This completes the intersection form:

$$R(B) = 0.229 \qquad R(B \cap D) = 0.122 \qquad R(B \cap D \cap G) = 0.042$$
$$R(D) = 0.383 \qquad R(B \cap G) = 0.076$$
$$R(G) = 0.310 \qquad R(D \cap G) = 0.154$$

Note that these magazines are not independent. Thus,

$$R(B \cap D) = 0.122 \neq [R(B)] \times [R(D)] = 0.229 \times 0.383 = 0.0877$$

Remember that these reaches may apply to target audiences numbering many millions, and therefore these differences are important.

From the intersection form one can reason in a straightforward way to get the logical form. Thus,

$$R(B \cap D \cap \overline{G}) + R(B \cap D \cap G) = R(B \cap D)$$

or
$$R(B \cap D \cap \overline{G}) = R(B \cap D) - R(B \cap D \cap G)$$
$$= 0.122 - 0.042$$
$$= 0.080$$

Proceeding in this way we can deduce the logical form:

$$R(B \cap \overline{D} \cap \overline{G}) = 0.073 \qquad R(B \cap D \cap \overline{G}) = 0.080 \qquad R(B \cap D \cap G) = 0.042$$
$$R(\overline{B} \cap D \cap \overline{G}) = 0.149 \qquad R(B \cap \overline{D} \cap G) = 0.034$$
$$R(\overline{B} \cap \overline{D} \cap G) = 0.122 \qquad R(\overline{B} \cap D \cap G) = 0.112$$

From the logical form simple addition gives the exposure distribution:

EXPOSURES	PROPORTION
0	0.388
1	0.344
2	0.226
3	0.042

This illustrates how, for three magazines, any desired breakdown can be calculated if complete information is given. Obviously, this gets more difficult as the number of magazines increases, but there is some consolation in the thought that here the difficulties are purely logical ones. Careful, logical thinking is all that is required, but it turns out to be remarkably hard to accomplish unless one uses Boolean algebra to help keep one's thoughts well-ordered.

108/ Boolean Programming

The preceding section showed that it can be useful to think about the effects of an advertising campaign in terms of logical classes. Given a defined target audience, each specific medium creates two classes: those persons reached by the medium and those persons not reached by the medium. The combination of a number of media produces a variety of classes which can be defined precisely in terms of the Boolean manipulations of logical classes. In the preceding section the emphasis was on two questions. First, what requirements must be satisfied in order to have complete information so that the number of persons in any specified class can be calculated? Second, how can any desired breakdown of the data be calculated from any particular presentation of complete information?

In this section we will use the Boolean apparatus developed in the preceding section to deal with a practical problem of great importance. This problem arises because it is often the case that in practice complete information is not available. In particular, almost any company with a large advertising budget will not have complete information.

We have repeatedly noted that each magazine produces, in effect, a logical dichotomy in the target audience: those persons who read the magazine and those persons who do not read it. This is the reason why n magazines produce 2^n logical classes in the target audience. Consider the implications of this in terms of the practical problem of measuring the size of each of the 2^n classes. If only twenty magazines are being measured there are more than one million classes. Yet most of the major organizations which undertake to supply these magazine (and other media) measurements rely on samples of 5,000 persons or less. It is painfully clear that one cannot obtain measurements on the numbers of persons in each of one million classes when less than 5,000 persons are measured. Therefore, for this reason if for no other, it would be ridiculous to attempt to provide a complete breakdown for even twenty magazines. This is still more the case when 40 or more magazines are being measured. In practice, then, the suppliers of media information never give anything approaching complete information.

Some illustrations of what the suppliers of media information do give may be useful. One major supplier formerly offered information concerning 17 magazines. Complete information here would require that 131,071 reaches be given. In fact, this supplier provided its regular subscribers with the reaches of each magazine alone, the reaches of each union of two magazines, and the reaches of the unions of each combination of three magazines—a total of 833 reaches. For an extra payment the subscribers could get the reaches of the union of each combination of four magazines and of each combination of five magazines—an additional 8,568 reaches. The total data made available, therefore, amounted to about 7.2% of the complete breakdown. This particular service is no longer available and we cite it simply because it did supply more nearly complete information than most of the other services. A more typical example is an organization which supplies information on about 40 magazines. However, the only data given are the reaches of each individual magazine and the reaches of each union of two magazines. Compared to the obviously unattainable complete breakdown, this is very little data indeed.[4]

---

[4] Of course, none of these remarks is intended to be critical of the suppliers of media data. There are a variety of good reasons why they present their data in the form they do. And while the data offered may be only a small part of some theoretical total, it is tremendously helpful to the advertisers in allocating their budgets.

This sets the stage for a critically important problem. Suppose the advertiser is considering the use of a group of magazines. Since complete information is not available, the advertiser is not able to determine directly from the data the exposure distribution he can expect to achieve. As long as the reaches of the individual magazines are known the advertiser can calculate his total tonnage, but this is rarely an adequate measure of advertising effectiveness. He will not be able to calculate the total reach he will achieve, and still less will he be able to use any weightings of successive exposures. Nonetheless, it is essential that the advertiser should have this information. Therefore, he must somehow estimate the unknown data from the data he does have. This is the media estimation problem and in this section we want to discuss one approach to it.

The importance of this problem is evidenced by the extensive literature devoted to it* and the great variety of methods of estimation which have been suggested for dealing with it. The problem has a fascinating complexity and an entire book could easily be devoted to its consideration. Not the least of the difficulties of dealing with this estimation problem is the fact that probability theory has very little to tell us about the structure of dependent events such as the readership of magazines. Any quantitative analyst who works on this estimation problem develops the feeling, amounting almost to certainty, that it ought to be possible to find extremely accurate estimates, if only he could adequately take into account the underlying structure of the magazine readership data. But to think this is one thing, to do it another. Therefore, it still remains true that there is no generally accepted best method for dealing with the media estimation problem.

Let us begin with a simple example of the problem. At the end of the preceding section the complete data were given for three magazines. Suppose, as would be the case very often in practice, that data are only available for individual magazines and for combinations of two magazines. In this case the advertiser would have six reaches instead of the seven needed for a complete breakdown. The available data might be given in any one of the forms discussed in the preceding section. Assuming that it was given in the union form, the advertiser would know only:

$$R(B) = 0.229 \qquad R(B \cup D) = 0.490$$
$$R(D) = 0.383 \qquad R(B \cup G) = 0.463$$
$$R(G) = 0.310 \qquad R(D \cup G) = 0.539$$

---

* J. M. Agostini, "Analysis of Magazine Accumulative Audience," *Journal of Advertising Research,* 2 (1962), 24–27; Richard A. Metheringham, "Measuring the New Cumulative Coverage of a Print Campaign," *Journal of Advertising Research,* 4 (1964), 23–28.

One piece of information is missing. As a result, there is no possible way to calculate, for example, the total reach that will be achieved by using all three magazines. Yet the advertiser needs to know this crucial quantity. How can he estimate it? This is the problem we want to consider in this section.

We will not review here the variety of procedures which have been proposed to accomplish estimations such as the one described above. Rather, we will develop an approach which has the merit of not making any assumptions about the underlying relationships among the magazines. This does not make it better than other proposed systems but it does make it impervious to criticisms based on challenges to its underlying assumptions.

Specifically, suppose we ask: What is the least total reach which the advertiser could possibly achieve? More precisely, what reaches for each of the eight logical classes established by these three magazines will meet all of the requirements of the given data and will minimize the total reach achieved? This sounds very much like one of the standard problem forms which we have discussed before—the minimization of some quantity, subject to various restrictions. As a matter of fact, it turns out that this problem is a straightforward linear programming problem—and of a particularly simple form. In order to show this it will be convenient to introduce some notational conventions. We want to be able to represent each of the logical classes by some convenient symbol. In the preceding section we did this by using the "cap" or intersection notation. Thus, to designate the class of adults who read B but do not read D and do not read G we use the logical intersection, $B \cap \overline{D} \cap \overline{G}$. For our present purposes this is unnecessarily complicated and it becomes very difficult to read when five or more magazines are involved. Therefore, let us use the convention that a small letter, as opposed to the capitals we have been using, will mean that the corresponding magazine was read. The absence of the small letter means that the magazine was not read. With this convention the class previously designated by $B \cap \overline{D} \cap \overline{G}$ becomes simply b. Other examples are

$$
\begin{array}{ll}
\overline{B} \cap D \cap \overline{G} & d \\
\overline{B} \cap \overline{D} \cap G & g \\
B \cap D \cap \overline{G} & bd \\
B \cap \overline{D} \cap G & bg \\
\overline{B} \cap D \cap G & dg \\
B \cap D \cap G & bdg
\end{array}
$$

The only problem this convention might cause would involve the class $\overline{B} \cap \overline{D} \cap \overline{G}$ because this class, according to the convention, ought to be designated by a blank space. However, it turns out that we never have occasion to refer to this class, so there is no difficulty. Our second new convention results from the fact that here we have no need to refer to a class apart from its reach. In other words, our only interest in a logical class is because of its reach. Therefore, R, used to designate reach, becomes redundant and we will eliminate it in this section. Thus, from now on b means what we previously denoted by $R(B \cap \overline{D} \cap \overline{G})$, and so forth.

With these conventions, what is the objective of our analysis? We want to minimize total reach, and total reach is simply the sum of the reaches of the seven logical classes which have at least one small letter. Therefore, we can formulate the objective thus:

$$\text{To minimize } z = b + d + g + bd + bg + dg + bdg$$

This objective is subject to the restrictions of the given data. Consider $R(B) = 0.229$. The logical class of readers of B includes, in our new notation, every logical class which has a b in it. Therefore, we must have

$$b + bd + bg + bdg = 0.229$$

Similarly,

$$d + bd + dg + bdg = 0.383$$

and

$$g + bg + dg + bdg = 0.310$$

The logical class $B \cup D$ includes each adult who reads B or D or both. In our new notation this means every class which includes b or d or both. We could, therefore, write the restriction which results from $R(B \cup D) = 0.490$ as

$$b + d + bd + bg + dg + bdg = 0.490$$

In fact, however, the same result can be achieved with a somewhat simpler analysis if the data are converted to their equivalent intersection form. Using the fundamental relation discussed in the preceding section we have

$$R(B \cap D) = 0.122$$
$$R(B \cap G) = 0.076$$
$$R(D \cap G) = 0.154$$

These can be converted to the corresponding restrictions:

$$bd + bdg = 0.122$$
$$bg + bdg = 0.076$$
$$dg + bdg = 0.154$$

We have, then, an objective function with seven variables to be minimized subject to six restrictions. The entire problem can be summarized in a table:

b	d	g	bd	bg	dg	bdg	
1			1	1		1	0.229
	1		1		1	1	0.383
		1		1	1	1	0.310
			1			1	0.122
				1		1	0.076
					1	1	0.154
1	1	1	1	1	1	1	z

The coefficients of the restricting equations are given in the body of the table, and the coefficients of the objective equation are given in the last row. Since all of the equations are linear it follows that this is a linear programming problem. Note that all of the coefficients are one. This suggests that this problem should have a rapid special algorithm, as did the transportation problem. There may be such an algorithm, but we have not yet discovered it. There are special tricks which speed up the solution for this kind of problem but they are not sufficiently general to justify attempting to describe them here. Anyone who has occasion to solve a number of these problems will undoubtedly discover a variety of helpful devices.

The problem can be solved in a straightforward way just like the linear programming problems of the preceding chapter. The minimizing solution is:

$$b = 0.031$$
$$d = 0.107$$
$$g = 0.080$$
$$bd = 0.122$$
$$bg = 0.076$$
$$dg = 0.154$$
$$z = 0.570$$

Therefore, we conclude that the worst reach the advertiser can possibly achieve is 0.570. It is logically impossible for him to do worse than this.

Obviously, it is also possible to find the maximizing solution. The table remains exactly the same but we maximize z instead of minimizing it. The maximizing solution is:

$$b = 0.107$$
$$d = 0.183$$
$$g = 0.156$$
$$bd = 0.046$$
$$dg = 0.078$$
$$bdg = 0.076$$
$$z = 0.646$$

The best the advertiser can do is to achieve a reach of 0.646. It is impossible for him to do better than this. It should be noted that the maximizing solution may give an answer with z greater than one. It is not necessary to add another restriction to avoid this since a maximum value of z greater than one means that it is logically possible for the advertiser to reach the entire target audience ($z = 1$).

By these two linear programming solutions we have found that the actual total reach the advertiser will achieve must lie between 0.570 and 0.646. Knowing these limits, is there any way to achieve an estimate of the actual reach that will be obtained? Yes, there is. An argument given by Polya suggests that the harmonic mean of the two limits should be used as the estimate.[5] In our case, this gives

$$H.M. = \frac{2(0.570)(0.646)}{0.570 + 0.646} = 0.6056$$

As we know that in our example the actual reach was 0.612, it will be seen that this estimate is very good indeed. Accuracy of this sort is not at all unusual but no generalizations can be made about the accuracy to be expected. It depends, in a complicated way, on the number of magazines involved and on the number of restrictions.

This seems to be a practical and useful way to approach the media estimation problem. A standard technique, linear programming, is used. Computer programs are readily available to handle the calculations. But a further executive consideration intervenes. We ought to investigate the kind of computer load which would result for large advertising budgets. Suppose ten magazines are under consideration and that the individual reaches plus the reaches of the unions of each pair of magazines are available. A quick calculation shows that this would require a linear program with 55 restricting equations and 1,023 variables. While this is well within the range of contemporary computer capacities, it is not the kind of calculation that should be lightly undertaken. If the number of magazines went to twenty—and this is not at all uncommon—then the linear program would have 210 restricting equations and 1,048,575 variables. For operational reasons alone, this is enough to give pause to possessors of even the mightiest computer systems. Therefore, these examples suggest that it would be useful to have available a simpler analogical procedure.

To develop such a system, let us recall the exposure distribution for the example used above, as given at the end of the preceding section:

---

[5] *American Mathematical Monthly*, 1950, p. 26. It will be recalled that the harmonic mean of two numbers, a and b, is given by

$$H.M. = \frac{2ab}{a + b}$$

Exposures	Proportion
0	0.388
1	0.344
2	0.226
3	0.042

For this distribution we can calculate the first and second moments about the origin. If we let exposures be i, where $i = 0, 1, \ldots n$, and the corresponding proportions be p_i, then the first moment about the origin (simply the mean) is defined as

$$\mu_1 = \sum_{i=0}^{n} i p_i$$

The second moment about the origin is

$$\mu_2 = \sum_{i=0}^{n} i^2 p_i$$

For our exposure distribution we find

$$\mu_1 = 0.922 \text{ and } \mu_2 = 1.626$$

The intersection form for these data—excluding $B \cap D \cap G$, which we assume we don't know—is

$R(B) = 0.229$	$R(B \cap D) = 0.122$
$R(D) = 0.383$	$R(B \cap G) = 0.076$
$R(G) = 0.310$	$R(D \cap G) = 0.154$

We will now define two new totals:

S_1 = sum of reaches of the individual magazines
S_2 = sum of reaches of intersections of magazine pairs

In our example we have

$$S_1 = 0.922$$
$$S_2 = 0.352$$

It will be seen that

$$\mu_1 = S_1 \text{ and } \mu_2 = S_1 + 2S_2$$

It can be proved that this always holds true for any group of magazines. Therefore, it follows that when we know S_1 and S_2—which requires knowing only the reaches of the single magazines and of *all* pairs of the magazines—we know the first two moments of the corresponding exposure distribution.

This knowledge permits us to construct a linear program based directly on the exposure distribution. We will now assume that we know only the above intersection form for our data. We have calculated S_1 and

S_2 and we therefore know that we must have, for the exposure distribution,

$$\mu_1 = 0.922 \text{ and } \mu_2 = 1.626$$

We can represent the unknown exposure distribution thus:

EXPOSURES	PROPORTION
0	x_0
1	x_1
2	x_2
3	x_3

We have three restrictions on the x's:

1. By definition, they must add up to one, or

$$x_0 + x_1 + x_2 + x_3 = 1$$

2. The first moment must equal $\mu_1 = 0.922$ or

$$x_1 + 2x_2 + 3x_3 = 0.922$$

3. The second moment must equal $\mu_2 = 1.626$ or

$$x_1 + 4x_2 + 9x_3 = 1.626$$

The total reach the advertiser will achieve is

$$z = x_1 + x_2 + x_3$$

Therefore, once again we have a linear programming problem: to minimize (or maximize) z, subject to the above three restrictions. This problem, however, is considerably simpler than the previous one, at least in terms of the number of equations and the number of variables.

We can use the standard procedure to find the minimum and maximum reaches. We find:

| | PROPORTION | |
| | MINIMUM | MAXIMUM |
EXPOSURES	REACH	REACH
0	0.430	0.3127
1	0.018	0.5700
2	0.552	0
3	0	0.1173
TOTAL REACH	0.570	0.6873

In this instance, the minimum reach found here (0.570) is the same as we found when we used all the available information. This is an "accident." Generally, the minimum reach found by this simplified procedure will be less than that found when all the available information is used. It will always be less than or equal to the minimum with all the available information. The maximum reach found by the simplified procedure will always be greater than or equal to the maximum reach found by using all the available information. Here we found 0.6873 as compared to the previous 0.646. The harmonic mean of the two simplified limits is 0.6172, very close to the actual 0.612.

Actually, it is not necessary to go through the linear programming solution of the simplified version. The structure is so simple that the solution can be worked out algebraically. The maximum and minimum reaches are expressed most conveniently in terms of S_1 and S_2, introduced above. For the maximum we find, where n is the number of magazines:

$$\text{maximum reach} = \left(S_1 - \frac{2S_2}{n} \right) \text{ or 1, whichever is smaller}$$

For the minimum reach, let k be the smallest integer greater than $(1 + \frac{2S_2}{S_1})$. Then

$$\text{minimum reach} = \frac{2}{k(k-1)} [(k-1)S_1 - S_2]$$

These expressions give exactly the same extreme reaches found above.

This simplified procedure is an eminently practical approach to the estimation problem. The estimates are always reasonable ones and the calculations are readily made.

109 / Brand-Share Model

The portion of the market that each company obtains is an important measure of the relative success of the respective brands. This portion is usually called the *brand share*. Certainly, one company can have 90 per cent of the market and still be making less profit than five other companies, each of which has 2 per cent of the market. But, in general, the executives of a company can tell whether or not they are making a reasonable profit on what they sell. They want to know whether they are selling as much as they should be selling, and how much more they could be selling. Brand-share measurements, which can be obtained from consumer surveys or by services that record brand sales in stores, provide some answers to these questions.

When a company introduces a change in strategy, it is often with the intention of achieving an increase in brand share. Sometimes, the change is made with the hope of reversing a downward trend in brand share. Perhaps a competitor introduces the first change, and the marketing decision-maker believes that it will result in a decreasing brand share for his company. However, changes in brand share can occur without any change at all in strategies, competitive strategies, and states of nature. A company that experiences a decreasing brand share may well be better off to wait and see, rather than take immediate action. The reason is that the decision-makers cannot be sure what effect their action may have on both short- and long-range profit. In other words, their first job is to predict what will happen if they do nothing to change their present course.

A useful model which helps to make this kind of prediction is called the brand-share model. This model attempts to determine what will happen to a company's brand share both in the short- and the long-run. Although brand share may not be as direct an outcome as short- and long-term profit, nevertheless, it is a most useful description of general conditions. It is also one way in which the effect of a change in a complex strategy, competitive strategy, or state of nature can be examined on both a short- and long-term basis.

To begin, we determine the brand shares of each of the several brands that are defined as the market. The definition of "the market" is not as straightforward as it might seem. The kind of problem that develops when we attempt to construct a brand-share model for automobiles is representative. Is it sufficient to consider cars that are in the same price field, or should we consider all prices of automobiles? Are small three-wheel cars part of the market? If so, are motor scooters also to be considered? Should we group all convertibles together? And so forth. Empirical data gathered from the consumer by surveys is one means of defining a product class. Once it is learned what the consumer considers to be competitive brands, the marketing executive can generally apply his experience and intuition to the job of defining the market.

One other kind of information is required. We need to know brand-switching characteristics. In other words, some consumers use one brand all of the time while others switch continually from one brand to another. Brand-switching may be influenced by a variety of factors, such as the effect of consumer leaders who cause consumer followers to imitate their choice. Meanwhile, the leader may meet up with an even more dominant leader who will succeed in switching the former to the latter's brand. Dissatisfaction with a product can lead to switching. The dissatisfaction may be caused by a chance event which occurs once in every n products. It may occur because of special circumstances, such as ill health or bad weather, which the consumer thereafter associates with the product. Another possibility is the effect of boredom with any brand after a given number of uses. Consumers have different tolerances for such boredom. No matter what the reasons, surveys detect the brand-switching phenomena by observing the last two purchases that the consumer has made. There are many refinements required in order to collect meaningful and useful data. We obviously cannot dwell on such topics because it would shift us from our purpose, which is to construct the general model.

Let us assume that five brands constitute "the market." These 5 brands, at the time we begin our study (t_0), have brand shares, $S_i(t_0)$. In this case i stands for the brand ($i = 1, 2, 3, 4, 5$). We know that the sum of the brand shares must equal 100 per cent of the market, or 1.00.

$$S_1(t_0) + S_2(t_0) + S_3(t_0) + S_4(t_0) + S_5(t_0) = 1.00$$

This granted, we need some device for representing the rate at which consumers are switching from one brand to another. As mentioned above, measurements of this are ordinarily obtained by observing the last two purchases made by the consumer. Suppose we have found 100 consumers who purchased Brand *1* on the first of these two purchase occasions. We tabulate the brands purchased on the second purchase and find:

BRAND	FREQUENCY
1	57
2	3
3	13
4	16
5	11
	100

We express these data as switching probabilities or proportions. We denote the proportion that switch from Brand i to Brand j by P_{ij}. From the above data we have:

$$P_{11} = 0.57; \ P_{12} = 0.03; \ P_{13} = 0.13; \ P_{14} = 0.16; \ P_{15} = 0.11$$

P_{11} represents the proportion who did not switch from Brand *1*. Note that the method of calculation guarantees that

$$\sum_{j=1}^{5} P_{ij} = 1$$

We must similarly obtain the other switching coefficients (P_{2j}, P_{3j}, P_{4j}, and P_{5j}). The total set of data can be conveniently summarized as follows:

i	$S_i(t_0)$	FROM BRAND i	1	2	3	4	5	
1	0.20	1	0.57	0.03	0.13	0.16	0.11	1.00
2	0.15	2	0.15	0.47	0.15	0.08	0.15	1.00
3	0.10	3	0.09	0.06	0.55	0.15	0.15	1.00
4	0.30	4	0.07	0.01	0.14	0.64	0.14	1.00
5	0.25	5	0.10	0.05	0.14	0.19	0.52	1.00
	1.00							

(TO BRAND j)

Each entry in the matrix is a switching proportion. Thus, the proportion of consumers who switched from Brand *2* to Brand *5* is $P_{25} = 0.15$. The diagonal of the matrix (0.57, 0.47, 0.55, 0.64, 0.52) shows the respective proportions of consumers who did not switch from their first purchase brand. The column headed $S_i(t_0)$ shows the original market share of each brand.

The matrix given above is called the *switching matrix* and sometimes the *transition matrix*. We can now use this matrix to deduce successive states of brand share under the assumption that the switching will remain constant. This is accomplished in the following way. Brand *1* starts out with 20 per cent of the market. For convenience, let us say that the market consists of 1,000 consumers. Then Brand *1* has 200 of these consumers at time t_0. What happens at time t_1? About 57 per cent of 200 consumers, or 114, do not change their brand. Brand *2* has 150 consumers at time t_0. Since 15 per cent of Brand-*2* users become Brand-*1* users, we calculate that 22.5 Brand-*2* consumers become Brand-*1* users. In the same way we find that 9 Brand-*3* consumers become Brand-*1* users, 21 Brand-*4* consumers become Brand-*1* consumers, and 25 Brand-*5* users become Brand-*1* consumers. This means that at time t_1, Brand *1* has

$$114 + 22.5 + 9 + 21 + 25 = 191.5$$

which represents a loss of 8.5 consumers. We can perform the same calculations for each of the brands and, in this way, determine brand share at time t_1. The operations to find brand share at time t_2 are identical in all respects. Of course, we begin with the brand-share situation of time t_1 instead of time t_0. For our assumed case, we find that brand share changes in the following way.

i	$S_i(t_0)$	$S_i(t_1)$	$S_i(t_2)$	$S_i(t_3)$	. . .	$S_i(t_L)$
1	20.00	19.15	18.41	17.93	. . .	17.29
2	15.00	9.80	7.72	6.88	. . .	6.32
3	10.00	18.05	21.31	22.63	. . .	23.54
4	30.00	29.85	30.06	30.27	. . .	30.63
5	25.00	23.15	22.50	22.29	. . .	22.22
	100.00	100.00	100.00	100.00		100.00

Three transitional steps are shown together with the limiting distribution. These limiting values picture the long-term situation that will occur if nothing happens to disturb the evolution of the system. The limiting values are derived by repeatedly going through the process that we described above to determine successive brand-share states. However, we must keep on doing this until no more change takes place in the brand shares. This procedure would be too time-consuming unless we used a computer. Fortunately it is possible to express this problem in mathematical terms. There are six relationships that we can write. The first five are the basic computations which are used to derive the next set of brand-share values. The sixth is the relationship we previously mentioned to describe the fact that the sum of the brand shares must equal 1.00.

$$S_1' = 0.57\ S_1 + 0.15\ S_2 + 0.09\ S_3 + 0.07\ S_4 + 0.10\ S_5$$
$$S_2' = 0.03\ S_1 + 0.47\ S_2 + 0.06\ S_3 + 0.01\ S_4 + 0.05\ S_5$$
$$S_3' = 0.13\ S_1 + 0.15\ S_2 + 0.55\ S_3 + 0.14\ S_4 + 0.14\ S_5$$
$$S_4' = 0.16\ S_1 + 0.08\ S_2 + 0.15\ S_3 + 0.64\ S_4 + 0.19\ S_5$$
$$S_5' = 0.11\ S_1 + 0.15\ S_2 + 0.15\ S_3 + 0.14\ S_4 + 0.52\ S_5$$

$$S_1 + S_2 + S_3 + S_4 + S_5 = 1.00$$

Under equilibrium conditions, the brand share at time t_{n+1} will be exactly the same as the brand share at time t_n. In other words, as much is going out as is coming in, and the brand share of each company remains the same. To express this fact mathematically, we set $S_i(t_{n+1}) = S_i(t_n)$. In the above equations, this means that $S_1' = S_1$, $S_2' = S_2$, $S_3' = S_3$, $S_4' = S_4$, and $S_5' = S_5$. From this, we derive a new set of equations.

$$-0.43\ S_1 + 0.15\ S_2 + 0.09\ S_3 + 0.07\ S_4 + 0.10\ S_5 = 0$$
$$0.03\ S_1 - 0.53\ S_2 + 0.06\ S_3 + 0.01\ S_4 + 0.05\ S_5 = 0$$
$$0.13\ S_1 + 0.15\ S_2 - 0.45\ S_3 + 0.14\ S_4 + 0.14\ S_5 = 0$$
$$0.16\ S_1 + 0.08\ S_2 + 0.15\ S_3 - 0.36\ S_4 + 0.19\ S_5 = 0$$
$$0.11\ S_1 + 0.15\ S_2 + 0.15\ S_3 + 0.14\ S_4 - 0.48\ S_5 = 0$$

$$S_1 + S_2 + S_3 + S_4 + S_5 = 1.00$$

(*Note:* $0.57\ S_1 - 1.00\ S_1 = -0.43\ S_1$; $0.47\ S_2 - 1.00\ S_2 = -0.53\ S_2$; and so forth.) It will be noted that we have six equations in five unknowns. In general this set of equations would be inconsistent. However, the first five equations are not independent. Any values of the S's which satisfy any four of these five equations will automatically satisfy the fifth one. Therefore, we can take any four of the first five equations plus the sixth one and solve them by ordinary algebra. The results are the brand shares in the limit. Figure 11.1 shows the alteration of brand shares in graphical form.

It is of some interest to note the changes in brand position that occur over time:

BRAND	RANKING AT t_0	RANKING AT t_L
1	3	4
2	4	5
3	5	2
4	1	1
5	2	3

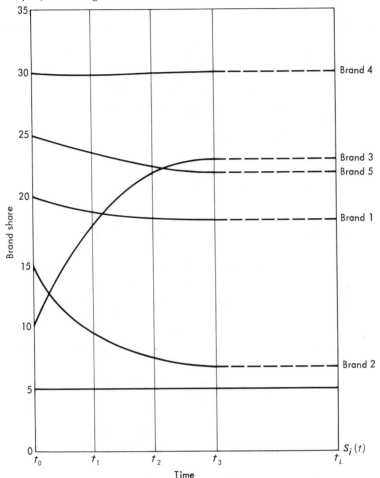

FIGURE 11.1 *Successive brand shares including the limiting shares at* t_L.

Brands 5, 1, and 2 drop one position in their rankings. Brand 3 climbs three steps, going from the lowest ranking to the position of second largest brand in the market. How long does it take for the change to occur? The answer to this question will depend on the characteristics of the switching probabilities, the initial brand distribution, and the speed with which switching takes place. Of major importance is the length of the purchase cycle. Obviously, equilibrium will be reached more rapidly—in calendar time—for a product which is purchased daily, like cigarettes, than it will be for a product which is purchased at intervals of one or more years, like automobiles.

Let us consider for a moment the problem of Brand 4. It is the leader in the market, with 30 per cent brand share. The sales manager observes that a decrease in sales takes place at time t_1. He asks himself whether the decrease is the first sign of a new trend for his company. After studying the brand-switching model, the sales manager knows that the setback is temporary. He also knows that if everything stays the same, his company will continue to obtain a little more than 30 per cent of the total market. This fact may not please him, in which case he will attempt to find a new strategy that will bring about a change in the brand-switching characteristics.

The conclusions which can be drawn from the use of brand-switching matrices are interesting and important. But are they likely to be right? It all depends on the correctness of the assumption that the transition proportions are unchanging. Unfortunately, successive consumer surveys often show changes in the transition proportions. In other words, there are transitions in the transition proportions for the various brands. The problem becomes much more complex when it is considered in this way, but the utility of the solution increases as well. In particular, the influence of a new strategy can be examined in terms of the changes it induces in the dynamic system of transition probabilities.

There may be changes in the transition proportions without any known specific external cause. But there are some situations in which such changes can be expected. For example, the exit from, or entry into, the market of a brand will surely produce such changes. Exit can occur because it may not be economical for a company to remain in business if its brand share drops below some specified level. Of course, the level will vary by industry, product, and many special circumstances. On Figure 11.1 we have drawn this level at 5 per cent. Brand 2 is not very far from being a marginal brand. It is therefore reasonable for the other companies to attempt to analyze what will happen to their respective shares of the market if Brand 2 should not survive. For this situation, data must be collected to indicate what would happen to Brand-2 users if Brand 2 ceased to exist. Another situation arises when a new brand is about to enter the market. Data from test markets can then be analyzed in this same way. The fact that a new brand starts out slowly does not mean that it will not succeed eventually in obtaining a reasonable share of the market. On the other hand, if a new brand obtains a substantial market position this does not mean that it will be able to keep it. Sometimes wide oscillatory behavior occurs before brand shares settle down to equilibrium values (see Figure 11.2). In this hypothetical case, only one brand exists initially and then two new brands enter the market. Especially in such oscillatory situations, observations of brand share that are limited to one particular interval of time can be misleading. It is possible to observe brand-share position at a time when brand share is swinging down or when it is very low, without considering the nature of such swings and with the misguided belief that they represent trends or permanent conditions. Many times, when a strong downtrend occurs, action is taken that alters the situation. Such action, since it is taken for the wrong reasons, will seldom improve upon the brand position that would have occurred at equilibrium under the original conditions.

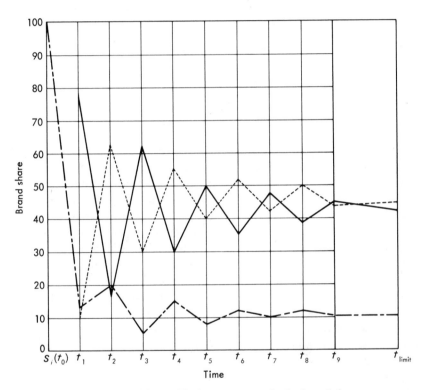

FIGURE 11.2   Wide oscillations can occur in the brand share over time.

One way of incorporating transitions of transitions is to represent the switching probabilities for each brand as lambda (λ) and mu (μ). We let λ_i be the probability that one or more consumers will switch to Brand i in some period of time and let μ_i be the probability that one or more consumers will switch from Brand i to some other competitive brand in the same period. The period of time is presumed to be small enough so that it is quite unlikely that more than one switch of either kind will take place. Figure 11.3(a) depicts the situation for Brand i. Both λ and μ will change over time, depending upon such factors as brand share, relative advertising expenditures, price changes, changes in quality, number of

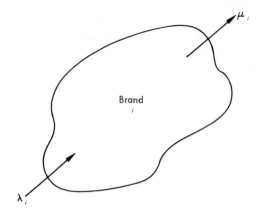

FIGURE 11.3(a)   *Representation of brand switching to and from* $(\lambda_i$ *and* $\mu_i)$ *brand i.*

competitors, strategies of competitors, degree of market saturation. The μ factor increases when competitive strategies are effective, with the result that more consumers flow out of the Brand-i set of consumers. In other words, μ represents, in part, the elements that are under the control of the competitors. At the same time changes can occur in states of nature that will result in an increased μ. However, it is important to note that a competitor's strategy may not be directed at increasing μ but rather at decreasing λ. Similarly, the decision-maker's strategy might be aimed at increasing λ, but it will usually also include strategic elements to decrease or stabilize μ. Changes in the state of nature can also affect λ.

The sales of Brand i can be put into terms of brand share, so that 100 per cent would be its maximum value at any time. One hundred per cent represents complete market domination and saturation. A mathematical model can be constructed to describe the probability that Brand i will have different shares of the market. We will not derive this model here, since it requires a complex derivation which does not shed additional light on the class of model with which we are dealing. It is worthwhile noting, however, that this class of model applies to general conditions which are known as birth and death processes. It is clear that the relevant analogy is that new customers are being born all the time as described by λ, while old customers pass along to other brands as described by μ. The mathematical model is

$$P_{S_i} = \frac{S!}{S_i!(S - S_i)!}\left(\frac{\lambda}{\mu}\right)^{S_i} P_0$$

S = market saturation limit,
S_i = brand share of i,
P_{S_i} = probability of Brand i obtaining a brand share S_i,

P_0 = probability of Brand i obtaining a zero brand share,
$S! = S(S - 1)(S - 2) \ldots (2)(1)$ and is read "S factorial."

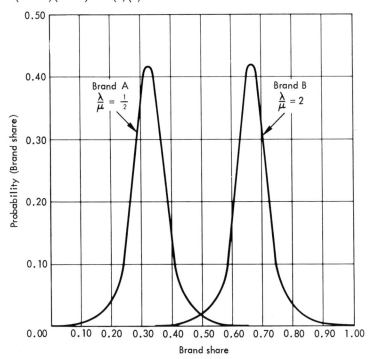

FIGURE 11.3(b)   ***Brand share probability distributions for Brands A and B.***

The market saturation limit is 100. Figure 11.3(b) depicts the resulting distributions for two competing brands A and B with (λ/μ) values of $\frac{1}{2}$ and 2 respectively. (With two brands the expected brand shares will sum to 1. When more than two brands are involved it is necessary to adjust the brand shares so that the expected values will sum to 1.) We can observe that the distributions in Figure 11.3(b) are quite narrow, indicating that the resulting brand shares will not vary by any great amount from the expected brand-share values, 0.33 for Brand A and 0.67 for Brand B. Models of this type can be used to simulate brand share in the limit. Therefore, they are essentially predictors of outcomes. It should be emphasized that λ and μ can be made dependent on the size of the brand share S_i, or they can be made independent of each other, and they can be dependent on time, and so on. Many of the relationships are complex feedback rules. The decision-maker can employ a model of this sort not only to try to obtain predictions of reality, but to determine the probable outcomes of strategies in a completely formal sense. It would be absurd to interpret the results derived from such models in any manner other than a qualitative one. Nevertheless, the extreme complexity of the marketing field normally prevents the decision-maker from tracing through complex interdependent situations. For this reason, qualitative interpretations of quantitative models can play an important role in assisting the marketing decision-maker.

110/ Pricing Problems

One of the fundamental marketing decision-problems is the determination of the "best" price for a product or service. This is also one of the most complex problems in the marketing field. The determination of price is, in classical economic theory, the result of supply-and-demand relations. But many factors which influence the demand for a product cannot be accounted for in such broad terms. It is not meaningful to consider a large number of brands as being differentiated solely by price. At the same time, any one brand is competing with every other choice that the consumer has as to where he should spend his money. In many cases, price is an integral part of the brand image. A change in price can shift the market to an entirely different group of consumers rather than add or subtract consumers from the same basic group. Psychological factors play an extremely important part in the determination of the value which a consumer imputes to any particular product. The values are not static and can change quite rapidly for reasons which are apparent only long after the effects of the change have been felt. It is clear that the heart of the pricing problem is broader than price alone. A wide spectrum of consumer values, most of which cannot be stated in numerical terms, are involved in every pricing decision. These are some of the reasons why, in spite of its importance, a genuine, practical pricing model has not yet been evolved. Some interesting aspects of pricing can be illuminated, however, by utilizing the brand-share model which we developed in the preceding section.

The switching probabilities of the brand-share model can be examined in terms of their responses to price changes. For example, in a given test area, it might be expected that as price is lowered, the changes in the switching probabilities would be proportional, in some sense, to the difference in price between the brands. Then an optimal change in price would be one which yielded the maximum profit. At least in theory, very large market shares could be obtained by lowering the price to cost or below. Such a situation might, in fact, be the objective of the marketing decision-maker who is willing to operate without profit for some period of time in the belief that competitors will be driven out of business. However, if we analyze this situation we see that the decision-maker is really not interested in brand share as an end, but rather as a means. The payoff that he is interested in is his competitors' profit.

We have assumed certain hypothetical relationships to hold between the switching probabilities and the prices of two competing brands such that an increase in the price of either brand increases the number of customers who will switch from that brand to the other brand. At the same time, it decreases the number of customers who will switch to the brand which has increased its price. Of course, a decrease in price works in the other direction. If both brands change their price there is a resultant influence on the switching probabilities. One other factor has to be considered. As the prices of the brands rise, the size of the total market decreases. Even when only one brand raises its price a significant amount, some customers in preference to switching their brand drop out of the market. On the basis of these assumptions, the brand-share model can be used to simulate profit positions for the brands in question.[6] We find that for any constant price of one brand, there is an optimal price for the other brand. That is, there is a price which yields optimum profit to the brand which varies its price. For example, where profit = market size × brand share × (price − cost):

PRICE OF BRAND A	BRAND SHARE	MARKET SIZE	(PRICE − COST)	BRAND A'S PROFIT
$1.00	0.560	100,000	$0.50	$28,000
1.10	0.517	100,000	0.60	31,000
1.20	0.477	99,000	0.70	33,100
1.30	0.434	98,000	0.80	34,000
1.40	0.388	96,000	0.90	33,500
1.50	0.336	94,000	1.00	31,600

We observe that at the price of $1.30, Brand A obtains maximum profit although it has less brand share than it would obtain at a lower price. Figure 11.4 illustrates the typical curve which occurs when Brand B holds its price constant. However, assuming that Brand A was originally priced at $1.00, Brand B also gained in profits. Brand A has increased its profit

[6] The price relationships which were used to determine brand switching and total market size are of the form:

$$P_{ij}(2) = f\left[\frac{P_i(1) - P_i(2)}{P_i(1)}, \frac{P_j(2) - P_j(1)}{P_j(1)}, P_{ij}(1)\right]$$

and

$$M(2) = g\left[\frac{P_i(1) + P_j(1)}{P_i(2) + P_j(2)}, M(1)\right]$$

where $P_i(1)$ = price of Brand i at time 1,
$M(1)$ = market size at time 1, and so on.

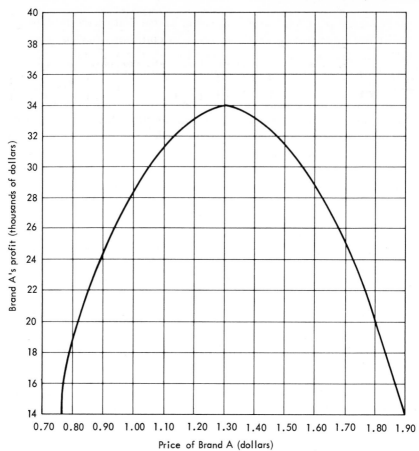

**FIGURE 11.4   The relationship of Brand A's profit to its price,
when brand B holds its price constant at $1.20.**

from $28,000 to $34,000 while Brand B's profits have been raised from
$25,000 to $30,000. This increase has taken place although Brand B has
done nothing. How can we explain this? Brand A has raised its price
and decreased its market share. Brand B has picked up this additional
market share. Of course, when the competitor's prices become unreasonably high a further increase in his prices will result in no advantage to
the competitor. If both brands are overpriced, a change by either one
can result in a considerable shrinkage in the size of the market and a loss
in profits to both. Figures 11.5 and 11.6 present "isoprofit lines" (lines
of equal profit) for each brand.

Figure 11.5 shows Brand A's profit for various combinations of Brand-
A and Brand-B prices. Figure 11.6 depicts Brand B's profits. Let us
first look at Figure 11.5. We will assume that the original prices of the

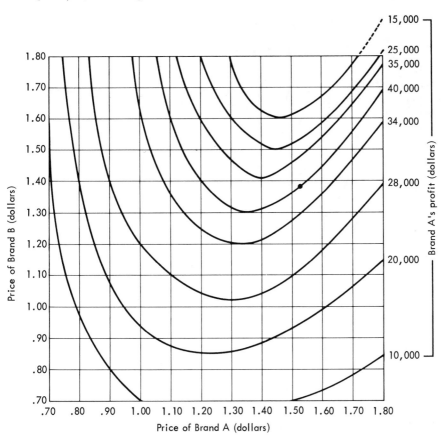

FIGURE 11.5 Lines of equal profit for Brand **A**, for different combinations of prices.

two brands are $P_A = \$1.00$ and $P_B = \$1.20$. Brand A changes its price from $\$1.00$ to $\$1.30$. This moves it to its optimal position with Brand B priced at $\$1.20$. We see that Brand A has raised its profit from $\$28,000$ to $\$34,000$. Figure 11.6 shows us that Brand B has experienced increased profits—from $\$25,000$ to $\$30,000$. Now Brand B wants to optimize its profit position with respect to A's new price of $\$1.30$. Accordingly, Brand B can move anywhere up and down the $\$1.30$ line of A's price, and it will choose a price of $\$1.48$ which optimizes its profit at $\$45,000$. Brand A now finds its profit level at $\$35,000$. However, once again, Brand A looks for its optimal position which occurs at either $\$1.16$ or $\$1.62$. The process of hunting and alternating would continue until a mutually satisfactory point was reached. In this example there is one point available at which both brands achieve their absolute maximum profits. That point is reached when A charges $\$1.52$ and B charges $\$1.38$. Their re-

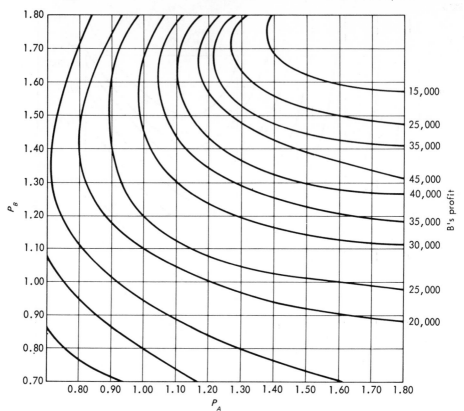

FIGURE 11.6 *Lines of equal profit for Brand B, for different combinations of prices.*

spective profits would then be $40,000 for *A* and $45,000 for *B*. A slight alteration in the shape of the curves could easily result, however, in a situation where the two brands could never simultaneously achieve their absolute maximum prices. In theory, under these circumstances each brand would indefinitely continue to shifts its price. In game-theory terms, we see that this is a nonzero-sum game; each set of strategies creates a different amount of wealth for each brand. We can also observe that if it were practical, a mixed strategy would be used by both the decision-maker and his competitors since their respective optimals do not coincide. For our example a mixed strategy is not necessary as the lines of optimal profit do cross each other at one point.

We have presented this example to illustrate the possible advantages to be gained by using a simulation model, such as the brand-share model, to investigate the effect of price on profit. At the same time, we must caution the reader that such models capture only a small part of reality.

The pricing problem is extremely complex. The model, with its artificialities, yields results that are conceptual aids and not solutions to
problems. If a brand could alter its price as frequently as desired, without creating side effects, it might be possible to begin to learn the real
nature of price-profit relationships.

111/ *Optimal Purchasing Policies*

Many businesses use one or more agricultural products as raw materials. Soybean processors, vegetable oil manufacturers, animal food producers, and many others can be cited as examples. For agricultural
products it is often the case that, due primarily to the growing season
and to storage problems, there is a fixed season each year during which
the product is marketed. The business firm in question can ordinarily
buy their next year's requirements at any time during the selling season
but they *must* make their purchase at some time within the selling
season. The price of the agricultural commodity varies throughout the
selling season and, usually, the firm has no way of predicting accurately
what the price will be. Obviously, the firm would prefer to buy the
commodity for less money, rather than more. This poses an interesting
problem: What purchasing policy should the firm follow in order to
minimize its total cost of buying the needed amount of the commodity?

Let us take an example. Suppose there are four months in the selling
season. Suppose the probability distribution of the price per unit has
been determined for each of the four months from historical data and
that these distributions are:

		MONTH		
PRICE	I	II	III	IV
2.00	0.02	0.04	0.05	0.03
2.25	0.09	0.12	0.08	0.08
2.50	0.14	0.18	0.13	0.12
2.75	0.19	0.24	0.18	0.15
3.00	0.23	0.22	0.20	0.20
3.25	0.16	0.09	0.26	0.13
3.50	0.08	0.07	0.10	0.11
3.75	0.06	0.03	0	0.10
4.00	0.03	0.01	0	0.08
ARITHMETIC MEAN	$2.95	2.81	2.90	3.06

With these data, how should the firm make its purchasing decisions? If
the price is $2.75 in the first month, should the firm buy or should it wait?

Before we undertake to discover the optimal purchasing policy let us
admit that this example is somewhat artificial. As a matter of fact, it is
worth specifying the three major reasons why the example is an artificial
one, together with some comments on the effect of the artificialities. First,

the division of the selling season into months is far too gross. Weekly, or perhaps daily, divisions would be more appropriate in most cases. But this is purely a pedagogical simplification and it has no effect on the analysis. If daily data were available we could accomplish the following analysis equally well, at the cost of some additional arithmetic. Second, the division of the prices into $0.25 intervals is undoubtedly too gross for real-world examples. However, again, this is simply a pedagogical device to avoid excessive data and arithmetic. If the data were available on a more precise basis we could use them equally well. Third, the above data assume the independence of one month's price from the prices of the other months. This is undoubtedly generally false. In reality, if the first month's price was high then the subsequent months would have increased probabilities of higher prices. This difficulty is a little more serious. But its major effect is to make it harder to get sufficient historical data from which to deduce the necessary conditional probabilities. If the data are available then a straightforward extension of the argument below will suffice to determine the optimal policy. Therefore, even though our example is artificial, the general line of reasoning needed to determine the optimal policy remains as it is in real-world examples.

Let us consider some typical policies which are sometimes used in practice. The naive approach would be to wait for some specified price which is deemed to be "satisfactory." Of course, the difficulty is that the specified price may never occur. Suppose the firm established the policy of purchasing only if the price is $2.50 or less. If they really stuck to this policy the firm might end up without any of the commodity. Specifically, from the table of probabilities it can be determined that the probability that the price is greater than $2.50 is 0.75, 0.66, 0.74, and 0.77 for the four months, respectively. Therefore, the probability that the price is never $2.50 or less is (0.75) (0.66) (0.74) (0.77) = 0.282. Obviously, the firm cannot accept a probability of more than .25 that none of the commodity will be purchased. Therefore, the firm will have to modify this policy. A plausible *modification* (and no longer naive) might be: Buy in the first three months if the price drops to $2.50 or less, otherwise buy in the fourth month at whatever price happens to obtain in that month. To determine the expected price which the firm will pay under this policy we may reason as follows. If the firm purchases in the first month it will pay an average price of

$$\frac{(2.00)(0.02) + (2.25)(0.09) + (2.50)(0.14)}{0.02 + 0.09 + 0.14} = \$2.36$$

Similarly, the firm will pay an average price of $2.35, if it purchases in the second month, an average price of $2.33 if it purchases in the third month, and we already know that the average price in the fourth month is $3.06. The probabilities of purchasing in each of the months are:

MONTH	PROBABILITY OF PURCHASE
1	0.25
2	(0.75)(0.34) = 0.255
3	(0.75)(0.66)(0.26) = 0.1287
4	(0.75)(0.66)(0.74) = 0.3663

Therefore, the expected purchase price under this policy is

$$0.25(2.36) + 0.255(2.35) + 0.1287(2.33) + 0.3663(3.06) = \$2.61$$

This is the average price entailed by the policy stated above.

Another naive policy would be to purchase one-quarter of the total requirements in each month. The expected price under this policy would be simply

$$\tfrac{1}{4}(2.95 + 2.81 + 2.90 + 3.06) = \$2.93$$

This is considerably worse than the modified policy above.

Perhaps the firm will consider a policy of "dollar averaging." The idea here is to spend a constant amount of dollars per month rather than to purchase a constant amount per month. By spending a constant amount of dollars per month the tendency will be to purchase more when the price is low so that the final average price paid ought to be lower. What would be the average price under this policy? To determine this requires the calculation of the harmonic means of the price distributions. We are dealing with a kind of rate here: dollars per unit. It will be recalled that the rule given in elementary courses in descriptive statistics is: when the second term in the rate is held constant calculate the arithmetic mean, when the first term in the rate is held constant calculate the harmonic mean. Here we are holding the first term in the rate, dollars, constant. So we need the harmonic means.* They are:

	MONTH			
	1	2	3	4
HARMONIC MEAN	$2.88	2.75	2.83	2.96

The harmonic mean of these four harmonic means is $2.85 and this is the average price which will be paid under a policy of dollar averaging.

Of the three policies we have considered the first one, as modified, is by far the best. But is it the best of all possible policies? How can the optimum policy be determined? This is a deceptive problem, but in a direction different from the usual way in which problems deceive us. Ordinarily, we are fooled because we think a problem is easy and it

* See footnote, p. 403.

turns out to be difficult. In the present case the problem looks difficult but it turns out to be remarkably easy, once the basic idea is put into focus. This kind of problem is sometimes cited as an example of dynamic programming and it is true that the basic idea on which the solution depends is a key idea in dynamic programming. However, it should be emphasized that dynamic programming is a much more powerful set of ideas than would be suggested by this particular problem.

The basic idea is already implicit in our calculations for the first suggested policy. The difficulty with finding the optimal policy is that there are so very many possibilities to be considered. Therefore, let us start our deductions from a point at which there is no choice at all— there is only one course of action open to the firm. In other words, let us begin at the end of the four-month season. Suppose that the first three months have gone by and the commodity has not been purchased. The firm has no alternative except to purchase in the fourth month, no matter what the price. In this case the firm must be content with an expected price of $3.06, the expected price for the fourth month.

With this in mind, let us consider what the firm ought to do in the third month. The firm knows that if it waits until the fourth month then it will have to pay an average price of $3.06. This granted, it is clear that there is no reason why they should pay more than $3.06 in the third month since they expect to get it at this price by waiting till the fourth month. On the other hand, the firm has no reason not to take a price lower than $3.06 in the third month, since they cannot expect to do as well if they wait until the fourth month. Therefore, their optimal policy in the third month is to buy if the price is less than $3.06 (meaning $3.00 or less) or wait until the fourth month. According to the probability distribution for the third month, the firm has probability 0.64 of buying in the third month (assuming that they have reached the third month) and probability 0.36 of having to wait until the fourth month. The expected price of the optimal policy for the third month is

$$0.05(2.00) + 0.08(2.25) + 0.13(2.50) + 0.18(2.75)$$
$$+ 0.20(3.00) + 0.36(3.06) = \$2.80$$

Therefore, if the firm has reached the third month without buying the commodity then the optimal policy for the firm to follow is to buy in the third month if the price is $3.00 or less, otherwise, wait. The expected price of this optimal third-month policy is $2.80.

Now we can consider the second month. In the second month, the firm has no reason to pay more than $2.80 since they can expect to get this price by waiting until the third month. On the other hand, the firm ought to purchase the commodity at any amount less than $2.80 in the second month since they cannot expect to do better by waiting.

Therefore, the firm's optimal policy in the second month is to buy if the price is $2.75 or less; otherwise, wait. According to the probability distribution for the second month, the firm has a probability of 0.58 of buying in the second month (assuming that the firm has reached the second month without buying) and the expected price of the optimal policy is

$$0.04(2.00) + 0.12(2.25) + 0.18(2.50) + 0.24(2.75) + 0.42(2.80) = \$2.64$$

Note that the term 0.42(2.80) results from a probability of 0.42 of having to wait until the third month and the $2.80 is the expected price of the optimal policy for the third month. We conclude that the optimal policy for the second month gives an expected price of $2.64.

We now consider the first month. Clearly, the optimal policy is to buy if the price is less than $2.64—this means $2.50 or less—otherwise, wait. The expected price of this policy is

$$0.02(2.00) + 0.09(2.25) + 0.14(2.50) + 0.75(2.64) = \$2.57$$

This is the expected price for the first-month optimal policy.

But this is exactly the answer we were attempting to find. We now have the optimal purchasing policy, since we know what to do in each month. Specifically:

MONTH	POLICY
1	Buy if $2.50 or less; otherwise, wait
2	Buy if $2.75 or less; otherwise, wait
3	Buy if $3.00 or less; otherwise, wait
4	Buy

It is this total policy which is optimal and which gives an expected price of $2.57. Obviously, the same reasoning could be used to discover the *optimal selling policy* for the supplier of the commodity.

The structure of the argument is a very important one. Much of the power of dynamic programming comes from the same general idea. It is: find a place in the decision process where the decision-maker has no choice —often the start of or, as here, the end of the process—and build from that fixed choice to a determination of the optimal policy.

112/ *Competitive Bidding*

Competitive bidding is another kind of pricing. In competitive bidding each firm bidding on a particular contract must submit a sealed bid, and the firm that submits the lowest bid, or price, is awarded the contract. This is a perfectly realistic and extremely illuminating kind of pricing problem. How should a firm determine price when engaged in competitive bidding, and what would constitute an optimal pricing policy?[7] Granted that this is a specialized marketing problem, it is, nevertheless, of crucial importance to firms that do not deal with a large number of consumers, and that have relatively few opportunities to sell their goods or services.

The best strategy for a firm depends, of course, on the objectives of the firm. We will assume that the firm's objective is the maximization of profits. This must be emphasized because other objectives may very well enter into consideration on a short-run basis. For example, a construction firm may have a backlog of work for its regular employees and a primary consideration may be the availability of additional workers.

Let us suppose that it will cost the firm c dollars to fulfill its obligations under the contract. If it makes a bid of x dollars—presumably $x > c$—then the firm will make $(x - c)$ contributory profit *if* it is awarded the contract. We ignore the cost of making the bid since it is a sunk cost when the bid is made.

Clearly, "*if* it is awarded the contract" is the important qualification. There is some probability, for a given bid x, that the firm will win the award. Let this probability be denoted by $P(w|x)$. This is the symbol for conditional probabilities and is to be read "the probability of winning the contract if the bid is x."

This is a decision problem under risk. The firm has as many strategies as there are amounts x which it can bid. As in any other decision problem under risk, the firm will want to select that strategy which has the best expected value—the maximum in this case. Obviously, the return is zero if the firm does not win the contract. Using our notation, the expected contributory profit with a bid of x is

$$(x - c)P(w|x) + 0[1 - P(w|x)] = (x - c)P(w|x)$$

Obviously, $(x - c)$ increases as x increases. However, it is intuitively clear that $P(w|x)$ decreases as x increases. On the one hand the firm could make a bid so high that the probability would be zero that they would be awarded the contract. And, on the other hand, the firm could make a bid so low, perhaps zero, that there would be a probability of one that they would be awarded the contract.) Therefore, there are opposing influences at work and we must discover how to determine the optimal bid.

The relationship between size of bid and probability of award can

---

[7] The competitive bidding model was developed by Lawrence Friedman. See his article, "A Competitive Bidding Strategy," *Operations Research*, 4, No. 1, February 1956, 104. We also want to thank our colleague, Professor Donald Morrison, whose incisive presentation of this model has helped us to eliminate some of the imperfections in our own exposition.

be conveniently expressed as a cumulative probability distribution. Suppose that all the necessary information was available and the relationship between the probability of award and the size of bid were known. What would the cumulative probability distribution look like?

Let us take an example. Assume that a firm is bidding on a contract which will cost $8,000 $(= c)$ to complete. For simplicity we will assume that all bids on this contract must be in thousand-dollar units. Then the relationship between the probability of award and the size of the bid might be presented as the following cumulative distribution.

Bid (x)	Probability of award (p)
$7,000	1.00
8,000	0.95
9,000	0.85
10,000	0.60
11,000	0.30
12,000	0.10
13,000	0.00

For each allowable bid there is a given probability of being awarded the contract if that bid is made. This probability gets smaller as the bid gets larger, as it should. An actual distribution, to be useful, would give probabilities of award for smaller intervals of the size of bid than we have done but the principle would be the same. The data indicate that a bid of $7,000 would certainly win the contract but that a bid of $8,000 has only a probability of 0.95 of winning the contract. Why? Because there is a probability of $1.00 - 0.95 = 0.05$ that there would be a competitive bid of $7,000, which would beat the bid of $8,000. Similarly, the probability of award at $9,000 goes down to 0.85 because there is a probability of $0.95 - 0.85 = 0.10$ of a competitive bid of $8,000. We can continue in this way and determine, by successive subtractions, the probability of each bid, as implied by the above cumulative distribution. We get:

Bid	Probability of bid
$7,000	0.05
8,000	0.10
9,000	0.25
10,000	0.30
11,000	0.20
12,000	0.10
13,000	0.00

This sort of presentation is the probability distribution with which we are familiar. The sum of the probabilities is 1 since one of these bids must occur—no other is possible. The relationship between the cumulative distribution and the corresponding probability distribution permits us, if we are given one of them, immediately to deduce the other. They simply represent two different ways of presenting the same information. Sometimes one is more useful, sometimes the other. In this case, the cumulative distribution is the probability of a bid of x dollars or greater which is the equivalent of the probability of award for a bid x if we ignore ties.

We have not given even a hint as to how a firm might have obtained the appropriate cumulative distribution, but let us continue to assume that, somehow, the firm does have it. Given this information we are able to calculate the expected profit for any bid. We will ignore the possibility of ties (equal bids) since they do not affect the principle involved, and since the possibility of ties looks more serious here than it would usually be because of the large interval of bids we have used in presenting our data. Consider a bid of \$9,000. If the firm is awarded the contract for this bid it will make \$9,000 − \$8,000 = \$1,000 profit. This corresponds to the $(x - c)$ we used above. Since we now know that the probability of the firm's being awarded the contract for this bid is 0.85, we can calculate the expected profit exactly as we did above. Our equation, given above, was

$$\text{Expected profit} = p(x - c)$$

For the \$9,000 bid we have, therefore, an expected profit of 0.85(\$9,000 − \$8,000) = \$850.

Proceeding similarly we can calculate the expected profit for each bid.

BID	EXPECTED PROFIT	
\$7,000	1.00(7,000 − 8,000) =	−\$1,000
8,000	0.95(8,000 − 8,000) =	0
9,000	0.85(9,000 − 8,000) =	850
10,000	0.60(10,000 − 8,000) =	1,200
11,000	0.30(11,000 − 8,000) =	900
12,000	0.10(12,000 − 8,000) =	400
13,000	0.00(13,000 − 8,000) =	0

The maximum expected profit is \$1,200, at a bid of \$10,000. This, therefore, is the bid the firm should make. Why? Because the firm has the stated objective of maximizing its expected profit and this bid, if repeated a large number of times under identical circumstances, would give the firm an average return of \$1,200 per bid. This is greater than that from any other bid.

We have made the assumption in our calculations that the cost of fulfilling the contractual obligations was known, in our example \$8,000. What effect does the undoubted fact that the decision-maker doesn't know the exact cost have on the problem? The answer is that if the wrong cost is used it can lead to the selection of a nonoptimal strategy. To avoid this, the decision-maker can accumulate information on the relationship between the estimates and the actual costs of the contracts which were awarded. This can be done, most conveniently, by recording for each completed contract the ratio between the estimated cost on which the bid was based and the actual final cost. By this means, a distribution of these ratios can be obtained which will be useful in many calculations concerning a firm's over-all position. Analytical methods can be used to determine the sensitivity of expected profit to errors in cost estimation. For example, we find the cost (c_1) which will switch the bid from $10,000 to $9,000 in the following way:

$$0.85(9,000 - c_1) = 0.60(10,000 - c_1) : c_1 = \$6,600$$

Similarly, we obtain the value of cost (c_2) which will switch the bid from $10,000 to $11,000.

$$0.30(11,000 - c_2) = 0.60(10,000 - c_2) : c_2 = \$9,000$$

We next take the ratios

$$\frac{8,000}{6,600} = 1.21$$

$$\frac{8,000}{9,000} = 0.89$$

and consult the distribution of ratios. Assuming that this distribution is stable, we can observe the probability that a ratio of 1.21 or greater will occur. In the same way, we can obtain the probability that a ratio of .89 or less will occur. If the probabilities of either or both eventualities are high, then it is quite likely that the decision-maker will initiate additional cost studies to refine the estimates. On the other hand, if it appears that the amount of error likely to occur will not affect the bid decision, then the decision-maker can ignore the uncertainty of cost as it does not affect his bidding strategy. Other techniques, including Monte Carlo, can be used if the sensitivity of expected profit to errors of estimation is high. In these cases, the variability of actual costs with respect to estimated costs can be included in the decision model. Consequently, the problems connected with estimation of cost can be handled. All that the decision-maker needs to know is the distribution of probabilities of award as a function of the amount of the bid; his firm can then utilize the procedures of this competitive bidding model to optimize its position.

But we can very well ask at this point: How can a firm determine the distribution? First, the *complexities* of trying to determine this distribution should be distinguished from the fundamental method as outlined above. The method itself is quite simple, at least in conception, despite any difficulties which may be involved in attempting to determine the crucial distribution of probabilities of award as a function of the amount of the bid.

We are, then, going to consider practical ways in which a decision-maker can obtain the necessary information about the distribution of the probabilities of award as a function of the amount bid. Since it is customary to announce the bids on contracts after they have been awarded, it is possible to learn the bidding behavior of competitors. We will consider three cases: *first,* the competitors for a particular contract are known; *second,* the identities of one's competitors are unknown but it is known how many there are; *third,* the competitors are unknown and their number is also unknown.

First we will consider the case where the competitors bidding for a particular contract are known. Let us study competitor *A.* The information we have about *A* consists of every previous contract on which *A* bid and for which the decision-maker's firm made a cost estimate. For every such contract we can determine the ratio of *A*'s bid to the decision-maker's *cost* estimate (not his "bid"). For example, part of the data on *A* might look like this:

Contract	Decision-maker's estimated cost	A's bid	Ratio
1	$8,500	$10,200	1.2
2	22,000	33,000	1.5
3	11,000	15,400	1.4
4	35,000	38,500	1.1
5	9,000	9,000	1.0

The ratio is simply *A*'s bid divided by the decision-maker's cost estimate. We would continue this procedure for all contracts on which we had the necessary information: the cost estimate and *A*'s bid. We would then summarize all of this information in a table in which we would give the total number of times that each ratio occurred. The table would look like this:

Ratio of A's bids to the decision-maker's cost estimates	Number of times it occurred	Probability of ratio
0.9	1	.02
1.0	3	.06
1.1	5	.10
1.2	11	.22
1.3	15	.30
1.4	8	.16
1.5	4	.08
1.6	3	.06
	50	1.00

Of course, we would search to discover some influence other than the variability of the decision-maker's costs to account for the differences in the ratios. It might turn out that A bid lower than the cost estimate when he had not obtained a contract award for 12 months or more; that he bid much more than the decision-maker's costs when he had recently won a contract that gave him a heavy backlog of work. We have a total of 50 such ratios, and this table gives the frequencies of the various ratios' occurrences and the corresponding probabilities.

We note that we have used a crude interval in our breakdown of the ratios. This is done solely for the purpose of simplicity in the example. In actual practice a more refined breakdown of the ratios would be used, but the principle would remain exactly the same.

From this table we can now determine the cumulative probability distribution for competitor A. This cumulative distribution will show the probability that a particular bid, expressed as a multiple of the decision-maker's cost estimate, will be lower than the bid of competitor A. Thus, for example, a bid of 0.9 times the cost estimate will be lower than the bid of competitor A with a probability of $1.00 - 0.02 = 0.98$. But this would leave the possibility of tie bids, chiefly because of the large interval we have used in presenting the ratios. To eliminate this possibility let us simply lower the bid slightly. Thus, we can say that a bid of 0.89 times the cost estimate wil be lower than A's bid with probability of 1.00. A bid of 0.99 times the cost estimate will be lower than A's bid with probability of $1.00 - 0.02 = 0.98$. A bid of 1.09 times the cost estimate will be lower than A's bid with probability of $1.00 - 0.02 - 0.06 = 0.92$. Proceeding similarly we can obtain the following table:

BID, AS MULTIPLE OF COST ESTIMATE	PROBABILITY THAT BID IS LOWER THAN BID OF A
0.89	1.00
0.99	0.98
1.09	0.92
1.19	0.82
1.29	0.60
1.39	0.30
1.49	0.14
1.59	0.06
1.69	0.00

This is the required cumulative probability distribution. For any given bid, expressed as a multiple of the cost estimate, it gives the probability that that bid will be lower than A's bid. Or, if A is the decision-maker's competitor in bidding for a particular contract, we can say that this table gives the probability of award as a function of the amount bid. This should mean that the decision-maker already has sufficient information to determine the bid which will give him the maximum expected profit, if A is his only competitor.

Let us see if this is so. Suppose the decision-maker is bidding on a contract and A is his only competitor. As usual, we will let c denote the cost estimate on this contract. Suppose the decision-maker bids $1.09c$ on this contract. According to the table the probability will be 0.92 that he will win the contract. If he wins the contract he will make a profit of $1.09c - c = 0.09c$. This, of course, is simply the $(x - c)$ we used above, where $(x = 1.09c)$. We know that the expected profit is the probability of award times $(x - c)$. In this case, then, $0.92(0.09c) = 0.0828c$. If he bids $1.19c$ we have

$$\text{Expected profit} = 0.82(1.19c - c) = 0.82(0.19c) = 0.1558c$$

Proceeding similarly, using the probabilities from the table above we obtain:

BID, AS MULTIPLE OF COST ESTIMATE	EXPECTED PROFIT WHERE A IS ONLY COMPETITOR	
0.89	$1.00(0.89c - c) =$	$-0.11c$
0.99	$0.98(0.99c - c) =$	$-0.0098c$
1.09	$0.92(1.09c - c) =$	$0.0828c$
1.19	$0.82(1.19c - c) =$	$0.1558c$
1.29	$0.60(1.29c - c) =$	$0.1740c$
1.39	$0.30(1.39c - c) =$	$0.1170c$
1.49	$0.14(1.49c - c) =$	$0.0786c$
1.59	$0.06(1.59c - c) =$	$0.0354c$

Clearly, a bid of $1.29c$ gives the maximum expected profit, $0.1740c$. If we use $c = \$8,000$, as in an earlier example, this would give a bid of $10,320 and an expected profit of $1,392. Consequently, it can be seen that empirically obtained information is sufficient to enable us to determine the bid which will maximize expected profit in the case where A is the only competitor.

What does the decision-maker do if there is more than one known competitor against him? Let us assume that he is faced with two competitors on a particular contract: A, as above, and B. We could go through precisely the same procedure for obtaining information about B as we did for A. We will not repeat these steps because they are the same as those illustrated for A above. Granting that we have done this, we would end up with a cumulative probability distribution for B which would be similar to, but different from, that for A. Now that we have this, it will be convenient to present the two cumulative probability distributions, one for A and one for B, in one table.

Bid, as multiple of cost estimate	Probability that bid is lower than bid of:	
	A	B
0.89	1.00	1.00
0.99	0.98	0.94
1.09	0.92	0.83
1.19	0.82	0.65
1.29	0.60	0.37
1.39	0.30	0.20
1.49	0.14	0.10
1.59	0.06	0.03
1.69	0.00	0.00

The distribution for A is the same one that was used before. From this table we are able to say immediately that, for example, a bid of 1.09 times the cost estimate has a probability of 0.92 of being lower than A's bid and a probability of 0.83 of being lower than B's bid. Can we deduce from this statement the probability that a bid of 1.09 times the cost estimate will simultaneously be lower than A's bid and B's bid, or, in short, that it will win the award of the contract? Yes, we can do this very simply. The probability of the joint occurrence of two independent events is the product of the probabilities of the two events separately. Therefore, the probability that a bid of 1.09 times the cost estimate will be simultaneously lower than A's and B's bids is $0.92 \times 0.83 = 0.76$. The probability that a bid of 1.19 times the cost estimate will be simultaneously lower than A's bid and B's bid is $0.82 \times 0.65 = 0.53$. Proceeding in this way we can obtain, for each bid, the probability that it is lower than both A's bid and B's bid. To do this requires only that we multiply the entries on the same row in the columns under A and B in the table above. This gives:

Bid, as multiple of cost estimate	Probability that bid is simultaneously lower than bids of A and of B
0.89	$1.00 \times 1.00 = 1.00$
0.99	$0.98 \times 0.94 = 0.92$
1.09	$0.92 \times 0.83 = 0.76$
1.19	$0.82 \times 0.65 = 0.53$
1.29	$0.60 \times 0.37 = 0.22$
1.39	$0.30 \times 0.20 = 0.06$
1.49	$0.14 \times 0.10 = 0.01$
1.59	$0.06 \times 0.03 = 0.00$
1.69	$0.00 \times 0.00 = 0.00$

The probability that the decision-maker's bid is simultaneously lower than the bids of A and of B is equivalent to the probability of award if A and B are the only competitors, as we are assuming. In other words, the table above gives the cumulative probability distribution for obtaining the contract as a function of the amount of the bid. Therefore, once again, we have the necessary information to enable us to determine which bid has the greatest expected profit. The calculations of the expected profit for each bid are made exactly as in the example we have given earlier. If we bid 1.09 times the cost estimate, the table shows that the probability of award will be 0.76. The expected profit is, therefore, $0.76(1.09c - c) = 0.0684c$. The expected profit from a bid of $1.19c$ is $0.53(1.19c - c) = 0.1007c$. The expected profit from a bid of $1.29c$ is $0.22(1.29c - c) = 0.0638c$. Similarly, the expected profit from each bid can be calculated. The maximum expected profit comes from a bid of $1.19c$ and is $0.1007c$. In terms of the earlier example, where $c = \$8,000$, this would mean that the bid should be \$9,520 with an expected profit of \$805.60.

We see that if we have the necessary data on the past performances of competitors, the method will work equally well for any number of known competitors. For each competitor we must obtain the appropriate cumulative probability distribution showing the probability that a given bid of the decision-maker will be lower than the bid of that competitor. The final cumulative probability of award distribution is then determined by multiplying, for each bid, the entries given for each competitor for that bid. This distribution gives the necessary information for calculating the expected profit for every bid, which then enables us to choose the bid with the maximum expected profit. This procedure, therefore, handles the case where the competitors are known.

What can the decision-maker do when he doesn't know who his competitors are? In this event we are no longer able to obtain specific information about the bidding behavior of each competitor as we did above. Our lack of information about the identity of the competitors on a particular contract forces us to utilize less precise information than otherwise. Instead of using information based on specific competitors we will have to be satisfied with information about an "average" or "typical" competitor. In other words, the best available information in this case is the past behavior of competitors on those contracts for which the decision-maker made cost estimates. The procedure to be followed is the same as before except that we lump all competitors together. We simply combine all the previous ratios of a competitor's bid to our cost estimate into one probability distribution. For example, A and B, as above, would be lumped into one probability distribution along with all the other competitors for which we had ratios. From this over-all probability distribution of ratios we can then obtain, as before, the cumulative probability distribution. The resulting cumulative probability distribution might look like this:

Bid, as multiple of cost estimate	Probability that bid is lower than bid of average competitor
0.89	1.00
0.99	0.97
1.09	0.90
1.19	0.79
1.29	0.58
1.39	0.35
1.49	0.21
1.59	0.08
1.69	0.02
1.79	0.00

This table is equivalent to the table for a single specific competitor given above. The only difference is that this table is for a single unspecified competitor—the average competitor. This table should, therefore, be interpreted as follows: for a bid of 1.19 times the cost estimate the probability is 0.79 that it would be lower than the bid of any single competitor picked at random.

Suppose, for example, that, on a particular contract, the decision-maker is faced with only one competitor but that he doesn't know the identity of this competitor. Then he would use this table to determine the expected profit for each bid. The calculations would be exactly the same as those which have been shown several times above. Notice that the important difference in using this table is that we do not know the identity of the competitor. If we knew that our only competitor was A then we would use the table for A. Otherwise *we must use the best information we have:* the cumulative probability distribution for the average competitor.

Suppose that the decision-maker does not know the identity of his competitors but that he does know how many of them there are on a particular contract. He can use the above table to determine the probability of award for each bid. He simply assumes that this average cumulative distribution applies to each of the unknown competitors. He then proceeds as in the case of known competitors. This table shows, for example, that a bid of 1.19 times the cost estimate has a probability of 0.79 of being lower than the bid of any one competitor picked at random. Suppose there are two such competitors. The probability that a bid of 1.19 times the cost estimate will be simultaneously lower than the bids of both the competitors is $0.79 \times 0.79 = 0.6241$. If there are three competitors the probability is $0.79 \times 0.79 \times 0.79 = 0.4930$. If there are four competitors the probability is $0.79 \times 0.79 \times 0.79 \times 0.79 = 0.3895$. And similarly for each other possible bid. For example, the necessary cumulative probability of award distribution based on three unknown competitors is:

BID, AS MULTIPLE OF COST ESTIMATE	PROBABILITY THAT BID IS LOWER THAN BIDS OF THREE UNKNOWN COMPETITORS
0.89	$1.00 \times 1.00 \times 1.00 = 1.0000$
0.99	$0.97 \times 0.97 \times 0.97 = 0.9127$
1.09	$0.90 \times 0.90 \times 0.90 = 0.7290$
1.19	$0.79 \times 0.79 \times 0.79 = 0.4930$
1.29	. . . 0.1951
1.39	. . . 0.0429
1.49	. . . 0.0093
1.59	. . . 0.0005
1.69	. . . 0.0000
1.79	. . . 0.0000

Of course, the probability that a bid is lower than the bids of three competitors is precisely the probability of award in bidding against the three competitors. Therefore, this table is the required cumulative probability of award distribution as a function of the size of the bid. We can immediately calculate the expected profit for each bid in the usual way.

The expected profit for a bid of $1.09c$ is $0.7290 (1.09c - c) = 0.0656c$
The expected profit for a bid of $1.19c$ is $0.4930 (1.19c - c) = 0.0937c$
The expected profit for a bid of $1.29c$ is $0.1951 (1.29c - c) = 0.0566c$

The maximum expected profit is $0.0937c$ and is obtained for a bid of $1.19c$. In terms of our earlier example, where $c = \$8,000$, this would mean that the maximum expected profit is \$749.60 and is obtained by bidding \$9,520. It is clear that the same procedure can be followed for any given number of competitors.

What should we do if we don't know the number of competitors on a particular contract? The answer is that we must find some way of obtaining an estimate of the number. Let us consider the effect on our bid as the number of competitors increases. It is easy to show that, as the number of competitors increases, the maximum expected profit will be obtained with lower bids. We can illustrate this using the cumulative probability distribution function of the "average" competitor given above. We calculate the following:

NUMBER OF COMPETITORS	BID WITH GREATEST EXPECTED PROFIT	AMOUNT OF EXPECTED PROFIT
1	$1.29c$	$0.1682c$
2	$1.19c$	$0.1386c$
3	$1.19c$	$0.0937c$
4	$1.19c$	$0.0750c$
5	$1.19c$	$0.0585c$
6	$1.09c$	$0.0478c$
7	$1.09c$	$0.0430c$
8	$1.09c$	$0.0387c$

It is clear that, as the number of competitors increases, the bid with the maximum expected profit becomes smaller and the amount of expected profit steadily becomes smaller. As the number of competitors gets even larger the amount of expected profit goes down steadily towards the break-even point. This means that the number of competitors is a most important variable in determining the bid with the maximum expected profit. In the case of an unknown number of competitors it is of paramount importance to obtain an estimate of the number. Once an estimate is available the above procedure is followed, using the estimated number of competitors.

We will not discuss in detail any of the various possible methods of estimating the number of competitors. It is similar to other estimation problems and has all the difficulties associated with such problems. One possibility is to determine whether there has been a relationship between the number of bidders and the size of the contract. If so, it would be possible to use estimated cost as a means for estimating the number of competitors. Perhaps the experience of the decision-maker will suffice to provide good estimates. Whatever the method of estimation, once the estimate has been obtained the procedure given above for a known number of competitors is then followed to determine the bid with the maximum expected profit.

113/ *Competition and Mixed Strategies*

One of the major characteristics of the marketing area is the fact that intelligent competition exists. Despite the great importance of competition in many marketing decision problems, our procedures for trying to incorporate the presence of rational opponents into our analysis leave a great deal to be desired. Several of our preceding sections have involved competition, either implicitly, as in the brand-share model, or explicitly, as in the preceding section on competitive bidding.

We have not yet, however, illustrated one of the most famous tools which has been developed for dealing with direct competitive struggles: game theory. In fact, game theory has by no means proved itself to be a technique adequate for the successful analysis of real-world competitive situations. Nonetheless, some of the concepts which have been developed and elucidated by game theory are of great importance for analyzing competitive situations even though the theory does not suffice to demonstrate the optimal course of action. We will, therefore, illustrate some of the ideas of game theory.

Sometimes, the effect of an intellgent competitor is to produce a situation in which the optimal strategy for the decision-maker is a mixture in time of the strategies that are available to him. If the decision-maker's strategies are such that he can use only one of the available alternatives at a time, then it sometimes occurs that a mixture of his alternatives over time is optimal. For example, if the available strategies are (1) raise the price, (2) keep the price unchanged, and (3) lower the price, then over a period of time it might be possible to employ each of these strategies in different proportions. The choice of which strategy to employ at a given time is made on a chance basis, but in keeping with specified proportions which have been determined to be optimal. This kind of long-range strategy may arise whenever the decision-maker and his competitor are in a repetitive situation. Let us assume that the decision-maker and the competitor are representatives of competing department stores. Each day the stores advertise in the local newspaper items which are on sale. Depending upon which items they advertise and the prices they ask, one store will gain sales at the expense of the other store. This assumption is necessary, as was discussed in an earlier chapter, in order to have a zero-sum game. Suppose that the following matrix applies:

DECISION-MAKER USES	COMPETITOR USES		
	$C1$	$C2$	$C3$
$S1$	-30	40	-32
$S2$	-60	20	-15
$S3$	35	-35	30
$S4$	65	25	-10

The matrix describes the gain in sales to the decision-maker. Negative entries signify a gain to the competitor and a loss to the decision-maker. Of course, a realistic matrix would be much larger, since a great number of items and prices for these items are involved. However, for our example, this matrix will suffice.

The decision-maker's maximin solution is the selection of strategy $S4$ with a payoff of -10. The competitor's minimax solution is $C3$ with a payoff of 30. Since these two payoffs are not the same, there will be two mixed strategies—one for the decision-maker and one for the competitor —which will result in an improvement in the payoff for both. It is the fact that the payoffs are not equal which determines that a mixed strategy should be employed in repetitive decision-making problems.

As we examine the matrix we observe that strategy $S4$ always yields a better payoff to the decision-maker than strategy $S2$. That is, no matter what the competitor does, $S4$ is better than $S2$. Therefore, the decision-maker will have no use for $S2$ and he discards it. We describe this situation by saying that $S4$ dominates $S2$. Whenever one strategy dominates another, it simplifies the decision problem. Next, as we continue our examination, we find that column $C3$ dominates $C1$. The dominating relationship does not hold in the original matrix, but it does hold after we discard $S2$.

	C1	C2	C3
S1	−30	40	−32
S3	35	−35	30
S4	65	25	−10

In this case, dominance is expressed in the reverse direction—because it is the competitor who is considering it and he prefers smaller payoffs. Since $C3$ always yields less payoff to the decision-maker than $C1$ does, the competitor will never choose to use $C1$. Thus, we can rewrite the payoff matrix:

		(Y_2) C2	(Y_3) C3
(X_1)	S1	40	−32
(X_3)	S3	−35	30
(X_4)	S4	25	−10

Dominance of strategies undoubtedly provides an intuitive means for discarding large numbers of strategies from consideration. However, we can see that with complex strategies and a great number of possibilities, it would be hard for the decision-maker to examine all the possibilities in his mind. Even on paper there can be difficulty in spotting dominance when the matrix includes many rows and columns.

We must now obtain the solution to this mixed strategy problem. We remember that the decision-maker's maximin is −10 and the competitor's minimax is 30. A mixed strategy will be some combination of the pure strategies which are chosen at random according to the probabilities which optimize the payoff for both parties. This mixed strategy will result in an equal value of the expected payoff for both the decision-maker and the competitor. To begin,

> let $S1$ be used X_1 per cent of the time by the decision-maker,
> $S3$ be used X_3 per cent of the time by the decision-maker,
> $S4$ be used X_4 per cent of the time by the decision-maker,
> $C2$ be used Y_2 per cent of the time by the competitor, and
> $C3$ be used Y_3 per cent of the time by the competitor.

Then we can write the following five inequations and two equations.

$$40X_1 - 35X_3 + 25X_4 \geq v \tag{1}$$
$$-32X_1 + 30X_3 - 10X_4 \geq v \tag{2}$$
$$X_1 + X_3 + X_4 = 1.00 \tag{3}$$
$$40Y_2 - 32Y_3 \leq v \tag{4}$$
$$-35Y_2 + 30Y_3 \leq v \tag{5}$$
$$25Y_2 - 10Y_3 \leq v \tag{6}$$
$$Y_2 + Y_3 = 1.00 \tag{7}$$

Where v is the expected value of the payoff after many repetitions of the decision problem. If the competitor uses either his pure strategy, $C2$, or $C3$, and the decision-maker uses the mixed strategy ($S1$ being used X_1 per cent of the time, $S3$ is used X_3 per cent of the time, and $S4$ is used X_4 per cent of the time), then either Equation (1) or Equation (2) results. These equations, which describe the expected value of the payoff to the decision-maker, are set equal to or greater than v since the decision-maker wants to maximize the payoff measure. The competitor, in turn, wants to minimize the size of the payoff measure, and so equations 4, 5, and 6 are set equal to or less than v. Thus the value of v will be as large as possible for the decision-maker and as small as possible for the competitor. Equations (3) and (7) express the fact that for both the decision-maker and the competitor, the per cent of time that each of their available strategies is used must sum to 100 per cent.

Since we are dealing with five inequations, the solution of the unknowns is not straightforward. One method is to treat the inequations as though they were equations and then to test the results to see if they violate the inequalities on v. We have seven equations and six unknowns. Therefore six equations can be solved at a time and the results tested by the seventh equation. This procedure can be quite lengthy, since each set of six must be solved until the solution does not violate the one remaining equation. For example, if we solve equations 1, 2, 3, 4, 5, and 7, we obtain the following values:

$$v = \frac{80}{137} = 0.585 \qquad X_1 = \frac{65}{137} = 0.474$$

$$Y_2 = \frac{62}{137} = 0.453 \qquad X_3 = \frac{72}{137} = 0.526$$

$$Y_3 = \frac{75}{137} = 0.547 \qquad X_4 = 0$$

When the appropriate values are substituted in Equation (6), we find

$$25\frac{62}{137} - 10\frac{75}{137} \leq \frac{80}{137}$$

or
$$\frac{1550 - 750}{137} = \frac{800}{137} \leq \frac{80}{137}$$

which is a violation of the restriction. Consequently, the values given above are wrong and a new attempt must be made. Equations 1, 2, 3, 5, 6, and 7 produce values which fulfill all of the requirements. These are

$$v = 4.00 \qquad X_1 = 0.00$$
$$Y_2 = 0.40 \qquad X_3 = 0.35$$
$$Y_3 = 0.60 \qquad X_4 = 0.65$$

When the appropriate values are substituted into Equation (4), we observe

$$40(0.40) - 32(0.60) \leq 4$$
or
$$- 3.2 \qquad \leq 4 \qquad \text{(which is true)}$$

The same solution for the Y and v values can be obtained by graphical methods. The reason is that, in this example, there are only two dimensions in the Y plane. Figure 11.7 portrays the graphical solution. Since $Y_2 = 1 - Y_3$, we rewrite equations 4, 5, and 6 in these terms.

$$40(1 - Y_3) - 32Y_3 = 40 - 40Y_3 - 32Y_3 = 40 - 72Y_3 = v_1$$
$$-35(1 - Y_3) + 30Y_3 = -35 + 35Y_3 + 30Y_3 = -35 + 64Y_3 = v_3$$
$$25(1 - Y_3) - 10Y_3 = 25 - 25Y_3 - 10Y_3 = 25 - 35Y_3 = v_4$$

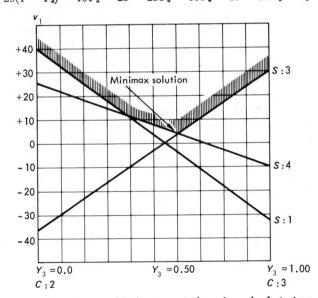

FIGURE 11.7 Graphical representation of a mixed strategy.

We determine v_1, v_3, and v_4 when $Y_3 = 0$ and when $Y_3 = 1$.

Y_3	v_1	v_3	v_4
0	40	−35	25
1	−32	30	−10

Next we plot these points, drawing straight lines to connect each v_i pair. The competitor prefers minus values, which represents his gains. Accordingly, he chooses the minimax solution. When we inspected the payoff matrix before deriving the mixed strategy result, we found the competitor's minimax payoff was 30, which he achieved with his strategy C_3. We can see that this is the top point on the right-hand side of the graph. Also, this point is lower than the top point on the left-hand side of the graph. That is why it is the minimax solution for pure strategies. But we observe that other points along the top surface lie still lower than the righthand point. The lowest top point falls at $Y_3 = 0.60$ and $v = 4$, which was the value of the solution we previously derived. The competitor will mix his strategies in order to obtain this large benefit. On the average, instead of losing 30 he will lose only 4. The decision-maker, on the other hand, by using his mixed strategy will change his maximin solution from a loss of 10 to a gain of 4. Although we cannot present the decision-maker's situation in a visual form, the same considerations apply and can, of course, be derived analytically.

Why should the competitor enter this competition with the decision-maker if he must expect a loss? Presumably, if he does not advertise in the newspaper, he will take an even greater loss. The competitor will search for new strategies which can be added to the decision matrix in an attempt to shift the advantage over to his side. Thus, a creative act is required on the competitor's part because nothing else will improve his lot. This is true if the decision-maker randomizes his mixed strategy. What might happen if he doesn't do so? Let us assume that he sets up a schedule to specify when each advertisement will appear and the competitor learns the information on this schedule. Then every time the decision-maker uses his $S3$, the competitor uses his $C3$, with a resultant gain each time of -35. Every time the decision-maker uses his $S4$, the competitor parries with his $C3$, and the resultant gain per time will be -10. Then, the decision-maker will lose—and the competitor will gain:

$$-35(0.35) - 10(0.65) = -18.75$$

which is an increase of 22.75 for the competitor at the expense of the decision-maker.

PROBLEMS

1. Two national coffee brands, B and C, are the major competitors of a regional brand, A. The regional company undertakes a market survey from which it obtains the following brand-share and brand-switching information.

BRAND SHARE		BRAND SWITCHING		
		A	B	C
0.12	A	0.1	0.3	0.6
0.40	B	0.1	0.5	0.4
0.48	C	0.1	0.3	0.6

What will be the limiting distribution of brand shares? If the switching matrix applies to a period of one month, how long will it take for the situation to come to equilibrium? If the market is of fixed size, say 100,000 sales per month, and each company makes a profit of $0.30 on every sale, what will be the average monthly profit at the end of six months for each of the three companies?

Brand *A*'s sales manager is distressed by the results of the analysis. He believes that the assumption of a fixed market size is unrealistic. He reasons that Brand *A* will be hard-pressed to take a larger share of customers from the two national brands but he feels that Brand *A* should obtain a larger share of new customers as they enter the market. The sales manager asks for a report on the change in population size by age groups for the region, as well as a report on population mobility, which will show how many consumers move in and move out of the marketing region. He receives the requested information from his marketing department. On the basis of these data the sales manager determines that 10,000 new sales will be made each month, while 5,000 sales from repeat customers will be lost to the market. The sales manager conceives of an advertising campaign which will bring Brand *A* the largest share of the new sales and the lowest loss, from attrition, of old customers. He sets down the situation in the following way:

NEW SALES PER MONTH	STARTING POINT (SALES PER MONTH)	LOST SALES PER MONTH
A: 5,000	12,000	1,000
B: 2,000	40,000	2,000
C: 3,000	48,000	2,000

Using the same switching matrix as before, determine the average monthly profits of each of the three companies over a period of six months. If the growth in the size of the market stops, what is the long-term outlook for Brand *A*? Assuming no growth in market size, compare the limiting distribution previously derived with the limiting distribution of the matrix shown below. What could account for such a change?

	BRAND SWITCHING		
	A	B	C
A	0.3	0.2	0.5
B	0.1	0.5	0.4
C	0.1	0.3	0.6

2. Two airline companies have many corresponding routes. Company *A* has followed a policy of replacing existing equipment as soon as significant improvements are available, while Company *B*'s policy has been to utilize existing equipment as long as possible. Company *B*'s management has always recognized the fact that their policy results in a smaller share of the market. On the other hand, Company *B*'s costs are lower than Company *A*'s, since Company *A* must borrow heavily in order to purchase new equipment. Company *B*'s competitive position requires that it replan its schedules every time Company *A* introduces new equipment on its routes: Let us assume that such a situation is about to occur. Company *B* reasons that Company *A* can use the equipment that it is about to receive in only four different ways. In its turn, Company *B* has five reasonable strategies available to it. Company .*B*'s objective is to minimize its loss while Company *A*'s objective is to maximize its gains. The following pay-offs are determined for each combination of strategies:

	B'S STRATEGIES				
A'S STRATEGIES	B_1	B_2	B_3	B_4	B_5
A_1	30	35	40	45	50
A_2	60	65	20	30	70
A_3	35	40	35	40	55
A_4	25	45	25	20	10

What is the optimal strategy for each company to follow? *B* discovers an error in the calculations of the row A_3 and makes the following changes:

$$A_3, B_1 = 38 \neq 35$$
$$A_3, B_3 = 38 \neq 35$$

What is the new solution and what has brought this about?

3. A manufacturer of ball-point pens ships them in quantities of 25 of each of two colors. He observes that many retailers place reorders for only one color. However, the total number of requests are about equally divided between the two colors. That is, some retailers order only the first color, others order only the second color. He speaks to a number of the retailers and they explain that only one color sold well. He can find no regional or other differences to account for this result. What is the manufacturer doing that creates this situation? What should he do to correct the situation? Hint: $P_j =$ the probability that j pens of either color will be in stock when the clerk discovers that the last pen of the other color has been sold. $N =$ the number of pens of each of the two colors which the retailer receives in the shipment, and

$$P_j = \frac{(2N-j)!}{N!(N-j)!} \frac{1}{2^{2N-j}}$$

4. When a manufacturer decides to sell his product in a foreign market he is confronted with a variety of decision problems. Most of these problems are analogous to the situations he faces in his home market. Generally, however,

the situations with which he has to deal are more extreme. Regional differences between consumers are relatively minor in comparison with national differences. We will consider a problem which confronts a manufacturer of radios. There are five countries in which he is considering marketing his line of products. His efforts in each country will produce different results because consumer taste varies in each country, different competitive products are sold in each country, and some of them compete more directly with the manufacturer's line of products. In the same way, advertising rates, media audiences, message effectiveness, tariffs, government regulations, and a host of other factors combine to yield different outcomes in each country. The manufacturer has allowed a budget of $200,000 for the international market. He sets up a table to indicate the estimated sales which might be expected for every $10,000 he allocates to one of the five countries. Because of diminishing returns, the rate at which sales volume increases with each additional dollar becomes less as more and more dollars are spent in one country. The table below compares the expected sales for the five countries, C_1, C_2, C_3, C_4, and C_5. How should the manufacturer allocate the sum of $200,000 to the five countries in order to maximize his expected sales? What will the expected sales be? If the manufacturer decides to budget the larger sum of $300,000, what will the new allocation be? What will be the revised estimate of expected sales? How do the ratios of sales to expenditures compare for the two different budgeted amounts?

AMOUNT SPENT ($)	EXPECTED SALES ($) FOR				
	C_1	C_2	C_3	C_4	C_5
10,000	18,000	15,000	15,000	20,000	16,000
20,000	36,000	25,000	30,000	40,000	32,000
30,000	49,000	35,000	45,000	60,000	42,000
40,000	62,000	45,000	56,000	80,000	52,000
50,000	75,000	55,000	67,000	97,000	62,000
60,000	88,000	65,000	78,000	114,000	72,000
70,000	101,000	75,000	89,000	131,000	82,000
80,000	114,000	85,000	100,000	145,000	92,000
90,000	127,000	95,000	111,000	155,000	102,000
100,000	140,000	105,000	121,000	165,000	112,000
110,000	150,000	111,000	131,000	175,000	122,000
120,000	160,000	117,000	141,000	185,000	132,000
130,000	170,000	123,000	151,000	195,000	140,000
140,000	180,000	129,000	161,000	205,000	148,000
150,000	190,000	135,000	171,000	215,000	156,000
160,000	197,000	139,000	181,000	225,000	164,000
170,000	204,000	143,000	186,000	230,000	172,000
180,000	211,000	147,000	191,000	235,000	176,000
190,000	218,000	151,000	196,000	240,000	180,000
200,000	225,000	155,000	201,000	245,000	184,000

5. Variety is an important variable which must be considered in many marketing studies. A frequent problem is to determine the optimal amount of variety. Let us assume that the following hypothetical relationship has been derived as

the result of a study conducted by a department store—namely, that the sales obtained from a specific counter are proportional to the expression $N^V V^N$, where V equals the number of varieties which appear on the counter and N equals the number of items of each variety which appear on the counter. It is assumed that it is the policy of the store to display equal numbers of whatever varieties are carried. We shall suppose that all of the items are of about equal size and the capacity of a counter is C. Then, $NV = C$.

What interpretation can be given for the relationship $N^V V^N$? What will the optimal variety be when the counter has a capacity of 120 items? ($C = 120$)

Hint: it is possible to rewrite the expression which we want to maximize in the following form:

$$\left(\frac{120}{V}\right)^V (V)^{120/V}$$

or

$$V(\log 120 - \log V) + \frac{120}{V} \log V$$

It is then possible to try different values of V until the maximum is found. However, note the shape of this function. There are two maxima. Try to plot this curve. The derivative of the function can be obtained and set equal to zero in order to derive the expression for the maxima. This result is given by

$$\log_e V = \frac{(120/V^2) + \log_e 120 - 1}{(120/V^2) + 1}$$

If the reader is familiar with natural logarithms (which have the base e), he can find the value of V which satisfies this equality. By substituting values other than 120 in the above expressions, the maxima can be found for counter capacities other than 120.

Comment on the credibility of the relationship $N^V V^N$, and whether its maximization would produce maximum sales.

6. Another variety problem can be formulated in the following terms. We are stocking $(V - 1)$ different items and we are considering adding one new variety. What is the probability that after S sales are made we will have sold none of this additional variety? The assumption is made that the sales of all varieties, including the new one, are equally likely.

The relationship we want is given by the equation

$$P = \left(\frac{V-1}{V}\right)^S$$

Let us suppose that we sell refrigerators at the rate of 20 per month. What is the greatest number of varieties, V, which will give us a probability of 0.05 or less of selling none of the newest variety in the line, in a month?

7. A company collects information about the amount of time that each of its salesmen spends with customers. It also has information concerning how much each one of the customers orders. These data are given below. What conclusion might be drawn about the relationship between salesmen's time and customer orders?

CUSTOMER	TOTAL TIME SPENT PER MONTH	TOTAL ORDERS RECEIVED PER MONTH
1	2	$3,500
2	2	2,000
3	3	1,500
4	3	4,000
5	4	2,500
6	4	3,000
7	4	4,500
8	5	5,000
9	6	500
10	6	3,500
11	7	3,500
12	7	1,500
13	8	2,500
14	9	4,500
15	9	3,500
16	10	1,500

8. A company which bids on many contracts has collected the following information:

COMPANY'S ACTUAL COST	COMPANY'S ESTIMATED COST	SIZE OF COMPETITOR'S BIDS
$16,000	$16,000	$24,000
18,500	15,400	20,000
10,000	10,000	16,000
28,300	25,700	36,000
10,500	15,000	24,000
10,000	12,500	15,000
15,300	13,900	25,000
12,000	12,000	18,000
8,300	9,200	12,000
9,000	10,000	14,000
5,000	5,000	10,000
8,600	6,600	8,000
4,600	4,200	8,000
3,400	4,300	6,000
9,600	10,700	15,000
36,700	36,700	55,000
32,300	26,900	35,000
18,000	20,000	22,000
3,800	3,800	6,500
11,000	10,000	15,000

How good a job has the company been doing in estimating contract costs? A new job presents itself which the company estimates will cost $10,000. What should the company bid on this job if there is only one competitor and assuming that the bids given above are those of that competitor? What should be the bid if there are two competitors and the bids given above represent both of them? What profit will the company make if it wins the award of the contract in each case? Develop a range of values within which the error in estimating costs is likely to fall. Use the extremes of this range to determine how profit might be affected.

9. A mail-order company buys lists for its direct-mail advertising. The population from which these lists are drawn is 20 million. The lists can be assumed to have been compiled by random selections from the population. If the company wants to mail 1 million pieces, which combination of lists should it select so as to minimize duplication? (We will ignore triplication, and so on, and assume that no duplication exists within a list.)

List 1	200,000
List 2	500,000
List 3	300,000
List 4	800,000
List 5	400,000
List 6	100,000

What is the least possible percentage of duplication?

10. Here are some actual magazine data for a particular demographic class, with the data in union form:

$$A = 0.161 \qquad\qquad BD = 0.490$$
$$B = 0.229 \qquad\qquad CD = 0.507$$
$$C = 0.220 \qquad\qquad ABC = 0.434$$
$$D = 0.383 \qquad\qquad ABD = 0.529$$
$$AB = 0.315 \qquad\qquad ACD = 0.549$$
$$AC = 0.332 \qquad\qquad BCD = 0.580$$
$$AD = 0.454 \qquad\qquad ABCD = 0.607$$
$$BC = 0.368$$

a. Find the complete breakdown for A, B, C.
b. Find the exposure distribution for B, C, D.
c. Find the intersection presentation of the data for all magazines.
d. Assuming you do not know $ABC = 0.434$, find the minimum and maximum reaches by both programming approaches.
e. Assuming you do not know $ABCD = 0.607$, find the minimum and maximum reaches by both programming approaches for all four magazines.

11. A market researcher reports on a study of the usage of three brands. He claims that of 1,000 households, 647 used Brand A, 582 used Brand B, 419 used Brand C, 284 used both Brand A and Brand B, 225 used both Brand A and Brand C, 212 used both Brand B and Brand C, and 123 used all three brands. Here "used" means purchased at least once in the period under consideration. Do you believe the market researcher?

Chapter 12

Of Finance

Marketing and production are line activities. Together they form the backbone of the majority of business organizations. Supporting these line activities are the great variety of staff functions which deal with information, personnel, money, policy, and other major decisions. Examples of operations research studies exist in each of these areas. The previous edition of this book, in a chapter called "Of Administration," examined a collection of examples of management science methods in this general area. But since the appearance of that edition, finance has become one of the most rapidly burgeoning areas of unique applications of modern quantitative methods. In this edition, therefore, we decided to focus our attention on examples in the field of finance.

Even when we confine our attention to financial applications it is impossible to discuss all of the major kinds of analyses that have been developed. Space limitations preclude such an attempt, and there are two other reasons for limiting the number of examples. First, some of the financial decision problems which have been analyzed are of such complexity that they cannot be realistically simplified for presentation. Second, some financial decision problems which have been analyzed require mathematical methods beyond the scope of this book.

Complexities of financial decision problems frequently result from their involvement with multiple objectives. Further, many of the objectives are difficult to quantify and relevant costs are often hard to estimate. Nonetheless, the framework which decision theory provides for the analysis of decision problems is just as applicable in finance as it is in marketing and production.

114/ *Some Simple Models Used in Finance*

How does a new approach, such as operations research, become accepted in an established area such as finance? The usual way is for area specialists to discover that some of the *simplest* ideas of the new approach are directly applicable *in an interesting manner* to some traditional problems in the area. This is certainly what happened in the case of operations research and finance.

It was discovered that a number of well-known operations-research tools, first developed in other fields, were (almost) immediately applicable to several important problems in the field of finance. This served to suggest the potential of operations-research methods in finance and led ultimately to the intensive efforts that are currently being reported in the literature. It is the purpose of this section to survey a few of these simple applications.

In an early article,[1] Edward G. Bennion called attention to the usefulness of some of the basic ideas of decision theory for the capital budgeting decision. The author used the notions of payoff matrix, probabilities of states of nature, and expected values that we have already developed, and he put them together in a distinctive way and showed clearly that this approach could make a valuable contribution to the analysis of a capital budgeting decision.

In another early article,[2] William J. Baumol used the optimal lot-size formulation (discussed on pages 319–326) for the analysis of the demand for currency. Assume that an individual pays out T dollars per year at a constant rate. Suppose that the interest cost is i per dollar per year, and that the individual withdraws cash in lots of C dollars, evenly spaced throughout the year. He pays a "broker's fee" of B dollars for each withdrawal. Then we can immediately write the equation for his total costs $T.C.$ per year:

$$T.C. = \frac{BT}{C} + \frac{iC}{2}$$

This is equivalent to the optimal lot-size equation and subject to the same assumptions of constant withdrawal, etc. (See pp. 322–324.) Minimization of the equation gives the optimal amount, C, which the individual should withdraw:

---

[1] Edward G. Bennion: "Capital Budgeting and Game Theory," *Harvard Business Review*, 34, No. 6 (Nov.–Dec., 1956), 115–123.

[2] William J. Baumol: "The Transactions Demand for Cash: An Inventory Theoretic Approach," *The Quarterly Journal of Economics*, LXVI, No. 4 (Nov., 1952), 545–556.

$$C = \sqrt{\frac{2BT}{i}}$$

The answer is identical to that of the optimal lot-size. Professor Baumol's article generated much interest because it dealt with an important theoretical problem in a simple and realistic way. As a matter of fact, the same formulation has been used by companies for the determination of their optimal cash balances.[3]

Another use of the optimal lot-size formulation was suggested by Harold Bierman and Alan K. McAdams.[4] They considered the problem of how much cash a company should seek in the market. Let Q be the optimal amount to be obtained, K the incremental fixed cost of obtaining money on a loan basis, and D the excess of cash disbursements over cash receipts in the next time period, which is assumed to be known. Finally, let k be the interest cost of keeping cash assets on hand. Then the total cost equation as a function of Q is:

$$T.C. = \frac{KD}{Q} + \frac{Qk}{2}$$

with the solution

$$Q = \sqrt{\frac{2KD}{k}}$$

This solution is also equivalent to the optimal lot-size formulation.

The potential usefulness of simulation was demonstrated in an article by Richard A. Byerly.[5] This approach was used to determine the optimal scheduling of the tellers in a bank. The total number of transactions per hour at a bank was determined and classified into seven types. For each of the seven types of transactions he determined the probability distribution of the time the teller took to accomplish the transaction. With this information he was then able to simulate teller operation and to determine the lengths of queues and customer waiting times under different teller operating procedures.

As might be imagined, linear programming uses were among the first ones suggested. A. Charnes, W. W. Cooper, and M. H. Miller developed the application of linear programming to financial budgeting—the allo-

---

[3] While we cannot cite a specific reference, we have seen various internal documents of companies using this approach.

[4] Harold Bierman and Alan K. McAdams: "Financial Decisions and New Decision Tools," *Financial Executive*, 32 (May, 1964), 23–26f.

[5] Richard A. Byerly: "The Use of Mathematical Models in the Analysis and Improvement of Bank Operations," *NABAC Research Bulletin*, 1, No. 5 (May, 1960), 12–19.

cation of funds within a company.[6] Using a form known as the warehousing model of linear programming they showed how restrictions due to facilities, financial restrictions, and transactions over time—hence involving the distinction between cash flows and accruals—could be incorporated in a linear programming formulation. They showed that part of the output from such a formulation would be the yields to the firm of the various possible changes in its asset structure and the opportunity cost of funds in the firm.

Over time, further applications were developed.[7] However, the cited instances are probably sufficient to show how operations research techniques began to be used in the field of finance.

115/ Investment Decision Trees

Generally, the payoff matrix for a decision problem is an apt and convenient way to summarize the relevant information in order to choose a course of action. And for most decision problems it is possible to construct the payoff matrix. However, it is often by no means obvious how to do it. Often, it is not clear how to define the strategies and the states of nature so that they can be put together into a meaningful payoff matrix.

Such difficulty is likely to occur when the analysis is of an initial decision which will entail a sequence of subsequent decisions that must be taken into account in order to correctly analyze the initial decision. This is precisely the structure of a large number of financial decisions so it is appropriate that we should consider how to deal with such situations. As an example, consider the decision problem of a company that has an option on the drilling rights for oil on a particular property. The company may commence drilling right away or it could first have a geological survey made and then decide whether or not to commence drilling. Or it could first have a seismic test made and then decide about drilling. Or it could first have a geological survey made and then a

[6] A. Charnes, W. W. Cooper, and M. H. Miller: "Application of Linear Programming to Financial Budgeting and the Costing of Funds," *Journal of Business*, XXXII (Jan., 1959), 20–46.
[7] Some interesting examples of linear programming include: Y. Ijiri, F. K. Levy, and R. C. Lyon: "A Linear Programming Model for Budgeting and Financial Planning," *Journal of Accounting Research*, 1 (Aug., 1963), 198–212; Joel Cord: "A Method for Allocating Funds to Investment Projects When Returns Are Subject to Uncertainty," *Management Science*, 10, No. 2 (Jan., 1964), 335–341; William J. Baumol and Richard E. Quandt: "Investment and Discount Rates Under Capital Rationing—a Programming Approach," *The Economic Journal*, LXXV, No. 298 (June, 1965), 317–329.

seismic test and then determine whether to begin drilling or not. How can this kind of decision problem (what should the company do?) be presented in payoff matrix form? A little experimentation is sufficient to demonstrate that it is not easy—and may be impossible—to find a payoff matrix form. Fortunately, we do not have to construct the payoff matrix for such a decision problem. There is an alternative kind of analysis which is remarkably easy to apply to complex sequential decisions.

The same kind of problem frequently arises in game theory. It is standard to distinguish between two different modes of representation of game structures: the normal form and the extensive form. The normal form is the familiar rectangular matrix which is equivalent to the payoff matrix (see page 438). The extensive form is frequently called the game tree. A similar distinction is made in the analysis of decision problems and the extensive form for a decision problem is called the decision tree. In this section we shall illustrate the construction of a decision tree and the subsequent analysis of it.

We will take the decision problem of the oil company mentioned above. Suppose that the necessary economic data is as follows:

Cost of geological survey	$ 5,000
Cost of seismic test	25,000
Cost of drilling	130,000
Value of oil	500,000

In addition, we need to know some relevant probabilities. Suppose that the best present estimate is that the probability of oil on the property is 0.2. If there is oil, the probability that the seismic test will show that there is oil is 0.9 and the probability that the geological survey will show that there is oil is 0.7. If there is no oil, the probability that the seismic test will show that there *is* oil (a mistake) is 0.2 and the corresponding probability for the geological survey is 0.3 (also a mistake). It will be convenient to use capital letters to designate the different variable outcomes:

G : Geological survey shows the presence of oil

$\bar{G}$: Geological survey does not show the presence of oil

S : Seismic test shows the presence of oil

$\bar{S}$: Seismic test does not show the presence of oil

O : Oil is present

$\bar{O}$: Oil is not present

With these symbols we can summarize the relevant probabilities conveniently by using the notation of conditional probabilities. It will be recalled that $P(A|B)$ means the conditional probability that A occurs, given that B has occurred. Using this notation, our information can be written:

$$
\begin{aligned}
P(O) &= 0.2; & P(\overline{O}) &= 0.8 \\
P(G|O) &= 0.7; & P(\overline{G}|O) &= 0.3 \\
P(G|\overline{O}) &= 0.3; & P(\overline{G}|\overline{O}) &= 0.7 \\
P(S|O) &= 0.9; & P(\overline{S}|O) &= 0.1 \\
P(S|\overline{O}) &= 0.2; & P(\overline{S}|\overline{O}) &= 0.8
\end{aligned}
$$

The left-hand values were given verbally above and the right-hand values are obtained from the obvious requirement that the two values must sum to one.

These are all the data. What should the company do? Give up its option? Drill immediately? Make a geological survey first and then drill if it shows oil? Or make a seismic test if the geological survey shows oil? Or perhaps take the seismic test first? Or do something else?

We suggest that the reader should stop here and try seriously to solve this problem—or at least try to decide how one ought to go about solving it. Remember, this is not a mathematical problem for which we are shortly going to present some high-powered mathematical technique. Rather, it is mainly a problem in logic which involves, at most, the calculation of some simple expected values. Further, the decision problem is a perfectly typical one, actually much less complicated than many analogous investment problems. Anyone who intends to deal with investment decision problems surely should be able to work his way through such a common example. This is why we suggest that the reader ought to try it. He will find that it is difficult. Most persons cannot find a way to begin the analysis and eventually feel that they are trapped in some intellectual hall of mirrors. Few people can deduce the correct answer without using the device we are going to present now: decision trees. Analysis by using decision trees is just about the only way to solve such sequential decision problems. That is why John F. Magee says: "The decision tree can clarify for management, as can no other analytical tool that I know of, the choices, risks, objectives, monetary gains, and information needs involved in an investment problem. We shall be hearing a great deal about decision trees in the years ahead. Although a novelty to most businessmen today, they will surely be in common management parlance before many more years have passed." [8]

It is necessary to emphasize the importance of decision trees for the following reason. As a technique we might classify decision trees as be-

[8] John F. Magee, "Decision Trees for Decision Making," *Harvard Business Review*, 42 (July–Aug., 1964), pp. 126–138. As the long-time head of Management Services Division of Arthur D. Little, Inc., Mr. Magee has had a great deal of experience with real-life decision problems so he well knows the users of whom he speaks.

ing an algorithm for the analysis of sequential decision problems. As an algorithm, this technique has in common with other algorithms (the dynamic-programming algorithm, the linear-programming algorithm, even the square-foot algorithm) the characteristic of sounding much more difficult than it really is. A good algorithm is, almost by definition, easy to apply. Yet algorithms often sound so complicated when they are first presented that the novice is likely to give up any hope of understanding the algorithm before he has even tried to use it. The reason is, of course, that words are clumsy and slow whereas thought is fast. An algorithm can be likened to a race track: the mind can take the hurdles at lightning speed and finish the course before the verbal description, hobbling along on crutches, has reached the first hurdle. So it is with decision trees. The analysis of our example can be completed and the optimal policy found in far less time than it takes to explain the basis for the argument. The reader must remember this during the remainder of this section. If there was ever an easy algorithm, then decision trees are an example of one. This is true regardless of how labored the reader may find its exposition.

There are three steps in a decision-tree analysis. First, the skeleton of the decision tree must be drawn. Second, the economic data and the various probabilities must be entered in the appropriate places on the tree. "Decision tree" means the result of these first two steps. Then, third, the decision tree must be analyzed to find the optimal course of action. Let us apply these three steps to our example.

The skeleton of a decision tree is made up of nodes, represented by small rectangles or circles, and line segments connecting the nodes. Most nodes will represent either an action which can be taken or a possible outcome from an action which is taken. However, some nodes may be used to represent states of nature. Line segments will join an action with each of its possible outcomes and an outcome with a subsequent action. The intention is to represent, by these means, every reasonable alternative. Every alternative course of action represented in the decision will eventually end in some terminal action. Each sequence of nodes and segments ending in a terminal action is called a branch. In the case of our decision problem there are only two possible terminal actions: drill for oil or give up the option. Therefore, every branch on our decision tree will terminate in one of these actions.

We begin at the top of the page with a node which represents the present situation—we can call it "Now." If it is possible, or relevant, we try to work from the more general to the more specific as we work down the skeleton. In our example, the most general aspect is certainly the presence or absence of oil. Therefore, we introduce two nodes to represent these two possibilities and connect them to the "Now" node by straight line segments. These three nodes represent states of affairs. The remainder of the nodes will represent actions or outcomes from actions. There are four actions which can be taken: give up the option (Quit), make a geological survey, make a seismic test, or drill. As we do not know which of the nodes, O and $\overline{O}$, is true, we must place nodes for the four actions under each of them. And, of course, they must be connected by line segments to the O and $\overline{O}$ nodes. This gives us the beginning of the skeleton as shown in Figure 12.1. The nodes marked "Quit" and "Drill" represent terminal actions, so there are already four completed branches on our skeleton.

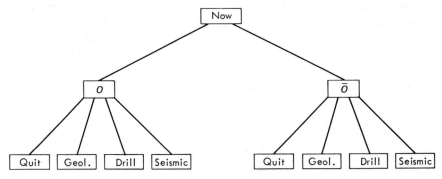

FIGURE 12.1

Let us consider the nodes which represent the action of taking a geological survey. Since all of the logical possibilities are the same for the O and $\overline{O}$ nodes it follows that all of the nodes and segments connected to one of the "Geology" nodes will appear in exactly the same way for the other "Geology" node. Therefore, we will only need to discuss the "Geology" node once. There are two outcomes possible from the geological survey: G and $\overline{G}$. We need, therefore, two nodes to represent these outcomes. Suppose G occurs. There are only two reasonable courses of action: drill or make a seismic test. Note that "Quit" is not included because if the company intended to quit if the geological test showed oil then it was a waste of money to make the survey. "Drill" is terminal so consider the node which represents making a seismic test. There are two outcomes: S and $\overline{S}$. If S, then the only reasonable action is "Drill." If $\overline{S}$, then the only reasonable action is "Quit." Note that it would be completely unreasonable to drill if $\overline{S}$ occurred. If this were intended then it follows that the company made a seismic test knowing that it would drill regardless of the outcome of the test.

We return to the other outcome of the geological survey, $\overline{G}$. Clearly, "Drill" would be unreasonable so the two alternatives are "Quit," a terminal action, and "make a seismic test." The two outcomes of the seismic test are S and $\overline{S}$. If $\overline{S}$, then the only reasonable course of action is "Quit." If S, then the only reasonable course of action is "Drill" because to quit would imply that the company took the seismic test while knowing that it would quit regardless of the outcome. This completes that part of the skeleton which stems from the "Geology" node. The result is shown in Figure 12.2.

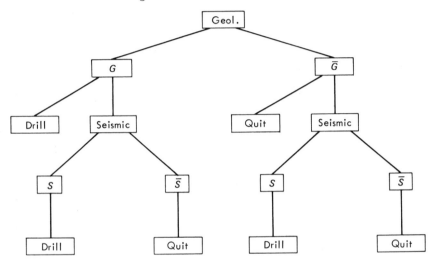

FIGURE 12.2

In the above development of part of the skeleton several times we used simple arguments to eliminate clearly unreasonable alternatives. But perhaps one might not notice such an argument or find it somewhat dubious—what then? The answer is that it will not affect the final conclusion in any way. One can construct the decision tree to include every logically possible alternative, regardless of its reasonability or lack of it. The analysis will eliminate the possibilities that are unreasonable. The advantage of using arguments to eliminate a few of the logical possibilities is that it decreases the amount of work required for the third step. In other words, it is a question of whether one chooses to do more thinking in the first step or in the third step.

An analogical argument must now be followed to develop that part of the skeleton which stems from the "Seismic" nodes. Again, there will be identical structures stemming from each of the two "Seismic" nodes. When this has been done the skeleton is complete. Of course, the same skeleton applies both to the O mode and to the $\overline{O}$ mode. The result is shown in Figure 12.3.

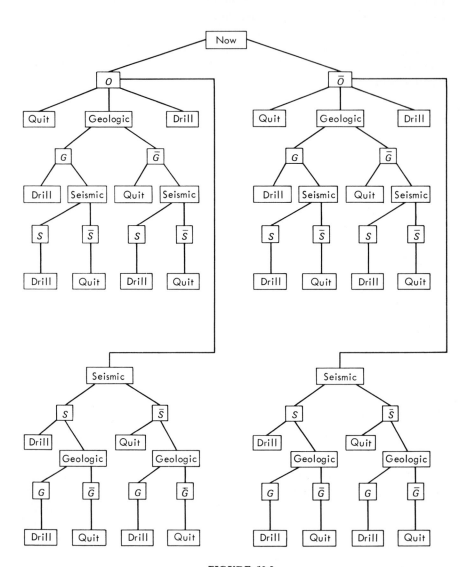

FIGURE 12.3

We are now ready for the second step, which will complete the decision tree. All of the data—probabilities and costs—must be entered at the appropriate points on the tree. The procedure is easy. Below each terminal node on the tree must be entered the net change in assets which will result from the actions taken on the branch leading to that node. If the terminal node is "Drill" then due account must be taken of whether the node stems from the O node or the $\overline{O}$ node. In the former case there will be income of \$500,000, which will not occur in the latter case. As an example, consider the three terminal nodes which stem from G on the O side of the tree. The terminal node "Drill" which stems directly from G has \$500,000 income from oil, minus \$130,000 cost of drilling, minus \$5,000 cost of the geological survey, for a net change in assets of \$365,000. The second terminal node "Drill" has the same \$365,000, but minus \$25,000 for the seismic test, or a net of \$340,000. The third terminal node is "Quit" and this has cost \$5,000 for the geological survey and \$25,000 for the seismic test for a net of −\$30,000. All of the terminal nodes must be similarly treated.

Next, each of the known probabilities is written beside the appropriate line segment on the decision tree. This means that the probability is to be written on the line segment leading to the corresponding outcome or state of nature. Thus, $P(O) = 0.2$, so 0.2 is written by the line segment leading from "Now" to O. Again, $P(S|O) = 0.9$, so 0.9 is written by each line segment on the O part of the tree which leads from "Seismic" to S. On the $\overline{O}$ part of the tree the corresponding line segments would have 0.2 since $P(S|\overline{O}) = 0.2$. All of the probabilities must be similarly entered on the tree. This completes the second step and the decision tree is now finished. It is shown in Figure 12.4. The zeroes were eliminated from the thousands for convenience.

We are now ready to begin the analysis, our third and final step. It will be seen that the completed decision tree has quite a few line segments with no probability associated with the segment. We are going to associate a probability with each line segment which does not have a probability in the completed decision tree. At the end of many of the branches it will be noted that there is only one line segment leading from a node—from S to "Drill," from $\overline{S}$ to "Quit," and so forth. Each of these receives the probability 1 because when only one line segment leads out of a node it is certain what the next node will be. To each remaining empty line segment we will now assign an unknown probability, x_i. In doing this we will observe two rules:

1. The x's are probabilities, so the sum of the x's on all the line segments leading out of a node must be 1 since one of the segments must be followed. Therefore, to conserve x's we can always assign a proba-

bility to one of the segments leading from a node which makes the relevant x's sum to 1.

2. In every case, the same x_i must be assigned to corresponding segments in the parts of the tree stemming from O and $\overline{O}$. This require-

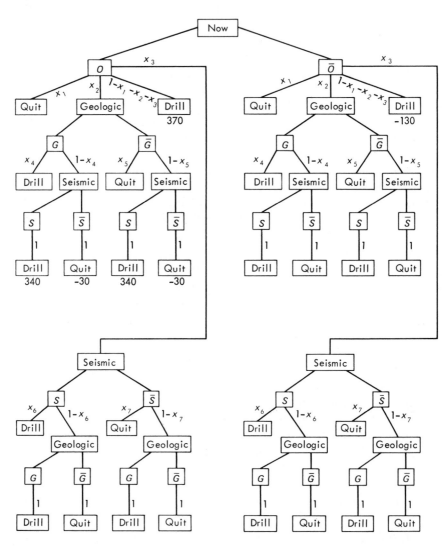

FIGURE 12.4

ment reflects the fact that the decision-maker does not know which part of the tree he is on, insofar as O and $\overline{O}$ are concerned.

Figure 12.5 shows the decision tree with these additions. It will be seen that the x's are always assigned to segments leading to courses of

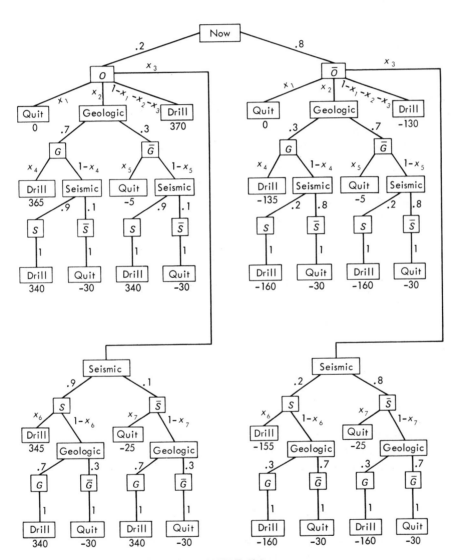

FIGURE 12.5

action which are under the decision-maker's control. This means that the numerical values of the x's are under the decision-maker's control, granted the proviso that since they are probabilities, they must be between zero and one. When we complete the analysis it will be found that each x is either zero or one.

The analysis is straightforward and it can be made simpler by thinking about each step as is it performed. However, it can be done in a completely routine way, at the cost of a modest amount of algebra. We will follow the routine procedure first and then see how the steps might be simplified. The routine procedure is to work one's way up the decision tree, calculating the expected value associated with each node. The expected value of a node is determined by summing the products of the probability on each line segment leading from the node multiplied by

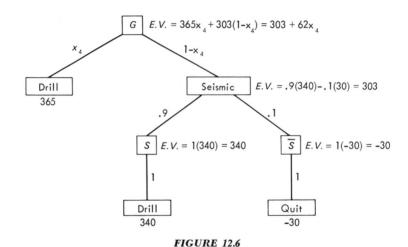

FIGURE 12.6

the expected value of the node to which the segment leads. Figure 12.6 shows the process for a typical part of the decision tree. This is continued upward until we finally reach the expected value of "Now." Figure 12.7 shows the calculated expected values of one of the last steps. The expected value of "Now" is:

$$-30 + 30x_1 + x_2[45.8 - 10.32x_4 + 10.08x_5] + x_3[20.6 + 7.12x_6 - 17.56x_7]$$

This expression represents the over-all expected value that can be achieved from our decision problem for any reasonable course of action, which will be determined by setting appropriate values of the x's. The decision-maker wants to make this as large as possible and he can choose the values of x which will best accomplish this. Of course, no x can be

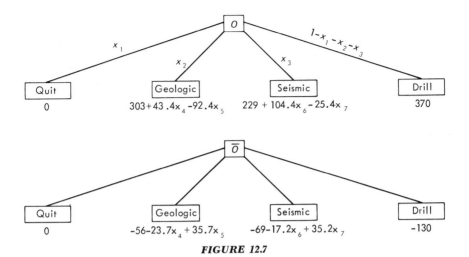

FIGURE 12.7

negative or larger than one. Furthermore, $x_1 + x_2 + x_3 \leq 1$ since these represent mutually exclusive courses of action. Obviously, x_4 and x_7 should be made zero as they would otherwise decrease the expected value. The values of x_5 and x_6 should be set at one since this can only increase the expected value. This gives

$$-30 + 30x_1 + 55.88x_2 + 27.72x_3$$

Since x_2 has the largest coefficient we should set $x_2 = 1$ and $x_1 = x_3 = 0$. This gives a maximum expected value of 25.88.

To find the optimal policy we return to Figure 12.5.
To identify the x's, we find

$x_2 = 1$ means first take the geologic survey
$x_4 = 0$ means that if G then make the seismic test
$x_5 = 1$ means that if $\overline{G}$ then quit

This is the optimal policy. The other x's are irrelevant once it is found that $x_3 = 0$.

It remains to note how the analysis can be simplified by thinking about the steps as they are performed. As an example, consider the calculations which involve x_4. Figure 12.8 shows all of the decision tree relevant to these calculations. At the point where the two expected values shown on the figure have been calculated we notice that all of the subsequent calculations involving x_4 will consist of the following:

$$(303 + 62x_4)(0.7)(x_2)(0.2) + (-56 - 79x_4)(0.3)(x_2)(0.8)$$

Since $x_2 \geq 0$ it follows that all we need do is to calculate

$$(0.2)(0.7)(62x_4) + (0.3)(0.8)(-79x_4) = -10.28x_4$$

Since x_4 has a negative coefficient we know immediately that it must be put equal to zero. Actually, it is easier than this because it is clear without multiplying that $(.14 \times 62)$ is less than $(.24 \times 79)$ and this is all we need to know in order to put $x_4 = 0$. Similar arguments can be used on x_5, x_6, and x_7. This simplifies the analysis considerably.

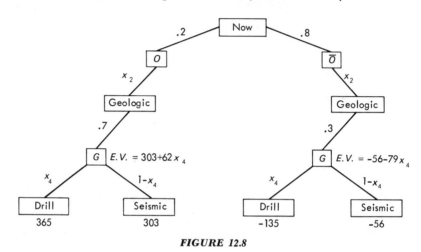

FIGURE 12.8

This entire analysis takes less than fifteen minutes. Remember our warning: the decision-tree algorithm is a great deal easier than it may appear from our description. It is far too useful a tool in the analysis of complicated sequential decisions to leave untried. The proof of its simplicity lies in its uses.

116/ Risk Analysis

The problem of capital investment is surely one of the major financial problems faced by most medium and large companies. The importance of the problem is suggested by the size of the capital investments made. David B. Hertz states that an estimated $65 billion will be committed to new capital investment projects in the course of 1968.[9] And this sum represents only those projects that will be accepted. An endless stream of possibilities, proposals, and projects—each representing a demand for capital investment—is constantly under analysis.

As a result of the importance of the capital investment problem there is a great deal of literature on the subject. A considerable variety of dif-

[9] David B. Hertz, "Investment Policies That Pay Off," *Harvard Business Review* (Jan.–Feb., 1968), pp. 96–108.

ferent analytical tools have been recommended, attacked, defended—
and used. Most large companies have extremely able analysts who devote
a major part of their time to analyzing investment projects. In addition, most projects have to go through a screening process in which successively higher echelons apply stringent standards to the project. By
the time a project is accepted by the executive committee of the company there is every reason to expect it to make a substantial contribution
to company earnings.

But the reality is all too often otherwise. A distressingly large number
of accepted investment projects—after all the winnowing described
above—fail to break even. And a very large proportion of projects fail
to achieve the returns on which their acceptance was based.[10] Why
should this be? Obviously, investments are usually made in situations
which involve considerable amounts of uncertainty or risk. But the methods of analysis are supposed to take this into account. Decisions in other
areas which involve risk are often successfully made without such glaring
differences between forecasts and facts. What analytical techniques might
help to improve the performance of the decision-makers?

We cannot answer this question here because we do not know the
answer. There are probably a variety of interacting causes, including
such factors as the natural optimism and enthusiasm of the proponents
of the project, which tend to make things look better than they are.
Perhaps the long-run improvement of the investment decision-making
process will require the careful disentangling of all causes of bias and
error. This is a task beyond our ability, so we have a more modest goal.
Dr. Hertz has argued persuasively in favor of one plausible explanation
of part of the discrepancy between anticipation and actuality in investment decision-making. In this section we want to present his suggestions
for the improvement of investment analysis.

Investment decisions are generally based on the application of one
or another criterion to the particular investment project under consideration. Some of the common criteria used as yardsticks are internal
rate of return, payback period, net discounted present value, and so
forth. Regardless of the specific criterion used, the over-all structure of
the analysis is likely to be the same. Using the prescribed criterion, the
analyst tries to produce a specific value for the investment proposal.
Following Hertz, we can call this the best-guess estimate for the project.

Let us consider an example. Suppose that an investment in a major
improvement of a production process is under consideration. Suppose
that the present production process produces 400,000 units per year at a
variable cost of $5 per unit. The market price is $10 per unit so the pres-

---

[10] For some examples, see Hertz, *op. cit.*

ent production process gives $2,000,000 in contributory profit (contribution to fixed charges and profit). We will assume that the criterion this company uses is return on investment (*ROI*). The best-guess approach proceeds by obtaining the best-guess at the value which will obtain for each of the variables which have an effect on the project's *ROI*. Thus, suppose that the best-guess estimates for the new production process are:

Project cost	$2,750,000
Variable cost	4.50 per unit
Production	475,000 units per year

It follows that the best-guess estimate for return on investment for this project would be

$$ROI = \frac{(475,000)(5.50) - 2,000,000}{2,750,000} = 22.3\%$$

where $5.50 = 10 - 4.50$ is the anticipated contributory profit per unit and the $2,000,000 is the current contributory profit which is subtracted to obtain the incremental contributory profit due to the investment.

If this company used, say, 18% as the required *ROI* for an investment proposal to be accepted, then this project would meet the requirement. A moment's thought is sufficient to suggest that this analysis is not a very sturdy foundation for an investment decision—very few companies would accept the above proposal solely on the basis of this analysis. The problem is that this decision problem is surely not one under certainty. It is extremely unlikely that any of the three best-guess estimates will turn out to be exactly right. What will be the effect of deviations from the best-guess estimates on the ultimate performance of the project, assuming that it is accepted? The major weakness of the best-guess analysis is that it does not provide any answer to this question.

In practice, companies usually take either or both of two approaches to help remedy the weakness of the best-guess analysis. One approach is simply to multiply the criteria used on each proposal. Thus, the company might demand an 18% *ROI* and a four-year payback period and a specified discounted cash flow return. The other approach is to try to get an idea of the effect on *ROI* of errors in the estimates. A common way of doing this is to make worst possible and best possible estimates for each of the relevant variables. Thus, suppose for our example that the extreme limits for each of the variables are:

	WORST	BEST
Project cost	$3,000,000	$2,500,000
Variable cost/unit	4.90	4.30
Production/yr	450,000	500,000

Then we can calculate, exactly as before, that the worst possible *ROI* is 9.8% and the best possible *ROI* is 34%.

Obviously, either of these approaches will help correct the possible errors which might result from reliance on the best-guess estimate analysis. However, neither of them really remedies its deficiencies. The first approach simply multiplies the number of hurdles a proposal has to negotiate. But the unfortunate fact remains that *errors in the best-guess estimates are likely to affect all the criteria in similar ways,* so the additional hurdles may not prevent accepting a dubious proposal. On the other hand, the second approach simply determines the maximum range within which the actual *ROI* should fall. It does not suggest anything about the likelihood that it will be in one part of the possible range rather than another. Often, the worst possible *ROI* is negative and the best possible *ROI* is clearly unattainable. What conclusion should management draw in such a case?

The suggestion is made that the investment proposal ought to be simulated so that an explicit probability distribution of the possible *ROI*'s can be given to management. This kind of simulation is called *risk analysis.* In the remainder of this section we want to consider the procedures needed to accomplish the risk analysis of our example.

Since we have previously discussed simulation, the general approach required should be clear. We need probability distributions for the relevant variables. Then numbers, in the indicated proportions, will be assigned to each of the possible values of each of the variables. By selecting random numbers, specific values of each of the three relevant variables can be determined. Any such randomly selected set of three values will represent the outcome of one simulated investment. The *ROI* can be determined for this simulated investment. By repeating the whole process a great many times we can obtain a probability distribution of *ROI*'s and this is the probability distribution which Dr. Hertz suggests should be considered by management in evaluating the investment proposal.

The only real problem in accomplishing this is the determination of the probability distributions for the three variables. The word "only" in the preceding sentence should not be misconstrued. The problem is both critical and difficult. Since the simulation depends on having these probability distributions we must briefly discuss procedures for obtaining them.

It is possible that historical records of analogous investments in the past will afford a basis for determining the probability distribution. For example, consider the cost of the proposal. It may be that the engineering department has prepared the best-guess estimate of the cost and that they have done the same for a number of prior investment proposals, many of which may have been accepted. In this case there would

be a historical record of the discrepancies between the engineering estimates and the actual costs. This record might permit the determination
of an appropriate probability distribution of the project cost of the investment proposal under current consideration. However, this possibility
would not usually exist. Only an exceptional company is likely to have
records of the relatively large number of past investments which would
be required in order to determine such a probability distribution. Further, conditions would probably be sufficiently different for any major
investment to make it doubtful whether past investments were similar
enough to justify using them as a basis for the desired probability distribution. For these reasons it is unlikely that the desired distributions can
be determined by any kind of frequency count. This means that the
distributions must be construed as measures of degrees of belief. In other
words, the probability distributions needed for risk analysis are almost
certainly going to be subjective distributions. This granted, how should
they be determined?

The problem of determining such subjective probability distributions
is a common one. PERT depends on probability distributions of the
time to completion of sub-projects; portfolio selection (see p. 475) depends on subjective probability distributions of yields of securities.
Many inventory decision problems require subjective probability distributions of demand; and, in general, the subjectivist approach to any
decision problem is quite likely to require the determination of such a
distribution. How can it be done? It is clear that it would be hopelessly
naive simply to ask the expert in one of the important variables to write
down the probability distribution which represents his beliefs about
the likelihood of occurrence of different possible values of the variable.
His degrees of belief do not come to his mind labeled with corresponding probabilities and he is not usually a professional statistician who
might be expected to be able to translate his feelings readily into probabilities. Therefore, it is generally accepted that the analyst must provide a good deal of assistance to the expert in eliciting the desired
probability distribution.

Two general principles are ordinarily followed in determining these
subjective distributions. First, a minimum number of questions is asked
the expert. This is desirable for the practical reason that one would like
to use less, rather than more, of the expert's time. And it is desirable for
the somewhat theoretical reason that the expert can rarely answer many
questions about his beliefs without contradicting himself. This by no
means implies that his beliefs are inconsistent. Rather, it suggests that
the expert, like most of us, is unable to make many relatively fine distinctions based on his subjective values or beliefs without falling into
error. He can, nonetheless, make some necessary major distinctions.

Second, the questions that are asked must be as free from ambiguity as possible. This only deserves to be called a principle because it turns out that it is difficult to avoid ambiguity of one sort or another. For example, it would often be helpful to ask the expert to indicate his estimate of the average value of the variable. Yet "average" is a most distressingly ambiguous term. The statistician recognizes that "average" is a layman's term and that it ordinarily encompasses the arithmetic mean (the center of gravity of the distribution), the median (the value such that half of the possible values are greater), and the mode (the most frequently occurring value). Admittedly, this can be clarified for the expert but it is by no means clear that he can successfully estimate any one of the three. It may be noted in passing that he is most likely to be unsuccessful in estimating the arithmetic mean.

In practice, then, we start with the assumption that the analyst must determine a "reasonable" shape for the subjective probability distribution of the expert and then find the specific distribution which has that shape by asking a small number of unambiguous questions. "Shape" means primarily whether it is or is not reasonable to assume that the distribution is symmetrical. A probability distribution is symmetrical if the probability of a given deviation above the arithmetic mean is the same as the probability of the same deviation below the mean. Suppose it is reasonable to assume that the distribution will be symmetrical and, furthermore, that it is expected that probabilities of small deviations from the mean are greater than the probabilities of large deviations. Under these circumstances the analyst might assume that the normal distribution could describe adequately the expert's opinions. A normal distribution is uniquely defined as soon as its mean and standard deviation are known. Therefore, the problem becomes one of eliciting this information from the expert. Since for the normal distribution the mean, median, and mode are all equal, it might be possible simply to ask the expert to state which value he thinks is most likely to occur (the mode). However, no comparable directness is possible for the standard deviation because even a professional statistician would have a hard time stating a good estimate of the standard deviation of a subjective probability distribution.

The procedure that is usually followed is based on the fact that, to continue our assumption of a normal distribution, the mean and standard deviation can be mathematically deduced from almost any two pieces of information about the subjective distribution given by the management expert. An approach is to ask the expert two questions, framed in terms of betting odds rather than in terms of probabilities. The reason for this is that it is commonly believed that many persons are able to think coherently in terms of bets who have no knowledge whatsoever about the probabilities which underlie the odds. Suppose we are interested in days to completion of a sub-project. We ask the expert to imagine a bet on the actual days to completion. The bet will be that the sub-project will be completed in x days or less. Further, if it is completed in x days or less then $1 will be won. If it is not completed in x days or less then $20 will be lost. The expert is instructed to pick x so that he would be equally happy to take either side of the stated bet.[11] Suppose he tells us that he would be indifferent between the two sides of the bet when $x = 42$ days. We now reason as follows. Since he is indifferent it must be an even-money bet. In other words, the expected value of the bet is zero. We are interested in the still unknown probability that the sub-project will be completed in 42 days or less. Letting this probability be represented by p, we have:

$$\$1p - \$20(1 - p) = 0$$

or
$$p = \frac{20}{21} = 0.952$$

In other words, the fact that this particular bet is an even-money bet for the expert imputes the fact that in his opinion the probability that the sub-project will be completed in 42 days or less is 0.952.

We now ask the expert another question of the same form. This time the bet is won if the sub-project is completed in y days or less but $20 is won. The bet is lost if the sub-project takes more than y days but only $1 is lost. The expert is asked to pick the value of y which would make him indifferent between the two sides of his bet. Suppose he says that he is indifferent when $y = 18$. Then, if r is the probability of completion in 18 days or less, we have:

$$\$20r - \$1(1 - r) = 0$$

or
$$r = \frac{1}{21} = 0.048$$

From this information we can deduce the mean and standard deviation of the (assumed) normal distribution. Since the probability that the days to completion will exceed 42 days is the same as the probability that it will be less than 18 days, it follows that these values are equidistant from the mean. Hence

$$mean = \frac{42 + 18}{2} = 30 \text{ days}$$

For any normal curve one must go 1.66 standard deviations above (or below) the mean in order to reach the measurement value which has a probability of 0.048 of being exceeded. Therefore,

---

[11] Attention is called to the standard gamble technique, p. 91.

$$42 = 30 + 1.66\sigma$$

or

$$1.66\sigma = 12$$

$$\sigma = 7.2$$

where σ is the standard deviation. We conclude that the expert's opinions about the days to completion of the sub-project can be summarized by stating that there is a normal distribution of days to completion, with mean equal to 30 and standard deviation equal to 7.2.

We would probably want to check the appropriateness of our assumption that the expert's opinions could be represented as a normal distribution of subjective probabilities. We might do this by asking the expert to tell us the value which he thought would be the most likely value of days to completion (the mode). If he says that approximately 30 days—say, between 28 days and 32 days—was the most likely value of the sub-project's days to completion we would probably be satisfied that, for all practical purposes, the normal distribution assumption was sufficiently close to reality. On the other hand, if he states that the most likely number of days to completion is, say, 24 days then we would have to recognize that his underlying subjective probability distribution is not symmetrical and, hence, not normal. Rather, it is some skewed distribution. To handle this kind of situation we need some mathematically specified family of skewed distributions; one such which is commonly used for this purpose is called the *beta distribution* (see page 295). Granted that *beta* is the specified form, then the procedure is analogous to the one we described above for the normal distribution.

It is certainly reasonable to assume that in a great many instances there *is* an "expert" who has rational and well-grounded opinions about the likelihood of occurrence of the various possible values of the variable of interest. If this is true then the approach outlined above should enable us to represent his opinions in the form of a probability distribution. The details of the procedure are not our major interest, but enough has been said to suggest that we can, in fact, obtain such a probability distribution. This is all that is required to accomplish the risk analysis of our investment proposal.

Suppose we have obtained the following probability distributions for our three variables:

PROJECT COST

Dollars (millions)	Probability
2.5	0.05
2.6	0.10
2.7	0.15
2.8	0.30
2.9	0.25
3.0	0.15
	1.00

VARIABLE COST

Dollars	Probability
4.30	0.05
4.40	0.15
4.50	0.20
4.60	0.20
4.70	0.20
4.80	0.10
4.90	0.10
	1.00

PRODUCTION

Units (thousands)	Probability
450	0.10
460	0.20
470	0.30
480	0.20
490	0.15
500	0.05

The indicated values should be construed as the class marks of the corresponding ranges of possible values. Thus, a project cost of $2.5 million represents the class mark (midpoint) of the range of values from $2.45 million to $2.55 million. We approximate this whole range of values by the class mark, $2.5 million. If this approximation is not adequate then we need only establish smaller classes.

Having the probability distributions, we assign Monte Carlo numbers to each class in proportion to the probability of the class.

INVESTMENT COST (MILLIONS)	NUMBERS	VARIABLE COST	NUMBERS	PRODUCTION UNITS (THOUSANDS)	PROBABILITY
$2.5	00–04	$4.30	00–04	450	00–09
2.6	05–14	4.40	05–19	460	10–29
2.7	15–29	4.50	20–39	470	30–59
2.8	30–59	4.60	40–59	480	60–79
2.9	60–84	4.70	60–79	490	80–94
3.0	85–99	4.80	80–89	500	95–99
		4.90	90–99		

We are now ready to simulate the result of this investment. Draw three two-digit random numbers, say 35–69–50. On the investment cost table 35 represents a cost of $2.8 million. On the variable cost table 69 represents a variable cost of $4.70. On the production table 50 represents a production of 470,000 units per year. This combination would give

$$ROI = \frac{(470,000)(10 - 4.70) - 2,000,000}{2,800,000} = 17.5\%$$

Similarly, the random numbers 84–08–86 give

$$ROI = \frac{(490,000)(10 - 4.40) - 2,000,000}{2,900,000} = 25.7\%$$

These are two simulated *ROI*'s for the investment proposal under consideration. The process is continued until a sufficiently large sample of *ROI*'s has been obtained. Obviously, a computer is extremely helpful in accomplishing this but the work is not so onerous as to preclude a sizable hand simulation. In our example, 1,000 simulations gave

ROI	FREQUENCY
9.0 – 12.9	40
13.0 – 16.9	228
17.0 – 20.9	380
21.0 – 24.9	265
25.0 – 28.9	75
29.0 – 32.9	11
33.0 – 36.9	1
	1,000

The mean *ROI* is 19.6% and the standard deviation is 4.1%. It is this frequency distribution which is the goal of the risk analysis of this investment project.

Clearly, the presentation of such a frequency distribution does convey a great deal of information which is surely not apparent from any other kind of summary. Thus, although the mean *ROI* is 19.6%, there is more than one chance in four that the *ROI* will turn out to be less than 17%. A relatively clear view of the inherent risk connected with the investment proposal is obtainable by means of this kind of simulation—hence its name, *risk analysis*.

The major advantages of *risk analysis* are highlighted when comparisons are made between alternative investments. The frequency distribution which results from the simulation will vary if the basic probability distributions change. The very same investment proposal, as viewed by different executives, might generate different sets of subjective probability distributions for the three variables. Totally different patterns of *ROI*'s could result and serve to explain any lack of executive consensus on a given investment proposal. In fact, putting these together, the mean *ROI* might well be the same but the dispersion might be greater, indicating a larger risk of getting a poor *ROI* if the investment is made.

The same sort of thing can happen because of seemingly slight changes in the conditions of the problem. As an instance of this we shall modify some of the data for our example. Suppose the production probability distribution remains unchanged, as does the variable cost distribution. However, the market price of the item becomes $6 instead of $10. This means that the current process—40,000 units at a variable cost of $5 per unit—is producing $400,000 in contributory profit. In order to obtain *ROI*'s of the same order of magnitude as above we must lower the distribution of investment costs to:

INVESTMENT COST (MILLIONS)	PROBABILITY
1.0	0.05
1.1	0.10
1.2	0.15
1.3	0.30
1.4	0.25
1.5	0.15
	1.00

Note that the probabilities remain the same, only the cost of investment has been changed by subtracting $1.5 million from each of the former costs. Therefore, the only changes made were to decrease the per unit contributory profit and to decrease the investment by a corresponding amount so that the mean *ROI* would remain at about the same level.

The simulation of this new investment proposal gives:

ROI	FREQUENCY
5.0 – 8.9	42
9.0 – 12.9	118
13.0 – 16.9	177
17.0 – 20.9	220
21.0 – 24.9	198
25.0 – 28.9	143
29.0 – 32.9	70
33.0 – 36.9	26
37.0 – 40.9	5
41.0 – 44.9	1
	1,000

The mean of this distribution is 20.1% and the standard deviation is 6.8. Even though the probability distributions were not modified in any way, these changes in profitability and investment have resulted in a much riskier investment. Here there is almost one chance in six of getting an actual *ROI* of less than 13% as compared to one chance in twenty-five for the previous investment. And this is true despite the fact that the new proposal has a higher mean *ROI*—20.1% as compared to the former 19.6%. Surely, management would want to take this increased risk into account when they make their decision about this investment.

Intuition is not a good guide for making correct investment decisions when minor changes in the economic conditions can produce major changes in risk. If the complexities of the interactions between the various subjective probability distributions are also taken into account it is clear why an explicit objective procedure is necessary. Simulation of the investment risks such as we have described is not difficult to accomplish. So there is little reason not to include risk analysis as a routine part of investment analyses.

117/ *Portfolio Selection*

The analysis of the buy and sell decisions involved in managing a portfolio of securities has been going on for at least as long as the buying and selling. Furthermore, for at least the past thirty years the analysts have used some fairly sophisticated quantitative techniques. Therefore, the claim that operations research has contributed something to the solution of the problems of portfolio management ought to be received with polite skepticism. Nonetheless, the claim is true and it is the purpose of this section to document this fact.

Clearly, the management of portfolios is becoming increasingly important. The steady growth of pension funds has in itself created enormous portfolios, very significant amounts of which are regularly invested in common stocks. But there has also been a tremendous increase in individual portfolios, which may have different objectives than the pension portfolios but which demand equally diligent management. Because of the growth in the importance of the portfolio management problem there has been an increasing amount of attention devoted to the problem by management scientists. This attention has been in two major areas.

First, a considerable amount of work has been done on the question of the degree to which computers can be used to handle all or many of the managerial decisions required by a portfolio. This kind of analysis requires painstakingly careful studies of the past decisions made by investment managers and the reasons for them. Then the analyst tries to encapsulate the human decision process in a form suitable for a computer.[12] If this can be done it is then possible to simulate portfolio

[12] Such an effort is frequently referred to as heuristic programming (see pp. 51, 186–193, and 212).

management by computer and to compare or contrast the resulting performance with that achieved by the human managers. Progress is being made but it does not appear likely that in the near future there will be extensive computer management of portfolios. Consequently, we shall not discuss such efforts here.

The second major area is the one which we wish to examine in this section. It has to do with the actual selection of securities for the portfolio. It is important to call attention to a distinction first made by Harry Markowitz in the first article which dealt with portfolio selection.[13] As Markowitz pointed out, there are really two stages in the process of selecting a portfolio. The first stage starts with everything we know, believe, or intuit about the various stocks—including any analysis of past behavior or forecasts of future performance—and ends up with our *beliefs* about their future performance. The second stage starts with our beliefs about future performance and ends with the selection of stocks for our portfolio. It is the second stage which will be our concern.

This is an important distinction because it suggests why there is no conflict between the extensive literature dealing with security analysis and the claim that operations research has added something to help deal with the problem of portfolio selection. The operations-research approach has added nothing to the battery of methods used in security analysis. Rather, it has concerned itself with the question of how the investor should select stocks to achieve his objectives, *granted his beliefs about the future performance of the stocks.* This is the problem we will consider, following the arguments of Markowitz[14] in our presentation.

We start with the fairly obvious statement that an investor generally has at least two objectives when he selects a portfolio. On the one hand, he certainly wants to get the largest return he can. But it must be remembered that the return from a portfolio is not a fixed and known quantity when the portfolio is purchased. Rather, there is some probability distribution of returns. Of course, the fact that we may not know this probability distribution does not raise any doubt that there is one. Therefore, we can say that the investor's objective is to achieve the largest possible expected return from his portfolio.

On the other hand, it is also true that most investors have an aversion to risk. This is (at least) true to the degree that the investor does not like to have a large risk of not achieving his objective of expected return.

[13] Harry Markowitz, "Portfolio Selection," *Journal of Finance,* 7, No. 1 (March, 1952), 77–91.

[14] Harry Markowitz, *op. cit.,* and Harry Markowitz, *Portfolio Selection: Efficient Diversification of Investments,* Cowles Foundation Monograph #16 (New York: John Wiley & Sons, Inc., 1959).

Consider, for example, two different probability distributions of expected percentage return on investment:

PERCENTAGE RETURN	PROBABILITY	PERCENTAGE RETURN	PROBABILITY
I		**II**	
18	0.2	−10	0.1
20	0.6	0	0.1
22	0.2	10	0.3
—		20	0.3
	1.0	60	0.2
			1.0

Each of these distributions has the same expected return: 20%. However, a large number of investors would unhesitatingly select I rather than II if they were given the choice. This is because there is greater risk associated with II than there is with I.

Descriptive statistics tells us that one measure of risk is the variance of the distribution. This is not the only measure and it is not necessarily the best such measure. However, it is the measure used by Markowitz and we will use it here. The variance, which is the second moment about the mean, is probably most familiar as the square of the standard deviation. If a random variable assumes the value x with probability p_x, then the equations for the expected value $\bar{x}$ and the variance σ^2 are:

$$\bar{x} = \sum_i x_i p_{x_i} \text{ and } \sigma^2 = \sum_i (x_i - \bar{x})^2 p_{x_i}$$

The variance of distribution I, above, is 1.6 while that of distribution II is 480. So the variance of II, being greater than that of I, does reflect the greater risk in the second case.

Our concern is with the typical investor who would like to maximize the expected return of his portfolio but who would like simultaneously to minimize the variance of the portfolio's return distribution. These objectives may be in conflict. It would be unusual to find that the same portfolio would simultaneously accomplish both objectives. How might the investor think about the resulting difficulty?

We can reformulate his objectives in two statements. First, if he has his choice between two portfolios with the same expected return, he will select that portfolio with the smaller variance. Second, if he has his choice between two portfolios with the same variance, he will select that portfolio with the larger expected return. These two statements have some important implications which we need to make explicit.

Suppose that we could calculate for every conceivable portfolio its expected return and its variance. This is obviously impossible in practice but there is nothing wrong with imagining that it could be done. If it were done then we could graph all the possible combinations of expected return and variance on a graph such as the one in Figure 12.9. All of

FIGURE 12.9

the points on the graph would fall within some kind of closed figure. Let us suppose it to be the circle shown on Figure 12.9. A rational investor would not be interested in the majority of the portfolios represented by points within the circle or on its circumference. The application of the two statements given at the end of the preceding paragraph is sufficient to eliminate every portfolio from consideration except for those portfolios represented by points on the lower right quarter of the circumference of the circle. These portfolios are called the efficient portfolios and the segment of the circumference on which they fall, shown in Figure 12.10, is called the *efficiency frontier*.

FIGURE 12.10

No rational investor would consider any portfolio not on the efficiency frontier. Why should he? For any portfolio not on the efficiency frontier the investor can find a portfolio which is on the frontier and which either has greater expected return for the same variance or else has smaller variance for the same expected return. This drastically reduces the number of portfolios which needs to be considered.

How should the investor select a specific portfolio from among the many represented by the efficiency frontier? For the efficient portfolios it is clear that additional expected return can only be achieved at the cost of additional risk. This means that a trade-off between expected return and risk is involved and this kind of trade-off is a matter for individual preference. The traditional economic approach to this kind of problem is to construct, at least in theory, the individual's indifference curves for expected return and variance. Three of the total family of indifference curves might look like the ones in Figure 12.11. These in-

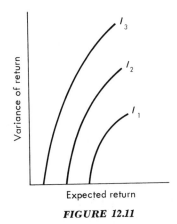

FIGURE 12.11

difference curves ought to curve upward to the right since the investor will not accept additional risk unless he gets more expected value and an additional increment of risk at a higher level of risk will require a greater additional increment of expected value than it would at a lower level of risk. Obviously, the investor prefers points on I_1 to points on I_2, points on I_2 to I_3, etc. However, by definition he is indifferent between any two points on the same indifference curve.

The traditional argument applies and, superimposing the indifference curves on the graph of the efficiency frontier as in Figure 12.12, the investor's optimal portfolio is given by the point of tangency of his indifference curve with the efficiency frontier. In our case it is the point of tangency of I_2 and the efficiency frontier. The optimal expected return and variance for this investor could be read directly from the graph.

This is the theory. Can we at least illustrate how it might be applied in practice? This would be perfectly straightforward up to the point at which the efficiency frontier is determined. We assume it is possible to obtain the relevant probability distributions for the percentage returns

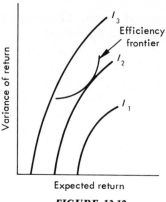

Expected return

FIGURE 12.12

expected for different common stocks. To illustrate, we could propose an arbitrary set of such probability distributions and launch into the necessary calculations. However, this would be misleading since it is often the determination of such probability distributions—ones which adequately reflect the beliefs of the analysts—which is the greatest difficulty.[15] Therefore, assuming that historical data is the only basis for the analyst's expectations of the future we will proceed directly from a hypothetical past history. It should be emphasized, however, that this does not imply that future expectations must be based on historical performance in such a simplistic fashion.

Let us consider two stocks. Portfolios will consist of all possible divisions of the total amount to be invested between the two stocks. Assume that the investor is interested only in the return on his investment for one year. Return on investment will be defined as the appreciation of stock price during the year plus any dividends, all divided by the initial price of the stock. Suppose, finally, that the investor is basing his expectations for the next year on the following historical information about the two stocks:

	BEGINNING PRICE		DIVIDEND	
Year	*Stock I*	*Stock II*	*Stock I*	*Stock II*
1	50	75	1	0
2	51	82	1	1
3	53	93	1	0
4	57	89	1	2
5	58	106	1	1
6	60	108	—	—

Our investor has come into the market at the beginning of the sixth year.

[15] Concerning this point see Denis J. Dwyer, "Using a Computer for Portfolio Selection," *Banking* (July, 1964), p. 45.

From these data we can calculate the yearly return on investment according to the definition given above. The end-of-the-year price for a stock is the price at the beginning of the following year. Thus, the percentage return for *II* in the first year is simply

$$\frac{82 - 75 + 0}{75} = 0.0933$$

There was no dividend for stock *II* in that year. For the fourth year the percentage return for *II* is

$$\frac{106 - 89 + 2}{89} = 0.2135$$

Proceeding similarly we find:

	RETURN	
Year	*I*	*II*
1	0.0400	0.0933
2	0.0588	0.1463
3	0.0943	−0.0430
4	0.0351	0.2135
5	0.0517	0.0283

Letting r_1 and r_2 represent the respective returns of the two stocks, we calculate the average returns as:

$$\bar{r}_1 = 0.0560$$
$$\bar{r}_2 = 0.0877$$

The return from *II* is larger, on the average, than the return from *I*. However, it is equally clear that the risk associated with *II* is considerably greater than that for *I*. How should the investor trade-off his desire for larger returns against his dislike for risk?

We have already agreed to measure risk by the variance of the returns. But before calculating the variances of the two stocks' returns let us recall that we are going to be interested in the variance of a portfolio—some combination of the two stocks. Common sense suggests, and statistical theory confirms, that there ought to be some relationship between the variances of the two stocks and the variance from any portfolio containing just these two stocks. Suppose two random variables, x_1 and x_2, have, respectively, variances V_1 and V_2. Let us define a new random variable, Y, equal to a weighted sum of x_1 and x_2:

$$Y = wx_1 + (1 - w)x_2$$

where $0 \leq w \leq 1$. Then it can be shown that *if x_1 and x_2 are independent* that the variance of Y is given by:

$$V_Y = w^2 V_1 + (1 - w)^2 V_2$$

If x_1 and x_2 are not statistically independent there is an analogous equation but it has to include a term based on the covariance, C_{12}, of x_1 and x_2. Those who have had a course in descriptive statistics will recall that the correlation coefficient, ρ_{12}, is often used to measure the dependence between two random variables such as x_1 and x_2. The covariance is simply related to the correlation coefficient:

$$C_{12} = \rho_{12}\sigma_1\sigma_2$$

where σ_1 and σ_2 are the standard deviations and, of course, are, respectively, $\sqrt{V_1}$ and $\sqrt{V_2}$. Alternatively, we can define the covariance directly as

$$C_{12} = E[(x_1 - \bar{x}_1)(x_2 - \bar{x}_2)]$$

where E means, as always, "expected value." The equation for the variance of Y in the general case is:

$$V_Y = w^2V_1 + (1 - w)^2V_2 + 2w(1 - w)C_{12}$$

This includes the situation when x_1 and x_2 are independent since in that case, $C_{12} = 0$.

Since stock returns are almost never independent we need to calculate the covariance as well as the two variances. It is simplest to work directly with the deviations of the returns from their means.[16]

$r_1 - \bar{r}_1$	$r_2 - \bar{r}_2$	$(r_1 - \bar{r}_1)^2$	$(r_2 - \bar{r}_2)^2$	$(r_1 - \bar{r}_1)(r_2 - \bar{r}_2)$
-0.01598	0.00562	0.00025536	0.00003158	-0.00008981
0.00282	0.05862	0.00000795	0.00343630	0.00016531
0.03832	-0.13068	0.00146842	0.01707726	-0.00500766
-0.02088	0.12582	0.00043597	0.01583067	-0.00262712
-0.00428	-0.05938	0.00001832	0.00352598	0.00025415
		0.00218602	0.03990179	-0.00730513

We are treating the measurements of return as if they were random samples from the population of returns for each stock. We want to estimate the variances and the covariance of the populations. As any book on statistics explains, to get unbiased estimates requires dividing the above totals by one less than the number of measurements. Then:

$$V_1 = \frac{0.00218602}{4} = 0.0005465$$

$$V_2 = \frac{0.03990179}{4} = 0.0099754$$

$$C_{12} = \frac{-0.00730513}{4} = -0.0018263$$

[16] We used the exact values for the mean returns: $\bar{r}_1 = 0.05598$ and $\bar{r}_2 = 0.08768$.

It should be noticed that the variance of *II* is much greater than that of *I*, thus reflecting the much greater risk associated with an investment in *II*. It should also be noted that the covariance between the two stocks' returns is negative. This means that there was a tendency for the return of stock *I* to be smaller when the return of stock *II* was larger, and similarly in reverse.

The fact that the covariance is negative is important. It means that the variance of a combined portfolio will be lower—since the term involving the covariance will be subtracted as a result of the negative covariance—because of the dependence between the two stocks' returns. *This is certainly in accord with one of the common motivations for diversification of portfolios.* If the investor can find stocks such that some of them get higher returns precisely when the others get lower returns then he has surely protected himself to some degree from adverse fortune. The model we are developing takes this explicitly into account and, to that degree at least, is in plausible accord with real behavior.

Any portfolio consisting only of stocks *I* and *II* can be represented as having a proportion, w, of the total investment in *I* and a proportion, $(1 - w)$, in *II*. We will assume that $0 \leq w \leq 1$ (although it is possible to interpret $w < 0$ as meaning that a "short" position should be taken and $w > 1$ as meaning that the investor ought to buy on margin). The expected return on the portfolio will be:

$$\bar{r}_p = w\bar{r}_1 + (1 - w)\bar{r}_2$$

In this example, we have

$$\bar{r}_p = 0.0560w + 0.0877(1 - w)$$
$$= 0.0877 - 0.0317w$$

Similarly,

$$V_p = w^2 V_1 + (1 - w)^2 V_2 + 2w(1 - w)C_{12}$$

For our data this is:

$$V_p = 0.0005465w^2 + 0.0099754(1 - w)^2 + 2w(1 - w)(-0.0018263)$$
$$= 0.0099754 - 0.0236034w + 0.0141745w^2$$

Now, if a value of w is specified we can immediately calculate the resulting portfolio's expected return and variance. Suppose the investor puts half his available funds in each stock. In this case $w = 0.5$ and we find $r_p = 0.0718$ and $V_p = 0.0017173$. Similarly, for any given w we can find the portfolio's expected return and variance.

How should the investor determine a value of w? Or, rather, how can he find the *specific* w which will give him the combination of expected return and variance which is *most in accord with his objectives?* One related question can be answered quite easily: What is the least possible variance which the investor can achieve with a portfolio? To answer this requires setting the derivative of V_p with respect to w equal to zero and solving for w:

$$\frac{dV_p}{dw} = -0.0236034 + 0.0283490w = 0$$

or $w = 0.83260$

Investing 83.25% of his investment funds in stock I and 16.74% in stock II minimizes the portfolio variance. Using the above equations, we find that this portfolio has an expected return, $E(R)$ of 0.0613 and a variance of 0.0001493. Notice that this portfolio is very much better than a portfolio consisting only of stock I, with expected return of 0.0560 and variance of 0.0005465. The minimum-variance portfolio has a higher expected return *and* a much lower variance than the portfolio consisting only of stock I. Therefore, it follows that no rational investor would be interested in a portfolio made up entirely of stock I. In other words, the portfolio which includes only stock I is not an efficient portfolio—it does not lie on the efficiency frontier.

In accordance with our earlier discussion of the underlying theory of portfolio selection, we ought to begin by finding the efficiency frontier for the set of all possible portfolios based on these two stocks. This is easy to do for our example because all of the possible portfolios fall on a smooth curve, as shown in Figure 12.13. The efficiency frontier is shown on the figure with a heavier line. See also Table 12.1. It is ap-

TABLE 12.1

w	$E(R)$	V_p
0	0.08768	0.0099754
0.1	0.08451	0.0077568
0.2	0.08134	0.0058218
0.3	0.07817	0.0041701
0.4	0.07500	0.0028019
0.5	0.07180	0.0017173
0.6	0.06866	0.0009162
0.7	0.06549	0.0003985
0.8	0.06232	0.0001644
0.83260	0.06129	0.0001493 ← Minimum
0.9	0.05915	0.0002136
1.0	0.05598	0.0005465

parent that none of the portfolios on the part of the curve which goes up to the left can be efficient since for each one of them there is a portfolio on the efficiency frontier which has the same variance and larger expected return.

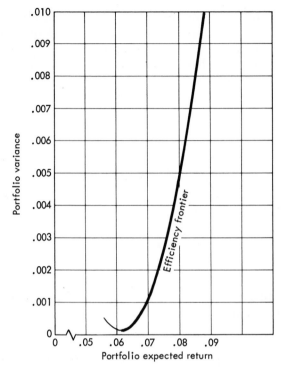

FIGURE 12.13

The efficiency frontier represents the very best that the investor can do. Consider an arbitrary efficient portfolio. The investor will not be able to achieve more expected return than that of the given portfolio without accepting more risk, as measured by the variance. The efficiency frontier shows the best trade-offs of risk for expected return that can be achieved. The investor's problem, then, is to select that point on the efficiency frontier which most nearly meets his requirements regarding expected return and variance.

One way to try to do this (an approach suggested by Markowitz) is for the investor to *contemplate* the efficiency frontier until he reaches a decision as to where he wishes to be on that curve. By carrying on a kind of internal dialogue and weighing benefits against costs, it is possible that an investor may be able to do this. It is, after all, analogous to what the executive must do with the optimal policy curve in the case of inventory problems with unknown costs.[17] No one would suggest that this is an easy task.

The only other approach is to use the argument we developed in terms of the investor's indifference curves for expected return and

[17] See Section 101, and particularly, p. 335.

variance. The major suggestion that has been investigated in this regard is indifference curves which are straight lines, as shown on Figure 12.14. Such indifference curves are approximations to the more plausible shape suggested in our theoretical discussion and as shown on Figure 12.11.

FIGURE 12.14

Straight-line indifference curves of this slope are equivalent to an investor's utility function for portfolios of this kind:

$$U = r_p - sV_p$$

Here, s is the parameter chosen by the investor to represent his dislike for risk. Obviously, the larger the s, the greater the aversion to risk. If this is the investor's utility function it is easy to find the optimal portfolio. His utility function for portfolios of two stocks will be:

$$U = w\bar{r}_1 + (1 - w)\bar{r}_2 - s[w^2V_1 + (1 - w)^2V_2 + 2w(1 - w)C_{12}]$$

which is maximized when:

$$w = \frac{\bar{r}_1 - \bar{r}_2 + 2s[V_2 - C_{12}]}{2s[V_1 + V_2 - 2C_{12}]}$$

In our case this gives

$$w = \frac{-0.0317 + 0.0236035}{0.028349s}$$

Now, if the investor will specify a value of s, then his optimal portfolio can be determined.

Of course, this only pushes the problem back another step. How is the investor to determine his value of s? Before he can hope to do this he has to get some insight into the meaning of s—what are the implications of different choices of this parameter? Unfortunately, this is not easy to answer. We can verify that when s takes very large values (approaches infinity) then $w = 0.8326$. It will be recalled that this is the value of w which gives the minimum-variance portfolio. The result is in accord with common sense since giving s a very large value is equivalent to placing all weight on the variance and ignoring expected return entirely. But the other end of the scale for *s* becomes somewhat confusing. The question is complex, both for determining a value for *s* and whether this particular form for the utility function is a reasonable one.[18]

While there is not too much help for the investor when it comes to selecting a point on the efficiency frontier, it is certainly helpful to be able to eliminate for him all of the inefficient portfolios. To do this for a large initial list of stocks is a major undertaking. The mathematical technique required is called *quadratic programming* since the objective function—like ours above—is a quadratic function. Markowitz has developed the necessary procedures[19] and IBM has a program for accomplishing his analysis which is available as a customer service. Furthermore, work is continuing in this area and alternative formulations and approaches are already available.[20] The problem of finding an optimal portfolio promises to be easier in the future than it has been in the past.

118/ *Dividend Policy*

One of the major objectives of management is to satisfy the stockholders for whom they work. It is generally maintained that this means that management should strive to *maximize the discounted present worth* of the company, either now or at some time in the future. Clearly, at some point, either now or in the future, the worth of the company will be translated into dividends to the stockholder. This does not mean that the company ought necessarily to pay dividends now. Provided the company is making a sufficient profit, it can pay a regular dividend at the average rate for its industry—or better—but it does not follow that the stockholders will be satisfied with such a policy.

Many times stockholders sell their holdings in a company which is paying a regular dividend and instead buy stock in a company which is paying no dividend at all. Why? Because the present worth of a company may be maximized by a company which does not pay dividends but which does reinvest its earnings in company expansion. Such a process is not expected to go on indefinitely. An alert management will take

---

[18] There is an interesting discussion of a similar utility function with a more straightforward meaning in William J. Baumol, "An Expected Gain-Confidence Limit Criterion for Portfolio Selection," *Management Science*, 10, No. 1 (Oct., 1963), 174–182. And Karl Borch questions the validity of the utility function we used above because it violates the requirements for Bernoullian utility. See Karl Borch, *The Economics of Uncertainty*, Princeton University Press, 1968.

[19] In his book, previously cited.

[20] For example, see William F. Sharpe, "A Simplified Model for Portfolio Analysis," *Management Science*, 9, No. 2 (Jan., 1963), 277–293.

advantage of a period which is particularly favorable for the company's expansion. The stockholder who is aware of the opportunities in his company's industry will ordinarily concur with management's decision to eliminate some dividends in order to maximize, in the longer run, the company's present worth.

The question of how much money management should pay out as a dividend and how much they should put back into the expansion of the company is very complex. A great variety of factors must be considered. As we shall explain, analytical methods can be used to obtain an approximate answer. The reason that the result is approximate and not exact is simply that it isn't feasible to include all of the factors which affect the solution. Furthermore, predictions are required which are difficult to make—particularly as these predictions move further into the future. But the solution does give some basic notions to the decision-maker. The objective of management is to maximize the dividend payout over a period of N years. Management has a great number of strategies which it can use to attempt to achieve the objective. But this is a case where the number of possible strategies is not so great that we cannot consider a reasonable number of them. Our payoffs will be the total dividend which can be paid to the stockholders at the end of N years. Normally, a variety of states of nature could occur. For example, the income of the company could vary each year, depending upon many conditions outside of the control of the company. Returns on additional investments could be treated as a probability distribution rather than as the expected value which we have used. Dividends to be paid in the future could be discounted to their present value. Market growth, new competitors, technological breakthroughs, rapidly changing economic conditions, and many other factors influence the decisions which must be made at each dividend period. In the same way, a number of strategic variations exist. The company could pay a stock dividend, or a combination of stock and monetary dividends could be used. The company might decide to raise additional capital for investment in expansion by means of a bond issue or through other stock issues. All of the possibilities we have mentioned could conceivably be included in the approach which we are about to explain. However, the number and complexity of computations which are required by this method when the problem is viewed in its expanded form would prove unsuitable for any example, and difficult for any real problem. For this reason we have included only the basic elements which underlie the problem. The method we will use is based upon the principles of dynamic programming which were developed by Richard Bellman.[21]

[21] Richard Bellman, *Dynamic Programming* (Princeton, N.J.: Princeton University Press, 1957).

A company has only A_0 dollars available at the beginning of a year. It can use all of this money for dividends, or it can use part of it for dividends and part for reinvestment, or it can use all of it for reinvestment. We will assume that the company pays a dividend only once a year since this assumption will further reduce the amount of computation which must be shown, without affecting the method. The company will pay out X_0 dollars as dividends at this initial time. The remainder of the A_0 dollars, which is an amount $(A_0 - X_0)$, will be used for the expansion of the company's facilities. We will assume that A_0 equals $500,-000. However, all numbers will be given in thousands of dollars. Therefore, $A_0 = \$500$. A year elapses. The company has earned another $500. In addition, it has earned a return on the amount $(A_0 - X_0)$ which it had reinvested. This means that at the end of the first year, $N = 1$, the company has an amount $A_1 = A_0 + (A_0 - X_0)R$. The return on reinvested money, R, decreases as the size of the reinvestment increases. In this way, we take account of the diminishing return on investment. Our assumption is that the return on reinvested money continues at the same rate over time and that the rate of return is reasonably constant over a period of years. As previously explained, it is mostly for computational

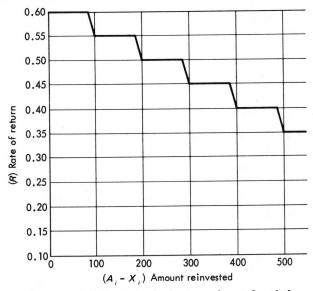

FIGURE 12.15   Rate of return on reinvested capital.

convenience that we have made assumptions of this kind. Figure 12.15 shows the return rate, R, as a function of reinvested money $(A_i - X_i)$. We can either use Figure 12.15 to provide us with all of the necessary return rates or the following table.

$(A_i - X_i)$ Amount reinvested	(R) Rate of return
$ 0 - 99	0.60
100 - 199	0.55
200 - 299	0.50
300 - 399	0.45
400 - 499	0.40
500 -	0.35

The way in which we will proceed is to examine what outcome results if we follow the strategy of paying no dividend, $X_0 = 0$; what outcome results if we pay out in dividends $100, $200, $300, $400, and $500. The required result is A_1: the amount of money on hand at the end of the first year. Thus, at $N = 1$:

X_0	$A_0 + (A_0 - X_0)R = A_1$
0	$500 + (500)0.35 = 675$
100	$500 + (400)0.40 = 660$
200	$500 + (300)0.45 = 635$
300	$500 + (200)0.50 = 600$
400	$500 + (100)0.55 = 555$
500	$500 + (0)0.60 = 500$

Now, if the company's objective is to maximize dividend payout for a one-year period, the policy that should be followed is to pay out $500 at each of the two dividend periods. We can see that result by looking at the table below.

If first dividend X_0 is	0	100	200	300	400	500
and total capital earned, A_1, is paid out as a dividend, X_1	675	660	635	600	555	500
then total paid to stockholders is . . .	675	760	835	900	955	1000

Since the last column represents the largest payout, that is the strategy which should be followed for a one-year objective. But let us suppose that the company wants to maximize the dividend payout over a two-year period. The amount earned at the end of the second year is A_2, and $A_2 = A_1 + (A_1 - X_1)R$. The second dividend paid is X_1, and R has the same meaning as before. Then we can compute the A_2 value for all possible values of X_0 and X_1 as follows:

	$X_0 = 0$ $A_1 = 675$			$X_0 = 100$ $A_1 = 660$
X_1	$A_1 + (A_1 - X_1)R = A_2$		X_1	$A_1 + (A_1 - X_1)R = A_2$
0	$675 + (675)0.35 = 911$		0	$660 + (660)0.35 = 891$
100	$675 + (575)0.35 = 876$		100	$660 + (560)0.35 = 856$
200	$675 + (475)0.40 = 865$		200	$660 + (460)0.40 = 844$
300	$675 + (375)0.45 = 844$		300	$660 + (360)0.45 = 822$
400	$675 + (275)0.50 = 813$		400	$660 + (260)0.50 = 790$
500	$675 + (175)0.55 = 771$		500	$660 + (160)0.55 = 748$
600	$675 + (75)0.60 = 720$		600	$660 + (60)0.60 = 696$

TABLE 12.2
Matrix of A_2

A_1

	675	660	635	600	555	500	
			X_0				
X_1	0	100	200	300	400	500	500
0	.911	.891	857	810	749	675	600
100	876	856	822	775	737	660	700
200	.865	.844	809	760	715	635	800
300	.844	.822	786	735	683	600	900
400	813	.790	.753	700	640	555	1000
500	771	748	.709	655	588	.500	
600	720	696	.656	.600			

Similar computations have been made for $X_0 = 200$, 300, 400, and 500. These results are compiled in the Table 12.2 which shows the resulting A_2 values for all possible combinations of X_0 and X_1. The diagonals each represent those combinations of X_0 and X_1, which sum to a particular value. In other words, the $400 diagonal results from $X_0 = 0$, $X_1 = 400$; $X_0 = 100$, $X_1 = 300$; $X_0 = 200$, $X_1 = 200$; and so on. The greatest value on each diagonal is marked with a dot.[22] That is the only value which needs to be considered. The reason that no other value is important can be understood if we assume we are stockholders for the moment. Let us consider the $400 diagonal. As stockholders we would have received $400 in some combination of payments, but our company would have more money left to work with if they had used the combination of payments $X_0 = 100$ and $X_1 = 300$. Therefore, that is the combination of dividend payments which is optimal for a total payout of $400. Any additional dividend X_2 will be added to $400, so it will not matter what combination was used. The company cannot possibly be better off by having less money. For this reason, we take only the dotted values from the matrix. If there is a tie for the maximum diagonal value, it does not matter. It is the same value, in either case, which is taken from the matrix.

If we assume the objective is to maximize dividend payout over a two-year period, $N = 2$, we find

$X_0 + X_1$	0	100	200	300	400	500	600	700	800	900	1,000
Max A_2	911	891	865	844	822	790	753	709	656	600	500
Total	911	991	1,065	1,144	1,222	1,290	1,353	1,409	1,456	1,500	1,500

[22] The method is suggested by Andrew Vazsonyi, *Scientific Programming in Business and Industry*, John Wiley & Sons, N.Y., 1958; pp. 219–254.

The optimal strategy yielding the largest payout is either the 900 or the 1,000 column. When $X_0 + X_1$ equals 900, A_2 equals 600. When $X_0 + X_1$ equals 1,000, A_2 equals 500. Both strategies produce a total of 1,500. We now go back to Table 12.2 and we find that the 600 value resulted when X_0 equals 300 and X_1 equals 600. In the same table we see that 500 resulted when X_0 equals 500 as before, and X_1 equals 500. Therefore, we observe that the optimal strategy for a two-year period does not necessarily begin in the same way as an optimal strategy for a one-year period.

We will go one step further. Our next set of computations is of the same type as our former ones. That is,

$$X_0 + X_1 = 0 \qquad\qquad\qquad X_0 + X_1 = 100$$
$$A_2 = 911 \qquad\qquad\qquad\qquad A_2 = 891$$

X_2	$A_2 + (A_2 - X_2)R = A_3$			X_2	$A_2 + (A_2 - X_2)R = A_3$		
0	911 + (911)0.35	= 1230		0	891 + (891)0.35	= 1203
100	911 + (811)0.35	= 1195		100	891 + (791)0.35	= 1168
200	911 + (711)0.35	= 1160		200	891 + (691)0.35	= 1133

Similar computations are carried out for all combinations of X_2 and $(X_0 + X_1)$. Table 12.3 is the result. Again, we see that the maximum value on each diagonal is dotted. And again, the same reasoning applies. We have now reached the end of the third year in our computations. We could continue indefinitely in the same fashion. Automatic

TABLE 12.3

Matrix of A_3

A_2

	911	891	865	844	822	790	753	709	656	600	500
						$(X_0 + X_1)$					
X_2	0	100	200	300	400	500	600	700	800	900	1000
0	1230	1203	1168	1139	1110	1067	1017	957	886	810	675
100	1195	1168	1133	1104	1075	1032	982	922	851	775	660
200	1160	1133	1098	1069	1040	997	947	887	838	760	635
300	1125	1098	1063	1034	1005	986	934	873	816	735	600
400	1090	1087	1051	1021	991	966	912	848	784	700	555
500	1075	1067	1029	999	967	935	880	814	742	655	500
600	1051	1037	998	966	933	895	837	769	690	600	
700	1017	996	956	923	889	844	785	714			
800	972	946	904	870	835						
900	918										

computing equipment would do the same job with less wear and tear and in much less time, once an appropriate program was fashioned.

Let us examine the result at the end of the third year, $N = 3$. This time the stockholder is going to be paid the A_i value since the objective is to maximize dividend payout for the end of the third year. Then,

$X_0 + X_1 + X_2$	0	100	200	300	400	500	600	700
A_3	1,230	1,203	1,168	1,139	1,110	1,087	1,067	1,037
TOTAL	1,230	1,303	1,368	1,439	1,510	1,587	1,667	1,737
$X_0 + X_1 + X_2$	800	900	1,000	1,100	1,200	1,300	1,400	1,500
A_3	999	967	935	895	844	785	714	600
TOTAL	1,799	1,867	1,935	1,995	2,044	2,085	2,114	2,100

The maximum total payout at the end of three years can be achieved by the combination, $X_0 + X_1 + X_2 = 1,400$. Because of our three-year objective, $X_3 = A_3$. In other words, our fourth dividend, paid at the end of the third year is a complete payout of the available capital of the company. $(A_3 - X_3) = 0$, and no money is going to be reinvested for expansion. Looking back at Table 12.3, we see that when $X_0 + X_1 + X_2 = 1,400$, then for the dotted value on the diagonal, $X_2 = 700$ and $X_0 + X_1 = 700$. We then return to Table 12.2 where we find that for the diagonal $X_0 + X_1 = 700$, the dotted value resulted when $X_0 = 200$ and $X_1 = 500$. This is the final solution of the problem.

$$X_0 = 200$$
$$X_1 = 500$$
$$X_2 = 700$$
$$A_3 = 714$$
$$\text{TOTAL PAYOUT:} \quad \overline{2,114}$$

Once again, we observe that the optimal dividend payout policy has been changed by the fact that an additional year has been included in the objective. As the rate of return increases, the optimal policy tends to shift from immediate payout to delayed payout so that advantage can be taken of the opportunities for reinvestment. Problem 1 in the problem section that follows is intended to demonstrate this effect.

PROBLEMS

1. The company which we discussed in the dividend example in this chapter begins to experience the effects of a rapidly expanding market. As a result, the

rate of return on its investment for expansion shifts upward. The following table gives the new rate-of-return schedule.

AMOUNT REINVESTED	RATE OF RETURN
$0 – 99	0.80
100 – 199	0.75
200 – 299	0.70
300 – 399	0.65
400 – 499	0.60
500 –	0.55

Using the amount $A_o = 500$, as before, determine the optimum dividend policy for $N = 1$ and $N = 2$.

2. Suppose an individual spends $5,000 per year at a constant rate. He keeps his money in a bank deposit which earns 5% per year. The only cost of a withdrawal is the time required to go to the bank and make the withdrawal. He values this time at $5.

    a. What is the optimal amount the individual should withdraw?

    b. The answer to (a) seems contrary to the typical behavior of individuals in the stated circumstances—which are by no means unreasonable. Perhaps one explanation is that most individuals fear the loss or theft of cash. How would you take this possibility of loss into account in determining the optimal amount to withdraw?

3. In the oil-drilling decision problem discussed on pp. 452–464, how is the optimal strategy affected by each of the following changes?

    a. $P(O) = 0.1$
    b. $P(O) = 0.3$
    c. $P(G|O) = 0.8$
    d. $P(\bar{G}|\bar{O}) = 0.5$

4. In a lot-acceptance decision problem, suppose there are only two states of nature:

$N1$: the lot is acceptable

$N2$: the lot is not acceptable

The probability of a defective item if $N1$ is true is 0.1. The probability of a defective item if $N2$ is true is 0.3. The opportunity cost of rejecting the lot if $N1$ is true is $2,000 and the opportunity cost of accepting the lot if $N2$ is true is $1,000. On the basis of historical records it is known that the probability that $N1$ is true is 0.6. A sample costs $10 per unit sampled. You can take a sample of two or no sample. Should you take the sample?

5. In the first example of risk analysis given in this chapter (pp. 464–475) suppose that each of the probability distributions is rectangular; each value is equally likely to occur. Run a simulation of 100 investments, determining the resulting frequency distribution of the ROI's.

6. Two stocks show the following five-year records:

Year	BEGINNING STOCK PRICE		DIVIDENDS	
	I	*II*	*I*	*II*
1	12	65	0	1
2	20	69	0	1
3	26	78	0	1
4	25	85	1	1
5	38	88	0	1
6	48	91	—	—

Determine the minimum variance portfolio for these two stocks and the efficiency frontier.

7. In the problem of portfolio selection, what would be the effect of considering a defensive stock (foods) and a glamour stock (electronics). In other words, what kind of expected returns, variances, and covariance would you expect to find?

8. In risk analysis a common problem is that some of the probability distributions are dependent on one another. For example, suppose the investment under consideration is for a new plant to produce a slight variant of an existing product. Then the price that would be set for the product might be related to the cost of the plant and demand would almost surely depend in part on the price. How would you handle this kind of situation?

9. In portfolio analysis it is often assumed that the investor's indifference curve for expected return and variance is a straight line:

$$U = r_p - sV_p$$

where U = utility, r_p = expected portfolio return, V_p = portfolio variance, and s is a constant to be determined by the investor. This means that the investor should be equally satisfied with any portfolio from among a set of portfolios, each with the same expected return and variance. The same would hold true for bets with the same expected return and variance. If this is so, the investor should be indifferent among:

> -1 with probability $\frac{1}{5}$, 1.5 with probability $\frac{4}{5}$
>
> -0.2 with probability 0.41, 1.83 with probability 0.59
>
> i with probability $\dfrac{1}{2.7183\, i!}$ $\left(\text{Poisson: } e^{-1}\dfrac{1^i}{i!} \right)$
>
> normal distribution with mean = 1 standard deviation = 1

Each of the four bets has mean and variance equal to one. Is this reasonable? How would you measure the differences among these bets?

10. Another major effort to apply quantitative methods in the general area of finance has been the attempt to evaluate credit risks, particularly in the area of extending credit to individuals. How would you measure the opposing costs involved in extending or not extending an individual credit? Contrast the case of a bank making a personal loan, an automobile dealer giving installment payment plans, and an airline offering time payments in the future for a trip now (with a down payment, of course).

PART V

THE EXECUTIVE
AND
OPERATIONS
RESEARCH

Chapter 13

Evaluation
of
Problems

The basic plan of this book is indicated by the titles of the five parts. Our first part dealt with organizations and decisions, showing some of the major features of the host of decision problems with which the executive must cope if he is to fulfill his function successfully. Our second part dealt with the theory of decisions. Here we tried to present an over-all view of the way in which operations research could contribute to the clarification or resolution of decision problems. The third part was concerned with the nature of models, exploring the broad range of attributes that characterizes the model-building function of management. The fourth part was devoted to actual decision problems, having some degree of generality. We tried to show how one can work one's way through to a solution of some of these decision problems by careful analysis of their various features. In other cases, one can only gain additional insights into the decision problem. But it has been our thesis that the decision-maker will always profit by using a rational approach to his decision problems.

These four parts have set the stage for the concluding part of the book: the executive and operations research. Several questions remain to be discussed. First, granted the general usefulness of operations research in decision problems, it still does not by any means follow that the executive needs an operations research analysis of every one of his decision problems. When, then, does he need such an analysis? This is the subject of Chapter 13, which will demonstrate the executive's need for a kind of broad gauge understanding of the methods and approaches of operations research. So, and second, it is the purpose of Chapter 14 to provide this overview of operations research. Finally, and third, certain problems involving the implementation and control of operations-research solutions merit the executive's attention. Chapter 15 provides a brief discussion of these problems.

119/ What Is a Problem?

We have no intention of trying to define completely what a problem is. The depth of that question is too great for us to attempt to sound it. We shall be content to mention only those few aspects of this question which appear to be most relevant for our discussion.

There is considerable agreement among people on some of the *general characteristics* of problems. Very often the existence and nature of a problem can be diagnosed by means of some obvious questions. Why should this activity be done? Why should it be done in that way? How else can this be done? How should this be done? When should this be done? Who should do this? These questions, and others like them, are *problem-pointers*. The act of questioning indicates the *possible existence* of a problem. By no means does it demonstrate the *real existence* of a problem. We usually use the word *problem* when someone is endeavoring to come to grips with one or more of these questions. To find suitable answers is to *solve the problem*. Generally, we recognize that the same questions can be asked simply from "idle curiosity," and we reserve the word *problem* for cases of "busy curiosity."

Frequently we refer to problems when the person involved is not aware there is any problem at all. For example, most businessmen would maintain that the president of a company that was steadily losing its share of the market had a problem. And they would maintain this even though the president might not know that the problem existed because a rising total market gave his company increasing sales. Of course, they would wonder how he could not know it—but that, for us, is another kind of organizational problem. Similarly, most accountants would hold that a small restaurant owner had a problem if the ratio of his liquid assets to his current liabilities was less than 10 per cent— even if the restaurant owner had never heard of this particular ratio. Any legitimate use of *problem* requires that *somebody must recognize* the problem, even if he is not the person involved. Perhaps we can say that this use of *problem* implies that the person involved *should* be coming to grips with it. One cannot come to grips with a problem until he is aware of its existence. The awareness of a problem is the first prerequisite for dealing with it.

How does one become aware of a problem? There are obviously a multitude of ways, and we do not propose to catalogue them all. But it will be worth mentioning a few of the more common ways.

120/ Head-On Confrontation

First, sometimes we become aware of a problem because reality is so obstreperous that it literally hits us head-on with the problem and there is no conceivable way that we could avoid being aware of it. Examples of this kind of awareness are, unfortunately, particularly numerous. Consider national problems. Only the erosion of millions of acres of farmland leads to an awareness of the problem of soil conservation. Or, the devastation of a hurricane is required before we become aware of the problem of lacking an adequate storm-warning system. Horrifying mid-air collisions produce an awareness of the need for total systems control of aircraft.

There are also many business examples. The manager who becomes aware of the problem posed by a new competitive product because his sales slump to the vanishing point is one case. But we do not mean to imply that all such problems are so catastrophic in their effects. An administrator might not become aware of the problems attendant upon an increasing size of organization until he is in the middle of them, but the effect of the administrator's obtuseness may only be unnecessary inefficiency and wastage. When the consequences are serious, however, becoming aware of a problem in this "head-on" way can be extremely costly. The attempts to cope with the problem must be on an emergency basis and there is no time for careful analysis. Such a situation can only result in a heightening of all the difficulties that surround the efforts to solve a problem even in calmer circumstances.

121/ Precautionary Monitoring

Second, some kinds of problems are highlighted by our way of looking at reality. With forethought we are always watching for certain signs. We have called our way of looking at reality "models" of reality. We are now saying that our models of reality generally put some kinds of problems into bold relief. An outstanding example is the administrator's accounting model of his organization. The accounting model is designed to call the administrator's attention quickly to problems signaled by unbalanced cash flow, decreased demand, unit cost increases, higher inventory investments, and a host of similar problems.

This problem-pointing characteristic of models deserves to be emphasized. The layman can be hard put to distinguish between real costs and accounting expenses. As a result he is unlikely to notice (become aware of) many problems which anyone familiar with the accounting model would be watching for. But there is a converse to this advantage of models which also deserves emphasis. This is that too great use of any one model is likely to lead to that philosophical error we called *hypostatization*—the confusion of our model with reality. A microscope is an excellent device for looking at bacteria, but useless for seeing stars. A telescope is fine for the stars but not suitable for seeing bacteria. And neither is any good for reading books. For adequately seeing the universe we need all three: microscopes, telescopes, and good vision. A person endowed with only microscopic vision would have a rather low survival index. It is even difficult to speculate on how his distorted picture of the universe would affect his behavior.

Our models can function as blinders instead of as aids to better vision. By giving the illusion of a "total" early-warning system, when in fact it is only "partial," a great disservice may be done. Susceptibility to such illusions is one of the greatest ills human minds are heir to. Classical economic theory is a good example. The classical economists had a model of the economic activities of society which included only market place phenomena. They were so delighted with this model that they resolutely refused to admit the relevance to economics of social problems that were a direct consequence of economic policies. The indefatigable persistence with which some of the classical economists adhered to this position can only be marveled at. Fortunately, the labor of subsequent economists has resulted in economic models that more adequately reflect reality.

The same kind of thing can happen in the business world. Let us consider the accounting model in this regard. Inventory carrying charges are reasonably accessible. There is, however, no entry for profit lost because of unfilled orders, nor is there an entry for the loss of customer goodwill because of out-of-stocks. All kinds of direct costs are emphasized, but there is no place for opportunity costs. Such examples can be multiplied easily. We are not criticizing the accounting model for omitting something it was never intended to include. Rather, we want to point out that an executive who leaned too exclusively on this one model would miss problems of which he should be aware. What would happen? His organization would continue along its path until reality brought him to a sharp realization of the problems—our first method of generating awareness. At that time it might be too late for satisfactory remedial action. The executive must always remember that all models should serve as problem-pointers, not as problem-blinders.

122/ External Perturbation

Third, awareness of a problem can result from the fact that someone whose role is external to the immediate system discovers its existence. Frequently, this effect is described as "not being able to see the wood for the trees." It also explains why consultants have increasingly participated in organizational affairs. In any case, the "outsider" becomes aware of the problem and presents his discovery with such irresistible logic that others become aware through his efforts. Such contributions to our perception of problems frequently reflect creative genius of a high order. As an example, we can cite Frederick W. Taylor's discovery of the "real" problems of production. The success with which he promulgated his concepts is recorded history. Perhaps it boils down to a question of converting "idle curiosity" into "busy curiosity"—changing problem-pointing questions into real problems that can be studied and solved. In such conversion the government occasionally takes a hand by means of legislation. Thus, a state may make employer contributions to unemployment insurance depend on the amount of use of the insurance by the employees. This is a pointed, and effective, way of making the employer treat the variability in his employment as a problem, rather than simply considering it to be an unfortunate accident of his line of business.

123/ Random Searching

Fourth, and last, one can become so problem-oriented that when no problems can be discovered by any other means one goes looking for them. Such a search is usually predicated on the proposition that "things can't be perfect." Few organizations are without some *problem-finding* group (it may be called a methods department or a value analysis group). Emphasis can be placed on efficiency experts, trouble-shooters or systems analysts—whatever the name—to stress preventive treatment; problem-spotting and problem diagnosis are ubiquitous. History provides ample evidence that functions such as these have a significant role to play. Nevertheless, the basis for "looking-for-trouble" is not without its own liabilities. The belief that organized searching will uncover real problems is, in the case of many organizations, only too often justified by the fact that *the searching process creates its own problems.* Such self-justifying processes provide continual reasons for their own existence without necessarily contributing to the organizational well-being. A number of subsequent remarks will be relevant to the question of when one can reasonably initiate a search for problems.

These are some of the major ways in which one can become aware of problems. But it is obvious that not all persons view the same things as problems even when they are faced with the same kinds of situations. Some persons will come to grips with the issues and attempt to resolve them. Others will ignore or defer the issues, i.e., they will not make any effort to solve the problem. For them there is only a problem-pointing question, not a real problem in our sense of the word. Let us consider the reasons for this difference.

124/ Problems and Objectives

We shall treat a particular kind of situation. In one form or another, it arises in a variety of circumstances. Some examples are: a bank manager observes the formation of long waiting lines in front of the open teller windows; the manager of a government tax office observes long waiting lines of citizens desiring assistance in preparing their tax statements; a doctor observes his waiting room filled with prospective patients.

The reactions of the three observers of this phenomenon are likely to be quite different. The bank manager will probably order additional windows to be opened, if any are available. If there are none available and the situation is repeated, he will come to recognize it as a problem and treat it as such. In this event he will consider such strategies as re-designing the bank to get more teller windows, expanding, opening a branch office, or relocating. In short, he will treat this situation as a genuine decision problem and take suitable action to resolve it.

The manager of the tax office is less likely to view the same type of situation as a problem. He will certainly take any available steps equivalent to opening additional teller windows, but he is not oriented to view repetition of the situation as an indication of a problem with which he must deal. Instead, he might view the queues as legitimate punishment for the dilatory citizens who waited until the last minute to fill out their forms. And the citizens themselves probably accept it as such.

The doctor will not have the equivalent of additional windows to open. He is unlikely to view the situation as a problem at all. On the contrary, in his system the waiting line is not undesirable. He can reason that the overcrowded waiting-room is proof to every patient (and other doctors) that he is sought after because he is a good doctor. This is merely confirmation of the patient's choice.

From the standpoint of queuing theory we can say that the doctor and the manager of the tax office are placing high values on their own time and a low value on the time of the people waiting. The bank manager, however, puts a higher value on the time of his customers. Why the difference? Why doesn't the bank manager use the same arguments as the other two? Like the manager of the tax office he could say that waiting lines are a form of punishment for customers who insist on coming to the bank from 12:00 to 1:00. If they would distribute themselves more evenly over the whole day they wouldn't have to wait. And like the doctor he could say that the waiting lines prove to his customers that it is a good bank and confirm the wisdom of selecting that bank. But he uses neither of these arguments. Instead, he views the situation as a *problem* to be solved. Why?

The answer to this question is that evidently, the objectives are different in the three cases. There may be other factors as well, but this appears to be the most important reason for the different responses to the same situation. The doctor will not view the waiting line as a problem. In most cases its absence would be a problem. The doctor's objective is to have a sufficient number of patients, and by his argument the waiting line can contribute to the achievement of his objective. His argument may be wrong but he has considerable *empirical data* which indicate that the waiting line is no impediment to the achievement of his objective. Therefore, he can, and does, ignore it as a problem.

The tax office manager has a variety of objectives—but they have no reference to the waiting line. One of his objectives is to provide assistance to the taxpayer, but this is in the nature of a free service. If the citizen will not come early and if the citizen wants this free service rather than paying for the advice of a tax consultant, he must wait. The waiting line, therefore, is not a problem. The objective of the tax office manager is, so to speak, a reasonable availability of advice for reasonable citizens. There is no objective for "unreasonable" citizens. The bank manager, like the doctor, has an objective of getting the maximum number of customers. He has many competitors who will be delighted to have his customers, and he thinks that long waiting lines are one of the quickest ways to lose customers. Faced with the doctor's argument, he would reply that the patients' payoff is deeply involved in his faith that he has a superb doctor. So the patient will wait, and the waiting line only confirms his evaluation of the quality of the doctor. The bank customer, on the other hand, has no such large payoff from one bank as compared to another. So he will not wait. This is particularly true, since, if anything, waiting is a sign of poor, rather than good bank management. Therefore, the bank manager views waiting lines as impinging directly on his objective and treats the situation as a problem.

This banker's sense of involvement with objectives is an attitude that generally accounts for our selection of the problems with which we try to cope. First and foremost are those problems which have the most direct effect on our objectives. We usually become aware of them first and act on them first. This is natural because we are objective-oriented. The models we find most congenial, and the ones we use the most, are those which help to point out and resolve the problems that have the greatest and the most direct effect on our major objectives. Problems that have a smaller or more indirect effect on our primary objectives are not noticed so quickly. They are not acted upon until priority problems with a more direct or larger effect have been considered.

We are not discussing the question of multiple objectives. Rather, we are considering *problems*. They may have an immediate, direct effect on our objectives or they may have a subsequent and indirect effect. No sharp line of demarcation can be drawn between "indirect" and "smaller." However, by "smaller" effects on our objectives we do not seem to convey all that we mean by "indirect" effects. For example, the entry of a local competitive product in one of our sales regions will have a smaller effect on our objective (maximum sales, maximum profit, and so on) than will the entry of a nationally distributed competitive product in all of our sales regions. But both of these effects are direct ones. On the other hand, an increasing labor turnover in our plant will have a more indirect effect on the objective of maximizing share of the market, although in the long run it could conceivably have a larger effect. This same problem of an increase in labor turnover would have a direct effect on the objective of maximizing profit. A problem relating to financial structure would have an indirect effect on most marketing objectives but a direct effect on the objective of paying a given, or maximum, dividend to stockholders.

As one would expect, the directness or indirectness of the effect of a problem on an objective depends on the objective as well as the problem. The difficulty involved in distinguishing between direct and indirect effects is illustrated by a problem in product quality. A slight decrease in product quality would probably have only an indirect effect on most objectives, but a large decrease would undoubtedly have a direct effect. It is useful to acknowledge that some differences can be defined only in terms of degree.

Let us attempt to define the difference between direct and indirect effects. There is clearly a differentiating element of temporal *immediacy*; the more immediate the more direct. But other characteristics are also involved. These reflect the fact that the awareness of problems increases as they become more related to the objectives. In other words, when objectives are *sensitive* to certain problems, these problems will be noted and acted upon before those with an indirect effect. And, of course, the *size of the effect* must be considered. Problems with a large effect are likely to be observed and acted upon before problems with a relatively smaller effect. With this in mind, why do we observe differences in the procedures that various organizations follow in dealing with problems? This observation remains true even when the problems are similar in type and in their effect on the organization's objectives. Let us consider why this is so.

125 / Problems and the Size of Organizations

The question we have raised above can be typified by an example. Company *A* produces electronic equipment for a *local market*. It is small and profitable. The company has a problem situation in the form of too high a turnover in the plant labor force. Having become aware of the problem, *A*'s plant manager calls a meeting of his foremen and discusses the problem with them for an hour. Finding no answers, he closes the meeting by ordering the installation of a suggestion box. Then he returns hastily to other, more pressing problems. Company *B* produces electronic equipment for the *national market*. It is large and profitable. It, too, has a problem in the form of too high a turnover in the plant labor force. Having become aware of the problem, *B*'s vice-president in charge of production calls in a team of consultants, which includes industrial psychologists, sociologists, and an applied anthropologist. After a reasonably lengthy investigation they will probably make some good recommendations as to how the problem can be resolved. The responses of the two companies to the same problem are totally different.

The kind of situation typified by this example is so common that similar examples are probably familiar to anyone acquainted with organizational realities. Our question is: Why does this difference occur in response to identical problems?

The answer, speaking generally, is that the *returns* that result from solving a problem *tend to be proportional to the size, income, sales, or profit* of the organization, while the *cost* of solving the problem *tends to be a fixed amount*. We want first to justify this answer and then to discuss how it affects organizational attitudes toward problems.

The first part of the answer is that the returns that result from solving a problem tend to be proportional to some measure of the organization's involvement in the area of the problem. Such measures are income, sales, budgets, operating costs, profit, and the like. This requires but little demonstration. An organization with extra labor costs of $100,-000 per year owing to high turnover may save $25,000 or $50,000 from cutting the amount of turnover. But they certainly can't save more than $100,000. Another organization with an extra labor cost of $1,000,000 owing to high turnover could easily save more than $100,000 by cutting the amount of turnover. Furthermore, comparable amounts of improvement in the two organizations would probably save comparable percentages of the respective total extra costs. This is what is meant by the statement that returns tend to be proportional to the measure of the organization involvement in the problem area. The measure of involvement here is the extra cost owing to the high turnover. And lest it be objected that this measure wouldn't be known, let us hasten to add that the same conclusion would follow if total labor costs were used as the measure.

The same kind of argument applies to most kinds of organizational problems. The solution of a marketing problem might increase sales by any reasonable range of amounts, but the increase would generally be proportional to the sales. A company with ten times the annual sales of another company that solved the same problem would probably get about ten times the amount of return in sales units, or about the *same percentage* return. It is exceptions to this statement that demand explanation rather than the statement itself.

The second part of the answer is that the cost of solving a problem tends to be a fixed amount. This requires justification because it is certainly an overgeneralization and is false in some cases. Nonetheless, it is generally a reasonable approximation to the facts. The important word is "tends"—we are not stating an equation. The major reason why the cost of solving a problem tends to be a fixed amount is that the amounts of information and analysis required are more nearly a *function of the problem than they are of the size of the organization* that has the problem.

Consider an analysis of an inventory problem as an example. A small firm may have two or three thousand items in inventory, whereas a large firm may have 200,000. But what will be typically required, in either case, will be a careful analysis of a relatively small selection of items. Once an inventory system has been worked out it will generally be up to the organization's personnel, with a little coaching, to get the system installed so that it covers all the items. Much of the time spent in analysis will be used in careful studies of generic problem characteristics as they apply to the special circumstances and needs of the organization. This represents a general cost of the study which will be applicable regardless of the number of items studied. Add to this the fact that a fair amount of the time will be spent in establishing the necessary working relationships and channels of communication. The result is that a large percentage of the cost of solving the inventory problem is fixed, and only a small percentage depends on the number of items. This is the hallmark of an essentially fixed cost, which is exactly our thesis. Simi-

larly, consider the case of a problem involving the allocation of salesmen's time. The fact that one company has ten times the number of salesmen another company has does not necessarily make the study of the first
company's problem more expensive. The study of customer characteristics will be required in either case and the same mathematical models
will be tried in both cases. The fixed costs, in short, are high. A great
number of organizational problems are of this sort.

There are, of course, problems for which the cost of a solution is
directly proportional to the size of the organization. An outstanding
example of this kind of problem is one in the area of information flow.
These are the problems that prompt systems analysis in the hope of improvement by redesign of the organization's communication network.
The communication network consists of links between various processors
of information. If all possible links existed (between every pair of information-processors) the number of links would increase in proportion
to the square of the number of information processors. Generally this
isn't the case, but the number of links certainly increases at least as fast
as the number of information-processors. The work, and hence cost, of
an analysis of such a system depends on the number of such links. Therefore, a large organization, having more information-processors and more
links, can expect a systems study to cost more money than it would for a
small organization. Despite exceptions, it appears that the majority of
problems are such that their *solutions involve high fixed costs.*

What does this imply in terms of company attitudes to problems?
The main consideration involves company size. Let's take a problem in
marketing for which a solution would involve a 2 per cent increase in
sales for one year. In accord with our argument we will suppose that a
solution will cost $50,000. If we assume a 10 per cent gross profit on sales,
it follows that a company's sales would have to be at least $25,000,000
per year—since ($25,000,000) (0.02) (0.1) = $50,000—before it would be
profitable to undertake the study. Smaller companies would be equally
delighted to gain 2 per cent of their sales by solving the given problem,
but it is simply not economical for them to have it solved. Similarly, in
the case of the two manufacturers of electronic equipment (*A* and *B*),
with which we began this section, equivalent percentage improvements
might result if the problem were solved in the two cases. But the difference in the amount of involvement in the problem area makes it
economical for the larger company to undertake an expensive analysis
of the problem, which would be completely uneconomical for the smaller
company.

This argument, then, serves to explain the reason behind the commonly observed difference in organizational responses to problems.
Managers can be acting with complete rationality but one will initiate an

extensive, and often expensive, search for a solution while another essentially ignores the problem.

Some further ramifications of the same argument are worth discussing. First, we have assumed in the above discussions that the solution to the problem is assured if only the search is undertaken. This, of course, is a bad assumption. A manager's life would be delightfully easy if he knew that each of his problems could be solved by retaining some suitable consultants or by employing his own specialists. Unfortunately, this is far from true. The manager may invest considerable sums in an attempt to solve a problem and may find no solution at all. In this event he still has his problem plus the realization that he has wasted resources in a vain effort to solve it.

In terms of the concepts we have been using, this situation can be expressed by saying that a search for a problem solution has some probability of being successful. The possibility of making an immediate and realistic estimate of this probability must be questioned, but we will reserve our discussion of this intricate subject for subsequent sections of this chapter. For the present it will be sufficient that there is some probability of finding a solution, whether we know what it is or not. Since there is usually a continual succession of problems in any business, it follows that the company has a succession of choices to make. For any problem it can attempt to find the solution, or it can ignore the problem, or it can handle the situation by utilizing its executives' intuition (we will discuss the various alternatives subsequently). At present let us note that there are two available possibilities: (1) undertake a search for the solution to the problem, which will cost some specified sum and which will have some specified probability of success, or (2) do something else that will not involve finding the solution to the problem. This choice is available for each problem and there is a constant succession of problems. So formulated, the situation of a company regarding its problems bears a striking resemblance to that of a gambler making wagers on some chance device. The problems are the successive wagers and, like the gambler, the company is not forced to make a bet. The sum required to search for the problem solution is the amount of the wager, and the return that results if the solution is found represents the amount won if the wager is successful. Finally, the probability that a solution will be found is the probability of winning. The analogy is complete and we might expect that probability theory, which has much to say about gamblers' chances, might have something to say about the company's policy regarding its problems. And in fact it does.

We have not yet taken account of two factors that must be introduced in order to have a reasonably realistic model of the company's situation regarding its succession of problems. However, it will be convenient here to discuss the main aspect of this situation which the probability-theory analysis suggests. In probability theory this problem is treated under the descriptive title, "The Problem of the Gambler's Ruin." The company that is establishing a policy for dealing with its problems is not a gambler, and it is not often in a position where it is really risking ruin by attempting to solve its problems. However, because of the analogies we have pointed out, it is possible to consider the company's situation in the light of the results available from an analysis of this intriguing comparison. The main result for the case of the gambler is that if he has C dollars and wagers one dollar each time with probability p of winning and probability $q = (1 - p)$ of losing, and if he intends to play the game until he has won some amount W, then his probability of ruin (i.e., he loses his C dollars) is

$$\text{Probability of ruin} = \frac{\left(\frac{q}{p}\right)^C \left[1 - \left(\frac{q}{p}\right)^W\right]}{1 - \left(\frac{q}{p}\right)^{C+W}} \qquad \text{(for } p \text{ not equal to } q\text{)}$$

where we are assuming he is playing against a gambling house or an opponent having essentially unlimited resources. The case where $p = q = \frac{1}{2}$, an even game, is much simpler. For this case, using the symbols as before, we have

$$\text{Probability of ruin} = 1 - \frac{C}{C + W}$$

As an illustration, a gambler who has $5 and wants to win $10 in the game of matching pennies for $1 per throw has a probability of ruin of $1 - 5/(5 + 10) = \frac{2}{3}$. In short, the probability that he will lose his $5 (ruin) is $\frac{2}{3}$ and, of course, the probability that he will win $10 is $1 - \frac{2}{3} = \frac{1}{3}$.

In analogy to the case of the company, however, suppose that the gambler has no set sum that he proposes to try to win. The company certainly is not going to stop attempting to solve its problems once it has succeeded in solving a given number of them. In other words, the gambler will play indefinitely. In the case where p does not equal q we find that the probability of ruin for the gambler becomes simply $(q/p)^C$. As would be expected, if q is greater than p (an unfair game) the gambler's ruin is certain (probability equals one). However, somewhat surprising is the fact that when $p = q = \frac{1}{2}$ the probability of ruin is also one. The basis from which this expression has been developed differs from the company's situation in two respects: first, we have assumed p was constant at every trial, which is not true for the company because the probability of achieving a solution will differ with each problem; and second, we have assumed a fixed stake at each wager, whereas for the company the amount risked by the attempt at a solution and the amount to be gained from a solution will differ for each problem. Despite these differences, however, we can still draw a conclusion from the parallel.

The company is not likely to put its entire resources into an effort to find the solution to a specific problem. But as a going enterprise faced with a succession of problems it will probably have a sum of money which it is willing to commit to such research activities. Any amount beyond that sum would require the utilization of funds needed for different purposes, and other company activities would suffer as a result. While the company is unlikely to be ruined, in any literal sense of the term, by the exhaustion of the research budget, it is certainly the case that the research director may be personally "ruined" (lose his job) by such exhaustion of his budget. Therefore, conservative executives could be expected to recognize, and take account of, the fact that the allocation of funds to a search for problem solutions bears a strong family resemblance to the problem facing a gambler with a limited capital. This does not mean that they need to be experts in probability theory. The point is simply that their allocation of such funds should be weighted in the direction indicated by the theory. This direction is given by the probability of ruin for an indefinite number of plays, $(q/p)^C$. In our derivation C represents the number of dollars the gambler has at the start of the game. Nothing is changed if we let the amount wagered be the unit of dollars (instead of one dollar), in which case C is simply the number of units (such as units of $100, $1,000, or $100,000) the gambler has. The probability of losing, q, is ordinarily smaller than the probability of winning, p. Otherwise, the executive would seldom commit his company's resources to the solution of a problem. For this reason the quantity (q/p) is generally less than 1. Therefore, as C gets larger and larger the quantity $(q/p)^C$ gets smaller and smaller. This is as it should be, since the probability of ruin would be expected to decrease as the initial capital, C, increases. But there are two implications we want to stress.

First, for fixed initial capital: as a specific problem requires larger amounts of money for a search for its solution, the probability of finding the solution must be larger in order to maintain a fixed probability of ruin. As an illustration of this, suppose a company has available $100,-000 (or 4 units of $25,000). Assume that the company requires that any research project should have a ruin probability of less than 0.05. Consider a search for a solution that costs $25,000 which would have a return of $50,000 if solved (this is an even-money bet since the net winnings would be $25,000). The company must have a probability of 0.68 or more of finding the solution in order to undertake this project since $\left[\dfrac{0.32}{0.68}\right]^4$ is approximately 0.05. On the other hand, for the same company, if the search costs $50,000 and the return is $100,000 then there must be a probability of more than 0.82 of a solution (since $\left[\dfrac{0.18}{0.82}\right]^2$ is approximately 0.05).

Second, a company with a larger initial capital can support more costly searches for a solution at the same probability of ruin. Alternatively, it can spend the same amount at a lower probability of solution and maintain the same probability of ruin. Thus, a company with $1,000,000 available for problem-solving could maintain the same probability of ruin on the $25,000 expenditure if the probability of a solution were only 0.52 (since $\left[\dfrac{0.48}{0.52}\right]^{40}$ is approximately 0.05). Similarly, the $50,000 expenditure would require the probability of a solution to be about 0.54.

In order to represent the relationships in a more meaningful way we need to generalize the ruin formulation to include the possibility of other than even-money bets. Clearly, we can always take the cost of the search for a solution as our measuring unit. If we do so, then we must express both capital and net return in terms of this unit. Therefore, let

$$C_r = \text{capital ratio} = \frac{\text{capital available for problem-solving}}{\text{cost of search for solution}}$$

and $\quad R_r = \text{return ratio} = \dfrac{\text{return from solution minus cost of search for solution}}{\text{cost of search for solution}}$

Then it can be shown that the probability of ruin will be $m_1{}^{c_r}$ where m_1 is the single root between *zero* and *one* of the equation

$$pm^{R_r+1} - m + q = 0$$

where p is, as previously, the probability of finding the solution and $q = 1 - p$. For any specific values of C_r, R_r, and p, this equation can be solved for m_1 and the probability of ruin will be given by $m_1{}^{c_r}$.

Figure 13.1 shows the relationship between the capital ratio and the return ratio for a probability of ruin fixed at 0.01. The capital ratio is placed on the ordinate scale. The return ratio is placed on the abscissa. Thus, a return ratio of one is the equivalent of an even-money bet. Lines of *iso-p* (equal probability for the successful solution of the problem) are shown in relation to the capital and return ratios. It is important to notice how these lines are asymptotic to particular capital and return ratios. As the p value decreases, the asymptotes move to larger capital and return ratios. On the basis of this figure we can draw several conclusions in addition to the observations we have made previously.

1. For a fixed probability of success (p), there is a return ratio below

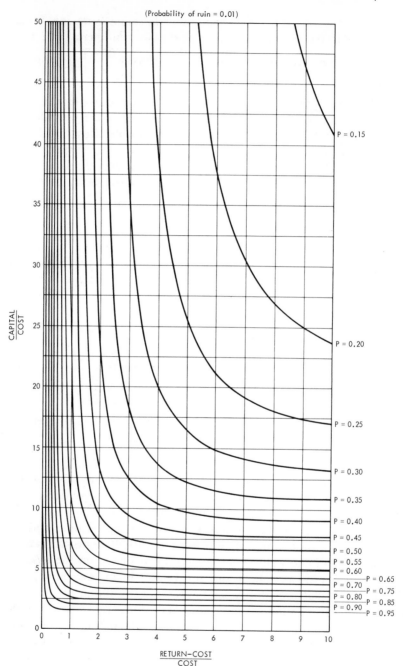

(Probability of ruin = 0.01)

CAPITAL/COST

RETURN−COST/COST

P = 0.15
P = 0.20
P = 0.25
P = 0.30
P = 0.35
P = 0.40
P = 0.45
P = 0.50
P = 0.55
P = 0.60
P = 0.65
P = 0.70
P = 0.75
P = 0.80
P = 0.85
P = 0.90
P = 0.95

*FIGURE 13.1   Lines of equal probability of successfully solving
a problem when the probability of ruin is fixed
at 0.01 for different capital and return ratios.*

which no amount of capital will suffice if a fixed probability of ruin is to be maintained. For example, when $p = 0.6$, then infinite capital would be required to maintain the probability of ruin at 0.01 when the return ratio is $\frac{2}{3}$ or below.

2. For any given capital ratio there is a probability of success that requires an infinite return ratio if the probability of ruin is to be maintained. For example, when the capital ratio is 5, an infinite return ratio is required to maintain the probability of ruin at 0.01, when $p = 0.6$.

Figure 13.2 (see p. 516) provides a different view of the same interrelationships by showing *iso-ruin* curves for a fixed probability of solution of 0.6. These curves illustrate how a demand for a smaller probability of ruin increases the capital required in order to undertake the search for a solution with a given return (and a probability of solution of 0.6). For example, if the return is 1.91, then a ruin probability of 0.01 is maintained when the capital is 6. If it is required that the ruin probability should be 0.0001, then a capital of 12 is required for the same return.

The conclusions that result from our discussion of the probability of ruin add further limits to the expenditures a smaller company can undertake in order to find problem solutions as compared to a bigger company. The introduction of the fact that solutions to problems are not certain results in further limitations on smaller companies because it introduces the possibility of a bad luck streak against which companies must maintain protection in the form of control over their probabilities of ruin.

We have assumed in this argument that there is a probability of finding a solution but that the solution, if found, will permit a fixed gain (or avoidance of a loss). Actually, of course, this is an unlikely state of affairs. Far more usual will be a case where there is some probability distribution of returns if a solution to the problem is found. The range of possible returns would probably start at zero in most cases, since we certainly hope that finding a solution to a problem will not result in a loss beyond the amount spent. For each possible return there would be a probability of achieving such a return if a solution to the problem were found. Such a distribution is difficult to determine but it is not impossible. For our argument above it is sufficient to use the expected or average return of this distribution as equivalent to the fixed return there assumed. However, it is straightforward to incorporate such a probability distribution of returns into the algebraic formulation of the ruin problem. This will produce an algebraic equation of some complexity which is no deterrent in view of computer capabilities.

Two other points remain to be mentioned in this discussion of the effect of company size on the approach to problems. First, most returns

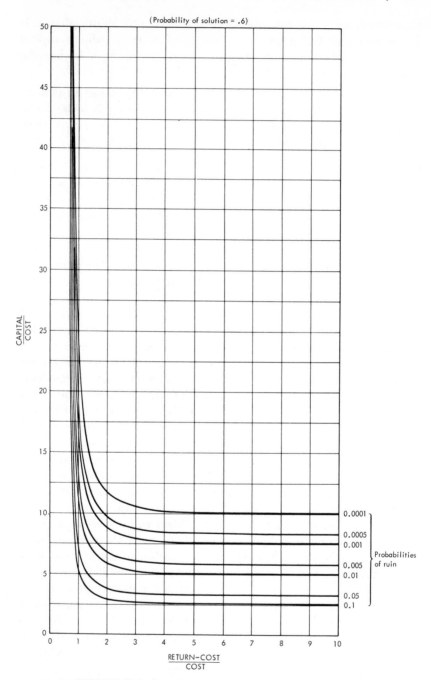

FIGURE 13.2   Iso-ruin curves for probability of solution = .6

from solutions to problems are not lump sums received upon implementation of whatever is indicated by the problem solution. Instead they are in the form of some increment to income over a period of years. Ordinarily, the number of years cannot be assumed to be too great because future changes in conditions will either require a new solution or will render the whole problem irrelevant. But, even so, the future income stream must be discounted back to present worth before any conclusions can be drawn concerning the advisability of searching for a solution. From the standpoint of the smaller company the effect is to require a greater margin of safety (as compared to the larger company) against the possibility of a bad luck streak. The spreading of the possible return over a number of years means that there is less chance of one good solution sustaining the available funds against several failures. Thus, the probability of ruin is increased. This requires a greater relative increase in the safety margin for the smaller company than it does for the larger company.

Second, as soon as probabilities of gains and losses enter the picture the question of the utility of money arises. The effect of the introduction of the utility of money was illustrated by our discussion of the self-insurance problem earlier (see pp. 78–82). The reader will remember that when due account was taken of differing utilities for money the company with larger resources could assume risks that a smaller company could not. Precisely the same effect results in the present case. The introduction of utilities for money will result in the smaller company's having to forego still more searches for solutions to problems which the larger company can undertake easily.

The net effect of all these various factors and influences is that there is a very strong relationship between company size and the problems for which the company can attempt to find solutions. We would not expect, then, to find smaller companies so often undertaking the solution of problems that have an indirect or smaller effect on their objectives. Only large companies can afford to assume the risk of undertaking solution to problems for which the probability of return is low or that have an attenuated, indirect effect on primary objectives.

This is the general background to the question of the allocation of funds for a search for a problem solution. We must now turn to a discussion of some of the specific questions that must be considered in reaching a decision concerning the allocation of such funds.

126/ *Problem-Solving: The Potential Gain*

The decision concerning the allocation of funds for problem-solving is, of course, a decision problem, and one that is similar to the many others we have discussed throughout the book. One difference, however, is that this decision problem is one that the manager often has to block out for himself. It is not uncommon to have a preliminary analysis performed in order to determine the desirability of undertaking some particularly expensive search for a problem solution, but even in this case the manager must himself reach the first decision: to undertake the preliminary investigation.

Having recognized that this is a decision problem, let us try to identify the usual components of a decision problem. First, what are the strategies? This depends on the kind of problem that has arisen. On the one hand it may be some aspect of an organization's operations that has never previously been considered as a problem. An example might be labor turnover in a small- to medium-sized plant. In this case the strategies might consist of (1) continuing to ignore the problem or (2) investing various sums of money in an attempt to solve the problem. On the other hand, there are problems that have always been treated as decision problems but that are now considered to be perhaps worthy of a more careful analysis. The past method of handling the problem may have been some established policy, or an executive may have decided each case on its merits. In this event, the strategies in the decision problem would include (1) the continuation of the previous procedure and (2) the allocation of various sums of money to the solution of the problem. The states of nature are the various possible situations that may pertain to the problem. The payoff is the return that results for the various combinations of strategies and states of nature. It is the payoff that we will now consider.

Many of the decision problems we have discussed have been of a kind in which something positive was definitely going to be done and it was a question of choosing the most profitable or the least costly "something" to do. For example, in an inventory problem there will be some kind of ordering policy. The relevant decision problem is to choose the least costly one. But in the present decision problem the question is, essentially, whether to invest in a search for a solution or not. Since the required investment will ordinarily be fairly well fixed, it follows that we will never make the search unless it is possible that the return can be larger than the cost of the search. We may not attempt to find the solution even if the return can be larger than the cost, but we certainly won't make the search if the return cannot possibly be larger than the cost. Therefore, a reasonable first step is to raise the question: What is the maximum possible return if this problem is solved?

The answer involves a comparison of how the organization stands with regard to the objective affected by the problem and what the organization might conceivably achieve if it tried. It is clear that the latter is more difficult to estimate than the former. But even knowing how the organization stands with regard to some objectives is quite difficult. Any objective that has a natural quantified measure causes no difficulties. A company's position with respect to profit is simply the amount or percentage of profit it is making. How it stands with regard to labor turnover is some suitable measure of turnover like the percentage of new employees per month. But what the company's position is with regard to labor relations, for example, is hard to define. We have already discussed this problem extensively and we will not repeat our remarks here. In the present context, if the objective cannot be quantified then the approach we are developing here cannot be used. We intend to find some measure of the distance separating the actual position of the company from its conceivable position. Distance implies measurement and if the objective cannot be quantified we cannot measure the distance. Therefore, we will assume that the objective in question has a quantitative measure and that the company's actual position with regard to the objective can be determined.

The more difficult part of the question is that dealing with what the company might conceivably achieve. There are two major ways (three, if we include executive experience and intuition) by which the best conceivable position of the company with regard to the objective might be determined. An analogy from a different field suggests the first method. An engineer who designs steam engines is interested in measuring their efficiency. He can do this very easily because the basic laws of thermodynamics imply a top efficiency beyond which no engine can possibly go. This, then, represents a theoretical maximum for any steam engine. Are there any such theoretical maxima for organizations? If there are any, then these would supply an upper (or lower) limit to the conceivable position of the company.

The answer is that there are such absolute maxima for organizations as well as for steam engines. As a matter of fact, there are quite a large number of them. Some of them are tritely obvious, but others are far from trite or obvious. Obvious ones come from areas where achievement can be measured in percentages of some total amount which cannot be bigger than 100 per cent nor smaller than 0 per cent. For example, labor turnover, readers of a magazine who notice an advertisement, potential customers reached by an advertising campaign, percentage defectives in production, and many similar kinds of measures have theoretical maxima or minima of 100 per cent or 0 per cent.

Many times, there is no such theoretical limit and it is necessary to try the second method: use data that show the positions of other organizations with regard to the objective in question. The maximum or minimum obtained in practice can be used as an approximation to the limit.

Such data are often available from trade associations; they sometimes appear in annual reports, or they may be found in special studies. The more similar the other organizations, the more reliable the extrapolation, but for many objectives it is possible to establish empirical limits on the basis of data from quite dissimilar organizations. For such measures as inventory turnover, sales per dollar of advertising, labor turnover, and many measures of rates of return it is usually possible to determine practical upper and lower limits in this manner.

Finally, of course, if no other limit can be obtained the manager can use his own experience as a guide for estimating the limit of possible improvement. It is important to have some kind of estimated limit because of the obvious, but sometimes overlooked, fact that no search for a solution should be undertaken unless it is at least possible to gain a return from the solution that exceeds the cost of the search. Once a limit has been established, the distance separating the actual position from the limit gives the maximum possible improvement as a result of solving the problem. Of course, the problem may not be solved, and even if it is solved the actual improvement will probably fall far short of the maximum possible improvement. But the knowledge that an upper bound exists to the return from a solution is, nonetheless, a necessary component of this decision problem. When the upper limit has been determined, it is then necessary to estimate the actual returns that may be achieved. We now proceed to a discussion of this difficult question.

127/ What Is a Problem-Solution Worth?

This question is obviously a complex one. But it is equally obvious that it is the key to a rational analysis of the decision problem of whether or not to undertake a search for a solution. The main difficulty results from the large variety of ways in which the manager might profit from a search for a solution. Let us list some of them.

1. He may profit from the mere fact of a search for a solution even if no solution is found. For example, a study of productive efficiency sometimes results in greater efficiency purely because of the response of the personnel to the fact that their efficiency is being studied.

2. He may profit from a search that doesn't find a solution by discovering that some factor he had been considering important is not so important. As a result, he will no longer have to worry about that factor. For example, a company that undertakes a study to minimize direct-mail duplication may not discover the solution, but

as a result of the investigation it may learn that duplication is not large enough to warrant further attention.

3. He may profit because the range of the possible states of nature is narrowed. Any successful search for improved predicting methods is an example.

4. He may profit because the number of strategies that he needs to consider is decreased. Often this results because the complex system involved in the problem is found to depend on some key component. Only those strategies which affect this key part need be considered. For example, a study of consumer response to product characteristics may show that some one aspect of the product is of overwhelming importance. This would eliminate the need to consider various marketing strategies that would otherwise be considered.

5. He may profit by discovering a more suitable measure of effectiveness.

6. He may profit by obtaining good estimates of the probabilities of the states of nature. An example would be that of a company considering a sizable expansion in a foreign country. Such a company might undertake a study to ascertain the probabilities of war, revolution, socialization, and other relevant states of nature.

7. He may profit by discovering the correct evaluation of the payoff measure. As an example we can cite studies made of the optimal allocation of salesmen's time in which it has been found that the payoff measure (sales, for example) is related to the allocation of time in ways that are far from obvious.

Still other kinds of returns from solutions could be given. But it is not worthwhile to try listing all of them, even assuming that this could be done. We cannot discuss every possible gain that might be derived from a search for a solution. The important thing to note is that the process of searching for a solution can produce peripheral benefits that help justify the decision to solve the problem. In other cases, the side effects may not be beneficial. This occurs, in particular, when an efficient process must be disturbed to collect information necessary for the solution of the problem. The decision-maker must consider the pros and cons of the side effects that might result from the decision to solve a problem.

Basically, the value of a solution can be treated in much the same way as any other value problem. We can distinguish at least three different types of value situations. In the first place, we have the situation in which the solution to a problem has a value determined by the supply and demand for solutions. For example, the demand for oil and the frequency with which varying quantities of oil are found permit us to specify the value of this solution. Similarly, the value of the solution to the problem of finding an adequate number of engineers depends upon the supply of engineers and the company's demand for them. The second type of value situation is the one in which there is an imputed value for the solution that is independent of the supply and demand for such solutions. For example, when an air-sea rescue operation is undertaken to locate a pilot downed at sea, the combined cost of all of the equipment and personnel employed in the search provides at least a lower bound for the imputed value of the pilot's life. In business, imputed values must be used when a numerical equivalent cannot be found. This is the case for employee morale, company goodwill, community relations, and so forth. The third type of value situation we will mention is one in which the value of the solution is basically a measure of improved efficiency. As we have previously stated, it is sometimes possible to estimate an upper limit for efficiency, in which case, if the organization knows its present efficiency it is able to estimate the probable value of a solution. The estimate depends upon the anticipated effectiveness of the strategies (techniques) that will be employed. Consequently, the appraisal of techniques is of great importance in the estimation of the value of a solution.[1] With standard techniques and methods, and an evaluation of the data that are used, it is possible to estimate the degree to which the best possible result will be approximated. With nonstandard techniques, it is necessary to approach this problem in stages. At each stage, the previous results and additional information gained can be used to reestimate the probable value of the solution that will result if the problem-solving procedure is continued.

It is not unusual for the solution of one problem to bring to light the value to be gained from solving another problem. However, many problems are not involved in such mutual relationships, and it is necessary to find still other means for estimating the worth of a solution.

The general procedure we would like to be able to follow is clear. We must attempt to estimate the payoffs that result from solutions. Since we will often have an estimate of the maximum possible improvement that could result, it may be most convenient to express the different payoffs as percentages of this maximum. Then, by determining the effect of a percentage-point improvement on some convenient dollar measurement (sales, costs, profit, and the like), it will be possible to convert the payoff measures to dollars, which can be included directly with the dollar cost of the search in evaluating the expected returns of the strategies. This,

---

[1] Chapter 14 presents such evaluation of O.R. techniques. Also, see Section 86 on the value of information.

of course, is far easier said than done, but it is quite straightforward for many problems. In estimating the payoffs it is often possible to utilize published studies showing the improvements that resulted from similar searches for solutions. In this context it may be noted that the smaller organization has an advantage here. In accordance with our previous argument it is likely that the smaller organization will be dealing with problems that have a direct and large effect on its primary objectives. These are the problems which have most often been handled by other organizations and, hence, for which the greatest amount of information on resulting improvements is available. The larger organization may be dealing with a specialized problem that has never, or rarely, been dealt with before. This makes it more unlikely that any significant amount of information concerning improvements will be available.

One rule of thumb is worth noting in connection with the fact that some problems have always been recognized as being decision problems (although no formal search has been made to find a solution); others have not been considered to be decision problems. The first kind of problem will have had the attention of a decision-maker. If he has had the benefit of an accurate measure of the payoff from his decisions he will have had the opportunity to develop his own methods for approaching an optimal selection of strategy. Under usual conditions he will have done so—and with a fair degree of success if the problem is not exceedingly complex. Thus, a solution for a problem of this kind is not likely to produce nearly so much improvement as will a solution to the other kind of problem.

To illustrate the difference we will contrast three problems. First, consider a transportation problem involving factories and warehouses. Here the costs are given and the total cost of any shipping strategy is immediately available. Any conscientious manager would approach the minimum-cost strategy for this problem, over a period of time, even for a large number of factories and warehouses. Second, consider an inventory problem. Here the manager will rarely receive the information necessary to completely evaluate his own decisions. He will not, therefore, be so likely to improve his decisions beyond a certain point—even with practice. Third, consider a problem in plant location that has never arisen before. Clearly, there is no basis for improving performance on such a unique problem. Generally speaking, the relative improvements resulting from solutions will be smaller in the first case, larger in the second, and largest in the third. We must emphasize the word "relative." It means the improvement as a percentage of the cost of the decision-maker's unaided decision. We cannot say anything about the absolute improvements because this measure depends on the specific circumstances of the problems. The moral is simple: Never underestimate the ability of the manager to approach the optimal strategy *if* he is given an adequate feedback of information.

In the attempt to evaluate the return from a solution, one of the greatest difficulties results from the fact that a solution may be found but the determining factors may be outside the manager's control. This would essentially eliminate the possibility of a return from the solution. For example, the labor-turnover problem might be analyzed at considerable expense only to find that the main contributing factors were sociological conditions over which the organization had no control. There is no certain way of handling this difficulty, but it is possible in many cases to estimate the hazard. Usually, the manager has reasonable knowledge of the factors that he controls. This being so, he may be able to discover, either from his own organization's experience or from that of similar ones:

1. That the quantitative measure of his objective in the past has varied, while the factors under his control remained essentially constant, or

2. That the quantitative measure of his objective in the past has remained fairly constant, while the factors under his control varied.

In either case, one can assume that the factors under his control are not sufficient to determine the objective measure (payoff). Hence, there is a good chance a solution will disclose that the important factors in determining his payoff are outside his control. However, it is known that feedback systems can produce variation although a constant strategy is being maintained. In this case, the lack of sufficient information about the system could mislead the decision-maker into believing that he has no control over the situation, when in fact he does have control but he doesn't know how it works.

Similarly, there is a problem with respect to the second point. The quantitative measure of the objective may remain constant while the control factors are varied, but the time lag may be so great that the effect of varying the controls cannot be observed. For example, changing advertising effort may not affect short-term sales but may profoundly affect long-term sales. Consequently, the manager must evaluate the kind of situation that prevails when he attempts to determine how much control he exercises in obtaining a solution. This question of control is examined at some length in Chapter 15.

Whenever a situation arises in which the decision-maker appears to have no strategy available that will permit him to utilize the results of a solution, the value of that solution would be nil. For example, the fact that a company knows who its potential customers are will be of limited value unless specific means are available for reaching these customers. If no medium exists that includes a larger proportion of potential customers in its audience than exists in the general population, the characterization of potential customers is valueless—at least for selecting optimal media. Sometimes persistence and imagination can succeed in devising a strategy that will give value to a solution. This depends on the caliber of the men who attempt to resolve the problem. It is not our intention to discuss such questions as the kind of men needed to provide creative and resourceful ideas with respect to the utilization of solutions. Still, the value of a solution will frequently increase because an ingenious way has been found for putting the result to work.

One additional factor should be mentioned that affects the value of a solution. Competitive incentives exist that are difficult to evaluate. Many times a value must be imputed for being the first to achieve something. Frequently, a company that is second, benefits at the expense of the first. In many other cases, the advantage of being first gives the company that pioneers the solution a lead that cannot be overcome. The position of a company with respect to its competitors and the characteristics of the market must, therefore, be considered when attempts are made to place a value on a solution.

We can see that the value of a solution is a function of many factors. If it can be represented on a single scale, such as dollars, then a direct decision can be made among possible alternative problems to be studied. If it is not possible to estimate the value of a solution on a single scale, then it is necessary to use the methods we have discussed for comparing outcomes in terms of the multiple objectives of the organization.

PROBLEMS

1. How does the right to obtain a patent affect the value of a company being first with a solution? Discuss.

2. Why do many large companies follow very liberal policies with respect to granting other companies the right to use the patents they hold? Discuss.

3. What advantages and disadvantages are there in letting a competitor have a large research budget while your company puts equivalent sums into advertising? Discuss.

4. Based on the effects of problem-solving on large and small organizations, what arguments pro and con can be developed for federal, state, or municipal government being responsible for:
   a. Pollution control?
   b. Medical research?
   c. Urban development?
   d. Transportation and communication regulation?

e. Outer space systems?

Now examine the same problem areas with respect to private industry, university participation, or private foundation operations.

5. How do small and large system considerations affect military research?

6. a. All of the hospitals in a large metropolitan area are overcrowded. Is this a problem? Discuss in rational terms.

b. Is overpopulation a problem in all parts of the world? Discuss.

c. Why is it that the pollution problem did not exist in the 1950's?

7. You are involved in seeking a site for a jet airport to service a large metropolitan center. Lay out the nature of the problem you face.

8. A severe water shortage is alleviated in a certain region of the country when Nature brings a long-standing drought to an end. As a result, all emergency procedures are canceled. What happened to the problem that existed before the rains came? *

9. What problems are brought to mind by the concept of desalinization?

10. How is problem-solving related to roulette?

11. Suppose you are responsible for the advertising and promotion of an expensive imported brandy. How would you assess the potential worth of a large-scale market study that undertakes to define your potential customers?

12. Suppose you must decide whether to accept or reject a lot of 100 expensive electrical components for use in our space exploration program. You can sample the lot, but each item sampled is destroyed by the test. Explain your analysis of this situation in order to decide how to proceed.

13. A company has $100,000 available for research in problem solutions. Use Figure 13.1 to determine the returns it would have to receive, for each of the probability curves, to justify the investment of $10,000 in a search for a solution. Do the same thing for an investment of $20,000. How does the ratio of the returns necessary in the two cases change as the probability of a return decreases?

14. For a constant investment of $10,000 and a constant return of $50,000, what amounts of capital are necessary for each of the probability curves?

15. For a fixed return of $50,000 and a capital of $100,000, what investment is justifiable for each of the probability curves?

16. A company with $100,000 available for research in problem solutions is willing to invest $10,000 in a search for a solution which will return $20,000 (its investment plus an equal amount) with probability of 0.574.

a. What probability of ruin is the company accepting?

b. What probability should this company expect for a return of $40,000 on an investment of $20,000 in order to have the same probability of ruin?

17. The reasoning we followed, based on the idea of the ruin probability, has a

---

* During the shortage it was maintained that more reservoirs were needed. To this suggestion someone responded "Why do we need more reservoirs? The ones we have aren't full!" Comment on this argument.

much more general applicability than the one we have emphasized in this chapter. Consider, for example, an investment in a small business. The business may be profitable over a long enough period of time but the earnings may be quite variable over any short period of time. We cannot reflect the actual situation very well with only the methods developed in this chapter but some of the characteristics of the situation can be approximated. We will assume that the payment of monthly costs of the business is the "bet" and that the return is an amount which equals the monthly costs plus gross profit. We will further assume that there is a fixed expected return, $E(R)$, which results from two possible outcomes: R with probability p, and o with probability $1 - p$. Then we can reflect different variabilities in return by selecting different values of R and p. Thus $R = 2,000$ and $p = \frac{1}{2}$; $R = 1,500$ and $p = \frac{2}{3}$; $R = 1,200$ and $p = \frac{5}{6}$; all have $E(R) = \$1,000$. Obviously, the variability is greater when the probability is smaller.

    a. Suppose monthly expenses are $1,000 per month. Suppose that the expected return is $1,200 per month (by our definition this means a gross profit of $200). How much capital would be required to maintain the probability of ruin at 0.01 in each of the following cases:

RETURN	PROBABILITY
$1,333	0.90
1,500	0.80
1,600	0.75
1,714	0.70
2,000	0.60
2,400	0.50
3,000	0.40
4,000	0.30

    b. Suppose a single owner has $10,000 and that monthly expenses are $1,000 per month. If he wishes to maintain a probability of ruin of 0.01, what combinations of amount, and probability, of return are satisfactory for him?

18. Many companies have stenographic pools to handle all dictation and typing required by their executives. On the one hand this saves money by cutting down the total number of typists and/or stenographers required. On the other hand this eliminates all, or the majority, of private secretaries for the executives. Since a private secretary is often considered to be a major symbol of a certain degree of status many executives intensely dislike such pools. How would you analyze the decision problem "To pool or not to pool"?

    a. How would you get rough estimates of the money savings?

    b. How does the size of the company affect the problem?

    c. Could executives be split into two classes: those who use the pool and those who have private secretaries? How would you draw the line?

19. The idea of status seems simple but it is difficult to define satisfactorily. We will assume that status is *solely* a function of position in the organizational

hierarchy. Suppose an organization has seven top executives, and consider the following three structures:

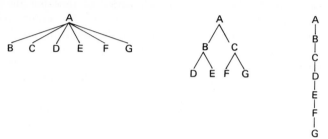

a. How would you define status? (Try to assign some kind of numerical measure.)

b. Which structure has the greatest total status (for all executives)?

c. Is the status of A different in the three cases?

d. Let us assume that executives at the second level hope to get increases in status during their professional life. Assume that a vacancy at the top level has a probability of $\frac{1}{4}$ of being filled outside the organization and that the remaining $\frac{3}{4}$ is divided equally among the subordinates of the immediately lower level. What structure gives the largest expected status for an executive of the second level?

e. Suppose the company has a total amount of $210,000 which it can pay these executives. How would you set the salary limitations for the various positions in the three structures? Are the salaries you assigned related to status as you defined it? If so, which is the cause and which is the effect, or what is the relationship, if not causal?

20. New York State (and several other states) has a lottery which is intended to produce income for education. About 30% of the money paid for lottery tickets is distributed as prizes. Obviously, the total amount paid out in prizes could be distributed in an enormous number of ways. For example, if there were to be prizes totalling $1 million, there could be one prize of $1 million; 10 prizes of $100,000; 100,000 prizes of $10; or any other arrangements.

a. How would you approach the problem of determining the optimal distribution of prizes?

b. Do you think the optimal distribution would change as the total amount to be distributed in prizes changes? If so, how?

c. If you were managing the lottery would you undertake a search for a solution to the problem of determining the optimal arrangement of prizes? What is your argument?

21. A bank manages a large number of pension portfolios. It has a huge total investment—say $100 million—in one large company's common stock. The bank has three analysts who are full-time analysts of the company's prospects and management argues that this is justified by the size of its investment. Is the argument correct? How should the total amount of analysts' time devoted to this company be determined?

22. You are the sales manager, in the United States, for an expensive imported French champagne. Your yearly advertising budget is $100,000 to support yearly sales of $2,000,000, with contributory profit of $200,000. There has never been a market study of the potential customers for this champagne. Such a study has been suggested. How could the total amount of analysts' time that should be devoted to such a study be determined?

Chapter *14*

Evaluation

of

Methods

In this chapter we want to present an overview of the various methods and models of operations research. Many of these operations-research methods were used in our analysis of some typical decision problems in Part IV but we did not emphasize there that certain specific operations-research techniques were being used.

One of the theses of this book is that operations-research methods can be understood only in terms of the broader subject of which they constitute a highly developed part. This broader subject is, of course, decision theory. We tried, in Part IV, to show how the logic of the decision problem in question accounted for the specific method used to solve the problem. This has naturally resulted in a greater emphasis on the structure of the decision problem and a lesser emphasis on the method of a solution as a separate subject.

In the last chapter, however, we saw that any evaluation of the probable returns resulting from a search for a solution to a decision problem requires some estimate of the likelihood that the problem will be solved. The estimate can hardly be made without some understanding of the kinds of tools and techniques available. These tools and techniques are the methods and models of operations research; we will try to present a description of them here.

128/ The Similarities of Problems

The reader has doubtless noticed some similarities among the various problems we discussed in Part IV. One of the most interesting and important characteristics of problems is the way in which they often fall into clusters. The problems within a cluster are by no means identical but they do have some basic, underlying, structural similarity. For example, the repairmen problem, discussed in Chapter 10, basically involves finding the right number of men to handle the work load created by machine breakdowns. And, of course, the "right number of men" is that number which minimizes the total cost. Now, problem 9 at the end of this chapter is a work-pool problem. Given a total number of men who are needed to operate a given number of machine tools, and given that some of the men are likely to be absent on any one day, it follows that the employer ought to have some extra number of men on the permanent payroll, so that all of the machine tools will have operators each day, despite absences. How many "extra" men should be hired? Clearly, this problem is structurally similar to the repairmen problem despite many differences in detail. Again, problem 8 at the end of this chapter, an over-time problem, is of the same general structure. The similarity of these problems results in the use of similar arguments in solving them. This, in itself, is a useful insight since it suggests that a procedure used in solving one problem may work for a different problem, provided it is "similar" in some sense to the first problem. It will be worth considering just what we mean by "similar" in this context.

It is clear that quite a great number of elements that distinguish one problem situation from another do not have any effect on the problem structure itself. For example, the inventory problem of one supermarket will be very similar to that of another supermarket, even though the second one is owned by a different company and is located in a different city, and it will be similar to the inventory problem of a large chain drug store, even though the items carried will be quite different. Furthermore, it will be similar to the inventory problem of a department store, or of a warehouse, or of a factory maintaining an inventory of its finished products. Yet the warehouse and the factory are not even meeting the demand of the ultimate consumer, as all the others are. Despite the differences there is an underlying similarity in all the cases. On the basis of this similarity we would all unhesitatingly refer to each of these cases as an *inventory problem*. And it is this similarity that we would like to understand a little better.

In the example we are considering, the similarities among the various specific cases cited are apparent. In every case the problem is the maintenance of a supply of some item or items, where the item is a physical thing. The reason for maintaining the supply is to meet future demand for the item. These two statements seem to outline the problem. The reason such things as store location, kind of store, and kind of item do not affect the problem is that they are irrelevant to the two characteristics we have abstracted. The relationship of demand to the problem is somewhat different. Demand is mentioned explicitly in the second statement and is therefore directly involved in the problem. The difference in kind of demand in the cases of the warehouse and the factory will therefore be incorporated in the analysis of the problem in the form of assumptions, or as empirically determined facts, about the nature of demand. In each of the cited cases, then, we find the same two characteristics: the maintenance of a supply of some physical item to meet future demand.

But do these two characteristics really describe the inventory problem? Those situations which have these two features appear to be inventory problems, but are there any inventory problems that do not have these two features? In mathematical terminology, we agree that the two characteristics in question are sufficient conditions (their occurrence is sufficient to ensure that we have an inventory problem) but are they necessary (must every inventory problem have these two features)? The answer to this question is mainly a semantic one. After all, we are only defining a term and we can define it pretty much as we please. But since we would like to be able to communicate ideas with other people it is desirable that our definitions of familiar terms, like "inventory problem," should not diverge too widely from accepted usage. With this in mind it appears that our two statements do represent necessary and sufficient features of an inventory problem. However, we can make one significant change in the first statement without distorting the usual conception of an inventory problem. We can remove the restriction that there must be a supply of some physical thing. Let us, instead, say that the problem may be one of maintaining a supply of anything at all. This change doesn't seem to affect the idea of an inventory problem in any significant way, but it does disclose the fact that there are a host of other kinds of situations that are inventory problems. As examples we can cite such things as a company's maintenance of liquid assets to meet future demand, the maintenance of an inventory of plant capacity, the maintenance of an inventory of able junior executives, the maintenance of an inventory of research projects, and many others. Problem 10, at the end of this chapter, provides another example. The problem deals with hotel reservations but it is clearly an inventory problem. The hotel must maintain a sufficient inventory of reservations. All of these diverse kinds of problems, together with the more usual ones mentioned earlier, fall into the general category of inventory problems.

Let us take another example of a class of problems with an underlying similarity. Consider the problem of having sufficient toll booths on a superhighway to receive the payments of all the drivers. First, let us note that this is clearly an inventory problem: to maintain a sufficient supply of toll booths to meet the demand of the motorists. The reason for discussing this particular subclass of the inventory problem separately will be given later in this chapter. The problem on the superhighway would certainly be essentially the same as the problem of having sufficient toll booths for a bridge or for a tunnel. Let us try to characterize the problem in general terms. Something (we aren't going to restrict it to motorists) comes to a facility at which the something in question is delayed for some reason. Then our something leaves the facility which is now free for any subsequent somethings. The problem is to determine the number of facilities necessary. Of course, the reason for the delay at the facility is that some kind of transaction takes place there. Since the transaction is often a service, this class of problems can be called *servicing problems*. Great numbers of problems fit our general description. As examples we can cite the supply of tables to restaurant customers, of teller windows to bank customers, of clerks to store customers, of landing strips to incoming airplanes, of loading docks to trucks, of berths for ships, of repairmen for broken machines, of telephone lines to callers, and many others. All of these problems have the general characteristics given above. In each case the "something" is different, the facility is different, and the service is different. Yet the underlying similarity remains. They are all examples of servicing problems.

The fact that we have shown two examples of classes of problems that are seemingly diverse and yet have an underlying similarity tells us very little about "similarity." How many other such classes of problems are there? How can we discover new ones? We would like to be able to answer questions such as these. But, to come right to the point, we cannot answer these questions. The two examples given above were chosen because analysis of these two kinds of similarity has led to a large number of methods and procedures for handling the corresponding decision problems. And there are some other classes of problems with an underlying similarity that have also permitted the development of some methods for handling the related decision problems. But there are many other classes of problems that seem to have the same kind of underlying similarity but that have not proved at all fruitful in terms of discovering procedures for coping with the corresponding decision problems. Thus, we can say that many companies are striving to minimize costs, or we can say that many are trying to maximize profit, or we can say that many are trying to utilize their total resources in an optimal manner, and we could cite numerous examples of each of these kinds of behavior, but none of these similarities leads to any kind of procedure for dealing with the decision problems.

Of course, discussion in terms of any one of these statements may give rise to some useful insights, but it doesn't lead to any specific methods for dealing with the decision problems. It may be observed that all three of these similarities among companies are of the nature of objectives rather than problems. This is true, but it does not explain the difference. By rephrasing, an objective can be converted into a problem. Thus, how should we minimize costs? How should we maximize profits? How should we utilize our resources? There are many other kinds of underlying similarities that are not related to objectives and that have not been fruitful in leading to procedures for handling the decision problems. For example, some industries take a basic raw material and process it into a number of products. Examples are oil refining, the dairy industry, the meat packing industry, and the lumber industry. Other industries take a number of components and assemble them into a finished product. The automobile industry is a sufficient example. Now, these are certainly two very basic underlying similarities among industries. Yet this fact has not led to the development of decision-problem methods, however much it may contribute to the understanding of one of the industries.

Examples of this sort could be multiplied indefinitely. There is no way of telling in advance which similarities will be fruitful and which will not. The reason seems to be related to a famous rule which was much quoted by medieval philosophers and logicians. They observed that a concept, "dog" for example, had two inversely related aspects. First, it covered a number of specific examples (all dogs, for our example). They called the number of specific exemplifications of a concept *the extension of the concept.* Second, there would be a number of things that could be said about the concept (all dogs are mammals, and so on). They called the number of things that could be said about the concept *the intension of the concept.* Now, their rule was: *the greater the extension, the less the intension and the greater the intension, the less the extension.* This is just another way of saying that if you talk about everything you can't say very much and if you say a great deal about something then you aren't covering very much. We can't say nearly as much about dogs in general as we can about the particular one at our heels (because everything we can say in general can be said about the particular dog) but what we say about the particular dog doesn't tell us about dogs in general (because that is what makes him particular). This little excursion in old-fashioned logic will serve to highlight the same kind of problem in our discussion of similarities. If we start with too general a similarity we can't say much about it. But if we start with too specific a similarity we don't cover many cases. The fruitfulness of an observed similarity depends on striking a happy medium (the medieval scholars would have called it a golden mean) between the extension and the intension of the similarity. And this depends on the creativeness of the observer and analyst of the similarity. What one person rejects as not being fruitful another person may use to develop a host of valuable insights and methods. We cannot hope to predict the kinds of similarities that may be found fruitful in the future. We must, therefore, be content to discuss those kinds of similarities which have been proved useful by considerable amounts of practice.[1]

This entire book is devoted to the development of one kind of similarity: the similarity among decision problems. This particular similarity covers an enormous range of cases (large extension) and yet a great deal can be said about it (large intension). It seems to have a very good balance between these opposing "costs" (extension and intension). This is why it can provide a unifying theory for so many different areas. But we now want to discuss some other similarities which have less extension but a correspondingly greater intension.

The most fruitful among such similarities are those which are at the roots of the best-known operations-research techniques. Each one is the nucleus from which have developed a number of specific techniques, methods, and models. We intend to discuss each of the major clusters of techniques with the dual purpose of providing a basic understanding of the techniques and of furnishing a basis for appraising the likelihood of successful applications of the techniques to specific decision problems.

129/ Inventory Models

We have already discussed various aspects of inventory models in our analysis of some kinds of inventory problems in Part IV, and we have considered other aspects in the preceding section. At the cost of some repetition we will summarize those earlier discussions here.

The underlying similarity of inventory models is that they all deal with problems associated with storing something to meet future demand. As we have seen, there is no need to restrict the application of these models to the storage of physical things, which is the most common kind of inventory problem. We can talk equally well of the storage of capital, of plant capacity, and of similar kinds of intangibles. The problem of inventory decisions is suggested by the following two questions. First, why store any of the things in question at all? Second, why not store an enormous amount, enough to meet any conceivable demand for a long period of time? The answer to these questions is that we can't act in either of these ways because there are costs associated with storing and costs associated with not storing. Either of these two extreme solutions would be too costly. Of course, in the general case the costs may have

---

[1] In Chapter 7 we attempted to catalogue some of these similarities according to their characteristics.

to be measured in utilities rather than in dollars, but the statement remains correct in either case.

The fact that there are costs associated with storing and with not storing immediately suggests that the decision problem of how much to store can be formulated in terms of the minimization of the sum of these two kinds of costs, which we can call the *total costs*. The costs associated with storing obviously increase as the amount stored increases. The costs associated with not storing decrease as the amount stored increases. The total costs are, therefore, a function of the amount stored, and the decision problem is to determine that amount to be stored which minimizes these total costs. Any specific inventory decision problem therefore requires the determination of the relationship between amount stored and these costs before it can be resolved. This requires three logically distinct steps: first, the identification of the relevant cost components; second, the measurement of the costs; and third, the determination of the relationship between the amount stored and the costs. We must now discuss these steps.

The identification of the relevant costs is not difficult ordinarily, but there is always a risk that one of them may be overlooked. This risk can be minimized by following a logical analysis of the costs and seeing which ones among the logical possibilities are applicable to a specific inventory problem. The basis of this logical analysis of costs is that one of the outstanding features of any inventory problem is its dependence on time. This much is implied by the very statement of the underlying structure: the maintenance of a supply to meet *future* demand. It is, therefore, always necessary in inventory problems to consider the effect on the costs of changes over time. Basically, the costs come in pairs: one increases as the amount increases, and the other decreases as the amount increases. There are two such pairs. We will phrase our discussion in terms of the usual kind of inventory problem.

The first arises from the fact that we have to maintain sufficient stock to meet demand, which may be either known certainly or else known only in the form of a probability distribution. Since demand occurs over time, we have a great number of ways in which to maintain stock. We could obtain small amounts very frequently, or we could obtain larger amounts less frequently. The two associated costs are the *procurement cost* and the *carrying cost*. The procurement procedure might be to produce the item in question, in which case we speak of the set-up cost involved in changing the production process to produce the item. Or it might be to order the item, in which case we speak of the ordering cost, which includes all the costs attendant upon processing an order. In either case, this cost increases as the amount ordered decreases since this requires more procurements per unit of time. The carrying costs include all costs of storage, insurance, depreciation, obsolescence, spoilage or theft, loss of interest on capital, and the like. These costs, and hence the total carrying cost, increase as the amount stored increases. Since loss of interest on capital is ordinarily expressed as a percentage of the amount invested it is important to consider any possible changes in price of the item in the future. It is also possible to decrease the amount invested by taking advantage of any quantity discounts or quantity savings on transportation charges. These, then, are the component costs of the pair of costs associated with the process of maintaining a supply to meet the demand over time.

The other pair of costs arise in those cases where demand is not known certainly. In this case two new possibilities arise. First, we may not have sufficient stock to meet the demand. Second, we may have too much stock, more than the demand. The first kind of cost is called the *back-order cost,* because in retailing any excess demand appears in the form of orders that cannot be filled until new stock is obtained by "ordering back" to get more stock. A variety of costs may be components of the back-order cost. First, the sale may be irrevocably lost with an attendant loss of the profit that could have been made. Second, there may be a considerable loss in the goodwill of the customer who was unable to obtain immediately what he wanted. Third, there is a cost associated with processing the special order required to get more stock and this cost, because of the speed required, may be greater than the usual order cost. Fourth, there will usually be expediting costs associated with trying to induce the supplier to act with more speed than usual. Fifth, there will usually be extra transportation costs. All of these costs enter into the back-order cost. This cost decreases as the amount of stock increases because there is clearly less chance of running out of stock in a period of time if there is a greater supply on hand.

The opposing costs here are the *carrying cost,* discussed before and still operative, and the *overstock cost* which results from having too much stock. Actually, we could achieve greater symmetry by defining the overstock cost to include the carrying costs but it is convenient to use the term "overstock cost" to designate a special, and important, cost which is not always relevant. For many items the only penalty for having too much stock is that it will be carried longer. The extra stock from one period can always be used in a subsequent period. However, for some items the demand is limited to a certain period of time and any stock on hand at the end of the period will have to be disposed of for a fraction of its cost. Examples are women's fashion goods, some kinds of children's toys, and the generator spare-part problem we discussed in Chapter 10. The cost associated with the disposal of such items is the overstock cost. Clearly, this cost increases as the amount carried increases. The two pairs of costs we have discussed include all the costs relevant to an inventory problem.

The next question concerns the measurement of the costs. Under ordinary circumstances the first pair of costs, carrying costs and procurement costs, can be determined from cost-accounting data. This means that for any inventory problem *where the demand is certain* the costs can be determined, since only these two costs are involved. Exceptions do occur, however. Thus, the cost which represents the loss of the use of the capital tied up in inventory can be difficult to measure satisfactorily because it is really an opportunity cost. Similarly, the procurement cost includes components that are opportunity costs. Since opportunity costs are defined in terms of the best possible use of resources it can be very difficult to estimate them if, as is usually the case, the best use of resources is not certain. In this case we have available the method presented in Chapter 10 which permits the executive to select directly the combination of total carrying costs and total procurement costs that he believes is most suitable for the company. In essence this procedure imputes a value to the ratio of the two costs but does not require direct estimates of the costs.

Let us consider the other pair of costs. In many cases the overstock cost can be determined directly from the records of losses suffered in past disposals of overstock items. Unfortunately, the situation with regard to the back-order cost is not so straightforward. All of the elements of this cost can be determined from cost-accounting data except for the cost due to the loss of customer goodwill. The lost goodwill is a highly important aspect of the back-order problem, and a good estimate of its cost is essential to the determination of the optimal amount of inventory to carry. Sometimes, ingenious methods can be devised to estimate this cost, but more often it is not possible to get a reliable estimate. In this case recourse must be made to the experience and intuition of the executive by methods analogous to those discussed in Chapter 10 for the other pair of costs. This is not the ideal procedure, but it may be the only one available.

The last question concerns the determination of the relationship between the amount stored and the relevant costs. This is essentially a mathematical problem and not too difficult, with one exception. Carrying costs and procurement costs vary with the amount ordered in an obvious way and it is easy to express the relationship in mathematical terms. The back-order cost and the overstock cost require the use of probability distributions to represent demand but there is no particular problem about handling these two costs mathematically. The exception noted, and the real difficulty in this part of the analysis of an inventory problem, is that it is necessary to know the probability distribution of demand. This requirement is a crucial one. We will discuss the matter more fully below in our evaluation of the usefulness of inventory models in the related decision problems.

This discussion has been in terms of the most common kinds of inventory problems. Later in this section we will briefly mention the additional difficulties that occur when we extend the inventory models to include supplies of intangible things. We can summarize our discussion by saying that the inventory models will provide solutions to the decision problems involving inventories, provided that the necessary information is available. Further, the necessary information is usually obtainable with the exception of the cost due to loss of goodwill and the probability distribution of demand, both of which may cause serious difficulties.

Now let us turn to an appraisal of inventory models from the executive's point of view. The first point that must be made—and it is an important one—is that there is often a semantic confusion between the executive who talks of his inventory problem and the operations-research analyst who talks of his inventory models. They often don't refer to the same inventory at all. This sounds like a surprising statement but it is true and the explanation is simple. The executive considers his inventory problem to consist of the whole process of predicting demand, ordering, and so on, and he feels he has an inventory decision problem if his total inventory is too high or his back-orders are too high, for whatever reason. Not so the analyst. He includes all of the executive's components except one: predicting demand. He has excluded that one by assuming in his formulation of the problem that the probability distribution of demand is known. The implications of this fact for the executive are enormous and we must discuss them briefly.

In assuming that the probability distribution of demand is known we are assuming that the average demand during the given future period is known and that the probabilities of deviations from that demand are known. Now, to be blunt, this is assuming quite a lot. To know the average demand by itself requires nothing other than the prediction or forecasting of demand, and this is subject to all the usual hazards attendant upon the notoriously backward art of forecasting. In the many cases where good forecasts of demand are available the inventory models will work perfectly well. But where there are no good forecasts of demand the use of inventory models will do very little to rectify the situation.

Let us take an example. When breaks are going badly in a retail business, say a department store, the situation will arise in which total inventory is too high and there is simultaneously a great number of back-orders. Now, this seems almost a contradiction in terms since we have already seen that the back-order cost should decrease as the amount maintained in stock increases. But it happens all too frequently. Why? Because the too-large inventory is in items for which the demand is small while supplies were too low in the fast-moving items and so these have had to be back-ordered. There is only one explanation for such a predicament: bad forecasting. If the harried executive of our department store were told that inventory models assumed demand forecasts, he would be likely to respond with a few choice expletives as preface to some such statement as: "If someone will give me some good forecasts I can manage the inventory myself!" The moral is simply that not all of an executive's inventory problems are solvable by the use of the inventory models we have been discussing.

It is necessary, then, to be certain of the nature of a given inventory problem before deciding to utilize inventory models in helping to solve it. It is not difficult to discover what aspects of the inventory procedure are at fault. For this purpose it is convenient to consider the actual inventory on hand to be the sum of three components:

1. The amount carried to meet average demand, assuming it to be known certainly in advance.

2. The amount carried as reserve stock to meet fluctuations in demand.

3. The excess amount that has resulted from forecasting errors.

For example, a typical inventory policy (before the utilization of inventory models) might be to order every item once a month and to maintain two months' supply as reserve stock. Consider an item with actual monthly demand of about 100 units. According to company policy there would be an average year-round inventory of half a month's demand, or 50 units, simply to meet the average demand. This is our first component. According to company policy there should be 200 units continually in stock to meet fluctuations in demand. This is the second component, reserve stock. The application of inventory models to this item might change the order period and it might change the amount of reserve stock maintained; any such change would be rationally based on the relevant costs and would save the company money. Further, such savings on hundreds or thousands of items can add up to very large amounts. But suppose that an inspection of the stock card for our item shows that the actual inventory is 1,100 units. This could only have resulted from a forecasting error, and inventory models can do nothing to avoid such errors. It is particularly important to be aware of this difference because many inventory problems in the executive's terms are forecasting problems in the terms of inventory models.

With this major provision about forecasting errors it appears that inventory models applied to the usual inventory decision problems can result in very significant savings. The formulation of the models is realistic, and due account can be taken of special circumstances such as storage space or capital limitations. The necessary information is usually available; if it is not there are procedures that can still produce significant improvements. It is, of course, the executive's problem, and responsibility, to estimate whether the total saving will justify the search for a solution. But in the case of inventory problems there is a high degree of likelihood that the solution will be found.

Further, methods are available for dealing with inventory problems for which the demand distribution is not completely known. Obviously, something has to be known about demand but it is remarkable how much can be done with only partial information about the demand distribution. For examples, the mean and standard deviation of demand or modal demand may be known, or it may be known that demand will never exceed some amount, and so forth. A considerable variety of methods are available to handle such cases as these.[2]

One warning must be given. Inventory theory has developed enormously in recent years and there is a very large and complex literature dealing with the great variety of inventory models. A major reason for the many periodical articles on the subject is simply that the field is a happy hunting ground for mathematicians looking for attractive (from a mathematical point of view) problems. It by no means follows that the resulting mathematical intricacies have any relevance to the real world of inventory problems. Simple approximate methods which are easy to apply often give results which are fully as good as those which can be obtained by launching a massive mathematical assault on the problem. Therefore, it is particularly important that the executive should endeavor to avoid the use of *excessive* refinements in the study of his inventory problem.

What about the application of inventory models to the supply of intangibles such as plant capacity, research projects, and the like? In these cases the fact that inventory models assume a forecast of demand is much more limiting. In such problems the forecast of demand is often, if not usually, the major obstacle. How, for example, does one forecast demand for liquid assets? And in the case of intangibles there is an additional difficulty because the relevant costs are not generally known and often can only be estimated within rather wide ranges. What, for example, is the cost of maintaining a supply of liquid capital, and what is the cost of being out of stock? Difficulties such as these rather sharply circumscribe the indefinitely wide applicability of inventory models. Nonetheless, when forecasts and costs can be had, the inventory models can be

---

[2] See Martin K. Starr and David W. Miller, *Inventory Control, Theory and Practice,* (Englewood Cliffs, N.J.: Prentice-Hall, Inc., 1961).

applied with good promise of success. We hope that the examples of the work-pool problem, the hotel-reservation problem, and the overtime problem[3] will serve to illustrate some of the possible applications of inventory models to decision problems other than those dealing with inventories of the more usual kinds of things.

130/ Waiting-Line Models

In the first section of this chapter we discussed an underlying similarity which we suggested could be called the "servicing" problem. This is the problem of providing sufficient facilities to meet the needs of persons or things that arrive at the facility, are given some "service," and then depart. An unexpectedly large number of processes meet this description, and there are a correspondingly large number of decision problems that depend upon the analysis of this kind of situation. We mentioned that this kind of problem is really a special case of the inventory problem, since it is obviously a question of maintaining a supply of facilities to meet future demand. However, the analysis differs sufficiently from that of other inventory problems to justify considering it to be a separate subclass. We must first attempt to discover the reason for this difference.

It will be instructive to compare three problems: the repairmen problem discussed in Chapter 10, and the work-pool problem and the overtime problem given as problems for the reader at the end of this chapter. All three of these problems are inventory problems where the thing being stored is time (in the form of men). Yet the work-pool problem and the overtime problem can be handled by straightforward applications of inventory models, while the repairmen problem requires analysis in terms of waiting lines. Why the difference?

The explanation in the case of the overtime problem is fairly obvious. In that problem the out-of-stock cost (equivalent to the back-order cost) is simply the extra labor costs required because the personnel have to work overtime in order to complete the day's workload. There is no cost caused by the fact that some of the workload had to wait until the overtime period before being completed. In short, in the overtime problem there was no waiting-time cost. Therefore, it could be handled directly as an inventory problem. However, this is not true of the other two problems. In both cases the out-of-stock cost is a penalty cost caused by not having a man available. In the repairmen problem this is the amount per hour that it costs to have a machine not working, and

---

[3] All problems at the end of this chapter (pp. 562–563).

in the work-pool problem it is the amount per day that it costs to have a position unfilled. At this level the problems are similar, although one is based on hours and the other on days.

The difference between these two stems from the fact that in the work-pool problem the positions can be filled the next day by the absent employees of the day before, whereas a broken machine must wait until it is repaired. In the work-pool problem an absent employee corresponds to a broken machine in the repairmen problem. In terms of this correspondence we can say that in the work-pool example "the machine can repair itself" by an employee's returning to work. The machines in the repairmen problem cannot repair themselves so they must wait until a repairman is available. Hence this problem requires analysis in terms of waiting lines. In any case where something requires some kind of service from one of a limited number of facilities and where there is a cost associated with any delay caused by the something's having to wait for a facility, we will have to use waiting-line analysis rather than the other inventory models.

A great variety of waiting-line models have been developed to handle the different cases that arise in practice. All of them are developed in terms of two measurable quantities: (1) the *arrival rate* of the things or persons to be serviced and (2) the *service rate* at the facility. The service rate is commonly called the *departure rate,* since at the conclusion of the service the thing or person departs from the facility. Both of these rates can be directly measured by an observer with a stop watch or some suitable recording device. Such measurements can be readily converted to probability distributions showing the probability of a given number of arrivals per time unit and the probability that a given time will be required to complete the servicing. These two distributions were given directly in our repairmen problem. As might be expected, it is the ratio of the average arrival rate to the average departure rate that governs the behavior of the waiting lines. Mathematical analysis which is sometimes of great complexity is used to determine various characteristics of the resulting process. Two of the more important measures of the behavior of the process are (1) the average number of things or persons in line waiting for service and (2) the average waiting time required in order to get service. The great variety of models that exist is required to handle all the variants of the fundamental waiting-line process that occur in practice. Some of the major variants are:

1. *Different probability distributions for arrivals.* For example, an assembly line delivers parts to a specific worker at a constant rate. Motorists arriving at a toll booth will have some probability distribution of arrivals.

2. *Different probability distributions for service times.* For example, a vending machine will service each customer with a constant service time but a doctor will require differing times (a probability distribution) to service his patients.

3. *Number of facilities.* For example, a single repairman must service all broken machines but a large airfield has several landing strips to service incoming planes.

4. *Servicing order.* This refers to the way in which the facility selects the next customer to be serviced. For example, a ticket office services the next customer in line, but a telephone operator chooses one of the waiting calls at random.

5. *Waiting-line discipline.* This refers to whether the waiting customers can switch to a shorter line (in the case of more than one facility). For example, a customer in line at a bank teller window will switch to a shorter line if he sees one, but a motorist in line for a toll booth usually cannot switch lines.

6. *Priorities.* There may be a set of priorities giving precedence to some customers over others. For example, broken machines might be repaired in the order of the cost of their being out of operation or in such order that shorter repair jobs are always done first.

Each combination of these variants, and of others not mentioned, requires separate mathematical analysis, so the profusion of waiting-line models is a necessity. The purpose of the mathematical analysis is, of course, to discover the important characteristics of the resulting waiting lines. It is worth noting that it is possible to determine the waiting-line characteristics by direct observation in the form of simulation samples. Any waiting-line process can be simulated. Enormous samples may have to be taken in order to get reliable results, but the use of computers makes this necessity less of a handicap than it would otherwise be.

Granting, then, an adequate description of the process being considered, it is possible to obtain either through mathematical analysis or through simulation methods the average waiting time that will result with various numbers of facilities. It is this waiting time that constitutes one of the two opposing costs of waiting-time problems. The average service time is one of the facts of the process and is accepted as such in the analysis. But the average waiting time decreases as the number of facilities increases and can, therefore, be controlled by management. The other cost is, evidently, the cost of the facility. For any given number of facilities the average waiting time can be determined. Given the cost per unit of waiting time and the cost of operating each facility, it is then simple to find the total cost for each number of facilities. The minimum such total cost then determines the optimal number of facilities.

The procedure outlined above is straightforward, and usually the only difficulty in obtaining the necessary data is in determining the waiting-time costs. Generally the cost of operating the facility is obtainable from accounting data, which may also yield the waiting-time cost. However, in the many cases where the waiting line consists of prospective customers it is difficult, or virtually impossible, to estimate the waiting-time cost. The possible cost of loss of customer goodwill is a major component which can only rarely be determined. However, in cases where the waiting-time cost cannot be estimated it is still possible to provide the decision-maker with the average waiting time that will result for any selection of number of facilities. This provides him with a quantitative basis for exercising his judgment as to acceptable waiting times.

Evaluated from the decision-maker's point of view there is no question whatsoever concerning the value of waiting-line models in analyzing decision problems involving this kind of situation. The necessary techniques are well developed and relatively easy to apply to specific problems, and no unrealistic assumptions or data requirements are involved. Further, waiting-line behavior is often contrary to an inexperienced intuition, so it is not easy to find the optimal strategy by judgment alone. The very nature of the waiting-line process implies that waiting lines can only be shortened by increasing the over-all idle time of the facilities. In order to have the facilities busy most of the time it is necessary to have waiting lines most of the time. Casual observation of such a process will generally lead to the wrong conclusions. A supervisor who walks repeatedly through the machine shop of our repairmen problem, for example, will find the two repairmen idle 75 per cent of the time. He might well decide to fire one of them because of this. Nonetheless, this was the optimal strategy, and firing one of the repairmen would increase total costs considerably. Only a careful analysis of the total costs of such situations in terms of waiting-line models can unequivocally determine the best strategy.

In our paradigm section we included only one problem involving waiting lines, the repairmen problem of Chapter 10. The reason was not that this kind of problem is unimportant. On the contrary, as our remarks above show, problems of this kind are frequent and important and the models are very valuable tools in resolving them. However, many of the most interesting of the waiting-line models are of a degree of complexity that puts them beyond the range of our discussion.

131/ Allocation of Resources

A large number of important decision problems involve the allocation of resources to various activities in such a way as to maximize profit or to minimize costs. Typically, there are a number of things to be done and there are not sufficient resources available to do each of them in the most effective way. If there were sufficient resources to do everything in the best possible way there could be no problem; one would simply do everything in the best way.[4] The problem arises because the limitation of resources requires that some things be done in a less-than-best way. The decision problem, then, is to assign the things that must be done to the available resources so that the total cost is minimized or the total profit maximized. The fact that some things must be done in a less-than-optimal way means that opportunity costs arise and suggests that one method for finding the best allocation would be to minimize these opportunity costs.

The simplest example of such a problem is the assignment problem, treated in Chapter 10. In the problem considered there it was necessary to assign a group of jobs for simultaneous processing to a group of machines, any one of which could do any one of the jobs. The cost of processing each job differs according to which machine processes it. The decision problem is to assign the jobs to the machines so that the total processing cost is minimized. The problem results from the fact that one machine does several jobs most cheaply but only one job can be assigned to it. The method of solution for this kind of problem is based on the determination of the opportunity costs of the various possible assignments. The problem used as an example in Chapter 10 typifies the assignment problem. The defining characteristic of this kind of problem is that each activity (job in our example) must be assigned to exactly one resource (machine in our example) and each resource must be assigned to exactly one job. Other examples of this kind of problem are: the assignment of salesmen to sales regions, the assignment of executives to positions, the assignment of consultants to clients, and similar ones. The procedure for determining the optimal assignments is so simple that there is no possible excuse for not using this model when it is applicable. However, its applicability is sharply limited by the difficulty of determining the necessary costs or other measures of utility. It is necessary to know the cost or measure of utility for each of the possible assignments. In the case of assignments of jobs to machines, these data can often be

---

[4] Of course, analysis may be required to determine the "best way."

obtained from cost-accounting reports, but usually it will be extremely difficult to determine the utilities involved in the other examples cited above.

A more frequently occurring kind of allocation problem is the transportation problem. An example of this kind of problem was given in Chapter 10. In a transportation problem there are a group of origins (the factories in our example) and a group of destinations (warehouses in our example). Each origin has a limited quantity (factory capacity) of the commodity that it can ship and each of the destinations has a requirement for a certain amount of the commodity (the warehouse requirements). Generally, any origin can ship to any destination, but this is not a requirement of the model. The cost of shipping a unit amount from each origin to each destination is fixed. The decision problem is to determine the minimum-cost shipping schedule that meets all the requirements of the destinations while remaining within the capacities of the origins.

The method of solution depends on an iterative process which evaluates the opportunity costs involved in specific shipping schedules and changes the schedules until a schedule is found that has an opportunity cost of zero. This, of course, is by definition the lowest-cost shipping schedule. The method of solution illustrated in our example requires that the total cost of any specific shipment should be simply the cost per unit times the amount shipped. In other words, quantity transportation discounts cannot be included if this method is to be used. However, in this case the procedure to be discussed below can be used. The simplicity of the method of solution and the fact that all the necessary cost data are easily available make this model an extremely useful one. Many actual transportation problems are far too large to be solved by hand, but the method of solution is well adapted for computers so the size of the problem is not an obstacle. This technique has been used repeatedly and has in many instances produced large transportation-cost savings.

Each of these two kinds of allocation problem is actually a special case of a far more general formulation of the allocation problem. This is the *linear programming model,* one of the most widely used of all operations-research models. We have given two examples of it (apart from the assignment and transportation examples which, as mentioned above, are special kinds of linear programming models). These examples were the media reach problem of Chapter 11 and the problem concerning the optimal utilization of plant capacity in Chapter 10. Linear programming models, in common with the other allocation models, are useful in situations where restrictions on the use of resources render it impossible to perform each activity in the same way it would be performed if it were the only activity to be performed. There is a conflict between activities; some of them must be performed, therefore, in less-than-optimal ways. Thus, opportunity costs are involved, and there is a problem of determining the best allocation of resources to activities. This kind of conflict is expressed in the model in the form of equations showing the limitations on the combinations of amounts of the various activities. For the problem involving the optimal utilization of plant capacity these limitations arose because of the limited capacities of the various plant departments. In other cases the limitations may take the form of minimum (or maximum) amounts prescribed because of space limitations, money limitations, or any other limitations.

Essential, however, for a linear programming model is the requirement that the expression showing each of the restrictions should be linear with regard to each of the activities in question. This is another way of saying that each additional unit of the activity must add a constant amount to the quantity being restricted. In our plant-capacity example an increase of one unit in the amount produced of either of the products required a constant amount of departmental capacity. Similarly, the expression that shows the relation of the activities to the objective must be linear with regard to the activities. That is, returns from the activities must be "to scale": twice as much of an activity produces twice as much profit, if the objective is to maximize profit; or twice as much of an activity costs twice as much, if the objective is to minimize costs. The fact that the restrictions and the objective function have to be linear with regard to the activities accounts for the name of the model, linear programming.

The decision problem is solved by finding the levels of the various activities that maximize (or minimize) the objective function while satisfying all the restrictions. Naturally, all the activities must occur either at a zero level or in some positive amount, since there is no meaning to a negative amount of an activity. It is usually the case that most of the restrictions in linear programming problems take the form of inequalities. In this event it is necessary to add one variable to each inequation to convert it to an equation. These variables are called *slack variables* and are activities just as much as the other activity variables in the equations. In our example, if a slack variable had occurred at a positive level in the optimal solution it would have meant that the corresponding productive facility was not utilized to its full capacity. One of the important conclusions of the mathematical analysis of this kind of problem is that the maximization (or minimization) of the objective function can be achieved with no more activities at positive levels than there are restrictions. For our example of the allocation of plant capacity we had two restrictions (for the two departments) and two activities (the two products). In our optimal solution some of each product was produced. However, we could equally well have started with 3, 5, 10, or any number of activities (products). The mathematical conclusion which we mentioned assures us that, no matter how many products were involved, we would never need to produce more than two in order to get maximum profit (since there are only two restrictions).

When there are only two activities it is possible to solve the decision problem geometrically. However, for more activities it is necessary to use an iterative algebraic procedure. Starting with a specific set of activity levels that meet the restrictions, we use a simple criterion to determine whether the solution can be improved. If the answer is affirmative we use another criterion to discover which activity should be replaced in our solution. We then replace it by the activity, which changes the objective function value in the desired direction. This series of steps is repeated until no further improvement is possible, which means that the optimal solution has been found. The best-known procedure for accomplishing this iterative process is called the *simplex* process. In our plant-capacity example, we showed the simplex procedure and an algebraic argument which is equivalent to the simplex method but which is somewhat easier to understand. The simplex method saves a good many pencil strokes but at the cost of a little greater difficulty in learning the elements of linear programming. Since many linear programming problems that arise include large numbers of activities and restrictions it is, in practice, necessary to take advantage of the saving in effort afforded by the simplex process—especially since the simplex process is well suited for use in computers.

A highly important mathematical fact concerning linear programming problems is that they really come in pairs. To every linear programming maximization (or minimization) problem there corresponds a linear programming minimization (or maximization) problem. The two problems thus paired are called *dual problems*. The dual of any linear programming problem is formed from the same data as the original but arranged in a different order. For example, any problem of the allocation of plant capacity that has two products and two departments, as did our example of Chapter 10, can be formulated thus:

To minimize $\qquad$ Profit $= p_1 x_1 + p_2 x_2$

Subject to $\qquad$
$$a_{11} x_1 + a_{12} x_2 \leq 100$$
$$a_{21} x_1 + a_{22} x_2 \leq 100$$
$$x_1 \geq 0$$
$$x_2 \geq 0$$

In this formulation a_{11} represents the percentage of capacity of Department 1 that the production of one unit of x_1 (the first product) requires, a_{12} represents the percentage of capacity of Department 1 that the production of one unit of x_2 requires, and so on. This formulation is precisely equivalent to the one we used in our example. Since this is a maximization problem the dual will be a minimization problem. The dual is written with the same constants but with different variables.

To maximize $\qquad\qquad Z = 100W_1 + 100W_2$

Subject to
$$a_{11}W_1 + a_{21}W_2 \geq p_1$$
$$a_{12}W_1 + a_{22}W_2 \geq p_2$$
$$W_1 \geq 0$$
$$W_2 \geq 0$$

A little study of how the constants have been rearranged in the dual will disclose the pattern better than will a lengthy verbal explanation, so we forego the latter. The main conclusion of the mathematical analysis of the relationship between the duals is that Z, the objective function of the dual, will have, for the optimal solution, the same value as the final value of the objective function in the original problem, profit in our case. A little dimensional analysis now suggests what the variables in the dual (W_1 and W_2) represent. Since Z is in dollars, it follows that the right-hand side of the objective function ($100W_1 + 100W_2$) must be in dollars too. But we know that the coefficients (100 and 100) are capacities, and not dollars, so it follows that W_1 and W_2 must be in dollars. In fact, they represent prices and, hence, are called "shadow prices." The shadow prices are the values that must be assigned to a unit of capacity in each of the departments in order to minimize the value of the output: the two products. In general, shadow prices represent the economic value per unit of the scarce resources involved in the restrictions of the problem.

The fact that any linear programming problem has a dual is of considerable importance in theoretical economics. And it has some important implications for the general problem of inter-divisional pricing within one parent company. Further, it is of direct practical importance, since the dual may be considerably easier to solve than the original linear-programming problem. Obviously, given the solution of either, it is quite straightforward to find the solution of the other.

Linear programming models are not the only models available for dealing with decision problems involving the allocation of resources. On the one hand there are various models that deal with cases where the linearity requirements cannot be assumed to hold. The quadratic programming model is an example, and there are other nonlinear programming models. On the other hand there are models that attempt to represent situations in which the allocation of resources is made in a sequence of decisions over time and the objective is to obtain the maximum return over the entire sequence of decisions. The best-known model of this kind is the dynamic programming model. We used dynamic programming in our example of dividend payout in Chapter 12 and in the determination of the optimal purchasing policy in Chapter 11.

The linear programming model, however, is the one that has been most used in practice. There is an extraordinary diversity of decision problems to which the linear programming model has been applied. A representative sample of such problems includes the optimal blending of gasoline, minimization of trim losses in the manufacture of paper, the minimum-cost diet meeting certain nutritional standards, smoothing production patterns, the optimal scheduling of airline flight crews, determination of an executive compensation plan, and even problems of structural design. All of these problems, together with those previously discussed and many others not mentioned, have the required linear programming structure: (1) a conflict between activities because of limited resources and (2) linearity of the restrictions and the objective function with regard to the activities.

From the executive's point of view linear programming models are of tremendous value. They provide expeditious means for solving decision problems of such complexity that it is almost impossible to find the optimal strategy by any other method. Two questions can be raised concerning the applicability of these models. First, can the costs that enter into the equations be reliably determined? The answer is that in the majority of frequently occurring linear programming problems, and particularly in those dealing with production, the cost figures can be determined from cost-accounting data. However, even if the cost figures are not really reliable, the linear programming procedure will still be based on the same data that management would use if it selected a strategy by some other means. Therefore, the use of linear programming will at least ensure the selection of the optimal strategy on the basis of the data management would use anyhow. When linear programming is applied to problems that arise in areas where cost data are not usually collected on a regular basis there can be considerable difficulties in determining the relevant costs. Under these circumstances linear programming can be used with each of a range of sets of costs and the effect of changing assumptions concerning costs can be determined. This in itself can provide the executive with a much sounder basis for handling his decision problem.

The second question is: What is the effect of the linearity assumptions that are required? Do these assumptions sharply limit the kinds of decision problems to which linear programming methods can be applied? The answer is a definite, but qualified, no. First, a great number of practical decision problems involve activities that are linear within the feasible range of levels of the activities. Second, when the activities are not linear over their entire feasible range it is very often possible to split the activity that is not linear into several activities, each of which is linear. Such a procedure can be used, for example, in handling transportation problems where there is a quantity discount. Thus, instead of having one activity that consists, say, of shipping from a specific factory to a specific warehouse, we have two activities. The first is the activity of shipping any amount up to the amount at which the discount applies, and the second is the activity of shipping any amount to which the discount applies. But if the nonlinearity cannot be remedied by this means it will be necessary to use some nonlinear programming model.

The major concern of the executive who is considering the use of linear programming must be with this question of linearity. The specialist in linear programming is very apt to hear a problem as if it were a linear programming problem whether it really is one or not. In this regard some linear programming specialists come dangerously close to that classic definition of the man who is too specialized: he is so good with a screwdriver that he cuts slots in the heads of nails.[5] Examples of questionable uses of linear programming are legion. One will suffice here. The media allocation problem is the problem of determining the optimal selection of media for a given advertising campaign. This problem can be construed as a linear programming problem only if each exposure has equal worth—the tenth exposure to a person having just as much worth as a first exposure to a different person with comparable demographic characteristics. Clearly this *might* be true of some campaigns. But, just as clearly, it is *not* true of most campaigns. Therefore, linear programming simply is not applicable to most advertising campaigns, despite claims to the contrary. The difficulty is that advertising exposures do not behave linearly: twice as many are generally not worth twice as much. Generally, the executive will have to defend himself against this kind of wrong interpretation of his problem. He can do this simply by sticking to his guns—if it doesn't sound linear to him then it isn't until someone can convince him that it is.

But, granted some difficulties, the best proof of the applicability of linear programming methods remains the great number of highly successful uses of these models in actual business decision problems.

132/ Competitive Models

The study of the decision problems underlying competitive strategies has been very highly developed under the title of the theory of games. Ordinarily we think of games as being purely recreational and not of importance to our more "serious" activities. In this sense, then, the name, "theory of games," is misleading. Actually, the essence of a competitive

---

[5] We owe this apt description to our colleague, Professor Samuel Richmond.

situation is that two or more persons or organizations are competing for some objective for which there is a conflict of interests. A game is the prototype of this kind of situation; for this reason the study of competitive decision problems is called the theory of games. The same theory underlies the playfulness of the decision problems in card games and the deadly seriousness of a struggle between two companies for greater shares of the market.

Despite the considerable body of theoretical results in the theory of games there have been few successful applications of the theory to practical decision problems involving competitors. We have included two examples of decision problems dealing directly with competitive behavior in Part IV.* The first was the problem concerning the advertising of two department stores in Chapter 11. This was a genuine "game" and was analyzed as such. The second was the competitive bidding model, also in Chapter 11. This was not handled as a "game" because all the game-like features were missing. The reason was that the situation was viewed as one company against a group of essentially anonymous competitors. The situation was, therefore, of the kind analyzed in classical economic theory, where no one buyer and no one seller has any influence on price. Game theory does not produce any new results or insights in this kind of situation. Our main question in this section, therefore, must be: Why hasn't game theory been found to be of greater usefulness in competitive decision problems? The subsidiary question will then be: What does game theory contribute to the executive who is faced with such decision problems?

We will be better able to answer these questions if we first discuss the main outlines of game theory as it is presently known. For our purposes it will be sufficient to note two main dichotomies in game theory. First, there are two kinds of games distinguished by the relationship that exists among the payoffs to the various players. Zero-sum games are those in which the sum of the payoffs to all the players is zero. In other words, what one player wins, another, or others, must lose. A typical example is the game of poker. The other kind of game is one in which the sum of the payoffs to all the players need not be zero. This kind of game is called, for obvious reasons, a nonzero-sum game. Examples will be given below. It may be noted that any nonzero-sum game can be converted to a zero-sum game by adding another hypothetical player, "Nature," who always receives a payoff calculated to make the sum of the payoffs equal to zero. This fact is important theoretically but it doesn't help in the analysis of any specific nonzero-sum game. The second dichotomy has to do with the number of players. Specifically, we want to distin-

---

* Without using the game theory model, the brand loyalty model, the brand share model, and the pricing problem model, all discussed in Chapter 11, also deal with competitive behavior.

guish between games with exactly two players and games with any number of players greater than two. We will now try to explain why these two dichotomies are important in understanding the present sharp limitations on the usefulness of game theory in competitive decision problems.

Let us consider the case of the two-person zero-sum game. In this case there is a complete conflict of interest; what one person gains the other loses. Analysis of this kind of game has led to a number of important conclusions. First, the decision criterion must be the maximin or minimax criterion. The use of any other criterion can lead only to a smaller payoff if the opponent uses the maximin criterion. Second, the value of the game to one player is the negative value to the other player if both of them use their maximin and minimax strategies. Third, to obtain this value it may be necessary to use a mixed strategy consisting of the random selection of one of several possible strategies. The method by which the optimal strategy is determined is known, and it may therefore be said that the theory of two-person zero-sum games is essentially complete.

What happens when we try to extend this analysis to some number of players greater than two, still assuming a zero-sum game? A major difficulty immediately arises. As soon as there are three or more players it becomes possible for coalitions of players to form. In a game of three players, for example, two of them may form a coalition against the third and by agreeing to their own selections of strategies may guarantee themselves payoffs greater than those which would result from their maximin strategies. Naturally, this gain is at the expense of the third player. Further, a coalition may be able to increase its total payoff by including a player who would sustain a loss by selecting the strategy desired by the coalition. In this case the coalition can offer him a side payment which may induce him to join. So coalitions, counter-coalitions, and counter-counter-coalitions can form in ways as numerous as they are fascinating and bewildering. The net effect of all these possibilities is that there is no generally accepted theory of zero-sum games with more than two players, although there are several extremely ingenious efforts in this direction.

Finally, consider a two-person nonzero-sum game. Here the difficulties are equally severe. First, the two players can form a coalition against "Nature," if necessary, with side payments, since there may be specific strategies for which they both receive positive payoffs (since the game is nonzero-sum). It may profit one of the two players to desert the coalition. Whether he does so or not will depend on whether the game is to be repeated and on the amount of retribution his opponent can subsequently inflict upon him. Finally, and most important, one player may be able to inflict large losses on his opponent at the cost of small losses to himself. He can then use this possibility as a threat to force his opponent to select strategies that afford him greater payoffs. This feature of two-person nonzero-sum games has led to extensive analysis of threats, bargaining positions, arbitration procedures, and so on. The results are usually of great interest but it seems that, for any general theory, games can be constructed for which the theory gives a solution that is contrary to common sense. As a result there is as yet no generally accepted theory of these games.

Now let us return to practical competitive decision problems. First, they usually have more than two opponents. Second, they are generally nonzero-sum. As a result, there is no general theory competent to analyze these problems. The fact that most competitive decision problems have more than two opponents is obvious, but the statement that they are usually nonzero-sum requires some defense. There are two reasons. First, the actual situation may be such that the payoffs do not sum to zero. For example, an advertising campaign may expand the whole market so that all opponents get larger amounts. Second, a competitive situation can only be zero-sum if all the opponents' utilities are measured by the same payoff measure. If they have different utilities for the various payoffs the game is automatically a nonzero-sum game. Yet, as we have noted before, there is good reason to believe that the utilities will be different for the different opponents. Finally, it may be noted that if the utilities are different it is necessary for each opponent to know the utilities of the other opponents for the various possible outcomes in order to even have a nonzero-sum game. If the utilities are unknown the situation becomes a game against "Nature," with decision-making under uncertainty. These various reasons explain why game theory has found few applications in practical competitive decision problems.

Nonetheless, game theory does provide some useful insights into competitive situations. One such is the fact that the decision criterion in competitive situations should be the maximin criterion. Another is the idea of mixed strategies. It is not at all obvious that it is sometimes necessary to randomly select a strategy in order to gain the maximum possible payoff. Yet this turns out to be the case in competitive situations. This realization can be of considerable value in competitive decision problems.

133/ Simulation

Simulation can be thought of as less a model than a procedure. If nothing else, the popularity of simulation as a decision-making tool is sufficient to justify a section to describe it. We used simulation in the analysis of the repairmen problem of Chapter 10. It will be recalled that the basic procedure was to assign numbers to different possibilities—in our example, to machine breakdowns and to hours taken to repair a breakdown—in accordance with the probabilities of each of the possible outcomes. Then by drawing random numbers it is easy to take a sample of the real-world process entirely on paper. This is the key to the power of simulation. (Also see pp. 178–193.) It is possible to take very large samples quickly and cheaply under circumstances in which it would be prohibitively expensive, or even impossible, to take a real-world sample. Thus, in our repairmen example we were able to investigate the effect of adding a second repairman without having to try it out in the real world at all. And consumer behavior was similarly investigated.

Generally, whenever various different probability distributions interact in some process under consideration it is likely that explicit mathematical analysis of the outcome will be painfully difficult. It is precisely here that simulation is most valuable. This general statement includes most of the innumerable variety of queuing, or servicing, problems. It is often easier to determine the optimal number of facilities, say, by simulation even when the theoretical solution is known. This is the case because of the truly formidable difficulties of the statements of many theoretical solutions in queuing theory. Particularly, now that computers are readily available through the conversational mode of time-sharing computers, simulation has become a flexible and admirably useful tool for the analysis of innumerable complex decision problems.[6]

Nonetheless, there is probably more misuse of simulation—due to misunderstanding its capabilities—than of any other operations-research tool. The great majority of the misuses of simulation are due to the forgetting of one crucial fact: *Simulation is not a substitute for knowledge.* This cannot be overemphasized. Simulation is not a method which, somehow, compensates for lack of knowledge. Unfortunately, the belief is all too prevalent that when the facts aren't known all that needs to be done is to simulate. Nothing could be further from the truth.

Consider our use of simulation in the repairman problem. In order to simulate we had to know the probability distribution of machine breakdowns per hour and the probability distribution of hours to repair a breakdown. Had these distributions not been known it would have been impossible to simulate the process. This ought to be completely clear from the method used in simulating the process. Yet in the field of marketing there is a widespread conception that consumer behavior must be simulated, and, as our own simulation example (pp. 186–193) shows, we know so little about consumer behavior! The simulation of consumer behavior requires complete information about that part of the behavior

[6] *Conversational Computers,* (ed.) William D. Orr (New York: John Wiley & Sons, Inc., 1968).

we are simulating. And, as a matter of fact, one of the major uses of simulation models of consumer behavior today is to force us to find out exactly what it is we need to know about consumer behavior in order to be able to simulate it.

Any executive who has to deal with a complex process is likely to find that simulation is a most valuable tool—as long as he remembers that its use requires complete information about the process.

134/ *Two Other Models*

The four models already discussed are, without doubt, the major models of operations research. There are, however, other models that are worthy of mention. Obviously, the question of what is a sufficiently general model is to a considerable degree a matter of taste. The models discussed above each cover a remarkable range of seemingly different problems. On the other hand, some models have been developed to handle a single decision problem arising for one company at one specific time. In between these two extremes are a great number of models covering different numbers of separate decision problems. We have selected two of these for brief comment.

The first one is known as the *replacement model*. This model is concerned with decision problems arising with reference to the replacement of parts or components of some complex system. Such problems arise in connection with things as diverse as light bulbs, machines, and executives. In any population of similar elements such as these an item that fails must be replaced by a similar item. Problems arise as to the expected number of replacements needed at various times in the future, the optimal replacement procedure, maintenance policies, and so on. In the case of a population of executives a desired age distribution may be an objective. What should be the hiring policy in order to achieve this age distribution? These and a variety of similar questions can only be answered on the basis of replacement models, which analyze precisely these kinds of problems. The models generally demand advanced mathematical treatment, so we have not included any examples of replacement problems here. The models are, however, available for the analysis of these kinds of decision situations.

The last model we will mention is the *search model*. It is less well developed than any of the other models we have discussed but it has promise of becoming very useful for a great variety of decision problems. People search for many different things: scientists search for hypotheses, decision-makers search for optimal strategies, advertising agencies search for customers, personnel departments search for good potential executives. All of the various searches have similarities, and the search model undertakes to determine and analyze the common elements. The first such model was developed during World War II to solve decision problems connected with air patrol searches for enemy submarines. The result of the application of the model was a considerable improvement in the effectiveness of the search system. There are a number of difficulties connected with the attempt to incorporate into the model the essential features of the kinds of searches mentioned above and, as a result, the model is not yet sufficiently developed. However, there appears to be no intrinsic reason why this model cannot eventually be further developed and applied to these other kinds of searches.

135/ *Operations Research: An Overview*

The preceding sections of this chapter have attempted to give a general picture of the various models of operations research together with some remarks about the value of the various models to the decision-making executive. The various models discussed were used in many of the problems we considered in Part IV, and the more general discussion in this chapter has been intended to supplement the more detailed analyses of Part IV. We will devote the final section of this chapter to some conclusions that may be drawn about the use of operations research in solving decision problems.

The reader noticed perhaps that the problems discussed in Chapter 11, on marketing, seemed more complicated and generally somewhat less precise than those treated in Chapter 10, on production. And the problems discussed in Chapter 12, on finance, are somewhat more tenuous than those considered in either of the other chapters. These differences are not accidental, and their explanation will give some insight into the process of evaluating the economics of a search for a solution to a specific decision problem. We will focus our discussion on two aspects of operations-research solutions.

First, all the solutions depend on some set of costs, whether measured in dollars or in utilities. The solutions generally depend on the accuracy with which these costs are measured; and as more costs are involved, the greater will be the cumulative effect of inaccuracies in the costs. In the case of the inventory model we were able to develop a procedure for describing all optimal solutions—for any carrying costs and ordering costs. However, this approach is not always available and even if it is there is clearly a considerable advantage in basing the analysis on a knowledge of the costs. Generally speaking, operations research does not have any magical means of estimating costs. Sometimes an ingenious method for estimating a specific cost is discovered but this is the exception rather than the rule. We would expect, then, that operations-research solutions would be most frequent in those areas where reliable cost estimates are most often available. This is exactly what we find. Cost estimates are readily available wherever cost-accounting systems have been used and, hence, most frequently in the areas of production and the clerical side of administration. In the areas of marketing and finance there are not generally any good estimates of the relevant costs. Therefore, there is either the additional problem of trying to estimate the costs or the problem of trying to avoid them. In either case the solution to the decision problem is one step further removed.

Second, solutions depend on the number of factors that must be taken into account. This statement does not refer to a simple count of the factors. Any large linear programming problem is sufficient to show that the mere size of the problem is no insurmountable obstacle, at least as long as computers are available. Rather, we have reference to the inter-relationships among the factors. And, again, we do not mean a simple count of the number of interrelationships. If a mathematical equation can be written that describes all the interrelationships some method will be found to use it. The problem is to write the equation. In order to do this we must know the form the interrelationship takes. And the form the interrelationship takes is not, to put it bluntly, generally known in the fields of marketing and finance. It is much more likely to be known in the production area. The major reason for this is simply the question of control. Most of the relevant factors are under the decision-makers's control in production, whereas many crucial factors are outside his control in marketing and finance. Even when the factors are under control it can be an extremely onerous task to disentangle the interrelationships. A case in point is the lengthy research effort required to determine the interactions among the umpteen factors that affect the growth of penicillin. Yet virtually any major marketing decision has as many, or more, factors and many of them are not under control of the decision-maker. He cannot set their level and then run experiments varying the factors one by one, two by two, and so on. Thus, in the marketing area a solution will often depend on laborious attempts to disentangle the interactions of the various factors and will, even then, usually require some rather ruthless assumptions, and the same kinds of problems arise in finance.

Both of these differences in these areas act to make operations-research solutions less likely and less reliable in the marketing and finance areas than in the production area. Other factors operate in the same direction. A major one, the difference between physical systems and behavioral systems in terms of stability, will be discussed in Chapter 15. None of these difficulties are intrinsically insuperable, but their resolution requires the accumulated experience of many different efforts to solve them. Here the argument of Chapter 13 enters the picture. Since the probability of a return from a search for a solution in the marketing area is smaller, it follows that fewer companies can afford to undertake the search. Thus, experience accumulates more slowly in the development of suitable marketing models.

However, the same reasoning has a happy side. The converse of all these arguments is that the models of operations research are particularly well developed in the production area. For decision problems in this area, and in others where the above arguments are less relevant, there is a very high probability of a return from a search for a solution, and many models are available, ready-made for the solution of these problems. Even small companies can profitably utilize these models in their decision problems. And, as experience accumulates, we can expect a steady increase in the number of adequate models available in the more difficult fields.

PROBLEMS

1. In our discussion of problems in the allocation of resources we stated that the transportation problem was a special case of this more general kind of problem. This suggests that the transportation problem might be solved by means of linear programming and, as a matter of fact, this is so. Consider the following simple transportation problem:

WAREHOUSES	FACTORIES			REQUIREMENTS
	I	II	III	
A	$5	4	6	600
B	6	7	8	400
C	8	7	6	500
CAPACITIES:	300	500	700	1,500

a. Determine the minimum cost transportation schedule by the method used previously.

b. Set up the equations which express this problem in linear programming form.

c. In "b" we refer to "equations." Shouldn't this be "inequations"? (Note that there are six restrictions but the answer to "c" implies that only five of them are necessary since if any five are fulfilled the sixth will be also. In mathematical terminology we say that only five of the equations are independent.)

d. Use the solution obtained in "a" and see whether the linear programming objective function shows that this is an optimal solution.

2. A company which manufactures dog food has a great number of different ingredients which it could use in mixing the final product. The final product must meet certain minimum nutritional requirements such as percentage of protein, percentage of fat, amount of vitamins, etc. The objective is to minimize the cost of the final product.

a. What information would be needed in order to formulate this as a linear programming problem?

b. Introduce whatever symbols you need and put this problem in linear programming form.

c. What does the requirement that the restrictions and the objective equation must be linear mean in this problem?

3. An oil company can mix its blending stocks in a variety of ways to make a corresponding variety of final products. There are a fixed number of different blending stocks and the total available amount of each blending stock is fixed. Per unit profits for the various final products are different. The company objective is to maximize profit.

a. What information is needed in order to formulate this as a linear programming problem?

b. Introduce whatever symbols you need and put this problem in linear programming form.

c. What does the requirement that the restrictions and the objective equation must be linear mean in this problem?

4. A company has large retirement plan funds which it invests. Top level policy has been established which places percentage limits on the amounts that can be invested in bonds, preferred stocks, and common stocks. The manager of the funds want to obtain the maximum possible returns from the investments.

a. Formulate this as a linear programming problem.

b. Why isn't this really a linear programming problem?

5. A company maintains inventories on 500 items. The average cost (total cost divided by total number of items used) to the company of these items is $2 per unit and the average monthly demand per item is 100 units. The company estimates its carrying costs at 10 per cent per year and its ordering costs at $10 per order. Over the last year the average inventory has been $250,000 and it is felt that this is too high. Company policy is to order each item once each month and to maintain a reserve stock of one month's demand for each item. What improvement do you think can be achieved through the use of inventory theory?

6. We have emphasized four kinds of costs which can be involved in inventory problems. Most inventory problems involve only these four costs or some subgroup of them. However, there are exceptions. One such is a department store inventory of women's fashion dresses. In this case the department store does not maintain an inventory of dresses in each style, color, and size combination. Instead, the store will use its "inventory" to increase the number of styles and colors which it has on its racks. In other words, an increase in "inventory" means an increase in variety rather than an increase in the number of each variety. The reason for this is that the variety and, hence, the

inventory, attracts customers. In our terms we can say that the inventory serves to create demand. How would you analyze this problem?

7. As an example of some of the difficulties involved in the analysis of two-person nonzero-sum games we can use the following:

	A's PAYOFFS				B's PAYOFFS	
	B1	B2			B1	B2
A1	1	−4		A1	1	5
A2	5	−2		A2	−4	−2

a. What are the players' maximin strategies? Should they use them?

b. Consider the difference if the game is played only once or if it is going to be played a number of times.

c. Consider the difference if communication is allowed between the players before the game is played.

d. Suppose A and B are competitors and the first strategy in such case is to leave price unchanged. The second strategy is to lower price. Do you think payoff matrices such as these might be reasonable representations of this situation?

8. A large mail-order house has found (through depth interviews of customers) that customer complaint letters should be promptly answered by a personal letter. For this purpose the company employs a number of women college-graduates who do nothing but answer these letters. The women are paid $3 per hour for regular time and $4.50 per hour for overtime. All incoming letters are answered on the same day even if it means overtime work. The average production of letters is 5 per hour per woman. The probability distribution of complaint letters per day is:

COMPLAINT LETTERS	PROBABILITY
120–139	.06
140–159	.13
160–179	.09
180–199	.21
200–219	.17
220–239	.12
240–259	.08
260–279	.14
	1.00

a. What is the optimal number of women the company should employ?

b. What kind of problem is this one, in terms of the operations-research techniques discussed in this chapter?

9. Suppose a company has 50 machine tools. Each tool needs a man to run it. But some men are likely to be absent on any given day, so if the company only maintains 50 men on its regular payroll then it is quite likely that some ma-

chines will be idle on each day. Therefore, it may be advantageous for the company to maintain a work-pool of more than 50 men. Suppose each man is paid $2.50 per hour and suppose the company estimates that it costs $60 if any one machine is idle for one day. If r is the absence rate per day and if there are N men in the work-pool then the probability that k men are absent on any one day is given by the Poisson distribution:

$$P(k) = e^{-Nr}\frac{(Nr)^k}{k!}$$

where $e = 2.7183$ and $k! = k(k-1)(k-2) \ldots (3)(2)(1)$ and $0! = 1$ by definition.

a. What is the optimal work-pool strategy if $r = 0.04$? A table of the Poisson distribution is helpful. Here are some relevant values of e^{-Nr}:

$$e^{-2} = 0.13534 \qquad e^{-2.12} = 0.12003 \qquad e^{-2.24} = 0.10646$$
$$e^{-2.04} = 0.13003 \qquad e^{-2.16} = 0.11533 \qquad e^{-2.28} = 0.10228$$
$$e^{-2.08} = 0.12493 \qquad e^{-2.20} = 0.11080 \qquad e^{-2.32} = 0.09827$$

b. What kind of problem is this, in terms of the operations-research techniques discussed in this chapter?

10. If hotels accept only a number of reservations equal to the number of rooms that are going to be vacant, then if some people ("no-shows") do not appear, the hotel will usually have some rooms vacant. Therefore, hotels usually accept more reservations than there will be vacant rooms. This occasionally results in an extremely indignant person who cannot obtain a room, despite his reservation. A hotel estimates that the cost of turning away a person who has a reservation is $60. The cost of a vacant room because of a "no-show" is $30. Hotel records show that 20% of their reservations are "no-shows." Thus, if the hotel accepts N reservations the probability that i persons will be "no-shows" is given by the binomial distribution:

$$P(i) = \binom{N}{i}(.2)^i(.8)^{N-i}$$

where
$$\binom{N}{i} = \frac{N(N-1)\ldots(N-i+1)}{i(i-1)\ldots(3)\,(2)\,(1)}$$

a. What is the optimal number of reservations for the hotel to accept for 12 vacant rooms?

b. What kind of problem is this, in terms of the operations-research techniques discussed in this chapter?

Chapter 15

Implementation
of Solutions
and Control

We have discussed the conditions that lead an executive to use operations research to help him resolve his decision problems. We would then expect that, having obtained a solution, the executive would proceed in his accustomed manner to implement the solution, observe the results, and make further decisions as they are required. However, as we observed in Part I, deciding and doing can be quite closely related to each other. We concluded, at that time, that it was entirely reasonable to consider decisions apart from actions for the purposes of formulating the decision framework. In this way, we were spared the problems that arise when a theoretical solution conceived on paper or in the mind of the executive must be converted into practice. We now want to consider what happens when the executive transforms solutions into decisions and decisions into actions.

136/ *Form of the Solution*

1. *The degree of specificity of the strategies.* Depending upon the nature of the problem solved, the executive may find that the strategies are completely explicit with respect to what actions he should take. However, this circumstance would be unusual. More often, the solution specifies a strategy that is stated in general terms. For example, the solution to an inventory problem might list the minimum amount of each item to keep in stock. The solution does not tell the decision-maker how he should go about maintaining the required levels. It does not tell him

what kind of records to keep, how the level should be measured, or what companies to order from. Similarly, the solution to the media allocation problem would not specify the form of the message, the dates on which each medium should be used, or the page on which the advertisement should appear. We can distinguish these multitudinous elements that produce the strategy as *tactics*.

It is inconceivable, in most circumstances, to include all relevant tactical factors in the decision problem, and it is generally not necessary to include them all since the assumption is made that the decision-maker has enough tactical means at his disposal to enable him to fulfill the strategy. However, at the point of implementation the decision-maker must reconsider the validity of this assumption. He could not detail all possible tactical approaches for each of a great number of alternative strategies. But now that the solution has indicated one particular strategy he must concentrate his attention on fulfilling that strategy. We must always bear in mind that deciding what to do is not the same thing as deciding how to do it. The solution to a decision problem can be to increase the variety of flavors sold under a single brand name. But the choice of which additional flavors may not be specified. Implementation of this decision requires tactical decisions that have as their objective the fulfillment of the strategic decision. It is clear that what may be a tactical decision in one case may be a strategic decision in another. Referring to our example of flavors, if the decision problem was conceived as the optimal selection of a set of new flavors then the strategies would be the various combinations of flavors that could be used. Many tactical problems would still remain after this decision was reached, such as: What color? What sweetness? What strength? Nevertheless, the form of any solution can be examined in terms of the extent to which the strategies offer explicit instructions for carrying out the decision.

2. *The degree of certainty of the outcome.* Another aspect of the form of the solution concerns the specificity of the outcome. When a solution is obtained under conditions of certainty, then the decision-maker knows exactly what will happen if he chooses to implement a specific strategy. On the other hand, if the solution is derived for conditions of risk or uncertainty, then the decision-maker does not know exactly what will occur. That is why he must utilize a decision criterion in order to produce a solution. Degree of certainty, we know, is the direct result of the way in which Nature takes part in the problem. States of nature, by definition, are not under the decision-maker's control, but they play a vital part in his evaluation of the solution. We will have occasion to go into this subject in much greater depth as this chapter progresses.

3. *Repetitive and nonrepetitive solutions.* From a purely theoretical point of view, we have not had to distinguish between decisions that are

made once and decisions that are made many times. Expected values provide the solution to risk problems, whether the problem arises once or frequently. However, when a solution must be implemented, the question of how often the decision will be made becomes important. In this regard, we can further differentiate the solution as to whether it will be the exact same decision that is made each time or a different solution based on the use of a general model. For example, the decision with respect to the location of a new plant is made only once. The decision of what level of inventory to carry is made only once but it is used over and over again, without change, until costs, demand, or some other factor is altered. The decision of how much stock to order can change at each order point, based on previous demand and forecasts of future demand. We will see that the repetitive character of the form of the solution influences the implementation phase.

4. *Degree of reversibility.* When something can be done that can be undone without any loss, the form of the solution is completely reversible. In some cases, the tactics used to put a decision into effect can vary widely in the way that they affect the reversibility of a decision. For example, renting additional space has a greater degree of reversibility than building a new warehouse. Similarly, renting computer equipment permits the decision-maker to return to the previous methods of data-processing if his decision to use computer equipment was not the best one. Temporary assignments to executive positions, test markets for redesigned products, and inventory test periods in which larger stocks are maintained until the reduced stocks required by the inventory decision have proved themselves to be adequate, are further examples of tactics with some degree of reversibility. In most of the cases, the decision-maker is willing to accept a lesser gain in the long run in exchange for increased security with respect to the soundness of his decision. The loss in his gain that the decision-maker is willing to take is related directly to his degree of belief in the solution and his degree of control in applying the solution. These two subjects will be treated in separate sections in this chapter.

5. *Degree of permanence of the solution.* The states of nature that exist at the time of the solution can change to other states at a later time. For example, an unexpected technological breakthrough can rapidly alter production and market conditions. The change does not have to be this extreme. It can occur gradually, and escape detection unless adequate means are set up to watch for this eventuality. In still other cases, because of feedback, strategies result in outcomes that alter the state of nature. For example, the decision to introduce variety will, in all likelihood, produce a number of responses that will permanently alter competitive strategies and states of nature. The decision-maker will, of

course, try to predict the changes, but his predictions may be poor for a number of effects other than his immediate profit. Consequently, the decision-maker must take appropriate steps in his implementation to allow for the lack of permanence in states of nature. In this respect, the executive problems of long-range planning tend to emphasize the uncertainties that exist with respect to the permanence of states of nature, while short-range plans are based on a relatively stable nature.

When states of nature change, in such a way that states that had zero probability of occurring take on a larger probability of occurring, it is almost implicit that different strategies will provide the optimal solution. For this reason, the decision-maker will consider the relative permanence of strategies. In fact, that is what is generally meant by long- and short-term planning. Long-term planning strategies are meant to provide relatively permanent strategies in the face of less permanent states of nature. Short-term plans are not intended to remain for long periods of time and are expected to be replaced when, for example, the likelihood of a specific state of nature shifts from .10 to .50. While these issues exist throughout the entire problem-solving phase, they gain most importance when the solution must be implemented. There is no question that the problem-solving effort can be directed to provide solutions with more or less permanence. But it is the decision-maker at the point of implementation who must contend with the problem.

There are, of course, still other ways in which the form of the solution can be characterized. But the ones that have been given represent the points of major interest to the executive when he thinks about the problem—and its solution—in terms of implementation.

137/ Degree of Belief

The fact that a solution has been obtained does not mean that the decision-maker will always have equal faith in the essential correctness of the solution. The word "solution" has a very final sound. It is the end point of a search process that has attempted to investigate all relevant factors and to combine them in such a way as to simulate the outcomes that would occur if the factors were actually combined. "Solution" implies that the outcomes have been transformed into payoffs reflecting the utility of the outcome to the decision-maker. "Solution" also connotes that a decision criterion has been employed to select the "optimal" strategy. The degree of belief that the decision-maker has in the soundness of the solution will vary. It will depend upon how many factors were investigated and combined—and how many were left out. The degree of belief will be affected by the extent to which the payoff measures actually reflect the decision-maker's utilities. His degree of belief will further depend upon the extent to which the decision criterion expresses his intuition and attitudes. We have shown that a number of different decision criteria exist, and we now want to emphasize that many more could be created. Since a choice must be made between different decision criteria, it is to be expected that frequently the decision-maker will not be 100 per cent satisfied with any of the available criteria. This dissatisfaction must be expressed in a lower degree of belief in the solution.

We can make the general statement that the executive's degree of belief in the goodness of a solution will always be affected by the assumptions that he knows have been made in order to reach the solution. Many times they will be his own assumptions—and for these he will know better than anyone else how much faith he places in them.

The extent to which error could influence the solution is another point on which the executive evaluates the "answer" to his problems. Errors can arise in many ways, but, in general, the executive does not include computational or technical mistakes as errors. Most important are errors of estimation and errors of prediction. For example, if the problem requires an estimate of the number of people between the ages of 25 and 40 who are blue-collar workers, the executive knows that the figure used will not be exact. As far as predictive errors are concerned, the forecasts of expected demand for a particular product are certain to include error. But the important point is how much error—and how sensitive is the solution to error? If the solution is very sensitive to error, and a small amount of error is likely to exist, then the executive will place less belief in the solution. On the other hand, if the solution is relatively insensitive to error, and only a small amount of error is likely to exist, then the executive can place a higher degree of belief in the solution. For example, in the competitive-bidding problem, we observed that, for the specific example used, a large error in the estimation of the cost of fulfilling the contract could be tolerated before the solution shifted to a different bid. Similarly, in linear programming problems, the shape and orientation of the solution polygon with respect to the payoff function can, at times, permit an entire range of optimal solutions (when the payoff function falls along a line of the polygon rather than first intersecting with a corner). In the same way, mixed strategies can result in which the minimax (or the maximin) is not a point but a line. Any combination of strategies that falls along such a line meets the requirements of the solution.

One of the most important factors influencing the decision-maker is his ability to control the solution. In other words, the problem-solvers will have told him that if he will use strategy x he should obtain the best possible payoff, y. The solution may contain all of the elements of control that the decision-maker deems necessary. But he will come to his conclusion after a careful evaluation of the solution. Generally, the degree of belief the decision-maker has for a solution will increase with the amount of control he is able to exercise.

138/ Degree of Control

The subject of control is complex. The reason is, partly, that "control" means many things to us. To begin with, we will distinguish between two kinds of control. First of all, there is the kind of control that depends on the degree to which the decision-maker can control his instruments. The instruments may be executives, machines, money, or other "instruments." This kind of control is associated with tactics and with the skill of the executive in handling his instruments. In essence, control of the first type concerns the ability of the decision-maker to fulfill his strategy.

The second kind of control we shall consider in some detail. It is independent of the executive's skill in carrying out a plan by means of the instruments and tactics available to him. It is the degree of control that is inherent in the solution to a problem. In other words, it is the manner in which a strategy and states of nature combine to yield a solution. Up to this point we have shown how an optimal strategy can be chosen subject to an objective such as to maximize profit or to minimize cost. But the decision-maker, being aware of the implementation phase, has an additional objective at all times—to maximize control. He will, therefore, examine the solution that is optimal with respect to cost, profit, or whatever and evaluate it with respect to control. He may decide that a less optimal solution offering greater control should be preferred to the optimal solution.

Frequently, the executive will evaluate a solution intuitively, but we will attempt to explain what is involved in this evaluation and to indicate what methods are available for performing this task. Let us look at the following decision matrix.

	0.5 $N1$	0.5 $N2$	EV
$S1$	11	90	50.5
$S2$	50	50	50.0
$S3$	30	69	49.5

If we could control states of nature we would select $N2$. But we have always said that we cannot control states of nature and, in this case, we see that each of the two states of nature is assigned a probability of 0.5. The states occur with equal likelihood, but which state will occur is no better known than whether a coin toss will result in a head or a tail. Then the only kind of control we can exercise is by the choice of a strategy. However, our objective is to maximize the payoff, and strategy S1 accomplishes this end. We have met this same type of situation before, when the farmer was trying to decide which strategy to use—asparagus or peas.

To restate the problem, strategy S1 offers the greatest expected value for the payoff, but if N1 should occur, then the decision-maker must accept a very low payoff. Perhaps it would mean ruin for him. In our present case, we see that S2 offers almost as good an expected payoff as S1. No rational decision-maker is going to choose S1 with its great extremes in preference to S2 which produces just 0.5 less expected payoff. As in the farmer's case, we know what the difficulty is and we know how to resolve it. Utilities must be substituted for the payoffs that are presently being used. Before we do this, let us slightly rearrange the decision matrix so that the basic quandary can be posed.

	0.5 N1	0.5 N2	EV
S1	10	90	50
S2	50	50	50
S3	30	70	50

On the face of it, no strategy is preferred—a ludicrous conclusion to any experienced executive who would immediately choose S2 because it offers him complete control. His payoff with S2 is independent of the state of nature. No matter what happens he will always get 50 with S2. His control if he chooses S2 is perfect. With S1 or S3 it is less than perfect.

We will convert to utilities by means of the standard-gamble technique. We let the smallest value 10 equal zero. We take the largest value in the entire matrix, which is 90, and replace it with 1. We then ask: For what probability that 90 will occur in a lottery between 10 and 90 would we be willing to accept either 50 with certainty or the lottery? Let us assume that the answer is $\frac{3}{4}$. We ask the same question for 30 with certainty or the lottery, and 70 with certainty or the lottery. Let us assume that the resulting matrix is as follows:

	0.5 N1	0.5 N2	EV
S1	0	1	0.50
S2	0.75	0.75	0.75
S3	0.625	0.875	0.75

It is clear that strategy *S*1 has been eliminated. But the problem remains. The expected values of the utilities for *S*2 and *S*3 indicate that they are equivalent. Again, the executive knows that this is not reasonable. Without question he prefers *S*2 to *S*3. It could be argued that the decision-maker did not properly choose his utilities. But this argument is relatively fruitless from an operational point of view because it can be demonstrated that the values assigned to the utilities are consistent and logical. That is, the decision-maker can hardly assign a value of $\frac{1}{2}$ to 50. Were he to do so, it would mean that he considered 50 with certainty to be the equivalent of a 50–50 lottery between 10 and 90 with an expected value of 50. He would, in other words, be placing no utility on control.

Obviously the executive wishes to express his preference for a stable situation over an unstable one. Therefore, the utility of 50 is greater than $\frac{1}{2}$, and $\frac{3}{4}$ is a reasonable choice. In other words, the reason that the executive assigns a utility of $\frac{3}{4}$ to 50 is precisely because he prefers certainty or control rather than uncertainty or lack of control. The distortion of the utility upward from $\frac{1}{2}$ is a function of the decision-maker's lack of certainty. Furthermore, the selection of $\frac{3}{4}$ instead of $\frac{1}{2}$ is implied by the diminishing utility of money. The utility sacrificed by foregoing $50 with certainty is greater than the utility gained by an additional $40 with uncertainty. Even in the case of an even-money bet, no rational person governed by diminishing utilities would ever participate. As for the other utilities, it is completely consistent that if 50 has a utility of $\frac{3}{4}$ or $\frac{6}{8}$ that 30, which is less than the expected value, will be worth a bigger gamble. Therefore, we have assigned it $\frac{5}{8}$. Similarly, to forego 70 with certainty we require more certainty. Therefore, we have assigned it a utility value of $\frac{7}{8}$. Although we have created this example with just the right values to illustrate our point, the fact remains that they could have been the executive's assignment of utilities.

Several things can be said about this problem. We will concentrate our remarks on the implications of the example for control. We can say that the decision-maker has not estimated his utilities correctly. If he is willing to re-evaluate his utilities, then the tie between *S*2 and *S*3 may be broken. The executives with the job of implementation will say that the decision-maker's revised utilities are correct only if *S*2 is chosen in preference to *S*3. But how can we be sure that the decision-maker's corrected utilities are the right ones? As in all problems of estimation, we can expect some amount of error. As we have previously stated, the solutions of different problems have various tolerances for error. But in the case of utilities, if the decision-maker insists that he has made no errors, then it is impossible to contradict him. What we can say, however, is that his utilities indicate that he has different objectives and different values from ours. If, for example, the decision-maker insists that the matrix with equal expected utilities for $S2$ and $S3$ is correct, then the conclusion can be drawn that he is not interested in the degree of control. The evaluation of the solution by the executive in charge of implementation will, in all probability, reject the decision-maker's solution.

Unfortunately, the situation is not always as clear as it is in this simple example. If the chosen utilities do not express the multiple objectives of obtaining the best possible combination of payoff and control, it is difficult to detect this fact. When the executive does not have the rare situation of choosing between two strategies that appear to offer equal expected utilities, but that have clearly different outcomes, how is he to know whether similar distortions have not appeared in the assignment of utilities? That is, how is he to tell whether the problem-solvers have included his objective of control?

In the problem section of Chapter 4, the reader was asked to use the standard-gamble technique. In that example, we suggested that comparisons should be made between the smallest and the largest values— but also with ranges falling between the extremes. In so doing, the reader was able to check his consistency in assigning utilities. If the elements of this comparison are now extended to the utility matrix, we will eliminate the 0 and 1 of $S1$ from our consideration. In other words, we will use the standard gamble to evaluate the utilities of $S2$ and $S3$. Then matrix 1

	0.5 $N1$	0.5 $N2$	EV
$S2$	0.75	0.75	0.75
$S3$	0.625	0.875	0.75

becomes matrix 2

	0.5 $N1$	0.5 $N2$	EV
$S2$	0.625	0.625	0.625
$S3$	0	1	0.50

We have taken the maximum and minimum values in the matrix and have set them equal to 1 and 0, respectively, as the method requires. Since 0.75 lies an equal distance from both 0.625 and 0.825, the probability that 0.875 will occur in a lottery with 0.625 should be greater than 0.50 to produce indifference between that lottery and 0.75 for certain. The reasons are the same as those given above for assigning more than 0.50 for the utility of 50. However, in order to obtain equal expected utilities as indicated by the original (matrix 1, above), we should have obtained matrix 3 (below) instead of matrix 2.

	0.5 *N*1	0.5 *N*2	*EV*
*S*2	0.50	0.50	0.50
*S*3	0	1	0.50

But matrix 3 is not reasonable since it assigns a utility of 0.50 to the value 0.75, and we have explained why a value of 0.50 for 0.75 is not justifiable. Why does this occur? Because the supposition of the standard gamble is that we can express any utility in terms of the two extremes. Using the standard-gamble method assumes that the individual, evaluating his utilities, is capable of assessing the multiple objectives that are involved in the problem—one of which is control. If the executive does not share this assumption, believing that it is beyond the realm of bounded rationality, then there is a means available for systematically including the control objective in the selection of a strategy. We have previously discussed this means—which is the use of the logarithmic measure of utility—but we must now express its importance in the area of control and implementation.

139/ Control and the Logarithmic Measure of Utility

Let us replace the outcomes in the decision matrix with the logarithms of the outcomes.

REPLACE		0.5 *N*1	0.5 *N*2	*EV*	APPROXIMATE EQUIVALENT *EV*
10 90	*S*1	1.000	1.954	1.477	30
50 50	*S*2	1.699	1.699	1.699	50
30 70	*S*3	1.477	1.845	1.661	46

We observe that the logarithms produce the highest expected value for *S*2—which is in keeping with the rational requirements for control. The tie between the expected values is broken by means of this measure of utility. The use of the logarithm insures the selection of the strategy with the best possible control whenever a tie occurs for the outcomes. Thus, the following relationship holds for any pair of values with the expected value of 50:

$$\log 99 + \log 1 < \log 98 + \log 2 < \log 97 + \log 3 < \ldots < \log 50 + \log 50$$

Using logarithms, the general form of the decision matrix can be written:

	p_1 $N1$	p_2 $N2$
$S1$	$\log O_{11}$	$\log O_{12}$
$S2$	$\log O_{21}$	$\log O_{22}$
$S3$	$\log O_{31}$	$\log O_{32}$

The expected value is then derived by the equations:

$$EV_1 = p_1 \log O_{11} + p_2 \log O_{12}$$
$$EV_2 = p_1 \log O_{21} + p_2 \log O_{22}$$
$$EV_3 = p_1 \log O_{31} + p_2 \log O_{32}$$

The largest EV_i, so calculated, determines the strategy to be selected, i. If we convert from this logarithmic form, we get

$$EV_1 = \log (O_{11}{}^{p_1}O_{12}{}^{p_2})$$
$$EV_2 = \log (O_{21}{}^{p_1}O_{22}{}^{p_2})$$
$$EV_3 = \log (O_{31}{}^{p_1}O_{32}{}^{p_2})$$

This is a form we certainly recognize. It is the logarithm of the relationship that we developed, at some length, when we were discussing dimensional analysis and multiple objectives (page 239). The fact that it is the logarithm of this familiar expression is of no particular consequence since the logarithm is simply a convenient way of evaluating the expression, $O_{11}{}^{p_1}O_{12}{}^{p_2}$, and so on. The greatest value of the logarithm will also be the greatest value of the expression. However, the form of the expression itself suggests an approach to the meaning of control.

The values p_1 and p_2 are the probabilities that the states of nature will occur. In our former discussion of dimensional analysis the corresponding powers represented the importance the decision-maker placed on the individual objectives. The interpretation of the present case can be made in these same terms. We observe that O_{ij} is raised to the p_j power, where the strategy is i and the state of nature is j. This implies that the objective is the state of nature and the importance of the objective to the decision-maker is the probability that the state of nature will occur. This is reasonable since the importance of the state of nature increases as its frequency increases. The value that the objective takes on is, in each case, the result of the strategy employed. Since the value is the utility of the outcome, the logarithm of the outcome is multiplied by the importance, p_j, of the state of nature that produced the outcome. In this way the utilities of the outcomes express the multiple objectives of wanting to maximize the payoffs and wanting simultaneously to maximize control.

When the decision-maker wishes to include control in his appraisal of the decision matrix he can use the logarithms of the outcomes as his measure of utility. The extent to which an individual approximates the values of the logarithmic utilities in his estimates of utility by the standard gamble, or by whatever means he uses, is evidence of the importance he places on control. This leads to the important question: How does the decision-maker exercise this control? States of nature have repeatedly been defined as falling outside the domain of the decision-maker's control. The answer to this question requires a careful inspection of states of nature.

140/ States of Nature and Control

States of nature were introduced at the very start of this book. At that time we presented a simple definition which adequately covered a great number of cases—but not all. The reader will have noticed that in a number of instances states of nature have been, in some sense, transformed into outcomes. We propose, now, to explore this kind of transformation and to explain what it means in terms of control.

The decision matrix, which we have studied at great length, can present situations where the states of nature appear under conditions of certainty, risk, or uncertainty. All three conditions require specific assumptions. First of all, with respect to certainty and risk, we must assume that the probabilities assigned to the states of nature are correctly chosen —which precludes the possibility that other states that are unknown could exist. In the second place, with respect to all three decision conditions, we must assume that the probabilities assigned to the states of nature will not change. The implications of these assumptions are far-reaching.

Let us consider decision-making under conditions of uncertainty. In a formal sense we know that our method guarantees we will obtain the best possible decision that our choice of a decision criterion permits. This selection of a decision criterion is, in a very real sense, a control decision. In other words, the decision-maker's choice of a criterion can be represented as a selection of p values. In this case the decision-maker is really rating the importance of the various states of nature but without the benefit of frequency observations. An executive faced with the problems of implementation could hardly be blamed for placing a relatively low degree of belief on a decision made in this fashion.

Because states of nature are, in many cases, difficult or impossible to determine—still less to place probabilities on their likelihood of occurring—an important transformation is used. In this transformation, states of nature are replaced by outcomes. Outcomes are usually much easier to observe. Furthermore, it is frequently possible to describe the complete universe of outcomes—an accomplishment which is much more difficult for states of nature. The transformation is used most often when the problem is one of uncertainty. That is, we do not know the states of nature but we can observe the outcomes. We can distinguish these transformed outcomes by calling them *outcome-states*. To illustrate, we will transform the matrix we used before.

| | | | | | OUTCOME-STATES | | | | | | |
	0	10	20	30	40	50	60	70	80	90	100
S1	—	0.5	—	—	—	—	—	—	—	0.5	—
S2	—	—	—	—	—	1.0	—	—	—	—	—
S3	—	—	—	0.5	—	—	—	0.5	—	—	—

The payoff entries are the probabilities that each outcome-state will result from a specific strategy. Now, in this sense we see that although the decision-maker cannot control the state of nature, he has some control over the outcome-states. *S2* gives him perfect control over one outcome-state. He may not like this particular outcome-state, and he can indicate this when he expresses his utility for it. But from the point of view of control, he could ask for nothing more.

Information theory tells us something about this aspect of the decision-maker's control. It will be remembered that H_{Max} was the condition of equally likely states—and that this represented complete disorder. In other words, it represents no control at all. When H was equal to zero—only one outcome-state possible—there would be complete order and perfect control. The information measures for this matrix would be (using bits):

$$H(S1) = -0.5 \log 0.5 - 0.5 \log 0.5 = 1.0 \text{ bit}$$
$$H(S2) = -1 \log 1 = 0.0 \text{ bit}$$
$$H(S3) = -0.5 \log 0.5 - 0.5 \log 0.5 = 1.0 \text{ bit}$$
$$H_{\text{Max}} = -\log (1/11) = 3.5 \text{ bits}$$

The redundancy value, R, gives a reasonable measure of control on the scale 0 to 1. Zero represents complete lack of control, while the value one stands for complete control.

$$R(S1) = 1 - 1/3.5 = 0.7$$
$$R(S2) = 1 - 0/3.5 = 1.0$$
$$R(S3) = 1 - 1/3.5 = 0.7$$

Using information theory gives us a "pure" measure of control. For this reason it suffers from the same defect—but at the opposite pole—that we previously observed when maximization of the payoff was accomplished without full consideration of control. In other words, information theoretic measures tell us nothing about which outcome-states appear. They do not permit the decision-maker to express his preference for one outcome-state over another. That is why $S1$ and $S3$ have the same redundancy measures. H_{Max} is based on the eleven outcome-states. If unit divisions had been employed, i.e., 0, 1, 2, . . . 50, . . . 98, 99, 100, there would have been 101 outcome-states. In this case, H_{Max} would be 6.6 bits. This would not have affected the R measure for $S2$, but the R measures for $S1$ and $S3$ would have been increased to 0.85. On the face of it this might seem absurd, but from a purely control point of view it is understandable. The number of possible outcome-states has increased. Therefore, more control would be required to maintain only two equally likely states out of a greater number of possibilities. This further illustrates the fact that, although information measures are descriptive of control, they are not well suited for the executive's evaluation of control.

We have explained how the outcome-state transformation allows for the possibility that we do not know or cannot observe all relevant states of nature. The transformation to outcome-states permits the decision-maker to encompass all of the reality with which he is concerned. For example, profit can be represented dollar by dollar between whatever bounds appear reasonably certain of containing all experience. Even more definitive are outcome-states given in percentages which range from 0 to 100. The brand-share model was an example of a transformation from states of nature to outcome-states. It would have been inconceivable to attempt to list, observe, or know all of the states of nature that affect brand share.

The outcome-state matrix can be used to obtain the logarithmic utility comparison by expressing the outcome states as logarithms. In the example given below, it should be noted how states $N1$ and $N3$ produce the same outcome, 3, when strategy $S3$ is used. This fact, which might be difficult to observe, is not required information for the outcome-state matrix.

	0.3	0.2	0.5		OUTCOME-STATES			
	$N1$	$N2$	$N3$		2	3	4	5
$S1$	5	4	3	$S1$	—	0.5	0.2	0.3
$S2$	2	5	3	$S2$	0.3	0.5	—	0.2
$S3$	3	4	3	$S3$	—	0.8	0.2	—

For the decision matrix, we have

$$EV(S1) = 0.3 \log 5 + 0.2 \log 4 + 0.5 \log 3$$
$$EV(S2) = 0.3 \log 2 + 0.2 \log 5 + 0.5 \log 3$$
$$EV(S3) = 0.3 \log 3 + 0.2 \log 4 + 0.5 \log 3 = 0.8 \log 3 + 0.2 \log 4$$

For the outcome-state matrix, we observe

$$EV(S1) = 0.5 \log 3 + 0.2 \log 4 + 0.3 \log 5$$
$$EV(S2) = 0.3 \log 2 + 0.5 \log 3 + 0.2 \log 5$$
$$EV(S3) = 0.8 \log 3 + 0.2 \log 4$$

And, in this sense, these forms are equivalent, even though we cannot retransform the outcome-state matrix back to the form of the usual decision matrix. Information is lacking as to which states produced which outcome-states.

The outcome-state transformation takes care of the first problem we mentioned, that is, the difficulty of assigning probabilities to states of nature and the possibility that unknown states exist. We will now consider the second problem that we raised, namely, the assumption that probabilities assigned to states of nature will not change.

141/ Stability and States of Nature

One of the most fundamental requirements of decision-making is that stability exist with respect to the states of nature. In its simplest form, stability refers to stationary probabilities for the states of nature. Stationary probabilities will not change values and, therefore, when we talk about decision-making under risk we assume that the probabilities for the states of nature are forever the same. Let us consider the following decision matrix, which applies to only one strategy, observing the probabilities of the states of nature over two periods of time.

	0.2	0.3	0.1	0.2	0.1	0.1
	$N1$	$N2$	$N3$	$N4$	$N5$	$N6$
$S1(t_0)$	10	4	10	4	8	10

	0.1	0.2	0.2	0.3	0.1	0.1
	$N1$	$N2$	$N3$	$N4$	$N5$	$N6$
$S1(t_1)$	10	4	10	4	8	10

We see that stability for the states of nature does not exist in this example. However, purely from the point of view of outcome states, the process appears to be stable. As long as only this kind of interchange takes place, we can consider the outcome-state distribution to be stable.

	OUTCOME-STATES									
	0	1	2	3	4	5	6	7	8	9	10
$S1(t_0)$	—	—	—	—	0.5	—	—	—	0.1	—	0.4
$S1(t_1)$	—	—	—	—	0.5	—	—	—	0.1	—	0.4

A most important statistical method exists that determines whether or not an in-time process is "under control" or stable. This is the method used in quality control. Because it is so difficult to observe states of nature—to find out how many states exist, to describe all of the states so that they can be identified and recognized, to observe which states produce the same outcome, and so on—quality control is based on the outcome-state matrix. Quality control enables the decision-maker to detect nonstationary probabilities for the outcome-states. Since so many decision methods, such as all decision-making under risk, standard-gamble or logarithmic evaluation of utilities, require stationarity, it is of the greatest importance that the decision-maker consider this aspect of control.

Statistical quality control is based on the sampling of outcome states. Each sample is examined to determine how much variability occurred within that sample. After a reasonable number of samples are taken, the average variability is determined. This average variability is then converted to an estimate of the variability of the population from which the samples were drawn. The measure of variability is used to establish control limits. Outcome-states that lie within the control limits are expected to occur. Outcome-states that fall outside of the control limits are unexpected events that appear to have so low a probability of expected occurrence that when they do appear it is taken as a signal that changes in the process may be taking place. Figure 15.1 shows a control chart in which outcome-state 90 appears. Since this outcome-state lies above the

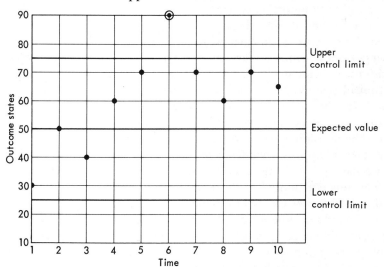

FIGURE 15.1 A control chart on which outcome-state 90 appears and signals that the process may not be under control.

upper control limit, its occurrence is unexpected and improbable unless a change in the process has taken place. Another sign that leads to the same conclusion appears on the chart. Starting with the fourth observation, all of the outcome states lie above the expected value. This is called a *run*. When a large number of successive values fall entirely on one side of the expected value, an improbable occurrence has been observed. Again, it is taken as a signal that a fundamental change may have occurred in the process.

It has not been our intention to develop the statistical methods of quality control except as they relate to the decision-maker's problems of evaluating his control. The most significant consideration, in this regard, is the fact that the conclusion that a process is out of control is not taken as an indication that the probabilities of the states of nature have changed. Instead it is interpreted as the fact that the definition of the strategy is incomplete. In other words, the conclusion is drawn that the decision-maker either lacks control over his instruments or else he has failed to consider an element that he could control if he found out what it was. Why is it that the assumption is made that no change occurred in the probabilities of the states of nature?

The answer is that quality control is applied mostly to physical processes. The assumption is far less applicable to behavioral processes. In a physical system Nature tends to exhibit constancy and consistency. When such a system does not exhibit constancy, then the most rewarding conclusion is the one we have drawn above. Under most circumstances it is possible to locate that element in the strategy which was either forgotten or changed. Clearly these sequential methods cannot be used when the strategy is changed with each decision (such as changing the settings on a machine as each new part is made), or when nonrepetitive decisions are being made. However, for repetitive decisions, this approach to control epitomizes the notions of an automatic decision-maker. The knowledge that a process is under control, and that an unknown change in strategy will be detected, adds immeasurably to the degree of confidence the decision-maker can place in the solution.

But what happens when the constancy of nature cannot be relied upon? As we have pointed out, this is particularly characteristic of behavioral systems, but not limited to them. It can be argued that if we could recognize the basic elements in economic, market, and personnel problems then we would be able to complete our strategies and thereby remove the apparent differences between physical and behavioral systems. Practically speaking, however, the point is purely philosophical, but the problem is real. The area that we are calling "behavioral" includes the greatest number of high-level decision problems.

First of all, we find a contradiction. States of nature, by definition, cannot be controlled. But in feedback systems, an input leads to an output which is fed back and causes a change in the state of nature. In that case, by selecting an input the decision-maker can indirectly control the state of nature, within whatever limits the system allows. For example, in the work-pool problem of Chapter 14, the decision-maker changed the probabilities of absenteeism by changing the size of the work pool. Further, it can be recognized that a stochastic process produces continual changes in the probability distribution of the outcome-states. But in this case, we will also observe that the matrix of transition probabilities could be constant. In that event, we would treat the transition probabilities as the outcome-states, and the decision-maker would be in a position to evaluate the degree of control in these terms. However, we have had occasion to suggest the use of the transition matrix.

It is evident that, lacking a stable system, we must hunt indefinitely through a maze of interdependent probabilities without ever finding our stable system upon which everything else could be based. Under these circumstances, lacking a permanent solution, the decision-maker can utilize the various methods available for reaching short-term decisions. His long-term decisions are achieved in a step-by-step process which continually evaluates what has happened—what can now be achieved—and how much control is available at each step along the way. If a limiting distribution is available, the stepping process can benefit from this information. However, states of nature with variable probabilities do not necessarily come to equilibrium. Some states oscillate continually in a periodic way, while others enter states from which there is no return and from which they lead to an entirely new set of companion states of nature. We can represent some of these conditions in the following way:

	$N1$	$N2$	$N3$	$N4$	$N5$	$N6$
$S1(t_0)$	0.10	0.50	0.40	0.20	—	0.80
$S1(t_1)$	0.20	0.40	0.40	—	0.20	0.60
$S1(t_2)$	0.30	0.50	0.40	—	0.20	0.45
$S1(t_3)$	0.20	0.40	0.40	—	0.20	0.34
$S1(t_4)$	0.10	0.50	0.40	—	0.20	0.26
$S1(t_5)$	0.20	0.40	0.40	—	0.20	0.20
$S1(t_6)$	0.30	0.50	0.40	—	0.20	0.15
.	.	.	.	.	.	.
.	.	.	.	.	.	.
.	.	.	.	.	.	.
$S1(t_i)$	—	—	0.40	—	0.20	0.08

The outcomes shown are the probabilities that the states of nature will appear. Each of the matrix columns is intended to represent a different type of condition for states of nature. $N1$ and $N2$ are periodic but oscillate with different frequencies. The periodic states may behave in this fashion because of feedback. A different strategy could produce different periods of oscillation or even stable states. $N3$ is an example of a stable state. Solutions for conditions in which all the states are stable can be regarded as relatively permanent. $N4$ and $N5$ are intended to represent a nonreversible change in the states of nature. We might suppose that under $S1$, $N4$ becomes $S5$ by means of some feedback connection. If, after $S1$ is removed, $N4$ does not reappear, then the implication is that some kind of threshold has been crossed from which there is no return. The issue of reversibility is an important one from the point of view of control. Catastrophe and ruin represent extreme situations from which the smallest chance of return exists. $N6$ is an example of a process that has a limit. Long range decision-making can be based on predictions of such an equilibrium state.

Another control characteristic of repetitive decision-making is worthy of mention. We have indicated previously how a mixed strategy changes the value of the payoff for both parties in a competitive situation. When the decision matrix does not have competitive strategies but only states of nature, the decision-maker can obtain complete control of a large range of outcomes by using a mixed strategy. For example,

	0.5 $N1$	0.5 $N2$	EV
$S1$	10	30	20
$S2$	70	90	80

If the decision-maker decides to use $S1$ exclusively over a great many repetitions he will obtain the expected value of 20. If he uses $S2$ exclusively, he will get 80. But suppose that the value he wishes to obtain is 50. Then, if he uses $S1$ half the time and $S2$ half the time, he will obtain an expected value of 50. Suppose that he would like to get 35. The answer is simply to use $S1$ three-fourths of the time and $S2$ one-fourth of the time. In this way, the decision-maker exercises control over the entire range of values between his minimum and his maximum expected values. If he knows how the probabilities of the states of nature will vary in the future, he can apply the same kind of mixed strategies in time. In all cases, this approach requires that the effects of the decisions should be cumulative over time. Repetitive decision-making allows for a learning process, and increased control can be gained by the decision-maker as he improves his knowledge of the situation.

These are some aspects of the problem of control that the decision-maker is faced with when he considers the solution in implementation terms. We are now in a position to answer the question: How does the decision-maker exercise control? Whether or not he can in any way affect

states of nature, the decision-maker's control is a function of the information he has about the problem and the solution. The decision-maker's
choice of a strategy—if predicated solely on some analytical maximization device—cannot include all of the elements pertinent to implementation. All of the elements cannot be included in a single maximization
technique. On the other hand, there are a variety of analytical methods
that can produce useful information with respect to this problem. The
decision-maker who puts full faith in his intuition alone is turning his
back on information that could substantially assist him in resolving his
control problems. For we see that the control problem is a question of
comparing complex multiple objectives under a variety of restrictive conditions imposed by nature. The decision-maker's only means of exercising control is by his choice of a strategy. Modifications of the strategy
can be made, based on information that went into obtaining the solution. Further modifications will result from additional information derived by auxiliary techniques. The decision-maker can then select that
strategy which promises the most rewarding degree of achievement of the
multiple objectives involved.

PROBLEMS

1. An executive has a choice of two alternative sets of tactics, x or y. His objective is to achieve the state of the system "E." The system has six states,
A, B, C, D, E, and F and no matter which tactics he uses he must begin with
A. The executive's ability to control the system is represented in matrix form
for each set of tactics. (That is, in x for example, there is perfect control, (1),
in changing F to B, but only 0.2 chance of changing D to C, with an 0.8 chance
of changing D to E.)

			x								y			
	A	B	C	D	E	F		A	B	C	D	E	F
A	0	0	0	0	0	1	A	0	0.5	0	0	0.5	0
B	0	0	0	1	0	0	B	0.2	0	0	0	0.8	0
C	0	0	0	0	0.6	0.4	C	0.1	0	0	0	0	0.9
D	0	0	0.2	0	0.8	0	D	0.1	0	0.9	0	0	0
E	0	0.3	0	0	0.7	0	E	0	0	0	0.5	0.5	0
F	0	1	0	0	0	0	F	0	0	0	0	1	0

a. What is the relative permanence of the outcome in each case?
b. What is the relative degree of reversibility with respect to the starting
point A in each case?
c. Which set of tactics offers greater control?
d. Which set of tactics should the executive choose?

2. An executive is faced with the following decision problem under uncertainty:

	N1	N2	N3	N4
S1	2	8	16	8
S2	8	8	8	4
S3	4	4	16	8

a. What will be his decision if he uses expected values?

b. What will be his decision if he considers the control aspects of the problem? How can he resolve the problem that arises?

c. Transform this matrix to an outcome-state matrix and obtain the entropy and redundancy of each strategy.

3. In what way can we interpret the four situations described below? $\bar{S}$ is the expected sales per week. S_u is the upper control limit so chosen that sales per week are greater than S_u less than 1 per cent of the time. S_L is the lower control limit which is not necessarily positioned an equal distance from the mean, $\bar{S}$.

     a. $S_u = 4.2,\ \bar{S} = 4.0,\ S_L = 3.8$
     b. $S_u = t/2 + 6,\ \bar{S} = t/2 + 2,\ S_L = t/2 - 2$
     c. $S_u = 2t/3 + 6,\ \bar{S} = t/2 + 2,\ S_L = t/3 - 2$
     d. $S_u = 4/2^t + 4,\ \bar{S} = 4.0,\ S_L = 4 - 4/2^t$

4. Assume the following repetitive decision situation:

	0.5 N1	0.5 N2	EV
S1	2	8	5
S2	4	8	6
S3	2	16	9

a. If the executive's objective is to achieve outcome values closest to 8 as often as possible, what is his optimal procedure?

b. If the objective is to obtain the expected value closest to 8 by following a pure strategy, what then is the optimal procedure?

c. If the objective is to obtain the expected value of 8 by following a mixed strategy, what is the best plan of action?

5. An executive makes n_i decision per day, where i stands for the day of the year. Over a period of time the executive collects enough *a posteriori* data concerning the correctness of each decision which he has made to determine that his expected fraction of incorrect decisions, $\bar{p}$, is 0.02. The executive prepares a control chart on which he marks the expected value. For each day he determines the control limits by using the equations:

$$(\text{Upper control limit})_i = \bar{p} + 3\sqrt{\bar{p}\,(1 - \bar{p})/n_i}$$
$$(\text{Lower control limit})_i = \bar{p} - 3\sqrt{\bar{p}\,(1 - \bar{p})/n_i}$$

What is the greatest fraction of incorrect decisions per day that the executive is prepared to accept as a chance possibility before he re-examines his own decision-making practices

     a. If he makes one decision per day?
     b. If he makes nine decisions per day?
     c. If he makes 100 decisions per day?
     d. How would you interpret the lower limit?

```
8 5 4 6 9 0 6 4 6 7 1 1 8 4 0 6 0 4 1 4 8 4
0 7 2 2 6 1 4 7 3 7 6 8 8 2 7 9 9 7 2 5 2 7
4 6 9 5 7 5 0 7 2 3 7 4 2 9 8 1 8 4 9 8 8 1
4 0 8 0 9 3 4 0 9 0 8 5 1 2 6 3 4 7 1 1 5 5
7 9 1 8 7 2 5 8 4 8 6 9 8 4 3 0 9 4 6 1 6 3
0 2 2 0 7 3 7 6 9 9 2 3 6 0 1 8 7 5 0 3 3 1
7 1 9 2 9 2 4 9 1 3 2 9 7 5 9 1 0 5 6 6 5 3
5 2 6 1 4 8 2 7 2 7 6 1 6 6 9 1 4 7 5 7 7 6
9 9 9 7 2 5 2 6 5 1 0 0 4 9 6 6 7 4 5 6 2 5
8 6 8 1 5 9 2 3 2 9 8 6 0 4 7 9 0 3 2 5 7 8
0 6 2 2 4 5 9 9 6 0 7 3 7 7 0 4 1 0 2 9 6 5
1 1 7 3 4 5 4 7 2 5 1 1 3 6 3 4 3 0 5 0 4 6
0 0 9 0 6 0 4 5 9 4 6 9 1 4 2 0 3 2 8 5 1 6
7 6 9 8 4 1 1 9 2 2 0 6 0 8 3 0 1 5 4 2 2 0
3 0 7 6 1 1 9 2 8 0 0 2 1 5 6 2 8 4 1 0 3 8
0 6 8 7 1 1 5 2 6 6 4 2 3 3 2 5 8 0 7 0 6 8
0 6 6 7 3 7 6 3 1 8 0 5 2 6 1 9 1 2 4 9 9 8
1 9 8 5 0 6 9 7 6 3 5 2 2 2 4 6 3 2 6 4 0 9
1 8 1 4 4 9 4 1 6 2 2 9 3 9 2 5 7 5 2 7 4 2
3 0 3 0 9 8 8 7 2 2 5 6 4 9 8 0 0 8 6 4 6 8
5 7 4 9 8 5 7 9 6 6 2 3 6 1 8 2 5 5 6 6 1 4
0 2 1 6 3 8 4 3 6 6 1 2 8 1 1 7 4 3 4 2 8 5
6 5 8 2 5 9 8 6 3 5 9 4 0 3 5 2 3 7 4 7 6 6
4 8 8 5 8 1 8 3 0 5 6 6 2 0 9 0 5 2 1 7 1 5
3 7 1 6 0 2 8 5 8 7 3 3 7 4 0 0 7 0 7 7 1 7
0 0 7 6 1 0 4 0 3 3 0 4 8 5 9 5 9 3 8 8 6 8
3 8 0 2 1 0 2 6 3 4 1 7 3 2 9 8 3 6 5 3 5 4
5 3 2 7 9 8 8 2 9 4 4 0 5 1 5 0 5 7 0 9 7 1
7 3 7 4 6 6 0 0 2 1 7 7 3 4 9 3 5 2 5 9 7 4
0 8 0 9 6 0 1 0 4 6 6 8 0 2 2 2 0 9 4 9 6 0
9 3 6 8 3 7 9 5 8 8 1 1 5 3 3 1 6 5 8 1 1 1
7 3 6 5 2 6 6 2 6 3 3 0 1 6 5 1 2 1 1 0 5 4
2 9 1 6 0 6 1 3 3 1 2 8 0 2 9 8 2 9 9 7 8 5
5 1 6 8 7 9 9 2 7 9 7 1 1 2 7 8 1 3 0 2 0 1
3 1 6 7 8 4 8 6 8 6 9 3 9 2 8 6 9 4 7 8 2 9
1 2 1 4 6 2 0 6 3 8 9 3 5 4 7 8 8 0 9 8 8 2
0 3 2 1 4 4 9 2 8 3 2 2 5 8 8 7 1 4 9 5 3 5
8 0 8 5 9 6 4 8 3 7 6 7 6 5 3 2 6 0 8 5 9 1
3 5 3 1 3 3 1 7 1 2 7 7 0 1 0 2 8 5 4 1 6 7
3 8 9 5 0 0 9 0 2 7 0 6 2 8 3 0 0 2 4 9 0 2
9 8 9 9 1 6 1 2 6 9 2 6 4 2 8 2 3 4 2 3 6 8
0 1 8 5 8 1 9 4 2 3 9 7 6 2 3 7 0 6 5 5 3 8
1 5 1 6 4 9 9 0 1 1 0 1 3 4 1 4 3 2 4 4 0 0
8 6 5 3 9 2 6 0 4 3 5 6 9 4 5 1 0 5 2 4 5 2
8 1 8 9 3 4 2 4 5 1 8 6 2 6 9 9 0 0 4 1 7 4
0 2 4 0 3 0 9 2 9 2 9 8 0 9 5 3 5 7 5 2 9 8
4 1 9 5 7 2 3 5 6 0 8 2 5 2 2 0 8 9 1 6 1 1
6 0 6 5 9 2 4 1 9 5 0 2 3 3 1 7 3 6 2 9 1 4
3 6 6 5 2 7 0 9 8 3 9 4 6 1 8 2 3 8 7 8 3 7
0 9 6 3 9 1 9 5 6 1 2 9 3 7 4 1 2 7 9 3 9 5
7 0 9 0 6 8 5 9 9 5 5 9 2 9 5 0 9 3 8 8 9 1 5
2 7 9 2 5 2 7 0 4 0 3 3 4 6 7 9 0 1 8 3 9 5
2 3 9 3 4 4 7 9 6 5 7 2 8 6 3 2 7 6 9 7 7 1
0 4 6 9 6 3 2 4 3 2 3 9 3 1 5 8 8 3 1 0 8 6
9 2 0 3 2 9 8 5 1 4 2 2 3 7 8 3 7 5 0 5 1 0
9 2 1 7 5 3 4 2 3 9 9 0 3 6 9 4 7 0 7 8 1 0
6 4 1 9 8 5 7 1 5 4 7 2 4 4 9 7 3 7 2 7 0 4
8 5 0 7 2 4 5 1 8 0 6 9 1 1 5 0 4 1 2 2 7 4
0 5 9 6 7 1 0 7 6 6 3 9 9 6 8 0 7 2 4 6 9 8
5 5 7 5 2 7 3 4 6 5 3 1 5 1 0 7 6 4 0 9 3 1
5 4 5 0 9 7 5 8 1 7 4 6 6 5 9 9 1 2 4 2 2 7
```

TABLE OF RANDOM NUMBERS (Cont.)

```
8 7 1 0 0 2 5 8 3 1 8 3 8 5 6 0 4 2 5 8 0 7
6 0 3 2 9 4 7 3 8 2 6 0 0 3 2 6 7 3 2 8 6 5
1 9 9 6 3 7 1 7 3 6 7 5 1 5 6 0 5 7 5 2 5 2
7 1 7 6 5 9 1 4 2 3 6 2 3 1 6 0 9 8 6 6 8 4
6 7 8 4 0 3 3 0 1 6 6 4 6 9 7 5 2 3 5 7 3 8
7 0 0 9 1 7 7 7 2 3 3 7 1 7 4 5 8 5 2 4 9 9
8 9 2 0 1 1 1 4 4 4 8 3 0 3 8 3 1 0 0 2 0 6
3 7 6 0 1 6 4 5 5 2 5 4 9 7 4 7 9 2 0 7 9 1
9 7 4 1 5 0 4 4 4 4 6 7 9 8 1 4 8 2 7 4 1 5
3 1 6 7 0 2 3 0 9 0 4 4 7 4 7 5 4 5 6 6 9 2
9 5 7 2 8 6 0 5 8 0 8 0 1 8 1 9 0 4 8 9 4 7
5 7 1 3 0 0 1 8 3 3 0 6 2 3 9 2 6 9 6 7 5 2
3 9 8 5 1 8 5 8 4 1 4 6 8 1 5 7 8 1 7 0 5 7
4 8 3 7 7 3 8 4 1 3 8 1 7 5 6 3 6 5 2 6 5 6
9 0 1 1 9 1 0 6 9 6 9 8 9 4 5 1 8 5 4 1 8 4
9 6 4 8 3 2 3 0 1 7 9 6 6 7 8 2 3 8 2 9 4 2
6 8 8 9 9 8 4 3 1 7 9 8 0 6 7 6 0 1 8 4 6 3
2 0 9 8 0 7 0 9 9 2 7 1 9 3 0 2 6 8 6 2 2 1
2 1 1 4 0 1 7 1 9 5 1 7 8 7 5 5 0 2 0 2 1 1
0 4 6 9 3 8 2 4 4 4 8 0 4 1 1 4 5 0 2 0 6 4
0 4 0 6 0 5 1 7 2 4 4 0 1 2 7 7 5 5 5 0 6 3
8 7 2 5 3 3 8 9 3 4 5 9 0 6 2 4 5 6 8 1 2 0
9 2 3 5 9 8 1 7 9 9 8 6 6 6 1 9 9 4 5 3 7 6
3 0 6 0 1 5 8 8 6 3 9 2 2 6 5 5 5 0 2 5 9 2
3 4 6 5 8 5 5 8 2 1 7 9 2 8 1 0 7 2 1 3 7 1
0 8 9 7 7 4 3 3 2 8 2 9 4 9 9 7 3 4 3 5 5 8
1 6 7 7 7 9 1 4 7 7 6 9 9 7 5 7 6 8 2 0 4 1
9 1 5 8 8 4 1 7 9 6 7 6 9 8 2 2 7 5 4 2 8 3
5 1 2 4 2 1 6 1 5 9 9 1 8 6 1 4 9 9 8 7 6 1
4 1 8 5 3 2 8 9 3 9 0 6 0 6 5 5 3 0 4 3 7 1
5 8 5 1 2 4 5 4 7 4 1 5 8 8 6 1 4 2 1 2 7 2
1 4 0 5 4 9 6 1 3 1 5 5 2 9 2 1 8 3 7 2 0 8
9 5 9 9 8 7 8 1 7 9 1 3 1 0 8 1 9 6 1 8 8 2
9 2 9 9 9 3 2 7 8 5 3 0 6 0 5 0 5 8 3 4 4 2
5 6 5 5 4 3 2 0 9 4 7 3 6 5 5 9 1 0 0 5 1 9
1 1 5 4 4 4 6 6 7 7 8 6 0 4 0 2 9 7 9 4 5 9
7 2 9 7 7 4 1 9 4 1 2 4 5 5 2 3 9 1 4 0 6 1
1 2 7 6 2 1 4 1 7 1 3 6 5 2 8 4 9 9 7 0 5 8
1 3 7 6 0 9 8 8 6 2 6 4 2 2 6 4 7 6 8 5 5 4
8 5 6 2 0 0 7 2 3 1 7 2 7 8 6 0 1 7 3 4 1 1
7 9 7 3 3 9 3 6 3 1 8 3 9 9 4 5 4 1 3 4 7 0
8 0 1 7 1 1 8 7 8 9 6 7 2 9 3 2 6 3 0 7 4 0
7 5 5 7 3 8 3 2 4 2 2 3 4 7 8 3 0 4 6 2 6 5
4 8 4 9 7 9 0 7 0 5 9 6 9 0 6 8 1 8 7 0 2 8
6 5 6 0 1 2 7 9 0 7 6 4 9 8 4 7 9 5 8 9 0 2
7 1 0 6 1 3 2 2 1 5 8 4 5 3 3 8 6 4 1 8 4 2
5 7 8 2 9 5 9 8 4 4 9 6 8 8 0 2 1 5 0 8 0 9
1 2 6 4 6 9 5 6 1 1 6 3 1 9 2 5 7 1 9 1 5 0
4 4 8 3 9 7 6 4 4 0 3 7 9 9 0 6 8 4 5 6 7 7
6 4 0 6 1 5 0 7 7 8 7 0 5 2 5 1 6 8 6 5 4 0
9 3 1 1 9 1 7 9 6 4 9 9 9 2 4 2 6 3 7 1 8 0
5 5 5 7 0 5 1 9 2 8 8 7 7 5 0 9 8 4 4 8 1 6
0 4 3 1 1 8 0 6 0 2 7 9 3 3 2 4 3 1 2 7 4 8
4 7 8 1 8 8 2 3 6 3 5 7 4 1 8 0 4 1 3 6 2 7
3 9 4 6 8 4 2 3 2 8 6 8 5 4 0 4 1 7 4 5 4 2
0 9 6 3 9 4 3 7 9 7 6 1 9 1 7 8 3 4 0 3 0 9
7 4 2 4 3 2 2 2 5 9 8 0 5 6 3 7 7 3 6 0 8 9
0 1 0 2 2 3 6 6 5 0 0 7 1 9 6 8 1 8 5 7 9 3
3 8 9 1 4 9 3 5 2 3 9 5 3 7 3 3 7 9 2 7 4 2
```

```
2 7 6 5 5 1 8 0 3 7 7 6 3 3 3 6 1 9 5 5 0 4
9 9 4 5 6 8 4 6 0 1 7 7 8 9 4 3 2 6 5 2 7 3
2 6 4 1 2 6 7 2 3 0 2 1 1 3 8 4 3 9 8 7 7 0
3 7 5 6 3 3 7 2 7 7 1 3 3 0 2 6 5 5 5 8 5 5
3 8 0 3 9 0 5 9 7 6 1 6 9 4 1 9 4 9 8 6 2 7
7 1 4 5 3 8 2 6 1 5 0 5 7 2 5 4 3 3 9 1 6 5
9 3 5 5 7 1 0 6 7 0 7 3 1 3 8 3 5 6 5 0 0 4
0 1 9 4 5 7 8 3 7 4 5 6 5 6 9 1 7 1 1 4 5 5
4 5 0 9 7 8 6 5 0 5 2 4 2 9 2 7 4 2 1 8 6 5
6 0 2 3 4 6 6 6 1 3 3 7 8 9 1 0 3 5 3 3 9 2
0 1 3 0 8 6 4 0 1 3 6 1 6 0 8 9 1 1 9 4 0 9
5 7 7 5 0 8 2 2 1 7 6 1 2 5 6 8 5 6 3 6 5 8
7 1 0 6 6 2 9 0 9 2 0 9 2 9 9 4 1 6 1 2 0 1
4 7 1 8 0 1 3 7 2 6 9 0 6 7 4 5 6 8 4 7 3 4
4 7 3 4 6 0 7 5 7 5 2 7 0 0 9 9 8 7 9 8 1 2
7 0 4 9 0 6 5 3 2 7 0 3 3 3 0 8 4 3 5 4 7 7
8 5 6 9 9 0 6 7 3 1 0 9 1 1 0 1 5 1 3 5 6 3
1 4 4 8 2 9 8 5 3 2 9 2 4 3 8 1 2 1 6 8 1 2
5 5 3 4 0 9 5 3 3 0 0 8 0 9 8 3 1 9 9 2 1 9
5 3 6 3 3 2 9 7 0 6 5 1 1 5 4 0 7 3 3 2 8 0
2 6 2 6 1 6 8 3 7 1 4 0 9 7 4 0 3 4 8 9 7 0
2 0 9 6 9 3 1 8 2 8 4 4 5 8 5 4 4 4 9 5 1 9
0 5 1 8 3 4 8 4 5 0 0 7 0 2 7 8 5 0 7 6 4 1
4 9 4 9 3 4 6 0 6 9 9 5 4 0 3 0 7 8 5 0 0 9
2 0 0 9 1 4 0 1 4 0 8 1 3 7 3 8 4 2 4 9 8 7
8 6 6 5 8 8 3 9 1 4 2 5 9 7 9 4 4 8 6 2 0 9
0 7 3 9 1 5 7 5 3 2 7 6 6 9 7 9 5 2 6 0 2 5
4 2 4 3 1 0 2 0 3 9 9 3 7 0 5 4 1 1 5 4 6 9
2 5 7 6 9 9 8 5 9 7 1 2 4 9 7 3 8 5 2 3 9 9
2 5 3 6 9 0 7 8 5 6 3 8 1 2 1 1 7 2 9 5 0 8
7 1 8 7 7 9 0 7 9 9 9 7 4 6 4 0 8 5 8 8 3 3
5 6 3 0 0 0 0 1 2 3 8 9 8 9 8 7 3 3 0 7 8 1
5 7 4 3 6 8 8 0 1 0 6 2 8 2 6 6 5 3 8 9 9 0
4 6 3 8 8 7 7 7 4 8 9 1 9 9 2 6 1 9 1 4 1 1
4 0 4 1 2 4 4 5 9 7 7 7 6 0 0 9 4 9 8 6 8 7
8 9 6 7 4 7 3 0 7 9 2 8 4 6 0 2 2 4 6 5 7 5
8 0 1 8 9 2 1 3 0 5 0 6 1 2 1 8 7 4 0 1 2 0
7 1 5 9 2 1 5 7 2 9 8 0 2 8 8 2 5 2 5 7 8 9
2 1 5 9 6 8 4 2 5 3 9 5 4 0 7 0 6 6 2 0 4 5
2 3 8 7 8 6 4 6 6 5 1 7 1 4 4 7 7 2 6 4 8 7
5 0 2 1 3 8 6 8 2 9 1 4 3 4 1 2 5 5 2 2 8 4
4 2 9 7 9 5 3 8 7 9 8 0 0 8 6 5 4 0 0 5 0 5
8 2 9 0 3 8 8 9 6 4 0 6 2 7 0 8 5 1 7 3 1 7
2 8 8 3 2 9 5 0 9 5 7 1 5 9 3 2 3 2 9 7 9 9
0 6 5 1 9 4 0 6 1 8 1 7 3 2 2 7 6 5 3 0 2 8
7 9 2 8 8 4 9 5 6 5 3 4 8 6 7 5 0 9 7 4 3 7
9 1 8 8 6 1 1 7 9 7 0 1 5 1 5 0 8 4 5 8 9 7
9 6 6 0 8 4 1 6 2 3 3 6 4 2 1 7 3 4 4 5 9 1
2 9 1 7 6 3 2 3 5 3 3 5 1 0 1 4 4 7 9 5 2 9
0 4 8 6 6 4 6 8 0 5 6 1 3 6 0 4 4 6 8 1 5 8 5
7 6 7 5 1 8 6 9 3 5 4 9 5 5 4 8 7 1 3 5 8 5
5 7 9 7 1 5 1 2 0 5 3 0 9 9 4 0 3 9 1 7 2 5
2 0 3 5 7 6 5 9 1 5 5 2 6 8 1 8 7 2 2 8 4 0
2 0 5 1 1 2 7 7 4 4 5 8 1 8 3 5 2 9 1 8 7 3
2 8 0 7 9 3 4 7 3 8 2 8 6 7 4 8 3 1 4 4 0 5
4 5 8 4 1 5 5 0 2 0 2 6 7 9 1 0 6 4 1 9 4 2
5 1 4 7 2 7 4 4 1 8 3 9 5 3 5 7 4 9 1 9 7 3
6 5 0 2 6 6 6 5 5 4 4 9 1 4 3 6 3 4 0 6 3 6
7 3 2 6 3 7 6 8 8 4 9 6 3 8 2 6 9 8 1 8 7 2
```

6	7	2	2	8	7	0	2	0	2	4	2	1	0	7	8	9	6	7	0	1	0
2	9	4	5	0	2	1	4	6	9	5	9	7	8	5	7	6	0	7	9	1	3
0	4	8	0	3	0	8	1	9	3	6	9	7	4	9	4	8	3	1	7	0	9
3	6	1	4	1	0	3	4	3	5	5	4	3	7	7	1	4	7	5	1	5	8
3	2	1	9	7	5	4	5	1	6	8	0	1	0	5	1	3	7	5	4	4	6
5	8	9	6	4	2	4	5	9	8	2	7	4	0	9	6	1	9	0	9	9	1
3	5	9	9	9	9	2	7	9	4	3	0	3	9	0	8	7	1	6	9	7	2
6	3	2	7	6	0	4	3	1	6	0	2	9	6	3	4	8	5	9	8	6	5
2	3	7	3	2	1	7	7	6	7	4	9	4	8	8	9	5	8	4	2	2	5
5	6	3	6	2	2	1	9	8	9	8	9	7	9	1	2	6	3	4	9	1	5
7	0	3	9	3	4	0	8	9	0	5	5	9	8	3	2	7	9	7	8	5	6
9	9	5	1	6	9	4	5	1	5	9	9	6	8	2	3	2	9	3	7	2	5
4	4	5	1	9	7	7	7	4	9	6	3	7	1	9	7	4	9	1	9	4	6
3	2	8	1	9	7	1	5	6	4	7	4	7	4	0	9	7	8	1	5	2	2
4	4	1	3	2	8	4	8	0	2	4	6	4	0	6	3	8	9	9	3	4	5
0	5	6	1	3	3	5	2	8	4	6	4	8	1	7	9	1	2	2	9	6	5
1	2	1	2	7	9	7	2	4	4	5	5	3	0	2	9	5	7	5	5	5	4
7	2	6	9	4	9	6	2	6	1	4	0	1	4	6	8	1	1	6	9	8	5
3	1	3	8	8	9	3	4	3	9	5	1	8	0	7	0	4	4	9	4	8	1
9	5	5	6	0	2	9	6	2	0	2	5	1	2	5	5	9	0	5	5	9	3
6	8	1	8	8	6	0	1	8	9	8	1	4	4	5	3	6	4	9	1	8	3
0	0	2	7	3	3	1	6	1	4	3	0	3	5	3	9	3	3	6	8	6	2
0	2	0	1	4	4	3	4	8	9	0	9	2	9	5	7	4	3	2	6	6	2
4	3	1	1	9	4	5	3	0	1	5	7	4	0	0	1	2	9	6	2	9	9
8	8	7	2	2	6	0	4	0	4	4	3	0	2	3	7	3	2	6	1	4	2
7	0	2	2	1	9	0	8	7	8	7	7	3	7	1	3	8	6	9	3	2	2
9	5	1	4	4	2	0	2	1	1	7	4	0	2	6	9	0	4	3	8	0	4
4	1	2	3	1	7	0	4	3	4	0	3	9	8	1	7	8	9	7	6	7	5
0	6	2	7	4	0	5	1	5	0	2	7	4	7	4	1	3	2	5	1	1	1
8	7	8	3	0	0	8	9	6	3	7	1	0	7	9	0	7	7	2	9	5	6
6	1	8	4	5	7	5	9	7	3	6	9	4	2	7	1	4	4	0	5	5	6
8	9	2	5	5	3	3	0	1	6	5	2	0	6	5	4	1	7	5	0	8	7
2	1	1	9	4	7	7	9	6	3	2	7	9	8	3	8	3	8	9	6	8	6
8	1	0	7	3	1	2	6	4	9	7	5	2	2	2	6	0	3	0	7	2	5
7	3	8	3	9	2	9	0	5	3	2	6	6	2	8	5	5	7	3	8	2	5
5	4	9	3	4	6	2	6	2	5	5	1	6	7	3	0	3	8	4	6	6	6
2	7	0	6	4	6	7	1	8	1	6	6	9	6	6	8	5	4	9	5	4	8
2	6	4	9	6	6	1	1	0	2	0	6	4	7	4	6	0	9	8	3	3	8
4	5	1	5	6	6	6	5	8	3	7	6	3	1	7	5	4	0	8	2	1	3
9	5	9	0	3	2	7	9	9	5	4	9	2	1	5	5	1	6	9	4	1	8
1	0	9	8	0	2	0	1	2	2	7	8	0	6	8	6	0	8	5	4	5	3
2	9	6	7	2	9	7	7	9	9	8	3	0	4	8	9	7	7	7	0	2	5
7	6	6	2	7	6	2	1	4	0	6	6	8	1	0	7	3	6	1	3	6	2
6	1	3	3	1	1	0	1	5	0	1	4	5	5	3	1	3	2	7	0	0	5
7	6	7	9	6	2	4	5	4	7	7	8	0	5	0	1	5	8	2	2	1	3
5	7	1	5	5	5	9	8	3	5	3	9	8	3	7	1	4	4	7	8	5	8
9	1	8	4	3	3	4	3	8	0	1	8	0	8	5	3	0	0	8	6	4	0
0	6	9	4	4	6	0	8	8	9	6	2	9	0	9	4	1	2	6	1	3	4

These random numbers have been generated by the authors.

Bibliography

Decision Theory

RAIFFA, HOWARD, *Decision Analysis*. Reading, Mass.: Addison-Wesley, 1968.

LUCE, R. DUNCAN, and HOWARD RAIFFA, *Games and Decisions*. New York: John Wiley & Sons, Inc., 1958.

BROSS, IRWIN D. J., *Design for Decision*. New York: The Macmillan Company, 1953.

EDWARDS, WARD, and AMOS TZERSKY, eds., *Decision Making: Selected Readings*. Penguin Books, Inc., 1967.

SCHLAIFER, R. ROBERT, *Analysis of Decisions Under Uncertainty*. New York: McGraw-Hill Book Company, 1967.

PRATT, JOHN, HOWARD RAIFFA, and ROBERT SCHLAIFER, *Introduction to Statistical Decision Theory*. New York: McGraw-Hill Book Company, 1965.

Introductions to Operations Research

BEER, STAFFORD, *Management Science*. New York: Doubleday & Company, Inc., 1968.

KAUFMANN, ARNOLD, *The Science of Decision Making*. New York: World University Library, 1968.

Operations Research

ACKOFF, RUSSELL L., and MAURICE W. SASIENI, *Fundamentals of Operations Research*. New York: John Wiley & Sons, Inc., 1968.

HILLIER, FREDERICK S., and GERALD J. LIEBERMAN, *Introduction to Operations Research*. San Francisco: Holden-Day, Inc., 1967.

RICHMOND, SAMUEL B., *Operations Research for Management Decisions*. New York: The Ronald Press Company, 1968.

SASIENI, MAURICE, A. YASPAN, and L. FRIEDMAN, *Operations Research, Methods and Problems*. New York: John Wiley & Sons, Inc., 1959.

CHURCHMAN, C. WEST, RUSSELL L. ACKOFF, and E. L. ARNOFF, *Introduction to Operations Research*. New York: John Wiley & Sons, Inc., 1957.

Marketing

MONTGOMERY, DAVID B. and GLEN L. URBAN, *Management Science in Marketing.* Englewood Cliffs, N.J.: Prentice-Hall, Inc., 1969.

BASS, FRANK M., CHARLES W. KING, and EDGAR A. PESSEMIER, eds., *Applications of the Sciences in Marketing Management.* New York: John Wiley & Sons, Inc., 1968.

Finance

HANSSMANN, FRED, *Operations Research Techniques for Capital Investment.* New York: John Wiley & Sons, Inc., 1968.

MARKOWITZ, HARRY M., *Portfolio Selection.* New York: John Wiley & Sons, Inc., 1959.

WEINGARTNER, H. MARTIN, *Mathematical Programming and the Analysis of Capital Budgeting Problems.* Chicago: Markham Publishing Company, 1967.

Operations Research, General Application

Mathematical Model Building in Economics and Industry. New York: Hafner Publishing Company, Inc., 1968.

MORSE, PHILIP M., ed., assisted by Laura W. Bacon, *Operations Research for Public Systems.* Cambridge, Mass.: The M.I.T. Press, 1967.

PIERCE, JOHN F., ed., *Operations Research and the Design of Management Information Systems.* New York: Technical Association of the Pulp and Paper Industry, 1967.

Applications in Various Sciences

BAILEY, NORMAN T. J., *The Mathematical Approach to Biology and Medicine.* New York: John Wiley & Sons, Inc., 1967.

BARTOS, OTOMAR J., *Simple Models of Group Behavior.* New York: Columbia University Press, 1967.

CHORLEY, RICHARD J., and PETER HAGGETT, eds., *Socio-economic Models in Geography.* New York: Barnes & Noble, Inc., 1968.

COLEMAN, JAMES S., *Introduction to Mathematical Sociology.* New York: The Free Press, 1964.

LUSTED, LEE B., *Introduction to Medical Decision Making.* Springfield, Ill.: Charles C. Thomas, 1968.

RASHEVSKY, NICOLAS, *Looking at History Through Mathematics.* Cambridge, Mass.: The M.I.T. Press, 1968.

SAATY, THOMAS L., *Mathematical Models of Arms Control and Disarmament.* New York: John Wiley & Sons, Inc., 1968.

TULLOCK, GORDON, *Toward a Mathematics of Politics.* Ann Arbor, Mich.: University of Michigan Press, 1967.

Inventory Theory

STARR, MARTIN K., and DAVID W. MILLER, *Inventory Control: Theory and Practice.* Englewood Cliffs, N.J.: Prentice-Hall, Inc., 1962.

BROWN, ROBERT G., *Decision Rules for Inventory Management.* New York: Holt, Rinehart & Winston, Inc., 1967.

Dynamic Programming

BECKMANN, MARTIN J., *Dynamic Programming of Economic Decisions.* New York: Springer-Verlag New York Inc., 1968.

KAUFMANN, ARNOLD, *Graphs, Dynamic Programming, and Finite Games.* New York: Academic Press, Inc., 1967.

JACOBS, O.L.R., *An Introduction to Dynamic Programming.* New York: Barnes & Noble, Inc., 1967.

BELLMAN, RICHARD E., *Dynamic Programming.* Princeton, N.J.: Princeton University Press, 1957.

Linear Programming

DORFMAN, ROBERT, PAUL A. SAMUELSON, and ROBERT M. SOLOW, *Linear Programming and Economic Analysis.* New York: McGraw-Hill Book Company, 1958.

BOULDING, KENNETH E., and W. ALLEN SPIVEY, *Linear Programming and the Theory of the Firm.* New York: The Macmillan Company, 1960.

HADLEY, G., *Linear Programming.* Reading, Mass.: Addison-Wesley Publishing Company, Inc., 1962.

Queuing Theory

COX, D. R., and W. L. SMITH, *Queues.* New York: John Wiley & Sons, Inc., 1961.

MORSE, P. M., *Queues, Inventories, and Maintenance.* New York: John Wiley & Sons, Inc., 1958.

SAATY, T. L., *Elements of Queueing Theory.* New York: McGraw-Hill Book Company, 1961.

Scheduling Problems

CONWAY, RICHARD W., WILLIAM L. MAXWELL, and LOUIS W. MILLER, *Theory of Scheduling.* Reading, Mass.: Addison-Wesley Publishing Company, 1967.

Cybernetics

BEER, STAFFORD, *Decision and Control.* New York: John Wiley & Sons, Inc., 1967.

ASHBY, W. ROSS, *An Introduction to Cybernetics.* New York: John Wiley & Sons, Inc., 1956.

DELATIL, PIERRE, *Thinking by Machine, a Study of Cybernetics.* Boston: Houghton Mifflin Company, 1957.

KLIR, J., and M. VALACH, *Cybernetic Modelling.* Princeton, N.J.: D. Van Nostrand Company, 1967.

Systems Theory

VON BERTALANFFY, LUDWIG, *General System Theory.* New York: George Braziller, 1969.

CHURCHMAN, C. WEST, *Systems Approach.* New York: Delacorte Press, 1968.

BERRIAN, F. KENNETH, *General and Social Systems.* New Brunswick, N.J.: Rutgers University Press, 1968.

Systems Analysis in Government

BLACK, GUY, *The Application of Systems Analysis to Government Operations.*
New York: Frederick A. Praeger, Inc., 1968.

McKEAN, ROLAND N., *Efficiency in Government Through Systems Analysis.* New
York: John Wiley & Sons, Inc., 1958.

QUADE, E. S. and W. I. BOUCHER, eds., *Systems Analysis and Policy Planning.*
New York: American Elsevier, 1968.

Cost-Benefit and Cost-Effectiveness Analyses

GOLDMAN, THOMAS A., ed., *Cost-Effectiveness Analysis.* New York: Frederick A.
Praeger, Inc., 1967.

HITCH, CHARLES J., and ROLAND N. McKEAN, *The Economics of Defense in the
Nuclear Age.* New York: Atheneum, 1966.

McKEAN, ROLAND N., *Public Spending.* New York: McGraw-Hill Book Company,
1968.

DORFMAN, ROBERT, ed., *Measuring Benefits of Government Investment.* Washington: D.C.: The Brookings Institution, 1965.

Game Theory

OWEN, GUILLERMO, *Game Theory.* Philadelphia: W. B. Saunders Company,
1968.

VON NEUMANN, JOHN, and OSKAR MORGENSTERN, *Theory of Games and Economic
Behavior.* Princeton, N.J.: Princeton University Press, 1947.

WILLIAMS, J. D., *The Compleat Strategyst.* New York: McGraw-Hill Book
Company, 1954.

Information Theory

GOLDMAN, STANFORD, *Information Theory.* Englewood Cliffs, N.J.: Prentice-Hall,
Inc., 1953.

JELINEK, FREDERICK, *Probabilistic Estimation Theory: Discrete and Memoryless
Models.* New York: McGraw-Hill Book Company, 1968.

Communications

CHERRY, COLIN, *On Human Communication.* Cambridge, Mass.: The M.I.T.
Press, 1957.

THAYER, LEE, ed., *Communication, Concepts and Perspectives.* Washington:
D.C.: Spartan Books, 1967.

Simulation

MARTIN, FRANCIS F., *Computer Modelling and Simulation.* New York: John
Wiley & Sons, Inc., 1968.

MEIER, ROBERT C., WILLIAM P. NEWELL, and HAROLD L. PAZER, *Simulation in
Business and Economics.* Englewood Cliffs, N.J.: Prentice-Hall, Inc., 1969.

MIZE, JOE H. and J. GRADY COX, *Essentials of Simulation.* Englewood Cliffs, N.J.:
Prentice-Hall, Inc., 1968.

EVANS, GEORGE W., GRAHAM F. WALLACE, and GEORGIA L. SUTHERLAND, *Simulation Using Digital Computers.* Englewood Cliffs, N.J.: Prentice-Hall, Inc.,
1967.

LOEHLIN, JOHN C., *Computer Models of Personality*. New York: Random House, Inc., 1968.
AMSTUTZ, ARNOLD E., *Computer Simulation of Competitive Market Response*. Cambridge, Mass.: The M.I.T. Press, 1967.

Bayesian Methods

FORESTER, JOHN, *Statistical Selection of Business Strategies*. Homewood, Ill.: Richard D. Irwin, Inc., 1968.
MORRIS, WILLIAM T., *Management Science, a Bayesian Introduction*. Englewood Cliffs, N.J.: Prentice-Hall, Inc., 1968.
SCHLAIFER, ROBERT, *Probability and Statistics for Business Decisions*. New York: McGraw-Hill Book Company, 1959.

Gambling

EPSTEIN, RICHARD A., *The Theory of Gambling and Statistical Logic*. New York: Academic Press, Inc., 1967.

Probability Theory

FELLER, WILLIAM, *An Introduction to Probability Theory and Its Applications;* Vol. I, 3rd ed. New York: John Wiley & Sons, Inc., 1968.
MORAN, P.A.P., *An Introduction to Probability Theory*. London: Oxford University Press, Inc., 1968.
PARZEN, EMMANUEL, *Modern Probability Theory and Its Applications*. New York: John Wiley & Sons, Inc., 1960.

Mathematics

STERN, MARK E., *Mathematics for Management*. Englewood Cliffs, N.J.: Prentice-Hall, Inc., 1963.
DEAN, BURTON V., MAURICE W. SASIENI, and SHIV K. GUPTA, *Mathematics for Modern Management*. New York: John Wiley & Sons, Inc., 1963.
KEMENY, J. G., J. L. SNELL, and G. L. THOMPSON, *Introduction to Finite Mathematics*. Englewood Cliffs, N.J.: Prentice-Hall, Inc., 1957.

The Mathematics of Optimization

WILDE, D. J. and C. L. BEIGHTLER, *Foundations of Optimization*. Englewood Cliffs, N.J.: Prentice-Hall, Inc., 1967.
DUFFIN, RICHARD J., ELMOR L. PETERSEN, and CLARENCE ZENGER, *Geometric Programming, Theory and Application*. New York: John Wiley & Sons, Inc., 1967.

Mathematical Methods of Operations Research

GUE, RONALD L. and MICHAEL E. THOMAS, *Mathematical Methods in Operations Research*. New York: The Macmillan Company, 1968.
TEICHROEW, DANIEL, *An Introduction to Management Science; Deterministic Models*. New York: John Wiley & Sons, Inc., 1964.
SAATY, THOMAS L., *Mathematical Methods of Operations Research*. New York: McGraw-Hill Book Company, 1959.

Measurement

CAMPBELL, NORMAN R., *Foundations of Science*. New York: Dover Publications, Inc., 1957.

TORGERSON, WARREN S., *Theory and Methods of Scaling*. New York: John Wiley & Sons, Inc., 1958.

Economic Theory

BAUMOL, WILLIAM J., *Economic Theory and Operations Analysis;* Second Edition. Englewood Cliffs, N.J.: Prentice-Hall, Inc., 1965.

LESOURNE, JACQUES, *Economic Analysis and Industrial Management*. Englewood Cliffs, N.J.: Prentice-Hall, Inc., 1963.

SPENCER, MILTON H. and LOUIS SELIGMAN, *Managerial Economics*. Homewood, Ill.: Richard D. Irwin, Inc., 1959.

Computers and Society

SACKMAN, HAROLD, *Computers, Systems Science, and Evolving Society*. New York: John Wiley & Sons, Inc., 1967.

MACBRIDE, ROBERT O., *The Automated State. Computer Systems as a New Force in Society*. Philadelphia: Chilton Book Company, 1967.

Men and Organizations

SIMON, HERBERT A., *Models of Man*. New York: John Wiley & Sons, Inc., 1957.

———, *Sciences of the Artificial*. Cambridge, Mass.: The M.I.T. Press, 1969.

———, *Administrative Behavior*, 2nd ed. New York: The Macmillan Company, 1957.

Index

Product class, 407
Production:
  batch type, 368
  serial-type, 368
Production department, 38
Production models, 374
Profit, contributory, 466, 474
Profit stream, 375
Programming, 302
  Boolean, 397
  dynamic, 424
Protein, 561
Proxy fight, 29
Purchase cycle, 411
Purchase diaries, 380, 383, 386
Purchasing, 319, 320
Purchasing behavior, 382
Purchasing policy, optimal, 421, 551
Purposes, 42

Q

Quadratic programming, 487, 550
Qualitative interpretations, 416
Qualitative measurements, 374
Quality, product, 506
Quality control, 579
Quandt, Richard E., 452
Quantum mechanics, 23
Queues, 451, 504
Queuing, 556
Queuing theory, 193, 352

R

Raiffa, Howard, 93, 113
R&D budget, 38
Random behavior, 42, 439, 448
Random numbers, 182, 467, 472, 556
Random sampling, 181
Ranking, 84, 223
Rate:
  of arrivals, 543
  breakdown, 359
  departure, 543
  of service, 543
Rate of return, 489
Ratio:
  capital, 513
  return, 513
Rational, 115
Rational approach, 499
Rational behavior, 42
Rationalist, 71
Rationality, 24, 25, 42, 43
  bounded, 49, 53, 63, 83, 97, 139, 150, 573

Rational opponents, 437
Reach, 379, 391
Reach objective, 393, 394
Reactions, compensating, 43
Readership, 376
  at-home, 376
  magazine, 392
  pass-along, 376
Receiving, 326
Recurrence relations, 363
Redhead, 365
Redundancy, 200, 576, 584
Refinery production, 180
Reflexive, 22
Refrigerators, 446
Region, permissible, 220
Regret, criterion, 115
Regulator, automatic, 37
Reliability, 341, 559
Renting, 566
Repairmen, 349
Repairmen problem, 531, 543, 556
Replacement, 278, 346
Replacement model, 557
Replacement time, 319
Rescue, air-sea, 522
Research:
  advertising, 380
  marketing, 380
  medical, 40
  military, 526
Research activities, 512
Research budget, 512, 525
Research projects, 541
Reservations, 563
Reserve stock, 540
Reservoir, 526
Responsibility, 47
Restrictions, 35, 36, 400, 403, 405, 441, 548
  financial, 452
Retirement plan, 561
Return on investment, 466
Returns, diminishing, 489
Returns to scale, 548
Reversibility, 582
  degree of, 566, 583
Reynold's number, 151
Richman, Barry, 5
Richmond, Samuel, 552
Risk, 320
  aversion to, 473
  credit, 495
Risk analysis, 464, 467, 471, 473, 494, 495
Risk problem, 426, 566
ROI, 466, 473, 474, 494
Rolls-Royce, 377
Roulette, 526